VOL. XXV, No. IV
Founded 1984

# The Yearbook of Experts®

## The Yearbook of Experts, Authorities & Spokespersons®

### An Encyclopedia of Sources®

# www.Yearbook.com

Yearbook of Experts®,
Volume XXV, Number IV

# The Yearbook of Experts®

## An Encyclopedia of Sources®

Broadcast Interview Source, Inc.
2233 Wisconsin Ave., N.W.
Washington, D.C. 20007-4132

Web site: www.Yearbook.com

Telephone: (202) 333-5000
Fax: (202) 342-5411
E-mail: Editor@Yearbook.com

Mitchell P. Davis, Editor & Publisher

Editor's Note: The purpose of the Yearbook of Experts® is to provide bona fide interview sources to working members of the news media. Great care is taken in the review and selection of sources for inclusion. Although all contacts have expressed interest in being available for interview, we do not guarantee the availability of any given participant for any given interview, nor is a warranty offered that every listed contact will be appropriate for a reader's particular purpose. Quotes are provided to show acceptance of the Yearbook of Experts by individuals who work in the news media, but should not be interpreted as endorsements by the named organizations. "America's Favorite Newsroom Resource" is based on tens of thousands of Yearbooks requested by journalists.

# Broadcast Interview Source, Inc.

2233 Wisconsin Ave., N.W.
Washington, D.C. 20007

Phone: (202) 333-5000
Toll-free: 1-800-YEARBOOK
Fax: (202) 342-5411
E-mail: Editor@Yearbook.com
Web site: www.Yearbook.com

29-Aug-06

Welcome to the fourth issue of the 25th volume of the Yearbook of Experts® -- now in a printed version to accompany the online version, Yearbook.com. This book is based on the live information provided by our member experts and groups, directly from the online database. Each expert has the ability to log in and update their information instantly, 24 hours a day.

You can always search the database at Yearbook.com for the most up-to-date information, but this book puts the information at your fingertips. Also, you can download new and revised Adobe PDF editions as they become available.

You may be reading this online from the Adobe PDF version, or you may be reading a printed edition. The content is the same, but when you read the book as the Adobe PDF from a Web enabled computer, you can click on links to take you directly to the experts' Web pages and see enhanced content.

From the Adobe PDF you can:
1) View news releases,
2) View Daybook.com events,
3) Jump to the participants' Web pages,
4) Listen to Real Audio.

**Bonus for registered journalists: Contact our experts via e-mail with our InterviewNet.com system.**

This Yearbook has five sections:
1) Introduction;
2) Topic Index, when viewed on your computer, these link directly to the profiles;
3) Profile Section, with descriptions of experts linked to their Yearbook.com sites;
4) Geographic Index, so you can find sources in your area;
5) Participant Index, to quickly find Participants.

Questions? Please contact us at (202) 333-5000 or Editor@Yearbook.com.

Sincerely,

Mitchell P. Davis, Editor & Publisher

# How does the Yearbook of Experts work for JOURNALISTS?

Journalists can access and use the Yearbook.com Web site free of charge, which includes the download of the Adobe PDF and other features. Also, they can create a profile in our News Media Yearbook. Journalists who choose to create a public profile in our News Media Yearbook also have free access to the News Media Yearbook for networking.

We print and mail copies of the Yearbook of Experts to thousands of leading journalists twice a year.

*Journalists -- You can visit Yearbook.com without registration, but some features require free registration.*

# Here's how to get all of our Journalist benefits:

FREE REGISTRATION: Go to Yearbook.com, and click on "JOURNALISTS."

Simply fill out the registration form.
This gives you greater access to our news sources.

# How does the Yearbook of Experts work for NEWS SOURCES?

*The annual membership cost of $995 includes:*

1) A listing in print and the Adobe PDF with 75 words of print text, indexing to nine topics and your contact information.

2) A complete profile at the www.Yearbook.com site with unlimited text, HTML, links to your audio -- *and the profile is also available via LexisNexis.*

3) Distribution of your news releases at www.NewsReleaseWire.com with **NO** per-release charge. News releases are transmitted six ways: 1) Immediately posted on our site; 2) Via our headline feed to over 20,000 journalists; 3) Via InstantNewsWire.com by topic; 4) Linked to your Yearbook.com profile; 5) As a custom URL link for your Web site that shows only your news releases; and 6) At the LexisNexis database.

4) Your event postings at www.Daybook.com, The Public Record of Today's Events®.

5) Talking News Releases on your profile page, on your news releases, and links from your Web site.

# Here's how to be included as a News Source Expert:

Go to **Yearbook.com,** and click on the "Sign Up" button on the lower left. You can view and print a PDF of our brochure. Then scroll down to the application form to sign up online.

Or call us at 1-800-YEARBOOK (800-932-7266), and *we will instantly create your profile.*

# Visit all the Yearbook of Expert's Web sites:

## Yearbook.com

*our main site*

## NewsReleaseWire.com

*read news from our experts and use the advanced features to segment geographically or by topic*

## Daybook.com

*for The Public Record of Today's Events[R] -- a future file of news and events -- perfect for print journalists who are working several months ahead*

# InterviewNet.com

*journalists can ask questions via e-mail and send them "one-to-one" or "one-to-many" to reach news sources*

# RadioTour.com

*listen to talking news releases via our audio system, to ensure you find the guests with the best sound for your program*

# ReviewBook.com

*registered journalists can request books for review*

# NewsMediaYearbook.com

*our directory of journalists available to news sources and journalists who register for networking in four ways: 1) on the Web; 2) Excel database for download; 3) Adobe PDF for download; and 4) Word document for press-on labels*

## *Broadcast Interview Source, Inc., was founded in July 1984.*

1984 -- Broadcast Interview Source publishes first edition of the Yearbook, mailing 750 copies of a 64-page booklet to talk radio shows. Talk Show Yearbook first released with contact information for the nation's talk shows.

1985 -- Broadcast publishes the second edition of the Yearbook with 20 paid listings from The Ad Council. The Associated Press requests 1,000 copies.

1986 -- The New York Times dubs the Yearbook, "Dial-An-Expert."

1987 -- Leading news/talk radio stations, "60 Minutes" and "Donahue" purchase copies of the Yearbook.

1988 -- Media circulation grows to 4,000 copies. The Wall Street Journal and The Washington Post publish reviews. The Associated Press calls it, "An Encyclopedia of Sources."

1989 -- Power Media Yearbook of top print journalists becomes another Broadcast Interview Source publication.

1992 -- Yearbook circulation grows to 12,000 copies a year.

1994 -- The White House, IRS and CIA place listings. 100,000 total copies in print.

1995 -- Newsweek and The New York Times Magazine run features on the Yearbook. Journalists request 9,000 print copies.

1996 -- Yearbook.com goes online and serves as the interactive companion to the printed Yearbook.

1997 -- Broadcast launches Daybook.com, an online calendar of the day's media events.

1998 -- LexisNexis includes the Yearbook in its extensive search engine.

1999 -- Free Library/BIS Publishing, Inc., now has 5 titles in print: Yearbook of Experts (Annual), Power Media Yearbook (Annual), Talk Show Yearbook (Annual), Baseball Goes to War (History), Family Words (Humor).

2001 -- NewsReleaseWire.com debuts, offering a secure way to send news releases. NewsMedia-Yearbook.com launches with live listings of journalists.

2002 -- Broadcast's RadioTour.com debuts as a targeted service with talking news releases, built to help TV and radio talk shows find the best guests for their programs. InterviewNet.com comes alive to offer direct e-mail contact, one-to-one or one-to-many.

2003 -- The Yearbook of Experts publishes as an Adobe PDF and printed editions.

---

*Yearbook: innovation & leadership for two decades.*

# Topic Index

**After School Programs**

**Aftercare**

**Afterlife**

**Age**

**Age Discrimination**

**Age Proof Your Brian**

**Agents**

**Aging**

**Aging and Fitness**

**Aging Anti-Aging**

**Aging Intervention**

**Aging Parent**

**Aging Parents**

**Aging Voices**

**Aging/Anti-Aging**

**Aging/Health**

**Aging/Marketing**

**Aging/Wellness**

**Agribusiness**

**Agriculture**

**AIDS/HIV**

**Aids/Religion/Church**

**AIDS/Women**

**Air & Water Quality**

**Air Accidents**

**Air Crash Law**

**Air Crash Litigation**

**Air Disasters**

**Air Disasters/Psychology**

**Air Frieght**

**Air Pollution**

**Air Quality**

**Air Quality/Indoor**

**Air Rage**

**Air Safety**

**Air Traffic Control**

**Air Travel**

**Aircraft**

**Aircraft Accidents**

**Aircraft Maintenance**
Volvo Group North America, 281
**Aircraft Safety/Design**
Experimental Aircraft Association (EAA), 282
**Airline Accidents**
Baum Hedlund, A Professional Corporation, 234
Magana, Cathcart & McCarthy, 234
Michael J. Pangia, 234
Rising Star Press, 324
**Airline Crash Forensics**
Dr. Dennis Dirkmaat — Mercyhurst College Archaeological Institute, 234
**Airline Crashes**
Baum Hedlund, A Professional Corporation, 234
Rising Star Press, 324
**Airline Disasters**
Diamond and Diamond LLC, Attorneys at Law, 230
**Airline Industry**
Alderman & Alderman, 228
Carmen Day -- Wealth4u In Spirit, 418
University of Portland, 180
**Airplane Crashes**
Baum Hedlund, A Professional Corporation, 234
Rising Star Press, 324
**Airplanes**
Aircraft Owners and Pilots Association -- AOPA, 284
Experimental Aircraft Association (EAA), 282
**Airports**
Aircraft Owners and Pilots Association -- AOPA, 284
Experimental Aircraft Association (EAA), 282
**Airshows**
Experimental Aircraft Association (EAA), 282
**Airspace**
Aircraft Owners and Pilots Association -- AOPA, 284
**Alan Berg**
Judith Lee Berg -- Human Resource Communication, 214
**Alcohol**
National Families in Action, 236
RID-USA, Inc. Remove Intoxicated Drivers, 203
**Alcohol Abuse**
Anheuser-Busch Companies, Inc., 268
Susan Neri-Friedwald CHT. (NGH, ABH, IMDHA, IACT) Behavior Modification Expert, 530
**Alcohol Abuse/Teenagers**
Robert R. Butterworth, Ph.D., 522
Susie Vanderlip -- Teen & Parenting Skills Expert, 531
Jeffrey S. Wolfsberg & Associates Inc., Alcohol & Other Drug Prevention Specialists, 522
**Alcohol and Drug Crimes**
William C. Head, 236
**Alcohol Counseling**
Robert DeLetis, Addictions Expert, 529

**Alcohol Drug Counselor**
Marilyn Redmond, Healing and Spiritual Growth, 525
**Alcohol Education**
Marilyn Redmond, Healing and Spiritual Growth, 525
Jeffrey S. Wolfsberg & Associates Inc., Alcohol & Other Drug Prevention Specialists, 522
**Alcohol Issues**
Anheuser-Busch Companies, Inc., 268
Susan Neri-Friedwald CHT. (NGH, ABH, IMDHA, IACT) Behavior Modification Expert, 530
**Alcohol Recovery**
Union Rescue Mission, 195
**Alcohol Recovery Program**
Robert DeLetis, Addictions Expert, 529
Susan Neri-Friedwald CHT. (NGH, ABH, IMDHA, IACT) Behavior Modification Expert, 530
**Alcohol/Drug Counselor**
Robert DeLetis, Addictions Expert, 529
Peter J. Killeen, 238
Susan Neri-Friedwald CHT. (NGH, ABH, IMDHA, IACT) Behavior Modification Expert, 530
**Alcohol/Drug Prevention**
Susie Vanderlip -- Teen & Parenting Skills Expert, 531
Jeffrey S. Wolfsberg & Associates Inc., Alcohol & Other Drug Prevention Specialists, 522
**Alcohol/Gambling**
Arnie Wexler — Arnie & Sheila Wexler Associates, 291
**Alcoholics at Work**
Stephen Viscusi - Workplace Expert , Life Coach , Career Coach & Headhunter, 394
**Alcoholism**
Robert DeLetis, Addictions Expert, 529
Marilyn Redmond, Healing and Spiritual Growth, 525
**Alcoholism Treatment**
Caron Foundation, 521
**Alcoholism/Drug Abuse**
Robert DeLetis, Addictions Expert, 529
Cindy Kubica, Stress Management & Communications Expert, 475
Susan Neri-Friedwald CHT. (NGH, ABH, IMDHA, IACT) Behavior Modification Expert, 530
Susie Vanderlip -- Teen & Parenting Skills Expert, 531
**Alcoholism/Substance Abuse**
Robert DeLetis, Addictions Expert, 529
Susan Neri-Friedwald CHT. (NGH, ABH, IMDHA, IACT) Behavior Modification Expert, 530
**Alcohol/Women**
Jean Cirillo, Ph.D. -- The Love Nanny, 530
**Alien Beings**
Fund for UFO Research, Inc., 544

**Aliens/Legal And Illegal**
Americans for Immigration Control, Inc., 253
**Alimony Maintenance**
Jamie S Lapin, CDP, CFP Risk Management Group, Inc., 278
**Alimony/Maintenance**
American Academy of Matrimonial Lawyers, 232
**Alkalize**
Networking By Images, 473
**All Star Game**
Sports Travel and Tours, 284
**Allergies**
Endometriosis Association, 518
Patricia Ann Hellinger, Expert on Immune System Deficiencies, 512
William A. Kent, THE TRUTH: Drugs Can Kill - Foods Can Heal, 498
Keith Nabe -- Flu Expert, 519
**Allergy**
American Academy of Allergy, Asthma & Immunology (AAAAI)., 514
Food Allergy Initiative, 267
Murray Grossan, MD — Tower Ear Nose Throat — Cedars Sinai, 516
**Allergy Diseases**
Food Allergy Initiative, 267
**Allergy Survival Tips**
American Academy of Allergy, Asthma & Immunology (AAAAI)., 514
**Alternative Cancer Treatment**
A.P. John Institute for Cancer Research, 512
**Alternative Careers-Actors**
Stephen Viscusi - Workplace Expert , Life Coach , Career Coach & Headhunter, 394
**Alternative Education**
Alternative Education Resource Organization, 184
Bo Lebo -- New Life Options -- Literacy Expert, 187
National Council for the Social Studies, 182
**Alternative Fuels**
Dr. Jay Lehr — TechnoFuturist, Environmental Scientist, 326
**Alternative Healing**
Independent Scholars of Asia, Inc., 247
David M. Jacobson, MSW, 474
Denise Lamothe, Psy.D, H.H.D. - Emotional Eating Specialist, 487
Evana Maggiore -- Fashion Feng Shui International, 452
Bo Martinsen, MD & Anne-Marie Chalmers, MD — Omega 3 Fish Oil Experts, 504
Medical Research Associaties, LLC, 506
Marilyn Redmond, Healing and Spiritual Growth, 525
**Alternative Health**
Dr. Charles Bens -- Health, Nutrition & Smoking Expert, 514
Dr. George V. Dubouch, Ph.D. -- Health & Wellness Expert, 490
Tim Ferriss - Fitness , Nutrition & Lifestyle Expert, 488
Loree Taylor Jordan, C.C.H., I.D, 496

**Bioinformatics**
Biotechnology Industry Organization, 204

**Biological Clock**
Bio Brite Inc., 520

**Biological Terrorism**
Dr. Jay Lehr — TechnoFuturist, Environmental Scientist, 326

**Biological Weapons**
American Industrial Hygiene Association, 502

**Biomedical**
UT Southwestern Medical Center, 505

**Biomedical Research**
Biotechnology Industry Organization, 204

**Biosecurity**
Institute of Food Technologists, 267

**Biosolids**
Water Environment Federation, 254

**Biotech**
Cerulean Associates LLC, 450
Tim Ferriss - Fitness , Nutrition & Lifestyle Expert, 488
Sol Weiss, Author, Inventor, Medical Doctor, 544

**Biotechnology**
American Academy of Anti-Aging Medicine, 519
Biotechnology Industry Organization, 204
ORYXE Energy International, 258
Technolytics -- Kevin G. Coleman, 342

**Biotechnology Patents**
Biotechnology Industry Organization, 204

**Biotechnology/Food**
Biotechnology Industry Organization, 204
Competitive Enterprise Institute, 206
Dr. Jay Lehr — TechnoFuturist, Environmental Scientist, 326

**Bioterrorism**
Dr. George V. Dubouch, Ph.D. -- Health & Wellness Expert, 490

**Bird Flu Cures**
Verona Fonte Ph.D. — Bird Flu Expert, 510

**Bird Flu Expert**
Verona Fonte Ph.D. — Bird Flu Expert, 510
Keith Nabe -- Flu Expert, 519

**Bird Flu Outbreak**
Verona Fonte Ph.D. — Bird Flu Expert, 510

**Bird Flu What To Do**
Verona Fonte Ph.D. — Bird Flu Expert, 510

**Birds**
World Wide Pet Industry Association, Inc., 264

**Birth Control**
American Life League, 216
Dave E. David, M.D., 510
Tom Nardone — Online Privacy Expert, 340

**Bishops**
Catholic Traditionalist Movement, Inc., 200

**Black Bears**
Center for Wildlife Information, 253

**Black Entrepreneurship**
Melvin J. Gravely, II, Ph.D. - Institute For Entrepreneurial Thinking, LTD., 422

**Black Families**
Lenora Madison Poe, Ph.D., 531

**Black Grandparents**
Lenora Madison Poe, Ph.D., 531

**Black History**
Veritas Institute, Inc., 368

**Black History Month Events**
Black Speakers Online, 328

**Black Leadership**
Carol M. Swain — Vanderbilt University Law School, 220

**Black Motivational Speakers**
Black Speakers Online, 328

**Black Speaker Bureau**
Black Speakers Online, 328

**Blackjack**
Frank Scoblete -- Casino Gambling Expert, 290

**Blacks in Advertising**
Dr. Marilyn Kern Foxworth, APR, Communications & Marketing Expert, 316

**Blacksmithing**
Doug Butler --Horseshoeing Expert, 263

**Blessing of Abraham**
Islam In Focus, 248

**Blind**
American Council of the Blind, 518
The Foundation Fighting Blindness, Inc., 516
The Seeing Eye, 516

**Blind Dates**
George B. Blake -- Single Again, 538

**Blind People/Dog Guides**
The Seeing Eye, 516

**Blindness**
National Library Service for the Blind and Physically Handicapped, 516

**Blog**
Carol Bradley Bursack - Caregiving Expert, 480
CityCast Media — Podcasts, Webcasts, Blogs, & RSS Technologies, 340
Shawn Collins — Affiliate Program Expert, 349
David Meerman Scott -- Strategic Internet Marketing Consultant, 348
Debbie Weil-- Corporate Blogging Expert, 349

**Blogging**
Room 214, Inc. - Social Media Experts, 436
Joan Stewart -- The Publicity Hound, 312
Denise Wakeman — The Blog Squad, 339

**Blogging for Business**
Joan Stewart -- The Publicity Hound, 312

**Blogs**
Denise Wakeman — The Blog Squad, 339

**Blood Donation**
American Red Cross, 192

**Blood Donors**
Pan American Health Organization, 192

**Blue Book**
Richard Marquis -- College Success Expert, 183

**Blues Music**
Chika Obodozie, 272

**Board Certified**
Byron J. Richards, CCN - Leptin & Nutrition Expert, 488

**Board Games**
Nicole Casanova - Entrepreneur & Relationship Expert, 537
Don't Quote Me -- Quote Experts, 292

**Board of Directors**
Executive Coaching & Consulting Associates, 308
Thin Book Publishing Company, 307

**Boarding Schools**
Independent Educational Consultants Association (IECA), 182

**Boating**
Sailboat Incorporated, 285

**Boating Accident**
TASA (Technical Advisory Service for Attorneys), 220

**Boating Engines**
Volvo Group North America, 281

**Body Fat Composition**
American Society of Bariatric Physicians, 490

**Body Image**
Joyce Knudsen, Ph.D., AICI, CIM, Image & Assessments, 455
Evana Maggiore -- Fashion Feng Shui International, 452
Carolyn Strauss- Entrepreneur/ Speaker, 482

**Body Image/Self-Acceptance**
Nili Sachs, Ph.D., 484

**Body Image/Self-Esteem**
Dianne M. Daniels, AICI, 484
Susan Neri-Friedwald CHT. (NGH, ABH, IMDHA, IACT) Behavior Modification Expert, 530

**Body Language**
Olivia Fox Cabane - Communications Expert & Networking Expert, 460
Maxine Lucille Fiel, B.A. -- Body Language Expert, 484
Gestech, Inc., 455
Heather Harder, Ph.D., Author, Speaker, and Consultant, 184
Lynne Marks, Image and Branding, 482
Patti Wood — Communication Dynamics, 466
Kate Zabriskie - Training Seminars, Workshops, and Keynotes, 390

**Body Language & Deception**
Stan B. Walters 'The Lie Guy', 228

**Body Language Expert**
Linda Talley, CSP -- Texas Leadership Coach, 455
Patti Wood — Communication Dynamics, 466

# C

Paul D. Slocumb, Ed.D., Educational
Crisis for Boys, 186
**Childhold**
F. Felicia Ferrara, Ph.D., 473
**Childhood**
Mary Ann LoFrumento, MD -
Pediatrician and Parenting Expert,
533
**Childhood Disease**
Mary Ann LoFrumento, MD -
Pediatrician and Parenting Expert,
533
**Childhood Diseases**
Food Allergy Initiative, 267
**Childhood Fears**
Mary Ann LoFrumento, MD -
Pediatrician and Parenting Expert,
533
**Childhood Obesity**
Caroline J. Cederquist, M.D., 488
Denise Lamothe, Psy.D, H.H.D. -
Emotional Eating Specialist, 487
Swimtastic Swim School, 486
**Childhood Trauma**
Robert R. Butterworth, Ph.D., 522
**Childhood Violence**
Robert R. Butterworth, Ph.D., 522
**Child-Parent Advocacy**
Myrna T. McCulloch, Director, The
Riggs Institute, 184
**Child/Parental Kidnapping**
Operation Lookout ® National Center
for Missing Youth, 188
**Children**
aha! Process, Inc. — Publishing &
training on economic diversity, 187
Cheli Cerra -- Child Success Expert,
191
CureSearch National Childhood
Cancer Foundation, 519
The Dream Factory, Inc., 188
Dream Merchant New Product
Guidance, 402
Dr. Frank Farley, 523
Debra Holtzman, J.D., M.A. -- Child
Safety Expert, 191
Institute for Childhood Resources, 292
International Nanny Association -- Pat
Cascio, President, 533
Debra Kimbrough -- Child Care Safety
Expert, 190
Dianne Linderman - Parenting Expert
& Author, 533
Mary Ann LoFrumento, MD -
Pediatrician and Parenting Expert,
533
Love and Logic Institute, 531
MENC: The National Association for
Music Education, 299
National Association of Social
Workers, 522
National Council for the Social
Studies, 182
Dr. Michael Nuccitelli, Licensed
Psychologist, 522
Swimtastic Swim School, 486
TeamChildren — Philadelphia Youth
Charity, 190
Young Marines, 246

**Children & Trauma**
Kaneta R. Lott, DDS -- Pediatric
Dentist, Banker, 532
**Children Advocates**
United Christian Services, Inc., 196
**Children and Youth**
Volunteers of America, 192
Young Marines, 246
**Children as Consumers**
Robert R. Butterworth, Ph.D., 522
Dr. Audrey Guskey, 430
**Children At Risk**
Gestech, Inc., 455
**Children Child**
Dr. Jamie Johnson -- The Dental Diva,
506
**Children Health**
Debra Holtzman, J.D., M.A. —
Corporate Spokesperson, 320
**Children In Poverty**
aha! Process, Inc. — Publishing &
training on economic diversity, 187
Association for Supervision and
Curriculum Development (ASCD),
181
**Children Massage**
TeamChildren — Philadelphia Youth
Charity, 190
**Children of Gay Parents**
Robert A. Bernstein -- Families of
Value, 198
**Children Security**
The Safety Minute Seminars, 239
**Children, Yours and Mine**
International Personal Development -
Ivan Burnell, 474
**Children/Adolescents**
100 Jobs For Kids & Young Adults—A
Self-Empowerment Tool, 366
**Children/Adoption**
National Adoption Center, 188
**Children/Advertising**
Robert R. Butterworth, Ph.D., 522
**Children/Art Materials**
The Art and Creative Materials
Institute, Inc., 291
**Children/Body Language**
Gestech, Inc., 455
**Children/Child**
Carole Lieberman, M.D., Media
Psychiatrist, 523
**Children/Cooking/Healthy**
Lynn Fischer's Healthy Living, Inc.,
487
**Children/Crime**
Paul D. Slocumb, Ed.D., Educational
Crisis for Boys, 186
**Children/Grandparents**
Lenora Madison Poe, Ph.D., 531
**Children/Guns**
Brady Campaign to Prevent Gun
Violence, 214
Mary Ann LoFrumento, MD -
Pediatrician and Parenting Expert,
533
**Children/Health**
The Dream Factory, Inc., 188
Debra Holtzman, J.D., M.A. -- Child
Safety Expert, 191

**Children/Marketing**
WonderGroup Youth Marketing and
Advertising, 438
**Children/Missing**
Operation Lookout ® National Center
for Missing Youth, 188
**Children/Nutrition**
Caroline J. Cederquist, M.D., 488
Mary Ann LoFrumento, MD -
Pediatrician and Parenting Expert,
533
Kaneta R. Lott, DDS -- Pediatric
Dentist, Banker, 532
**Children/Parenting**
Elayne Savage, Ph.D., The Rejection
Expert, 528
**Children/Parents**
Institute for Creative Solutions --
Randy Rolfe, 524
**Children/Recreation**
The Dream Factory, Inc., 188
**Children's Activities**
Young Marines, 246
**Children's Books**
Deb Capone, 190
Debra Kimbrough -- Child Care Safety
Expert, 190
Brian Taylor, Publishing Industry
Consultant & Book Marketer, 322
**Children's Education**
Educational Adventures, 190
**Children's Entertainment**
Educational Adventures, 190
**Children's Literature**
Marymount University, 180
**Children's Music**
Debra Kimbrough -- Child Care Safety
Expert, 190
**Children's Products**
Debra Holtzman, J.D., M.A. —
Corporate Spokesperson, 320
Debra Holtzman, J.D., M.A. -- Child
Safety Expert, 191
Institute for Childhood Resources, 292
Keith E. Nabe - Management
Consultant/Public Speaker, 412
**Children/Self-Esteem**
Debra Kimbrough -- Child Care Safety
Expert, 190
**Children/Television**
Dr. Toni Leonetti — Founder, Human
Potential International, 475
Mary Ann LoFrumento, MD -
Pediatrician and Parenting Expert,
533
**Children/Trauma**
Dr. Elizabeth Carll, Stress and Trauma
Expert, 476
**Children/Violence**
Dr. Elizabeth Carll, Stress and Trauma
Expert, 476
Mary Ann LoFrumento, MD -
Pediatrician and Parenting Expert,
533
**China**
Association on Third World Affairs
(A.T.W.A.), 246
Chin-Ning Chu —- Asian Marketing
Consultants, 428
Radio Free Asia, 301

**Civil Society**
Center for Civil Society & Governance at AED, 250
Forums Institute for Public Policy, 203

**Civil War**
History Publishing Company, LLC, 303

**Civil War Battles**
History Publishing Company, LLC, 303

**Civility**
Etiquette International, 453
Humanists of Florida Association, 199

**Civility and Desk Rage**
Laura Stack, MBA, CSP, The Productivity PRO, 395

**Civility/Manners**
Dr. John E. Mayer -- Expert on Youth & Parenting, 532

**Claims Adjuster**
R. A. Martinez, Homeowners Insurance Expert, 270

**Claims Representative**
R. A. Martinez, Homeowners Insurance Expert, 270

**Clairvoyant**
Petrene Soames, author of The Essence of Self-Healing, 544

**Class Actions**
Baum Hedlund, A Professional Corporation, 234
Eliot Disner -- McGuireWoods LLP, 222
Paul Young -- Securities Arbitration Commentator, 228

**Classes**
National Association of Tax Professionals (NATP), 360

**Classical Education**
Calvert School, 186

**Classroom Tips**
National Education Association - NEA, 179

**Clean Air Issues**
Edison Electric Institute, 258
ORYXE Energy International, 258

**Clean Comedian**
Lola Gillebaard - Humorist & Motivational Speaker, 380

**Clean Water Act**
Dr. Jay Lehr — TechnoFuturist, Environmental Scientist, 326
Water Environment Federation, 254

**Clergy/Episcopal Priest**
R. Brent and Company Publishing, 307

**Clergy's Abuse of Religion**
R. Brent and Company Publishing, 307

**Clergy's Abuse of Religions**
Zoe Rastegar — Talk Show Host, 248

**Clidren's Health Care**
Dr. Marlene M. Coleman, M.D. - Harbor Pediatric Medical Group, 190

**Client Loyalty**
Andrew Sobel, 444

**Client Relationships**
Andrew Sobel, 444

**Client Retention**
Stan Craig — Performance Leadership Speaker, 350

Andrew Sobel, 444

**Client Service**
Stan Craig — Performance Leadership Speaker, 350

**Climate**
NOAA Public Affairs, 262

**Climate Change**
Alliance to Save Energy, 256
Jim Reed - Severe & Unusual Weather, 261

**Clinical Guidelines**
American Thoracic Society, 515

**Clinical Insanity**
Leon Pomeroy, Ph.D., 212

**Clinical Nutritionist**
Byron J. Richards, CCN - Leptin & Nutrition Expert, 488

**Clinical Psychologist**
Dr. John M. Presley - Peace Advocate, 250

**Clinical Supervision**
National Board for Certified Counselors, Inc. and Affiliates, 524

**Clinical Trials**
Breast Care Specialists, 512
MCMC llc., 500

**Cloche**
Headwear Information Bureau — Bush Casey, 296

**Clockwise Pattern**
Frank Jakubowsky, Author, 542

**Cloning**
American Life League, 216
International Academy of Anti-Aging Medicine, 519
Dr. David Stevens — Christian Medical Association, 506

**Closed Circuit TV**
James M. Atkinson, 242

**Closing a Law Practice**
Edward Poll, J.D., M.B.A.., CMC -- Law Firm Management Expert, 223

**Closing The Sale**
Jim Meisenheimer — Creator of No-Brainer Selling Skills, 460

**Clover**
Carolyn Finch — Body Language Expert, 484

**Cluster Headache**
National Headache Foundation, 510

**Clutter**
Dorothy Breininger - Center for Organization and Goal Planning, 472
Carol M. Olmstead -- Feng Shui For Real Life, 452
The Procrastinator's Handbook — Rita Emmett, 471
PUBLISIDE Personal Publicity, Gail Sideman, 318

**CMC**
Institute of Management Consultants USA, Inc., 411

**Coach**
Patricia R. Adson, Ph.D., Adson Coaching and Consulting, 404
Terry L. Anna CDMP - Professional Business & Life Journey Coach, 448

Olivia Fox Cabane - Communications Expert & Networking Expert, 460
Coach and Grow R.I.C.H., 404
Coaching Insider, 400
Marsha Egan, Success & Executive Coach, 405
Loren Ekroth - Conversation & Communications Expert, 460
Ms. Bert Fife - Consultant, Speaker, Coach, 468
Laura Berman Fortgang - The Life Blueprint Institute, 446
Gary Griffin - On Turnaround Management, 410
Jim Jacobus — Human Performance Improvement Expert, 424
Terri Levine, CEO of Comprehensive Coaching U. Inc., 408
Mariposa Leadership, 405

**Coach Credentialing**
International Coach Federation, 405

**Coach Training**
Laura Berman Fortgang - The Life Blueprint Institute, 446

**Coaches**
Dr. Maynard Brusman - Workplace Expert, 376

**Coaches with PCC's**
Dr. Maynard Brusman - Workplace Expert, 376

**Coach/Executive**
Michael R. Martorella, Executive Coach & Advisor — MMI Communication, 408

**Coaching**
AchieveMentors, Inc., Leslie Furlow, RN, Ph.D., 384
Patricia R. Adson, Ph.D., Adson Coaching and Consulting, 404
Attention Deficit Disorder Association, 186
Barry Demp Coaching, LLC — Detroit Life Coach, 449
Dorothy Breininger - Center for Organization and Goal Planning, 472
Karma Brown, The Strategic Coach, 404
Career Coach Institute, 366
Nicole Casanova - Entrepreneur & Relationship Expert, 537
Dr. Alden M. Cass, President of Catalyst Strategies Group, 406
Change Masters Incorporated, 396
Coach and Grow R.I.C.H., 404
Coaching Insider, 400
Coaching Makes a Difference, 398
June Davidson, American Seminar Leaders Association, 330
Aviva Diamond — Blue Streak/A Communications Company, 471
Diane DiResta — Training Coach, 471
Loren Ekroth - Conversation & Communications Expert, 460
Giant Leap Consulting, 448
Robert S. Grossman — Business Performance Expert, 388
International Coach Federation, 405
Ruth King - BusinessTVChannel.com, 422

# E

# G

# H

**Horse Welfare**
Doug Butler --Horseshoeing Expert, 263

**Horses**
Doug Butler --Horseshoeing Expert, 263
Equissage, Inc., 263

**Horseshoeing**
Doug Butler --Horseshoeing Expert, 263

**Hospice**
Carol Bradley Bursack - Caregiving Expert, 480
M. Tray Dunaway, MD, FACS, CSP, CHCO Healthcare Driving Doctors Crazy, 502
J. Shep Jeffreys, Ed.D. -- Grief Expert, 541

**Hospital**
Helen Hayes Hospital, 502

**Hospital Cost Expert**
Nan Andrews Amish —-  Health Care Cost Expert, 500

**Hospital Security**
The Safety Minute Seminars, 239

**Hospital-Doctor Relations**
M. Tray Dunaway, MD, FACS, CSP, CHCO Healthcare Driving Doctors Crazy, 502

**Hospitals**
CureSearch National Childhood Cancer Foundation, 519
M. Tray Dunaway, MD, FACS, CSP, CHCO Healthcare Driving Doctors Crazy, 502
Pete Silver — Marketing Communications Writer, 450

**Hosptials/Good/Bad**
Joseph Werner -- Creator of the term: Silent Majority, 212

**Host**
Dave E. David, M.D., 510

**Hostile Workplace**
Lynda McDermott, Author, Expert on Leadership & Teams, 422

**Hosting**
Christopher Faulkner, C I Host, 342

**Hot Water**
National Oilheat Research Alliance, 258

**Hotel Construction**
Theodore W Garrison, III - Construction Expert - Strategic Planning, 279

**Hotels**
www.YourSpaGuide.com, 492

**Hotels and Hospitality**
Harriet Lessy - BuzzCommunications, 318

**House Cleaning**
CommuniCard, 462

**House Fluffing**
Debra Gould - The Staging Diva ™, 272

**House Stager**
Debra Gould - The Staging Diva ™, 272

**House Staging**
Debra Gould - The Staging Diva ™, 272

**House Staging Business**
Debra Gould - The Staging Diva ™, 272

**House Staging Course**
Debra Gould - The Staging Diva ™, 272

**House Staging Seminar**
Debra Gould - The Staging Diva ™, 272

**House Staging Training**
Debra Gould - The Staging Diva ™, 272

**Household Chemicals**
KHB Consulting Services, 260

**Household Employer Taxes**
Stephanie Breedlove - Household Employment Tax Expert, 360

**Household Employment Law**
Stephanie Breedlove - Household Employment Tax Expert, 360

**Household Help**
Stephanie Breedlove - Household Employment Tax Expert, 360
Marta Perrone - Domestic Connections Publications, 252

**Household Payroll**
Stephanie Breedlove - Household Employment Tax Expert, 360

**Household Planning**
John Longenecker — Author and Columnist on Personal Sovereignty., 214

**Household Privacy/Authority**
John Longenecker — Author and Columnist on Personal Sovereignty., 214

**Household Staff**
Stephanie Breedlove - Household Employment Tax Expert, 360

**Housekeeper Taxes**
Stephanie Breedlove - Household Employment Tax Expert, 360

**Housekeepers**
Marta Perrone - Domestic Connections Publications, 252

**Housewife**
EllynAnne Geisel -- Not So Desperate Housewife a/k/a the Apron Lady, 303

**Housewives**
EllynAnne Geisel -- Not So Desperate Housewife a/k/a the Apron Lady, 303

**Housing**
Alternative Living for the Aging, 520
The Financial Services Roundtable, 354
Habitat for Humanity International, 276
National Multi Housing Council, 276
Timberland Design, 270

**Housing Alternatives**
Alternative Living for the Aging, 520

**Housing Finance**
National Multi Housing Council, 276

**Housing for the Elderly**
Alternative Living for the Aging, 520

**Housing Policy**
National Multi Housing Council, 276

**Housing Prices/Values**
Massachusetts Association of Realtors, 270

**Housing Starts**
Anthony Hsieh - Loans and Personal Finance Expert, 352

**Houston Cultural Tourism**
WorldFest-Houston, 298

**How to Flirt**
Dr. Susan Campbell, Dating & Relationship Coach, 535

**How to get a Raise**
Stephen Viscusi - Workplace Expert , Life Coach , Career Coach & Headhunter, 394

**How to Get Rich**
Gail Howard -- Lottery Expert, 291

**How to Win**
Gail Howard -- Lottery Expert, 291

**How's Your Laugh Life?**
Karen Susman — Karen Susman & Associates, 376

**How-To Ideas**
Debra Holtzman, J.D., M.A. — Corporate Spokesperson, 320

**HR-Process**
Sven Ringling — iProCon GmbH, 416

**Human Behavior**
Jim Jacobus — Human Performance Improvement Expert, 424

**Human Capital**
David Nour -- Relationship Economics Expert, 458

**Human Capital and Empowerment**
Brenda Campbell — Management Consulting and Information Technology, 368

**Human Capital Management**
Financial Voyages, LLC., 430

**Human Embryo**
Dr. John A. Henderson M.D. - God & Religion Expert, 199

**Human Performance**
American Academy of Anti-Aging Medicine, 519

**Human Potential**
American Academy of Anti-Aging Medicine, 519
Jeff Korhan -- Grow from What You Know, 406
Dr. Toni Leonetti — Founder, Human Potential International, 475
Geela Parish, Author, 332

**Human Potentials**
American Academy of Anti-Aging Medicine, 519

**Human Resource Consulting**
Abbott, Langer & Associates, Inc. — Salary and Benefits Survey Experts, 373
Astron Solutions - Human Resource Consulting, 386
Sven Ringling — iProCon GmbH, 416

**Human Resource Management**
Kevin Joyce, Management Consultant and Organizational Change Expert, 384

**Human Resources**
AchieveMentors, Inc., Leslie Furlow, RN, Ph.D., 384

# K

**K-12 Teaching and Learning**
Association for Supervision and Curriculum Development (ASCD), 181

**Kahuna**
Personal Transformation Press, 500

**Karma**
Lissa Coffey -- Lifestyle Designer, 534
Walter Semkiw, MD -- Reincarnation Expert, 546

**Kashmir**
Imran Anwar / IMRAN.TV, 248

**Kennedy/Unseal Files**
Joseph Werner -- Creator of the term: Silent Majority, 212

**Kern-Foxworth**
Dr. Marilyn Kern Foxworth, APR, Communications & Marketing Expert, 316

**Ketogenic Diet**
Epilepsy Foundation, 515

**Keynote**
Diane DiResta — Training Coach, 471
Wolf Rinke Associates, 475

**Keynote Presentations**
Dan Stockdale — Business Relationship Expert, 402

**Keynote Speaker**
Ageless Lifestyles Institute - Dr. Michael Brickey, 476
Esther M. Berger -- The MoneySmart Expert, 356
Dr. Joyce Brothers, 522
Frank C. Bucaro & Associates, Inc., 202
Chin-Ning Chu —- Asian Marketing Consultants, 428
Debra Holtzman, J.D., M.A. — Corporate Spokesperson, 320
John Patrick Dolan - Negotiate like the Pros, 382
Laura Berman Fortgang - The Life Blueprint Institute, 446
Polly Franks - Crime Victim Advocate & Child Safety Expert, 188
Lola Gillebaard - Humorist & Motivational Speaker, 380
Melvin J. Gravely, II, Ph.D. - Institute For Entrepreneurial Thinking, LTD., 422
International Academy of Anti-Aging Medicine, 519
Jim Jacobus — Human Performance Improvement Expert, 424
Diana Kirschner, Ph.D. - Psychologist & Love Expert, 538
Cindy Kubica, Stress Management & Communications Expert, 475
Sylvia L. Lovely — Expert on Cities, 276
National Speakers Association, Washington D.C. Area Chapter, 378
Jay Platt — Inspiring People To Be Unstoppable...No Matter What!, 468
Peter Ressler & Monika Mitchell Ressler, 424

Wolf Rinke Associates, 475
Nili Sachs, Ph.D., 484
Dan Stockdale — Business Relationship Expert, 402
Linda Talley, CSP -- Texas Leadership Coach, 455
Thin Book Publishing Company, 307
Jim Thomas, Negotiate to Win, 412
Norma Tillman -- Private Investigator, 240
Jodi Walker, Certified Professional Speaker, 468
Steve Waterhouse, 460
Wiest & Associates Inc.,The Customer Acquisition and Retention Company™, 444
Mikki Williams Unltd. * Vistage International * Coaching, etc..., 330

**Keynote Speakers**
Carol Grace Anderson, M.A., 454
Carol Bradley Bursack - Caregiving Expert, 480
Olivia Fox Cabane - Communications Expert & Networking Expert, 460
Prof. William Crossman - Futurist & Talking Computers ExpertTalking Computers Expert, 341
Debra Benton -- Leadership Development Expert, 313
Speaker Bank — Your Professional Keynote Speaker Source, 326
SpeakerLeads.com, 328
Dottie Walters — Walters Speaker Services, 330

**Keynote Speaking**
Nelson Motivation, Inc., 386

**Keynotes Speaker**
Ellen A. Kaye and Perfect Presentation, 470

**Keys to Confidence**
Carolyn Stein -- The Training Express, 388

**Keyword**
Broadcast Interview Source, Inc. — Publisher of the Yearbook of Experts, 460

**Kidnapping**
SWS Security, 242

**Kidnapping Help**
Jeffery M. Leving — Fathers' Rights, 540

**Kidney Health**
American Kidney Fund, 508

**Kidney Stones**
American Kidney Fund, 508

**Kidney Transplants**
American Kidney Fund, 508

**Kids**
100 Jobs For Kids & Young Adults—A Self-Empowerment Tool, 366
Debra Holtzman, J.D., M.A. — Corporate Spokesperson, 320
WonderGroup Youth Marketing and Advertising, 438

**Kids Consultant**
WonderGroup Youth Marketing and Advertising, 438

**Kids Games**
Don't Quote Me -- Quote Experts, 292

**Kids/Advertising**
WonderGroup Youth Marketing and Advertising, 438

**Kids/Marketing**
WonderGroup Youth Marketing and Advertising, 438

**Kinesics**
Gestech, Inc., 455

**King/Unseal Files**
Joseph Werner -- Creator of the term: Silent Majority, 212

**Kitchen Appliances**
Donald Silvers, CKD--Author, Kitchen Design With Cooking in Mind,, 268

**Kitchen Consultant**
Donald Silvers, CKD--Author, Kitchen Design With Cooking in Mind,, 268

**Kitchen Design**
Donald Silvers, CKD--Author, Kitchen Design With Cooking in Mind,, 268

**Kitchen Designer**
Donald Silvers, CKD--Author, Kitchen Design With Cooking in Mind,, 268

**Kitchen Expert**
Donald Silvers, CKD--Author, Kitchen Design With Cooking in Mind,, 268

**Kitchen Remodeling**
American Lighting Association, 271

**Kitchens**
EllynAnne Geisel -- Not So Desperate Housewife a/k/a the Apron Lady, 303
Donald Silvers, CKD--Author, Kitchen Design With Cooking in Mind,, 268

**Kiwanis**
Civitan International, 195

**Knowledge Management**
Brenda Campbell — Management Consulting and Information Technology, 368

**Knowledge Workers**
Thin Book Publishing Company, 307

**Korea**
Radio Free Asia, 301

**Korean Healing**
Dahn Yoga, 499

**Kyoto**
Dr. Jay Lehr — TechnoFuturist, Environmental Scientist, 326

# L

**La Nina**
Alliance to Save Energy, 256

**Labels & Warnings**
KHB Consulting Services, 260

**Labor**
Americans for Democratic Action, 208
National Writers Union, 301
U.S. Chamber of Commerce, 205

**Labor & Emply Relations Law**
Dow Lohnes PLLC, 218

**Labor and Employment**
BNA, Inc., 216

**Labor Economics**
Utica College, 181

**Labor Issues**
The Herman Group -- Strategic Business Futurists, 328

# M

**Riddles**
Mensa, 181

**Right of Self-Defense**
John M. Snyder, Gun Law Expert, 214

**Right to Bear Arms**
John M. Snyder, Gun Law Expert, 214

**Right to Die**
The Funeral Help Program, 541
National Right to Life Committee, 216

**Right to Life**
National Right to Life Committee, 216

**Rights**
Americans for Free Choice in
Medicine, 364

**Rights of Individual**
Leon Pomeroy, Ph.D., 212

**Rights of Society**
Leon Pomeroy, Ph.D., 212

**Risk**
Cheryl Perlitz - Life Change and
Survival Expert, 470

**Risk Assesment**
Threat Assessment, 239

**Risk Assessment**
Outsecure, Inc. Information Security
Consultant, 244

**Risk Management**
Dan Borge — Risk Consultant, 362
Patricia D. Galloway — The
Nielsen-Wurster Group, Inc., 278
LogistiCare, Non-Emergency
Transportation, 281
Jim Lorenzen, CFP®, AIF® - The
Independent Financial Group, 354
Susan M. Mangiero, Ph.D. AVA, CFA,
FRM -- Business Consultant, 362
Keith E. Nabe - Management
Consultant/Public Speaker, 412
National Association of Professional
Insurance Agents, 362
Projectize Group, 428

**Risk Management/Sports**
Alan Goldberger — Referee Law
Expert, 222

**Risk Strategic Management**
Dan Borge — Risk Consultant, 362

**Risk Taking**
Dr. Frank Farley, 523
Giant Leap Consulting, 448
Louis Levy, 480

**Rites**
Masonic Information Center, 201

**Ritual**
Masonic Information Center, 201

**Riverdale, NY**
Eugenia Foxworth, President of The
Greater New York Council of
FIABCI-USA, 274

**Road Rage**
C. Leslie Charles, Author, Speaker,
Consultant, 472
The Safety Minute Seminars, 239

**Roaring 20's Art**
International Coalition of Art Deco
Societies (ICADS), 291

**Robert Louis Stevenson**
Dale Powell - Christmas Storyteller,
Tradition Sharer & Christmas
Trivia, 302

**Rock and Roll**
Dale Bowman — The Life and Death
of Lynyrd Skynyrd bassist Leon
Wilkeson, 299

**Rock Music**
Renee Grant-Williams --
Communication Skill Training
Expert, 466
Music City Community Chorus, 279
Son of the Soil, 279

**Rocky Mountains**
Center for Wildlife Information, 253

**Rodents**
National Pest Management
Association, 262

**Rodin**
Alma H. Bond, Ph.D., 538

**Rogaine and Hair Loss**
Tom Nardone — Online Privacy
Expert, 340

**Roger Mason**
Safe Goods Publishing, 324

**Roid Rage**
Rick Collins, Esq., 521

**Rolfing**
TeamChildren — Philadelphia Youth
Charity, 190

**Roller Coasters**
SeaWorld, Busch Gardens and the
Anheuser-Busch Adventure Park,
286

**Roman Empire/America/Civic**
R. Brent and Company Publishing, 307

**Roman Republic/America**
R. Brent and Company Publishing, 307

**Roman Republic/Civic Virtue**
R. Brent and Company Publishing, 307

**Romance**
George B. Blake -- Single Again, 538
Dr. Ava Cadell, 535
Dandelion Books, LLC - Dynamic
Literature Experts!, 307
Gestech, Inc., 455
International Personal Development -
Ivan Burnell, 474
Dr. Nancy Kalish -- Lost Love Expert,
536
Judith Sherven, Ph.D. & Jim
Sniechowski, Ph.D. — Fear of
Success, 535

**Romance at Work**
Superb Speakers and Consultants
Bureau - Joyce Scott, CEO, 395

**Romance Compatibility Expert**
Kerrin Carleen Hopkins - Personality
Profile Expert, 524

**Romance in the Workplace**
Stephen Viscusi - Workplace Expert ,
Life Coach , Career Coach &
Headhunter, 394

**Ronnie Van Zant**
Dale Bowman — The Life and Death
of Lynyrd Skynyrd bassist Leon
Wilkeson, 299

**Roommate Compatibility Expert**
Kerrin Carleen Hopkins - Personality
Profile Expert, 524

**Roosevelt**
The Bonus Army — An American
Epic, 303

**Rosacea**
Jan Marini -- CEO, Jan Marini Skin
Research, Inc., 492

**Ross, Betsy**
National Flag Foundation, 302

**Roswell**
Fund for UFO Research, Inc., 544

**Rotary**
Civitan International, 195

**Rotator Cup Cuff**
William A. Kent, THE TRUTH: Drugs
Can Kill - Foods Can Heal, 498

**Roulette**
Frank Scoblete -- Casino Gambling
Expert, 290

**Royalty**
Craig Conroy, Conroy Research
Group, 314

**RSS**
CityCast Media — Podcasts,
Webcasts, Blogs, & RSS
Technologies, 340
Room 214, Inc. - Social Media
Experts, 436

**Rubies**
Gemological Institute of America, 294

**Ruby K. Payne**
aha! Process, Inc. — Publishing &
training on economic diversity, 187

**Rudeness**
C. Leslie Charles, Author, Speaker,
Consultant, 472

**Rudeness on the Phone**
Nancy Friedman, Telephone Doctor,
336

**Rules**
Dr. John E. Mayer -- Expert on Youth
& Parenting, 532

**Run**
Jack Nirenstein -- Running Technique
Expert, 486

**Runaways/Street Kids**
Operation Lookout ® National Center
for Missing Youth, 188

**Running**
Mercury Masters — The Running
Team for Women 50+, 518
Jack Nirenstein -- Running Technique
Expert, 486

**Rural**
National Rural Electric Cooperative
Association, 256

**Rural Development**
Sylvia L. Lovely — Expert on Cities,
276
National Rural Electric Cooperative
Association, 256

**Rural Economic Development**
Sylvia L. Lovely — Expert on Cities,
276

**Rural Issues**
Sylvia L. Lovely — Expert on Cities,
276

**Russia/Eastern Europe**
NCSJ: Advocates on Behalf of Jews in
Russia, Ukraine, Baltic, etc, 196

**Russia/Politics**
Utica College, 181

**Satellite Navigation**
Aircraft Owners and Pilots
Association -- AOPA, 284
**Satellite TV tours**
Rick Frishman -- Planned Television
Arts, 314
**Satellites**
NOAA Public Affairs, 262
**SATs**
Steven Roy Goodman, M.S., J.D. —
College Admissions Expert, 182
**Saving Money**
Dr. Audrey Guskey, 430
**Say What You Mean**
Meryl Runion, CSP-- Communication,
Management Leadership Speaker,
470
**SBA**
Penny Pompei — National Women's
Business Center, 218
**Scams**
Cynthia Bercowetz, Identity Theft
Expert, 349
James E. White — Honest Inventor
Help, 396
**Scams/Writing/Publishin**
Brian Taylor, Publishing Industry
Consultant & Book Marketer, 322
**Scenario Analysis**
Arik Johnson — Competitive
Intelligence Consultant, 244
**Scenario Planning**
Arik Johnson — Competitive
Intelligence Consultant, 244
**Scenic Photography**
Greg Lawson -- Worldwide Scenic
Photography, 296
**Scholarship**
Steven Roy Goodman, M.S., J.D. —
College Admissions Expert, 182
**Scholarships**
American Council of the Blind, 518
Bari Meltzer Norman, Ph.D. —
College Admissions Expert, 182
Overseas Press Club of America, 300
**School**
Cheli Cerra -- Child Success Expert,
191
Mary Ann LoFrumento, MD -
Pediatrician and Parenting Expert,
533
**School Bus Accidents**
Baum Hedlund, A Professional
Corporation, 234
**School Bus Safety**
C.A.N.D.I.D.-Citizens AgaiNst Drug
Impaired Drivers, 236
**School Choice**
Bari Meltzer Norman, Ph.D. —
College Admissions Expert, 182
**School Counseling**
Independent Educational Consultants
Association (IECA), 182
National Board for Certified
Counselors, Inc. and Affiliates, 524
Bari Meltzer Norman, Ph.D. —
College Admissions Expert, 182
**School Crisis**
Craig Conroy, Conroy Research
Group, 314

National School Safety and Security
Services -- Ken Trump, 239
Merrill Vargo, Ph.D. — Executive
Director of Springboard Schools,
180
**School Desegregation**
Marymount University, 180
**School Disasters**
Craig Conroy, Conroy Research
Group, 314
**School Discipline**
Dr. John E. Mayer -- Expert on Youth
& Parenting, 532
**School for Romanian Children**
St. Andrew's Foundation of Romania,
191
**School Improvement**
Merrill Vargo, Ph.D. — Executive
Director of Springboard Schools,
180
**School Issues**
Cheli Cerra -- Child Success Expert,
191
**School Leader Preparation**
Merrill Vargo, Ph.D. — Executive
Director of Springboard Schools,
180
**School Loans**
Equal Justice Works (formerly
NAPIL), 228
**School Problems**
Marilyn Redmond, Healing and
Spiritual Growth, 525
Merrill Vargo, Ph.D. — Executive
Director of Springboard Schools,
180
**School Programs**
Merrill Vargo, Ph.D. — Executive
Director of Springboard Schools,
180
**School Reform**
Merrill Vargo, Ph.D. — Executive
Director of Springboard Schools,
180
**School Safety**
National School Safety and Security
Services -- Ken Trump, 239
The Safety Minute Seminars, 239
**School Security**
Howard Services, Security, 244
National School Safety and Security
Services -- Ken Trump, 239
The Safety Minute Seminars, 239
**School Shootings**
Judith Lee Berg -- Human Resource
Communication, 214
Robert R. Butterworth, Ph.D., 522
Howard Services, Security, 244
**School Shopping**
Dr. Audrey Guskey, 430
**School Success**
Cheli Cerra -- Child Success Expert,
191
**School Systems**
Merrill Vargo, Ph.D. — Executive
Director of Springboard Schools,
180
**School Terrorism**
National School Safety and Security
Services -- Ken Trump, 239

**School Violence**
Dr. Elizabeth Carll, Stress and Trauma
Expert, 476
Craig Conroy, Conroy Research
Group, 314
Great Potential Press, Inc., 186
Dr. John E. Mayer -- Expert on Youth
& Parenting, 532
National School Safety and Security
Services -- Ken Trump, 239
Paul D. Slocumb, Ed.D., Educational
Crisis for Boys, 186
**School-Based prevention**
Jeffrey S. Wolfsberg & Associates Inc.,
Alcohol & Other Drug Prevention
Specialists, 522
**School/Boredom**
Merrill Vargo, Ph.D. — Executive
Director of Springboard Schools,
180
**Schools**
The Consummate Consumer, 359
Steven Roy Goodman, M.S., J.D. —
College Admissions Expert, 182
National Council of Teachers of
Mathematics, 179
National Education Association -
NEA, 179
Merrill Vargo, Ph.D. — Executive
Director of Springboard Schools,
180
**Schools and Drugs/Drinking**
Dr. John E. Mayer -- Expert on Youth
& Parenting, 532
**Schools and Parents**
Dr. John E. Mayer -- Expert on Youth
& Parenting, 532
Merrill Vargo, Ph.D. — Executive
Director of Springboard Schools,
180
**Schools/Music**
MENC: The National Association for
Music Education, 299
**Schools/Private**
Independent Educational Consultants
Association (IECA), 182
Bari Meltzer Norman, Ph.D. —
College Admissions Expert, 182
**Schools/Safety**
National School Safety and Security
Services -- Ken Trump, 239
**Schools/Technology**
On-Tech E-Rate Services, 181
PhoChron Yearbooks, 310
**School-Work Transition**
American Association for Career
Education (AACE), 369
**Science**
American Association of
Pharmaceutical Scientists, 505
American Speech-Language-Hearing
Association, 515
Fund for UFO Research, Inc., 544
Bob Heck & Jim Thielman -- The
Theory of Wrong, 536
Frank Jakubowsky, Author, 542
National Science Foundation, 261
NOAA Public Affairs, 262
Leon Pomeroy, Ph.D., 212

**Self-Help Spirituality**
David M. Jacobson, MSW, 474
Denise Lamothe, Psy.D, H.H.D. - Emotional Eating Specialist, 487
Marilyn Redmond, Healing and Spiritual Growth, 525
Lauren Thibodeau, Ph.D. / Princeton Consulting & Therapy, LLC, 464

**Self-Image**
Barbara Thompson -- Personal Empowerment Expert, 487

**Self-Improvement**
Gestech, Inc., 455
Dr. Kenneth S. Kallin-PhD, 191
Robert Paisola's Western Capital Corporate Training Services, 454

**Self-love**
Dandelion Books, LLC - Dynamic Literature Experts!, 307

**Self-Marketing**
Marjorie Brody, CSP, CPAE Speaker Hall of Fame, PCC, 456

**Self-Mastery**
Nicole Casanova - Entrepreneur & Relationship Expert, 537

**Self-Publishing**
AGM Books — Parvez Abedin (India), 306
iUniverse Inc. Book Publisher, 318
National Writers Union, 301
Dan Poynter -- Book Publishing Industry Expert, 305
Small Publishers Association of North America, 306
Cathy Stucker — The Idea Lady, 430

**Self-Publishing Service**
iUniverse Inc. Book Publisher, 318

**Self-Reliance**
Leon Pomeroy, Ph.D., 212

**Sell Ipod**
PodSwap, 305

**Sell My Law Practice Expert**
Edward Poll, J.D., M.B.A.., CMC -- Law Firm Management Expert, 223

**Selling**
Dave Jensen, MS - Sales & Productivity Expert, 370
Jill Konrath -- Selling to Big Companies, 369

**Selling a House**
Randall Bell, Real Estate Damages, 270

**Selling a Law Practice**
Edward Poll, J.D., M.B.A.., CMC -- Law Firm Management Expert, 223

**Selling to Big Companies**
Jill Konrath -- Selling to Big Companies, 369

**Selling Yourself**
Patricia Fripp, 466

**Seminar Leader**
Vincent Muli Kituku, Ph.D., CSP --- Motivational Leadership Speaker, 482

**Seminar Leaders**
David M. Jacobson, MSW, 474
Walter Semkiw, MD -- Reincarnation Expert, 546
Lauren Thibodeau, Ph.D. / Princeton Consulting & Therapy, LLC, 464

**Seminar Leaders/Speakers**
June Davidson, American Seminar Leaders Association, 330

**Seminar Training**
M. Sean Agnew Enterprises LLC, 372
Marjorie Brody, CSP, CPAE Speaker Hall of Fame, PCC, 456
Patricia D. Galloway — The Nielsen-Wurster Group, Inc., 278
David M. Jacobson, MSW, 474
Kris R. Nielsen — The Nielsen-Wurster Group, Inc., 278
The Safety Minute Seminars, 239
Norma Tillman -- Private Investigator, 240

**Seminar Training/Seminars**
June Davidson, American Seminar Leaders Association, 330

**Seminars**
Cerulean Associates LLC, 450
Carol Dunitz, Ph.D -- Effective Business Communication Expert, 333
Joseph F. Dunphy, M.B.A., 356
Live the James Bond Lifestyle, 322
National Speakers Association, 330
Robert Paisola's Western Capital Corporate Training Services, 454
Peter Ressler & Monika Mitchell Ressler, 424
Timothy A. Dimoff — High Risk Security Expert, 238
Dottie Walters — Walters Speaker Services, 330

**Seminars/Parenting**
Love and Logic Institute, 531

**Senior**
Carol Bradley Bursack - Caregiving Expert, 480

**Senior Citizen Jobs**
Stephen Viscusi - Workplace Expert , Life Coach , Career Coach & Headhunter, 394

**Senior Citizen/Gambling**
Arnie Wexler — Arnie & Sheila Wexler Associates, 291

**Senior Citizens**
Alternative Living for the Aging, 520
Jacqueline Marcell - Elder Care, Alzheimer's, Caregiving Expert, 542
Barbara Morris, Pharmacist, Anti-Aging Expert, 480

**Senior Communities**
Alternative Living for the Aging, 520
Stonewall Communities, Inc. - Gay and Lesbian Aging Issues, 520

**Senior Health**
Jacqueline Marcell - Elder Care, Alzheimer's, Caregiving Expert, 542

**Senior Housing**
Alternative Living for the Aging, 520

**Senior Issues**
Dr. David J. Demko, Gerontologist and Editor, AgeVenture News, 478
Jacqueline Marcell - Elder Care, Alzheimer's, Caregiving Expert, 542

**Senior Issues/Cooking/Health**
Lynn Fischer's Healthy Living, Inc., 487

**Senior Leadership Team**
Michael R. Martorella, Executive Coach & Advisor — MMI Communication, 408

**Senior Marketing**
Dr. David J. Demko, Gerontologist and Editor, AgeVenture News, 478
Dr. Audrey Guskey, 430

**Seniors**
Dorothy Breininger - Center for Organization and Goal Planning, 472
The Funeral Help Program, 541
Dr. Nancy Kalish -- Lost Love Expert, 536
Jacqueline Marcell - Elder Care, Alzheimer's, Caregiving Expert, 542
National Association of Social Workers, 522

**Seniors Housing**
Michael Dwight -- Real Estate Speaker, 276

**Sensory**
Sensory Resources, Conferences & Publications on Sensory Dysfunction, 518

**Sensory Dysfunction**
Sensory Resources, Conferences & Publications on Sensory Dysfunction, 518

**Sensory Integration**
Sensory Resources, Conferences & Publications on Sensory Dysfunction, 518

**Sensory Integration Dysfunction**
Sensory Resources, Conferences & Publications on Sensory Dysfunction, 518

**Sensory Messaging**
Sensory Resources, Conferences & Publications on Sensory Dysfunction, 518

**Sensory Processing**
Sensory Resources, Conferences & Publications on Sensory Dysfunction, 518

**Sensory Processing Disorder**
Sensory Resources, Conferences & Publications on Sensory Dysfunction, 518

**Sensory Seeking**
Sensory Resources, Conferences & Publications on Sensory Dysfunction, 518

**Sensory-based Motor Disorder**
Sensory Resources, Conferences & Publications on Sensory Dysfunction, 518

**SEO Expert**
Marc Harty -- PRTraffic.com, 342

**SEO Marketing**
Marc Harty -- PRTraffic.com, 342

**Separated**
Today's Relationships — Russell Price, Jr., 537

**Urban Renewal**
Sylvia L. Lovely — Expert on Cities, 276

**Urban Revitalization**
Sylvia L. Lovely — Expert on Cities, 276

**Urban Sprawl/Smart Growth**
Sylvia L. Lovely — Expert on Cities, 276

**U.S. Bilateral Alliances with Japan**
National Committee on American Foreign Policy, 248

**U.S. Congress**
Advocacy Associates, LLC., 216
Mark Dankof's America, 210

**U.S. Flags**
National Flag Foundation, 302

**U.S. Government**
Advocacy Associates, LLC., 216
Dr. John M. Presley - Peace Advocate, 250

**U.S. Labor History**
National Writers Union, 301

**U.S. Marine Corps**
Networking By Images, 473

**U.S. Postal Service**
Association for Postal Commerce, 203

**U.S. Supreme Court**
Southwestern University School of Law, 220

**U.S. Treasury Department**
William E. Donoghue -- The Father of Safe Money Investing, 350

**U.S. Veterans Reform**
Dr. John M. Presley - Peace Advocate, 250

**USA Film Festivals**
WorldFest-Houston, 298

**Usability**
Mequoda Group — Helping Publishers Harness The Internet, 342

**Usability Guidelines**
Mequoda Group — Helping Publishers Harness The Internet, 342

**U.S.-China-Taiwan Relations and the**
National Committee on American Foreign Policy, 248

**Used Ipods**
PodSwap, 305

**USF**
On-Tech E-Rate Services, 181

**Usher Syndrome**
The Foundation Fighting Blindness, Inc., 516

**Utah**
Robert Paisola's Western Capital Corporate Training Services, 454

**Utilities/Environment**
Edison Electric Institute, 258

**Utilities/Natural Gas**
American Gas Association, 260

**Utility Deregulation**
Edison Electric Institute, 258

**Utility Restructuring**
Alliance to Save Energy, 256
Nuclear Energy Institute (NEI), 258

**Utiltiy Safety**
Carl Potter, CSP, CMC, Certified Safety Professional, 192

# V

**VA Hospitals**
Dr. John M. Presley - Peace Advocate, 250

**VA Medical Centers**
Dr. John M. Presley - Peace Advocate, 250

**Va Statute Religious Freedom**
Council for America's First Freedom, 210

**Vacation Homes**
Hideaways International, Inc., 285
Massachusetts Association of Realtors, 270

**Vacations**
Craig Conroy, Conroy Research Group, 314
Hideaways International, Inc., 285
Sailboat Incorporated, 285
XANADU Enterprises -- Get Paid to Travel, 286
www.YourSpaGuide.com, 492

**Vaccine/Drug Reactions**
National Child Abuse Defense & Resource Center, 189

**Vaccines**
Association of American Physicians and Surgeons, 506
Mary Ann LoFrumento, MD - Pediatrician and Parenting Expert, 533

**Vagus Nerve Stimulator**
Epilepsy Foundation, 515

**Valentine's Day**
Ric Edelman - Radio/TV/Author/ Columnist, 352
Bob Heck & Jim Thielman -- The Theory of Wrong, 536
Diana Kirschner, Ph.D. - Psychologist & Love Expert, 538
Pam Little — Editor - WomensWallStreet.com, 356
Tom Nardone — Online Privacy Expert, 340
Barbara Pachter, Communications Expert, 453
The Procrastinator's Handbook — Rita Emmett, 471
Elayne Savage, Ph.D., The Rejection Expert, 528

**Valentine's Day**
Amy Schoen, CPCC - Dating & Relationship Expert, 537

**Valuation**
Susan M. Mangiero, Ph.D. AVA, CFA, FRM -- Business Consultant, 362
Strategic Management Partners, Inc. - Turnaround Management & Equity Investing Experts, 410

**Value**
Strategic Management Partners, Inc. - Turnaround Management & Equity Investing Experts, 410

**Values**
Frank C. Bucaro & Associates, Inc., 202
Carolyn Finch — Body Language Expert, 484

**Values and Morals**
Leon Pomeroy, Ph.D., 212

**Vantage Score**
Robert Paisola's Western Capital Corporate Training Services, 454

**Vatican**
Seton Hall University, 179

**Vatican Council II**
Catholic Traditionalist Movement, Inc., 200

**Vegetables**
International Fresh-Cut Produce Association, 266
Produce Marketing Association, 266

**Vehicle Maintenance**
National Institute for Automotive Service Excellence (ASE), 281

**Vehicles/Commercial**
Volvo Group North America, 281

**Vehicles/Homeland Security**
Volvo Group North America, 281

**Vendor Fraud**
Intelysis — Fraud Investigators, 242

**Venture Capital**
Intelysis — Fraud Investigators, 242
Strategic Management Partners, Inc. - Turnaround Management & Equity Investing Experts, 410

**Verbal Communication**
Meryl Runion, CSP-- Communication, Management Leadership Speaker, 470

**Verdict Search**
ALMExperts, 220

**Verona Fonte**
Verona Fonte Ph.D. — Bird Flu Expert, 510

**Verry Funny Speaker**
Bob Heck & Jim Thielman -- The Theory of Wrong, 536

**Vertical Search**
Vertical Search Engine, 348

**Very Funny Speaker**
Dale Irvin — Very Funny Speaker, 377

**Veteran Hospitals**
Dr. John M. Presley - Peace Advocate, 250

**Veterans**
The Bonus Army — An American Epic, 303
Networking By Images, 473

**Veterans Advertising**
Veteran's Vision, 246

**Veterans advocacy**
Veteran's Vision, 246

**Veterans Advocacy Organizat**
Veteran's Vision, 246

**Veterans Affairs**
Dr. John M. Presley - Peace Advocate, 250

**Veterans Budget Priorities**
Veteran's Vision, 246

**Veterans Day**
National Flag Foundation, 302

**Veterans Endorsements**
Veteran's Vision, 246

**Veterans Issues**
Daniel New, 210

# LISTINGS

**NATIONAL EDUCATION
ASSOCIATION - NEA**
Washington, DC USA
http://www.nea.org

The National Education Association was founded in 1857 to elevate the character and advance the interest of the profession of teaching and to promote the cause of education in the United States. NEA membership currently stands at 2.6 million. Members include teachers, college faculty, education support professionals, retired educators and students.

Andrew Linebaugh
*Director*
National Education Association
Washington, DC
*Contact Main Phone:* 202-822-7200
*Cell:* 202-550-9428
**Click to Contact from Web Site**

**NATIONAL COUNCIL OF TEACHERS
OF MATHEMATICS**
Reston, VA USA
http://www.nctm.org

NCTM President Francis (Skip) Fennell has experience as a classroom teacher, a principal, and a supervisor of instruction. Dr. Fennell is currently Professor of Education at McDaniel College. Widely published in articles and textbooks related to elementary and middle-grades mathematics education, he has also authored chapters in yearbooks and resource books published by NCTM. Dr. Fennell has been recognized as Maryland's Outstanding Mathematics Educator, McDaniel College's Professor of the Year, and the Carnegie Foundation Professor of the Year.

Gay Dillin
*Media Relations Manager*
National Council of Teachers of Mathematics
Reston, VA
*Contact Phone:* 703-620-9840
*Contact Main Phone:* 703-620-9840
**Click to Contact from Web Site**

**SETON HALL UNIVERSITY**
South Orange, NJ USA
http://www.shu.edu

For 150 years, Seton Hall University has been a catalyst for leadership, developing the whole student - mind, heart and spirit. Only 14 miles from New York City, Seton Hall combines the resources of a large university with the personal attention of a small liberal arts college. A Catholic university, Seton Hall embraces students of all races and religions, challenging each to better the world through integrity, compassion and a commitment to serving others. www.shu.edu

Jill Matthews
Seton Hall University
South Orange, NJ USA
*Contact Phone:* (973) 378-2695
**Click to Contact from Web Site**

## UMASS, AMHERST
Amherst, MA USA
www.umass.edu

A leading center for public higher education in the Northeast, the University of Massachusetts Amherst has gained a reputation for excellence in a growing number of fields, for its wide and varied academic offerings, and for its expanding historic roles in education, research, and public service. The flagship campus of the Commonwealth's University system, the University of Massachusetts Amherst is a major research university enrolling 24,000 students, from all 50 United States and over 100 countries. Its 10 schools and colleges offer 88 undergraduate majors, 68 master's and 48 doctoral programs. Sponsored research activities total more than $100 million a year. Located on 1,450-acres in the scenic Pioneer Valley of Western Massachusetts, the campus provides a rich cultural environment in a rural setting close to major urban centers. As a member of the Five College consortium, the university shares a mutually rewarding relationship with students from Amherst, Hampshire, Mount Holyoke, and Smith colleges.

Cristina Geso
*Executive Director, Alumni Association*
UMass Amherst
Amherst, MA USA
*Contact Phone:* 413-545-2317
**Click to Contact from Web Site**

## HOFSTRA UNIVERSITY
Hempstead, NY USA
www.hofstra.edu

Hofstra University, a private college located approximately 25 miles east of Manhattan, has Schools of Business, Law, Communications, Education and Liberal Arts and Sciences. Faculty experts can address issues such as the Middle East; economics, ethics, relationship issues; constitutional and criminal law; and education. Experts appear in a wide variety of local and national broadcast outlets, newspapers and magazines. The Hofstra Web site at www.hofstra.edu features a newsroom with video clips of top faculty experts.

Ginny Greenberg
Hofstra University
Hempstead, NY USA
*Contact Phone:* 516-463-6819
**Click to Contact from Web Site**

## MERRILL VARGO, PH.D. — EXECUTIVE DIRECTOR OF SPRINGBOARD SCHOOLS
San Francisco, CA USA
http://www.SpringboardSchools.org

Dr. Merrill Vargo, Executive Director of Springboard Schools, is both an experienced academic and a practical expert in the field of school reform. She has taught English, managed her own consultancy, and has directed several education programs, including in the California Department of Education. A tireless advocate for learning and for public schools, Dr. Vargo consistently champions the needs of children, including children growing up in poverty, children of color, and English Language Learners.

Ben Delaney
*Director of Marketing and Communications*
Springboard Schools
San Francisco, CA USA
*Contact Phone:* 415 348-5508
*Contact Main Phone:* 415 348-5500
**Click to Contact from Web Site**

## MARYMOUNT UNIVERSITY
Washington, DC USA
www.marymount.edu

Marymount University in Arlington, Virginia, has media-savvy faculty experts who can speak with authority on a wide variety of topics. Areas of expertise include business ethics, school desegregation, Irish-American history, forensic science and forensic psychology, healthcare issues, Arthurian legends, the effects of media on children, child development and children's literature, presidential debates, and college admissions trends. For assistance finding an expert in a particular field, contact Laurie Callahan at 703-284-1648 or laurie.callahan@marymount.edu.

Laurie Callahan
*Director of Public Relations*
Marymount University
Arlington, VA USA
*Contact Phone:* 703-284-1648
**Click to Contact from Web Site**

## ANTIOCH NEW ENGLAND GRADUATE SCHOOL
Keene, NH USA
http://www.antiochne.edu

Antioch New England Graduate School is a pioneer in the education of adult learners. It offers scholarly, innovative, practice-oriented masters programs in clinical psychology, education, environmental studies, and management; and doctoral programs in applied psychology and environmental studies. Faculty are academicians and practicioners with disciplinary expertise in mental health practice, educational reform, environmental issues and resource management, and organizational leadership, including the non-profit sector. In addition, faculty experts with media experience can be provided on a wide variety of topics including professional training; adult development; life structure relationships; affective, behavioral and cognitive domains; and experiential learning.

Elizabeth BelleIsle
*Director of PR & Marketing*
Antioch New England Graduate School
Keene, NH
*Contact Phone:* 603-357-3122
**Click to Contact from Web Site**

## UNIVERSITY OF PORTLAND
Portland, OR USA
www.up.edu

The University of Portland is one of the major private institutions on the West Coast. The faculty includes national experts on aging, airline industry, Chilean politics, criminology, Eastern European business investment, hate crimes, consumer behavior and property taxes.

John Furey
*Associate Director of Media Relations*
University of Portland
Portland, OR
*Contact Phone:* 503-943-7202
**Click to Contact from Web Site**

## GLOBAL ACADEMY ONLINE
Washington, DC USA
http://www.GlobalAcademyOnline.com

Global Academy Online is the premier provider of online transparent, private label, curriculum and instruction to colleges, universities and distance learning institutions. The Academy also consults and delivers stratigic planning advise and assistance to organizations seeking to start or expand online education resources. With degree and certificate programs in 31 higher education fields of study and a renowned international faculty, the Academy is a unique, one of a kind, education source.

LaFonda Oliver
*Vice President, Communications*
Global Academy Online, Inc.
Center for Ethics & Free Enterprise
Washington, DC USA
*Contact Phone:* (202)-580-8755
*Contact Main Phone:* (505)-397-9769
*Cell:* (806)-239-8289
**Click to Contact from Web Site**

## UTICA COLLEGE
Utica, NY USA
http://www.utica.edu

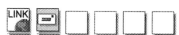

At Utica College, expert opinion is offered by more than 100 faculty and staff experienced in media relations, including: George Curtis, J.D., Director, Economic Crime Investigation Institute; Theodore Orlin, J.D., Clark Professor of Human Rights Scholarship & Advocacy; Stephen Neun, Ph.D., Professor of Economics; David Habbel, Ph.D., Associate Professor of Communication Arts; Thomas Crist, Ph.D., Associate Professor of Physical Therapy; Nathaniel Richmond, Ph.D., Professor of Government and Politics; and Mary Katharine Maroney, Ph.D., Professor/Director of Nursing.

Christine LeoGrande
*Coordinator of Media Relations*
Utica College
Utica, NY USA
*Contact Phone:* 315-223-2519
**Click to Contact from Web Site**

## ON-TECH E-RATE SERVICES
Red Bank, NJ USA
http://www.on-tech.com/erate

On-Tech (www.on-tech.com) is a technology consulting firm focused on managing the E-Rate process for schools and libraries. Dan Riordan, President of On-Tech, has been involved with the E-Rate since 1997, when he was trained by the New Jersey Department of Education to offer expertise to schools. He is also a certified network engineer, a former school technology coordinator and a former purchasing officer for the U.S. government, giving him unique insight into the program's rules.

Dan Riordan
On-Tech Consulting, Inc.
Red Bank, NJ USA
*Contact Phone:* 732-530-5435
**Click to Contact from Web Site**

## READERS ARE WRITERS, INC
Atlanta, GA USA
http://readersarewriters.org

My sons can read. As parents, we are very fortunate that they read all the time and at very high levels. They read so much that when we need their attention, we restrict them from their books. What my children don't like to do is write. Readers Are Writers focuses on the imaginative talents of children; created to take the entire fifth grade class through the series of steps that a book or story must transverse before it reaches their library shelves. Designed to provide an arena in which they can be creative and grow, it gives them the experience of producing a written manuscript and turning that manuscript into a book.

H. Christine Lindblom
Readers Are Writers, Inc.
Social Circle, GA USA
*Contact Phone:* 770-464-0454
**Click to Contact from Web Site**

## MENSA
Arlington, TX USA
http://www.us.mensa.org

American Mensa is the high IQ society. One of every 50 Americans qualifies for membership. Mensa provides social interaction, mental stimulation and much more for anyone who scores in the top two percent of the general population on a standardized intelligence test. Mensa has 134 chapters across the United States and hosts gatherings, meetings, symposia, and colloquia on a regular basis. Mensa has programs for gifted and talented children as well as for adults. Members range from 4 to 101 years of age. There are more than 150 special interest groups.

Catherine Barney
*Marketing Director*
American Mensa
Arlington,
*Contact Main Phone:* 817-607-0060
**Click to Contact from Web Site**

## ASSOCIATION FOR SUPERVISION AND CURRICULUM DEVELOPMENT (ASCD)
Alexandria, VA USA
http://www.ascd.org

Founded in 1943, ASCD, an international, nonprofit association, is one of the largest professional development organizations for education leaders. It provides world-class education information services, offers cutting-edge professional development for effective teaching and learning, and supports activities to provide educational equity for all students. ASCD's 165,000 members reside in more than 140 countries and include principals, teachers, superintendents, professors of education, and their educators.

Barbara Gleason
*Public Relations Coordinator*
Association for Supervision and Curriculum Development (ASCD)
Alexandria, VA
*Contact Phone:* 703-575-5608
**Click to Contact from Web Site**

## NATIONAL COUNCIL FOR THE SOCIAL STUDIES
Silver Spring, MD USA
http://www.ncss.org

National Council for the Social Studies, founded in 1921, is the largest association in the nation devoted solely to social studies education. Its membership is organized into a network of more than 110 affiliated local, state, and regional councils and associated groups composed of pre-K-16 classroom teachers, college and university professors, school officials, supervisors and consultants, publishers, and other social studies professionals.

Al Frascella
*Director, Communications*
National Council for the Social Studies
Silver Spring, MD USA
*Contact Phone:* 301-588-1800
*Contact Main Phone:* 301-588-1800
**Click to Contact from Web Site**

## CHERYL L. WILD, PH.D., EDUCATION AND CERTIFICATION TESTING CONSULTANT
Newark, NJ USA
www.WildandAssociates.com

Cheryl Wild, Ph.D., is the nation's foremost psychometrician and quality consultant in the test publishing industry. Dr. Wild helps organizations improve their tests and surveys. Education and certification tests often make the news for the wrong reasons-- errors, bias, or failures in security. Dr. Wild can explain the causes of these problems and how to prevent them!

Cheryl L. Wild, Ph.D.
*President*
Wild & Associates, Inc.
Avon by the Sea, NJ USA
*Contact Phone:* 732-774-5188
**Click to Contact from Web Site**

## INDEPENDENT EDUCATIONAL CONSULTANTS ASSOCIATION (IECA)
Fairfax, VA USA
http://www.iecaonline.com

IECA represents experienced professionals providing private counseling for families on school placement issues. Knowledgeable authority on wide range of education issues, including: college admission trends, individual learning styles, learning disabilities, single sex vs. coed education, wilderness therapy programs, private school considerations, the changing face of boarding schools.

Mark Sklarow
*Executive Director*
Independent Educational Consultants Association (IECA)
Fairfax, VA United State
*Contact Phone:* 703-591-4850
*Cell:* 703 591-4850
**Click to Contact from Web Site**

## STEVEN ROY GOODMAN, M.S., J.D. — COLLEGE ADMISSIONS EXPERT
Washington, DC USA
http://www.topcolleges.com

College Admissions Consultant: Selective Colleges, Graduate Programs, Business, Law Schools and Medical Schools, Educational Planning and Career Strategies. He is an Admissions Commentator/Expert Witness: Applicant Pool Generation, Recruiting Strategies, Interview Process, Socioeconomic Diversity, Evaluation of Applicants. As one of the foremost education consultants in the United States, Steve Goodman lectures about the college admissions process and privately consults with applicants to selective colleges and universities, graduate programs and professional schools.

Steven Roy Goodman, M.S., J.D.
Washington, DC
*Contact Phone:* 202-986-9431
**Click to Contact from Web Site**

## BARI MELTZER NORMAN, PH.D. — COLLEGE ADMISSIONS EXPERT
Miami, FL USA
http://mycollegecounselor.com

As a former Barnard College admissions officer and high school guidance counselor, Bari Norman, Ph.D. has worked on both sides of the college admissions desk. As an educational consultant, she is uniquely qualified to advise students and their families through the college application process. Dr. Norman writes the Ask the College Advisor column for the Miami Herald, and has been featured in the New York Times, Wall Street Journal, New York Daily News, Washington Post, and other outlets. She also lectures about college admission to audiences across the country.

Bari Meltzer Norman, Ph.D.
www.MyCollegeCounselor.com
*Contact Phone:* (954) 456-0761
**Click to Contact from Web Site**

**MARY CAMPBELL GALLAGHER, J.D., PH.D. - - BARWRITE SCHOOLS & BARWRITE PRESS**
New York, NY USA
www.barwrite.com

Expert on the bar exam and education Mary Campbell Gallagher, J.D., Ph.D., is a graduate of Harvard Law School, Ph.D. in linguistics, professional speaker, consultant, and president of BarWrite (TM and SM). The mission of BarWrite is applying linguistic systems to teaching writing, including legal writing. Author of Scoring High on Bar Exam Essays and co-author of texts on education, Dr. Gallagher has been published in The Weekly Standard, Legal Times, The Nation, and Student Lawyer.

Mary Campbell Gallagher, J.D., Ph.D.
BarWrite Schools & BarWrite Press
New York, NY USA
*Contact Phone:* 212-327-2817
**Click to Contact from Web Site**

**RICHARD MARQUIS -- COLLEGE SUCCESS EXPERT**
Detroit, MI USA
http://www.richardmarquis.net

Richard Marquis, MA, is a college success expert, author and speaker. He shows students how to work smarter, learn more and supercharge their college performance. This enables them to stay in school, earn a higher GPA and secure their degrees. He is an award-winning scholar and researcher who has taught Western Civilization and American and World History at the college level. There he encountered students for whom his insightful and "to-the-point" ideas proved life changing. These insights became the inspiration for his book, Grade Grabbers: Improve Your GPA. Richard is no smarter than most people, yet his name consistently appeared on the dean's list. He earned Associate and Bachelor of Arts degrees with highest honors, served as a graduate assistant and received the prestigious Graduate Deans' Award for Research Excellence for his Master of Arts degree thesis. For students seeking college success, Richard Marquis knows "you can do it!"

Richard Marquis
Marquis Advantage, LLC
Plymouth, MI USA
*Contact Phone:* 800-223-2403
**Click to Contact from Web Site**

**MINDPICTURE COMPANY**
Bejing, China
www.MindPicture.net

MindPicture, Inc. is the first mover in the world that has developed visual and multisensory learning system in the study guides field. In Sept of 2005, the MindPicture project that integrates technologies of IT and edgy theories of brain and cognition was incorporated and MindPicture, Inc. was born. We have applied the visual+multisensory learning theories to study guides field to such depth that we have successfully developed effective visual expression system and further use it to transform series of verbal books into intuitive visual and multisensory learning systems.

Sherham Lu
MindPicture Company
Bejing, China
*Contact Phone:* 86-10-82561826
**Click to Contact from Web Site**

**INTERNATIONAL READING ASSOCIATION**
Newark, DE USA
http://www.reading.org

The world's leading literacy organization provides educators with a wealth of resources to foster reading success for all learners. With more than 90,000 individual and institutional members worldwide, the International Reading Association is the only professional education organization that has reading and literacy instruction as the primary focus. It sponsors programs that address emerging global issues and promotes literacy for all nations. Alan E. Farstrup, Ph.D. Executive Director, serves as the official spokesperson on all aspects of literacy and education.

Beth Cady
*Public Information Associate*
International Reading Association
Newark, DE
*Contact Phone:* 302-731-1600
*Contact Main Phone:* 302-731-1600
**Click to Contact from Web Site**

## THE HIP HOP EDUCATOR
Los Angeles, CA USA
http://www.HipHopinTheClass.com

The Hip-Hop Educator Alan Lawrence Sitomer, California Literacy's TEACHER OF THE YEAR, is reaping tremendous success in urban schools by using Hip-Hop as a means of elevating the literacy skills of multicultural students. By tying Tupac to Tennyson and building bridges to classics through contemporary musical artists, Alan has empowered schools to raises test scores and helped students gain admissions to prestigious colleges like Stanford, Berkeley and USC. Interviews welcomed.

Alan Lawrence Sitomer
Milk Mug Publishing
Beverly Hills, CA USA
*Contact Phone:* 310-278-1153
**Click to Contact from Web Site**

## FRIENDS OF LIBRARIES U.S.A.
Philadelphia, PA USA
www.folusa.org

Friends of Libraries U.S.A. is a membership organization of more than two thousand individual and group members. Our mission is to motivate and support local Friends groups across the country in their efforts to preserve and strengthen libraries, and to create awareness and appreciation of library services by assisting in developing Friends of the Library groups in order to generate local and state support, providing guidance, education, and counsel throughout the Friends network, and promoting the development of strong library advocacy programs.

Sally G. Reed
Friends of Libraries, U.S.A.
Philadelphia, PA USA
*Contact Phone:* 215-790-1674
**Click to Contact from Web Site**

## MYRNA T. MCCULLOCH, DIRECTOR, THE RIGGS INSTITUTE
Portland, OR USA
http://www.riggsinst.org

Millions of adults/children still can't read! Millions more can't spell! McCulloch will light up phone lines, spice up your copy, provide an op-ed piece, or help the brave hearts win a Pulitzer!! 27 years' experience, street-smart observations, & ability to simplify a complex subject make her invaluable. Her recommendations: (1) discover root causes? (2) change methods/content / training to what works (3) do relevant research (4) accommodate all 'learning styles' (5) examine time management (6) broadcast exemplary model classrooms.

Myrna T. McCulloch
*Director*
The Riggs Institute & Riggs' Literacy & Learning Center
Riggs' Literacy & Learning Center
Beaverton, OR USA
*Contact Phone:* 503-646-9459
*Contact Main Phone:* 800-200-4840
**Click to Contact from Web Site**

## LAWRENCE HALL YOUTH SERVICES
Chicago, IL USA
www.lawrencehall.org

Today in Illinois, one in five children lives in poverty, and fifteen percent of the state's children are considered seriously at risk. The children — and families — served by Lawrence Hall are more than statistics. They are survivors of circumstance, of neglect, of physical and emotional abuse. The story of Lawrence Hall is written every day in their healing, growth, and accomplishments. One of the oldest child-welfare agencies in Illinois, Lawrence Hall delivers an essential continuum of care — a lifeline of action, hope, and opportunity — that enables children to build more promising futures. And their own success stories. We invite you to learn more about the work of Lawrence Hall. From foster care to therapeutic day school, residential treatment, and supervised independent living programs, we're answering the needs of the least fortunate - and least able - in our communities, and changing lives.

Julie Youngquist
*Vice President for Institutional Advancement*
Lawrence Hall Youth Services
Chicago, IL USA
*Contact Phone:* 312-456-6506
**Click to Contact from Web Site**

## HEATHER HARDER, PH.D., AUTHOR, SPEAKER, AND CONSULTANT
Chicago, IL USA
http://www.heatherharder.com

Heather Harder, Ph.D., challenges parents, children, and individuals to recognize, and release behaviors both personally and professionally. As author, speaker, and authority on learning, leadership, and human behavior, Heather combines advanced academic research with common sense, and spiritual truth to create inspired, often controversial and always thought provoking material. With humor and logic, Heather has delighted audiences on hundreds of radio and television shows across this country including CNN, CSPAN, MTV, NBC, and CBS news.

Heather Harder, Ph.D.
Growth on the Go
Crown Point, IN USA
*Contact Phone:* 219-662-7248
**Click to Contact from Web Site**

## ALTERNATIVE EDUCATION RESOURCE ORGANIZATION
Roslyn Heights, NY USA
http://www.edrev.org

AERO founder and alternative education expert Jerry Mintz has appeared on FOX's Hannity and Colmes, CBS, CNBC, WPIX, All Things Considered, and Talk of the Nation. He is editor in chief of The Education Revolution Magazine, and the Almanac of Education Choices. AERO has helped many to start homeschooling, create alternative schools or homeschool resource centers. His new book is No Homework and Recess All Day. AERO is a non-profit organization dedicated to supporting and promoting alternative education around the world.

Jerry Mintz
*Director*
Alternative Education Resource Organization
Roslyn Heights, NY
*Contact Phone:* 800-769-4171
**Click to Contact from Web Site**

## GREAT POTENTIAL PRESS, INC.

Scottsdale, AZ USA
http://www.giftedbooks.com

Winner of the 2003 Glyph Award for Excellence in Publishing! We specialize in books for parents, teachers, and educators of gifted and talented children. Within our website, you can order our award-winning books and videos, read articles about gifted issues, find information about upcoming conferences and events, and much more. Check back often for updates and special online sales!

Alicia F. Markham
*Marketing Associate*
Great Potential Press, Inc.
Scottsdale, AZ USA
*Contact Phone:* 1-877-954-4200
*Contact Main Phone:* 602 954-4200
*Cell:* 623 695-2153
**Click to Contact from Web Site**

## PAUL D. SLOCUMB, ED.D., EDUCATIONAL CRISIS FOR BOYS

Houston, TX USA
www.ahaprocess.com

The inherent goodness of boys frequently is masked by the statistics—bullying, school violence, dropouts, and adolescents committing adult crimes. 'Hear Our Cry: Boys in Crisis' examines the what, how and why of boy behaviors and reveals the keys to dealing with them. Dr. Slocumb's groundbreaking work examines the relationship between brain structure and the varied social influences boys face. 'Hear Our Cry: Boys in Crisis' is a must read for both educators and parents.

Paul D. Slocumb
*Author / Consultant*
aha! Process, Inc.
Highlands, TX USA
*Contact Phone:* 281-844-5346
*Contact Main Phone:* 800-424-9484
**Click to Contact from Web Site**

## CALVERT SCHOOL

Baltimore, MD USA
http://www.calvertschool.org

Celebrating 100 years of service helping nearly 500,000 children, Calvert School provides a complete homeschool curriculum to Pre-K—8 students in the U.S. and abroad. About 30,000 courses are shipped worldwide each year. As homeschooling's first formal curriculum provider, starting in 1906, Calvert's hallmark remains its detailed, step-by-step lesson manuals. Its classical, integrated and proven curriculum is used in many charter schools, cyber schools, and other institutions. Calvert's experts have participated in numerous radio, TV and print interviews.

Bob Graham
*Public Relations*
Calvert School
Hunt Valley, MD
*Contact Phone:* 888-487-4652
*Contact Main Phone:* 410-785-3400
**Click to Contact from Web Site**

## ATTENTION DEFICIT DISORDER ASSOCIATION

Philadelphia, PA USA
http://www.add.org

ADDA is a nonprofit organization that provides information, resources and networking opportunities, as well as advocacy, to help adults with Attention Deficit/Hyperactivity Disorder (AD/HD) lead better lives. ADDA also helps professionals stay current on significant developments. Contacts: Michele Novotni, PhD, CEO; Evelyn Polk Green, Sr. Exec. Officer; David Giwerc, MCC, President. (484) 945-2101.

Victoria Sandoe Burkhart
Burkhart Group
Attention Deficit Disorder Assn.
Pottstown, PA USA
*Contact Phone:* 610-970-9143
*Contact Main Phone:* 484-945-2101
**Click to Contact from Web Site**

## ARTISTS OF AMERICA

Los Angeles, CA USA
www.artists-of-america.org

Artists of America (AOA) is an IRS recognized 501(c)(3) non profit organization. Our mission is to provide art classes to Inner City Children. Our goal is to improve lives, one child at a time. WE PROVIDE: Art teachers and supplies for schools. A "Learn to read program" designed for children up to 3rd grade to help them read better. The Key to a Good Life is a love of reading. It opens doors that no one can close. The Cultural Experiences for Inner City Students, introducing them to the cultural life.

Diedre Hopkins Burke
Artists of America
Los Angeles, CA USA
*Contact Phone:* 310-809-5277
**Click to Contact from Web Site**

## KATHRYN SEIFERT, PH.D., TRAUMA EXPERT

Baltimore, MD USA
http://www.careforusall.com/

Kathryn Seifert, Ph.D. is a psychotherapist, author, speaker, and researcher with over 30 years of experience in the fields of mental health, addictions, and criminal justice. An expert in family violence and trauma, Dr. Seifert is Founder and CEO of Eastern Shore Psychological Services (www.ESPSMD.com), and her debut book, How Children Become Violent: Keeping Your Kids out of Gangs, Terrorist Organizations, and Cults will be available this fall from Acanthus Publishing.

Kathryn Seifert, Ph.D.
*CEO*
ESPS, LLC
Sailsbury, MD USA
*Contact Phone:* 410-334-6961
*Contact Main Phone:* 410-334-6961
**Click to Contact from Web Site**

## AHA! PROCESS, INC. — PUBLISHING & TRAINING ON ECONOMIC DIVERSITY
Houston, TX USA
http://www.ahaprocess.com

aha! Process, Inc. was founded by Ruby K. Payne Ph. D., with an emphasis on educational issues facing children from poverty and the impact of 'hidden rules of economic class.' aha! Process instructs and enlightens educators, social workers, employers, and law enforcement through 30+ books, videos and workshops. aha! Process addresses critical social and educational issues - foster parenting, welfare-to-work education, identifying gifted students from poverty, and the challenges facing boys to receive an education equal to girls.

Paula Nicolella
aha! Process, Inc.
Washington, PA USA
*Contact Phone:* 724-225-7568
**Click to Contact from Web Site**

## BO LEBO -- NEW LIFE OPTIONS -- LITERACY EXPERT
Los Angeles, CA USA
mindspan.bizland.com

How well you can read determines your health, finances, and social achievement. Misread a sign on the freeway and you may never get there. Reading skills matter in daily life. Processing information correctly is vital to achievement. Discover Mindspan, an award-winning program, using music to revitalize communities by making school standards cool. Ask about the Wind in the Willows CD bringing cognitive research to at risk readers by literacy donations and sales in California.

Cynthyny 'Bo' Lebo
New Life Options
Sherman Oaks, CA USA
*Contact Phone:* 818-990-5410
*Cell:* 818-742-5099
**Click to Contact from Web Site**

## LIFETIME ADOPTION FOUNDATION — LET'S TALK ADOPTION RADIO SHOW
Sacramento, CA USA
http://www.LetsTalkAdoption.com

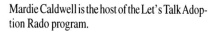

Mardie Caldwell is the host of the Let's Talk Adoption Rado program.

Mardie Caldwell
Nevada City, CA USA
*Contact Phone:* 530 265-2645
**Click to Contact from Web Site**

## CHILD FIND OF AMERICA
New Paltz, NY USA
www.ChildFindofAmerica.org

Child Find of America Inc. is a national not-for-profit organization that: locates issing children through active investigation prevents child abduction through education resolves incidents of parental abduction through mediation. Founded in 1980 by the mother of a missing child, Child Find has helped locate, return to a legal environment and positively impacted the lives of thousands of children. In the 2002-2003 fiscal year, 90 cents of every dollar Child Find received was spent on its programs: Location, Mediation and Public Information. Worth Magazine named Child Find one of America's 100 Best Charities in December 2001, and Child Find received an A+ Top Charity rating by the American Institute of Philanthropy, a nonprofit charity watchdog.

Public Relations Director
Child Find of America
New Paltz, NY USA
*Contact Phone:* 845-691-4666
**Click to Contact from Web Site**

## THE CHILD SHARE PROGRAM
Los Angeles, CA USA
childshare.org

Child SHARE (Shelter Homes: A Rescue Effort) was founded by Dr. Mary Rotzien in 1985 with seed funding and key leadership from Westwood Presbyterian Church. The program was a direct response to thousands of foster children, including infants and toddlers, languishing in institutional care in Los Angeles. Convinced that the faith community could provide families for these children, Child SHARE began building a wrap around ministry with foster parents, respite homes, babysitters and volunteers from local churches. Today, Child SHARE works with over 400 local congregations representing 30 denominations to find families and friends for abused children. Over 600 children lived in Child SHARE's foster or adoptive homes in LA or Orange County last year, with around 200 new placements each year! Even more exciting, two out of three children placed in a Child SHARE home stay with the SAME family until they are reunited with a relative or adopted. One in three Child SHARE children is ADOPTED, usually by their foster parents— more than twice the national average!

Joanne Feldmeth
The Child SHARE Program
Glendale, CA USA
*Contact Phone:* 818 243-4450
**Click to Contact from Web Site**

## THE DREAM FACTORY, INC.
Louisville, KY USA
http://www.DreamFactoryInc.com

The Dream Factory, Inc. (a 501(c)(3) organization) was founded in 1980 in Hopkinsville, Kentucky, by Charles Henault, a South Central Bell employee, who wanted to create a volunteer organization dedicated to granting the dreams of children with critical or chronic illnesses. Currently, there are more than 30 chapters across the United States with over 5,000 volunteers who work to produce and deliver dreams, visit children and their families in the hospital and their homes, arrange special celebrations and conduct fundraising events for individual children. This volunteer support ensures that the maximum percentage of donations are used for the procurement and distribution of dreams. The Dream Factory is a member of the Association of Wish Granting Organizations (AWGO), which has 20 members across the nation all serving the needs of children diagnosed with life-threatening illnesses.

Kelly Cummings
The Dream Factory, Inc.
Louisville, KY USA
*Contact Phone:* 502-637-8700
**Click to Contact from Web Site**

## POLLY FRANKS - CRIME VICTIM ADVOCATE & CHILD SAFETY EXPERT
Richmond, VA USA
http://franksfoundation.org

A nationally recognized advocate for victims of crime, especially childhood sexual abuse, Franks is the mother of two children who were attacked by a former neighbor who turned out to be a convicted serial rapist from another state. Despite being in a wheelchair, he became a licensed private investigator for the sole purpose of bringing this predator to justice. Franks has testified before congress and been interviewed by national T.V., radio and print media regarding protecting America's children from sexual predators.

Polly Franks
National Coalition of Victims in Action
*Contact Main Phone:* 804-564-9196
**Click to Contact from Web Site**

## NATIONAL ADOPTION CENTER
Philadelphia, PA USA
www.Adopt.org

Expands adoption opportunities for children throughout the United States, particularly for minority children and children with special needs. Has a Web site and access to adoptive parents, adopted children and adoption professionals and can address important adoption and child welfare issues. Has placed more than 20,000 children since 1972.

Gloria Hochman
*Dir., Communications & Marketing*
National Adoption Center
Philadelphia, PA
*Contact Phone:* 215-875-0324
*Contact Main Phone:* 215-735-9988
**Click to Contact from Web Site**

## OPERATION LOOKOUT ® NATIONAL CENTER FOR MISSING YOUTH
Everett, WA USA
http://www.operationlookout.org

OPERATION LOOKOUT was founded in 1984 as a private nonprofit (501)(c)(3) child-search center to provide free services to parents searching for their missing children. We provide expert interviews, fact sheets, the latest statistics on family and stranger child abductions, runaways, and unexplained disappearances, anti-victimization resources, photographs, PSAs, and other referrals for the general public and the media. Contact: www.operationlookout.org or 1-800-LOOK-OUT(566-5688)

Melody Gibson
*Executive Director*
OPERATION LOOKOUT ®; National Center for Missing Youth
Everett, WA
*Contact Phone:* 425-771-7335
*Contact Main Phone:* 800-LOOKOUT
**Click to Contact from Web Site**

## NATIONAL COALITION FOR THE PROTECTION OF CHILDREN & FAMILIES
Cincinnati, OH USA
http://www.nationalcoalition.org

The National Coalition for the Protection of Children & Families (formerly the National Coalition Against Pornography) features experts who can speak on a variety of topics related to the sexualized messages of the culture including pornography, homosexuality, sex education, teens and sex, sexually oriented businesses, child pornography, and legal matters related to the above.

Francesca Jensen
*Director of Communications*
National Coalition for the Protection of Children & Families
Cincinnati, OH
*Contact Phone:* 513-521-6227
**Click to Contact from Web Site**

## JOAN JOHNSON, B. S. - DOMESTIC VIOLENCE EXPERT
Scottsdale, AZ USA
http://www.joanjohnson.tv

Joan formerly hosted a radio talk show in Atlanta, Georgia. She has appeared on numerous TV and radio talk shows in America. She has ghost authored two books, conducts keynotes for The SHARE Committee for The Arizona Coalition Against Domestic Violence. Expert and authority on dynamics of Domestic Violence and recovery. Currently writing her book - a 31 day spiritual recovery guide after domestic abuse. Coaching, keynotes, and workshops available.

Joan Johnson
*Bachelor of Science*
Scottsdale, AZ USA
*Contact Phone:* 602-225-8422
*Cell:* 602-377-3004
**Click to Contact from Web Site**

## NATIONAL CHILD ABUSE DEFENSE & RESOURCE CENTER
Toledo, OH USA
http://www.falseallegation.org

False allegations child abuse/neglect—mistaken, mischievous, malicious—continue dismembering innocent families. 'Shaken Baby' and 'Munchausen Syndrome by Proxy' theories lack scientific validity. Faulty interviewing techniques, too rarely taped, inspire molestation 'disclosures' devastating the guiltless, traumatizing unabused children for life. Internationally recognized strategist Kimberly Hart adds science to suspicions of crimes. Former investigative reporter Barbara Bryan exposes law, policy, practice and family courts. Educational resource NCADRC supplies 'victims,' objective experts for programs/panels seeking 'whole' or hidden truth.

Kimberly Hart
*Executive Director*
National Child Abuse Defense & Resource Center
Holland, OH
*Contact Phone:* 419-865-0513
**Click to Contact from Web Site**

## DIANNE POST
Phoenix, AZ USA

Dianne Post is an attorney and writer who has spent twenty years representing battered women and children and advocating for equality and human rights in the U.S. and abroad.

Dianne Post
*Attorney*
Dianne Post
Phoenix, AZ
*Contact Phone:* 602-271-9019
**Click to Contact from Web Site**

**DEB CAPONE**
Montauk, NY USA
www.simpleasthat.com

As Simple As That's™ founder, Deborah Capone, recognized the great need for intelligent and sensitive material that would empower children to respect and celebrate all cultures choices and 'abilities' after she and her Chinese daughter became a family through adoption in 2000. The dramatic shifts in the US population underscored the urgency to provide an empowering set of role models to enable all children to navigate their place in the world regardless of their race, ethnicity or family structure/formation.

Deb Capone
As Simple As That™
Montauk, NY USA
*Contact Phone:* 631-668-3578
**Click to Contact from Web Site**

---

**TEAMCHILDREN — PHILADELPHIA YOUTH CHARITY**
Philadelphia, PA USA
www.TeamChildren.com

TeamChildren's mission is to transform how we relate to and raise babies and children such that every child is given both the opportunity and the tools to reach their full potential. By tranforming the tecnological divide and through our Project Playground we bring the benefits of massage and rolfing for babies and children. These benefits are a happier, smarter, child through touch, care, better blood circulation and better personal bonding. The majority of children when given the opportunity for massage will choose it.

Robert Toporek
TeamChildren
Norristown, PA USA
*Contact Phone:* 610-666-1795
**Click to Contact from Web Site**

---

**DR. MARLENE M. COLEMAN, M.D. - HARBOR PEDIATRIC MEDICAL GROUP**
Newport Beach, CA USA
http://www.harborpediatric.com/Dr/Coleman/index.htm

Born in Los Angeles, California.. Received B.S. and M.S. degrees from University of Southern California and M.D. degree from the University of California Irvine Medical School; residency training at White Memorial Medical Center in Los Angeles; Associate Clinical Professor of Family Medicine at USC School of Medicine, teaching freshman medical students Introduction to Clinical Medicine; Captain, United States Naval Reserve Medical Corps, served in Operation Desert Storm in Washington D.C.; Attending Physician, Cal Tech. Board certified in Pediatrics.

Marlene M. Coleman, M.D.
Harbor Pediatric Medical Group
Los Angeles, CA USA
*Contact Phone:* 949-645-4670
**Click to Contact from Web Site**

---

**EDUCATIONAL ADVENTURES**
Charlotte, NC USA
www.educationaladventures.com

With the start of summer underway, parents need to be extra cautious when traveling this summer and teach their children how to be safe on the beach. 20-year veteran Children's Safety Expert and co-Founder of "The Danger Rangers", Mike Moore, has developed the following tips that every family should know before setting off to the beach.

John Falkenbury
Educational Adventures
Charlotte, NC USA
*Contact Phone:* 704-334-7474
*Contact Main Phone:* 704-334-7474
*Cell:* (704) 904-0108
**Click to Contact from Web Site**

---

**DEBRA KIMBROUGH -- CHILD CARE SAFETY EXPERT**
Houston, TX USA
www.DebraKimbrough.com

Seeking A Child Care Safety Expert? Child Care Safety Expert, Debra Kimbrough, protects children by teaching their caregivers better guidance skills. According to Debra, 'an unskilled adult is a risk to children'. Debra wrote 'The Guidance Series' - A set of skills needed by adults responsible for the safety of children in out-of-home care. Her expertise comes from being an abuse/neglect investigator, child care center director, state licensing representative, and assistant in over 100 cases as a consultant, and expert witness.

Debra Kimbrough
Houston, TX USA
*Contact Phone:* 281-339-4507
**Click to Contact from Web Site**

**DEBRA HOLTZMAN, J.D., M.A. -- CHILD SAFETY EXPERT**
Hollywood, FL USA
www.thesafetyexpert.com

Debra Holtzman, JD, MA, is an internationally recognized child safety and health expert and award-winning parenting author. Frequently appears on regional and national television and radio, she has been recently featured on The Today Show, Dateline, CNBC, MSNBC, and The Associated Press Radio, and in USA Weekend Magazine. Debra is the safety expert on the Discovery Health Channel's popular TV series, Make Room for Baby. Her latest book, The Safe Baby: A Do-it Yourself Guide to Home Safety, is in bookstores everywhere.

Debra Holtzman, J.D., M.A.
*Contact Phone:* 954-963-7702
**Click to Contact from Web Site**

**CHELI CERRA -- CHILD SUCCESS EXPERT**
Miami, FL USA
www.chelicerra.com/

As a child success specialist, Cheli works with parents whose children are having problems academically or behaviorally. Some of them have concerns over high stakes testing or choosing a school for their child. She has appeared on numerous radio and several news shows. Many of her articles and resources can be found on her website: http://www.chelicerra.com. She is the co-author of the School Talk! Success Series. This is a series which provides a practical down-to-earth approach to handling common education issues. Cheli is currently a school principal in Miami-Dade County, Florida. Working in public education for over 22 years and a mother of two, Cheli knows first hand the real education issues currently in the trenches.

Cheli Cerra
Miami, FL
*Contact Main Phone:* 305-978-6108
**Click to Contact from Web Site**

**DR. KENNETH S. KALLIN-PHD**
Pompano Beach, FL USA
http://www.timeoutforkids.org/

Dr. K. S. Kallin-Nissen-Duame is, currently, the conceptualizer and founder of the evolving non-profit, charitable, organization, known as TIME-OUT FOR KIDS, Inc. (TOFK). He is also the author of the revealing, impacting, exposing book, entitled In Fear Of My Child . . . a dramatic, real-life-experience, literary masterpiece from which the impetus and need for such a solution precept was realized. The book is but a powerful, representative, true example of what tens-of-thousands of other families and innocent children, caused to go awry, have to deal with . . . including all the trauma and tragedies inherent. For sure, what is contained in its pages will evoke all the emotions and even curl-your-toes at what this troubled child came to manifest or do. However, the book is more important as an eye-opener to realize and understand the length and breadth of a major social problem that is not only affecting our now but tapping our future viability as a nation.

Dr. K. S. Kallin- Ph.D.
Pompano Beach, FL USA
*Contact Phone:* (954) 537-3635
**Click to Contact from Web Site**

**ST. ANDREW'S FOUNDATION OF ROMANIA**
Washington, DC USA
www.StAndrewKids.org

The St. Andrew's Foundation of Romania is set up to fund programs in Romania for street children and other children who have fallen through the cracks, educationally. A key target for our funding is the Back to School Foundation (Fundatia Inapoi la Scoala) which runs a school in Bucharest, Romania for bright, motivated street children living in shelters, as well as disadvantaged children who have dropped out of school. The school successfully teaches a grade 1-8 academic program. St. Andrew's is also set up to finance the living arrangements of those youngsters who cannot or should not be living with their families.

Wendy Graham
St. Andrew's Foundation of Romania
Washington, DC USA
*Contact Phone:* 202-342-3351
**Click to Contact from Web Site**

## CARL POTTER, CSP, CMC, CERTIFIED SAFETY PROFESSIONAL
Tulsa, OK USA
www.carlpotter.com

Carl Potter is a Certified Safety Professional who works with organizations that want to put safety first on the minds of their employees so that everyone can go home everyday without injury. Carl is a nationally known expert who writes articles, presents keynotes, seminars and consults to organizations with high-risk environments. As a motivational safety speaker Carl challenges employees to take personal responsibility for their own safety and those around him. In his seminar Safety and the Supervisor he challenges frontline leaders to create an environment of trust so that employees can take personal responsibility for safety.

Carl Potter, CSP, CMC, CSP
Potter and Associates International, Inc.
Tulsa, OK USA
*Contact Phone:* 800-259-6209
**Click to Contact from Web Site**

## CONGRESS OF RACIAL EQUALITY — CORE
New York, NY USA
http://www.core-online.org

Founded in 1942, CORE is the third oldest and one of the Big Four civil rights groups in the United States. From the protests against Jim Crow laws of the 40's to the Sit-ins of the 50's and the Freedom Rides of the 60's; through the cries for Self-Determination in the 70's and Equal Opportunity in the 80's to the struggle for community development in the 90's, CORE has championed true equality for all people. As the shock troops and pioneers of the civil rights movement, CORE has paved the way for the nation to follow. As we approach the end of the 20th century, CORE has turned its focus to preparing minorities for the technical and skills demands of the new millennium.

Corinne Innis, Publicist
Congress of Racial Equality — CORE
New York, NY USA
*Contact Phone:* 212-598-4000
**Click to Contact from Web Site**

## PAN AMERICAN HEALTH ORGANIZATION
Washington, DC USA
www.paho.org

The Area of Public Information assumes the main responsibility for the public relations function in PAHO. It serves as the link between PAHO and the general public, as well as specialized audiences. It publishes and produces materials about PAHO including Perspectives in Health magazine and PAHO Today newsletter; creates and produces multimedia material on PAHO, such as Public Service Announcements, for use by the media; and provides media training and assistance with communication strategies and tactics to PAHO staff. The Area also coordinates PAHO's Speakers Bureau.

Daniel Epstein
*Information Officer*
Pan American Health Organization
Office of Public Information
Washington D.C., DC USA
*Contact Phone:* 202 974 3459
*Contact Main Phone:* 202 974 3000
**Click to Contact from Web Site**

## AMERICAN RED CROSS
Washington, DC USA
http://www.redcross.org

Get Life-Saving Answers from America's Most Trusted Humanitarian Organization. * Disaster Relief and Preparedness * Blood Donation * Biomedical Research * First Aid and CPR * Swimming and Lifeguard Training * HIV/AIDS Education * International Disaster Relief * International Development * Geneva Conventions * Americans trust the American Red Cross to get them reliable information that can help save lives, and you can, too. Additional Web Site: www.disasterrelief.org

Deborah Daley
American Red Cross
Washington, DC
*Contact Phone:* 202-639-3500
**Click to Contact from Web Site**

## THE VOLUNTEER CENTER OF SW FAIRFIELD COUNTY
Stamford, CT USA
ucanhelp.org

The Volunteer Center of Southwestern Fairfield County serves nonprofit organizations, employers and individuals by coordinating their talents and resources, to build the capacity of agencies with the goal of enhancing the quality of life in our communities through volunteerism.

Roberta Eichler
The Volunteer Center of SW Fairfield County
Stamford, CT USA
*Contact Phone:* 203 348-7714
**Click to Contact from Web Site**

## VOLUNTEERS OF AMERICA
Alexandria, VA USA
http://www.volunteersofamerica.org

Volunteers of America is a national, nonprofit, spiritually based organization providing local human service programs, and opportunities for individual and community involvement. Each year, more than 1.7 million people across the nation feel the helping hand of Volunteers of America. Its programs help abused and neglected children, at-risk youth, seniors and the elderly, people with disabilities, the homeless and people with alcohol and drug addiction.

Julie Anderson
*Public Relations Manager*
Volunteers of America
Alexandria, VA
*Contact Phone:* 703-341-5031
*Contact Main Phone:* 800-899-0089
**Click to Contact from Web Site**

# CHELI CERRA, M. Ed.
## Family Education Specialist

Is Your Child Truly Happy? Is Your Child Maximizing Their Academic Potential? Are You Doing Everything You Can To Help?

YOUR CHILD'S ACADEMIC PERFORMANCE HELPS DETERMINE HIS OR HER FUTURE! ARE YOU PREPARED TO HELP MAXIMIZE THAT PERFORMANCE?

As a Parent or Guardian, do you know:

- What to expect from your child's teacher.

- How to pick the right programs and school.

- Ways to enhance your child's confidence.

- How to evaluate your child's learning style.

As a school Principal in Dade County, Florida, Cheli Cerra has been working in public education for more than 20 years. She is also the coauthor of the *School Talk! Success Series* which provides a practical approach to handling common education issues.

Dedicated to helping parents become constructive participants in their child's daily academic development, Cheli provides a practical approach to common educational issues, such as:

- Effective Parent/Teacher Communication.

- Improving your child's grades.

- Enabling your child to succeed in high-stakes tests.

- Improving your child's study skills.

- How to be a strong, effective voice in support of your child.

Cheli Cerra is a working mother of two, an author, a member of the National Speakers Association, and a member of the Screen Actors Guild. She has been featured in *Women's Day* and is a national media contributor as an expert on education. She is also currently a school principal in Miami-Dade County, Florida.

CONTACT CHELI CERRA at (305) 978-6108
9737 NW 41st Street, #356 • Miami, Florida 33178

www.CHELICERRA.com

## GOODWILL INDUSTRIES INTERNATIONAL, INC.
Rockville, MD USA
http://www.goodwill.org

Goodwill Industries International is a network of 205 community-based agencies in 22 countries, providing education and career services to people seeking employment. Each agency serves people with disadvantages such as welfare dependency and homelessness, as well as people with physical, mental and emotional disabilities.

Christine Nyirjesy Bragale
*Director, Media Relations*
Goodwill Industries International, Inc.
Rockville, MD
*Contact Phone:* 240-333-5264
*Pager:* 888-434-8066
*Cell:* 301-928-9536
**Click to Contact from Web Site**

## AMERICAN JEWISH JOINT DISTRIBUTION COMMITTEE, INC.
New York, NY USA
http://www.jdc.org

An American-Jewish Rescue and Relief NGO serving the needs of Jewish communities in more than 50 countries. Established in 1914, JDC has been on the cutting edge of emergency rescue and long term relief during wars and in peach-time. Current programs include renewal of Jewish community life in the former Soviet Union and Central Europe, Social programs in Israel and assistance to communities in Latin America, Asia and Africa. Major funds are provided by the United Jewish Community campaign and by private donations.

Claire Schultz
*Assistant Exec. V.P., Marketing & Communications*
American Jewish Joint Distribution Committee, Inc.
*Contact Phone:* 212-885-0818
*Contact Main Phone:* 212-687-6200
**Click to Contact from Web Site**

## GREATER MILWAUKEE FOUNDATION
Milwaukee, WI USA
greatermkefdn.org

Since 1915, the Greater Milwaukee Foundation has been helping donors make a difference. We are one of the oldest and largest community foundations in the world with over 900 funds and more than $462 million in assets. Grants made through the Foundation's leadership efforts touch the lives of thousands of people in Greater Milwaukee everyday. We help donors create a legacy of giving, and our stewardship ensures donor giving will last their lifetimes and beyond.

Doris H. Heiser
Greater Milwaukee Foundation
Milwaukee, WI USA
*Contact Phone:* 414 272-5805
**Click to Contact from Web Site**

## SISTER TO SISTER - NATIONAL WOMAN'S HEART DAY
Washington, DC USA
www.sistertosister.org/

Do you know that women's heart disease is the number one killer of women in the United States? One out of every three women will die of heart disease. That's the bad news. . .but, the good news is that women's heart disease is often preventable. Sister to Sister, a national grassroots nonprofit organization, exists solely to bring free heart disease screenings and heart-healthy prevention information and support to all women in order to prevent heart disease, the number one killer of women today. Each year, Sister to Sister sponsors National Woman's Heart Day. At Sister to Sister's request, the Federal Government has proclaimed the third Friday of every February to be National Woman's Heart Day.

Janet Staihar
Staihar & Associates
Washington, DC USA
*Contact Phone:* 202-237-2080
**Click to Contact from Web Site**

## ASSOCIATION OF FUNDRAISING PROFESSIONALS
Alexandria, VA USA
http://www.afpnet.org

AFP (formerly the National Society of Fund Raising Executives) is the leading association for professional fundraisers, representing 27,000 individuals who work for a variety of local, national and international nonprofit organizations. Founded in 1960, AFP generates news and research regarding ethical fundraising and the future of philanthropy. AFP can provide information and insight on topics related to fundraising, giving, volunteerism, e-philanthropy and the Internet, ethics, provincial/state and federal legislation, and other nonprofit sector issues.

Walter Sczudlo
*Executive V.P.*
Association of Fundraising Professionals
Alexandria, VA usa
*Contact Phone:* 800-666-3863
*Contact Main Phone:* 800-666-3863 (VA)
**Click to Contact from Web Site**

## SALVATION ARMY NATIONAL HEADQUARTERS
Alexandria, VA USA
www.salvationarmyusa.org

The Salvation Army is a humanitarian organization and an evangelical part of the universal Christian church. One of the largest charitable and service organizations in the world, The Salvation Army has been in existence since 1865, supporting those in need without discrimination. The Salvation Army serves local communities nationwide, touching the lives of one in every 10 Americans in a variety of ways. The Army provides food for the hungry, clothing and shelter to the homeless, companionship to the elderly and ill, opportunities for underprivileged children, relief for disaster victims, and other services to assist those in need.

Theresa Whitfield
Salvation Army National Headquarters
Alexandria, VA
*Contact Phone:* (703) 519-5893
*Contact Main Phone:* 703-684-5500
**Click to Contact from Web Site**

## MIRIAM'S KITCHEN
Washington, DC USA
http://miriamskitchen.org

Since 1983, Miriam's Kitchen has served homeless individuals in the District of Columbia. Approximately 75 percent of our guests are sleeping on the streets and in shelters. This means that Miriam's may be the only place that they go for help. Our mission is to provide individualized services that address the causes and consequences of homelessness in an atmosphere of dignity and respect both directly and through facilitating connections in the Washington, DC community.

John Jordan
Principor Communications
Washington, DC USA
*Contact Phone:* 202-595-9008
**Click to Contact from Web Site**

## CIVITAN INTERNATIONAL
Birmingham, AL USA
http://www.civitan.org

Civitans are everyday citizens, just like you and me, who come together in communities throughout the world to make life better for their neighbors. Family, friends, neighbors and co-workers meet at local Civitan clubs to socialize, learn and serve in their communities. Starting with just a single club, and a vision for helping others, Civitan has grown to over 40,000 members in 24 countries, including youth and college programs. Founded on the most basic moral and spiritual values, Civitans' commitment to identify and address needs in their communities have set them apart from other social and service organizations.

David Bledsoe
*Director of Communications & PR*
Civitan International
Birmingham, USA
*Contact Phone:* 205-591-8910
*Contact Main Phone:* 205-591-8910
**Click to Contact from Web Site**

## UNION RESCUE MISSION
Los Angeles, CA USA
http://www.unionrescuemission.org

Union Rescue Mission (URM) is a non-profit organization dedicated serving the poor and homeless. Established in 1891, URM is the largest rescue mission of its kind in the United States and the oldest in Los Angeles. It provides a comprehensive array of emergency and long-term services, including food, shelter, clothing, medical and dental care, recovery programs, transitional housing, legal assistance, education, counseling and job training to needy men, women, children and families.

Karen Kilwein
*Director of Public Relations*
Union Rescue Mission
Los Angeles, CA
*Contact Phone:* 213-347-6319
**Click to Contact from Web Site**

## PLAN USA
Warwick, RI USA
www.planusa.org

Plan USA is part of a unique, global alliance of caring individuals like you—a worldwide community sharing a common agenda for child-centered development and the well-being, rights and interests of the world's children. Our mission: We strive to achieve lasting improvements in the quality of life of deprived children in developing countries through a process that unites people across cultures and adds meaning and value to their lives by: enabling deprived children, their families, and their communities to meet their basic needs and to increase their ability to participate in and benefit from their societies; fostering relationships to increase understanding and unity among people of different cultures and countries; promoting the rights and interests of the world's children.

Hugh Minor
Plan USA
Warwick, RI USA
*Contact Phone:* 800-556-7918, 1177
**Click to Contact from Web Site**

## TOM LEE — EXPERT ON CATHOLIC CHURCH HISTORY
Phoenix, AZ USA

Mid-70s, the late Peter Levi, former Jesuit, and professor of Poetry at Oxford University, declared: The Church has painted itself into a corner by declaring as dogma things that man can never know and which God is quite unlikely to be worried about. In his pending book, The Invention of Christianity and the Papacy, Tom Lee explores the turbulent history of the first five hundred years when those far-fetched and contentious doctrines were formulated.

Tom Lee
Star Concepts, LLC
Phoenix, AZ USA
*Contact Phone:* 602-595-1946
**Click to Contact from Web Site**

## BUSTEDHALO.COM
New York, NY USA
http://www.bustedhalo.com

BustedHalo.com Mission Statement — We live in an age filled with seekers in their twenties and thirties who are desperately trying to find deeper meaning in their lives but whose journey has little to do with traditional religious institutions. BustedHalo.com believes that the experiences of these pilgrims and the questions they ask are inherently spiritual. Based in wisdom from the Catholic tradition, we believe that the joys and the hopes, the griefs and the anxieties of the people of this age are the joys and hopes, the griefs and anxieties of all God's people. Nothing genuinely human fails to raise an echo in their hearts. BustedHalo.com strives to reveal this spiritual dimension of our lives through feature stories, reviews, interviews, faith guides, commentaries, audio clips, discussions and connections to retreat, worship and service opportunities that can't be found anywhere else.

New York, NY
*Contact Phone:* 212 265 3209
**Click to Contact from Web Site**

## REV. ROY A. TEEL JR.
Moorpark, CA USA
http://www.narrowaypress.com

Rev. Roy A. Teel Jr. author of The Way, The Truth, and The Lies How the Gospels mislead Christians about Jesus' true message. The Way, the Truth, and the Lies cuts through oft-repeated myths to reveal a remarkably human Jesus. It breaks down the walls that have separated believers from non-believers to show Jesus' true message to humanity—a message so simple and so pure that He had to die for teaching it.

Roy A. Teel Jr.
*Reverend*
NarroWay Publishing LLC
Moorpark, CA USA
*Contact Phone:* 818-970-4859
*Pager:* 818-801-4859
**Click to Contact from Web Site**

## THE FELLOWSHIP PRESS - PUBLISHING WORKS BY M.R. BAWA MUHAIYADDEEN
Philadelphia, PA USA
http://www.bmf.org/

Muhammad Raheem Bawa Muhaiyaddeen is best remembered for his efforts to bring unity through understanding to the faithful of all religions through Sufism. What is Sufism? Sufism is understanding. It is understanding right from wrong. It is understanding that each of us is responsible for our actions. It is understanding that we cannot hurt one another without hurting ourselves. It is understanding Islam and that Islam means kindness, care, compassion, tolerance and submission to God.

Muhammad Lateef Hayden
*Publisher*
The Fellowship Press
Philadelphia, PA USA
*Contact Phone:* 610-937-2457
*Cell:* 610-937-2457
**Click to Contact from Web Site**

## NCSJ: ADVOCATES ON BEHALF OF JEWS IN RUSSIA, UKRAINE, BALTIC, ETC
Washington, DC USA
http://www.ncsj.org

NCSJ represents 50 national organizations and over 300 federations and community relations councils. It is the mandated central coordinating agency in the organized American Jewish community for advocacy on behalf of the Jewish minority residing within the 15 nations of the former Soviet Union.

Mark B. Levin
*Executive Director*
NCSJ: Advocates on Behalf of Jews in Russia, Ukraine, Baltic, etc
Washington, DC USA
*Contact Phone:* 202-898-2500
**Click to Contact from Web Site**

## UNITED CHRISTIAN SERVICES, INC.
Tampa Bay, FL USA

United Christian Services, Inc. is a Florida based 501c3 charitable organization dedicated to public service, teaching, counseling, religious instruction, and community based services. The director of the center, Dr. Maggie Faulkner is a pastor and a counselor who works with children and families in all areas of needs. She specializes in foster, adoptive, and teenage issues. She has over 30 years of multi-dimensional counseling experience. Kathleen Mohr is an award winning teacher with a background of 20 years of teaching at levels k-college. She has her master's degree in counseling and pursing her doctorate. She currently counsels children and families, tutors, and teaches.

Dr. Maggie C. Faulkner
United Christian Services, Inc.
Palm Harbor, FL USA
*Contact Phone:* 727-771-1112
**Click to Contact from Web Site**

**Advocates on behalf of Jews in Russia, Ukraine, the Baltic States & Eurasia**

NCSJ: Advocates on behalf of Jews in Russia, Ukraine, the Baltic States and Eurasia is the mandated central coordinating agency of the organized American Jewish community for policy and activities on behalf of the estimated 1.5 million Jews in Russia and Eurasia. NCSJ (originally founded as the National Conference on Soviet Jewry) encompasses nearly 50 national organizations and more than 300 local federations, community councils and committees. Through this extensive network, NCSJ mobilizes the resources, energies and talents of millions of U.S. citizens and also represents the American Jewish community in dealings with similar national groups in international arenas.

NCSJ:
Advocates on behalf of
Jews in Russia, Ukraine,
the Baltic States &
Eurasia
2020 K Street, NW,
Suite 7800,
Washington, D.C.
20006

*Robert J. Meth, M.D.,
Chairman*

*Mark B. Levin,
Executive Director*

**202.898.2500**
**202.898.0822 (fax)**
ncsj@ncsj.org
www.ncsj.org

## THE UNITED SYNAGOGUE OF CONSERVATIVE JUDAISM
New York, NY USA
http://www.uscj.org

International policy-making organization of 760 synagogues, comprising one and a half million Jews, working to formulate a religious response to pressing social and religious issues such as intermarriage, religious pluralism, and economic injustice. Commissions address needs in many vital areas—education, youth, substance abuse, Israel, access for the disabled—and work to further religious observance.

JoAnne Palmer
*Director of Public Affairs*
The United Synagogue of Conservative Judaism
New York, NY
*Contact Phone:* 212-533-7800
**Click to Contact from Web Site**

## WOMENSPATH—CHRISTIAN PRODUCTS & WORKSHOPS FOR & ABOUT WOMEN
Chicago, IL USA
www.womenspath.com

Women Protected in Christ (WPIC) is an interactive study book to remind women how Christ loves and protects women. WPIC challenges the view that Christian women are doormats or second-class citizens and highlights how women are encouraged to support, forgive, and be compasionate with one another and our differences. Dr. Denise Fraser Vaselakos, a clinical psychologist, and Ms. Joan Fraser Scannicchio are sisters and business partners in real life, familiar with media work (radio, television, newspaper)experienced speakers, workshop leaders,presenting with both humor and common sense.

Denise Fraser-Vaselakos
Homer Glenn, IL USA
*Contact Phone:* 708-645-0300
**Click to Contact from Web Site**

## ROBERT A. BERNSTEIN -- FAMILIES OF VALUE
Bethesda, MD USA
http://www.pgw.com/catalog/catalog.
asp?DBKey=79&CatalogKey=
172813&Action=View&Index=Page&Book=
181751&Order=58

GAY MARRIAGE AND RELIGIOUS VALUES -- Robert A. Bernstein is the author of the award-winning Straight Parents, Gay Children: Keeping Families Together (Thunder's Mouth Press, 2d ed. 2003) (Introduction by Robert Mac-Neil of MacNeil-Lehrer Productions) and of Families of Value: Personal Profiles of Pioneering Lesbian and Gay Parents (Marlowe and Co., 2005). He is currently writing a book on religion and homosexuality. Bernstein is a former U.S. Department of Justice supervisory trial attorney and law professor. As a free-lance writer, his articles have appeared in more than 60 daily newspapers, such as the New York Times, Washington Post and Los Angeles Times. In 1996, he was a "Parent of the Week" on the Oprah Winfrey Show. His first book, Straight Parents, Gay Children, won an award for best scholarship on the subject of intolerance from the Gustavus Myers Center for the Study of Human Rights in America.

Robert A. Bernstein
Bethesda, MD USA
*Contact Phone:* 301-530-4015
**Click to Contact from Web Site**

## DR. ROBERT MOREY - RELIGION & CULT EXPERT
Orange, CA USA
http://www.faithdefenders.com/ministry/

Dr. Robert A. Morey is the author of over 45 books, some of which have been translated into French, German, Italian, Dutch, Danish, Swedish, Spanish, Arabic, Farsi, Polish, and Finnish. He is listed in The International Authors and Writers Who's Who and Contemporary Authors. He earned a B.A. in philosophy from Covenant College, an M.Div. in theology from Westminster Seminary, a D.Min. in apologetics from Westminster Seminary, and received a D.D. in Islamic Studies from Faith Theological Seminary and a Ph.D from LBU in Islamic Studies for his groundbreaking research on the pre-Islamic origins of Islam. Some of his books have been nominated for Book of the Year, and have been included in the annual Best of the Good Books. They are textbooks in many colleges and seminaries around the world. He was elected chairman of the membership committee of the Evangelical Theological Society for several years.

Dorothy Kusch
*Secretary*
Faith Defenders
Orange, CA USA
*Contact Phone:* 1-800-418-7884
*Contact Main Phone:* 1-800-41-Truth
**Click to Contact from Web Site**

## DR. JOHN A. HENDERSON M.D. - GOD & RELIGION EXPERT

Asheville, NC USA

http://www.johnhenderson-god.com/home.shtml

John A. Henderson M.D. is a retired Air Force Flight Surgeon and General Surgeon and he and his wife, Ruth live in Asheville, North Carolina. Henderson graduated with honors from the University of Illinois College of Medicine in 1945. He interned at the Research and Educational Hospital, Chicago, Illinois; and was surgical resident at Scott and White Clinic, Temple, Texas. During his Air Force career, he served in England, Spain, and Japan. Within the United States, he was stationed in various states from New York to California.

John A. Henderson M.D.
God.com
Asheville, NC USA
*Contact Phone:* 828-285-2346
**Click to Contact from Web Site**

## HUMANISTS OF FLORIDA ASSOCIATION

Bradenton, FL USA

http://www.floridahumanist.org

HFA is a democratic membership organization, promoting Humanism in the State of Florida. We work to promote Humanism and the use of reason and compassion in solving Human problems. We achieve our goals through, education, example and progressive social action, and are dedicated to working in collaboration with others to achieve our goals. Our focus is to make Humanism an active force for positive social change. We engage in progressive social activism to promote Humanism.

Jennifer Hancock
*Executive Director*
Humanists of Florida Association
Bradenton, USA
*Contact Main Phone:* 941-745-7181
**Click to Contact from Web Site**

## CHRISTIAN-MUSLIM STUDIES NETWORK

Chicago, IL USA

http://www.christian-muslim.net

Christian-Muslim Studies Network is dedicated to promoting and improving the study of Christian-Muslim relations! Here students will soon find resources for choosing a quality program of study, opportunities for hands-on experience, options for tailoring your studies, and possibilities for using your skills around the world. Educators will find suggestions for building a more effective program. Administrators of study programs, internships, and other opportunities will have the opportunity to describe and link their programs to this site. Considerations for other school personnel incorporating Muslim students in a Christian-Muslim study program will also be available.

Le Anne Clausen
Chicago, IL USA
*Contact Phone:* 773-656-4745
**Click to Contact from Web Site**

**HUMANITY'S TEAM**
New York, NY USA
http://www.HumanitysTeam.org

Humanity's Team is a spiritual movement whose purpose is to communicate and implement the belief that we are all one, one with God and one with life, in a shared global state of being, so that the behavior of humanity may shift to reflect this understanding. Dubbed a civil rights movement for the soul, the movement has some 15,000 adherents from more than 90 countries on six continents. It was created by the spiritual author Neale Donald Walsch in 2003 in response to the crisis that he saw the human race facing following the 9/11 tragedy.

Gerry Harrington
*Worldwide Team Communications Coordinator*
Humanity's Team
Kingston, NY USA
*Contact Phone:* 845-331-7168
*Contact Main Phone:* 541-482-0126
*Cell:* 845-389-9201
**Click to Contact from Web Site**

**CATHOLIC TRADITIONALIST MOVEMENT, INC.**
Westbury, NY USA
http://www.latinmass-ctm.org

The grassroots Catholic Traditionalist Movement, was publicly launched in New York City on March 15, 1965, to provide Catholics with information necessary for correct understanding and implementation of the Second Vatican Council's decisions, in full conformity with the traditional doctrine and practices of the Roman Catholic Church. Ever since 1968, when the centuries-old Sacrifice of the Mass became threatened with extinction, the C.T.M. has concentrated its efforts on maintaining the completely unchanged Roman Catholic Latin Tridentine Mass.

Richard Cuneo
Catholic Traditionalist Movement, Inc.
Westbury, NY
*Contact Phone:* 516-333-6470
**Click to Contact from Web Site**

**TRINITY FOUNDATION, INC./THE WITTENBURG DOOR MAGAZINE**
Dallas, TX USA
http://www.Trinityfi.org/mission

The foundation regularly provides assistance to print and electronic journalists investigating suspected fraud or other abuses of the public trust by members of the religious media. The foundation maintains a private investigative license with the State of Texas and frequently provides undercover operatives to news programs like Prime-Time Live, 60 Minutes, Dateline, CNN Special Reports, 20/20, British Broadcasting Corporation, Canadian Broadcasting Corporation, and Inside Edition, among many others. Check out their religious satire magazine at http://www.TheDoor-Magazine.com

Ole Anthony
*President/Publisher*
Trinity Foundation, Inc./The Door Magazine
Dallas, TX
*Contact Phone:* 214-827-2625
*Contact Main Phone:* 214-827-2625
**Click to Contact from Web Site**

## MASONIC INFORMATION CENTER
Silver Spring, MD USA
http://www.msana.com

The Masonic Information Center is a division of the Masonic Service Association. Its purpose is to provide information on Freemasonry to Masons and non-Masons alike. The Center is directed by a Steering Committee of distinguished Masons geographically representative of the Fraternity throughout the United States and Canada.

Richard Fletcher
*Director*
Masonic Information Center
Silver Spring, MD
*Contact Phone:* 301-588-4010
**Click to Contact from Web Site**

## COMMON SENSE FOR TODAY
Ringgold, GA USA
www.cstnews.com

Dr. Don Boys is International Director of Common Sense for Today, an agency that presents 'another view' on subjects such as Islam, evolution, welfare, gay rights, pornography, abortion, death penalty, crime and punishment, Fundamentalism, affirmative action, etc. Boys dealt with most of those issues as a member of the Indiana House of Representatives, on talk shows, and in newspaper columns. Boys has written 13 books, edited over 100 school texts, wrote columns for USA Today from 1985 to 1993, and has appeared on numerous network and regional television shows.

Donald Boys, Ph.D.
Common Sense for Today
Ringgold, GA USA
*Contact Phone:* 706-965-5930
**Click to Contact from Web Site**

## DIANA CORNELIUS, NON-RELIGIOUS SPIRITUALITY EXPERT
San Jose, CA USA
http://www.dianacornelius.com

In 1992, a profound mystical experience changed the life of Diana Cornelius forever. Something 'other worldly' wanted her attention. Learning the power of the mind through the study of metaphysics, her life took on new dimension and clarity of purpose. Her exceptionally personal and instructional book, AL.I.F.E. BLUEPRINT: Spirituality Designed for the Non-Religious, gives readers step-by-step directions for learning how to manifest rich, meaningful lives. Her story, her exuberant attitude, and her valuable information guarantee a great interview.

Diana Cornelius
Cupertino, CA USA
*Contact Phone:* 408-725-1495
**Click to Contact from Web Site**

## FOUNDATION FOR A COURSE IN MIRACLES
Temecula, CA USA
http://www.facim.org

A nonprofit teaching foundation directed by Dr. Kenneth and Gloria Wapnick, and sister organization to the Foundation for Inner Peace, publishers of the spiritual text 'A Course in Miracles'®. Dr. Wapnick worked extensively with Dr. Helen Schucman, scribe of the Course, in preparing the original manuscript for publication. The Foundation's purpose is to further understanding and application of the Course principles of forgiveness by means of workshops, classes, publications, and electronic media.

Kenneth Wapnick
*President*
Foundation for A Course in Miracles
Temecula, CA
*Contact Phone:* 951-296-6261
*Contact Main Phone:* 951-296-6261
**Click to Contact from Web Site**

## STEVEN GAFFNEY — HONESTY EXPERT
Arlington, VA USA
www.stevengaffney.com

We provide skills to achieve honest, effective communication with anyone. These tools open lines of communication, enable people to express withheld information and ideas as well as resolve any difficult problem. Our clients have experienced immediate and sustained increases in motivation and productivity as well as exceptional leadership that resulted in achieving their goals. We produce results and you can hold us accountable to do the same for you. — Steven Gaffney, President of Steven Gaffney Company

Steven Gaffney
Steven Gaffney Company
Arlington, VA USA
*Contact Phone:* 703-241-7796
**Click to Contact from Web Site**

## JACK MARSHALL — PROETHICS, LTD.
Alexandria, VA USA
http://www.proethics.com

Writer, speaker, and innovator in legal and business ethics. President of ProEthics, a training and consulting firm applying the lessons of history, literature, philosophy, and popular culture to everyday ethical dilemmas. A Harvard and Georgetown educated attorney, his dynamic presentations utilize his skills as a professional theatrical director and actor. Call ProEthics at 1-877-PRO-ETHX.

Grace Marshall
*PR Director*
ProEthics, Ltd.
Alexandria, VA
*Contact Phone:* 877-776-3849
*Contact Main Phone:* 703-548-3754
**Click to Contact from Web Site**

## FRANK C. BUCARO & ASSOCIATES, INC.
Bartlett, IL USA
http://www.frankbucaro.com

Frank's unique approach blends the serious subject of ethics with a humorous and high-energy presentation style. The result is a riveting and fun experience for the entire audience. Frank's successful teaching career provided a smooth transition to full-time keynote and seminar presenter. The ethics scandals rocking Wall Street throughout the 90's served to further propel his career as an increasing number of organizations identified a need for ethics training. Fortune 500 companies, associations, and educational organizations have requested his upbeat, content rich keynote and seminar programs. These presentations highlight ethics as a powerful ally for growth and sustainability in the marketplace. Now a business owner, author, speaker and consultant, Frank explains, unwavering attention to ethical practices and behaviors is necessary. For example, this attention reduces vulnerability to costly and embarrassing legal problems, supports employee morale and retention, and fosters quality customer relationships. An ethical environment helps to create fertile ground for growth and productivity. A member of the National Speakers Association, Frank is a recipient of the CSP (Certified Speaking Professional) designation and the CPAE (Council of Peers Award of Excellence) Speaker Hall of Fame award.

Meg Wojtas
*Director of Marketing*
Frank C. Bucaro & Associates, Inc.
Bartlett, IL USA
*Contact Phone:* 847-742-8107
*Contact Main Phone:* 1-800-784-4476
**Click to Contact from Web Site**

## CHRISTOPHER BAUER, PH.D. -- BUSINESS ETHICS TRAINING
Nashville, TN USA
http://www.Bauerethicsseminars.com

Ethics expert Dr. Christopher Bauer's training as a clinical psychologist gives him a unique perspective on how individuals manage matters of ethics. It also allows him to provide equally unique commentary and analysis. As a speaker, seminar leader and consultant, he helps individuals and companies make more ethically-informed decisions while maximizing their bottom line. Bauer Ethics Seminars provides keynotes, breakouts, seminars, retreats, and consultation. Each helps individuals, teams and companies take effective responsibility for 'walking the talk' of ethical behavior.

Christopher Bauer, Ph.D.
Bauer Ethics Seminars
Nashville, TN USA
*Contact Phone:* 615-385-3523
**Click to Contact from Web Site**

## RID-USA, INC. REMOVE INTOXICATED DRIVERS
Schenectady, NY USA
http://www.rid-usa.org

Doris Aiken initiated the first effective anti-DWI campaign in the U.S. A celebrated award-winning leader in advancing anti-DWI laws, a former TV public affairs producer and host, she is a popular talk show guest and feisty victims' advocate. Aiken's organization RID-USA (Remove Intoxicated Drivers), active in 41 states, published the first citizen action manual, initiated the first victim impact panels and victim impact court statements (now mandated in most states), victim rights manuals, and many other programs.

Doris Aiken
*President/Founder*
RID-USA, Inc. Remove Intoxicated Drivers
Schenectady, NY
*Contact Phone:* 518-393-4357
**Click to Contact from Web Site**

## NATIONAL POLICY INSTITUTE
McLean, VA USA
http://www.nationalpolicyinstitute.org

The National Policy Institute (NPI) provides investigative studies and exclusive research papers addressing critical legal, regulatory, and cultural questions that impact on the interests of the USA's historic majority population. NPI analyzes immigration and demographic trends, crime and community safety issues, affirmative action and civil rights initiatives, and education and economic policies in the same way that hundreds of research/ educational foundations review the consequences of public policy on minorities, immigrants, and other special interest groups.

Kevin T. Lamb
*Publications Director*
National Policy Institute
McLean, VA United States
*Contact Phone:* 703-442-0558
*Contact Main Phone:* 703-442-0558
**Click to Contact from Web Site**

## FORUMS INSTITUTE FOR PUBLIC POLICY
Princeton, NJ USA
http://www.forumsinstitute.org

Forums Institute for Public Policy is a nonpartisan organization committed to promoting sound public policymaking through education, communication and research. Forums Institute administers the New Jersey Policy Forums on Health and Medical Care. For more than a decade, these Forums have brought together state policymakers with national and state experts for candid, off-the-record dialogue about timely health care policy issues. A trained facilitator moderates every Forum; original issue briefs are prepared especially for the events.

Nancy Cavallo
*Communications Director*
Forums Institute for Public Policy
Princeton, NJ United States
*Contact Phone:* 609-720-0136
*Cell:* 609-306-3775
**Click to Contact from Web Site**

## NATIONAL ASSOCIATION OF GOVERNMENT COMMUNICATORS
Washington, DC USA
http://www.nagc.com/

The National Association of Government Communicators (NAGC) is a national not-for-profit professional network of federal, state, local, military and other government employees who disseminate information within and outside government. Its members are government communications officers working as editors, writers, graphic artists, video professionals, broadcasters, photographers, information specialists and agency spokespersons.

Michael C. Sheward, APR
National Association of Government Communicators
Fairfax, VA USA
*Contact Phone:* 703-691-0377
**Click to Contact from Web Site**

## AMERICAN SOCIETY OF ASSOCIATION EXECUTIVES (ASAE)
Washington, DC USA
http://www.asaenet.org

Headquartered in Washington, DC, the American Society of Association Executives (ASAE) and its partner organization, The Center for Association Leadership, exist to enhance the power and performance of the association community worldwide through resources, education, ideas and advocacy. Its more than 23,000 members manage trade associations, professional societies, and philanthropic organizations across the United States and in 50 countries.

Chris Vest
*Media Relations*
ASAE & The Center for Association Leadership
Washington, DC
*Contact Phone:* 202-626-2798
**Click to Contact from Web Site**

## ASSOCIATION FOR POSTAL COMMERCE
Arlington, VA USA
http://www.postcom.org

The Association for Postal Commerce (PostCom) is a national association representing those who use or support the use of mail for business communication and commerce. PostCom pursues its mission by representing its members before Congress, the U.S. Postal Service, the Postal Rate Commission, other governmental agencies, associations and organizations.

Dr. Gene A. Del Polito
*President*
Association for Postal Commerce
Arlington, VA
*Contact Phone:* 703-524-0096
**Click to Contact from Web Site**

## INTERNATIONAL ASSOCIATION OF FACILITATORS
Minneapolis, MN USA
http://www.iaf-world.org

The International Association of Facilitators (IAF) is the largest global association for facilitators. The IAF promotes, supports and advances the art and practice of professional facilitation through methods exchange, professional growth, practical research, collegial networking and support services. The IAF offers professional accreditation, conferences and resources for both the professional facilitator and to managers, leaders, and professionals who apply facilitation within their work and lives.

Betty Kjellberg
*Executive Director*
International Association of Facilitators
St. Paul, MN USA
*Contact Phone:* 480-874-9919
*Cell:* 602-743-5019
**Click to Contact from Web Site**

## WHARTON SCHOOL CLUB OF WASHINGTON
Washington, DC USA
www.whartondc.com

Outstanding programs, such as our Annual Conference and Joseph Wharton Gala Dinner, now in its 38th year, that honors area business and public sector leaders, offer sponsors, members and attendees the opportunity to develop valuable business opportunities and expand critical knowledge. Our 2006 Conference on March 24, 2006 will focus on a timely topic for all business executives who want their company to survive potential natural and man-made disasters and major business disruptions: Powerful Leadership in Perilous Times: Preparing Your Business.

Alan N. Schlaifer
*President & CEO*
Wharton School Club of Washington
Bethesda, DC USA
*Contact Phone:* 301-365-8999
**Click to Contact from Web Site**

## RALPH J. BLOCH & ASSOCIATES, INC. -- ASSOCIATION PROGRAMS AND CONSULTING
Chicago, IL USA

We are dedicated to helping trade associations become more effective and more relevant to their members. We accomplish this by consulting in critical performance areas, and by providing development, professional sales and management of association programs. Our approach to consulting is practical, personal and results-oriented. Our clients appreciate the way our principal, Ralph Bloch, works with their volunteer leaders and management staffs in the areas of strategic planning, leadership development, management assessment and issues resolution.

Ralph J. Bloch
Ralph J. Bloch & Associates, Inc.
Chicago, IL USA
*Contact Phone:* 312-640-0465
**Click to Contact from Web Site**

## BIOTECHNOLOGY INDUSTRY ORGANIZATION
Washington, DC USA
www.bio.org

The Biotechnology Industry Organization (BIO) represents more than 11,000 biotechnology companies, academic institutions, and state biotechnology centers across the United States and 31 other nations. BIO members are involved in the research and development of health care, agricultural, industrial and environmental biotechnology products.

Kim Coghill
*Director of Communications*
Biotechnology Industry Organization
Washington, DC
*Contact Phone:* 202-962-9200
**Click to Contact from Web Site**

## ALABAMA DEPARTMENT OF ECONOMIC AND COMMUNITY AFFAIRS
Montgomery, AL USA
http://www.adeca.alabama.gov/

Larry J. Childers
Alabama Department of Economic and Community Affairs
Montgomery, AL United States
*Contact Phone:* 334-242-5525
**Click to Contact from Web Site**

## NATIONAL TAXPAYERS UNION
Alexandria, VA USA
http://www.ntu.org

The National Taxpayers Union is the nation's largest non-profit, non-partisan organization representing American taxpayers. Its spokespeople often appear on national television and radio news programs on issues of importance to the nation's taxpayers. Their expertise includes: state and federal tax policies, state and federal budget policies, Social Security and Medicare programs and citizen activism as well as many other areas of concern.

Pete Sepp
*Vice President, Communications*
National Taxpayers Union
Alexandria, VA
*Contact Phone:* 703-683-5700
**Click to Contact from Web Site**

## JOSEPH ZODL—WORLD TRADE
Phoenix, AZ USA
http://www.zodl.net

Author of Export-Import (Phoenix, IIEI Press, $39.95, Fourth Edition), Joseph Zodl is an expert in international business, exporting, importing, and helping American business succeed in the global marketplace. His topics include starting a company, overcoming barriers, increasing profits, decreasing costs, and political analysis. More than twenty years practical experience and ten years teaching at college and MBA level. Excellent resource and media guest.

Joseph Zodl
Joseph Zodl—World Trade
Phoenix, AZ
*Contact Phone:* 602-667-5690
**Click to Contact from Web Site**

## ERIC DE GROOT -- GLOBAL PROBLEM SOLVER
Atlanta, GA USA
http://www.globaleducationmatters.com

Eric possesses a current and critical understanding of both the U.S. and European cultures and this unique perspective is evident in all of his presentations. As of 9/11, the global angle that Eric will deliver is all the more significant for American associations and corporations. De Groot's expertise will help you to avoid cultural, lingual, and geographic goof-ups; saving you time, money, face, and goodwill. Furthermore, Eric, who is fluent in Dutch, German, French, and English, and a veteran of 17 marathons worldwide, will help you speed up global market penetration and corporate growth through his Change and Shape worldly approach. Upon conclusion of his presentations, the necessity of change toward a global minded organization to achieve further success will be clear. Eric will have you laughing and learning as he teaches you to become a Global Player with a Global Mindset

Eric de Groot
Global Education Matters
Atlanta, GA USA
*Contact Phone:* 404-250-1709
**Click to Contact from Web Site**

## U.S. CHAMBER OF COMMERCE
Washington, DC USA
www.uschamber.com

The United States Chamber of Commerce is the world's largest business federation, representing 3,000,000 businesses, 2,800 state and local chambers of commerce, 830 business associations and 98 American chambers of commerce in 83 countries.

Linda Rozett
U. S. Chamber of Commerce
Washington, DC USA
*Contact Phone:* 202-463-5682
**Click to Contact from Web Site**

## FOREIGN-TRADE ZONE CORPORATION
Mobile, AL USA
www.ftzcorp.com

The Foreign-Trade Zone Corporation is the only nationally recognized consulting firm that limits its practice to FTZ consulting, software systems, and management. Its range of consulting work in the FTZ program is all-encompassing, with services extending from cost-benefit analysis, Board applications, activations with CBP, to the operation and management of nine FTZ projects. With involvement in over 150 projects located in 35 states and Puerto Rico, the Foreign-Trade Zone Corporation has in-depth experience in virtually every industry imaginable.

Craig M. Pool
*President*
Foreign-Trade Zone Corporation
Mobile, AL
*Contact Phone:* 251-471-6725
**Click to Contact from Web Site**

## THECAPITOL.NET
Washington, DC USA
http://www.thecapitol.net/

TheCapitol.Net is a non-partisan firm that provides training and publications that show how Washington works for people who work in Washington. TM Our publications are written by current Washington insiders who are all independent subject matter experts in the federal legislative and budget process, media training, and advocacy and persuasion. We also offer practical legislative, federal budget, communication, and media training. TheCapitol.Net came out of Congressional Quarterly, which had offered many of our training courses since the late 1970s. TheCapitol. Net is the exclusive provider of Congressional Quarterly Executive Conferences.

Chug Roberts
*Publisher*
TheCapitol.Net
Alexandria, VA USA
*Contact Phone:* 202-678-1600
*Contact Main Phone:* 877-228-5086
**Click to Contact from Web Site**

## WINNING CAMPAIGNS — ALAN LOCKE
Washington, DC USA
www.winningcampaigns.org

Alan L. Locke is publisher of WINNING CAMPAIGNS, the largest monthly direct circulation magazine serving the political community. He was associated with William Colby, former director of Central Intelligence for the United States. He is an expert on Media Relations/Crisis Management and Political Campaigning. Locke has been an analyst on the American political scene for international political, business and academic leaders visiting the United States.

Alan L. Locke
EJM Consulting/Winning Campaigns
Falls Church, VA USA
*Contact Phone:* 703-534-5645
**Click to Contact from Web Site**

## COMPETITIVE ENTERPRISE INSTITUTE
Washington, DC USA
www.cei.org

The Competitive Enterprise Institute is a non-profit public policy organization dedicated to the principles of free enterprise and limited government. We believe that consumers are best helped not by government regulation but by being allowed to make their own choices in a free marketplace. Since its founding in 1984, CEI has grown into a $3,000,000 institution with a team of nearly 40 policy experts and other staff.

Jody Clarke
Competitive Enterprise Institute
Washington, DC USA
*Contact Phone:* 202-331-2252
**Click to Contact from Web Site**

## RENANA BROOKS, PH.D, SOMMET INSTITUTE FOR THE STUDY OF POWER
Washington, DC USA
www.renanabrooks.com

Presidential consultant, author, psychologist, media commentator, and therapist to Washington insiders, Dr. Renana Brooks has unparalleled access to the private lives and public faces of America's political and business leaders. She advises when they are challenged by scandal or political mistake. Brooks also has conducted extensive research on the sequelae of culture wars, eroding values, epidemic infidelity, escalating depression and anxiety, increasing delay of adult responsibility, bullying and discourses of contempt, and increasing language of demonization of differences. Brooks advises politicians, organizations, and families. She has been featured in many major newspapers and NBC, CBS, ABC, Fox, CNN, CSPAN, and talk radio.

Renana Brooks, Ph.D
*Founder and Director*
The Sommet Institute
Washington, DC
*Contact Phone:* 202-783-0775
**Click to Contact from Web Site**

## SENATOR DON BENTON, POLITICAL EXPERT
Portland, OR USA
http://www.donbenton.com

Elective Office: Elected to state Senate, 1996 and 2000; Washington state House of Representatives, 1994. Community Involvement: Clark County American Red Cross, 20-year volunteer; Republican precinct committeeman; Vancouver Moose Lodge, life member; College of the Canyons, past president, board of trustees; The Jaycees, SCV Chapter, past president; Assistant Scout Master, Pack 358, Boy Scouts of America and Member, Financial Literacy Public-Private Partnership.

Don Benton
Vancouver, WA USA
*Contact Phone:* 360-754-7369
**Click to Contact from Web Site**

# Eric de Groot
# Global Problem Solver

The world has become smaller, closer and faster — *and* significantly more complex for those who do business around the globe. Global Problems require a Global Problem Solver.

Everyday, businesses worldwide lose billions of dollars as well as an abundance of time and goodwill, because they do not fully understand different cultures or customs. Globalization depends on the success and the expansion of the world economy, led by the U.S.A. Not enough American managers receive proper training, have the right tools or use cultural knowledge to build market share abroad.

Therefore, you need laser-sharp precision, and you need to know where you are on the map. You need a GPS. De Groot is that virtual problem locator and solver. A multi-lingual executive and cultural connoisseur with two decades of hands-on experience as an importer and exporter and international busines strategist, he will help you solve your global problems.

Eric possesses a current and critical understanding of both the U.S. and European cultures, and this unique perspective is evident in all of his presentations. De Groot — who is fluent in Dutch, German, French and English — will instruct you and your corporate team on how to avoid cultural, linguistic and geographic goof-ups, saving you time, money, face *and* goodwill. Through his "Change and Shape" worldly approach, Eric will have you laughing and

learning as this Global Problem Solver shows you how to become a Global Player with a Global Mindset.

A native of Amsterdam, the Netherlands, and now a U.S. citizen, de Groot is the real deal when it comes to entrepreneurship, counting more than 20 years of ideas, concepts, visions and master plans. As an author of several published articles on "Cultures2Go™," and co-author of "Irresistible Leadership," Eric is working to finish his own book on "Global Education Matters and Global Goof-Ups™." Contact this GPS 24/7 to solve your problems globally and/or learn "How to avoid international cultural misunderstanding."

*Clients that have benefited from Eric's services include the Department of Justice (FBI), Society of Former Special Agents of the FBI, the Edison Electric Institute, the Weather Channel, the Home Depot, the Coca-Cola Company, Bellsouth, Time Warner, Macy's, Bloomingdale's, Saks Fifth Avenue and hundreds of commercial and non-profit organizations.*

■ *Eric is very active in the community and has served on many boards. He has raised funds in the "race to end world hunger" (18 marathons), received a state award for a recycling road race, was nominated twice as "Member of the Year" and received the Presidential Award from his NSA speaking chapter.*

**MEMBER**
**NSA**™
NATIONAL SPEAKERS ASSOCIATION

**Eric de Groot**
Global Education Matters™
P.O. Box 720400
Atlanta, Georgia 30358

404-250-1709
404-808-2073 Direct
404-256-5437 Fax
866-SPEAKER-55

**www.globaleducationmatters.com** ◆ **eric@globaleducationmatters.com**

## AMERICANS FOR DEMOCRATIC ACTION
Washington, DC USA
http://www.adaction.org

ADA is America's oldest independent liberal lobbying organization. In the spirit of the New Deal and ADA founders Eleanor Roosevelt, renowned economist John Kenneth Galbraith, and former Senator and Vice President Hubert Humphrey we lobby through coalition partnerships, through direct advocacy, and through the media. Our lobbying philosophy is based on democratic action - motivating our grassroots members to lobby their senators and representatives as constituent-advocates. With 65,000 members nationwide, numerous state and local chapters, and its headquarters in the District of Columbia actively engaging in the political process, ADA continually strives to push for democratic and progressive values and ideals in American policy.

Don Kusler
*Communications*
Americas for Democratic Action
Washington, DC USA
*Contact Phone:* 202-785-5980
**Click to Contact from Web Site**

## WILLIAM S. BIKE -- POLITICAL COMMENTATOR
Chicago, IL USA
www.anbcommunications.com

As a political commentator, William S. Bike, senior vice president of public relations, writing and political consulting firm ANB Communications, uses his encyclopedic knowledge of history to add an unusual depth to discussions of current events. Bike has made frequent radio and television appearances and literally wrote the book on politics: Winning Political Campaigns, a how-to handbook on political campaigning, Political-book-reviviews.com said: from a practical, political standpoint, it is the best book out--yet.

William S. Bike
ANB Communications
Chicago, IL USA
*Contact Phone:* 773-229-0024
*Cell:* 312-996-8495
**Click to Contact from Web Site**

## PAUL A. LONDON
Washington, DC USA
http://www.aei.org/book802

Paul A. London, former Clinton administration deputy undersecretary of commerce, defies conventional political wisdom and outlines a blueprint for U.S. economic resurgence in The Competition Solution: The Bipartisan Secret behind American Prosperity [Publication date: March 3, 2005/AEI Press, publisher for the American Enterprise Institute for Public Policy Research (AEI)]. He identifies increased competition in the health care and education sectors as far more critical to the economy than Social Security reform and tax cuts.

Sam Thernstrom
*Publications*
American Enterprise Institute
Washington, DC USA
*Contact Phone:* 202-862-5870
*Contact Main Phone:* 202-862-5800
**Click to Contact from Web Site**

## ALAN CARUBA — PUBLIC RELATIONS EXPERT
South Orange, NJ USA
http://www.caruba.com

Alan Caruba is a veteran public relations expert and counselor whose clients have included corporations, associations, professionals, celebrities and authors. Respected by the media for his candor and by clients for his emphasis on the truth as the only basis for PR.

Alan Caruba
South Orange, NJ USA
*Contact Phone:* 973-763-6392
**Click to Contact from Web Site**

# FOREIGN-TRADE ZONE
## C O R P O R A T I O N

A Foreign-Trade Zone is a specially designated area in, or adjacent to, a U.S. Customs Port Of Entry, which is considered to be outside the Customs Territory of the U.S.

The following is a partial list of the many benefits you can attain when using Foreign-Trade Zones or Foreign-Trade Zone Subzones:

- No duty is ever paid on merchandise re-exported from a Foreign-Trade Zone;
- If the merchandise is sold domestically, no duty is paid until it leaves the Zone or Zones;
- Generally, no duty is paid on waste or yield loss in a Foreign-Trade Zone or Subzone;
- Duty on scrap is eliminated or reduced in a Foreign-Trade Zone;
- Generally, if foreign merchandise is manufactured within a Foreign-Trade Zone or Subzone into a product with a lower duty rate, then the lower duty rate applies on the foreign content when duty is paid;
- Merchandise in a Foreign-Trade Zone may be stored, repackaged, manipulated, manufactured, destroyed or otherwise altered and changed.

The Foreign-Trade Zone Corporation is the only nationally recognized consulting firm that limits its practice to Foreign-Trade Zone consulting, FTZ software systems and management.

Its range of consulting work in the FTZ Program is all-encompassing, with services extending from Foreign-Trade Zones cost-benefit analysis, Board applications, activations with Customs and Border Protection, to the operation and management of nine U.S. Foreign-Trade Zone projects.

With involvement in more than 150 FTZ projects located in more than 35 states and Puerto Rico, the FTZ Corporation has in-depth experience in virtually every industry imaginable.

SmartZone® is the complete FTZ inventory control solution offered by the FTZ Corporation. It is the only software package designed by FTZ experts and experienced operators. With more than 250 companies currently using SmartZone®, and with the SmartZone® team's hands-on experience operating both manufacturing and distribution Zones, the company has developed a reputation as the experts in this field.

**Foreign-Trade Zone Corporation**: 2062 Old Shell Road, Mobile, Alabama 36607

Tele: (251) 471-6725
Fax: (251) 471-6727
E-mail: ftzconsultinginfo@ftzcorp.com
Web site: ftzcorp.com

## COUNCIL FOR AMERICA'S FIRST FREEDOM

Richmond, VA USA
www.firstfreedom.org

The Council for America's First Freedom (CAFF) is a non-denominational, non-political, non-profit organization based in Richmond, Virginia. CAFF's mission is to champion religious freedom worldwide through education and to strengthen appreciation for America's protection of this fundamental human right. Currently, CAFF is developing the First Freedom Center, a world-class facility that will offer a dynamic visitor experience with state-of-the-art, interactive exhibits exploring the development of religious freedom in America, and today's related national and international issues.

Maureen Rosenbaum
*Manager of Community Affairs & Development*
*Contact Phone:* 804-643-1786
**Click to Contact from Web Site**

## PATRICK WOOD - THE AUGUST REVIEW

Rathdrum, ID USA
www.augustreview.com/

Patrick M. Wood edits and publishes The August Review, which is a critical analysis of globalization and the nucleus of people who drive it. His work spans over 30 years. Between 1978 and 1981, Wood co-author of Trilaterals Over Washington, Volumes I and II with the late Antony C. Sutton, who had been a Senior Fellow at the Hoover Institution at Stanford University. Wood is available for appearance on talk radio and television programs.

Patrick M. Wood
The August Review
Rathdrum, ID USA
*Contact Phone:* 208-712-0170
**Click to Contact from Web Site**

## MARK DANKOF'S AMERICA

San Antonio, TX USA
http://www.MarkDankof.com

Areas of Interest/Expertise: The American Right; Paleo-Conservatism; Libertarianism; Constitutionalism; Christianity; Lutheranism; Dispensationalism; the Israeli lobby; Iran; Central Asia and the Caspian; U. S. Congressional Roll-Call analysis. Profile: Paleo-conservative political writer and consultant; Christian clergyman. Agencies: Breaking All the Rules (BATR) [BATR's Neo-Con Watch, Old Right Pundits, and American Memory divisions]; Senior Editor of Old Right Topic News; FreedomWriter; DixieInternet.com; Strike the Root, Iran Dokht; PersianMirror; Rozaneh Magazine; Sarbazan; CASCFEN (Azerbaijan); American Nationalist Union; and Mark Dankof's America.

Mark Dankof
*Investigative Journalist*
Mark Dankof's America
San Antonio, TX USA
*Contact Phone:* 210-563-4584
*Cell:* 210-563-4584
**Click to Contact from Web Site**

## DR. ADRIAN H. KRIEG, CFMGE

Bradenton, FL USA
www.a2zpublications.com

Dr. Krieg was born in 1938 in Switzerland, and immigrated to the US in 1952. His doctorate is in manufacturing science. He has authored over 500 published articles relating to science, history, politics, economics, and the environment. He served in the US army European theater. He is the author of numerous published books relating to the 19th and 20th century history. He had done over 200 radio and numerous TV interviews. His latest book is: Our Political Systems, available from all booksellers worldwide.

Dr. Adrian H. Krieg, CFMGE
Bradenton, FL USA
*Contact Phone:* 941-322-2739
**Click to Contact from Web Site**

## DANIEL NEW

Iredell, TX USA
www.mikenew.com

Daniel New is the father of Army Spc. Michael New, the soldier court-martialed in 1996 for disobeying an order to wear a United Nations uniform, report to a general from Finland, and deploy as a U.N. mercenary to Macedonia. He has become an articulate spokesman for American sovereignty and has developed initiatives for local, state and national legislation to protect us from the encroachment of the United Nations into areas, which are the very definition of sovereignty.

Daniel New
Iredell, TX
*Contact Phone:* 254-796-2173
**Click to Contact from Web Site**

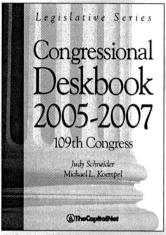
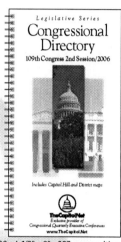
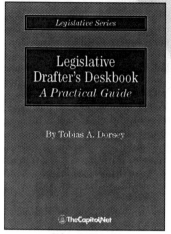
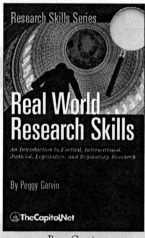
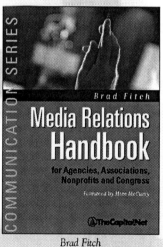

**JOSEPH WERNER -- CREATOR OF THE TERM: SILENT MAJORITY**
Setauket, NY USA
http://www.josephwerner.com

Mr. Werner created and extensively used the term SILENT MAJORITY well before it found its way into Pres. Nixon's speech. He is the only known person in the world who operates as he does - "30+" years of LONE, "Completely" self-financed, Not-For-Profit - CATALYTIC CAMPAIGNS at the LOCAL, NATIONAL and INTERNATIONAL levels - in Quest for "BETTERMENT OF MANKIND." Major Areas of Involvement (some of which have lasted more than "10" years): Turmoil years of the 60s-70s (a positive force during an era of polarization); Teacher's Union (unrealized national power); Illegal Aliens (America's health, wealth, safety and future at stake); Affirmative Action (Un-American-dividing our country); American Spirit Award (Established this Annual-National Award in 1996 - Americans Helping Americans); Unseal Kennedy & King Files (Held in national archives - we owe it to the future to get the facts today); Berlin Wall (LONE "Catalytic" Campaign - One segment, annual all-day, lone vigils at the checkpoint Charlie entrance to the Berlin Wall with writings, give-a-ways, etc. plus "international" involvement so "VAST" one must see web site.) Berlin Airlift (Honorary Life Member of Veterans Association; plus writer of tribute entitled, Berlin Airlift: Peace Warrior's Eternal Echo and book entitled, Berlin Airlift: Brides & Grooms Created); Miscellaneous (30+ years of continuous involvements.

Joseph Werner
Setauket, NY
*Contact Phone:* 631-751-8170
**Click to Contact from Web Site**

**LEON POMEROY, PH.D.**
Washington, DC USA
http://www.e-valuemetrics.com

Dr. Pomeroy's interdisciplinary doctoral dissertation involved work in the fields of psychology, computer science, computer-assisted data processing, biochemistry and nutrition, and biomedical engineering funded by several government and university entities. During this period he had offices at the Clayton Foundation Biochemical Institute as well as the Department of Biomedical Engineering of the Electrical Engineering Department at UT Austin, and headed up a team of electrical engineers with whom he worked in the computer extraction of information from brain waves employing sophisticated statistical models. This interdisciplinary research resulted in several publications appearing in such prestigious scientific journals as the Proceedings of the National Academy of Sciences of the USA, and Journal of Electroencephalography and Clinical Neurophysiology. During his graduate studies he was privileged to have studied under Raul Hernandez-Peon, M.D., Director, Brain Research Institute, 445 Moras, Mexico City, D.F.

Leon Pomeroy, Ph.D.
Woodbridge, VA United States
*Contact Phone:* 703 730 9357
**Click to Contact from Web Site**

**LOIS ANGELL**
Washington, DC USA

Lois Angell — A.K.A. 'Washington's Angell' — gives a humorous insider's looks at D.C. Her work as a top staffer in all three branches of government provides material from places the press can't go.

Lois Angell
Washington, DC
*Contact Phone:* 202-965-5568
**Click to Contact from Web Site**

**DAVID DEBATTO - FORMER COUNTERINTELLIGENCE SPECIAL AGENT**
St. Petersburg, FL USA
http://www.davedebatto.com

David DeBatto's unit served in Iraq's Sunni Triangle where some of the worst fighting of Operation Iraqi Freedom has occurred. As leader of a Tactical Human Intelligence Team, David was responsible for tracking down and capturing high level Iraqi fugitives and Al-Qaeda terrorists and in seizing numerous weapons caches and top secret government documents. The hard work of his team and the extensive network of informants they were able to develop led to capture of one of the top '55 Playing Card' fugitives from Saddam's regime.

David DeBatto
St. Petersburg, FL USA
*Contact Phone:* 727-944-5445
*Cell:* 978-809-0521
**Click to Contact from Web Site**

*When you need a solid insight into Politics, International Relations, Government Affairs and the Media, contact:*

# ALAN L. LOCKE

publisher of *Winning Campaigns*, the largest direct circulation monthly magazine serving the political world with offices in Falls Church, VA, four miles from the White House. He has been acclaimed as a consultant on politics, national and international government affairs and the media.

**H**e was associated with the late Ambassador William Colby, former director of Central Intelligence for the United States, and has been involved in a number of political campaigns on national and local levels. These include presidential, gubernatorial and down ballot campaigns ranging from statewide to local level.

**H**is clients have included Campaigns & Elections magazine where he was Vice President of Operations, the National Leadership Forum on Global Affairs of which he is a member of the Board of Directors, Congressional Quarterly Inc., KCI Publishing Inc., the United States Naval Reserve and the United States Coast Guard. He had organized, directed and managed all political training programs nationwide for *Campaigns & Elections* magazine and *Congressional Quarterly* for a number of years.

**A** national speaker on Media Relations/Crisis Management and Political Campaign Management Techniques, he has been called upon as an analyst on the American political scene and foreign affairs for international political, business and academic leaders visiting the United States.

**A**mong his areas of expertise are Political Campaign Management and International Political Affairs and Developments. He has served as a television guest commentator on political and business matters for a national financial newsletter.

**M**r. Locke has been publisher of Business Magazine, a chain of business-related magazines with a circulation in excess of 100,000 in the East Coast and Mid-Atlantic regions and was owner/publisher of a weekly newspaper in Boston, Ma. He had also been an editor, writer and columnist for several newspapers including the Boston Herald as well as other publications in Pennsylvania and Massachusetts. He has also served as Director of Public Affairs and Education for the Association of Trial Lawyers of America.

**H**e has been an adjunct professor of management and marketing techniques, media relations and communications at Boston University, Boston, MA, Trinity College in Washington, D.C., Suffolk University School of Management, Boston, MA, The Washington (DC) Center and Northern Virginia Community College. He is a graduate of Boston University with a degree in Public Relations.

For speaker bookings, interviews and sounds bites, he can be reached at:

Alan L. Locke, EJM Consulting/WINNING CAMPAIGNS, 221 S Virginia Ave., Falls Church, VA,

22046 or call 703-534-5645, FAX 703-534-1008 or e-mail at info@winningcampaigns.org.

His websites are www.winningcampaigns.org or www.ejm-consulting.com

## JUDITH LEE BERG -- HUMAN RESOURCE COMMUNICATION

Denver, CO USA

Judith dissects and analyzes the anatomy and disease of hate, hate groups and hate crimes. She confronts the sociopathic nature of choosing to hate, as the pathological background noise of the 1984 assassination of her husband, Alan Berg, who was a criminal trial attorney and talk radio personality. Judith relates the Turner Diaries, militia mentality, and the Aryan Nation's neo-nazi pathology to the demise of America. Judith, as a educator, public speaker and journalist, covered the Oklahoma Bombing Trial; she has been interviewed by journalists and newspapers, and has appeared on major radio and television shows.

Judith Lee Berg
Human Resource Communication
Denver, CO
*Contact Phone:* 303-322-6229
*Pager:* 303-207-8566
**Click to Contact from Web Site**

## JOHN LONGENECKER — AUTHOR AND COLUMNIST ON PERSONAL SOVEREIGNTY.

Los Angeles, CA USA
www.transferofwealth.net

Are America's Anti-Crime Policies further looting the Amercan Household? John Longenecker says the Household is the Stronghold of resistance to adversity in America, and that erosion of privacy, personal authority and power are no accident of good intentions, but a tactical move to loot America hundreds of ways. Author and Columnist John Longenecker identifies the ways household privacy, authority and power are dissolved in a major transfer of our greatest wealth: our way of life.

John Longenecker
Lakewood, CA USA
*Contact Phone:* 800-507-8240
**Click to Contact from Web Site**

## BRADY CAMPAIGN TO PREVENT GUN VIOLENCE

Washington, DC USA
www.BradyCampaign.org

The Brady Center to Prevent Gun Violence is a national, non-profit, education, legal advocacy, and research organization working to reduce gun deaths and injuries. The Center, in conjunction with its lobbyingl affiliate, the Brady Campaign to Prevent Gun Violence, has a comprehensive, multi-faceted approach to stemming America's gun violence epidemic. The Center was created in 1983 to educate the American public about the scope of gun violence and to develop solutions to the problem. Sarah Brady, wife of James Brady, former White House press secretary, is chair of the Center. Jim Brady is on the Center's Board of Trustees.

Peter Hamm
Brady Campaign to Prevent Gun Violence
Washington, DC
*Contact Phone:* 202-289-5792
*Contact Main Phone:* 202-898-0792
**Click to Contact from Web Site**

## JOHN M. SNYDER, GUN LAW EXPERT

Washington, DC USA
www.gunsaint.com

Named "Dean of gun lobbyists" by The Washington Post and The New York Times, gun law expert John Snyder is the author of GUN SAINT, a book about a canonized Catholic saint who used handguns in 1860 to rescue Italian villagers from a gang of terrorists. Snyder is Public Affairs Director of the Citizens Committee for the Right to Keep and Bear Arms, Chairman of the St. Gabriel Possenti Society and Vice President of the National Association of Chiefs of Police.

John M. Snyder
Telum Associates, LLC
Arlington, VA USA
*Contact Phone:* 202-326-5259
*Cell:* 703-212-9863
**Click to Contact from Web Site**

### BNA, INC.
Washington, DC USA
http://www.bna.com/

Founded in 1929 to report, interpret, and explain the increasingly complicated workings of the federal government and their far-reaching impact on the economic life of the nation, BNA is today Washington, D.C.'s largest private news publisher, reporting on the full range of government regulations, legislation, court opinions, and laws that dictate the ways America does business. Completely free of advertising, BNA's more than 200 print and electronic publications are known and valued for their unbiased reporting.

Karen James Cody
*Communications Director*
BNA, Inc.
Washington, DC
*Contact Phone:* 202-452-4169
**Click to Contact from Web Site**

### ADVOCACY ASSOCIATES, LLC.
Washington, DC USA
http://www.AdvocacyGuru.com

Stephanie Vance, former hill staffer and current Advocacy Guru has joined forces with Jason Jordan, formerly the chief lobbyist and head of government relations for the American Planning Association, to form Advocacy Associates, LLC. Advocacy Associates, LLC, provides its clients with a new approach to creating policy change, focusing on advocacy training and consulting, lobby day coordination, grassroots network and campaign development, and consulting round local initiative and ballot measure campaigns.

Stephanie Vance
*Advocacy Guru*
Advocacy Associates, LLC.
Washington, DC
*Contact Phone:* (202) 244-4866
**Click to Contact from Web Site**

### NATIONAL RIGHT TO LIFE COMMITTEE
Washington, DC USA
http://www.nrlc.org

The National Right to Life Committee is the nation's largest pro-life group, with affiliates in all 50 states and some 3,000 local chapters nationwide. Through education, legislation, political action and communications, NRLC works against abortion, infanticide and euthanasia. NRLC spokespeople are available for interviews and debates on all life-related issues.

Megan Dillon
*Director of Media Relations*
National Right to Life Committee
Washington, DC
*Contact Phone:* 202-626-8825
**Click to Contact from Web Site**

### AMERICAN LIFE LEAGUE
Stafford, VA USA
http://www.all.org

Judie Brown is entering her 20th year as president of American Life League. With 300,000 supporters nationwide, American Life League is the country's largest pro-life grass-roots educational organization. American Life League believes all innocent human life deserves respect and protection. Judie is ready to offer fresh insight on Abortion, Assisted Suicide, Birth Control, Cloning, and Fetal Research.

Amber Dolle
*Director of Gov., & Media Relations*
American Life League
Stafford, VA
*Contact Phone:* 540-659-4171
**Click to Contact from Web Site**

### CENTER FOR WOMEN POLICY STUDIES
Washington, DC USA
http://www.centerwomenpolicy.org

The Center for Women Policy Studies, founded in 1972, was the first feminist policy research center offering expertise on women's issues: education for girls/women; women's health; economic opportunity/low-income women; work/family policies; violence against women and sexual harassment; women and AIDS. Broad expertise on women's equity agenda, focus on women of color.

Dr. Leslie R. Wolfe
*President*
Center for Women Policy Studies
Washington, DC
*Contact Phone:* 202-872-1770
**Click to Contact from Web Site**

# JOHN M. SNYDER, GUN LAW EXPERT

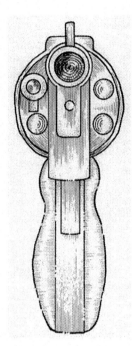

Named "Dean of gun lobbyists" by the Washington Post and the New York Times, gun law expert John Snyder is the author of "Gun Saint," a book about a Catholic saint who used handguns in 1860 to rescue Italian villagers from a gang of terrorizing soldiers.

He has been quoted extensively by national and local media, testified before Congress and state legislatures in defense of carrying firearms and written about the merits of ordinary, responsible citizens bearing arms to protect themselves and their communities. He makes for a thoughtful and provocative interview.

Snyder is public affairs director of the Citizens Committee for the Right to Keep and Bear Arms, chairman of the St. Gabriel Possenti Society and vice president of the National Association of Chiefs of Police.

**John M. Snyder**
Telum Associates, LLC
Arlington, Virginia, U.S.A.
Contact Phone: 202-326-5259
Cell #: 703-212-9863

info@possentisociety.com
GunDean@aol.com

P.O. Box 2844
Arlington, Virginia 22202

For more information about the St. Gabriel Possenti Society and the right to armed self-defense, write or e-mail Possenti Society founder John M. Snyder at the address above.

**RACHEL BONDI --**
**WWW.EARNINGPOWER.ORG**
Los Angeles, CA USA
www.EarningPower.org

Men Matter. Men are still in charge. The statistics prove their influence. About 99% of the FORTUNE 500 CEOs, 85% of corporate boards, 70-90% of congress, news editor, and college faculty are men. Since women must work with men, why do they still use mothers' outdated strategies to get ahead? The truth about equality is many men are interested in empowering women. We've identified the types and their personal and business reasons for doing so.

Rachel Bondi
Dana Point, CA USA
*Contact Phone:* 949-394-1811
**Click to Contact from Web Site**

## PENNY POMPEI — NATIONAL WOMEN'S BUSINESS CENTER
Washington, DC USA
www.wbiznet.biz

Penny Pompei founded a multi-million dollar architecture firm and an award-winning vineyard. Now she heads the National Women's Business Center and trains other women (and men) in what it takes to make it as an entrepreneur. From finance to marketing, executive development to government contracting, NWBC under Pompei's leadership is bringing sophisticated business strategy to America's next generation of small businesses by showing women (and men) how to start and grow successful companies.

Penny Pompei
*President & CEO*
National Women's Business Center
Washington,
*Contact Phone:* 202.464.1401
*Contact Main Phone:* 202-785-4922
**Click to Contact from Web Site**

## PUBLIC PATENT FOUNDATION (PUBPAT)
New York, NY USA
http://www.pubpat.org

Wrongly Issued Patents and Unsound Patent Policy Harm the Public ... by making things more expensive, if not impossible to afford; ... by preventing scientists from advancing technology; ... by unfairly prejudicing small businesses; and ... by restraining civil liberties and individual freedoms. PubPat presents the Public's Interests Against Wrongly Issued Patents and Unsound Patent Policy.

Dan Ravicher
Public Patent Foundation (PUBPAT)
New York, NY USA
*Contact Phone:* (212) 796-0570
**Click to Contact from Web Site**

# DOW LOHNES

## DOW LOHNES PLLC
Washington, DC USA
http://www.dowlohnes.com

Dow Lohnes PLLC provides expert commentary and background to local, national and international broadcast and media outlets on legal and technical issues. With more than 140 lawyers in Washington, D.C., and Atlanta, Dow Lohnes has an 88-year history of providing services to communications businesses and other businesses in highly regulated industries. Our lawyers have participated in the evolution of the telecommunications and media industries.

Katharine A. Voldal
*Director, Special Projects*
Dow, Lohnes & Albertson, PLLC
Washington, DC
*Contact Phone:* 202-776-2490
*Contact Main Phone:* 202-776-2000
**Click to Contact from Web Site**

## PATTISHALL, MCAULIFFE, NEWBURY, HILLIARD & GERALDSON LLP
Chicago, IL USA
http://www.pattishall.com

Pattishall, McAuliffe, Newbury, Hilliard & Geraldson LLP is one of the most experienced intellectual property firms in the country, representing major corporations in domestic and international litigation and transactions involving brands, packaging, computer software, domain names and Internet advertising. Internationally recognized by peers as leaders in their field, firm partners have served as advisors to the United States government and are well-known as law professors, authors and speakers on trademark, copyright and unfair competition issues.

Mark V.B. Partridge
*Partner*
Pattishall, McAuliffe, Newbury, Hilliard & Geraldson LLP
Chicago, IL USA
*Contact Phone:* 312-554-8000
**Click to Contact from Web Site**

# We Make Communications Our Business

Since handling and resolving one of the nation's first communications law cases in 1923, Dow Lohnes has witnessed and participated in the evolution of the telecommunications and media industries. Our attorneys are exceptional, informed resources offering legal advice on the far-reaching impact of broadcast and media technology on today's business environment, including:

- Communications and Media Law
- Cable Television
- Commercial Television/ Radio Broadcasting
- Computer/Information Technology
- Internet
- Libel/First Amendment

- New/Online Media
- New Technology
- Newspaper/Magazine Publishing
- Public Broadcasting/Educational Telecommunications
- Satellite
- Telecommunications

With more than 140 lawyers in Washington, D.C., and Atlanta, Dow Lohnes also provides superior corporate, transactional, regulatory and litigation services to businesses in other highly regulated industries.

For more information on all of Dow Lohnes' practice expertise, please contact our Business Development Department at 202.776.2490 or info@dowlohnes.com.

## Ꝺ DowLohnes PLLC

Washington, DC

1200 New Hampshire Avenue, NW, Suite 800
Washington, DC 20036-6802
T 202.776.2000    F 202.776.2222

Atlanta, GA

Six Concourse Parkway, Suite 1800
Atlanta, GA 30328-6117
T 770.901.8800    F 770.901.8874

**www.dowlohnes.com**

## ALMEXPERTS
New York, NY USA
http://www.almexperts.com

ALMExperts is a leading expert witness directory with 15,000 listings from qualified experts, expert witnesses, investigators, court reporters and litigation support professionals. The ALMExperts Directory is designed to help lawyers find the special expertise they need and to help experts and consultants spread the word about their services and qualifications. It's organized by 3300 specialties for easy browsing and features powerful keyword searching to permit lawyers to quickly find the expertise they need.

Amy Hochhauser
ALM
New York, NY USA
*Contact Phone:* 212-313-9021
**Click to Contact from Web Site**

## TASA (TECHNICAL ADVISORY SERVICE FOR ATTORNEYS)
Blue Bell, PA USA
http://www.tasanet.com

TASA (Technical Advisory Service for Attorneys) provides outstanding Technical Consultants and Testifying Experts in over 10,000 categories, including over 900 medical fields through TASAmed. Technical consultants are available as speakers and advisors to the news media. Our experienced Referral Advisors will personally identify top-caliber local and national experts who match your unique requirements. TASA's independent Expert Witnesses advise on technical merits, investigate, research, test, educate, and testify for plaintiffs or defendants. Services include prompt, customized searches; unlimited referrals; resumes; and your initial interview calls with experts. More than 45 years of unparalleled referral experience to legal, insurance, government, and corporate clients. TASA is a division of The TASA GROUP, Inc.

Patricia Pinciotti
*Marketing & Communications Manager*
TASA (Technical Advisory Service for Attorneys)
Blue Bell, PA
*Contact Phone:* 800-523-2319
**Click to Contact from Web Site**

## CAROL M. SWAIN — VANDERBILT UNIVERSITY LAW SCHOOL
Nashville, TN USA
http://www.carolmswain.com

Carol M. Swain is professor of political science and law at Vanderbilt University. Her media appearances include ABC News, Fox News Live, CNN's News from the Headlines, C-SPAN's Washington Journal, PBS's Lehrer News Hour, NPR's Here & Now, NPR's Talk of the Nation, NPR's Morning Edition, and Daybreak USA Today. Her recent books are The New White Nationalism in America: Its Challenge to Integration (2002) and Contemporary Voices of White Nationalism (2003).

Carol M. Swain
*Prof: Law & Political Science*
Vanderbilt University Law School
Nashville, TN USA
*Contact Phone:* 615-322-1001
*Contact Main Phone:* 615-310-8617
**Click to Contact from Web Site**

## DICKSTEIN SHAPIRO MORIN & OSHINSKY
Washington, DC USA
http://www.dicksteinshapiro.com

Dickstein Shapiro Morin & Oshinsky LLP, founded in 1953, is a multiservice law firm with more than 375 attorneys in offices in Washington, DC, New York City, and Los Angeles. The Firm represents more than 100 Fortune 500 companies as well as start-up ventures, entrepreneurs, leading financial institutions, charitable organizations and government officials in high-profile investigations. Dickstein Shapiro's five core practice groups - Corporate & Finance, Energy, Intellectual Property, Legislative & Regulatory Affairs, and Litigation & Dispute Resolution, with additional experience in Insurance Coverage, Securities Litigation, State Attorney General issues, Energy Regulatory matters, White Collar Crime, Government Contracts, and Antitrust - involve the Firm in virtually every major form of counseling, litigation, and advocacy.

Ali Bayler
Dickstein Shapiro Morin & Oshinsky
Washington, DC USA
*Contact Phone:* 202-777-2583
*Contact Main Phone:* 202-785-9700
**Click to Contact from Web Site**

## SOUTHWESTERN UNIVERSITY SCHOOL OF LAW
Los Angeles, CA USA
http://www.swlaw.edu

Southwestern faculty members are valuable sources of information and commentary on more than 150 legal issues. Many have been interviewed by national press and broadcast media. Several are nationally recognized experts. Topics of expertise include constitutional law, criminal law, entertainment law, intellectual property, antitrust, international law, internet legal issues, juries, bankruptcy, and the U.S. Supreme Court.

*Public Information Office*
Southwestern University School of Law
Los Angeles, CA
*Contact Phone:* 213-738-6766
**Click to Contact from Web Site**

## THE JOHN MARSHALL LAW SCHOOL
Chicago, IL USA
http://www.jmls.edu

The John Marshall Law School is forging a future of unparalleled achievement as Chicago's urban law school. Its programs offer students expertise not only at the J.D. level, but through specialty degrees in employee benefits law, international business and trade law, information technology and privacy law, real estate law, tax law and trial advocacy. It has the only Fair Housing Legal Clinic in the country. John Marshall's faculty regularly provide legal commentary for print, radio and TV.

Marilyn Thomas
*Director of Public Relations*
The John Marshall Law School
Chicago, IL
*Contact Phone:* 312-360-2661
**Click to Contact from Web Site**

## ELIOT DISNER -- MCGUIREWOODS LLP
Los Angeles, CA USA
www.mcguirewoods.com

Partner at Los Angeles law firm of McGuire-Woods LLP, Eliot Disner makes Antitrust Law understandable. Antitrust Trial Lawyer (millions in verdicts), former Chairman of California State Bar Antitrust Section, frequent speaker and commentator on Microsoft and other antitrust issues. Author of Antitrust For Business Lawyers (www.ali-aba.org), and other antitrust law and litigation publications. He has been referred to as a heavy hitter, a bulldog trial lawyer, name-brand and an antitrust guru. Also Knowledgeable about intellectual property, franchise law, trial practice and federal courts.

Eliot Disner
McGuireWoods LLP
Los Angeles, CA USA
*Contact Phone:* 310-315-8299
**Click to Contact from Web Site**

## ALAN GOLDBERGER — REFEREE LAW EXPERT
Clifton, NJ USA
http://www.RefLaw.com

Attorney: New Jersey — New York — Maryland Bars Speaker: Sports Law — Sports Officials' Training — Risk Management/Liability — Association Law Basketball Referee Football Official Baseball Umpire Author: Sports Officiating: A Legal Guide Co-Author: Sport, Physical Activity and the Law President: North Jersey Board of Approved Basketball Officials, Inc. Chairperson: National Association for Girls and Women in Sport Committee on Legal Issues.

Alan Goldberger
Alan Goldberger/Goldberger & Goldberger
Clifton, NJ
*Contact Phone:* 973-471-9200
*Contact Main Phone:* 973-471-9200
**Click to Contact from Web Site**

## NATIONAL DISTRICT ATTORNEYS ASSOCIATION
Alexandria, VA USA
www.ndaa-apri.org

The National District Attorneys Association (NDAA) was formed in 1950 in response to crime and the need for community protection. It has become the nation's largest organization representing local prosecuting attorneys who handle 95% of all cases and 99% of cases involving violent crime. It has a current membership of more than 7,000 including many of the nation's local prosecutors, along with assistant prosecutors, investigators, victim/witness advocates and paralegals. NDAA is the Voice of America's prosecutors and supports their efforts to protect the rights and safety of the people. Establishing the truth, ensuring that justice prevails and protecting victims of crime is the mantra of those who serve as our local prosecutors. Through its affiliates — APRI, NCDA, and the NAC — NDAA provides training and expertise on many legal issues including, anti-terrorism, crime control, capital litigation, community prosecution, DNA technology, ethics, child abuse, juvenile justice, violent crime, etc. NDAA is dedicated to enhancing the professional knowledge and skills of prosecutors, and improving prosecutorial and criminal justice practices.

Velva Walter
*Director, Media Relations*
National District Attorneys Association
Alexandria, VA
*Contact Phone:* 703-519-1689
**Click to Contact from Web Site**

## DR. IRA WILLIAMS, THE CURE FOR MEDICAL MALPRACTICE
Greenville, SC USA
www.cureformedicalmalpractice.com

Tort reform gives patients only two alternatives: Sue or forget it. Dr. Ira Williams offers another view for curing a leading cause of injury and death — medical malpractice. In his recent book, 'First Do No Harm: The Cure for Medical Malpractice,' Dr. Williams outlines a solution for fair regulation of the medical profession and discipline of negligent doctors by doctors, not courts. Tort reforms regulates litigation only, not medical care. It is a mirage.

Dr. Ira Williams
Greenville, SC USA
*Contact Phone:* 864-235-4069
**Click to Contact from Web Site**

## NATIONAL MEDICAL FOUNDATION FOR ASSET PROTECTION
Provo, UT USA
http://www.nationalmedicalfoundation.org/

When Jay W. Mitton opened his first law office in 1972, he was the first attorney in the country to specialize in the field known today as asset protection. Over thirty years later, his foundations continue to protect individuals and families from the devastating effects of lawsuits through education, research and publicity campaigns. The National Medical Foundation, The National Dental Foundation, and The National Foundation for Tax Planning and Asset Protection can be reached at 800-375-2453.

Spencer McKay Sessions
*Public and Media Relations*
National Medical Foundation for Asset Protection
National Dental Foundation
Provo, UT USA
*Contact Phone:* 800-296-7009
**Click to Contact from Web Site**

## EDWARD POLL, J.D., M.B.A.., CMC -- LAW FIRM MANAGEMENT EXPERT
Los Angeles, CA USA
http://www.LawBiz.com

Edward Poll, coach, consultant, author and speaker. Ed, known as Your Practical Guide to Profit, guides lawyers to expand their client market share and increase repeat business with less stress. He is the author of eight management books including Attorney & Law Firm Guide to the Business of Law, 2nd ed. (ABA 2002), called the "Bible of running a law practice" and Collecting Your Fee: Getting Paid from Intake to Invoice (ABA 2003), among others.

Edward Poll, J.D., M.B.A.., CMC
*Principal*
LawBiz Management Company
Venice, CA USA
*Contact Phone:* 800-837-5880
**Click to Contact from Web Site**

## PHILIP BELL, JD CPA LL.M
Houston, TX USA
http://www.Flyntbell.com

In his 25+ years as a JD CPA consultant, Phil has coached entrepreneurs and businesses in engaging their creativity to Forward an organization. Phil received his LL.M in International Law from St. Thomas University and is currently in Ph.D research for Psychology in organizations. Designing a legal learning systems model + macro-g financing to step-up an organization is a highly effective means to utilize all tools available to maximize your organization's potential. Topics & seminars evoke individual change dynamics-Etching Ethics in Corporations+ Financing Integrity+ Small Steps for the Entrepreneur. He is a partner with FlyntBell+ and a member of the banking group- Ed Bell & Associates. He also serves on the advisory board for the Schumacher Foundation.

Philip Bell JD CPA LL.M
FlyntBell +
Houston, LA USA
*Contact Phone:* 713 942-7147
**Click to Contact from Web Site**

## NATIONAL ASSOCIATION OF LEGAL ASSISTANTS, INC.
Tulsa, OK USA
http://www.nala.org

Established in 1976, the National Association of Legal Assistants, Inc., is the leading professional association for paralegals, dedicated to advancing the growing legal assistant/paralegal career field. The association represents more than 18,000 paralegals through individual members and 91 affiliated associations. It administers the Certified Legal Assistant credentialing programs, conducts occupational research, offers continuing education programs, publishes the quarterly journal Facts & Findings, and offers NALA NET, a national database of state ethical codes and guidelines for paralegals.

Marge Dover, CAE
*Executive Director*
National Association of Legal Assistants, Inc.
Tulsa, OK
*Contact Phone:* 918-587-6828
**Click to Contact from Web Site**

*Celebrating 35 Years*

## ASSOCIATION OF LEGAL ADMINISTRATORS
Lincolnshire, IL USA
http://www.alanet.org

Since 1971, the Association of Legal Administrators has provided educational opportunities, publications support and services to law office administrators who manage such areas as technology, finance, human resources, facilities, marketing and practice development. ALA has more than 10,000 members representing more than 6,000 employers, including private law firms and corporate and government legal departments, in 30 countries.

Steve Carasso
*Sr. Communications Specialist*
Association of Legal Administrators
Lincolnshire, IL
*Contact Phone:* 847-267-1378
*Contact Main Phone:* 847-267-1252
**Click to Contact from Web Site**

## STETSON COLLEGE OF LAW CENTERS FOR EXCELLENCE
Gulfport, FL USA
http://www.law.stetson.edu/Centers/

Stetson University College of Law, Florida's first law school, is a leader in international legal education. Stetson offers a welcoming environment for lawyers around the world, with renowned professors who share the knowledge and skills needed to succeed in the global marketplace. Legal experts teach International Law in the areas of business transactions; litigation and arbitration; sales; banking and finance; commercial, criminal and environmental law; human rights; intellectual property; trade regulation; and tribunals.

Frank Klim
*Executive Director of Communications*
Stetson University College of Law
Gulfport, FL USA
*Contact Phone:* 727-562-7889
*Contact Main Phone:* 727-562-7800
**Click to Contact from Web Site**

## VICTORIA RING, LEGAL MARKETING
Columbus, OH USA
http://www.50statenotary.com

Victoria Ring is an author, publisher and entrepreneur with over 20 years experience in the small business marketing field. She has self-published and authored 22 books, hundreds of articles and training videos centered on the topic of marketing and building a successful freelance business. Victoria Ring is a Certified Paralegal who currently serves as the CEO for 50 State Notary and Graphico Publishing, both of which were built from the ground up by Victoria.

Victoria Ring
*Certified Paralegal*
50 State Notary
BankruptcyProcessorTraining.Com
Columbus, OH USA
*Contact Phone:* 614-875-4496
*Cell:* 614-214-8734
**Click to Contact from Web Site**

## ASUNCION C. HOSTIN, ESQ. - EVIDENCE AND COURTROOM TRIAL TECHNIQUE
New York, NY USA

As a former federal prosecutor and law professor, Ms. Hostin is an expert in Evidence and Courtroom Trial Technique. Ms. Hostin is a former Assistant U.S Attorney for the District of Columbia. She received her B.A. from Binghamton University and her J.D. from the University of Notre Dame Law School, where she was a Notre Dame Law Scholar, a member of the National Trial Team, and the recipient of the American Jurisprudence Award in Trial Advocacy. At the U.S. Attorney's Office, Ms. Hostin was responsible for all phases of investigation and prosecution of federal and local crimes in the District of Columbia. Ms. Hostin appeared before the District of Columbia Court of Appeals as lead appellate counsel in several cases, and tried numerous cases to verdict. Ms. Hostin received a Special Achievement Award in 1999, was named EEO Mediator in 2000, and was nominated for the U.S. Department of Justice's Director's Award in 2001.

Asuncion C. Hostin
*Counsel*
Dickstein, Shapiro, Morin & Oshinsky LLP
New York,
*Contact Phone:* 212-896-5457
*Cell:* 914-720-5357
**Click to Contact from Web Site**

## CENTERS FOR EXCELLENCE
Gulfport, FL USA
http://www.law.stetson.edu/Centers/

Stetson University College of Law, Florida's first law school, has Centers for Excellence in advocacy, elder law, higher education law and policy, and international law. Stetson is ranked by U.S. News & World Report as the nation's top school for trial advocacy and is the home of the National Clearinghouse for Science, Technology and the Law, the central resource for legal professionals, scientists and law enforcement studying the intersections of science, technology and the law.

Frank Klim
*Executive Director of Communications*
Stetson University College of Law
Gulfport, FL USA
*Contact Phone:* 727-562-7889
*Contact Main Phone:* 727-562-7800
**Click to Contact from Web Site**

COLLEGE OF LAW

*Florida's First Law School*
## STETSON UNIVERSITY COLLEGE OF LAW
Tampa Bay, FL USA
http://www.law.stetson.edu/

Stetson University College of Law, Tampa Bay, Florida, offers experienced legal experts in Advocacy, Bankruptcy Law, Business Law and International Trade, Civil and Criminal Procedure, Constitutional Law, Consumer Protection, Courtroom Technology, Elder Law, Ethics, Family Law, Forensic Evidence, Higher Education Law and Policy, International Law, Jurisprudence, Latin American Law, and Legal Writing and Language. Stetson is ranked number 1 in trial advocacy for 2007 by U.S. News and World Report.

Frank Klim
*Executive Director of Communications*
Stetson University College of Law
Gulfport, FL USA
*Contact Phone:* 727-562-7889
**Click to Contact from Web Site**

# Law Firm Management Expert

## *Edward Poll, J.D., M.B.A., CMC*

Edward Poll -- coach, consultant, author and speaker -- is known as "Your Practical Guide to Profit" and guides lawyers to expand their client market share and increase repeat business with less stress.

He is the author of eight management books including, *Attorney & Law Firm Guide to the Business of Law*, 2nd ed. (ABA 2002), called the "Bible of running a law practice," and *Collecting Your Fee: Getting Paid from Intake to Invoice* (ABA 2003), among others.

Since 1990, Ed has been coaching and consulting lawyers and law firms in strategic planning, profitability analysis, and practice development. He has practiced law on all sides of

the table for 25 years - as a corporate general counsel, government prosecutor, sole practitioner, partner, and law firm chief operating officer.

His firm, LawBiz® Management Company, works with lawyers to increase their profits and their effectiveness in the way they practice law. Services provide possible solutions to law practice management challenges and include legal coaching, customized consulting services, speaking and training seminars, assistance for buying and selling a law practice, law firm retreats, managing partners roundtables, articles, and other resources, including an e-zine and blog.

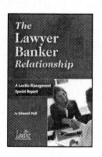

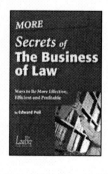
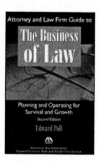

Edward Poll, J.D., M.B.A., CMC · Principal, LawBiz® Management Company
Edward Poll & Associates, Inc.
421 Howland Canal · Venice, California 90291-4619
Office # (310) 827-5415 · Order # (800) 837-5880 · Fax # (310) 578-1769
edpoll@lawbiz.com · www.LawBiz.com

**AMERICA'S DUMBEST CRIMINALS**
Jacksonville, FL USA
www.AmericasDumbestCriminals.com

Here, you will find the ultimate collection of incredibly stupid and painfully dumb attempts at crime ever brought together.

John A. Palumbo
*Executive Producer*
America's Dumbest Criminals
Jacksonville, FL USA
*Contact Phone:* 904-448-1100
**Click to Contact from Web Site**

**PRISON MINISTRY TASK FORCE, EPISCOPAL DIOCESE OF MARYLAND**
Annapolis, MD USA
http://www.prisonministry.ang-md.org

The Prison Ministry Task Force was created by convention resolution in 1998 when delegates learned that prisoners had become the fastest-growing segment of the population. Sixty percent of the 2.2 million inmates in prisons and jails will return behind bars within three years unless reentry -- education, job training and drug treatment -- programs are applied inside and after release. The Task Force brings programs and people together; encourages advocacy nationally, and disseminates information about ministries, policies, legislation, court cases and programs that can help reform the criminal justice system. The Task Force sponsors a camp for inmates' children because a child of a prisoner has a 70 percent chance of going to prison. The Task Force also sponsors Prison Ministry Sundays in the Diocese and the 250-member Prison Ministry Network News. To join the twice-monthly, blind-copied online news service covering prison ministry and criminal justice reform issues, write PrisMinNet@aol.com or valhymes@aol.com For resources, contacts, events, books, www.prisonministry.ang-md.org.

Val Hymes
Prison Ministry Network News
Annapolis, MD United States
*Contact Phone:* (410) 224-2478
**Click to Contact from Web Site**

**JUSTICE ON TRIAL**
Las Vegas, NV USA
www.justiceontrial.org

Justice On Trial, a California Non-Profit corporation, formed in April of 2002, is a defense-of-innocence advocacy organization whose motto is Organized Opposition to the Declaration of Guilt. The company's website, www.JusticeOnTrial. org, its affiliation with mainstream media and a planned television series are devoted to accomplishing: Review of cases for prosecutorial and/or law enforcement improprieties; Dramatic presentation of cases to national broadcast audiences; Publicize cases nationally and locally in other media; Assist in the defense of those wrongly accused/imprisoned; Collect leads/clues on selected cases and investigate where applicable; Reduce the number of innocent people in; or going to; jail/prison; Reduce crime through public education about the justice system; Lobby for reason and national equity in sentencing; Help create more humane conditions & rehabilitation for all prisoners; Establish acceptable standards for those incarcerated but not convicted, Offer suggestions as to how to improve or help repair the system. Justice On Trial is actively seeking cases to review. Contributions can be made by contacting John Bradley at 1-800-631-5931 or JJB@ JusticeOnTrial.org.

John J. Bradley
*Director*
Justice on Trial
Glenbrook, NV USA
*Contact Phone:* 775-749-5522
**Click to Contact from Web Site**

## ALDERMAN & ALDERMAN
Hartford, CT USA
www.alderman.com/Presskit.html

Myles H. Alderman, Jr. Esq. is the author of Chapter 11 Business Reorganizations: For Business Leaders, Accountants and Lawyers. Attorney Myles Alderman has been representing debtors, creditors and other parties in interest in Chapter 11 Business Reorganizations and alternative business solutions since 1986. His clients include professional services firms, manufacturers, distributors, retailers and financial institutions ranging in size from closely held businesses to some the largest corporations in the world. In 2006, Mr. Alderman was designated one of the top lawyers in the area of Business Bankruptcy Law by the Law and Politics Magazine.

Rosemary Mahan
*Public Relations*
Alderman & Alderman
Hartford, NY USA
*Contact Main Phone:* 860.249-0090
**Click to Contact from Web Site**

## PAUL YOUNG -- SECURITIES ARBITRATION COMMENTATOR
Los Angeles, CA USA
www.SecuritiesGuy.com

Securities arbitration expert Paul Young is a noted All-Money Matters commentator who runs L.A. and Company, LLC - a national organization dedicated to Main Street consumers dealing with money matters. 1. LAC's Debt Settlement Initiative provides debt settlement services to individuals, families, small businesses. We work to tangibly reduce debt and to avoid collections or bankruptcy. 2. Securities Arbitration enables investors burned by Wall Street to recover when they've been victimized. Managing Director Paul N. Young brings 23 years of experience and a successful track record. Fully media experienced.

Caren Gellman
*Media Relations*
Securities Arbitration Group
Los Angeles, CA USA
*Contact Phone:* 800-222-4724
*Contact Main Phone:* 310-826-0278
**Click to Contact from Web Site**

## EQUAL JUSTICE WORKS (FORMERLY NAPIL)
Washington, DC USA
http://www.equaljusticeworks.org

Equal Justice Works (formerly The National Association for Public Interest Law) was founded in 1986 by law students dedicated to surmounting barriers to equal justice that affect millions of low-income individuals and families. Today, Equal Justice Works leads the country in organizing, training and supporting public service-minded law students, and in creating summer and postgraduate public interest jobs.

Dottie Li
*Director of Communications*
Equal Justice Works (formerly NAPIL)
Washington, DC
*Contact Phone:* 202-466-3686
**Click to Contact from Web Site**

## STAN B. WALTERS 'THE LIE GUY'
Lexington, KY USA
http://www.kinesic.com/MediaAccess.htm

Stan B. Walters 'The Lie Guy®' is one of the world's leading authorities on interviewing and interrogation. He consults for some of the world's largest corporations, governments and law enforcement agencies. Stan is called upon regularly by the media to comment on some of the top stories of the day. His books, 'The Truth About Lying,' and 'Principles of Kinesic Interview and Interrogation,' are required reading at colleges and for training programs across the country.

Stan B. Walters
Stan B. Walters & Associates, Inc
Versailles, KY USA
*Contact Phone:* 800-847-4774
*Cell:* 859-421-1088
**Click to Contact from Web Site**

# THE HIT TV SHOW!

# AMERICA'S DUMBEST CRIMINALS

## John A. Palumbo,
### Executive Producer

"America's Dumbest Criminals" was originally conceived and syndicated in 1996. It was a hit immediately as it led the way for what is better known today as "reality TV." Ahead of its time, and a common household name, the show has been seen by almost everyone, and they can still recall some of the hilarious and outrageous videos from this popular TV show.

"America's Dumbest Criminals" racked up high ratings in its first four seasons in the United States and in syndicated airings in more than 30 countries, according to New York-based Lacey Entertainment, which markets and distributes the show worldwide.

Along with the New York Times best-selling book, "America's Dumbest Criminals," executive producer John Palumbo brings priceless archival and new footage of the show to the media, including interviews with police officers.

Palumbo is a savvy talk show guest, and -- as you can imagine -- he has some of the most uproarious stories and footage to reveal about "America's Dumbest Criminals."

Also a keynote speaker, Palumbo is accessible coast-to-coast.

**Available for Media Interviews:**

### John A. Palumbo,
### Executive Producer
### America's Dumbest Criminals

*10175 Fortune Parkway, Suite #101
Jacksonville, Florida 32256*
*904-448-1100     Fax: 904-448-1112*

*www.AmericasDumbestCriminals.com*

*E-mail:
info@AmericasDumbestCriminals.com*

### PATRICK DE CAROLIS, JR. — FIRM SPECIALIZES IN FAMILY LAW
Los Angeles, CA USA
www.TropeandTrope.com

Trope and Trope is a law firm that has been in existence for more than half a century. Our practice is focused primarily in the area of family law and handles cases in the greater Southern California area.

Patrick De Carolis, Jr.
Trope and Trope
Los Angeles, CA USA
*Contact Phone:* 310-488-6082
**Click to Contact from Web Site**

### HANNAH BENTLEY, ATTORNEY AT LAW
Los Angeles, CA USA

California attorney practicing environmental, municipal and land use law. She brought and settled some of the first known citizen enforcements of federal and California state environmental labeling requirements and also has experience regarding disclosure laws. She has significant experience litigating financial and other public law disputes affecting the interests of municipalities and local government agencies. Her cases have been covered by CNN, the New York Times, and the Los Angeles Times among others.

Hannah Bentley
Law Office of Hannah Bentley
Manhattan Beach, CA USA
*Contact Phone:* 310-697-3996
*Cell:* 310-904-5264
**Click to Contact from Web Site**

### JAMES YANG — INTELLECTUAL PROPERTY ATTORNEY
Los Angeles, CA USA
http://ContactJamesYang.blogspot.com

Journalists and organizations may contact James Yang for interviews and public speaking engagements regarding patents, trademarks, copyrights and trade secrets for news articles. James Yang is a patent attorney. He helps inventors and small businesses create, maintain and profit from their intellectual property so that they may gain a competitive edge. Small businesses and inventors rely on his services to assist them in procuring patents, trademarks and copyrights in their inventions, brand names and creative works.

James Yang
Irvine, CA USA
*Contact Phone:* 562-556-4048
*Cell:* 562-556-4048
**Click to Contact from Web Site**

### DIAMOND AND DIAMOND LLC, ATTORNEYS AT LAW
New York, NY USA
http://www.diamondanddiamondlaw.com

Mark Diamond is a seasoned trial lawyer with years of experience as a legal commentator. You can depend on him to provide crisp, informed and entertaining conversation. Mark has made hundreds of appearances on ABC, CBS, NBC, FOX, COURT-TV, and many other television and radio stations nationwide. He was a repeat guest host of "The Barry Gray Show," WOR-AM, and has been quoted in The New York Times, The New York Daily News, Gannett papers, Smart Money, CBS MarketWatch, National Law Journal, American Lawyer, USA Today, and elsewhere. He is past Chairman of the American Bar Association Criminal Law Committee and the Association of Trial Lawyers of America Indoor Environment Litigation Group. He is the author of legal articles in American Bar Association Journal, California Lawyer, Connecticut Law Journal, GQ, Investor's Business Daily, New York Law Journal, Parade, USA Today, and other publications. Mark served as news editor of WPIX-TV, NYC, and producer of Paramount Pictures/BusinessWeek's weekly TV show "Taking Advantage."

Mark Diamond
Diamond and Diamond LLC, Attorneys at Law
New York, NY USA
*Contact Phone:* 212-227-3377
**Click to Contact from Web Site**

### TOM OWEN - OWL INVESTIGATIONS, INC.
Colonia, NJ USA
www.owlinvestigations.com

Owl Investigations, Inc. offers one of the most sophisticated digital audio and video processing laboratories presently available. Thomas J. Owen, a nationally known expert, served for many years on the Board of The International Association for Voice Identification. He currently serves as Chairman of the Audio Engineering Society's Standards Group WG-12 on Forensic Audio, and is the Chairman of the American Board of Recorded Evidence. Tom Owen is also the Head Instructor for the New York Institute of Forensic Audio from 1992 to the present.

Tom Owen
OWL Investigations, Inc.
Colonia, NJ USA
*Contact Phone:* 732-574-9672
**Click to Contact from Web Site**

### LARRY S. GREENFIELD — MEDIATION-COMPLEX BUSINESS & ENTERTAINMENT LAW
Los Angeles, CA USA
www.LarrySGreenfield.com

Larry S. Greenfield
Los Angeles, CA USA
*Contact Phone:* 310-657-7122
**Click to Contact from Web Site**

# Paul Young
## Securities Arbitration Commentator
### www.SecuritiesGuy.com

Paul Young, an 18-year securities arbitration commentator and burned investors' representative and advocate nationwide, is also a stock market and investments expert whose authoritative, knowledgeable, unbiased commentary provides all media outlets the best information for Main Street investors across the nation.

Without conflicts of interest or other affiliations, media can be assured of, and trust in, Young's useful, insightful, straight-forward air and print presentations, involving the stock market, investing and, in fact, all money matters.

*Here are some points to consider:*

■ Securities arbitration enables investors burned by Wall Street to recover when they've been victimized. In 2005, 25 new securities arbitration cases were filed each day; 9,000 plus for the year.

■ When MainStreeters are burned and abused by Wall Street, the viable mechanism exists for MainStreeters to recover funds lost due to Wall Street misdeeds (suitability, risk, misrepresentations, other failures – call!). The recovery system not only exists, but it also works well for real people in the real world. While securities fraud and investor abuse reaches into all corners of the nation and all demographic sectors, burned investors can fight back and win!

■ A MainStreeter's financial present and future well-being is always a crucial and timely topic. Young has provided meaningful and authoritative, provocative and entertaining, informative commentary for broadcast and print outlets for many years.

### Need Expert Quotes and Quick Response?

CONTACT: Caren Gellman,
Media Relations
Main Phone: 1-310-826-0278
1-800-222-4724

Direct email to Paul Young:
FraudFight@aol.com
Securities Arbitration Group
Los Angeles, California

■ *PAUL N. YOUNG brings a combined 24-plus years of dedicated experience and a successful track record. Paul is fully media experienced.*

**NANCY GRAY — GRAY & ASSOCIATES, P.C.**
Los Angeles, CA USA
www.GrayFirm.com

Nancy Gray
Gray & Associates, P.C.
Los Angeles, CA USA
*Contact Phone:* 310-226-2410
**Click to Contact from Web Site**


**AMERICAN ACADEMY OF MATRIMONIAL LAWYERS**
Chicago, IL USA
http://www.aaml.org

The American Academy of Matrimonial Lawyers was founded in 1962. Its 1,600 fellows are the top lawyers concentrating in the field of matrimonial law, including divorce, prenuptial agreements, custody, legal separation, annulment, property evaluation, division and support. Authoritative spokespersons are available throughout the U.S. to furnish accurate and objective information about legal aspects of newsmaking events, transactions and proceedings.

Richard Auletta
*c/o P.C. Auletta & Co. LLC*
American Academy of Matrimonial Lawyers
New York, NY
*Contact Phone:* 212-355-0400
**Click to Contact from Web Site**

**RALPH MARTINEZ — MARTINEZ LAW GROUP**
Los Angelex, CA USA
www.MartinezLawOffice.com

The Martinez Law Group tradition of legal guidance in commercial/real estate transactions and litigation is founded on personal trust, integrity, experience, and the forging of long-term relationships with clients. Located in Orange County, California, MLG has an impressive track record spanning three decades in both transactional law and litigation. MLG works alongside your internal team to provide an unmatched level of personalized and comprehensive legal advice for the future of your business

Laurie
Martinez Law Group
Irvine, CA USA
*Contact Phone:* 949-450-0123
**Click to Contact from Web Site**


**FRED L. COOVER, ESQUIRE**
Columbia, MD USA
http://www.cooverbarr.com

Coover & Barr, LLC is strategically located along the Baltimore/Washington corridor in the heart of the Mid-Atlantic region. Our practice areas include litigation, corporate and business law, real estate, land use and zoning law, construction law, government contract law, commercial law, family law, and personal injury. Our clients include businesses, nonprofit organizations, local governments and individuals throughout the Mid-Atlantic region of the U.S. Fred L. Coover, known to all as "Chip," has spent over 20 years building a highly respected practice with an emphasis in real estate and construction law; business law and litigation; local land use and zoning law; divorce and custody law, and general civil litigation before all courts throughout the central Maryland region.

Fred L. Coover
Coover & Barr, LLC-Attorneys at Law
Columbia, MD USA
*Contact Phone:* (410) 995-1100
**Click to Contact from Web Site**

**ED SHERMAN -- NOLO PRESS OCCIDENTAL**
San Francisco, CA USA
http://www.nolotech.com

Ed Sherman, a family law attorney since 1970, founded Nolo Press and started the self-help law movement with How to Do Your Own Divorce. Through his several books on divorce and relationships, creation of the independent paralegal movement, and his co-founding of Divorce Helpline and Couples Helpline, he has made it his life's work to keep family problems out of the adversarial court system by making the legal process understandable, affordable and accessible for all.

Sandra Borland
*Publicist*
Nolo Press Occidental
Santa Cruz, CA USA
*Contact Phone:* 800-464-5502
**Click to Contact from Web Site**

## MICHAEL J. PANGIA
Washington, DC USA
www.michaelpangia.com

Attorney, Pilot, Licensed Aircraft Mechanic, Aviation Accident Litigator, Lecturer, Recognized Expert on many aviation matters; appearances on CNN, NBC, ABC, CBS, BBC, FOX. Former chief trial lawyer for FAA now representing victims and families in air disasters. FAA accident prevention counselor; expert witness in Congressional safety hearings; U.S. and international lecturer on aircraft safety, litigation; Council to International Society of Air Safety Investigators; knowledgeable in air traffic control matters, FAA, and causes of plane crashes.

Michael J. Pangia
Washington, DC
*Contact Phone:* 202-955-6450
**Click to Contact from Web Site**

## MAGANA, CATHCART & MCCARTHY
Los Angeles, CA USA
http://www.mcmc-law.com

Representing the seriously injured and families of persons tatally injured in major aircrash and mass disaster lawsuits for over 40 years, our staff includes seven trial attorneys, an appellate lawyer, a full-time investigator and a registered nurse. Daniel C. Cathcart, who obtained a verdict in the State of Hawaii exceeding $20 billion is Of Counsel. William H. Wimsatt has been a military and civilian pilot in both helicopters and airplanes. He owns and flies his own plane.

Carter P. Spohn
*Director of Business Affairs*
Magana, Cathcart & McCarthy
Los Angeles, CA
*Contact Phone:* 310-553-6630
**Click to Contact from Web Site**

## LITIGATION MANAGEMENT & TRAINING SERVICES, INC.
Long Beach, CA USA
www.PreventLitigation.com

Many employers are unaware of the legal pitfalls inherent in managing their workplaces. Worse yet, those who are informed are often pressured into inaction by fear of lawsuits. We help managers lead within legal limits without paralysis. As experienced litigation attorneys, we know firsthand the value of paying attention to prevention. Services include policy development, employment practices evaluations and training to recognize potential legal landmines before they explode into lawsuits. Our business is keeping companies out of court.

Patricia S. Eyres, Esq.
*President/CEO*
Litigation Management & Training Services, Inc.
Long Beach, CA
*Contact Phone:* 562-495-0098
*Contact Main Phone:* 562-495-0098
*Cell:* 310-994-2081
**Click to Contact from Web Site**

## FULCRUM FINANCIAL INQUIRY LLP — LITIGATION CONSULTING SERVICES
Los Angeles, CA USA
http://www.fulcruminquiry.com

Fulcrum Financial Inquiry LLP offes litigation consulting services. Our analysis and research combined with unique presentation techniques have resulted in an unequaled track record in successful court cases and client recoveries. Our personnel are full time and focused on the services we provide. We incorporate technology into our work to provide great results at a more reasonable cost. Our expertise encompasses damages analysis, lost profit studies, business & intangible asset valuations, fraud investigations, forensic economic analysis, analysis of computerized data and computer forensics.

David Nolte
Fulcrum Financial Inquiry LLP
Los Angeles, CA USA
*Contact Phone:* 213.787.4111
*Contact Main Phone:* 213.787.4100
**Click to Contact from Web Site**

## DR. DENNIS DIRKMAAT — MERCYHURST COLLEGE ARCHAEOLOGICAL INSTITUTE
Erie, PA USA
http://mai.mercyhurst.edu/

Dr. Dennis Dirkmaat is director of a forensics program. He is consulted regularly by law enforcement during criminal cases and is an airline crash specialist for the National Transportation Safety Board.

Dennis Dirkmaat, Ph.D.
*Director of Forensic Anthropology*
Mercyhurst College Archaeological Institute
Erie, PA
*Contact Phone:* 814-824-2105
*Contact Main Phone:* 814-824-2000
**Click to Contact from Web Site**

## BAUM HEDLUND, A PROFESSIONAL CORPORATION
Los Angeles, CA USA
http://www.baumhedlundlaw.com

Expert media source for aviation, airline, train, bus and truck accidents. Former airline captain and current fighter pilot attorneys on staff. Expert source for antidepressant injuries and other defective drugs. For many years the media has turned to this national preeminent victims' law firm specializing in mass disasters and mass torts. They offer articulate technical analysis of all types of major transportation accidents and are authorities in air safety, commercial airline procedures, truck, train and bus accidents and certain drug injuries. They have represented thousands of victims and their attorneys have appeared in hundreds of newspaper, magazine, radio, documentaries and TV media including Fox News, CNN, Larry King, NY Times, Wall St. Journal, USA Today and Newsweek. Listed in Who's Who in the World, Who's Who in American Law and the Bar Register of Preeminent Lawyers and one of their attorneys was recently twice awarded Lawyer of the Year.

Robin McCall
*Media Relations Director*
Baum Hedlund, A Professional Corporation
Los Angeles, CA
*Contact Phone:* 310-207-3233
**Click to Contact from Web Site**

## NATIONAL FAMILIES IN ACTION
Atlanta, GA USA
http://www.nationalfamilies.org

Since 1977 National Families in Action (NFIA) has provided leadership for the substance abuse prevention field through its help to families and communities wanting to prevent drug use among children. President & CEO Sue Rusche is NFIA's spokesperson. A nationally recognized expert on prevention, drug legalization, and drugs and the brain, she is the director of the Parent Corps, a national volunteer program for parents who want to protect their children from drugs. She is co-director of the Addiction Studies Program for Journalists with Wake Forest University School of Medicine.

Paula Kemp
*Executive Vice President*
National Families in Action
Atlanta, GA
*Contact Phone:* 404-248-9676
**Click to Contact from Web Site**

## C.A.N.D.I.D.-CITIZENS AGAINST DRUG IMPAIRED DRIVERS
Milwaukee, WI USA
http://www.candid.org

Citizens AgaiNst Drug Impaired Drivers is dedicated to reducing the number of injuries and fatalities due to drug-impaired drivers. A grassroots organization, we create lifesaving awareness about driving impaired from illegal drugs, prescription and over-the-counter medications, and impairing products that are inhaled. We advocate safe use of medications and personal responsibility behind the wheel by raising consumer awareness, encouraging patient education, and supporting law enforcement training. Our award-winning, ground-breaking work is creating road safety for you.

Karen Tarney
*Co-Founder & Executive Director*
C.A.N.D.I.D.-Citizens AgaiNst Drug Impaired Drivers
Milwaukee, WI
*Contact Phone:* 414-352-2043
**Click to Contact from Web Site**

## DONALD J. RAMSELL — DUI & DRUNK DRIVING DEFENSE ATTORNEY
Chicago, IL USA
www.dialdui.com

DUI Drunk Driving Defense Attorney — Chicago, Illinois — www.dialdui.com —Why is a breath test inaccurate? Why are sobriety tests considered voodoo science? This nationally prominent DUI Attorney has the answers. Ramsell, known as 'DUI Don', has defended over 12,000 cases spanning 19 years. Ramsell recently defended a DUI in the US Supreme Court. Ramsell is a NHTSA-certified field sobriety instructor. Clients include Lovin' Spoonful, political figures, police officers.

Donald J. Ramsell
*President*
Attorneys- DUI and Criminal Defense
Wheaton, IL United States
*Contact Phone:* 630-665-8780
**Click to Contact from Web Site**

**William C. Head**
*Senior Partner*

Head, Thomas, Webb & Willis, LLC
*Attorneys at Law*
750 Hammond Drive, Bldg. 5
Atlanta, GA 30328
404-250-1113 / Fax: 404-250-1494
Toll Free: 888-8WC-HEAD (892-4323)
wchead@absolutely-not-guilty.com

www.GeorgiaCriminalDefense.com
www.Absolutely-Not-Guilty.com
www.DrunkDrivingDefense.com

## WILLIAM C. HEAD
Atlanta, GA USA
http://www.drunkdrivingdefense.com

William C. Head is a Legal Expert on criminal law, particularly alcohol & drug defense nationally recognized as one of the leading authorities on defense of persons charged with 'drunk driving.' After practicing 30 years in criminal law, he operates America's largest criminal defense firm emphasizing DUI/DWI litigation. He is also a leading author on the subject. In 2003, he was named "Top DUI Lawyer in America" by the National College for DUI Defense, Inc., the leading non-profit group of DUI-DWI attorneys.

William C. Head
*President*
William C. Head
Atlanta, GA
*Contact Phone:* 404-250-0306
**Click to Contact from Web Site**

# William C. Head, Esq.
## *Drunk Driving Defense Expert*

William C. Head of Atlanta, Georgia, is nationally recognized as one of the leading authorities on the legal defense of persons charged with "drunk driving."

A practicing attorney for 30 years, he operates America's largest criminal defense firm emphasizing DUI/DWI litigation. He has authored books, seminar materials and articles for legal publication and portions of legal treatises.

A veteran of more than 100 television and radio interviews, and approximately 50 newspaper articles, Mr. Head speaks for the rights of accused criminals, including drinking drivers.

A LIFE member of the National Association of Criminal Defense Lawyers, the Georgia Association of Criminal Defense Lawyers and the South Carolina Association of Criminal Defense Lawyers, Mr. Head has lectured on the subject of DUI/DWI defense in more than 200 cities in the U.S., Canada and the Caribbean. One of the 12 original "founders" of the National College for DUI Defense, Inc., Mr. Head is well known nationally by criminal defense specialists. In 2003, Mr. Head was named "Top DUI Lawyer in America" by the National College for DUI Defense.

William C. Head, President
Atlanta, Georgia
Contact Phone: 404-250-0306

NATIONWIDE: 1-800-DUI-LAWS
(1-800-384-5297)

**www.DrunkDrivingDefense.com**

**wchead@absolutely-not-guilty.com**

**Georgia Criminal Defense**
Sponsored by: Head Thomas Webb & Willis LLC

Head Thomas Webb & Willis,
Attorneys at Law
750 Hammond Dr., Building 5
Atlanta, Georgia 30328
Phone: 404-250-1113
Fax: 404-250-1494

**EMERGENCY: 800-695-0040**
**www.GeorgiaCriminalDefense.com**

## PETER J. KILLEEN
Little Falls, NJ USA
http://www.ThePoliceConnection.org

Former Police Officer. Police Psychotherapist, 9/11 Trauma Expert, Former Franciscan Friar-,Peter Killeen has a unique and extensive background in the law enforcement field.Peter Killeen holds master's degrees in both Counseling Psychology and Theology, and is a former police officer for the Port Authority of New York and New Jersey. He has done extensive trauma work with the Port Authority of NY and NJ following the September 11 attacks. He is a recognized expert on PTSD.

Peter Killeen
*Host/Director*
Peter J. Killeen
Little Falls, NJ
*Contact Phone:* 973-819-8537
*Cell:* 973-819-8537
**Click to Contact from Web Site**

## MIKE KNOX — YOUTH VIOLENCE AND GANG EXPERT
Houston, TX USA
www.gangguy.com

A nationally recognized authority and author on gangs and juvenile crime, Mike Knox provides solutions to one of America's fastest growing problems — gangs. In addition to his book, Gangsta in the House: Understanding Gang Culture, Mike Knox has been interviewed by ABC News Nightline, CNN, Day & Date, Geraldo, New York Newsday, The Detroit News, The Houston Chronicle, The Daily Tribune, National Education Association Today, Women's Day, ABC's Jay Monihan Show, Talk America's Probing America, People's Radio Network and National Public Radio. An articulate and experienced speaker, he combines powerful and motivating information with commentary about the gang world, why our children are attracted to gangs and how we can get these youths out of these violent gangs.

Helen Matthews
Cutting Edge Communications
Houston, TX USA
*Contact Phone:* 713-465-6500
**Click to Contact from Web Site**

## INTERNATIONAL ASSOCIATION OF EMERGENCY MANAGERS (IAEM)
Falls Church, VA USA
http://www.iaem.com

IAEM is an international association whose members include 2,700 local, state, federal, military, and private industry emergency management coordinators. Members protect their localities from disaster, coordinate response & recovery efforts, provide expertise on topics such as terrorism, natural disasters, and related public safety preparedness issues.

Elizabeth B. Armstrong, CAE
*Executive Director*
International Association of Emergency Managers (IAEM)
Falls Church, VA
*Contact Phone:* 703-538-1795
**Click to Contact from Web Site**

## ROGER TURNER — EMERGENCY RESPONSE TRAINING EXPERT
Dallas, TX USA
http://pertacinc.com/

PERTAC inc. is the Professional Emergency Response Training And Consultation company for the 21st century! Founded by emergency workers for emergency workers, PERTAC is available to the various emergency response disciplines and the professionals who work within them. Whether you work in the criminal justice field, EMS, fire, or hospitals; you are at your best when people are at their worst. PERTAC is there to help you so you can better serve those persons in need. As our name implies, we provide professional emergency responders with both training and consultation, and more.

Roger Turner
PERTAC, Inc.
Fort Worth, TX USA
*Contact Phone:* 817.691.8965.
**Click to Contact from Web Site**

## CRUSADE AGAINST FIRE DEATHS, INC. — RICHARD M PATTON
Citrus Heights, CA USA
www.firecrusade.com

Richard M. Patton, Fire Protection Engineer, realized years ago that fire codes and certifications for fire related products and systems were often oriented to benefit those who profited from fire at the expense of the consumer. For example, fire sprinkler systems are regulated by code to be priced at two to four times as much as a properly engineered system would cost. To create a market for smoke detectors costing one dollar to manufacture and selling for ten dollars up, certification tests were falsified and codes were rigged to hide an excess of a 50 percent failure rate. Patton exposes fire related frauds and aids those being harmed by the system.

Richard M Patton
*President*
Crusade Against Fire Deaths, Inc.
Citrus Heights, CA U.S.A.
*Contact Phone:* 916-721-7700
**Click to Contact from Web Site**

## TIMOTHY A. DIMOFF — HIGH RISK SECURITY EXPERT
Akron, OH USA
http://www.timothydimoff.com/

Timothy Dimoff is a nationally known security expert, author and speaker who specializes in high-risk security and human resource issues. He provides assessments, tactics, procedures and programs to corporate America, the media, associations and other groups. His expertise includes violence and crime prevention, human resource and labor issues, business security, premises liability and personal safety. He is the author of six books, including 'Life Rage', an insightful examination into the various rages pervading American society today.

Carol Saferin
Mart Saferin & Assoc.
Cleveland, OH USA
*Contact Phone:* 440-461-6753
**Click to Contact from Web Site**

**NATIONAL SCHOOL SAFETY AND SECURITY SERVICES -- KEN TRUMP**
Cleveland, OH USA
http://www.SchoolSecurity.org

National School Safety and Security Services is a Cleveland-based, national consulting firm specializing in K-12 school security and emergency preparedness issues. Kenneth S. Trump, President, has over 20 years school safety experience in 45 states. Ken is one of the most widely quoted school safety experts and has appeared on all cable and network news.

Kenneth S. Trump, M.P.A.
*President*
National School Safety and Security Services
Cleveland, OH
*Contact Phone:* 216-251-3067
**Click to Contact from Web Site**

**THREAT ASSESSMENT**
San Diego, CA USA
http://www.threatassessors.com

Whether it is case management or building a threat management team, getting started is essential in today's world. IAS will get you going down that path. Drs. Turner and associates have extensive experience in the management of threats in business and in government. IAS will give you the roadmap. Threat management can be an organizational nightmare, but it is an essential part of your operations.

James T. Turner, Ph. D.
*President*
International Assessment Services, Inc.
San Diego, CA
*Contact Phone:* 760-789-9484
*Contact Main Phone:* 415 512-1299
*Pager:* 800 407-1959
**Click to Contact from Web Site**

**IAC SECURETECH — INFORMATION SECURITY COMPANY**
Houston, TX USA
www.iacsecuretech.com

IAC SecureTech provides flexible, round the clock network security risk management services that improve the integrity, availability and confidentiality of our client's information and business processes by adapting invisibly and proactively to unexpected, rapidly evolving threats. We deal daily with network intrusion, data forensics, viruses, spyware, and regulatory issues which impact information security infrastructure thus becoming an adjunct security force that reduces our clients' need to hire while keeping their security budgets fixed and low.

Aaron Hughes, CISSP
*CEO*
IAC SecureTech
Houston, TX USA
*Contact Phone:* 832-615-3523
**Click to Contact from Web Site**

**BRIAN YOUNG — SEXUAL ASSAULT PREVENTION INSTRUCTOR**
San Francisco, CA USA
empoweringwomendvd.com

'It's a unique DVD, because it responds to the fact that the vast majority of sexual assaults are perpetrated by someone the victim knows,' said Brian Young, President of Metamorphosis Productions. 'Cliche approaches such as 'poking the eyes' and 'kicking the groin' are difficult even in ideal training, much less with an acquaintance in close quarters.' Differentiating itself from the pack, this breakthrough DVD demonstrates a series of effective yet simple-to-learn assault prevention techniques that teach women to defend themselves while on their backs; their most vulnerable position. 'No! - Empowering Women' delivers more than twenty-five easy to learn, easy to practice, instinct driven sexual assault prevention techniques. Armed with this video every woman has a fighting chance.

Brian Young
Metamorphosis Productions, LLC
San Francisco, CA USA
*Contact Phone:* 415-308-7088
**Click to Contact from Web Site**

**THE SAFETY MINUTE SEMINARS**
Boston, MA USA
http://www.safetyminute.com

Identity Theft and Personal Security Expert. Commenting on issues regarding personal security for a variety of industries including real estate, nurses, teachers and student. Presenting programs on travel safety, workplace violence, computer security and identity theft.

Robert L. Siciliano
*Personal Security Consultant*
The Safety Minute Seminars
Boston, MA
*Contact Phone:* 800-243-8723
**Click to Contact from Web Site**

## KESSLER INTERNATIONAL
New York, NY USA
http://www.investigation.com

Michael G. Kessler is the President and CEO of Kessler International, a corporate investigation and forensic accounting firm headquartered in New York with offices worldwide. A graduate of St. John's University, Mr. Kessler has held a number of distinguished government positions throughout his notable career, including Chief of Investigations for the New York State Department of Taxation and Finance, and Assistant Chief Auditor for the NYS Attorney General. Since founding Kessler International in 1988, Mr. Kessler has become globally recognized as one of the foremost experts in the field of forensic accounting, and has presided over thousands of complex fraud audits, counterfeiting investigations, computer forensics engagements and a wide array of additional white collar crime related inquiries. Mr. Kessler has also helped develop government training programs, is often employed as an expert witness in a courtroom setting, has served as a consultant for numerous corporations and agencies, speaks frequently at professional organizations and is a published author.

Michael G. Kessler
*President & CEO*
Kessler International
New York, NY
*Contact Phone:* 212-286-9100
*Contact Main Phone:* 212 286-9100
**Click to Contact from Web Site**

## sequence inc.®
Forensic Accounting Answers

### SEQUENCE INC. FORENSIC ACCOUNTING
Milwaukee, WI USA
http://www.sequence-inc.com

Specializing in corporate fraud and financial investigations. Tracy Coenen is a CPA, MBA, and Certified Fraud Examiner. Her top-notch investigative intuition and exceptional technical expertise have made her a nationally-recognized expert on fraud and financial investigations. Forensic accounting services and financial investigations provided for the following: corporate fraud and embezzlement, financial statement fraud, contract disputes, shareholder disputes, accountants' professional liability, tax controversy - civil and criminal, insurance fraud, criminal defense, misappropriation of fiduciary duty. Offices in Chicago and Milwaukee.

Tracy L. Coenen, CPA, MBA, CFE
*President and Forensic Accountant*
Sequence Inc. Forensic Accounting
Milwaukee, WI USA
*Contact Phone:* (414)727-2361
**Click to Contact from Web Site**

### FIDELIFACTS
New York, NY USA
http://www.fidelifacts.com

Employment screening and background checks; credit, driving and criminal history checks. Due Diligence investigations. Educational and employment verifications and interviews of former supervisors. Caregiver, nanny, home companion and tenant background checks.

Tom Norton
*President*
Fidelifacts
New York, NY
*Contact Phone:* 800-678-0007
**Click to Contact from Web Site**

### NORMA TILLMAN -- PRIVATE INVESTIGATOR
Nashville, TN USA
http://www.get-in-touch.com

Norma Tillman defies all stereotyped private investigators. With over twenty years experience she has worked on almost every type of investigation. Her specialty is locating and reuniting separated families and friends for television shows. She is never at a loss for an interesting story based on her true experiences. Her behind the scenes look at the real world of private investigation is informative, entertaining, inspirational, and motivating.

Norma Tillman
*Author/Private Investigator*
Norma Tillman Enterprises
Nashville, TN USA
*Contact Phone:* 615-661-0929
**Click to Contact from Web Site**

# *School Security Consultant:*
# *Kenneth S. Trump*

K ENNETH S. TRUMP, M.P.A., is President of National School Safety and Security Services, a Cleveland-based national consulting firm specializing in school security and emergency preparedness training, school security assessments and related school safety and crisis consulting services. Ken is one of the nation's leading school safety experts with more than 20 years of school security experience working with education and public safety officials in 45 states.

Ken is author of the 1998 best-selling book, "Practical School Security: Basic Guidelines for Safe and Secure Schools" (Corwin Press), and more than 45 articles on school security and crisis issues. His book, "Classroom Killers? Hallway Hostages? How Schools Can Prevent and Manage School Crises," was released in July 2000. In May 1999, he testified before the U.S. Senate Committee on Health, Education, Labor and Pensions on school safety.

Ken is one of the most widely quoted national expert consultants on school security and crisis issues. He has been interviewed by all network and cable news outlets, top 50 U.S. daily print newspapers and radio stations nationwide.

**Kenneth S. Trump, M.P.A.**
**President**
**National School Safety**
**and Security Services**
**Cleveland, Ohio**

**(216) 251-3067**

**kentrump@aol.com**
**www.schoolsecurity.org**

## GARY M. BARNBAUM CPA CMC
Los Angeles, CA USA
http://www.gmbarnbaum.com

Full time accounting firm specializing in servicing individuals and small and medium-size businesses, including sole proprietorships, corporations, and partnerships. We provide business accounting, tax return preparation for individuals, partnerships, corporations, estates, and trusts. Financial consulting is offered in the areas of new business start-ups, turnaround for businesses in trouble, investigative and forensic accounting including occupational fraud matters, government audit problems, and litigation support functions. We prepare partial and complete business plans including business projections. CMC - Certified Management Consultant is the highest level of accreditation in the management consulting field.

Gary M. Barnbaum CPA CMC
Woodland Hills, CA USA
*Contact Phone:* (818)340-4511 X 101
*Cell:* (818)606-6200
**Click to Contact from Web Site**

## INTELYSIS — FRAUD INVESTIGATORS
Philadelphia, PA USA
http://www.intelysis.com

Intelysis provides litigation support, corporate investigative services and competitive research to the business and legal communities. Our team of investigators, forensic accountants, computer forensic experts, lawyers and researchers assist in solving commercial fraud cases, fire and arson matters, computer security breaches, e-mail threats, electronic discovery issues and provide in-depth background checks for businesses seeking critical information about their employees, business partners or acquisition targets. Principals: Bashir Rahemtulla, Sandy Boucher, Jeffrey Brenner, Jack Mattera, David Ziegler.

Jeffrey S. Brenner, Esq.
Intelysis
Cherry Hill, NJ USA
*Contact Phone:* 856 667-4180
*Contact Main Phone:* 888 610-8783
**Click to Contact from Web Site**

## ROBERT KEITH WALLACE, PH.D. - HOMELAND SECURITY AND CONFLICT RESOLUTION EXPERT
Fairfield, IA USA
http://www.victorybeforewar.com

Dr. Wallace's early research published in Science and Scientific American began the field of mind-body medicine. An expert on meditation and other peace strategies from the Vedic tradition of India (the source of Yoga and Ayurveda), he has lectured on peace throughout the world, including at Harvard, MIT, UCLA, Oxford, and Cambridge. He is the author of many professional articles and four books, including a new book on preventing terrorism, Victory Before War (June, 2005).

Jay B. Marcus
Center for Science & Crime
Fairfield, IA USA
*Contact Phone:* 641-472-5945
**Click to Contact from Web Site**

## JAMES M. ATKINSON
Boston, MA USA
www.tscm.com

Founded in 1987 and located near Boston Massachusetts, Granite Island Group, is the internationally recognized leader in the field of Technical Surveillance Counter Measures (TSCM), Bug Sweeps, Wiretap Detection, Surveillance Technology, Communications Security (COMSEC), Counter-Intelligence, Technical Security, and Spy Hunting. Granite Island Group provides expert technical, analytical and research capability for the detection, nullification, and isolation of eavesdropping devices, technical surveillance penetrations, technical surveillance hazards, and physical security weaknesses.

James M. Atkinson
Granite Island Group
Gloucester, MA USA
*Contact Phone:* 978-546-3803
**Click to Contact from Web Site**

## SWS SECURITY
Street, MD USA
http://www.swssec.com

Steve Uhrig is the President of SWS Security, a multi-national manufacturer of electronic surveillance equipment. Formerly in government service, he is a popular talk show guest and media expert with 75 appearances as of August 2006. Steve is an expert witness, a security consultant to Tom Clancy, a regular consultant to the History Channel, and also was the technical advisor and an actor in the movie Enemy of the State. He has a sense of humor, exhaustive technical knowledge and an ability to explain surveillance history, concepts, practices, uses and abuses in layman's terms.

Steve Uhrig
*President*
SWS Security
Street, MD
*Contact Phone:* 410-879-4035
*Contact Main Phone:* 410-879-4035
**Click to Contact from Web Site**

### JANUS ASSOCIATES, INC. -- INFORMATION SECURITY
Stamford, CT USA
http://www.janusassociates.com

JANUS, with over fifteen years in the business, is one of only a few independent firms nationwide that specializes in the computer security field. Serving as a consultant to federal and state government agencies, and to major domestic and international corporations on computer abuse, misuse, forensics, theft and fraud, JANUS is regarded as the 'expert's expert' by both its clients and competitors alike.

Lyle A. Liberman
*Director of Marketing*
JANUS Associates, Inc.
Stamford, CT USA
*Contact Phone:* 203-251-0200
**Click to Contact from Web Site**

### HOWARD SERVICES, SECURITY
Franklin, MA USA
www.expertsecurity.com

What were once unimaginable security threats are becoming more commonplace. Major terrorist acts on US soil, violence in our schools, malls and sidewalks concern us all. From Main Street to Wall Street expert explanations and solutions allow us to face these challenges. Howard Services provides independent and non-product affiliated consultations. To increase public awareness we work closely with the media to inform the public of pertinent and current information to address these issues.

Howard Levinson, CPP
*President*
Howard Services, Security
Franklin, MA USA
*Contact Phone:* 508-520-1500
**Click to Contact from Web Site**

### OUTSECURE, INC. INFORMATION SECURITY CONSULTANT
Bridgeport, CT USA
www.Outsecure.com

How Secure Are You? As a company, Information Security is of vital importance for survival. In today's context, whether you are in a regulated industry or not, determining adequacy and level of security is becoming more and more challenging. Security now, more than ever has become a business concern. It can only be effectively implemented by a structured and holistic approach. With a staff of certified security professionals, in the US, Asia Pacific and India we seek to help you assess the effectiveness of your security measures against global security standards and offer remediation processes if required.

Pamela Gupta
Outsecure Inc.
Bridgeport, CT USA
*Contact Phone:* 203-333-3344
**Click to Contact from Web Site**

### KRISTA BRADFORD — BRADFORD EXECUTIVE RESEARCH, LLC
New York, NY USA
http://www.bradfordresearch.com

Krista Bradford is Founder and Principal of Bradford Executive Research, LLC, which provides competitive intelligence (CI) for executive search and technology recruitment for some of the world's most profitable and successful corporations. Prior to founding the company in 1997, she worked as a three-time Emmy Award-winning television journalist and investigative reporter for more than two decades. Ms. Bradford has written extensively in the areas of jobs, careers, executive search, adoption, journalism, and competitive intelligence.

Krista Bradford
*Founder and Principal*
Bradford Executive Research, LLC
Westport, CT USA
*Contact Phone:* 203-227-8615
*Contact Main Phone:* 203-227-8615
*Cell:* 203-247-2281
**Click to Contact from Web Site**

### MILITARY OFFICERS ASSOCIATION OF AMERICA
Alexandria, VA USA
http://www.moaa.org

Military Officers Association of America (MOAA) is an independent, nonprofit organization located in Alexandria, VA, and operated to benefit the Nation, its uniformed services personnel, their families, and survivors. It is the largest veterans organization in the U.S. for active duty and retired military officers, with nearly 360,000 members. It has 415 U.S. and overseas chapters.

Col. Marvin J. Harris, USAF (Ret.)
*Director of Public Relations*
Military Officers Association of America
Alexandria, VA
*Contact Phone:* 703-838-0546
**Click to Contact from Web Site**

### ARIK JOHNSON — COMPETITIVE INTELLIGENCE CONSULTANT
Minneapolis, MN USA
http://www.aurorawdc.com

Intelligence matters to the world's elite companies and author of Enabling the Need-to-Know Enterprise, his unique philosophy for Competitive Intelligence best practices in research, analysis and infrastructure development. Since 1995, Arik's team of advisors and analysts at his firm, Aurora, have helped clients see clearly the risks and rewards around and ahead of them, connecting the dots with Aurora's ReconG2 suite of CI products and services.

Arik Johnson
Aurora WDC
Minneapolis, MN USA
*Contact Phone:* 715-720-1616
**Click to Contact from Web Site**

## RESEARCH/INTELLIGENCE ANALYST PROGRAM
Erie, PA USA
http://www.mercyhurst.edu/academics/ac_28.htm

Mercyhurst offers the only training program for research/intelligence analysts employed by federal agencies, law enforcement and corporations. Director Robert Heibel was former deputy director of counterterrorism for the FBI.

Robert J. Heibel
*Director, Mercyhurst College*
Research/ Intelligence Analyst Program
Erie, PA
*Contact Phone:* 814-824-2117
*Contact Main Phone:* 814-824-2000
**Click to Contact from Web Site**

## YOUNG MARINES
Washington, DC USA
http://www.youngmarines.com

The Young Marines is a non-profit youth education and service program for boys and girls, ages 8 through completion of high school. The Young Marines strengthens the lives of America's youth by teaching self-confidence, academic achievement, honoring our nation's veterans, responsible citizenship, community service and the importance living a healthy, drug-free lifestyle. The program focuses on character building and leadership and promotes a lifestyle that is conducive to being productive members of society.

Janelle Johnsen
*Director of Public Relations, Young Marines*
*National Headquarters*
Washington, AZ USA
*Contact Phone:* 1-866-702-5480
*Contact Main Phone:* 1-800-717-0060
**Click to Contact from Web Site**

## NAVY LEAGUE OF THE UNITED STATES
Arlington, VA USA
www.navyleague.org

The Navy League of the United States offers its 'Military and Sea Services Experts' for journalists, with sources and commentary on a wide range of maritime and defense topics such as Navy, Marine Corps, Coast Guard and Merchant Marine operations, various ships, submarines, equipment and technology used by the sea services, quality of life matters for active duty military personnel, public policy issues and appropriations, current events and breaking news.

Janet Mescus
*Senior Director of Communications*
Navy League of The United States
Arlington, VA
*Contact Main Phone:* 703-528-1775
**Click to Contact from Web Site**

### VETERAN'S VISION
Washington, DC USA
www.vetsvision.org

As the president of three nationwide veterans' organizations, MAJ Brian Hampton, USAR (ret) has developed a reputation for being a forceful, intrepid and controversial national advocate for veterans' causes. In city rallies around the country, Hampton has challenged federal elected officials for spending $70 billion on benefits for illegal aliens, while investing 1/10 of 1% of that to help 300,000 homeless veterans. A Vietnam Veteran, Hampton earned a Masters' Degree from Michigan State University.

Brian Hampton
*Founder and Publisher*
Veteran's Vision
Falls Church, VA USA
*Contact Phone:* 703-237-8980
*Contact Main Phone:* 800-528-5385
**Click to Contact from Web Site**

## AMERICAN FOREIGN SERVICE ASSOCIATION
Washington, DC USA
http://www.afsa.org

AFSA speaks for the 23,000 Foreign Service professionals about the importance of vigorous American leadership in international affairs; international trade facilitation and American prosperity; dangers of isolationism; role of diplomacy in ensuring national security; safety of Americans abroad; political ambassadorial appointments; budget allocations for diplomacy, foreign aid, and other foreign affairs activities.

Tom Switzer
*Director of Communications*
American Foreign Service Association
Washington, DC
*Contact Phone:* 202-944-5501
**Click to Contact from Web Site**

## ASSOCIATION ON THIRD WORLD AFFAIRS (A.T.W.A.)
Washington, DC USA
http://www.atwa.org

An independent membership organization, ATWA promotes fresh approaches to, and clearer understanding of, societies undergoing major transitions. Working with countries in Asia and Eastern Europe, as well as Africa, Middle East, South Asia and Latin America, ATWA brings together policy and opinion makers, diplomats, and other VIPs. Activities include Capitol Hill conferences where Members of Congress, ambassadors and other experts discuss timely topics; holding seminars at embassies; publishing conference reports; providing expert consultants and speakers. Topics: US foreign policy; the Islamist-Jihadist threat; Islam today; the US-China-Taiwan tangle; promoting and building democracy; the Middle East; Africa; promoting sustainable development; benefits of fair trade.

Lorna Hahn, Ph.D.
*Executive Director*
Association on Third World Affairs (A.T.W.A.)
Washington, DC
*Contact Phone:* 202-973-0157
**Click to Contact from Web Site**

## NATIONAL DEFENSE UNIVERSITY PRESS
Washington, DC USA
http://www.ndu.edu/inss/press/nduphp.html

NDU Press publishes books, policy briefs, occasional papers, monographs and special reports on national security strategy, defense policy, national military strategy, regional security affairs, and global strategic problems. These publications reflect the output of NDU research and academic programs as well as contributions by outside analysts and experts. Joint Force Quarterly is a professional military journal published by NDU since 1993 for the Chairman of the Joint Chiefs of Staff.

Col Merrick Krause, USAF
National Defense University Press
Washington, DC USA
*Contact Phone:* 202-685-4221
**Click to Contact from Web Site**

## NAVAL INSTITUTE PRESS -- U.S. NAVAL INSTITUTE
Annapolis, MD USA
www.navalinstitute.org

The United States Naval Institute, with more than 130 years of sea service history, works through our unique independent forum to: * Support the professional development of Sailors, Marines, and Coast Guardsmen * Honor America's enduring sea service heritage * Advance a strong national defense * Challenge convention by encouraging debate on critical defense issues

Susan Artigiani
*Publicity Manager*
Naval Institute Press
Annapolis, MD
*Contact Phone:* 410-295-1081
*Contact Main Phone:* 410-268-6110
**Click to Contact from Web Site**

## U.S. ARMY WAR COLLEGE
Carlisle, PA USA
http://www.carlisle.army.mil

The U.S. Army War College is the senior education center of the Army. College expertise emphasizes strategic leadership and the landpower. See military security studies at www.carlisle.army.mil, or contact these experts: regional military assessments, strategic issues of leadership and management and ethics, defense strategy analysis, campaign planning, Homeland defense, Peace keeping and stability operations, Strategic logistics, Force development, Strategic communications, Military History, Executive [over 40] Health and Fitness.

Carol Kerr
*Public Information Officer*
U.S. Army War College
Carlisle, PA
*Contact Phone:* 717-245-4389
**Click to Contact from Web Site**

## NAVAL INSTITUTE
Annapolis, MD USA
http://www.USNI.org

The mission of the U.S. Naval Institute is to provide an independent forum for those who dare to read, think, speak, and write in order to advance the professional, literary, and scientific understanding of sea power and other issues critical to national defense.

Ivan Scott
Naval Institute
Ananpolis, MD USA
*Contact Phone:* 410-268-6110
**Click to Contact from Web Site**

## INDEPENDENT SCHOLARS OF ASIA, INC.
Berkeley, CA USA
http://www.hypersphere.com/isa

Independent Scholars of Asia Inc. represents scholars and institutions who work in Asia in the fields of anthropology, arts, economics, ethno medicine, folklore, geography, Asian languages and literatures, social and political sciences. ISA also organizes local, national and international conferences and has so far published twenty-two proceedings of our annual conferences.

Ruth-Inge Heinze
Independent Scholars of Asia, Inc.
Berkeley, CA United States
*Contact Phone:* 510 849-3791
**Click to Contact from Web Site**

## COUNCIL ON HEMISPHERIC AFFAIRS
Washington, DC USA
www.coha.org

For over 25 years, COHA director Larry Birns and its researchers have been turned to by the national media for analysis on fast-breaking Latin American political and economic issues and Canadian developments. They have been cited on scores of occasions in The New York Times and The Washington Post, plus over every network news program.

Alex Sanchez
Council on Hemispheric Affairs
Washington, DC
*Contact Phone:* 202 223 4975
**Click to Contact from Web Site**

## ISLAM IN FOCUS
Fairhope, AL USA
www.islam-in-focus.com

Anis Shorrosh, D. Phil. in Islamic Studies, Oxford Graduate School, D. Min. in Theological Studies, member of Oxford Society of Scholars. Author of 10 books: 'Islam: A Threat or a Challenge?', 'Islam Revealed', 'The True Furqan' - all best sellers. Debater with Muslims, lecturer on Islam, Middle East and Prophecy.

Mrs. Anis Shorrosh
*Secretary*
Islam In Focus
Fairhope, AL
*Contact Phone:* 251-680-7770
*Contact Main Phone:* 251-680-7722
**Click to Contact from Web Site**

## WINSTON MID EAST ANALYSIS & COMMENTARY
Chicago, IL USA

Mid-East regional conflicts, weapons, war, technology and oil. Forecasts of probable scenarios; relations between Washington & Jerusalem. Radio and TV interviews — good with live call-ins. 150 interviews during Gulf War. Have published over 3,500 related articles in USA Today, Washington Post, U.S. Defense News, Boston Globe and Chicago Tribune. Articles available by e-mail.

Emanuel A. Winston
*Analyst & Commentator*
Winston Mid East Analysis & Commentary
Chicago Area, IL
*Contact Phone:* 847-432-1735
**Click to Contact from Web Site**

## ZOE RASTEGAR — TALK SHOW HOST
Washington, DC USA
accentproductions.org

Born in Shiraz, Iran, Zohreh Rastegar was raised in an upper middle class, educated, urbane family. Her mother was owner and headmistress of a private school in Tehran before retiring. Her father was an executive at the National Oil Company. He was also a poet and published a book of poetry just prior to his death in December, 2001.

Zoe Rastegar
Washington, DC USA
*Contact Phone:* 202-333-4373
*Cell:* 202-841-8733
**Click to Contact from Web Site**

## IMRAN ANWAR / IMRAN.TV
New York, NY USA
http://WWW.IMRAN.COM

Imran Anwar is a published writer, respected global affairs analyst, well-known media expert on technology & international business and popular commentator on TV. He is a regular guest on CNN, Fox News Channel and other TV/radio channels to discuss foreign policy, international affairs, South Asia & the Middle East, and the war on terror. As an Internet pioneer, high-tech CEO and respected visionary Imran is a popular public speaker delivering keynote addresses at conferences worldwide.

Imran Anwar
*President*
IMRAN INTERNETional
IMRAN.TV
Heron Pointe, NY USA
*Contact Phone:* 516-909-6800
*Contact Main Phone:* 631-289-0999
*Cell:* 516-456-6700
**Click to Contact from Web Site**

## NATIONAL COMMITTEE ON AMERICAN FOREIGN POLICY
New York, NY USA
www.ncafp.org

When vital U.S. Foreign Policy interests are at stake, contact Dr. George D. Schwab, President & Co-Founder with Hans J. Morgenthau of the National Committee on American Foreign Policy, for up-to-date, credible analysis and interpretation. Dr. Schwab, professor emeritus of history (CUNY) and author of numerous books and articles, is an expert on U.S. National security interests relating to Afghanistan, global terrorism, Islamic Fundamentalism, prospects for Middle East Peace, U.S.-China-Taiwan relations and the cross-strait issue, North Korean nuclear issue, U.S. bilateral alliances with Japan and South Korea, Central Asia, transatlantic relations and Northern Ireland.

Daniel Morris
*Program Director*
National Committee on American Foreign Policy
New York, NY
*Contact Phone:* 212-224-1146
*Contact Main Phone:* 212-224-1120
**Click to Contact from Web Site**

# Independent Scholars of Asia, Inc.
## *Professional, Non-profit Group*

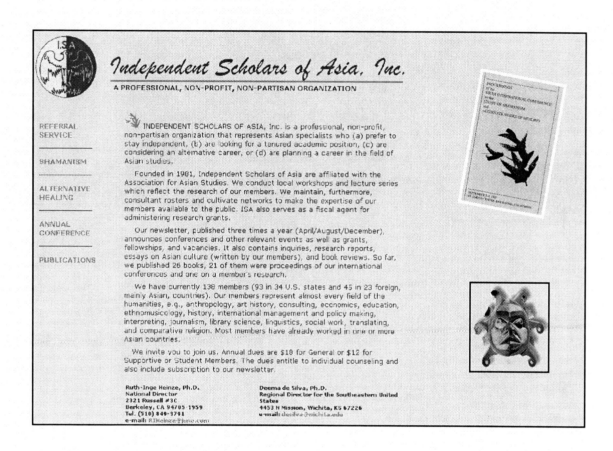

**Independent Scholars of Asia, Inc.**
**Berkeley, Calif. -- U.S.A.**
**Ruth-Inge Heinze**
**Contact Phone: 510-849-3791**

# www.hypersphere.com/isa/

## CODEPINK: WOMEN FOR PEACE
Los Angeles, CA USA
http://www.codepinkalert.org

CODEPINK is a women-initiated grassroots peace and social justice movement working to end the war in Iraq, stop new wars, and redirect our resources into healthcare, education and other life-affirming activities. CODEPINK rejects the Bush administration's fear-based politics that justify violence, and instead calls for policies based on compassion, kindness and a commitment to international law. With an emphasis on joy and humor, CODEPINK women and men seek to activate, amplify and inspire a community of peacemakers through creative campaigns and a commitment to non-violence.

Dana Balicki
CODEPINK: Women for Peace
Venice, CA USA
*Contact Phone:* 310 827 4320
**Click to Contact from Web Site**

## ASSOCIATION OF WORLD CITIZENS
San Francisco, CA USA
http://www.worldcitizens.org

The Association of World Citizens is a San Francisco based international peace organization with branches in over 30 countries. NGO status with the United Nations. Goals include: Strengthened and democratic United Nations, Economic policies to end poverty and save the environment, Abolition of nuclear weapons with priority in removing U.S. and Russian nuclear warheads of the current hair trigger alert status. Elimination of the war system through the establishment of world law to resolve conflicts.

Douglas Mattern
*President*
Association of World Citizens
San Francisco, CA
*Contact Phone:* 650-326-1409
**Click to Contact from Web Site**

## DR. JOHN M. PRESLEY - PEACE ADVOCATE
Daytona Beach, FL USA

Dr. Presley, philosopher, psychologist, administrator, teacher, creative thinker; Participant/ significant seminars; solo speaker, hundreds of civic clubs, churches, various organizations, women's groups; interviewed by Diane Sayer, Larry King, Hard Copy, many local TV stations; Select Pepper Commission, Juvenile Crime; authority several areas: world peace (author book Code 3-M Roadmap for Peace); peace impact of religious extremist; mentally challenged; Juvenile offenders; VA medical systems; youth camps; member Mensa; sleep Research; patented invention owner. Teaching: special education, HS band Director, FSU, Auburn graduate faculty, UVA Medical School adjunct faculty; Leadership positions. CEO Florida P.H. churches, Executive Director Retarded Children Assoc.(Miami), Supt. (State Institution (MR) Ft. Myers, FL), Supt./ Creator model program/ designed facility, Sunland, Miami - recognized by U.S. News & World Report w/article, facility dedicated by Rose Kennedy; attended Two Mr. Expert banquets with President Kennedy/family; editorial changes/ Encyclopedia Britannica requested by owner, Benson; CEO three VA Medical Centers.

Dr. John M. Presley
Port Orange, FL USA
*Contact Phone:* 386-304-8102
**Click to Contact from Web Site**

## AMNESTY INTERNATIONAL
Chicago, IL USA
http://amnestyusa.org

Founded in London in 1961, Amnesty International is a Nobel Prize-winning grassroots activist organization with over 1.8 million members worldwide. Amnesty International undertakes research and action focused on preventing and ending grave abuses of the rights to physical and mental integrity, freedom of conscience and expression, and freedom from discrimination, within the context of its work to promote all human rights. Amnesty International USA (AIUSA) is the U.S. Section of Amnesty International.

Queta R Bauer
*President*
Cultural Communicatrions, LLC
Chicago, IL United States
*Contact Phone:* 773-285-1055
**Click to Contact from Web Site**

## CENTER FOR CIVIL SOCIETY & GOVERNANCE AT AED
Washington, DC USA
www.aed-ccsg.org

The AED Center for Civil Society and Governance (CCSG) supports citizens to mobilize effectively to influence policy, improve lives, and build peace. Building democracy requires mobilizing diverse groups of citizens. CCSG addresses critical issues by organizing people around shared interests and problems on local, regional, and national levels. CCSG believes that the process of connecting individuals and groups to work together for change is both a significant end in itself and a means to the shared goals of peace, democracy, and development.

Michael Kott
*Director*
Center for Civil Society & Governance
Academy for Educational Development
Washington, DC USA
*Contact Phone:* 202-884-8241
*Contact Main Phone:* 202-884-8000
**Click to Contact from Web Site**

# ASSOCIATION OF WORLD CITIZENS

## MOBILIZING FOR PROGRESSIVE CHANGE AS RESPONSIBLE CITIZENS OF THE WORLD

Douglas Mattern is co-founder and president of the Association of World Citizens, a San Francisco based peace organization with branches in over 30 countries and NGO status with the United Nations

Douglas Mattern is available to lecture or interview on the greatest challenge of our time. This is to <u>rid the world of nuclear weapons before it is too late</u> and mobilize to end the war business. Only then can we lay the foundation for a world community and a new civilization for the 21st century that is based on respect for life, respect for the environment, and respect for each other.

Mattern, in addition to his peace work for more than 30 years, was a senior engineer/manager in the largest commercial computer companies in Silicon Valley for over 25 years.

Mattern has appeared on scores of radio and TV interview programs, including the NBC Today show. He has more than 130 published articles on peace related issues.

Mattern is listed in Marquis Who's Who in America and Who's Who in the World. He received the Albert Einstein Peace Award from the International Association of Educators for World Peace, 2001. He has met with presidents, nobel peace laureates, UN officials and other world leaders in pursuing the goal of a better world.

## World's number one crime: The War Business

*Every gun that is made, every warship launched, every rocket fired signifies, in the final sense, a theft from those who hunger and are not fed, those who are cold and not clothed. This world in arms is not spending money alone. It is spending the sweat of its laborers, the genius of its scientists, the hopes of its children. This is not a way of life at all in any true sense. Under the cloud of threatening war, it is humanity hanging from a cross of iron.*

President Eisenhower

Number of people living in poverty on less than $2 a day: 3 billion
Number of people who die every day from hunger: 24,000
Number of nuclear weapons stockpiled: 30,000 - including thousands of nuclear warheads on hair-trigger alert, ready to be launched in a few minutes notice
World military spending: $1 trillion per year

## World's number one hope: Moblizing for Change

ASSOCIATION OF WORLD CITIZENS, 55 New Montgomery St. #224
San Francisco, CA 94105 Tel: 415 541 9610 email: worldcit@best.com

**DONNA POISL, IMMIGRANT EXPERT, AUTHOR**
Charlotte, NC USA
www.howtoliveandthrive.com

Donna Poisl is a leading authority on the problems immigrants face learning to live in a new country. She has written a beginner's guide for immigrants, based on her own experiences as an immigrant and years helping clients as a real estate and insurance agent. Poor quality education and healthcare are often the results of low paying jobs and poverty in the immigrant community. She tells how helping immigrants succeed will make a stronger country for everyone who lives here.

Donna Poisl
*Author*
Live & Thrive Press
Gastonia, NC USA
*Contact Phone:* 704-861-9500
*Cell:* (704) 747-2238
**Click to Contact from Web Site**

**NATIONAL IMMIGRATION FORUM**
Washington, DC USA
http://www.immigrationforum.org

The leading pro-immigration organization in the country. Quoted by every major U.S. newspaper and on national radio and television shows. Expert spokespeople in English and Spanish, immigrants and refugees who can put a human face on your story. Clear and concise written materials on legal and illegal immigration, the impact of recent laws on immigrant communities, citizenship, and public benefits. Publications on the fiscal impact of immigration and how immigrants are assimilating into American society.

Douglas Rivlin
*Director of Communication*
National Immigration Forum
Washington, DC
*Contact Phone:* 202-347-0040
**Click to Contact from Web Site**

**MARTA PERRONE - DOMESTIC CONNECTIONS PUBLICATIONS**
Encino, CA USA
http://domestic-connections.com/

What are your obligations as a domestic employer as it relates to immigration, tax, health, contract and labor laws? What are the psychology, chemistry and personality issues that flow from that relationship? How can you be assured that you are making the right decisions when hiring household employees? Marta Perrone has nearly 20 years of experience in this area and has written a comprehensive guide with forms, advice and guidelines for childcare, housekeeping and emergency procedures.

Marta Perrone
Domestic Connections Publications
Encino, CA USA
*Contact Phone:* 818-784-8102
**Click to Contact from Web Site**

## AMERICANS FOR IMMIGRATION CONTROL, INC.
Monterey, VA USA
http://www.immigrationcontrol.com

Americans for Immigration Control, Inc. is the nation's largest grassroots lobby for immigration reform. With more than 250,000 members, AIC is leading the fight to reduce overall immigration levels, end welfare and affirmative action benefits for aliens, and protect America's borders from illegal entry by foreign populations. Besides lobbying for immigration control, AIC conducts public education campaigns through direct mail, paid advertisements, opinion surveys, and public appearances by its spokesmen on radio and television.

Robert Goldsborough
*President*
Americans for Immigration Control, Inc.
Monterey, VA
*Contact Phone:* 540-468-2023
**Click to Contact from Web Site**

## FEDERATION FOR AMERICAN IMMIGRATION REFORM (FAIR)
Washington, DC USA
http://www.fairus.org

FAIR is the largest and most effective organization in America working on the issue of mass immigration and has testified before Congress on every major piece of immigration legislation. FAIR's expert spokespeople have appeared on hundreds of radio and television talkshows. Television appearances have included 60 Minutes, NBC Nightly News, Crossfire, The Today Show, 48 Hours, and Dateline. They are available via telephone or will travel by arrangement.

Ira Mehlman
*Media Director*
Federation for American Immigration Reform (FAIR)
Washington, DC
*Contact Phone:* 310-821-4283
*Contact Main Phone:* 202-328-7004
**Click to Contact from Web Site**

## NEGATIVE POPULATION GROWTH - NPG, INC
Washington, DC USA
www.npg.org

Negative Population Growth (NPG) is a national membership organization founded in 1972 to educate the American public and political leaders about the detrimental effects of overpopulation on our environment, resources and quality of life. NPG advocates a smaller and truly sustainable United States population accomplished through smaller families and lower, more traditional immigration levels.

Craig Lewis
NPG, Inc
*Contact Phone:* 703-370-9510
**Click to Contact from Web Site**

## SURVIVAL CENTER — FAMILY PREPAREDNESS, HEALTH, SURVIVAL SUPPLIES
Seattle, WA USA
http://www.survivalcenter.com

Richard Mankamyer Uncle Richard Author, Lecturer and General Manager of the Survival Center has over 35 years experience helping people prepare for most any emergency that may come their way. We have helped thousands of families to prepare. We have worked with Federal Reserve Bank locations to prepare, nuclear power plants, various business and governmental agencies as consultants and suppliers. We have the knowledge and experience to help you prepare. Survival Center, America's Premier Preparedness Center, is helping Americans prepare for most any emergency that may come their way with survival supplies, emergency preparedness, disaster kits, disaster preparedness supplies, MRE's, food storage, water filters, medical kits, and Under Ground Shelters.

Richard Mankamyer
*Director of Preparedness and Emergency Planning*
Survival Center
Preparedness/Emergency Supplies
McKenna, WA USA
*Contact Phone:* 1-360-458-6778
**Click to Contact from Web Site**

## ANGELO A PAPARELLI, US IMMIGRATION LAW SPECIALIST
Irvine, CA USA
www.entertheusa.com

Angelo Paparelli is named the World's Leading Lawyer for Corporate Immigration Law by The International Who's Who of Business Lawyers (2005 edition). He advises Fortune 50 companies, entrepreneurs, investors, educators and families. He regularly serves as an expert witness and speaker on immigration topics. Paparelli's professional leadership roles have included chairman of the Immigration and Nationality Committee, ABA Section of International Law and Practice. He is president of the Academy of Business Immigration Lawyers and a member of the National Speakers Association.

Jowilla Rabor
Paparelli & Partners, LLP
Irvine, CA USA
*Contact Phone:* 949-955-5562
*Contact Main Phone:* 949-955-5555
**Click to Contact from Web Site**

## CENTER FOR WILDLIFE INFORMATION
Missoula, MT USA
http://www.BeBearAware.org

General H. Norman Schwarzkopf, is a national spokesperson for this group which is involved with grizzly bear conservation and education and the wildlife stewardship campaign. They are concerned with hiking and camping in bear, mountain lion and rattlesnake country and with urban wildlife-bears, mountain lions and coyotes returning to the city. Some topics include: Saving the Grizzly Bear, What to Do if Attacked by a Wild Animal and Bear Pepper Spray-Does it Work? Their professional speakers include bear management specialists and forest and park rangers.

Chuck Bartlebaugh
*Executive Director*
Center for Wildlife Information
Missoula, MT
*Contact Phone:* 406-721-8985
*Contact Main Phone:* 406-523-7750
**Click to Contact from Web Site**

### INTERSTATE COMMISSION ON THE POTOMAC RIVER BASIN
Rockville, MD USA
http://www.potomacriver.org

The ICPRB is an advisory agency established by Congress to "Enhance, protect, and conserve the water and associated land resources of the Potomac River and its tributaries through regional and interstate cooperation." The ICPRB coordinates environmental protection activity within the basin, stimulates federal and state action, conducts research, serves as a liaison with citizens, disseminates information about the Potomac, and provides technical support to participating state and local governments and citizens groups.

Curtis Dalpra
Interstate Commission on the Potomac River Basin
Rockville, MD USA
*Contact Phone:* 301.984.1908 x 107
**Click to Contact from Web Site**

### THE NATIONAL ANXIETY CENTER
South Orange, NJ USA
http://www.anxietycenter.com

Global Warming? Urban Sprawl? Endangered Species? Pesticides? Ozone 'Holes'? Are these and other issues real or just 'scare campaigns'? Since 1990, the Center has been a clearinghouse for information about scare campaigns that create widespread anxiety and drive public policy, generating countless new laws, regulations, and international treaties, affecting all aspects of life in America. Talkers Magazine calls this veteran science and business writer, 'one of the great guests of talk radio.' Print journalists value his expertise.

Alan Caruba
The National Anxiety Center
South Orange, NJ
*Contact Phone:* 973-763-6392
**Click to Contact from Web Site**

### AMERICAN WATER WORKS ASSOCIATION
Denver, CO USA
http://www.awwa.org

The American Water Works Association is the authoritative resource for knowledge, information and advocacy to improve the quality and supply of water in North America and beyond. With over 57,000 members and 4,700 utility members, AWWA is the largest and oldest organization of water professionals in the world. AWWA strives to advance public health, safety and welfare by uniting the efforts of the water community. Our technical experts are proud to be the best resource for information on drinking water issues.

Greg Kail
*Sr. Public Affairs Manager*
American Water Works Association
Denver, CO USA
*Contact Phone:* 303-734-3410
*Contact Main Phone:* 800-926-7337
**Click to Contact from Web Site**

### THE OCEAN CONSERVANCY
Washington, DC USA
www.OceanConservancy.org

The Ocean Conservancy's mission is to protect ocean ecosystems and conserve the global abundance and diversity of marine wildlife. Through science-based advocacy, research, and public education, The Ocean Conservancy informs, inspires, and empowers people to speak and act for the oceans. Headquartered in Washington, DC, The Ocean Conservancy has offices in Alaska, California, Florida, Maine and Virginia and the U.S. Virgin Islands. More than half a million members and volunteers support The Ocean Conservancy's mission.

Tom McCann
*Director of Media Relations*
The Ocean Conservancy
Washington, DC USA
*Contact Phone:* 202-429-5609
*Contact Main Phone:* 1-800-519-1541
**Click to Contact from Web Site**

### WATER ENVIRONMENT FEDERATION
Alexandria, VA USA
http://www.wef.org

Do you cover issues like the Clean Water Act reauthorization, pollution prevention, infrastructure financing and security, watershed management, or wastewater residuals and biosolids management? The Water Environment Federation is an international nonprofit technical and educational organization that preserves and enhances water quality worldwide. With nearly 40,000 members, we can put you in touch with local, national and international water quality experts.

Lori Burkhammer
*Director, Public Information*
Water Environment Federation
Alexandria, VA
*Contact Phone:* 703-684-2480
**Click to Contact from Web Site**

### GARY MOORE — DIRECT SALES & MARKETING EXPERT
Chicago, IL USA
www.PlayingWithTheEnemy.com

Gary Moore is an entrepreneur and business executive, exciting speaker/sales trainer, musician and author. As president of Covenant Air & Water, LLC www.aquativa.com, he provides solutions to water problems. Gary's most recent accomplishment is author of Playing with the Enemy: A Baseball Prodigy, a World at War, and a Field of Broken Dreams (September 2006). Inspired by true events, it is a heartwarming story about baseball, WWII, destiny, character, family, and second chances www.playingwiththeenemy.com.

Carole V. Batholomeaux
Bartholomeux/Public Relations, LLC
Phoenix, AZ USA
*Contact Phone:* 602-404-8018
**Click to Contact from Web Site**

## FRANCISCO PATINO — INVENTOR
New York, NY USA

Francisco Patino, 19, was born in Barranquilla, Colombia. After his sister passed away at the age of 7, he became determined to make something great of his life. He came to America at age 12 to live with his father in New York City. He is currently a student at Queens College in New York and also runs a carpet cleaning business with his uncle. Francisco was inspired to create the Double Traction Bike because all of the kids in his neighborhood ride on each other's bike handlebars to get around. He is a passionate inventor and also hopes to go to law school in the future.

Jill Lublin
Promising Promotion
Novato, CA USA
*Contact Phone:* 415-883-5455
**Click to Contact from Web Site**

## NATIONAL RURAL ELECTRIC COOPERATIVE ASSOCIATION
Arlington, VA USA
http://www.nreca.coop

NRECA is the national trade organization representing the nation's more than 900 private customer-owned electric cooperatives providing electric service to 39 million people in 47 states. Electric cooperatives own and maintain nearly half the nation's power lines, spanning three quarters of the United States. Electric co-op consumers live in 2,600 of the nation's 3,136 counties. NRECA provides programs and services to ensure that electric cooperatives remain a vital segment of the electric utility industry.

Patrick Lavigne
*Director of Media & Public Affairs*
National Rural Electric Cooperative Association
Arlington, VA
*Contact Phone:* 703-907-5732
**Click to Contact from Web Site**

## AMERICAN PUBLIC POWER ASSOCIATION
Washington, DC USA
http://www.APPAnet.org

The American Public Power Association is the national trade association for the nation's 2,000 community-owned, locally controlled, not-for-profit electric utilities. They provide power to 43 million Americans. APPA can give you information on issues facing the electric utility industry.

Madalyn Cafruny
*Director of Communications*
American Public Power Association
Washington, DC
*Contact Phone:* 202-467-2952
**Click to Contact from Web Site**

## ALLIANCE TO SAVE ENERGY
*Creating an Energy-Efficient World*

## ALLIANCE TO SAVE ENERGY
Washington, DC USA
http://www.ase.org

The Alliance to Save Energy is a coalition of prominent business, government, environmental, and consumer leaders who promote the efficient use of energy worldwide to benefit consumers, environment, the economy, and national security. The Alliance offers expertise on: Energy, Energy Efficiency, Energy Policy, Environment, Climate Change/Global Warming, Consumer Money-Saving Tips, Utility Restructuring, Energy Prices, Pollution, Disasters—Rebuilding Efficiently, "Green Schools" - Energy Efficiency in School Buildings and Curricula. Alliance President Kateri Callahan brings 20 years of experience in policy advocacy, fundraising, coalition building, and organizational management.

Ms. Ronnie J. Kweller
*Deputy Director of Communications*
Alliance to Save Energy
Washington, DC
*Contact Phone:* 202-530-2203
*Contact Main Phone:* 202-857-0666
*Cell:* 202-276-9327
**Click to Contact from Web Site**

# Angelo A. Paparelli,
## *U.S. Immigration Law Specialist*

## Angelo Paparelli
## Paparelli & Partners, LLP
## Irvine, Calif. -- U.S.A.
## Main Phone: 949-955-5555
## Contact Phone: 949-955-5575
## www.entertheusa.com

## ORYXE ENERGY INTERNATIONAL
Irvine, CA USA
http://www.oryxe-energy.com

ORYXE Energy International (www.oryxe-energy.com) was founded in 2001 to solve the world's dual need for dependable fuel supplies and a cleaner environment. By focusing on a specific challenge-cleaner-burning fossil fuels-we have developed innovative additive technologies that improve fuel performance and make a meaningful reduction in toxic emissions from conventional and reformulated fossil fuels. Our proprietary products are proven, safe and cost-effective. ORYXE Energy was named a Top 100 Innovator by Red Herring.

Kristen Reilly
ORYXE Energy International
Irvine, CA USA
*Contact Phone:* 949-452-9272 x224
**Click to Contact from Web Site**

## NUCLEAR ENERGY INSTITUTE (NEI)
Washington, DC USA
http://www.nei.org

NEI is the media's source for news about nuclear energy. We are the nuclear industry's policy organization with nearly 300 member organizations worldwide. We provide analysis of nuclear issues: energy, environment, economics, new nuclear plants, nuclear plant safety and security, power uprates, license renewal and used nuclear fuel management. We offer access to regional, national and international experts. Spokespeople are immediately available when you need insightful commentary quickly.

NEI Media Relations
Nuclear Energy Institute (NEI)
Washington, DC
*Contact Phone:* 202-739-8000
**Click to Contact from Web Site**

## NATIONAL OILHEAT RESEARCH ALLIANCE
Washington, DC USA
www.nora-oilheat.org

The National Oilheat Research Alliance (NORA) is a collaborative effort among Oilheat companies in 22 USA states and regions. NORA supports research and development, technical training of Oilheat personnel, and consumer education projects. To date, NORA has provided scholarships to students studying oil-powered heating systems; supplied new educational materials to technicians; supported equipment development to bring more efficient and environmentally friendly systems to market; and developed consumer materials explaining the advances in the latest Clearburn Science™ Oilheat technologies.

Lee Yaffa
Greystone Services
Peabody, MA USA
*Contact Phone:* 978-535-9185
**Click to Contact from Web Site**

## EDISON ELECTRIC INSTITUTE
Washington, DC USA
http://www.eei.org

Edison Electric Institute (EEI) is the association of United States shareholder-owned electric companies, international affiliates, and industry associates worldwide. Our U.S. members serve 97 percent of all the ultimate customers in the shareholder owned segment of the industry, and 71 percent of all electric utility ultimate customers in the nation. They generate almost 60 percent of the electricity produced by U.S. electric generators. EEI provides information on energy and environmental issues of national importance. For the story behind the story, call EEI's media Department.

Jim Owen
*Media Relations*
Edison Electric Institute
Washington, DC
*Contact Phone:* 202-508-5659
**Click to Contact from Web Site**

## TED ROCKWELL -- ENGINEER & NUCLEAR POWER EXPERT
Washington, DC USA
http://members.authorsguild.net/tedrockwell

Ted Rockwell's books describe his 60+ years continuous involvement in the birth and development of nuclear technology, beginning with the wartime atomic bomb project, then as Admiral Rickover's Technical Director, building the nuclear Navy and the world's first commercial atomic power plant under Eisenhower's Atoms for Peace program. Rockwell is experienced in explaining in simple terms nuclear power, radiation, nuclear waste, and other aspects of technology that may benefit or threaten our health and environment.

Theodore Rockwell
Author/Engineer
Chevy Chase, MD USA
*Contact Phone:* 301-652-9509
**Click to Contact from Web Site**

# Center for Wildlife Information

## Be Bear Aware
## and Wildlife Stewardship Campaign

### General H. Norman Schwarzkopf, National Spokesperson

The Center for Wildlife Information works in partnership with state and federal wildlife and land management agencies to reduce human-wildlife conflicts that can result in people and animals being injured and killed. To address this issue, the Center for Wildlife Information is coordinating the Be Bear Aware and Wildlife Stewardship Campaign. The Campaign provides public information and educational materials about how to avoid conflicts with all wildlife, with an emphasis on bears, cougars, alligators and venomous snakes. We coordinate bear avoidance and wildlife stewardship training workshops and presentations for youth groups and community organizations.

Many visitors to our parks, forests and refuges have a false sense of security around wild animals. They mistake passiveness and the appearance of domestication as an invitation to approach and interact. This false sense of security has led to an increase in serious maulings and fatalities. Chuck Bartlebaugh has more than 30 years of experience studying human-wildlife conflicts — what causes them and how to avoid them.

## Special Topics:

- ■ *Hiking and Camping in Bear, Cougar and Rattlesnake Country*

- ■ *Urban Wildlife: Bears, Cougars, and Coyotes in Residential Areas*

- ■ *Grizzly Bear Delisting*

- ■ *Bear Spray: What it is and when and how to use it*

- ■ *How to Avoid Conflicts with Wild Animals*

- ■ *What to Do in an Encounter with a Wild Animal*

### Center For Wildlife Information
A 501 (c) (3) Non-profit Organization

Chuck Bartlebaugh
Executive Director,
Center for Wildlife Information
P.O. Box #8289
Missoula, Montana 59807
406-721-8985

bearinfo@qwest.net • www.bebearaware.org

## SONOCO PRODUCTS COMPANY
Hartsville, SC USA
http://www.sonoco.com
NYSE SON

Sonoco, founded in 1899 and headquartered in Hartsville, South Carolina, is a $3.5 billion global manufacturer of industrial and consumer products and provider of packaging services. The Company's 17,600 employees at over 300 locations in 35 countries serve customers in 85 nations on six continents. Sonoco is one of the world's largest packaging companies and users of recovered/recycled paper.

Allan V. Cecil
*VP, Invest. Rel./Corp. Affairs*
Sonoco Products Company
Hartsville, SC
*Contact Phone:* 843-383-7524
**Click to Contact from Web Site**

## AMERICAN GAS ASSOCIATION
Washington, DC USA
http://www.aga.org

The American Gas Association represents 197 local energy utility companies that deliver natural gas to more than 56 million homes, businesses and industries throughout the United States. AGA's members account for roughly 83 percent of all natural gas delivered by the nation's local natural gas distribution companies. AGA is an advocate for local natural gas utility companies and provides a broad range of programs and services for member natural gas pipelines, marketers, gatherers, international gas companies and industry associates. Natural gas meets nearly one-fourth of the United States' energy needs. For more information, please visit www.aga.org.

Daphne Magnuson
*Director, Public Relations*
American Gas Association
Washington, DC
*Contact Phone:* 202-824-7205
*Contact Main Phone:* 202-824-7000
**Click to Contact from Web Site**

## SRI CONSULTING
Menlo Park, CA USA
www.sriconsulting.com

SRI Consulting is the world's leading provider of value-added information services for the International chemical industry. Publishing continuously for almost 60 years, SRI Consulting is the preeminent source for in-depth business and process analyses offered in a variety of printed and electronic formats. In addition to these continuing information services, SRI Consulting also offers advisory services and a broad range of techno-economic services for the global chemical industry.

Linda R. Henderson
*Director of Sales & Marketing*
SRI Consulting
Menlo Park, CA USA
*Contact Phone:* 650-384-4300
*Contact Main Phone:* 650-384-4300
**Click to Contact from Web Site**

## AMERICAN CHEMISTRY COUNCIL
Arlington, VA USA
www.americanchemistry.com

The American Plastics Council is a national trade association representing 23 of the nation's largest resin producers, including monomer and polymer production and distribution. Founded in 1988, APC works to make plastics a preferred material by demonstrating they are a responsible choice in a more environmentally conscious world.

Chris VandenHeuvel
*Director of Communications*
American Chemistry Council
Arlington, VA
*Contact Phone:* 703-741-5587
**Click to Contact from Web Site**

## KHB CONSULTING SERVICES
Evanston, IL USA
http://www.khbconsulting.com

Dr. Kenneth H. Brown has over thirty years experience in the paint & coatings industry and in the chemical specialty products industry. He is the former Vice President of Technology at Roman Adhesives, Inc., the former Technical Director of Rust-Oleum Corporation, and the former Executive Director of Paint Research Associates at Eastern Michigan University. Dr. Brown is currently a consultant and expert witness, specializing in hazardous materials, household chemical products, industrial chemicals, paint & coatings, aerosols, and laboratory testing & analysis. Brown has also published articles and patents in the fields of polymers, chemicals, and paint & coatings. He also has taught organic chemistry part-time at local universities.

Dr. Kenneth H. Brown
KHB CONSULTING SERVICES
Evanston, IL USA
*Contact Phone:* 847-475-2755
**Click to Contact from Web Site**

## ROBERT C. BYRD NATIONAL TECHNOLOGY TRANSFER CENTER
Wheeling, WV USA
www.nttc.edu

The National Technology Transfer Center (NTTC) provides access to federal technology information, technology and market assessment services, technology marketing and assistance in finding strategic partners. The NTTC fosters relationships with federal clients, showcases technologies and facilitates partnerships between clients and U.S. industry.

Robert Reid
*Media/Public Affairs*
Robert C. Byrd National Technology Transfer Center
Wheeling, WV
*Contact Phone:* 304-243-2158
**Click to Contact from Web Site**

## LAWRENCE LIVERMORE NATIONAL LABORATORY
Livermore, CA USA
http://www.llnl.gov

Established in 1952, Lawrence Livermore National Laboratory is a premier research and development institution for science and technology applied to national security. We are responsible for ensuring that the nation's nuclear weapons remain safe, secure, and reliable. The Lab also applies its expertise to prevent the spread and use of weapons of mass destruction and strengthen homeland security.

Susan Houghton
*Director, Public Affairs Office*
Lawrence Livermore National Laboratory
Livermore, CA USA
*Contact Phone:* 925-422-4599
*Contact Main Phone:* 925-422-4599
**Click to Contact from Web Site**

## NATIONAL SCIENCE FOUNDATION
Arlington, VA USA
http://www.nsf.gov

The National Science Foundation (NSF) is an independent federal agency providing financial and other support for basic research, education and related activities in the various disciplines of science, mathematics and engineering. NSF awards grants and contracts to academic institutions, private research firms, industrial labs and major research facilities and centers. Informative films, video news releases and B-roll footage are available on a variety of topics.

Dena Headlee
*A/V Specialist*
National Science Foundation
Arlington, VA
*Contact Phone:* 703-292-7739
**Click to Contact from Web Site**

## AMEC EARTH & ENVIRONMENTAL SPECIALISTS
Philadelphia, PA USA
www.amec.com/earthandenvironmental

AMEC Earth and Environmental provides a broad range of environmental, geotechnical, infrastructure, water resources and materials services to public and private clients in the U.S. and worldwide. The company has won awards for excellence from state and national environmental regulators for its work. It offers expertise in the full range of earth and environmental issues, from mold and asbestos assessment to the cleanup of eveything from military firing ranges to nuclear and hazardous waste facilities.

Brad Christensen
*Media Relations Director*
AMEC Earth & Enviromental
Tempe, AZ USA
*Contact Phone:* 480-940-2320
*Contact Main Phone:* 480-940-2320
*Cell:* 602-432-1339
**Click to Contact from Web Site**

## JIM REED - SEVERE & UNUSUAL WEATHER
Columbia, SC USA
www.jimreedphoto.com

Jim Reed is co-author of Hurricane Katrina: Through the Eyes of Storm Chasers (Farcountry Press). He is a 15-year professional storm chaser and award-winning extreme-weather photographer who specializes in documenting the full force of nature at close range. Reed, whose clients include National Geographic, The New York Times, and NOAA, is an expert in discussing the subjects of America's changing climate, storm chasing, and severe weather preparedness.

Jim Reed
Jim Reed Photography - Severe & Unusual Weather
Columbia, SC USA
*Contact Phone:* 803-782-6226
*Cell:* 316-371-9621
**Click to Contact from Web Site**

## NOAA PUBLIC AFFAIRS
Washington, DC USA
http://www.publicaffairs.noaa.gov

NOAA Public Affairs is the media/public relations office for the National Oceanic & Atmospheric Administration. NOAA is a Federal science agency that includes: The National Weather Service, National Marine Fisheries Service, National Environmental, Satellite, Data and Information Service, National Ocean Service, and the Office of Oceanic & Atmospheric Research. With 12,500 employees and an annual budget of $3.5 billion, we seek to understand and improve the Nation's environmental and economic health and security, and provide real and tangible products and services.

Robert Hansen
NOAA
Washington, DC USA
*Contact Phone:* 202-482-4594
**Click to Contact from Web Site**

## NEW JERSEY PEST MANAGEMENT ASSOCIATION
Livingston, NJ USA
www.njpestcontrol.com/nj

The New Jersey Pest Management Association was founded in 1941 and is one of the oldest trade associations representing the industry. Members of NJPMA are also dual members of the National Pest Management Association.The insect and rodent pest problems, as well as others, that occur in New Jersey are common to other States. . Journalists are encouraged to contact Alan Caruba at (973) 763-6392, the Association's longtime public relations counselor for any assistance.

Leonard Douglen
Livingston, NJ USA
*Contact Phone:* 1-800-524-9942
**Click to Contact from Web Site**

## NATIONAL PEST MANAGEMENT ASSOCIATION
Washington, DC USA
http://www.pestworld.org

Representing the interests of the structural pest management industry. The NPMA's mission is to communicate the role of our industry as protectors of food, health, property, and the environment, and affect the success of our members through education and advocacy. The NPMA has guided its members and the industry through legislative and regulatory initiatives on the federal and state levels, the creation of verifiable training and changing technologies used by the industry.

Cindy Mannes
*Director of Public Affairs*
National Pest Management Association
Fairfax, VA USA
*Contact Phone:* 610-585-3203
*Contact Main Phone:* 703-352-6762
**Click to Contact from Web Site**

## UNITED POULTRY CONCERNS, INC.
Machipongo, VA USA
http://www.upc-online.org

United Poultry Concerns is the nation's leading authority on the treatment of chickens and other domestic fowl in food production, science, education, entertainment, and human companionship situations. Provides up-to-date information on the ways poultry are used. Addresses the treatment of ostriches and emus. Ready resources include a magazine, books, videos and fact-sheets.

Karen Davis, Ph.D.
*President*
United Poultry Concerns, Inc.
Machipongo, VA
*Contact Phone:* 757-678-7875
**Click to Contact from Web Site**

## THE HUMANE SOCIETY OF THE UNITED STATES
Washington, DC USA
http://www.hsus.org

The Humane Society of the United States is the nation's largest animal protection organization. Our professional staff of veterinarians, investigators, researchers, and policy experts are located in the Washignton, D.C., area, in regional offices across the country. They are available to comment on all animal issues: Pets and Equine Protection, Disaster Relief for Animals, Humane Solutions to Conflicts with Wildlife, Animals in Research, Farm Animals and Sustainable Agriculture, Animal Cruelty Investigations, Anticruelty Legislation, Domestic and International Wildlife Protection.

Rachel Querry
*Media Relations Deputy Director*
The Humane Society of the United States
Washington, DC
*Contact Phone:* 301-258-8255
*Contact Main Phone:* 202-452-1100
**Click to Contact from Web Site**

## ADVOATES FOR EMS LEADERSHIP
Kansas City, MO USA
advocatesforems.org

After the September 11th attacks, the country focused its attention on terrorism preparedness and first responders - described as police, fire and other. There was no voice for emergency medical services (EMS) in Washington policy discussions. To speak up for the EMS community, Advocates for EMS (AEMS) was founded as a not-for-profit organization on October 22, 2002 by the National Association of EMS Physicians and the National Association of State EMS Directors. In a short two-year time frame, AEMS has grown into an organization with over 50 corporate, organizational and individual members and has succeeded in establishing relationships with members of Congress and staff on Capitol Hill. In addition, AEMS has also worked to establish relationships within the various agencies that have jurisdiction over EMS issues, including the National Highway Transportation Safety Administration through Department of Transportation, Department of Health and Human Services and the Department of Homeland Security bringing to light many of the issues surrounding EMS.

Dede Gish-Panjada, MBA
Advoates for EMS Leadership
Lenexa, KS USA
*Contact Phone:* 913-492-5858
**Click to Contact from Web Site**

## EQUISSAGE, INC.
Round Hill, VA USA
http://www.equissage.com

Since 1990, Equissage has been the nation's leading trainer of equine and companion animal massage therapists. Graduates work for many of the top trainers and owners in the country. The Equissage Certificate Program boasts more than 7,000 graduates from all 50 states and 17 foreign countries. This program has been featured in major publications throughout this country and Europe.

Mary A. Schreiber
*President*
Equissage, Inc.
Round Hill, VA
*Contact Phone:* 540-338-1917
**Click to Contact from Web Site**

## DOUG BUTLER --HORSESHOEING EXPERT
LaPorte, CO USA
www.DougButler.com

DBE's newest release, The Principles of Horseshoeing (P3), is one of the sharpest tools in the hands of aspiring and experienced farriers and an important reference for horse owners. If you are a farrier, this 1000 page reference book can help you be at the top of your profession. If you are a horseowner, The Principles of Horseshoeing (P3) will help you learn about your horse and show you how to choose and work with the right farrier.

Doug Butler
Doug Butler Enterpriscs, Inc.
LaPorte, CO USA
*Contact Phone:* 800-728-3826
*Contact Main Phone:* 970-221-0516
**Click to Contact from Web Site**

## AMERICAN VETERINARY MEDICAL ASSOCIATION
Schaumburg, IL USA
http://www.avma.org

AVMA is the National Professional Association of Veterinarians, advancing the science and art of veterinary medicine and its relationship to animal health and welfare, public health, and agriculture.

Sharon Granskog
*Media Relations*
American Veterinary Medical Association
Schaumburg, IL
*Contact Phone:* 847-285-6619
**Click to Contact from Web Site**

## INTERNATIONAL ASSOCIATION OF CANINE PROFESSIONALS, MARTIN DEELEY
Orlando, FL USA
http://www.dogpro.org

The International Association of Canine Professionals is an organization established to maintain the highest standards of professional and business practice among canine professionals. The IACP commitment is to develop professional recognition, communication, education, understanding and co-operation. With over 750 members worldwide it has an extensive knowledge and related experience on all dog matters. Martin Deeley the President, has been working with dogs for over 30 years. Information can be obtained from www. martindeeley.com

Martin Deeley
*President*
International Association of Canine Professionals
Montverde, FL USA
*Contact Phone:* 407-469-2008
**Click to Contact from Web Site**

## CAPTAIN HAGGERTY & BABETTE HAGGERTY
Jupitter, FL USA
http://www.haggertydog.com

Captain Haggerty wrote the book on How to Get Your Pet Into Show Business. He has more experience and knowledge of dogs than anyone else worldwide. He is the man who trained the trainers. He has been featured on Letterman 26 times and has impressed audiences with his outstanding presence in print, television and radio for over 40 years. Babette Haggerty has been called Palm Beach's Favorite Dog Trainer and the Miss Porter's of Dogs.

Captain Haggerty CA
*Contact Phone:* 561-747-8181
**Click to Contact from Web Site**

## WCFO, INC THE WORLD CANINE FREESTYLE ORGANIZATION
Brooklyn, NY USA
www.worldcaninefreestyle.org

WCFO, INC. is a non-profit corporation, founded to globally promote the joys and fun of responsible pet ownership through musical canine freestyle, both as a sport and an entertainment medium.

Patie Ventre
WCFO, INC The World Canine Freestyle Organization
Brooklyn,, NY USA
*Contact Phone:* 718-332-8336
**Click to Contact from Web Site**

## BASH DIBRA — DOG TRAINER TO THE STARS
Riverdale, NY USA
http://www.pawsacrossamerica.com/index.html

Need information on pets, animal behavior, or dog training? Contact Bashkim (Bash) Dibra, best selling author, animal behaviorist, pet authority and dog trainer to the stars. Clients include Henry Kissinger, Kim Basinger, Matthew Broderick, Sarah Jessica Parker, Kathleen Turner, Mariah Carey and Jennifer Lopez. Bash's two bestselling books are Dog Training by Bash, and Teach Your Dog to Behave. He also has a new book, DogSpeak He has appeared on Today, The Tonight Show, CBS This Morning, CNN and Good Morning America.

Bash Dibra
Dog Trainer to the Stars
Riverdale, NY
*Contact Phone:* 718-796-4541
**Click to Contact from Web Site**

## DIANA L. GUERRERO'S ARK ANIMALS
Big Bear Lake, CA USA
http://www.dianalguerrero.com

Diana L. Guerrero shares thirty years of cutting-edge techniques and innovative services. This pet pioneer is an animal expert, professional speaker and author. Offers: 'What Animals Can Teach Us about Spirituality,' 'Blessing of the Animals,' FREE monthly electronic newsletter, animal career teleseminars, animal disaster preparedness education, animal behavior modification and training for wild animals and domestic pets. This Latina travels from California and publishes many websites including www.arkanimals.com. Credentials at www.dianalguerrero.com or call (800) 818-7387

Diana L. Guerrero
*Animal (Pet) Expert*
Ark Animals
Big Bear Lake, CA
*Contact Phone:* Upon Inquiry
*Contact Main Phone:* 800.818.7387
*Cell:* Upon Inquiry
**Click to Contact from Web Site**

## PET FOOD INSTITUTE
Washington, DC USA
http://www.petfoodinstitute.org

The Pet Food Institute is the voice of the U.S. pet food manufacturers and is dedicated to supporting initiatives to advance industry quality of dog and cat food, educating the public on pet feeding and care, representing the pet food industry to government officials and promoting overall pet care and well-being.

Stephen E. Payne
Pet Food Institute
Washington, DC
*Contact Phone:* 202-367-1120
**Click to Contact from Web Site**

## WORLD WIDE PET INDUSTRY ASSOCIATION, INC.
Los Angeles, CA USA
http://www.wwpia.org

World Wide Pet Industry Association, Inc. of Arcadia, California, is a nonprofit membership association for manufacturers, distributors, retailers and consumers In addition, WWPIA produces SuperZoo trade shows annually held in Las Vegas, and America's Family Pet Expo, the world's largest consumer pet expo, held annually in California and Michigan. The 55-year-old WWPIA, whose mission is to promote responsible pet care worldwide, also sponsors numerous education programs for the industry and the consumer.

Doug Poindexter
*Executive Vice President*
World Wide Pet Industry Association Inc.
Arcadia, CA USA
*Contact Phone:* 800-999-7295
**Click to Contact from Web Site**

## CHARLOTTE REED — INTERNATIONAL PET & MEDIA EXPERT
New York, NY USA
www.charlottereed.com

Charlotte Reed is an international pet expert. Renowned for her pet know-how, energy and wit, she is a popular television and radio guest, writer, spokesperson and lecturer. She is also the owner of four dogs, three cats, one parrot and a cage full of finches. As a pet care specialist, Charlotte's advice on responsible pet ownership and her recommendations on how to ensure living with a happy and healthy pet always includes the newest pet products. As a columnist for many of the nation's most widely read pet publications, she is also always able to discuss current pet trends, the business of pets and the unleashing of the pet industry. She writes the Luxury Unleashed column for Dog Fancy, the dog column for Pet Business and Miss Fido Manners for Fido Friendly.

Charlotte Reed
Two Dogs & A Goat, Inc.
New York, NY USA
*Contact Phone:* 888-286-6475
**Click to Contact from Web Site**

"From coast to coast, from celebrities to casting
directors, from in front of the camera to behind
the scenes, the 'movers-and-shakers' in the industry
know to contact BASH DIBRA, author, pet expert
and celebrity trainer-to-the-stars, who is fast
becoming the 'PET LAUREATE' of our times!"

**BashDibra**

 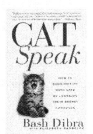    

# Bash Dibra
# 718-796-4541

## www.PawsAcrossAmerica.com or www.StarPet.com

BASH DIBRA, internationaly renowned animal
behaviorist, author of 5 best selling books, video
and soon to be published "STARPET" How to make
your pet a star (Simon&Schuster).

Contact:  Bash Dibra
Dog Trainer to the Stars
Riverdale, NY
Phone: 718-796-4541
E-Mail: Bash@StarPet.com

## AMERICAN FLORAL INDUSTRY ASSOCIATION
Dallas, TX USA
www.afia.net

The American Floral Industry Association (AFIA) is the nation's only organization representing the permanent botanical, gift and decorative accessories industry. Its members are manufacturers, importers, and wholesalers of permanent florals, trees, plants, containers, and other floral-related products. Members are also continually developing new products in coordinated home decor, including candles, candleholders, picture frames, tabletop lamps, bookshelves and chests, decorative boxes, accent tables and chairs, wall art, kitchen accessories, pre-made floral arrangements and much more.

Marsha Bills
*Marketing Director*
American Floral Industry Association
Dallas, TX USA
*Contact Phone:* 214-742-2747
**Click to Contact from Web Site**

## AMERICAN FEED INDUSTRY ASSOCIATION
Arlington, VA USA
www.afia.org

AFIA is the only national organization devoted exclusively to providing strong, highly qualified leadership representing the business, legislative and regulatory interests of the animal feed and pet food industries and their suppliers. AFIA and its Industry Committees work consistently with Congress and various federal and state agencies to ensure the feed industry's voice is heard on important policy matters.

Rex A. Runyon
*V.P. Public Relations*
American Feed Industry Association
Arlington, VA USA
*Contact Phone:* 703-524-0810
**Click to Contact from Web Site**

## PRODUCE MARKETING ASSOCIATION
Newark, DE USA
http://www.pma.com

The Produce Marketing Association, founded in 1949, is a not-for-profit global trade association serving more than 2,100 members who market fresh fruits, vegetables, and related products worldwide. Its members are involved in the production, distribution, retail, and foodservice sectors of the industry.

Lee Mannering
Produce Marketing Association
Newark, DE
*Contact Phone:* 302-738-7100
**Click to Contact from Web Site**

## TOM NASSIF, PRESIDENT & CEO — WESTERN GROWERS
Orange County, CA USA
http://www.wga.com

Thomas A. Nassif, a Southern California native, was named President and CEO of Western Growers in 2002. Originally an attorney, one of the many highlights of his career was serving as a member of the Reagan administration, first in 1981 as Deputy Chief of Protocol (A) for the White House, later as Deputy Assistant Secretary of State for Near East and South Asian affairs in 1983, and finally in 1985 when he was named United States Ambassador to the Kingdom of Morocco by President Reagan.

Jason Burns
*Sr. Communications Director*
Western Growers
Irvine, CA USA
*Contact Phone:* 949-885-2257
**Click to Contact from Web Site**

## INTERNATIONAL FRESH-CUT PRODUCE ASSOCIATION
Alexandria, VA USA
http://www.fresh-cuts.org

IFPA is the ultimate resource for the fresh-cut produce industry. Our services include educational programs, procedural manuals, information on technological innovations and raw product sourcing, regulatory updates, trend tracking, an annual conference and trade show and a network of industry leaders. IFPA's members are fresh-cut producers and their service providers and customers.

Sean Handerhan
*Marketing Services*
International Fresh-Cut Produce Association
Alexandria, VA
*Contact Phone:* 703-299-6282
**Click to Contact from Web Site**

## CALORIELAB, INC.
Las Vegas, NV USA
http://calorielab.com

CalorieLab, Inc., operates an independent diet and weight loss web site at calorielab.com. Our news blog at http://calorielab.com/news covers the world of weight loss, including weight loss; diet books; business aspects of the weight loss dieting industry; weight loss in the popular media; Nutrition Facts disclosure by food manufacturers and restaurants; public policy obesity and food issues; environmental and sociological contributors to obesity; school lunch programs; and the wacky side of obesity.

Mark Schrimsher
*President*
Las Vegas, NV USA
*Contact Phone:* 1 (702) 866-9006
**Click to Contact from Web Site**

## FOOD ALLERGY INITIATIVE
New York, NY USA
http://www.FoodAllergyInitiative.org

The Food Allergy Initiative (FAI) is a 501 (c) (3) non-profit organization dedicated to supporting research towards the effective treatment and cure for food allergies and anaphylaxis. Today, it is estimated that 11,000,000 Americans are affected by food allergies, at least 30,000 experience episodes of food-induced anaphylaxis, and hundreds die each year in the United States.

Rachel Sanzari
*Administrative Director*
Food Allergy Initiative
New York, NY
*Contact Phone:* 212-572-8428
**Click to Contact from Web Site**

## INSTITUTE OF FOOD TECHNOLOGISTS
Chicago, IL USA
www.ift.org

Founded in 1939, the Institute of Food Technologists is a non-profit scientific society with 22,000 members working in food science, technology and related professions in industry, academia and government. Its Food Science Communicators are university-based experts, able to deliver credible insight and commentary to media worldwide, bringing sound science to the discussion of food issues. IFT conducts the world's largest annual convention on food grown, processed, manufactured, distributed and eaten worldwide.

James N. Klapthor
*Media Relations Manager*
Institute of Food Technologists
Chicago, IL
*Contact Phone:* 312-782-8424
**Click to Contact from Web Site**

## ANIMAL AGRICULTURE ALLIANCE
Arlington, VA USA
http://www.animalagalliance.org

The Animal Agriculture Alliance's mission is to communicate the important role of animal agriculture to our nation and improve understanding that animal well-being is central to producing safe, high-quality, affordable food and other products essential to our daily lives. The Alliance, a 501(c)(3) tax-exempt organization, is a broad-based coalition of farmers, ranchers, their suppliers, their customers and retailers.

Kay Johnson
*Executive Vice President*
Animal Agriculture Alliance
Arlington, VA USA
*Contact Phone:* 703-562-5160
*Contact Main Phone:* 703-562-5160
**Click to Contact from Web Site**

## NATIONAL CHICKEN COUNCIL
Washington, DC USA
http://www.nationalchickencouncil.com

NCC represents companies that produce and process more than 90 percent of the nation's chicken. Contact us for information about industry's commitment to food safety, worker safety, and environmental protection; and data on consumption, production, expenditures and other facts of America's favorite food at the center of the plate.

Richard L. Lobb
*Director of Communications*
National Chicken Council
Washington, DC
*Contact Phone:* 202-296-2622
**Click to Contact from Web Site**

## SUGAR ASSOCIATION, INC.
Washington, DC USA
http://www.sugar.org

The Sugar Association is a nonprofit organization established in 1943. We seek to create and maintain an understanding that the benefits of sugar contribute to the flavor, quality and functionality of wholesome foods. Sugar is a natural form of human energy and has only 15 calories in a teaspoon. The Association also seeks to increase appreciation of the non-food value of sugar. In pursuit of educating consumers, policy makers and the media, the Sugar Association is committed to integrity and sound scientific principles.

Richard Keelor, PhD
*President & CEO*
Sugar Association, Inc.
Washington, DC
*Contact Phone:* 202-785-1122
**Click to Contact from Web Site**

## SALT INSTITUTE
Washington, DC USA
http://www.saltinstitute.org

The Salt Institute, a non-profit association of North American salt producers, is the world's foremost source of authoritative information about salt. Primary among its estimated 14,000 uses are chemical production, highway deicing, human and animal nutrition and water conditioning. Salt Institute experts are authoritative on issues of roadway traffic safety (especially winter driving), nutrition and dietary guidelines (including all medical research on sodium and health and iodine nutrition) and production and environmental issues concerning salt.

Richard L. Hanneman
*President*
Salt Institute
Alexandria, VA
*Contact Phone:* 703-549-4648
*Cell:* 571-331-7563
**Click to Contact from Web Site**

## DREYER'S GRAND ICE CREAM
Oakland, CA USA
http://www.dreyers.com

If you think that getting paid to eat ice cream every day is too good to be true, you haven't met John Harrison and his talented taste buds! As the Official Taster for Dreyer's/Edy's Grand Ice Cream, John has dipped his golden spoon into more than 200 million gallons of America's favorite frozen treat during his sweet career. In fact, John's taste buds are such a cool asset that they are insured for One Million Dollars and provide the final word on what new flavors ice cream lovers scoop up in the freezer aisle each year. John's job isn't always Peaches 'N Cream...some days it's Rocky Road or Butter Pecan. But John's mission remains the same...to make sure Dreyer's/Edy's ice cream meets the highest quality standard before it tops waffle cones, builds sweet foundations in sundae dishes or plays center stage in banana splits.

Kim Goeller-Johnson
*Media Relations Manager*
Dreyer's Grand Ice Cream
Oakland, CA
*Contact Phone:* 510-601-4211
**Click to Contact from Web Site**

## ANHEUSER-BUSCH COMPANIES, INC.
St. Louis, MO USA
www.beeresponsible.com

Anheuser-Busch Companies, Inc. is a St. Louis-based diversified corporation with subsidiaries that include the world's largest brewing organization, the country's second-largest manufacturer of aluminum beverage cans and one of the largest theme park operations in the world. It has been an industry leader in the use of environmentally sound packaging and in the reclamation and reuse of brewing and manufacturing by-products. The company also has provided major support for a wide range of environmental efforts.

Teresia H. Vogt
*VP, Public Communications*
Anheuser-Busch Companies, Inc.
St. Louis, MO
*Contact Phone:* 314-577-7750
*Contact Main Phone:* 314-577-2000
**Click to Contact from Web Site**

## MARIA LIBERATI
New York, NY USA
http://www.marialiberati.com

A lifestyle journey through the past and to the future of Italian living. Enjoy Maria's family recipes, cooking tips and decorating ideas today.

Joan Campbell
art of living, PrimaMedia, Inc.
Harleysville, PA USA
*Contact Phone:* 215-721-6661
**Click to Contact from Web Site**

**DONALD SILVERS, CKD--AUTHOR, KITCHEN DESIGN WITH COOKING IN MIND,**
Los Angeles, CA USA
http://www.donsilvers.com

Don Silvers is a Certified Kitchen Designer for both residential and commercial kitchens, a professional chef, author, lecturer and university instructor. CNN calls him: the only Certified Kitchen Designer and chef in (residential) industry today. His book Kitchen Design with Cooking in Mind tells how to design a kitchen that is functional and useful for preparing everything from a single cup of tea to dinner for twenty (St. Petersburg Times). His new book co-authored with Moorea Hoffman Kitchen Appliances 101 (What Works, What Doesn't and Why), gives the consumer the information needed on major kitchen appliances to make informed buying decisions.

Donald Silvers and Moorea Hoffman
*Co-authors of Kitchen Appliances 101: What works, What doesn't and Why*
Kitchen Design With Cooking in Mind
Los Angeles, CA
*Contact Phone:* 800-900-4761
**Click to Contact from Web Site**

## OLSON COMMUNICATIONS, INC.
Chicago, IL USA

Olson Communications is a full service marketing communications company specializing in the foodservice industry, the business that feeds America away from home. Olson Communications concentrates on foodservice markets, trends, issues, and communication strategy. They are experts on chain and independent restaurants, supermarket delis, meal solutions, and international foodservice.

Sharon M. Olson
*President*
Olson Communications, Inc.
Chicago, IL
*Contact Phone:* 312-280-4573
**Click to Contact from Web Site**

## DR. REESE HALTER — TREE SCIENTIST
Los Angeles, CA USA
www.drreese.com

Dr. Reese Halter researches, protects, and conserves forests and wildlife worldwide. As an award-winning conservation biologist, he is founder and president of Global Forest Science. he organization opens facilities, drafts legislation, and takes other actions to protect threatened habitats and animals. Dr. Halter also spends time with his family, encourages educational conservation children's programs, and has written a best-selling children's book titled Forest Adventures with Bruni the Bear.

Mike Nason
Nason Group
Laguna Niguel, CA USA
*Contact Phone:* 949-661-6031
*Cell:* 949-500-1180
**Click to Contact from Web Site**

# SALT: Answer Your Questions

- Where is salt produced and how? How much salt is produced in the U.S.? In the world?
- You say there are 14,000 known uses of salt; what are the major ones?
- The U.S. has suffered a rash of mine injuries and fatalities. What is the salt industry's worker safety record?
- Is salt intake related to blood pressure and to people having heart attacks and strokes?

- How many billions of IQ points are lost in the world each year through failure to iodize salt – a top UNICEF and WHO public health priority?
- Are we eating more salt than we used to? Putting more on roads?
- Is it safe to store oil, gas and radioactive wastes in salt deposits?
- What's the difference between table salt and kosher salt? Sea salt?

*Richard L. Hanneman,*
*President*
*Cell: 571/331-7563*
*dick@saltinstitute.org*
***www.saltinstitute.org***

- Dick speaks frequently, does TV/ radio appearances; his articles have appeared in such diverse journals as *Water Conditioning & Purification*, the *British Medical Journal* and *Public Works* magazine. Expert on performance of winter highways, salt supplies during winter storms, environmental issues and all aspects of salt and health.

Richard L. Hanneman, left, and Morton Satin

*Morton Satin, Technical*
*Director*
*Cell: 240/481-7337*
*morton@saltinstitute.org*

- Morton joined the Salt Institute in 2006 after 16 years as director of the U.N. Food and Agriculture Organization (FAO) in Rome. He is a biochemist with CEO-level experience in the food industry who is fast becoming an expert in mine safety and salt production technology. Frequent presenter and prolific author, including three books.

*Salt Institute: 700 N. Fairfax Street, Suite 600, Alexandria, VA 22314-2040 Phone: 703/549-4648 FAX: 703/548-2194*

*The Salt Institute is the world's foremost source of authoritative information about salt (sodium chloride) and its more than 14,000 known uses. The Institute is a non-profit association of salt producers (manufacturers), founded in 1914.*

To have salt-related information delivered via RSS, subscribe to our feeds at http://www.saltinstitute.org/rss/use_own_newsreader.html.

## LEONARD LEWIN, FURNITURE CONSULTANT
Sacramento, CA USA
www.NewFurnitureIdeas.com

Leonard Lewin is a 40-year veteran of the furniture industry who is dedicated toward educating consumers about furniture shopping. His goal is to provide the retail customer with the tools and information they need to become confident, savvy furniture shoppers. His book, Shopping For Furniture: A Consumer's Guide, and website, www.newfurnitureideas.com, are packed with useful industry-insider information, covering topics such as furniture quality, understanding retail pricing, furniture care, and working with designers.

Kent Sorsky
*Marketing Director*
Linden Publishing
Fresno, CA USA
*Contact Phone:* 559-233-6633
**Click to Contact from Web Site**

## RANDALL BELL, REAL ESTATE DAMAGES
Laguna Beach, CA USA
www.RealEstateDamages.com

Randall Bell is an applied economist who has consulted on the world's worst disasters and their impacts on real estate values. His cases include the World Trade Center, the Flight 93 crash site, Jon Benet Ramsey and OJ Simpson crime scenes, Heaven's Gate Mansion, Bikini Atoll nuclear test sites, along with landslides, floods, fires and oil spills. Randy's career has been profiled by the Wall Street Journal to People Magazine and all the major networks.

Randall Bell
Real Estate Damages
Laguna Beach, CA USA
*Contact Phone:* 949-497-7600
**Click to Contact from Web Site**

## TIMBERLAND DESIGN
St. Louis, MO USA
http://www.timberlanddesign.com

Our Bob Timberlake Log Home Collection offers the most authentic home available. Hand-hewn naturally tapered logs are selected for each home. The craftsmanship and natural logs make each Timberlake home unique.

Tammy Donelson
Timberland Design
Ballwin, MO USA
*Contact Phone:* 636-391-8833
**Click to Contact from Web Site**

## TOLL BROTHERS, INC
Philadelphia, PA USA
http://www.tollbrothers.com
NYSE TOL

Toll Brothers, Inc. is the nation's leading builder of luxury homes. No other builder is as committed to quality as Toll Brothers. The Company is the only public home builder to receive the three most coveted awards in the home building industry: America's Best Builder, National Builder of the Year, and the National Housing Quality Award. Toll Brothers is proud to have been recognized for its dedication to quality and customer service.

Kira McCarron
Toll Brothers, Inc
Horsham, PA USA
*Contact Phone:* 215-938-8220
**Click to Contact from Web Site**

## MASSACHUSETTS ASSOCIATION OF REALTORS
Waltham, MA USA
http://www.marealtor.com

As the largest real estate trade organization in Massachusetts, the MAR compiles housing market data and conducts programs which promote the business activities, professional growth and public image of its 21,000 members. As an industry watchdog, MAR also works to protect private property rights and consumer interests in all real estate transactions through legislative and regulatory initiatives.

John J. Dulczewski
*Communications Director*
Massachusetts Association of Realtors
Waltham, MA
*Contact Phone:* 781-839-5507
*Contact Main Phone:* 781-890-3700
**Click to Contact from Web Site**

## R. A. MARTINEZ, HOMEOWNERS INSURANCE EXPERT
San Diego, CA USA
www.missionclaims.net

R. A. Martinez is a licensed, expert adjuster in the field of homeowners insurance. Whether you have questions about mold, wild fires, the homeowners insurance crisis, or any other aspect of this important subject matter, he will provide qualified answers and explanations to your most compelling inquiries. Appeared live on San Diego's Local-8 News. Listed as an expert contributor with several news media outlets. Author of 'Mold, Fire, Flood, & Other Topics: Homeowners Insurance Explained' (available in libraries and our website). President of Mission Claims & Mission Inspections, offering claims and underwriting services to insurance companies and the general public.

Rafael Martinez
*President*
Mission Claims
San Diego, CA USA
*Contact Phone:* 619-282-0988 x11
*Contact Main Phone:* 619-282-0988
*Cell:* 619-865-0767
**Click to Contact from Web Site**

## PROJECT MANAGEMENT INSTITUTE (PMI)
Philadelphia, PA USA
http://www.pmi.org

With more than 225,000 members in over 150 countries, Project Management Institute (PMI) is the global advocacy organization for the project management profession. PMI is actively engaged in setting professional standards, conducting research and providing access to a wealth of information and resources. PMI also promotes career and professional development and offers certification, networking and community involvement opportunities. For more than 35 years, PMI has advanced the careers of practitioners who have made project management indispensable in achieving business results. For more information, please visit www.pmi.org.

James D. McGeehan
Project Management Institute
Newtown Square, PA USA
*Contact Phone:* 610-356-4600
*Contact Main Phone:* 610-356-4600
**Click to Contact from Web Site**

## WTCA - REPRESENTING THE STRUCTURAL BUILDING COMPONENTS INDUSTRY
Madison, WI USA
www.sbcindustry.com

Established in 1983, WTCA - Representing the Structural Building Components Industry is an international not-for-profit trade association of structural building component manufacturers. Its growing membership also includes truss plate and original equipment manufacturers, computer engineering and other service companies, lumber mills, inspection bureaus, lumber brokers and distributors, and professional individuals in the fields of engineering, marketing and management.

Melinda Caldwell
WTCA - Representing the Structural Building Components Industry
Madison, WI USA
*Contact Phone:* 608-310-6729
**Click to Contact from Web Site**

## DON ZEMAN, AMERICA'S HOME IMPROVEMENT EXPERT
Columbia, MO USA
www.homefront.com

A Leading Source for Home Improvement News and Advice One of the most dynamic and fastest-growing sources for home improvement and home maintenance advice in the country, Homefront is the brainchild of builder and contractor Don Zeman. Based in Columbia, Mo., Homefront was founded in 1995 by Don and now includes a radio show and website. A native of St. Louis, Mo. who cut his teeth in the construction industry by working on the renovation of the historic homes in south St. Louis, Don has logged more than 25 years of experience building and renovating homes in the Midwest and Southeast.

Nancy Zeman
Homefront with Don Zeman
Columbia, MO USA
*Contact Phone:* 573-256-5108
**Click to Contact from Web Site**

## AMERICAN LIGHTING ASSOCIATION
Dallas, TX USA
http://www.americanlightingassoc.com

The American Lighting Association is a trade association representing the lighting industry. Its membership includes lighting and fan manufacturers, retail showrooms, sales representatives and lighting designers dedicated to providing the public with the proper application of quality residential lighting.

Larry Lauck
*VP, Communications*
American Lighting Association
Dallas, TX USA
*Contact Phone:* 800-605-4448
**Click to Contact from Web Site**

## KWASNY FLOORING
Detroit, MI USA
http://www.kwasnyco.com

Kwasny Flooring and Lining Systems is a manufacturer and installer of SaniCrete, providing a single source flooring system. SaniCrete is a heavy-duty polyurethane floor system designed to provide excellent resistance to abrasion, chemical attack and thermal shock. SaniCrete can be installed over wet concrete and installed quickly for returning the area to service in less than 24 hours. SaniCrete will help assure that your facility floors are sanitary and meet all USDA guidelines.

Keith Kwasny
*President*
Kwasny Flooring & Lining Systems
Farmington Hills, MI USA
*Contact Phone:* 248-893-1000
**Click to Contact from Web Site**

## TOM KRAEUTLER — HOME IMPROVEMENT EXPERT
Oakhurst, NJ USA
www.888moneypit.com

Veteran home inspector and host of the nationally syndicated home improvement radio show "The Money Pit," Tom Kraeutler understands the threats to a home's health, including costly termite damage, mysterious leaks, cracked foundations and more. His unique blend of home improvement expertise and media savvy allows him to take homeowners through complicated issues step-by-step, explaining what the problem is, how to spot it, why it's occurring, and what they need to do to fix it.

Ian Heller
Media Management Group
New York, NY USA
*Contact Phone:* 212-545-8383
**Click to Contact from Web Site**

## DR. WILLIAM S. TURNER III, PROJECT MANAGEMENT CONSULTANT
Vienna, VA USA
www.wstech.com

In a world where programs and projects are the normal way of doing business, Dr. Turner has more than 25 years international experience as program/project manager and consultant. He works with organizations to achieve their business goals by effective use of IT. He achieves cooperation by being a catalyst in mobilizing teams of client personnel. These teams identify barriers to success and find creative solutions. Results are measurable and there is a transfer of knowledge.

Dr. William Turner III
*President*
Worldwide Service Technology Ltd.
Vienna, VA USA
*Contact Phone:* 703-938-2465
*Cell:* 703-626-4270
**Click to Contact from Web Site**

## DEBRA GOULD - THE STAGING DIVA
TM

Toronto, Ontario Canada
www.stagingdiva.com

Internationally recognized home staging expert Debra Gould is President of Six Elements and creator of The Staging Diva™ Home Staging Business Training Program. Debra staged hundreds of homes priced from $190,000 to $1.5 million, and trains others in the US, Canada, Australia and South Africa. She is the only home staging trainer with an MBA in marketing, 20 years experience as an entrepreneur, and a track record of growing her own successful home staging business.

Debra Gould
*President*
Six Elements, Inc.
Toronto, Ontario Canada
*Contact Phone:* 416-691-6615
**Click to Contact from Web Site**

## FIABCI-USA — FIABCI, THE INTERNATIONAL REAL ESTATE FEDERATION
Washington, DC USA
http://www.fiabci-usa.com/frgetcountrypage.php

Through our individual and association members in 57 countries, FIABCI membership gives you access to 1.5 million potential contacts. FIABCI-USA (the US Chapter) is the only international real estate organization representing the entire spectrum of the real estate industry in the US. Our mission is to open the international community to our members on a local, national, and international level, so that they may develop a broad base of real estate contacts that will translate into increased business opportunities and ultimately financial success. People connecting people to create one global marketplace. The most valuable resource of FIABCI is our members.

Susan Newman, Secretary General
FIABCI-USA
Arlington, VA USA
*Contact Phone:* 703/524-4279
**Click to Contact from Web Site**

## NATIONAL ASSOCIATION OF INDUSTRIAL & OFFICE PROPERTIES — UTAH CHAPTER
Salt Lake City, UT USA
http://www.naiop.org/UTAH/index.cfm

Our mission is to provide developers,owners, investors and affiliated professionals involved in industrial, office and related commercial real estate with effective support and guidance to create, protect and enhance property values. We facilitate communication, networking, and business opportunites; provide a forum for continuing education; and promote effective grassroots public policy related real estate development, investment and property rights.

Melissa Clyne
Salt Lake City, UT USA
*Contact Phone:* 801.486.6763
**Click to Contact from Web Site**

**CHIKA OBODOZIE**
Lanham, MD USA

Chika Obodozie, is a Realtor with Century21 Advantage Realty, licensed in Maryland, Washington, DC and Virginia. He is also a concert promoter.

Chika Obodozie
Lanham, MD USA
*Contact Phone:* 301-484-8030
**Click to Contact from Web Site**

# Indispensable for business results

Project Management Institute is the global standard-setting organization
and worldwide advocate for the project management profession.
By providing organizations with the necessary knowledge, tools and
resources to connect corporate strategy with results, PMI positions you
to achieve the desired bottom line and execute meaningful change.

## www.pmi.org/yearbook.htm

**Project Management Institute**

Making project management indispensable for business results.®

| **Regional Service Centre** | **Global Operations Center** | **Regional Service Centre** |
|---|---|---|
| Asia Pacific | Newtown Square, Pennsylvania | Europe – Middle East – Africa (EMEA) |
| Singapore | USA | Brussels, Belgium |
| Tel:+ 65 6330 6733 | Tel: +1-610-356-4600 | Tel: +32-2-743-15 73 |

## JERRY BOUTCHER - RESIDENTAL REAL ESTATE INVESTMENT
Washington, DC USA
www.askjerryboutcher.com

Washington's Only Real Estate Call-In Show! Hosted by Washington's most recognized real estate authority. Join Jerry Boutcher each week as he examines the local market, interviews top producing local agents, builders and lenders and takes your calls live in the studio. Jerry also answers callers' questions about financing options, interest rates, choosing a Realtor, writing a winning sales contract, understanding title insurance, buying a new versus a resale home and the hundreds of other issues that face every home buyer, seller and owner. For More Information: www.askjerryboutcher.com Real Advice, Real Insight and Real Answers to Your Real Estate Questions™

Frank Felker
*Director, Business Development*
Monarch Title, Inc.
McLean, VA USA
*Contact Phone:* 703-852-3145
*Contact Main Phone:* 703-852-1730
*Cell:* 703-401-3170
**Click to Contact from Web Site**

## EUGENIA FOXWORTH, PRESIDENT OF THE GREATER NEW YORK COUNCIL OF FIABCI-USA
New York, NY USA
www.EugeniaFoxworth.com

Eugenia Foxworth is a unique Realtor "without borders", specializing in exceptional Properties in New York City, Riverdale, NY and internationally. She has acquired a reputation with both buyers and sellers as someone who can make a deal happen through her tenacity, knowledge of the market, professionalism and personality. She is licensed with REBNY and is a member of the Manhattan Association of Realtors, NAR and FIABCI. She has been chosen as a member of Elite 2003, 2004, 2005 and 2006 by Unique Homes Magazine and is a Coldwell Banker Certified Previews Property Specialist and a Certified International Property Specialist. Eugenia resides in New York and has lived and traveled extensively throughout the world.

Eugenia Foxworth
New York, NY USA
*Contact Phone:* 212-327-1200 ex 263
**Click to Contact from Web Site**

## COUNCIL OF RESIDENTIAL SPECIALISTS
Chicago, IL USA
http://www.crs.com

The Council of Residential Specialists is the largest not-for-profit affiliate of the National Association of Realtors. Founded in 1976, the Council provides superior member benefits that enable residential specialists to maximize their professional performance. The Council offers the CRS Designation to REALTORS who have completed advanced educational and professional requirements.

Sara Patterson
*Director of Communications*
Council of Residential Specialists
Chicago, IL
*Contact Phone:* 312-321-4445
*Contact Main Phone:* 312-321-4400
**Click to Contact from Web Site**

# Don Zeman:
## America's Home Improvement Expert

One of the most dynamic and fastest-growing sources for home improvement and home maintenance advice in the country, Homefront, now marking its 11th year, is the brainchild of builder and contractor Don Zeman.

Based in Columbia, Mo., Homefront was founded in 1995 by Don and now includes a radio show, 90-second daily radio hints, 90-second television news and Web site.

A native of St. Louis, who cut his teeth in the construction industry by working on the renovation of the historic homes in south St. Louis, Don has logged more than 25 years of experience building and renovating homes in the Midwest and Southeast.

"Our focus has always been educating homeowners and consumers," Zeman said. "The more information homeowners have, the better decisions they can make about their homes and projects. That's what we do here at Homefront."

Since the explosion of the radio show across the country and the addition of 90-second daily hints, Homefront has added a unique television franchise: 90-second news stories designed to run in local news programs. These news segments are being shown in morning, noon and early evening news shows as well as local programs.

"It's just another way for us to educate homeowners," Zeman said.

Don Zeman, 601 W. Nifong, Suite 5C, Columbia, Missouri 65203
Phone: 573-256-5108     Fax: 573-256-5127
www.homefront.com        don@homefront.com

## MICHAEL DWIGHT -- REAL ESTATE SPEAKER
Los Angeles, CA USA
www.stearnsdwightassts.com

Specializes in Operations and Marketing Management: Creative Development, Start-up Organizations, Expansion Planning and Implementation, Restructure/Reorganization. Mr. Dwight's broad Management background has been developed through a results-oriented track record demonstrated by successful and profitable accomplishments. Key strengths and problem-solving skills have been honed through hands-on operations in diverse and competitive environments enabling Dwight to speak on the following business topics: Sales and Marketing Management and Operations, Strategic Planning, Business Development.

Pat Dwight
SDA & Associates
Laguna Beach, CA USA
*Contact Phone:* 949-494-0424
**Click to Contact from Web Site**

## HABITAT FOR HUMANITY INTERNATIONAL
Americus, GA USA
http://www.habitat.org

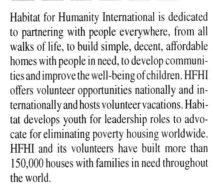

Habitat for Humanity International is dedicated to partnering with people everywhere, from all walks of life, to build simple, decent, affordable homes with people in need, to develop communities and improve the well-being of children. HFHI offers volunteer opportunities nationally and internationally and hosts volunteer vacations. Habitat develops youth for leadership roles to advocate for eliminating poverty housing worldwide. HFHI and its volunteers have built more than 150,000 houses with families in need throughout the world.

*Director of Public Relations*
Habitat for Humanity International
Americus, GA United States
*Contact Phone:* 1-800-422-4828
**Click to Contact from Web Site**

## NATIONAL MULTI HOUSING COUNCIL
Washington, DC USA
http://www.nmhc.org

The National Multi Housing Council (NMHC) is acknowledged as the preeminent source of apartment-related information. Apartment trends, market conditions, resident demographics, owning versus renting, rent control, apartments and the smart growth movement, industry structure, legislative and regulatory issues, and the impact of policy on market supply and demand are just a few topics NMHC addresses.

Michael Tucker
*Communications Manager*
National Multi Housing Council
Washington, DC
*Contact Phone:* 202-974-2300
**Click to Contact from Web Site**

## SYLVIA L. LOVELY — EXPERT ON CITIES
Lexington, KY USA
http://www.newcities.org

Sylvia Lovely was born in the Appalachian hills of Kentucky and grew up poor but she has risen to become a nationally recognized expert on cities and the power of people to create positive change. Ms. Lovely speaks across the country about cities, downtown revitalization, business environment, public policy, community leadership, voting, and what she calls Building New Cities for the 21st Century. Ms. Lovely's first book is New Cities in America: The Little Blue Book of Big Ideas. Ms. Lovely is President of the NewCities Institute, Adjunct Faculty Member UK Martin School of Public Policy and Administration and Executive Director of the Kentucky League of Cities. She is a regular contributor to newspapers and publications and a featured commentator on various TV and radio programs. She recently appeared on the Lou Dobbs Tonight show on CNN and is publisher of City magazine. Sylvia Lovely was named one of one of Kentucky's Top Women of Influence and Appalachian Woman of the Year.

Bobbie S. Bryant
Kentucky League of Cities
Lexington, KY USA
*Contact Phone:* 888-352-0922
**Click to Contact from Web Site**

## MICHAEL A. COVINO
Westchester, NY USA
http://www.luxmac.com

Michael A. Covino is president of the national mortgage banking firm, LUXMAC Covino & Company, dba: LUXMAC Home Mortgage. Michael has specialized in the financing of luxury homes and estate properties for 23 years. This extensive experience has earned him the title of Leading Expert in the field of super jumbo loans. His success is a combination of hard work and an experienced, personable and capable staff. The LUXMAC Home Mortgage Team will see each high-end loan transaction through to a successful closing.

Michael A. Covino
*President*
LUXMAC, Covino and Company
Tarrytown, NY United States
*Contact Phone:* 914-703-6400
*Contact Main Phone:* 914-703-6400
**Click to Contact from Web Site**

# Sylvia L. Lovely
## *New Cities & Citizens Expert*

Sylvia Lovely was born in the Appalachian hills of Kentucky and grew up poor, but she has risen to become a nationally recognized expert on cities and the power of people to create positive change.

Ms. Lovely speaks across the country about cities, downtown revitalization, business environment, public policy, community leadership, voting, and what she calls "Building New Cities for the 21st Century." Ms. Lovely's first book is "New Cities in America: The Little Blue Book of Big Ideas."

Ms. Lovely is president of the NewCities Institute, adjunct faculty member, University of Kentucky, Martin School of Public Policy and Administration, and executive director of the Kentucky League of Cities.

She is a regular contributor to newspapers and publications and a featured commentator on various TV and radio programs. She recently appeared on CNN's "Lou Dobbs Tonight" and is publisher of City magazine.

Sylvia Lovely was named one of one of Kentucky's "Top Women of Influence" and "Appalachian Woman of the Year."

*NewCities Institute*
*Kentucky League of Cities*
*100 East Vine Street, Suite 800*
*Lexington, Kentucky 40507*
*800-876-4552*

*www.NewCities.org*

## JAMIE S LAPIN, CDP, CFP RISK MANAGEMENT GROUP, INC.
Montgomery County, MD USA
www.rmgfinancial.com

Jamie Lapin is a Certified Divorce Planner, Certified Financial Planner (25 years), and a veteran of the "divorce wars". Clients, lawyers & judges have a limited understanding of money, taxes and the long-term economics of divorce. Her focus on the "business" of divorce maximizes familial dollars and saves thousands in costs. An engaging speaker, Jamie is an excellent resource for sound bytes, quotes, interviews, articles and speaking engagements.

Jamie S. Lapin, CDP, CFP
*President*
Risk Management Group, Inc.
Rockville, MD
*Contact Phone:* 301-838-4111
*Cell:* 301-442-5111
**Click to Contact from Web Site**

## GUIDO CAMPELLONE — CITIPACIFIC MORTGAGE
Irvine, CA USA
www.citipacificmortgage.com

Guido Campellone, co-host of the KLSX radio Los Angeles mortgage show, founded CitiPacific Mortgage in Irvine, California. Campellone, is known for combining technology with financing, building deals with Microsoft, Citrix, MCI and HBO as VP of Mendelsen Associates. CitiPacific was nominated for the 2005 Stevie Award Technology Innovator of the Year for unique lead generation and management software shared by partners. Guido's expertise in financing real estate increases clients' personal wealth creation and retirement earnings.

Guido Campellone
*CEO*
CitiPacific Mortgage
Irvine, CA USA
*Contact Phone:* 1-866-220-2121
**Click to Contact from Web Site**

## KRIS R. NIELSEN — THE NIELSEN-WURSTER GROUP, INC.
Princeton, NJ USA
http://www.nielsen-wurster.com

Kris R. Nielsen, Chairman of The Nielsen-Wurster Group, Inc. has extensive experience as a project manager, project risk manager, expert witness, negotiator and arbitrator in construction litigation. An engineer, an attorney and Certified Project Management Professional, Nielsen is consulted regularly by counsel on resolution of construction disputes.

Kris R. Nielsen
*Chairman*
The Nielsen-Wurster Group, Inc./Kris R. Nielsen
Princeton, NJ
*Contact Phone:* 609-497-7300
**Click to Contact from Web Site**

## PATRICIA D. GALLOWAY — THE NIELSEN-WURSTER GROUP, INC.
Princeton, NJ USA
http://www.nielsen-wurster.com

Patricia Galloway is the CEO and Principal of The Nielsen-Wurster Group, Inc. A P.E. in Civil Engineering (BSCE, Purdue University) and recognized expert on construction scheduling. She prepares delay analysis for construction litigation, writes articles on construction scheduling and delay analysis, and testifies extensively as a scheduling expert.

Patricia D. Galloway
*CEO*
The Nielsen-Wurster Group, Inc./Patricia D. Galloway
Princeton, NJ
*Contact Phone:* 609-497-7300
**Click to Contact from Web Site**

## MICHAEL W. MCLAUGHLIN
San Francisco, CA USA
http://www.GuerrillaConsulting.com

Michael W. McLaughlin is a Principal with Deloitte Consulting LLP and has worked with companies of all sizes, from America's highest-profile companies to start-ups. He is the co-author with Jay Levinson of Guerrilla Marketing for Consultants and publisher of Management Consulting News. In addition to broadcast appearances, McLaughlin's perspectives have generated interviews from national publications. He has written extensively and also presented frequently at national onferences.

Media Contact
*Contact Main Phone:* 415 388 1871
**Click to Contact from Web Site**

## EDWARD BOND, PROFESSIONAL CERTIFIED CONSTRUCTION MANAGER
Boston, MA USA
www.bondbrothers.com

Bond Brothers is a fourth generation, 98-year professional construction management firm providing construction management for building, civil, and utility clients around New England. Their expertise resides in providing value informed design (VID) strategies from preconstruction through design and construction into commissioning for academic, commercial, energy, health care, institutional, industrial and utility clients. A highly diversified construction firm, they use their broad range of expertise to help owners maximize their return on investment, resulting in abundant repeat clients.

Edward Bond CCM, CMC, FSMPS
*CEO*
Bond Brothers
Everett, MA USA
*Contact Phone:* 617-387-3400
**Click to Contact from Web Site**

## THEODORE W GARRISON, III - CONSTRUCTION EXPERT - STRATEGIC PLANNING
Daytona Beach, FL USA
http://www.TedGarrison.com

Ted Garrison has cemented his reputation as THE expert in construction to call when you need a construction speaker. As the author of Strategic Planning for Contractors, Ted provides expert advice on strategic planning and strategic thinking in areas of planning, marketing, leadership, systems and project management. When you need an expert on construction operations - Ted is the expert you need to speak to.

Theodore W. Garrison, III
Garrison Associates
Ormond Beach, FL USA
*Contact Phone:* 800-861-0874
*Cell:* 386-846-5954
**Click to Contact from Web Site**

## APICS THE ASSOCIATION FOR OPERATIONS MANAGEMENT
Alexandria, VA USA
http://www.apics.org

APICS The Association for Operations Management is the global leader and premier source of the body of knowledge in operations management, including production, inventory, supply chain, materials management, purchasing, and logistics. Since 1957, individuals and companies have relied on APICS for its superior training, internationally recognized certifications, comprehensive resources, and worldwide network of accomplished industry professionals. To learn more about the APICS community, visit www.apics.org.

Mary King
*Senior Manager, Multimedia*
APICS The Association for Operations Management
Alexandria, VA USA
*Contact Phone:* 703-354-8851
*Contact Main Phone:* 800-444-2742
**Click to Contact from Web Site**

## SHAKESPEARE OXFORD SOCIETY
Washington, DC USA
http://www.shakespeare-oxford.com

Founded in 1957, the Shakespeare Oxford Society is a non-profit, educational organization dedicated to exploring the Shakespeare authorship question and researching the evidence that Edward de Vere, the 17th Earl of Oxford (1550 - 1604) is the true author of the poems and plays of 'William Shakespeare.' Doubters of the 'Stratfordian' theory include Mark Twain, Henry James, Sigmund Freud, Supreme Court Justice John Paul Stevens, and Shakespearean actors Derek Jacobi, Michael York, and Jeremy Irons.

Matthew Cossolotto
*President*
Shakespeare Oxford Society
Silver Spring, USA
*Contact Phone:* 914-245-9721
*Cell:* 914-645-7228
**Click to Contact from Web Site**

## SON OF THE SOIL
Irvine, CA USA
http://www.sonofthesoil.com

Son of the Soil is a 3 piece band, performing all original Hard Pop Punk Rock! The songs are generally melodic, some heavier than others. Listen and Enjoy!

Zafar Amin
Son of the Soil
Irvine, CA USA
*Contact Phone:* 949 752 0424
**Click to Contact from Web Site**

## OPERA BOSTON
Boston, MA USA
http://www.operaboston.org

Opera Boston is New England's most innovative opera company, named Best of Boston for eight consecutive years by the Boston Globe. Opera brings together music, theater, singing, costumes, drama, dance and visual arts in a multi-media event like no other. From our season of fully-staged productions with live orchestra presented at the Cutler Majestic Theatre in the Boston Theatre District, to special performances of opera, operetta and Broadway musicals in unique venues, Opera Boston events are attractions for tourists and Bostonians.

Fusco & Four Associates
West Roxbury, MA USA
*Contact Phone:* 617-363-0405
**Click to Contact from Web Site**

## MUSIC CITY COMMUNITY CHORUS
Nashville, TN USA
http://www.musiccitycommunitychorus.com/

MC to the third power stands for the Music City Community Chorus, a non-profit, broad-based volunteer performing chorus, to be formed in Nashville, Tennessee under the direction of Renee Grant-Williams. The overall goal is to create an organization that will build a bridge between disparate Nashville music communities and styles.

Elaine Collins
Music City Community Chorus
Nashville, TN USA
*Contact Phone:* 615-259-4900
**Click to Contact from Web Site**

## BOSTON CENTER FOR THE ARTS
Boston, MA USA
http://www.bcaonline.org

The BCA is located in Boston's South End, the largest landmark district in the United States. The BCA is a four acre complex that includes: The Cyclorama, built in 1884 to display a panorama painting, is on the National Register of Historic Places. The 23,000 square foot Cyclorama rotunda is now the site of exhibitions, performances and community events and houses the Community Music Center of Boston, the Art Connection, the Boston Ballet Costume Shop, three small theaters and a rehearsal studio. The Tremont Estates Building, originally an organ factory built in 1850, now houses over 50 artist studios, the Mills Gallery, two rehearsal spaces and Hamersley's Bistro. Boston Ballet's headquarters, a 1991 building designed by noted architect Graham Gund, houses rehearsal and administrative spaces, and a ballet school.

Fusco & Four Associates
West Roxbury, MA USA
*Contact Phone:* 617-363-0405
**Click to Contact from Web Site**

## ZIMBABU T. HAMILTON - EXPERT PERCUSSIONIST JAZZ RADIO PRODUCER
Chicago, IL USA
http://www.zimprov.com

Introducing the last Funkateer, Zimbabu, aka known as the Bruce Lee of Drums. Zimbabu T. Hamilton (Zim) is the bandleader of ZIMPROV. The concept of ZIMPROV is to focus on the sound that allows the inner spirit to speak harmoniously, melodically and in rhythm with the universe.

Zimbabu T. Hamilton
Zimprov
Chicago, IL USA
*Contact Phone:* 773-320-9111
**Click to Contact from Web Site**

## THE AMERICAN WATERWAYS OPERATORS
Arlington, VA USA
http://www.americanwaterways.com

AWO is the national association representing the inland and coastal tugboat, towboat and barge industry. Comprised of nearly 4,000 tugboats and towboats and over 27,000 barges, the industry safely and efficiently moves over 800 million tons of cargo each year, including over half of America's export grain, energy sources such as coal and petroleum, including most of New England's home heating oil and gasoline, and other bulk commodities that are the building blocks of the U.S. economy. Recognized leaders in marine safety, all AWO members must participate, as a condition of membership, in The Responsible Carrier Program, an award-winning, third-party audited safety and environmental protection regime. AWO provides expert information on issues affecting this vital economical and environmentally-friendly segment of America's commercial transportation system.

Anne Burns
*Vice President - Public Affairs*
The American Waterways Operators
Arlington, VA
*Contact Phone:* 703-841-9300
**Click to Contact from Web Site**

### DAVID G. DWINELL, MASTER BROKER
Phoenix, AZ USA
www.TransportationExpert.com

David G Dwinell is an expert in surface transportation. He is a Transportation Broker, who has been a Driver, an Owner Operator, a Motor Carrier, and a Motor Carrier/Broker. commonly called a Truck Broker. He has been in transportation as an entrepreneur since he was 14 years and still can't get it out of his system. Transportation is the largest single industry in the world. In the US, 1/3 of the GDP is from transportation. He is allowed as an expert for testimony before the United State Justice Department, as well as a Contract Mediator in over 5,000 disputed Claims. He is an author, lecturer and Professor of Transportation since 1987. He teaches transportation professionals, using his text books, in his own school and in seminars throughout North America. He is a consultant to some of this nations largest transportation corporations, investment companies, mutual fund and capital managers, as well as thousands of graduates who have received the Master Broker Certification upon graduation. He has created several transportation innovations, from the first online transportation auction website back to transportation capacity coordination. (finding tomorrows' trucks- today) He has tracked the economics of transportation pricing, wholesale and retail, since 1987 to today and accurately predicts market trends. He is an engaging public speaker, equally at home in board meetings, before cameras, and large audiences.

David Dwinell
QT Investments
loadtraining.com
Youngtown, AZ USA
*Contact Phone:* 800-776-7067
*Contact Main Phone:* 623 974 2232
*Cell:* 623 332 5199
**Click to Contact from Web Site**

## JOSEPH VRANICH, AUTHOR & RAIL TRAVEL EXPERT
Irvine, CA USA
http://www.aei.org/publications/bookID.
798,filter.all/book_detail.asp

Joseph Vranich is author of 'End of the Line: The Failure of Amtrak Reform and the Future of America's Passenger Trains' (AEI Press, December 2004). Vranich's career includes working to create Amtrak in 1970-71, president/CEO of the High Speed Rail Association, and a U.S. Senate appointee to Amtrak Reform Council. He has appeared on ABC, BBC, C-SPAN, CBS, NBC, CNN, Fox News, MSNBC, PBS, NPR and on more than 200 local talk shows.

Joseph Vranich
*Author & Speaker*
Irvine, CA USA
*Contact Phone:* 949-551-3150
**Click to Contact from Web Site**

## AMERICAN PUBLIC TRANSPORTATION ASSOCIATION
Washington, DC USA
http://www.apta.com

APTA is a nonprofit international association of 1,600 member organizations including public transportation systems; planning, design, construction and finance firms; product and service providers; academic institutions; and state associations and departments of transportation. APTA members serve the public interest by providing safe, efficient and economical public transportation services and products. APTA members serve more than 90 percent of persons using public transportation in the United States and Canada.

Virginia Miller
*Manager - Media Relations*
American Public Transportation Association
Washington, DC
*Contact Phone:* 202-496-4816
**Click to Contact from Web Site**

## LOGISTICARE, NON-EMERGENCY TRANSPORTATION
Atlanta, GA USA
http://www.logisticare.com

Atlanta-based LogistiCare is the nation's leading provider of specialized, non-emergency transportation network management. Clients include state Medicaid agencies, school boards and transit authorities, hospital systems and many of the nation's largest managed care organizations. As an outsourcing solution, LogistiCare's services are based on a medical case management model and include utilization management, risk management and quality assurance reporting. This results in better quality, cost containment, reduced fraud and enhanced access to services.

Edward Domansky
*Director, Corporate Communications*
LogistiCare
Atlanta, GA USA
*Contact Phone:* 770-994-4579
**Click to Contact from Web Site**

## NATIONAL INSTITUTE FOR AUTOMOTIVE SERVICE EXCELLENCE (ASE)
Leesburg, VA USA
http://www.asecert.org

ASE is a national, non-profit organization dedicated to improving the quality of automotive repair through voluntary testing and certification of automotive repair professionals. There are more than 400,000 ASE-certified professionals nationwide. Spokespersons, available for broadcast and print interviews, can discuss finding good auto repairs, the benefits of technician certification, maintenance tips, etc.

Patricia Serratore
*Vice President*
National Institute for Automotive Service Excellence (ASE)
Leesburg, VA
*Contact Phone:* 703-669-6633
**Click to Contact from Web Site**

## VOLVO GROUP NORTH AMERICA
New York, NY USA
www.volvo.com
NASDQ VOLVY

The Volvo Group is a global provider of commercial transport solutions, as well as the world's leading producer of heavy diesel engines. The Volvo Group holds leading positions in each of its business areas, which include trucks, buses, construction equipment, marine and industrial power drives, aerospace engines and components, as well as financial services. In 2001, the Volvo Group acquired Renault VI and Mack Trucks, to make it the second largest heavy truck manufacturer in the world.

Marjorie Meyers
*Manager, Corporate Communications*
Volvo Group North America
New York, NY USA
*Contact Phone:* 212-418-7434
*Contact Main Phone:* 212-418-7400
*Cell:* 646-246-8606
**Click to Contact from Web Site**

## NATIONAL AUTOMOBILE DEALERS ASSOCIATION
McLean, VA USA
http://www.nada.org

The National Automobile Dealers Association, founded in 1917 represents 20,000 new-car and -truck dealers with 43,000 separate franchises. NADA represents dealers on Capitol Hill, to automobile manufacturers and to the public. The association offers a variety of products and services, including educational training, to help dealers improve their businesses. NADA also publishes the N.A.D.A. Official Used Car Guide.

David Hyatt
*Vice President and Chief Public Affairs Officer*
National Automobile Dealers Association
McLean, VA
*Contact Phone:* 703-821-7120
**Click to Contact from Web Site**

## LAUREN FIX -- AUTOMOTIVE EXPERT & CONSULTANT
Buffalo, NY USA
http://www.laurenfix.com

Lauren Fix an automotive analyst on safety, vehicles and repair. Appearing on Oprah, Today, The View, MSNBC, CNN, FOX News, NBC, ABC, CBS, and NPR. Authored: Driving Ambitions and The Performance Tire and Wheel Handbook. Hosting Talk 2 DIY-Automotive, in-depth demonstrations and tips for auto repair. Lauren's syndicated segments: The Car Coach®, car care tips and His Turn-Her Turn™, car reviews a male/female perspective. Lauren provides information on marketing, sales training and consumer awareness.

Lauren J. Fix
*Automotive Consultant/Expert*
Lancaster, NY
*Contact Phone:* 716-636-1128
*Contact Main Phone:* 716-636-1128
*Cell:* 716-440-3888
**Click to Contact from Web Site**

## THE DRIVING COMPANY, LLC
Washington, DC USA

Miriam Schottland is an instructor in accident avoidance, car control techniques, high performance driving and counter terrorism techniques, with 16 years experience in working with the most highly recognized advanced driver training school in the country. She is chief instructor for the BMW Club, the Audi Club and senior instructor for the Ferrari Club as well as many other organizations. Driving is the most dangerous and complicated thing we will ever do, and yet we know so little about it. There are many myths regarding driving, and a little knowledge of applied physics can go long way in explaining why cars do what they do when we drive them. This is why the Driving Company has been created. Infamous in her outspoken criticism of the poor quality of drivers and the training they receive, she is a frequent guest lecturer on nation wide radio and TV talk shows as well as an expert witness and consultant in the area of driving.

M. Schottland
Washington, DC USA
*Contact Phone:* 202-265-3438
**Click to Contact from Web Site**

## RECREATION VEHICLE INDUSTRY ASSOCIATION (RVIA)
Reston, VA USA
http://www.rvia.org

Recreation Vehicle Industry Association (RVIA) is the national trade association of RV manufacturers and component parts suppliers producing 98% of American RVs, including motorhomes, travel trailers, truck campers, folding camping trailers, and conversion vehicles. RVIA has numerous industry spokespeople available to address RV travel topics and trends. David J. Humphreys is RVIA's president and primary spokesperson. A leisure travel expert, he can address topics related to RV and general travel, tourism and outdoor recreation.

Jim Lubinskas
*Marketing Communications Manager*
Recreation Vehicle Industry Association (RVIA)
Reston, VA
*Contact Phone:* 703-620-6003
*Contact Main Phone:* 703-620-6003
**Click to Contact from Web Site**

## EXPERIMENTAL AIRCRAFT ASSOCIATION (EAA)
Oshkosh, WI USA
www.eaa.org

International 170,000-member aviation organization dedicated to recreational flying. Members include pilots and non-pilots, designers, builders, restorers and enthusiasts of vintage, experimental, ultralight, rotorcraft and warbird aircraft. Hosts annual EAA AirVenture at Oshkosh, Wisconsin, with 750,000 attendees and 12,000 aircraft. More than 1,000 chapters worldwide.

David Berkley
*Director of Communications*
Experimental Aircraft Association (EAA)
Oshkosh, WI
*Contact Phone:* 920-426-6295
*Contact Main Phone:* 920-426-4800
**Click to Contact from Web Site**

# *Lauren Fix:* *Automotive Expert,*
## *The Car Coach® / Car Smarts®*

A highly credible automotive and lifestyle expert, Lauren Fix provides solid information on safety and a wide range of automotive topics and issues. Her motivational speeches, such as the "Carma Coach," will help you find the "vehicle" that gets you "where you want to go." Fix toured with O Magazine for "Oprah's 2005 Live Your Best Life Tour," presenting motivational inspiration, consumer information and automotive advice.

## TV & Radio

■ Oprah, Today, The View, CNN, Fox News, Headlines News, MSNBC, Inside Edition, The Early Show, NBC, ABC, CBS, WB, UPN, The Weather Channel, ESPN, Discovery, Speed, B. Smith Style, National Public Radio.
■ Host, auto expert for Talk 2 DIY Automotive on Scripps Do-It-Yourself Network (DIY); 65 one-hour shows.
■ Syndicated segments: The Car Coach® (car care tips) and His Turn–Her Turn™ (car reviews from a male and female perspective).

## Print & Internet

■ Automotive editor for YourLifeMagazine.com; contributing to USA Today; Good Housekeeping; Woman's World; Redbook; Self; InTouch Weekly; Essence; Marie Claire; Prevention; Intellichoice; Motor Trend; Truck Trend; Hot Rod; Car Craft; TheCarConnection.com; family-car.com; and more.

## Books

■ "Driving Ambitions: A Complete Guide to Amateur Auto Racing" and "The Performance Tire and Wheel Handbook."
■ Soon: "The Carma Coach" and "Just Drive It!"

## Promotions

■ Spokesperson for the "Be Car Care Aware" program.

**Lauren J. Fix**

80 Rotech Drive,
Lancaster, N.Y. 14086

646-475-4357
Fax: 501-639-9360

thecarcoach
@laurenfix.com

www.laurenfix.com

### AEROSPACE INDUSTRIES ASSOCIATION
Arlington, VA USA
http://www.aia-aerospace.org

The Aerospace Industries Association is the trade association representing the nation's manufacturers of commercial, military, and business aircraft, helicopters, aircraft engines, missiles, spacecraft, and related components and equipment. AIA publishes a monthly newsletter and industry statistics, all of which are available to the news media. AIA was founded in 1919; early members included Orville Wright, Glenn H. Curtiss, and nearly every important aircraft manufacturer at that time.

Matt Grimison
*Manager, Communications*
Aerospace Industries Association
Arlington, DC
*Contact Phone:* 703-358-1076
**Click to Contact from Web Site**

### AIRCRAFT OWNERS AND PILOTS ASSOCIATION -- AOPA
Frederick, MD USA
http://www.aopa.org

As the world's largest civil aviation organization, AOPA represents more than 400,000 U.S. pilots and aircraft owners. Information and policy perspective on General Aviation, safety, airspace regulations, airports, air traffic control and air navigation.

Chris Dancy
*Media Relations Director*
Aircraft Owners and Pilots Association
Frederick, MD
*Contact Phone:* 301-695-2162
*Contact Main Phone:* 301-695-2000
**Click to Contact from Web Site**

### APPALACHIAN TRAIL CONSERVANCY (ATC)
Harpers Ferry, WV USA
http://www.appalachiantrail.org

The Appalachian Trail Conservancy, along with more than 5,000 volunteers and government partners, manages the 2,175-mile Appalachian Trail that stretches across 14 states from Maine to Georgia. The trail, which is within a day's drive for more than two-thirds of the U.S. population, is America's premier hiking trail and the world's longest footpath.

Brian B. King
*Associate Director of Communications*
Appalachian Trail Conservancy (ATC)
Harpers Ferry, WV
*Contact Phone:* 304-535-6331
*Contact Main Phone:* 304-535-6331
**Click to Contact from Web Site**

### SPORTS TRAVEL AND TOURS
Springfield, MA USA
http://www.sportstravelandtours.com

Sports Travel and Tours is a growing niche in the travel industry; where fans see their favorite sports teams in action or visit a stadium or arena. Jay Smith, President of Sports and Travel & Tours, has been in the travel industry since 1974. His involvement in the sport travel niche has been since 1990 and he has the behind-the-scenes info on this growing travel segment.

Jay F. Smith
*President*
Sports Travel and Tours
Hatfield, MA USA
*Contact Phone:* 413-247-7678
*Contact Main Phone:* 800-662-4424
**Click to Contact from Web Site**

## PASSPORTER TRAVEL PRESS
Ann Arbor, MI USA
www.passporter.com/

PassPorters are unique, all-in-one travel guides that offer comprehensive, expert advice and innovative planning systems of built-in worksheets and organizer 'PassPockets.' The PassPockets help you organize your vacation by building trip itineraries on the front before you go, storing maps, passes, and receipts inside while you're there, recording memories and expenses on the back to enjoy when you return.

Dave Marx
*Author*
PassPorter Travel Press
Ann Arbor, MI
*Contact Phone:* 734-332-7801
**Click to Contact from Web Site**

## SAILBOAT INCORPORATED
Washington, DC USA
www.Sailboat.com

Sailboat.com offers lots of sailing ideas.

Mitchell Davis
Universal Coupon Corporation
Washington, DC USA
*Contact Phone:* 202-333-5000
**Click to Contact from Web Site**

## BILL HINCHBERGER - BRAZIL EXPERT
Sao Paulo, SP Brazil
www.BrazilMax.com

Bill Hinchberger is editor and publisher of Brazil-Max, www.BrazilMax.com, 'the hip guide to Brazil.' A former correspondent for The Financial Times and Business Week, he gives private 'understanding Brazil' sessions to visiting executives of a leading European bank and is a frequent public speaker. He holds an M.A. in Latin American Studies from the University of California, Berkeley, and is the former president of the Sao Paulo Foreign Press Club (1995-99).

Bill Hinchberger - BrazilMax
*Editor and Publisher*
BrazilMax
Sao Paulo, SP, CA Brazil
*Contact Phone:* +(55-11) 5507-4150
*Cell:* +(55-11) 9976-6623
**Click to Contact from Web Site**

## HONEYMOON CARD CORPORATION
Washington, DC USA
www.HoneymoonCard.com

That's right we've built The Honeymoon Card to appeal to the cost-conscious couple seeking an affordable honeymoon destination. With people getting married later in life, once they are solvent, and how most hotels have already burned though all the gold and Platinum people in their programs, what better financial customer can you have than a new household. The Honeymoon Card is designed to help properties reach the new buyer of condos — the newly wed.

Mitchell P. Davis
Honeymoon Card Corporation
Washington, DC USA
*Contact Phone:* 1-800-HONEYMOON
**Click to Contact from Web Site**

## HIDEAWAYS INTERNATIONAL, INC.
Portsmouth, NH USA
http://www.hideaways.com

When Mike Thiel talks, you can count on a lively exchange. He's traveled the world in search of out-of-the-ordinary getaways for his travel club membership. Mike says, 'You can vacation like the rich and famous, without being either!' He is founder, publisher and editor in chief of Hide-aways.com, Hideaways Guide, Hideaways Newsletter and author of Villa Vacations Made Easy, and 102 Tips for Renting Your Vacation Home.

Tammy Ciolfi
*Marketing Associate*
Hideaways International, Inc.
Portsmouth, NH
*Contact Phone:* 603-430-4433
*Contact Main Phone:* 800-843-4433
**Click to Contact from Web Site**

## TED CELENTINO, BUSINESS TRAVEL EXPERT
San Francisco, CA USA
www.airrage.com

This leading expert on business travel, stress reduction, and air rage is the author of the popular book for business travelers, Combating Air Rage. Readers learn tips on reducing stress from travel, ways to work more efficiently on the road, and methods for handling airline snafus with ease. Mr. Celentino is effective and professional in interviews and is a useful resource on all aspects of business travel.

Ted Celentino
*Business Travel Expert*
San Francisco, CA
*Contact Phone:* 415-990-2354
**Click to Contact from Web Site**

### TRAVEL EXPERT GLORIA BOHAN — CEO OF OMEGA WORLD TRAVEL

Washington, DC USA
http://www.OmegaTravel.com

Gloria Bohan is one of the most successful women in business today and a leading figure in the travel industry as Founder and President of Omega World Travel - the top woman-owned business in the U.S. Well known as a successful entrepreneur, businesswoman mentor, and industry trendsetter, she boasts many business awards, is a pioneer in the field of space tourism, and a frequent public speaker on topics like business diversity and travel industry trends.

Michael Jordan
*Public Relations Manager*
Omega World Travel
Fairfax, VA USA
*Contact Phone:* 703-359-0200
**Click to Contact from Web Site**

### DR MICHAEL BREIN... PUBLIC TRANSPORTATION TOURISM EXPERT & TRAVEL PSYCHOLOGIST

Ashland, OR USA
http://www.michaelbrein.com

Michael Brein publishes travel books and guides-the world's first and only travel guide series specifically designed to show travelers how to go to the top 50 visitor attractions by public transportation in the world's most visited cities. Michael also is a travel psychologist writing a book and MP3 audio series on the psychology of travel as revealed through the best travel stories of more than 1,000 world-travelers.

Michael Brein
*Pres / CEO*
Michael Brein's Travel Adventures (sm)
Ashland, OR USA
*Contact Main Phone:* 541-535-9971
**Click to Contact from Web Site**

### MAN FROM THE MIDDLE OF NOWHERE, TEXAS

Amarillo, TX USA
www.middleofnowheretexas.com

Middle of Nowhere, Texas is located in the Panhandle of Texas. Anyone in the world can become a Certified Citizen of Middle of Nowhere. Just click online at www.middleofnowheretexas.com and order a certificate which is shipped with 1 of inspiration (100% Texas Dirt) paper weight and bragging rights as proud Texan. Our goal is to establish a Guinness Book World Record by recording the largest population of citizens in the world without having the problems of crime, taxes and political unrest.

Glenn Baxter
*Man from Middle of Nowhere*
Middle of Nowhere Texas
Acton, TX USA
*Contact Phone:* 817-326-2158
**Click to Contact from Web Site**

### MR. LAURIE PANE — CHASING SUNSETS — SAIL AROUND THE WORLD

Los Angeles, CA USA
www.chasingsunsetsthebook.com/

'Chasing Sunsets' is a real reality show, a light-hearted, novel-like recounting of how a family of three circumnavigated the world in six-and-a-half years, written from the very different perspectives of macho-male, co-captain/wife, and growing son (8 to 14 years old). Normal family life, if normal includes being arrested by secret police, surviving a lightning strike, dealing with depth-charges, finding hidden Roman mosaics, riding long-tails, camels and elephants, walking under water-falls, sailing under venting volcanoes, and being stalked by whales.

Mr. Laurie Pane
Los Angeles, CA USA
*Contact Phone:* 818-729-1954
**Click to Contact from Web Site**

### SEAWORLD, BUSCH GARDENS AND THE ANHEUSER-BUSCH ADVENTURE PARK

Clayton, MO USA

The Anheuser-Busch Adventure Parks — one of the largest theme park operations in the world — are owned and operated by Busch Entertainment Corporation. Adventure Parks include Sea World, Busch Gardens and the new Discovery Cove. In addition to featuring state-of-the art roller coasters, spectacular shows and up-close animal encounters, the parks are leaders in wildlife conservation and have the most-widely recognized animal rescue and rehabilitation programs in the world.

Fred Jacobs
*Senior Director, Communications*
Busch Entertainment Corporation
Clayton, MO
*Contact Phone:* 314-613-6077
**Click to Contact from Web Site**

### XANADU ENTERPRISES -- GET PAID TO TRAVEL

Evansdale, IA USA
http://www.roadrat.com/media

When was the last time that you saw a brand-new RV being delivered somewhere on the back of a vehicle-carrying truck, the way new cars are? An ambulance? Or even a limousine? Perhaps never, because recreational and specialty vehicles almost always transported by ordinary people (not truck drivers) who simply drive them to the dealerships where they're sold, and to customers, all over the continent. It's the Virtually-Unknown Travel Job that Audiences Love to Learn About!

Craig Chilton
XANADU Enterprises
Evansdale, IA
*Contact Phone:* 319-234-0676
**Click to Contact from Web Site**

# Mike Thiel
## "The Luxe Travel Guru"

*Contact Mike Thiel for a lively exchange and insider's insight on alluring getaways (international villas, boutique hotels and resorts, executive retreats, private islands, yacht-like cruise ships, city center oases), the world's most exceptional destinations, and up-and-coming travel trends.*

Since 1979, Mike has been traveling the world in search of its best . . . and sharing his finds with the discerning and independent travelers of The Hideaways Aficionado™ Club. Mike is the founder, president, and editor-in-chief of *Hideaways Life* newsletter, *The Hideaways Collection™* directory, several electronic newsletters, *Villa Vacations Made Easy* how-to guide, and www.Hideaways.com. "The Luxe Travel Guru" brings a strong point of view to any discussion and is sure to educate, entertain, and inspire with travel stories . . . and secrets!

### Mike is the expert on:

- Vacation home rentals
- Honeymoon destinations
- Executive retreats
- Barge and yacht charters
- Multigenerational travel
- Off-the-beaten path
- Top travel destinations
- And much more!

Mike has been featured in *The Wall Street Journal, New York Times, The Boston Globe,* and on *CNN, CNBC, The Travel Channel,* and others. He is a a trusted, quotable resource for TV/radio producers, authors, editors, columnists, and writers.

**PR Contact**
Tammy Ciolfi
Hideaways International, Inc.
Portsmouth, New Hampshire
603-430-4433 ext. 178
www.Hideaways.com

## BRIAN G. DALZELL — PERFORMANCE ADVANTAGE
Toronto, Ontario Canada
www.BDalzell.com

If your organization requires new perspectives and understanding to help it Achieve its Vision through a meaningful and lasting transformation of personnel, we can help. If your organization is struggling or overwhelmed with the challenge of upgrading the knowledge, skills and attributes of Your Most Important Asset - Your People, we can help. If your organization needs additional resources, expertise and perspective to bring about meaningful and lasting change to Achieve its Vision, we can help.

Brian G. Dalzell
The Performance Advantage, Inc.
Brampton, Ontario Canada
*Contact Phone:* 905-459-2496
**Click to Contact from Web Site**

## HERBERT DEGRAFFE, JR., SPORTS & ENTERTAINMENT MARKETING & ADVERTISING
New York, NY USA
http://www.thesaagroup.com

SAA SPORT AND ENTERTAINMENT GROUP has created an operating infrastructure, with well-recognized brands, customer letters of intent, proprietary content, satisfied business communities, strategic partners, distribution channels and outsourced production. Sports Advertising Associates, Inc. is now transforming its products and services, as well as its fundamental business model, to take full advantage of the newest business performance management, Internet-based technologies, current market trends and recent changes in the global arena.

Herbert J. DeGraffe, Jr.
*CEO*
SAA Sports & Entertainment Group
New York, NY USA
*Contact Phone:* 212-206-3811
*Cell:* 603-498-1109
**Click to Contact from Web Site**

## HOMERUN SOFTWARE — 800-HOMERUN.COM, INC.
Washington, DC USA
www.Homerun.com

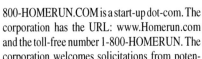

800-HOMERUN.COM is a start-up dot-com. The corporation has the URL: www.Homerun.com and the toll-free number 1-800-HOMERUN. The corporation welcomes solicitations from potential partners. Such soliciations should be faxed to (202) 342-5411.

Mitchell P. Davis
800-Homerun.com Inc
Washington, DC USA
*Contact Phone:* 1-800-HOMERUN
**Click to Contact from Web Site**

## PERFORMANCE RESEARCH
Newport, RI USA
http://www.performanceresearch.com

Performance Research is the world's leader in the evaluation of corporate sponsorship of sports, special events, theme parks, the arts, charitable causes, and web-based programs. Having conducted more than one million surveys and hundreds of focus groups related to sponsorship, Performance Research is the most trusted source for interpreting the marketing impact and consumer response to corporate sponsorship

Jed Pearsall, Ed.D.
*President*
Performance Research
Newport, RI
*Contact Phone:* 401-848-0111
**Click to Contact from Web Site**

## PERSONAL BEST CONSULTING, LLC — DR. LEIF H. SMITH
Hilliard, OH USA
http://www.PersonalBestConsulting.com

Leif H. Smith, Psy.D. has worked with hundreds of athletes, coaches, teams, and executives to quickly improve on-the-job results and performance. He is also the publisher of 'Personal Bests,' a monthly newsletter designed to offer tips and techniques to immediately improve personal productiveness. Dr. Smith has been published in magazines such as 'Pure Power' and 'Small Business Digest,' and has appeared on shows such as 'Sports Pulse' on the Comcast Network.

Dr. Leif H. Smith
*President*
Personal Best Consulting, LLC
Hilliard, OH USA
*Contact Phone:* 614-870-8742
**Click to Contact from Web Site**

## SPORTS MEDIA CHALLENGE
Charlotte, NC USA
http://www.sportsmediachallenge.com

In sports, reputations are easy to gain and hard to lose. Whether there's an emerging star, looming crisis or major endorsement deal, Kathleen Hessert's one of the nation's leading experts in preparing sports personalities and organizations for public scrutiny in both good times and in bad. Whether on the Internet or face to face with the fans and media, Sports Media Challenge helps protect and enhance sports brands. Kathleen has become the leader in sports online word-of-mouth and Fan Generated Media™. Clients include NBA, Peyton Manning, Longhorns football, Nascar's Kasey Kahne, etc.

Kathleen Hessert
*President*
Sports Media Challenge
Charlotte, NC
*Contact Main Phone:* 704-541-5942
**Click to Contact from Web Site**

 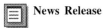

# Explore North America in an RV, While *Someone Else* Pays for It!

More than 90 percent of your viewers, listeners and readers already are fully qualified to join them. They just don't know about them yet. What can be better than a topic that has been proven as a real audience-pleaser? This one has been fascinating people for 25 years.

Most people love to travel, and here is a way to do it as adventure travel with a twist: **The people who do it this way get *paid* for it.**

In 1979, the first complete guidebook that had ever been written about this job came off the press -- and today is *still* the only book of its kind -- and continues to serve as the primary gateway for our firm.

Its author Craig Chilton has been a guest on more than 1,000 radio and TV shows across the U.S.A. and Canada -- from Honolulu to St. John's (and even once, in-studio, in Moscow, Russia). Nearly 100,000 copies of the book have helped tens of thousands of its readers to add a whole new travel dimension to their lives.

Think about this: When was the last time that you saw a brand-new RV being delivered somewhere on the back of a vehicle-carrying truck, the way new cars and pickups are? What about a brand-new school bus? A UPS route truck? An ambulance? Even a limousine? If you answered, "Perhaps never," that's not surprising. *Here's why:*

It's North America's great "sleeper" travel job.

Recreational and specialty vehicles almost never are transported on trucks. Instead, ordinary people (not truck drivers) simply drive them to the dealerships where they are sold. They blend in perfectly with the rest of the traffic. These vehicles are manufactured and modified in 3,800 places. It takes a big workforce to deliver them: about 100,000 people. Of those, 30 percent are women, 40 percent are couples and about one-third are aged 65 to 80, making this North America's most senior-friendly industry.

This is a job for people of all ages, though, from 18 on up. The job can be done full-time, part-time, during vacations and even just on weekends. Weekenders who have regular "9-to-5" jobs make up 10 percent of all these drivers. Realistic earnings for full-timers is $35-55k/yr. for singles, and $45-75k/yr. for couples. College students and teachers doing this typically earn $8,000-$12,000/summer.

---

🚐 *Audience response and more details:*
***Visit our unlinked media page at http://www.roadrat.com/media.***
🚐 *Availability: In-studio in Midwest, and elsewhere by arrangement; phoner almost anytime.*

## BOBBY LOPEZ AND THE G-TEAM
Richmond, VA USA
http://www.bobbylopezgolf.com

Bobby Lopez, PGA Golf Professional and former Touring Professional on the European Tour offers a one day school guaranteed to cut 7 strokes in 24 hours! How? My golf instruction is personalized to your specific golf swing needs, no cloning, no complicated swing theory.

Bobby Lopez
Richmond, VA USA
*Contact Phone:* 757-382-5500
**Click to Contact from Web Site**

## JEFF BUKANTZ -- US OLYMPIC FENCING TEAM CAPTAIN
New York, NY USA
www.JeffBukantz.com

Jeff Bukantz is Captain of the U.S. Fencing Team and a former top-ranked medalist in the sport. At the Athens Olympics in 2004, Jeff led his team to their first gold medal in 100 years. He's an expert on the topics of fencing, Olympic terrorism, coaching, youth sports, father-son relationships, teamwork, and the contributions of Jewish athletes. Jeff just published a sentimental memoir entitled Closing the Distance: Chasing a Father's Olympic Fencing Legacy.

Jeff Bukantz
Livingston, NJ USA
*Contact Phone:* 973-533-1845
*Cell:* 973-615-2150
**Click to Contact from Web Site**

## AROUND THE RINGS.COM
Atlanta, GA USA
http://www.aroundtherings.com

World's leading trade publication focusing on business, politics of Olympic Movement. News, information services include media guides, radio, internet. Newsmaker Breakfasts provide major source of news, interview opportunities during games.

Sheila S. Hula
*Publisher*
Around the Rings.com
Atlanta, GA USA
*Contact Phone:* 404-874-1603
**Click to Contact from Web Site**

## FRANK SCOBLETE -- CASINO GAMBLING EXPERT
New York, NY USA
http://www.goldentouchcraps.com

Frank Scoblete, casino gambling's #1 best-selling author of 20 books, and Dom Dice Dominator LoRiggio,the world's greatest controlled shooter at craps, have been beating the casinos for two decades. And they are now telling everyone how to do it! In their new book Golden Touch Dice Control Revolution! Frank and Dominator discuss how to beat the casino game of craps by using a controlled dice throw which changes the probabilities to favor the players. They also teach a new blackjack advantage-play method that is so easy to learn that most blackjack players can get an edge in a few hours of class time. Frank and Dominator have appeared on numerous television programs including the History Channel, A&E, the Travel Channel, CNN, the Learning Channel, Discovery Channel and TBS. They have also done hundreds of radio interviews. To get in touch with Frank Scoblete and Dice Dominator call 1-800-944-0406 or 516-596-0406.

Frank Scoblete
Frank Scoblete Enterprises
Malverne, NY USA
*Contact Phone:* 516-596-0406
*Cell:* 516-655-0575
**Click to Contact from Web Site**

## ARNIE WEXLER — ARNIE & SHEILA WEXLER ASSOCIATES
Bradley Beach, NJ USA
http://www.aswexler.com

Work with all aspects of compulsive gambling: counseling, referrals, public awareness, education, treatment, court cases, colleges, employee assistance programs, judicial systems, legislators, and gaming organizations. They have presented workshops and training seminars internationally. Arnie is the most quoted expert on compulsive gambling. Arnie is writing a book on gambling in America. They have authored many articles on compulsive gambling and sell a video tape on compulsive gambling. They have trained over 35,000 casino workers.

Arnie Wexler
Arnie & Sheila Wexler Associates
Bradley Beach, NJ
*Contact Phone:* 732-774-0019
*Cell:* 954-501-5270
**Click to Contact from Web Site**

## GAIL HOWARD -- LOTTERY EXPERT
Las Vegas, NV USA
www.gailhoward.com

Gail Howard has a solid background in the lottery. She has been a weekly columnist for 23 years for New York Lottery News. Publisher of Lottery Advantage monthly for six years, she was also the former lottery editor of Gambling Times Magazine. She is the author of seven books including Lottery Master Guide. Featured or quoted in Newsweek, US News & World Report, Family Circle, Playboy, The Wall Street Journal, Chicago Tribune, Newsday, The New York Times, and The Los Angeles Times to name just a few.

Gail Howard
Las Vegas, NV
*Contact Phone:* 800-945-4245
*Contact Main Phone:* 702-365-9270
**Click to Contact from Web Site**

## INTERNATIONAL COALITION OF ART DECO SOCIETIES (ICADS)
Boston, MA USA
http://decoicads.com/

Barbara Baer Capitman, founder of the Miami Design Preservation League (MDPL), created the concept for the World Congress on Art Deco® in 1989. During an organizing symposium held shortly before Ms. Capitman's death in 1990, the National Coalition of Art Deco Societies, later renamed the International Coalition of Art Deco Societies (ICADS), was born. ADSW is a member of ICADS. The enthusiastic response to the first World Congress, hosted by MDPL, led to the decision to continue the World Congress as a biennial event. ICADS, which selects the sites, adopted a policy of alternating between U.S. host cities and cities around the world. The most recent World Congress was held in NEW YORK CITY in 2005.

Fusco & Four Associates
West Roxbury, MA USA
*Contact Phone:* 617-363-0405
**Click to Contact from Web Site**

## THE ART AND CREATIVE MATERIALS INSTITUTE, INC.
Hanson, MA USA
http://www.acminet.org

ACMI certifies that art materials are nontoxic or properly labeled with any needed health warnings. ACMI creates a positive environment for art and creative materials usage, promotes safe use of these materials, and serves as an information and service resource. Look for the ACMI seals on art and creative materials.

Deborah M. Fanning, CAE
*Executive Vice President*
The Art and Creative Materials Institute, Inc.
Hanson, MA
*Contact Phone:* 781-293-4100
**Click to Contact from Web Site**

## WIZARD ENTERTAINMENT
New York, NY USA
www.wizarduniverse.com

Wizard Entertainment, with its monthly publications Wizard: The Comics Magazine, ToyFare: The Toy Magazine, InQuest Gamer: The Gaming Magazine and Anime Insider, serves as the leading authority in the areas of pop culture and collectibles. Whether you need to know the value of the hottest collectibles or want to gauge the temperature of fans about the next Spider-Man film, our staff can offer expert commentary on subjects including comics, toys, anime/manga, video games, movies, DVDs and the Internet.

Mel Caylo
Wizard Entertainment
Congers, NY USA
*Contact Phone:* 845-268-2000
**Click to Contact from Web Site**

## TIM WALSH — TOY EXPERT
Tampa, FL USA
http://www.theplaymakers.com

Interview game inventor and toy historian Tim Walsh, author of Timeless Toys (formerly The Playmakers). Tim shares rare playthings on TV, toy sound effects on radio, and toy stories galore from his book, including... How the creator of Slinky left his toy fortune and family to join a cult. How a doll made as a gag gift for men confirmed that the creation of Barbie was possible. Why PEZ candy first appeared in "cigarette lighter" dispensers. How a gold medalist in the 1908 Olympics later invented the Erector Set. And why Frank Lloyd Wright's son invented Lincoln Logs. Tim is the co-inventor of the TriBond and Blurt!, games which have sold over 4 million copies. He is a fifteen-year veteran of the toy industry and a sought-after speaker, having appeared on numerous TV and radio programs including CBS This Morning and NPR's All Things Considered. Find out more at: www.theplaymakers.com.

Tim Walsh
Sarasota, FL USA
*Contact Phone:* 941.926.8004
**Click to Contact from Web Site**

## DON'T QUOTE ME -- QUOTE EXPERTS
London, Ontario Canada
http://www.dontquoteme.com/

Don't Quote Me® harnesses the universal popularity of quotes in branded and co-branded products and services that include awardwinning games, merchandise and an interactive website. Don't Quote Me® has partnered with leading industry publishers - Sports Illustrated, TIME For Kids and TV Guide - to develop board games that are informative, fun to play and rich in content. Available to Journalists - syndicated radio and newspaper programs, interviews with the president, studio games for on-air play, prize giveaways, daily quote subscription, and more. Great games, great quotes! It's all at www.dontquoteme.com.

Nancy Joyal
*Director of Communications*
Don't Quote Me
London, ON Canada
*Contact Phone:* 519-439-0440
*Contact Main Phone:* 1-866-801-4263
**Click to Contact from Web Site**

## INSTITUTE FOR CHILDHOOD RESOURCES
San Francisco, CA USA
http://www.drtoy.com

Resources,expertise in play, toys, and children's product selection; child care; family issues. Author, consultant and frequent speaker. Dr. Stevanne Auerbach,Director, is popular contributor to media. Dr. Auerbach/Dr. Toy™ was Director of the world's first museum to promote play and appreciation of toys, The San Francisco International Toy Museum. Books include Dr. Toy's Smart Play/Smart Toys:How to Raise a Child with a High P.Q. (Play Quotient), Toys for a Lifetime: Enhancing Childhood Through Play,The Toy Chest, Choosing Child Care. Produces annual reports, 'Dr. Toy's 100 Best Children's Products' 'Best Vacation Products', 'Best Classic Products' and others on www.drtoy.com. Writes Dr.Toy syndicated column.

Stevanne Auerbach, Ph.D. (Dr. Toy)
*Consultant/Author/Speaker*
Institute for Childhood Resources
San Francisco, CA
*Contact Phone:* 415-864-1169
**Click to Contact from Web Site**

# Lottery Expert

## Gail Howard

### Solid Background in All Aspects of Lottery World

- Weekly columnist for 21 years for *New York Lotto News*
- Publisher of monthly *Lottery Advantage®*
- Former Lottery Editor of *Gambling Times* magazine
- Author of seven books including *Lottery Master Guide*, with foreign language editions in French, German, Spanish, Norwegian, Latvian, Chinese, Korean and Japanese

### Widely Quoted as Leading Authority on Lotteries

- Featured or quoted in *Newsweek, US News & World Report, Family Circle, Playboy, The Wall Street Journal, Chicago Tribune, New York Daily News, Newsday, The New York Times, Los Angeles Times, Washington Times* and dozens of others

### World Famous for Her Scientific Lottery Systems

- Developed scientific lottery systems in 1982 that have won more than $97 million for 74 first prize jackpot winners—all documented and on file
- Her remarkable track record in helping people become millionaires has led to appearances on hundreds of radio and television shows, including *The Today Show* and *Good Morning America*
- She tracks all Lotto games daily with her Smart Luck® software, enabling her to provide tips and valuable information on specific Lotto games for any state or country at any time

**Contact:**
**Gail Howard**
**SMART LUCK** Publishers & Software
Dept.Y-1, PO Box 81770
Las Vegas, Nevada 89180-1770

**1-800-945-4245 • 1-702-365-1818**

**1-702-365-9270**

**www.smartluck.com**
or **www.gailhoward.com**

## SCOTT TRAVERS - RARE COIN EXPERT
New York, NY USA
http://www.PocketChangeLottery.com

Find a fortune in your pocket change with Scott A. Travers -- the nation's number one most quoted coin expert. One of the most influential coin experts in the world. Author of best-selling, award winning books: The Coin Collector's Survival Manual --Fourth Edition; How to Make Money in Coins Right Now -- Second Edition (Random House); The Investor's Guide to Coin Trading (Wiley); One-Minute-Coin Expert -- Third Edition (Random House).

Scott A.Travers
*Rare Coin Expert*
Scott Travers Rare Coin Galleries, LLC
New York, NY
*Contact Phone:* 212-535-9136
**Click to Contact from Web Site**

## ANTOINETTE MATLINS, P.G.
Woodstock, VT USA
http://www.gemstonepress.com

Antoinette Matlins, P.G. (Professional Gemologist) is an internationally respected gemologist and jewelry expert and leading consumer advocate. She is available for interviews and to answer questions about diamonds, colored gems, pearls and jewelry in general. An independent expert, former gemology editor for National Jeweler Magazine and noted columnist, Matlins has been featured on ABC, CBS, NBC, CNBC and CNN, as well as in USA Today, US News & World Report and many national and international consumer and trade publications. She is author of seven leading books in the field, including Jewelry & Gems: The Buying Guide; Diamonds: The Antoinette Matlins Buying Guide; and The Pearl Book: The Definitive Buying Guide. Unaffiliated with any jewelry industry organization, Matlins' qualifications are unsurpassed. Her unique background has given her a vast knowledge of all aspects of the field and a keen understanding of what people really don't know, what they want to know and, perhaps most important, what they need to know-both good and bad. Whether the story is fashion, glamour, bridal, investment or consumer affairs-whether you're looking for a sparking newsmaker or a startling expose-Matlins' input can provide the brilliant angle you are searching for.

Antoinette Matlins, P.G.
*Author*
Gemstone Press
Woodstock, VT
*Contact Phone:* 802-457-5145
**Click to Contact from Web Site**

## GEMOLOGICAL INSTITUTE OF AMERICA
Carlsbad, CA USA
http://www.gia.edu

An independent nonprofit organization, the Gemological Institute of America (GIA) is recognized as the world's foremost authority in gemology. Established in 1931, GIA has translated its knowledge into the most respected gemological education available. In 1953, GIA created the International Diamond Grading System™. Through research, education, gemological laboratory services, and instrument development, GIA is dedicated to ensuring the public trust in gems and jewelry by upholding the highest standards of integrity, academics, science, and professionalism.

Alexander Angelle
*Senior Manager, Public Relations*
Gemological Institute of America
Carlsbad, CA
*Contact Phone:* 760-603-4112
**Click to Contact from Web Site**

## ACCESSORY BRAINSTORMS
New York, NY USA
http://www.accessorybrainstorms.com

Joan Lefkowitz is the president of Accessory Brainstorms, NYC. The company helps inventors with products in fashion, beauty, and lifestyle accessory categories get their products to market. We are the original marketers of TOPSY TAIL which sold $100,000,000 worldwide. As a licensing agency, we do sales and consulting from our New York showroom. Accessory Brainstorms is listed as a Good Guy on the UIA fraud website.

Joan Lefkowitz
Accessory Brainstorms
New York, NY USA
*Contact Phone:* 212 379-6363
**Click to Contact from Web Site**

# Tim Walsh, Toy Expert

Interview game inventor and toy historian Tim Walsh, author of "Timeless Toys" (formerly "The Playmakers: Amazing Origins of Timeless Toys"). Tim shares rare toys on TV, his "Sounds Like Fun" CD on radio and toy stories galore from his breathtakingly beautiful book, including . . . How in 1960, the creator of Slinky left his wife and six kids to join a cult in Bolivia. How Lilli, a doll made as a sexy gag gift for men in 1955,

confirmed that the creation of Barbie was possible. Why PEZ candy first appeared in dispensers that looked like cigarette lighters. How A.C. Gilbert won a gold medal at the 1908 Olympic games and later invented the Erector Set. And why Frank Lloyd Wright's son invented Lincoln Logs. Tim is the co-inventor of TriBond and Blurt!, board games which have sold more than 4 million copies around the world. He is a 15-year veteran of the toy industry and a sought-after speaker on toys, having appeared on TV and radio programs across the country, including CBS This Morning, CNN News and NPR's All Things Considered.

**www.theplaymakers.com**
**Tim Walsh**
**Sarasota, Florida**
**941.926.8004**

## HEADWEAR INFORMATION BUREAU — BUSH CASEY
New York, NY USA
http://www.hatsworldwide.com

As founder of the Headwear Information Bureau (HIB), Casey Bush is an articulate, knowledgeable, entertaining speaker and magazine fashion columnist who has been quoted extensively in newspapers and on TV. Representing the women's/men's hat industries, she started HIB 10 yeas ago as a resource for press, retailers and consumers. She has created several venues for hats: April as Straw Hat Month, September as Fall Hat Month, etc. which garner a wide range of publicity.

Casey Bush
Headwear Information Bureau
New York, NY USA
*Contact Phone:* 212-627-8333
**Click to Contact from Web Site**

## ENCORE STUDIOS
Clifton, NJ USA
http://www.encorestudios.com

Encore Studios is an industry leading manufacturer, designer and printer of wedding, Bar Bat Mitzvah and other social invitations, birth announcements, fine stationery and holiday cards. Their standards of quality, attention to detail, diversity of rich papers, striking type faces have inspired hundreds of thousands of consumers to choose an Encore invitation for their lifestyle event. They revolutionized their industry as the first company to offer envelope calligraphy addressing including being able to personalize each invitation with the guest's name. Noted individuals that purchased Encore include Star Jones Reynolds, Kevin Costner, Robert DeNiro, and Howard Stern. Their designs have won numerous International Greeting Card Association Awards including "Card of the Year".

Brian Lawrence
*Vice President of Sales and Marketing*
Encore Studios
Clifton, NJ USA
*Contact Phone:* 800-526-0497 x538
*Cell:* 2014461038
**Click to Contact from Web Site**

## GREG LAWSON -- WORLDWIDE SCENIC PHOTOGRAPHY
San Diego, CA USA
http://GregLawsonGalleries.com

Greg Lawson's travel itinerary is constant and purposeful: Taste the fruits of the earth. Savor them. Capture them. Share them. Worldwide landscape, nature, scenic and wildlife imagery have been his pursuits for some four decades. His work is not contrived and is always shot on location. Lawson has authored numerous photographic books (latest: Natural States™ ISBN 0-9762197-6-X). Visitors to his Walls of the World™ galleries are powerfully impacted by his strong and unique image presentations.

Kristina Lawson
Walls of the World
Ramona, CA USA
*Contact Phone:* 760-789-0543
**Click to Contact from Web Site**

## PHOTOSOURCE INTERNATIONAL
Osceola, WI USA
www.photosource.com

We are the meeting place for photographers who want to sell their stock photos, and for editors and art directors who want to buy them. For more than twenty-five years we've been helping photographers and photobuyers from our worldwide connected electronic cottage on our farm in western Wisconsin. Photo researchers seeking highly specific pictures use our free service to locate the SOURCE of images from our two million keywords at www.photosource.com.

Rohn Engh
*Director*
PhotoSource International
Osceola, WI USA
*Contact Phone:* 800-624-0266
**Click to Contact from Web Site**

## CONNIE BRANSILVER, NATURE PHOTOGRAPHER, WRITER, INSPIRATIONAL SPEAKER
Naples, FL USA
www.conniebransilver.com

Internationally known nature photographer, artist, author and speaker, Connie Bransilver, has photographed on all seven continents. She brings images and inspirational prose to audiences seeking clarity, passion, and purpose. Wild Love Affair: Essence of Florida's Native Orchids, and Florida's Unsung Wilderness: The Swamps, offer personal and spiritual explorations of wilderness. Her fine-art prints hang in institutions throughout the world. She captures the emotion of nature and brings it to viewers, readers and listeners.

Connie Bransilver
Naples, FL USA
*Contact Phone:* 239-649-6235
**Click to Contact from Web Site**

## BILL MEAD — BASEBALL GOES TO WAR
Bethesda, MD USA

Bill Mead is the author of Baseball Goes to War, a humorous and surprising account of our national pastime as it was played during World War II. With Williams, DiMaggio and other stars off to war, the major leagues featured a one-armed outfielder, a 15-year-old pitcher and aging retreads such as Pepper Martin and Jimmie Fox. Mead has also authored six other baseball books. He has appeared on The Today Show, and Good Morning America.

Bill Mead
Baseball Goes to War
Bethesda, MD
*Contact Phone:* 301-657-2234
**Click to Contact from Web Site**

# SCOTT A. TRAVERS
## RARE COIN EXPERT

**Find a fortune in your pocket change with Scott A. Travers. The world's Number One most quoted coin expert.**

WORTH $1,000

### THE MOST INFLUENTIAL COIN EXPERT ANYWHERE

▓ Author of bestselling, award-winning books: The Coin Collector's Survival Manual® (Random House), Find a fortune in your pocket change—One-Minute Coin Expert® (Random House), How to Make Money in Coins Right Now (Random House), The Investor's Guide to Coin Trading (Wiley), Travers' Rare Coin Investment Strategy (Simon & Schuster), Scott Travers' Top 88 Coins Over $100 (Random House), and the Insider's Guide to U.S. Coin Values 2007 (Random House).

### WIDELY QUOTED AND RESPECTED AS THE LEADING COIN AUTHORITY

▓ Interviewed on shows from Good Morning America to Inside Edition. Television network appearances include CNN, MSNBC, CNBC, FOX, Bloomberg, ABC, NBC, CBS, New Tang Dynasty, Univision, Telemundo, Reuters and Associated Press. Online features include the AOL Welcome screen. Radio interviews include Sirius Satellite Radio, National Public Radio, CBC Canada, NYSE Radio Network, Bloomberg and affiliates of CBS, ABC and NBC. Print includes the New York Times, Wall Street Journal, Barron's, Newsweek, Business Week and Christian Science Monitor.

SCOTT A. TRAVERS
RARE COIN EXPERT
NEW YORK, N.Y.
212-535-9136

TRAVERS@
POCKETCHANGELOTTERY.COM

## PAUL DICKSON — BASEBALL COMMENTATOR & AUTHOR

Washington, DC USA
PaulDicksonBooks.com/

Paul Dickson is a 63-year old writer with more than 40 books and several hundred magazine articles to his credit. Dickson loves to talk about baseball. He is author of The New Dickson Baseball Dictionary, The Joy of Keeping Score, Baseball's Greatest Quotations and Baseball, The President's Game. He is eager to grant interviews on his newest (June 2003) book entitled, The Hidden Language of Baseball: How Signs and Sign-Stealing Have Influenced the Course of Our National Pastime.

Paul Dickson
*Contact Phone:* (301) 942-5798
**Click to Contact from Web Site**

## CONNIE GORDON — GORDON GLOBAL CREATIVE CENTER

Miami, FL USA
http://www.connigordon.com

Conni Gordon, Certified Speaking Professional, has taught over 15,000,000 individuals around the world how to tap into their creative potential through her orginal, four-step art and TILS method. Her dynamic programs unlock the mind. They give everyone the power to believe in themselves, accomplish more, and become innovative problem-solvers. Best of all, Conni's sessions are FUN! Whether your event is for international dignitaries, executives, sales professionals, medical or legal professionals, entrepreneurs, students, spouses, and children Create with Conni is a proven winner....

Conni Gordon
Gordon Global Creative Center
Miami Beach, FL USA
*Contact Phone:* 305-532-1001
**Click to Contact from Web Site**

## BARBARA GARRO -- ELECTRIC ENVISIONS, INC.

Saratoga Springs, NY USA
http://www.ElectricEnvisions.com

ELECTRIC ENVISIONS supports your desire to commission images you choose, explore your desire to create art through painting, and maximize the ambiance of your living and working spaces. Subscribe to our Free GARRO TALK E-Newsletter

Barbara Garro
*Artist/Writer/Teacher -- GarroTalk*
Electric Envisions Art & Art Services
Electric Envisions Publications
Saratoga Springs, NY USA
*Contact Phone:* 518-587-9999
*Contact Main Phone:* 518-587-9999
**Click to Contact from Web Site**

## WASHINGTON ITALIA FILM FESTIVAL

Washington, DC USA
www.washingtonitalia.com

The festival, celebrating the Italian cinema in America, is produced by the Capri in the World Institute. In association with Cinecitta Holding (the Italian corporate film giant), Rai Trade and Lazio Region. In collaboration with Istituto Luce, A.I.P.-Audiovisual Industry Promotion, Union Camere, Italy-America Chamber of Commerce and Camera di Commercio, Agricoltura, Artigianato, Industria - Napoli. Under the patronage of the Presidenza del Consiglio dei Ministri, Italians Around the World Ministry, Italian Ministry of Culture, Campania Region, City di Capri, City of Anacapri, and the National Italian American Foundation.

Janet Staihar
Staihar & Assoc.
Washington, DC USA
*Contact Phone:* 202-237-2080
**Click to Contact from Web Site**

## NAMM, THE INTERNATIONAL MUSIC PRODUCTS ASSOCIATION

Carlsbad, CA USA
www.namm.com

Over the past century, NAMM has proudly represented the industry that brings the gift of music into people's lives. What started in May of 1901 as a small, grassroots organization of 52 founding Members has since blossomed into an international association representing nearly 9,000 retailers and manufacturers of musical instruments and products from 85 countries worldwide. Everything NAMM does is intended to serve its Members and realize its mission of unifying, leading and strengthening the global music products industry and increasing active participation in music making.

Scott Robertson
NAMM, The international Music Products Association
Carlsbad, CA USA
*Contact Phone:* 760-438-8007
*Contact Main Phone:* 800-767-NAMM
*Cell:* 760 4388001
**Click to Contact from Web Site**

## WORLDFEST-HOUSTON

Houston, TX USA
http://www.worldfest.org

WorldFest was founded 46 years ago as Cinema Arts, an International Film Society in August, 1961. WorldFest became the third competitive international film festival in North America, following San Francisco and New York. WorldFest is the oldest Independent Film & Video Festival in the World. It evolved into a competitive International Film Festival in April, 1968. It was founded by award-winning producer/director Hunter Todd to present a quality film festival for the Independent filmmakers. The mission/vision statement of WorldFest is to recognize and honor outstanding creative excellence in film & video, to validate brilliant abilities and to promote cultural tourism for Houston, to develop film production in the region and to add to the rich cultural fabric of the city of Houston.

Hunter Todd
WorldFest
Houston, TX USA
*Contact Phone:* 713-965-9955
**Click to Contact from Web Site**

## MENC: THE NATIONAL ASSOCIATION FOR MUSIC EDUCATION
Reston, VA USA
http://www.menc.org

The world's largest arts education organization and the only association that addresses all aspects of music education. Nearly 120,000 members represent all levels of teaching from pre-school to graduate. Best resource for information on music education trends, advocacy, research and publications, including National Standards for Arts Education. Advocacy initiatives include The National Anthem Project, Music In Our Schools Month, and the World's Largest Concert.

Elizabeth W. Lasko
*Director, Public Relations*
MENC: The National Association for Music Education
Reston, VA
*Contact Phone:* 703-860-4000
**Click to Contact from Web Site**

## AZITA ZENDEL — INDEPENDENT HOLLYWOOD FILM MAKER
Los Angeles, CA USA
www.TheHollywoodApprentice.com

Azita Zendel is the writer-producer-director of the movie CONTROLLED CHAOS, a hilarious tale of a Hollywood Assistant based on her four years as Oliver Stone's assistant, when he directed JFK, HEAVEN & EARTH, NATURAL BORN KILLERS and NIXON. Azita Zendel is also the author of the career guidebook HOLLYWOOD APPRENTICE: How to Break Into Hollywood & Survive the Toxic Boss Syndrome. Azita Zendel has appeared as a guest expert on numerous national radio and local TV shows, with hosts of such varied opinion as National Public Radio's Warren Olney and KABC's Larry Elder. Azita Zendel has been extensively featured in several books, The New Yorker magazine, The New York Times, The International Herald Tribune, The Los Angeles Times, and many other newspapers. Azita Zendel's talking points are just as varied, and reflect her diverse background and experience. Azita Zendel has lectured for prestigious organizations like the Simon Wiesenthal Center and the Jewish Federation of Greater Los Angeles.

Azita Zendel
New York, NY USA
*Contact Phone:* 310-475-3773
**Click to Contact from Web Site**

## DALE BOWMAN — THE LIFE AND DEATH OF LYNYRD SKYNYRD BASSIST LEON WILKESON
Jacksonville, FL USA
leonsmurder.com

To Be a Final Friend: The life and death of Lynyrd Skynyrd Bassist Leon Wilkeson. Take a look behind the scenes of a band that was one of the originators of the Southern Rock sound. Get to know the real Leon, a talented but simple man with a kind, generous, fun-loving soul. Told from the viewpoint of Leon's friend and manager, Dale Bowman, this is a tale that will be cherished by Skynyrd fans and enjoyed by everyone. Available June, 2005, ISBN 0-971809-98-4. USA
**Click to Contact from Web Site**

## BIG HORSE INCORPORATED
San Francisco, CA USA
www.bighorse.com

Fortune Magazine, The Philadelphia Inquirer, USA Today, The Black Film Report, 20th Century Fox, Walt Disney Company, Eastman Kodak, the Institute for Independent Film Finance and a host of indie producers recognize Big Horse Inc. as the only analyst with a complete understanding of the film business landscape, from the economics of marketplace performance through demographics for independents and the studios alike.

Jeffrey N. Hardy
*President*
Big Horse Incorporated
San Francisco, CA USA
*Contact Phone:* 310 593 4616
*Contact Main Phone:* 310 593 4616
**Click to Contact from Web Site**

## OSIE JACKSON & LONDA WOODY, ENTERTAINMENT PROMOTER FOR ELVIS PRESLEY
Franklin, NC USA
http://www.osiejackson.com

Osie Jackson, famed entertainment manager/promoter for Elvis, The Stamps, The Blackwoods, Alabama, and other famous county western/gospel stars of the 60s and 70s is releasing his autobiography in time for Elvis Presley's 70th birthday, January 2006. Mr. Jackson's book, Shaking Hands with Fame: Memoirs of an Entertainment Promoter, will include personal stories from the road and backstage with the stars. Also included are over 75 never-before-seen photos from his personal collection. Jackson is availble for interview.

Osie Jackson & Londa Woody
*Entertainment Promoter for Elvis Presley*
Osie Jackson
Axiom Publishing
Franklin, NC USA
*Contact Phone:* 828-349-3722
**Click to Contact from Web Site**

## SPECIALIZED INFORMATION PUBLISHERS ASSOCIATION, FORMERLY NEPA
Washington, DC USA
www.sipaonline.com

The association formally announced it is changing its name to the Specialized Information Publishers Association, a change the board agreed to earlier this year. Mayer said that name change is symptomatic of the broader shifts in the industry and the association. The deeper the board delved into the objections prospective companies had to joining our association — companies that do all the things yours and mine do — the more even I came to appreciate that the term newsletter was no longer an attraction to these companies, he said. That doesn't mean they don't produce newsletters or that the association won't continue to provide support and services to newsletter publishers, he said. Incoming President Nancy McMeekin echoed Mayer at another presentation during the conference, noting that the association's reason for being has not changed. Let no one say newsletters are no longer important to us, she said. It's just that most of us are doing so much more.

Patricia Wysocki
Specialized Information Publishers Association
McLean, VA USA
*Contact Phone:* 703-610-0260
**Click to Contact from Web Site**

## OVERSEAS PRESS CLUB OF AMERICA
New York, NY USA
www.opcofamerica.org

The OPC, founded in 1939, is a professional organization that sponsors awards in journalism, actively upholds freedom of the press globally, supports student scholarships, maintains a network of reciprocal press clubs worldwide, and presents panel discussions, book nights, and prominent world figures. It publishes a monthly newsletter and an annual awards journal.

Sonya K. Fry
*Executive Director*
Overseas Press Club of America
New York, NY
*Contact Phone:* 212-626-9220
**Click to Contact from Web Site**

## AMERICAN SOCIETY OF JOURNALISTS AND AUTHORS (ASJA)
New York, NY USA
www.asja.org

The nation's leading organization of freelance non-fiction writers offers unparalleled services tailored to the unique needs of independent writers: Network via 2 online special interest groups. Our monthly newsletter includes a confidential survey of magazine payment rates, book advances, contract provisions as well as candid evaluations of individual editors. ASJA Writers Search matches members with lucrative writing projects with corporations, publishers and nonprofit organizations that have ranged from the DuPont Company to the Harvard School of Public Heath, Reader's Digest and the Pew Charitable Trusts. ASJA Contracts Committee, the nation's premier information clearing-house on publishing contracts, sponsors Contracts Watch, our most up-to-date electronic report on contract terms, copyright issues and industry developments. ASJA's Annual Writers Conferences attract the nation's leading writers, editors, agents and publishers for candid and wide-ranging discussions of markets and trends in book and magazine publishing and new media. ASJA is also your best source for comment on media-related issues: * Writing contracts * Electronic Rights * Copyright Issues * Freelance earnings * Censorship Issues * New Media * 1st Amendment Issues * Journalistic Ethics * Publishing Industry

Anne Peace
*Executive Director*
ASJA (American Society of Journalists and Authors)
New York, NY USA
*Contact Phone:* 212 997-0947
**Click to Contact from Web Site**

## SOCIETY OF PROFESSIONAL JOURNALISTS
Indianapolis, IN USA
http://www.spj.org

The Society of Professional Journalists works to improve and protect journalism. The organization is the nation's largest and most broad-based journalism organization, dedicated to encouraging the free practice of journalism and stimulating high standards of ethical behavior. Founded in 1909 as Sigma Delta Chi, SPJ promotes the free flow of information vital to a well-informed citizenry, works to inspire and educate the next generation of journalists, and protects First Amendment guarantees of freedom of speech and press.

Terry Harper
*Executive Director*
Society of Professional Journalists
Indianapolis, IN
*Contact Phone:* 317-927-8000
**Click to Contact from Web Site**

## THE NEWS COUNCIL CORPORATION
Washington, DC USA
www.NewsCouncil.org

We identify important public affairs issues which may require public relations help — issues that, with greater information, can increase better understanding by all Americans. We ask public relations executives to donate non-peak time to assist non-profits. We match non-profits with public relations execs willing to volunteer their expertise. We ask firms which provide public relations services to donate or provide reduced prices for their services, bandwidth, advertising space and executive time for assistance: Addiction, Adoption, Credit Awareness, Crime, Diabetes, Diet, Education, Heart Attack, Homelessness, Families, Heart Attack, Pets as Therapy, Suicide.

Mitchell Davis
News Council Corporation
Washington, DC USA
*Contact Phone:* 202-333-5000
**Click to Contact from Web Site**

## NATIONAL WRITERS UNION
Davie, FL USA
http://www.nwuatlarge.org

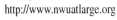

Helping Freelance Writers Succeed is the central promise of the National Writers Union's At-Large chapter, also known as UAW Local 1981. Benefits of membership include contract and grievance advice; access to valuable collective resources; colleagueship and community; training opportunities; a national voice in conversations that matter; an open invitation to participate in local, state and national political activism; freelance press credentials; and membership in the labor movement through our affiliation with International Union, UAW.

Seth Eisenberg
*Co-Chair*
National Writers Union
At-Large Chapter
Davie, FL USA
*Contact Phone:* (877) 411-2539
*Contact Main Phone:* (954) 252-9090
*Cell:* (954) 554-3306
**Click to Contact from Web Site**

## LINDA HUNT — MEDIA CRITIC
Washington, DC USA

Provocative commentary on TV news, media ethics, women in television. This former CNN reporter and author of Secret Agenda: The U.S. Government, Nazi Scientists and Project Paperclip (St. Martin's Press) is available on short notice for talk shows or commentary. Recent appearances include ABC's PrimeTime Live, MSNBC, NPR. Current media topics are a specialty.

Linda Hunt
*Media Critic*
Washington, DC
*Contact Phone:* 305-292-2784
**Click to Contact from Web Site**

## THE NEWSEUM
Washington, DC USA
http://www.newseum.org

The Newseum - the interactive museum of news - is scheduled to open in 2007 at its new address on Pennsylvania Avenue in Washington, D.C. The 215,000-square-foot museum will help further the public's understanding of news media through six levels of visitor experiences including an Interactive Newsroom and an extensive News History Gallery. The Newseum's operations are funded by the Freedom Forum, a nonpartisan foundation dedicated to free press, free speech and free spirit for all people.

Michael Fetters
*Director of Communication*
Newseum
Arlington, VA USA
*Contact Phone:* 703-284-2895
**Click to Contact from Web Site**

## THE FREEDOM FORUM
Arlington, VA USA
http://www.freedomforum.org

The Freedom Forum is a nonpartisan foundation dedicated to free press, free speech and free spirit for all people. The foundation focuses on three priorities: the Newseum, First Amendment and newsroom diversity. The Freedom Forum funds the operations of the Newseum, an interactive museum of news under construction in Washington D.C.; the First Amendment Center; and the Diversity Institute. It was established in 1991 and is supported by income from an endowment of diversified assets.

Michael Fetters
*Director of Commnications*
Newseum
Arlington, VA
*Contact Phone:* 703-284-2895
**Click to Contact from Web Site**

## RADIO FREE ASIA
Washington, DC USA
http://www.rfa.org

Radio Free Asia (RFA) is a private, nonprofit news organization dedicated to broadcasting news and information to people in those Asian countries where thorough, objective, and balanced news reporting is unavailable. RFA can offer extensive expertise on international broadcasting, international newsgathering, and a range of Northeast Asian and Southeast Asian issues and countries, including China.

Sarah Jackson-Han
*Director of Communications*
Radio Free Asia
Washington, DC USA
*Contact Phone:* 202-530-7774
*Cell:* 202-907-4613
**Click to Contact from Web Site**

## ON THIS SPOT PRODUCTIONS — WASHINGTON D.C. HISTORIAL INFORMATION
Washington, DC USA

On This Spot Productions to Publish Local/ Regional History. Paul Dickson and Douglas Evelyn announce the formation of On This Spot Productions as a publisher of local history, concentrating initially on Washington, D.C. and the Capital Region. The Washington area's rich history is interconnected with national history yet underrepresented in new books, educational publications, and materials for students and families.

Paul Dickson
On This Spot Productions
Garrett Park, MD USA
*Contact Phone:* 301-942-5798
**Click to Contact from Web Site**

## ELSA MCKEITHAN — LIVING HISTORY CONSULTANT
Winston-Salem, NC USA
http://www.TalkingStonesPublishing.com

Our theme is change, transformation and personal growth that radiates from the individual into the world. We publish books that bring you inspiration for self-expression, practical wisdom and how-to knowledge. For more about Talking Stones Publishing and our projects, see the Talking Stones page. Are you writing a memoir or autobiography? Sign up for our free newsletter, Stone Soup. We work cooperatively and interactively with memoir writers. If you would like to find out about our coaching and editing services, see the Writers page or click here to go directly to Writing with Elsa.

Elsa McKeithan
Winston-Salem, NC USA
*Contact Phone:* 336-774-7655
**Click to Contact from Web Site**

## DALE POWELL - CHRISTMAS STORYTELLER, TRADITION SHARER & CHRISTMAS TRIVIA
Lucasville, OH USA
www.dalepowell.com

Dale Powell is a educator who has become an edutainer. He still teaches at a middle school and a university, but manages to bring his speaking, acting, and storytelling talents via radio and TV as well as traveling up 50 days per year. Dale's expertise lies in holidays (particularly Christmas, but he does them all) and is the author of the Dickens World sequel to A Christmas Carol. His one man shows include The Transformation of Ebenezer Scrooge and Poe for Tonight.

Dale Powell
Lucasville, OH USA
*Contact Phone:* 1-888-750-4802
**Click to Contact from Web Site**

## QSTAT USA INC — DR. PHILIP TRUSCOTT — STATISTICS EXPERT
New York, NY USA
http://www.TheDataAlmanac.com

Dr Philip Truscott, Statistics Expert is the chief programmer of the ultra fast statistical program, QStat, which was independently assessed as the fastest available statistical program by British Census users. He is Editor of The Data Almanac which packages a fact book with the largest collection of survey data ever published on a single CD-ROM disk. His work focuses on making statistical data access to the layman/woman emphasizing data on health, crime, housing, education and consumer spending.

Philip Truscott
Jersey City, NJ USA
*Contact Phone:* 201-626-6243
**Click to Contact from Web Site**

## NATIONAL FLAG FOUNDATION
Pittsburgh, PA USA
www.americanflags.org

Flags - Our Most Articulate Symbols. Why did the founders of the Republic call it: a new constellation? What about Betsy? When and how do I half-staff? Can I fly it at night? Hoist your phone and let your listeners' flag questions fly to NFF, the world's largest flag association at Flag Plaza, The Flag Heart of America! The Library of Congress and The US Information Agency send Flag etiquette questions to NFF. Enjoy inspiring Americana stories and ... Be sure to learn what happened on July 4, 1788 to Liberty's Five Flags!

Joyce Doody
*Executive Director*
National Flag Foundation
Pittsburgh, PA
*Contact Phone:* 412-261-1776
**Click to Contact from Web Site**

## ANGELS OVER AMERICA
Columbia, MD USA
www.AngelsOverAmerica.org

Angels Over America, 9/11 Memorial DVD, celebrates victims and heroes. A spectacular tribute to 9/11 victims and heroes, Carolyn Long's video, Angels Over America, brings an entirely new perspective to this pivotal moment in our nation's history. "It is dedicated to an America that lost its innocence on this day—but never its hope," says Long, poet and executive producer of this stirring memorial DVD. "The events of 9/11 will be a part of the American consciousness forever. How they are held there will shape our future," says Long. Angels Over America celebrates the courage and resilience that are the hallmarks of the American Spirit, while providing perspective, healing, and hope. Award-winning New York arranger and producer Mark Freeh created the video from Ms. Long's poem, Angels Over America, against the backdrop of his stirring arrangement of America the Beautiful, and moving renditions of Amazing Grace, and My Country 'Tis of Thee. A free, preview version of the video can be viewed or downloaded from the website at www.AngelsOverAmerica.org. The final version of the DVD with poem, or a printed copy of Angels Over America, can be ordered online from the website, by email from Carolyn@AngelsOverAmerica.com or by calling 410-730-2345. Carolyn Long is a professional speaker, consultant and writer based in Columbia, MD. She can be reached at Pratt Publishing, Inc., 410-730-2345, or via email to Carolyn@AngelsOverAmerica.com

Carolyn Long
*Author, Executive Producer*
Angels Over America
Columbia, MD USA
*Contact Phone:* 410-730-2345
*Contact Main Phone:* 410-730-2345
*Cell:* 443-250-0222
**Click to Contact from Web Site**

## HISTORY PUBLISHING COMPANY, LLC
New York, NY USA
http://www.historyscope.com

An experienced speaker, author, political campaign director, business leader and historian, Don Bracken serves as Senior Editor of the History Publishing Company, a firm dedicated to the study of American history through modern technology. A witness to and a participant of historical events, he brings to any forum in which he appears, first hand accounts of stories that will both inform and entertain. He is the author of the recently released book Times of the Civil War and the co-editor of the widely acclaimed Civil War Historyscope Series.

Don Bracken
History Publishing Company,LLC
Palisades, NY USA
*Contact Phone:* 845-359-1765
**Click to Contact from Web Site**

## ELLYNANNE GEISEL -- NOT SO DESPERATE HOUSEWIFE A/K/A THE APRON LADY
Pueblo, CO USA
www.ApronMemories.com

Essayist, storyteller and artifact guardian, EllynAnne Geisel, a/k/a The Apron Lady, lives on Not So Desperate Lane, Pueblo, Colorado. She is the writer and apron curator for her traveling exhibition APRON CHRONICLES: A Patchwork of American Recollections, a touring speaker with her platform program APRON MEMORIES, and the owner/designer of APRON MEMORIES®, her collection of inventive vintage and inspired nostalgia aprons. EllynAnne's national press includes Time, Good Housekeeping, Country Living,Chicken Soup for the Soul magazine and the Wall Street Journal. THE APRON BOOK: MAKING, WEARING AND SHARING A BIT OF CLOTH AND COMFORT by EllynAnne Geisel and Foreward by Ellen Levine, Editor-in-Chief Good Housekeeping magazine, will be published by Andrews McMeel, September 2006.

Ellyn Anne Geisel
Apron Memories
Pueblo, CO USA
*Contact Phone:* 719-545-5704
**Click to Contact from Web Site**

## THE BONUS ARMY — AN AMERICAN EPIC
Garrett Park, MD USA
http://www.thebonusarmy.com

The Bonus Army: An American Epic. During the Depression summer of 1932, some 45,000 World War I veterans marched on Washington, D.C. to demand immediate payment of a cash bonus promised eight years earlier. They lived in shantytowns, white and black together, and for two months protested peacefully. Then, on July 28, Army Chief of Staff Douglas MacArthur, going beyond orders from President Herbert Hoover, drove out the veterans with tanks, tear gas, and bayonets. His reluctant aide was Major Dwight D. Eisenhower and among the cavalry troops swinging sabers was Major George S. Patton. The eviction helped to defeat Hoover and elect Franklin D. Roosevelt. But he also opposed the bonus, offering them only work camps. In 1935, some 250 of them, trapped on Florida keys, were killed by the worst hurricane ever to strike the United States. Their epic story went on, however, and out of tragedy came triumph: the GI Bill, the most important social legislation in American history. As America will soon be dealing with a new group of veterans from a new war the story of the Bonus Army has timely overtones.

Paul Dickson
*Co-Author*
Garrett Park, MD USA
*Contact Phone:* 301-942-5798
**Click to Contact from Web Site**

## HOLLIS PR ANNUAL

Teddington, Middlesex United Kingdom

http://www.hollis-pr.com

Widely acclaimed as the bible of the P.R. industry in the United Kingdom. It's the shop window for all U.K. PR consultancies, and the source for thousands of in-house PR contacts. Also - Hollis Europe (guide to consultancies throughout the continent), Hollis Sponsorship (guide to major sponsoring companies and events) and Hollis Business Entertainment (annual guide to corporate hospitality). A.S.K Hollis - The Directory of UK Associations; Advertisers Annual; Marketing Handbook; Showcase - International Music Business Guide.

Gary Zabel
*Managing Director*
Hollis PR Annual
Teddington, Middlesex, England
*Contact Phone:* + 44 20 8977-7711
**Click to Contact from Web Site**

## SOURCES

Toronto, Ontario Canada

http://www.sources.com

Sources is Canada's directory for journalists, writers and researchers. Sources provides 5,000 experts and spokespersons ready to answer questions on thousands of topics, including: Canadian trade with Cuba, universal Medicare coverage, cultural protectionism, U.S.-Canada trade issues, cross-border pollution, wilderness preservation, Arctic air masses, gun control, Quebec separatism, dealing with crime, public broadcasting, agricultural subsidies, and drug smuggling — plus a selection of links to the best Internet sites for journalists and researchers.

Mr. Ulli Diemer
Sources
Toronto, Ontario Canada
*Contact Phone:* 416-964-7799
**Click to Contact from Web Site**

## NATIONAL CARTOONISTS SOCIETY

Orlando, FL USA

http://www.reuben.org

We know cartoonists! Looking for information on comics, cartoons, cartoon history, humorous illustration, greeting cards, and the people who draw and write all that funny stuff? The National Cartoonists Society has it all. We're the oldest, largest organization of cartoonists in the U.S. Contact us if you need a resource for a story, a quote, or just background information about the business and the people in it.

Mary Anne Grimes
National Cartoonists Society
Kansas City, MO
*Contact Phone:* 212-293-8626
**Click to Contact from Web Site**

## BOB STAAKE

Catham, MA USA

http://www.BobStaake.com

Cartoonist Bob Saake's has published 17 books, including Jay Leno's Headlines, Humor and Cartoon Markets, and children's books such as POP!, BOING and SPLISH. His work has appeared on everything from mugs to Hallmark cards to The Ren and Stimpy Show. Another animated series, Cop and Donut Show, based entirely on Bob's drawings and character designs, will debut soon on Nickelodeon.

Bob Staake
Catham, MA
*Contact Phone:* 508-945-0191
**Click to Contact from Web Site**

## AMY BORKOWSKY, AUTHOR AND COMEDIAN

New York, NY USA

http://www.SendAmy.com

The witty and insightful creator of the hit CDs and book AMY'S ANSWERING MACHINE: MESSAGES FROM MOM , and author of STATEMENTS: TRUE TALES OF LIFE, LOVE, AND CREDIT CARD BILLS has made appearances from 'Today' to NPR. Amy's collection of hilarious phone messages from her overprotective mother offer perspective on how mothers refuse to acknowledge we're adults, and she's an engaging authority on how credit card bills are a diary, chronicling how we literally spend our lives.

Amy Borkowsky
Amy Borkowsky Productions, Inc.
New York, NY USA
*Contact Phone:* 212-481-2979
**Click to Contact from Web Site**

**HOLLAND COOKE -- PODCASTING EXPERT**
Block Island, RI USA
http://www.HollandCooke.com

In the thirty five years Mr. Cooke has toiled in the radio/TV vineyard, he's survived a variety of on-air and management positions, not the least of which was his 7 storied years as Operations Manager of WTOP/Washington, during which time 1500AM scored its highest ratings ever as an all-news station. Ever! Undaunted, HC then became a founding partner of USA TODAY Sky Radio, the live-via-satellite News, Sports, and Talk audio channels heard on Delta, Northwest, and United Airlines. Though he consistently declines comment when asked if he's the same Holland Cooke heard on WBIG-FM/Washington, Cooke smiles wistfully when remembered as WPRO/Providence evening DJ in the '70s. Today, his tireless work includes programming and marketing strategies for Talk radio stations from Alaska to New Zealand, career counseling for radio talent, and Internet development for entrepreneurs, companies, and radio personalities.

Holland Cooke
Block Island, RI USA
*Contact Phone:* 401-330-6868
**Click to Contact from Web Site**

**PODSWAP**
Miami, FL USA
http://www.podswap.com

The PodSwap staff are experts in the use, trouble-shooting, repair, market pricing, and consumer satisfaction levels of the iPod portable music player. We are the first and foremost name in the emerging industry of iPod recycling, repair, re-use, and salvagability. We were the first company to sell used, warrantied iPods to the retail public. Podswap singlehandedly created and continues to innovate the used iPod and iPod upgrade market. More information about our company is available at http://www.podswap.com.

Gregg Radell
Podswap.com
Miami, FL United State
*Contact Phone:* 305.256.5905
**Click to Contact from Web Site**

**DAN POYNTER -- BOOK PUBLISHING INDUSTRY EXPERT**
Santa Barbara, CA USA
http://ParaPublishing.com

Book writing, publishing/self-publishing expert. Dan Poynter: Author (100+ books), Publisher (since 1969), Speaker (CSP). Web site has more than 500 pages of helpful information including statistics on the book publishing industry. History, trends and predictions on printed books and eBooks. Author of Writing Nonfiction, Is There a Book Inside You?, The Self-Publishing Manual, The Skydiver's Handbook, The Parachute Manual, The Expert Witness Handbook and many more.

Dan Poynter
*Author-Publisher-Speaker*
Para Publishing
Santa Barbara, USA
*Contact Phone:* 805-968-7277
*Cell:* 805-448-9009
**Click to Contact from Web Site**

### HARRY HUSTED
Bronx, NY USA

Creating Words is a b2b media company that is dedicated to helping people learn to be better communicators. We are in the market to help your business grow by providing consulting services in the form of writing or other types of communication. We are about helping your business achieve your main goal - to be more profitable. We also help individuals who wish to better their writing for personal or business reasons.

Harry Husted
Creating Words
Bronx, NY USA
*Contact Phone:* 3473989787
*Cell:* 7183081566
**Click to Contact from Web Site**

### SMALL PUBLISHERS ASSOCIATION OF NORTH AMERICA
Colorado Springs, CO USA
http://www.spannet.org/

SPAN is a nonprofit trade association dedicated to advancing the interests and expertise of independent publishers through educational opportunities and discounted services. Publishing is a business, and we strive to help our members flourish in this competitive market. SPAN helps publishers gain increased visibility, more sales, and larger profits.

Scott Flora
Small Publishers Association of North America
Colorado Springs, CO USA
*Contact Phone:* 719-475-1726
**Click to Contact from Web Site**

### AGM BOOKS — PARVEZ ABEDIN (INDIA)
Mumbai (Bombay), India
http://www.agmbooks.com

AGM BOOKS, Mumbai, INDIA A young and dynamic self publishing consultancy based in India invites first-time aspiring authors/experts to explore the self-publishing route at highly affordable costs. International writers / experts exploring Indian market are welcome ! WE OFFER: 1) Highly affordable book design-production-editing-printing & POD services. Unbeatable cost, world class quality. 2) Nation-wide book distribution/marketing, backed by India's largest book distributors. Email us : feedback@agmbooks.com or visit us at www.agmbooks.com

Parvez Abedin
*Proprietor*
AGM BOOKS
Mumbai, AL INDIA
*Contact Phone:* 91-22-56315170
*Cell:* 9.19821E+11
**Click to Contact from Web Site**

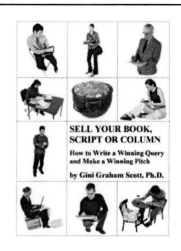

### PUBLISHERSANDAGENTS.NET
San Francisco, CA USA
www.PublishersandAgents.net

Publishers and Agents.Net connects writers with publishers, literary agents, syndicates, film producers, production companies, and film agents. We also have two additional services to connect screenplay writers with the film industry through www.screenplaywritersconnection.com and songwriters with music publishers, record labels, and music agents and managers at www.songwritingconnection.com. Additionally, we now connect entrepreneurs with venture capitalists through www.venturecapitalconnection.com. We can also help you write book proposals and film scripts. Call 510-339-1625 for details on additional services.

Gini Graham Scott
*Creative Director*
PublishersandAgents.net
Oakland, CA USA
*Contact Phone:* 510-339-1625
**Click to Contact from Web Site**

### EXPERT AUTHORS
San Francisco, CA USA
http://www.roninpub.com/rn_mediacontact.html

Books for Independent Minds. Ronin authors are leading experts in their respective fields and happy to assist you with your research.

Beverly Potter
*Contact Phone:* 510-420-3669
**Click to Contact from Web Site**

## DANDELION BOOKS, LLC - DYNAMIC LITERATURE EXPERTS!
Tempe, AZ USA
http://www.dandelionbooks.net/

Amazing, Shocking News & Views. . . Conscious Solutions: Learn how to turn every crisis into a creative challenge. . . Tap in to Secrets of the Ancients for living longer, healthier and better! Learn about alternatives to expensive, potentially dangerous, life-threatening medical procedures. . . Audacious, Outrageous Fiction. . . The Human Experience in the raw! Rip-Roaring Adventure. . . Belly-Laugh Books that will make you howl & and hold your sides!!

Carol Adler, MFA
*President*
Dandelion Books, LLC
Tempe, AZ USA
*Contact Phone:* 1-800-861-7899
**Click to Contact from Web Site**

## R. BRENT AND COMPANY PUBLISHING
Asheville, NC USA
www.rbrent.com

R.BrentandCompany, a publishing and consulting company since 1995, has served more than 100 clients. We empower individuals and companies to create and share their legacies through books, the internet, and other interactive media. We publish works that reflect our clients' expertise, passion and mission. Our authors have extensive experience and knowledge in their fields, and are highly articulate, educated and passionate. All are available for interviews, articles, speaking engagements and other media events.

Robbin Brent Whittington
R. Brent and Co. Publishing
Asheville, NC USA
*Contact Phone:* 828-299-0977
**Click to Contact from Web Site**

## THIN BOOK PUBLISHING COMPANY
Bend, OR USA
http://www.thinbook.com

We are dedicated to providing you with easy to read books that deliver information about how organizations work. We are experts in Appreciative Inquiry and change management. Enjoy our newest book, Appreciative Inquiry in the Catholic Church by Susan Star Paddock.

Rand Hammond
Thin Book Publishing Co.
Bend, OR USA
*Contact Phone:* 1-888-316-9544
*Cell:* 541-390-7364
**Click to Contact from Web Site**

## TERRI KAY
Elkhart, IN USA
http://www.terrikay.com

The author, a graduate of Indiana University and University of Wisconsin Law School, used her legal and medical expertise to create the crime story series, A Promise of Revenge, consisting of thriller books, and more. Her book guides and web site include topics like relationships, bullying, domestic abuse, and self esteem. From discounts to book clubs, to crossword puzzles and word search activities, to online promotion of guest authors, the series offers education and entertainment.

Terri Kay
*Contact Phone:* 574 875-0866
**Click to Contact from Web Site**

## MARILYN ROSS — SELF-PUBLISHING RESOURCES
Denver, CO USA
http://SelfPublishingResources.com

Self publishing can be a wonderful solution for getting into print. It puts you in control of your own destiny and positions you to be a lot more profitable than going with a typical royalty publisher. In self publishing you keep approximately 60% of the profits instead of less than the $1 most royalty publishers offer. You control percentages, order fullfillment, promotiom, book marketing, sales, and negotiate your own rights and after market deals. Yet it involves a lot of details, decisions, and determination. For some people it feels overwhelming. That's why Self Publishing Resources exists! We've Been there, Done that over and over to save you from making expensive mistakes. We're like a handy Swiss Army knife: we have all the tools to lead you to greater success and profits. Marilyn and Tom Ross, considered the gurus of self publishing, welcome you! You can trust these highly experienced, award-winning professionals. Since 1977, they have self-published 13 of their own books. With their consulting help, thousands of writers just like you have produced and sold millions of books. Their best-selling Complete Guide to Self-Publishing has racked up book sales of over 100,000 copies and continues to receive rave reviews.

Marilyn Ross
Buena Vista, CO USA
*Contact Phone:* 719-395-8659
*Cell:* 719-395-2227
**Click to Contact from Web Site**

## EXECUTIVE COACHING & CONSULTING ASSOCIATES
Washington, DC USA
www.exe-coach.com

Will your organization's culture develop healthy leader-follower relationships or frustrated whistle-blowers? Ira Chaleff, President of Executive Coaching & Consulting Associates and author of The Courageous Follower: Standing Up To and For Our Leaders poses this challenging question. Ira is one of the few thought-leaders in the world on 'leader-follower' relations. The second and expanded edition of his classic book has just been released (Berrett-Koehler, 2003). He is available for interviews, speeches, workshops and executive coaching.

Ira Chaleff
*President*
Executive Coaching & Consulting Associates
Kensington, MD USA
*Contact Phone:* 301-933-3752
**Click to Contact from Web Site**

## YEARBOOK OF EXPERTS ®
Washington, DC USA
www.Yearbook.com

1984 First edition of the Yearbook published -- The Talk Show Guest Directory -- 750 copies of a 64 page booklet mailed to talk radio shows. Talk Show Yearbook first published with contact information for the nation's talk shows. 1985 The 2nd edition of the Yearbook published with 20 paid listings from the Advertising Council. The Associated Press requests 1,000 copies. 1986 The New York Times dubs the Yearbook Dial-An-Expert. 1987 Copies purchased by more than 90 percent of the leading news talk radio stations, 60 Minutes and Donahue. 1988 Media circulation grows to 4,000 copies. The Wall Street Journal and The Washington Post publish reviews. AP calls it An Encyclopedia of Sources. 1989 Power Media Yearbook of top print journalists becomes another Broadcast Interview Source publication. 1992 Yearbook circulation grows to 12,000 copies. 1994 Clinton White House, IRS and CIA place listings. 100,000 total copies in print. 1995 The Yearbook featured in Newsweek and The New York Times Magazine. 9,000 print copies requested by journalists. 1996 Yearbook.com goes online and serves as the interactive companion to the printed Yearbook. 1997 Daybook.com becomes an online calendar of the day's events.

Mitchell P. Davis
Broadcast Interview Source, Inc.
Washington, DC USA
*Contact Phone:* 202-333-5000
**Click to Contact from Web Site**

## FEATURES USA — COPYRIGHT FREE NEWS
Washington, DC USA
www.FeaturesUSA.com

Features USA offers links to copyright free articles.

Mitchell P. Davis
Broadcast Interview Source, Inc.
Washington, DC USA
*Contact Phone:* 202-333-5000
**Click to Contact from Web Site**

## DAWN JOSEPHSON -- CAMEO PUBLICATIONS, PUBLISHING & EDITORIAL SERVICES
Hilton Head Island, SC USA
http://www.cameopublications.com

Whether you're sending a sales letter to a prospect or a press release to the media, your writing skills (or lack thereof) can make or break your business. Editor, ghostwriter, and writing consultant Dawn Josephson coaches people to improve their writing skills so they can deliver the best written messages every time. With over 1500 published articles and 20 published books, she helps people transform their current writing into a work of art that engages readers and presents the topic both logically and informatively.

Dawn Josephson
*the Master Writing Coach*
Cameo Publications, LLC
Ridgeland, SC USA
*Contact Phone:* 843-645-3770
**Click to Contact from Web Site**

## PHOCHRON YEARBOOKS

Bristow, VA USA
http://www.phochron.com

Our state-of-the-art digital printing facility provides the full range of yearbooks for primary
schools, secondary schools and colleges. Let us
deliver your most memorable yearbook, ever!
Find out how much you can save using our revolutionary automation.

Manoel Amado
PhoChron Yearbooks
Bristow, VA USA
*Contact Phone:* 877-330-0537
**Click to Contact from Web Site**

## IRWIN ZUCKER — PROMOTION IN MOTION PUBLIC RELATIONS

Los Angeles, CA USA
www.promotioninmotion.net

The IRWIN Award, named for Book Publicists of
Southern California founder Irwin Zucker, was
introduced in 1995 as a way to formally and publicly recognize BPSC members who conduct the
best book sales/promotion campaigns. Honorees
share with the BPSC audience the steps they took
that led to the success of their book promotion
campaigns.

Irwin Zucker
*President*
Promotion In Motion
Hollywood, CA USA
*Contact Phone:* 323-461-3921
*Pager:* 310-497-4001
*Cell:* 310-927-1134
**Click to Contact from Web Site**

## PARTYLINE, PUBLIC RELATIONS MEDIA NEWSLETTER

New York, NY USA
http://www.Partylinepublishing.com

PartyLine is the premier media placement newsletter for the public relations trade. Each week,
their skilled researchers ferret out what the media
need from PR sources. They explain just who has
gone online and what types of information are
needed. Year after year, the most respected names
in public relations, promotion, marketing and
management, from top public relations and advertising agencies, corporations, universities, hospitals, associations, publishers, travel bureaus,
health and government agencies, hotels, the entertainment industry use their services.

Betty Yarmon
*Vice President*
PartyLine, Public Relations Media Newsletter
New York, NY
*Contact Phone:* 212-755-3487
**Click to Contact from Web Site**

## MAHASH GROSSMAN — THE AUTHORS TEAM

San Francisco, CA USA
AuthorsTeam.com

Mahesh Grossman has been called a ghostwriting
guru by the Fox News Channel and America's
leading expert on ghostwriting by Jim Christofer-
son of KWKC-AM. Grossman has been involved
in the development of 45 books as ghostwriter or
editor. He is the author of a new book called Write
a Book Without Lifting a Finger, which is available at bookstores nationwide. Grossman has appeared on over fifty radio and television shows.
Audiences enjoy his tales of ghostwriting as it
relates to American history as well as sordid tid-
bits about greedy authors and vengeful ghostwrit-
ers. Best of all, they come away with knowledge
of how to hire a ghostwriter to write their tales, no
matter what their budget. A graduate of Columbia
University, Mr. Grossman writes a column called
Be the Change for Imagine magazine. He is also
nationally known for teleseminars on How to Get
a Six-Figure Book Advance, and was personally
selected by Mark Victor Hansen, author of the
Chicken Soup for the Soul series, to speak at Hans-
en's Mega Book Marketing University.

Mahash Grossman
The Authors Team
Soquel, CA USA
*Contact Phone:* 561-434-9044
**Click to Contact from Web Site**

# Marilyn Ross, Expert
# Self-Publishing Resources

*Marilyn Ross—*
*Self-Publishing Resources*
*Expert / Author / Speaker*

## Self-Publishing Myth Busters

♦ ***Self-publishing is only for losers.*** Really? Then why have bestselling authors Stephen King, Robert Kiyosaki, Richard Nelson Boyles, Marlo Morgan, Richard Paul Evans, Louise Hay, Spenser Johnson, and thousands of others done it?

♦ ***Self-published books are shunned by reviewers and booksellers.*** Not so – if done properly. You must have a quality message, professional editing, a striking cover, and quality printing. With that criteria – and following normal publishing conventions – the playing field is leveled.

♦ ***Self-publishing is strictly an ego trip.*** For some, yes; all publishing can be an ego trip. But for savvy businesspeople who produce niche books targeted to specific and reachable audiences, it can be very lucrative.

♦ ***Self-published books are hard to sell.*** Any book can be hard to sell. Yet when you realize that 52% of all books are NOT sold in bookstores, a whole horizon of fresh opportunities emerge. What about on the Web, in nontraditional retail outlets, through book clubs, via mail order, in catalogs, as corporate premiums?

♦ ***Self-publishing is just a fad.*** It's not a fad. It's not a trend. It's a revolution! Authors are seizing control of their destiny by the thousands. In 2004, title output increased by 14% over the previous year to an all-time high of 195,000 new titles. Guess who is responsible for the leap?

### To discuss this and other publishing-related topics, contact Marilyn Ross today!

### About the Author / Speaker / Expert

Marilyn Ross—and her passion for publishing—has been featured in *The New York Times, The Los Angeles Times, The Denver Post, Chicago Tribune, Globe & Mail, The Wall Street Journal, Investors Business Daily, Success, U.S. News & World Report, Newsweek,* and hundreds of other national magazines and newspapers.

*Entrepreneur* called her a "trend tracker." A reporter on NPR's All Things Considered remarked, "The bible of this self-publishing craze is *The Complete Guide to Self-Publishing* by Tom and Marilyn Ross."

Her lively, irreverent, yet credible comments have graced hundreds of radio and TV shows, plus Internet sites. This media savvy book coaching professional "preaches what she practices" and continues to be in demand as a speaker, publishing consultant, and expert interview source.

A member of the National Speakers Association, the Authors Guild, and the American Society of Journalists and Authors (ASJA), Marilyn is the award-winning author of hundreds of articles and 13 books including the saucy *Shameless Marketing for Brazen Hussies.* Contact her today!

### Call Marilyn Ross 24/7 at: 719-395-8659 or 719-395-2227
### E-mail her at: Marilyn@MarilynRoss.com    URL: www.SelfPublishingResources.com
Availability: Denver, CO, nationwide by arrangement, and via telephone or e-mail.

## POWER MEDIA BLUEBOOK
Washington, DC USA
www.PowerMediaBlueBook.com

The Power Media BlueBook is a benefit to listed experts from the Yearbook of Experts. Also journalists who register to create a profile may download the book in Adobe PDF format, free of charge. The BlueBook uses a direct-connect e-mail system that ensures listed journalsits do not get unwanted spam, and have control of who can e-mail to them.

Mitchell P. Davis
Broadcast Interview Source, Inc.
Washington, DC USA
*Contact Phone:* 202-333-5000
**Click to Contact from Web Site**

## NEWS RELEASE WIRE
Washington, DC USA
www.NewsReleaseWire.com

News Release Wire was built for the Experts listed in the Yearbook of Experts. There is no charge for Yearbook experts to send news releases. Get the full brochure about this service www.Yearbook-Brochure.com.

Mitchell P. Davis
Broadcast Interview Source, Inc.
Washington, DC USA
*Contact Phone:* 202-333-5000
**Click to Contact from Web Site**

## TOM HENNIGAN — PROMOTIONS USA, LLC
New York, NY USA
http://www.pr-omotion.com

Integrated radio and web promotions, guerrilla marketing, product launches, contests and sweepstakes - and hopefully things never heard of before. . .. We pride ourselves in creative planning. Yes, we think outside the box. Bring us the project and we will set it in motion or call on us for a brainstorming session. Give us your wish list - one of us just might have a favor to call in from our fairy godmother. It's all about knowledge... From individual states' legal requirements to who gets red carnations or chocolate donuts with the permit request - we know. Our knowledge is the key to your success. And if we don't know - it doesn't take us long to find someone who does.

Tom Hennigan
Promotions USA LLC
Guttenberg, NJ USA
*Contact Phone:* 201-223-1602
**Click to Contact from Web Site**

## JOAN STEWART -- THE PUBLICITY HOUND
Milwaukee, WI USA
http://www.PublicityHound.com

Publicity expert Joan Stewart shows you how to use free publicity to establish your credibility, enhance your reputation, position yourself as an expert, sell more products and services, promote a favorite cause or issue, and position your company as an employer of choice. She worked as a newspaper editor and reporter for 22 years and accepted and rejected thousands of story ideas, so she knows what the media want.

Joan Stewart
The Publicity Hound
Port Washington, WI USA
*Contact Phone:* 262-284-7451
**Click to Contact from Web Site**

### DEBRA BENTON -- LEADERSHIP DEVELOPMENT EXPERT
Denver, CO USA
www.DebraBenton.com

Debra Benton is a leading expert in Executive Effectiveness Development, author of seven business books frequently highlighted in the Wall Street Journal, Harvard Business Review, New York Times, and USA Today. Organizations around the world have been seeking her advice for two decades from Fortune 100 companies to the White House to Crystal Cathedral to the U.S. Border Patrol. She presents standards that exceptional leaders use to work differently and be different at work - standards that take you from promise to prominence. She gives immediately applicable straightforward ideas with a fresh perspective and a lively but humorous-in-the-right-places delivery. "You can not go wrong by starting with Debra," says Jeff Cunningham, publisher at Forbes.

Debra Benton
Livermore, CO USA
*Contact Phone:* 970-484-4687
**Click to Contact from Web Site**

### DIRECTORY OF EXPERTS
Washington, DC USA
pages.zdnet.com/biswire/directoryofexperts/

This Directory of Experts page has been developed to assist searchers who are looking for our Yearbook of Experts. The old name of the book was Directory of Experts, and while we moved to Yearbook of Experts, Authorities & Spokespersons, many people still remember us as the Directory of Experts.

Mitchell P. Davis
Directory of Experts
Washington, DC USA
*Contact Phone:* 202-333-5000
**Click to Contact from Web Site**

### JAMES SPENCER — EXPERT — VIDEO LEARNING LIBRARY
Scottsdale, AZ USA
www.videomarketplace.com

Videomarketplace.com, founded in 1988, offers the largest collection of in-stock how-to, special interest and hard-to-find videos and dvds in North America. We offer video programs produced and/or distributed by more than 1,500 independent producers and studios. Our vast collection exceeds 30,000 titles within 42 title categories and 350 subcategories. All in-stock products are shipped within 24-48 hours via First Class Mail.

James Spencer
*President*
Video Learning Library
Scottsdale, AZ US
*Contact Phone:* 480-596-9970
**Click to Contact from Web Site**

### PAIGE STOVER HAGUE
Boston, MA USA
http://www.IctusInitiative.com

Paige Stover Hague is the President of The Ictus Initiative, a distinguished public relations and marketing firm that specializes in promoting speakers, authors, and business executives. Paige offers the specialized skills, perspectives, and professional leadership experience that make her an invaluable partner, advisor, and consultant in building a client's image. An attorney and a former senior executive for numerous publicly traded and multinational publishing houses, she founded Ictus in 2002 and has enjoyed tremendous success.

Paige Stover Hague
*President*
The Ictus Initiative
Boston, MA USA
*Contact Phone:* 508-577-0271
*Contact Main Phone:* 617-230-2167
**Click to Contact from Web Site**

### JUANELL TEAGUE, CONSULTANT, AUTHOR, SPEAKER
Dallas, TX USA
www.juanellteague.com

Juanell Teague is a message development consultant and positioning expert for leaders who want to be a successful professional speaker and for speakers who want to increase their market demand and fees. As a speaker coach, Juanell provides a variety of speaker services. 'Through the years, I began to look for speakers of great character who were the cream of the crop. I saw people from diverse walks of life - business, industry, entertainment, sports - use professional speaking to affect positive social change. I've been privileged to help a number of them take off and succeed.' - Juanell

Juanell Teague
Dallas, TX USA
*Contact Phone:* 972-231-2831
**Click to Contact from Web Site**

**RICK FRISHMAN -- PLANNED TELEVISION ARTS**
New York, NY USA
http://www.PlannedTvArts.com

Rick Frishman, president of Planned Television Arts, since 1982 is the driving force behind PTA's exceptional growth. In 1993 PTA merged with Ruder-Finn and Rick serves as an Executive Vice President at Ruder-Finn. While supervising PTA's success, he has remained one of the most powerful and energetic publicists in the media industry. Rick continues to work with many of the top editors, agents and publishers in America including Simon and Schuster, Random House, Harper Collins, Pocket Books, Penguin Putnam, and Hyperion Books. Some of the authors he has worked with include Mitch Albom, Bill Moyers, Stephen King, Caroline Kennedy, Howard Stern, President Jimmy Carter, Mark Victor Hansen, Nelson DeMille, John Grisham, Hugh Downs, Henry Kissinger, Jack Canfield, Alan Deshowitz, Arnold Palmer, and Harvey Mackay.

Rick Frishman
Planned Television Arts
New York, NY USA
*Contact Phone:* 212-593-5845
*Contact Main Phone:* 212-593-5820
**Click to Contact from Web Site**

---

**REBECCA O'MEARA**
New Orleans, LA USA

Rebecca O'Meara Communications represents renowned experts in all areas of health, medicine, fitness, dieting, psychology, psychiatry, business, law, entertainment, travel, cooking, men and women's issues and more. Our seasoned experts are available for interviews, columns and as spokesmen.

Rebecca O'Meara
Rebecca O'Meara Communications LLC
New Orleans, LA USA
*Contact Phone:* 504-861-2188
*Cell:* (504) 231-6858
**Click to Contact from Web Site**

**CRAIG CONROY, CONROY RESEARCH GROUP**
Gibsonia, PA USA
http://www.craigconroy.com

Animated authority, author and a great guest, two books, numerous trade publication articles. 'A producer's dream, talk show host's ideal guest.' He speaks in soundbites, great source for reporters. Material backed by market research. Book him today for your next sweeps. 'He lights up switchboards like a Christmas tree.'

Terry or Rosa
*Marketing*
Craig Conroy, Conroy Research Group
Gibsonia, PA
*Contact Phone:* 800-344-1492
*Contact Main Phone:* 724-443-6876
**Click to Contact from Web Site**

---

**CUSTOMER REFERENCE FORUM**
Dallas, TX USA
www.customerreferenceforum.com

We provide information and networking opportunities designed to help marketing professionals turn customers into sales people. We deliver these through live events, our newsletter Reference Point, teleconferences and other media.

Bill Lee
*President*
Customer Reference Forum
Dallas, TX USA
*Contact Phone:* 214-559-4380
**Click to Contact from Web Site**

**PUBLIC RELATIONS SOFTWARE**
Washington, DC USA
www.PublicRelationsSoftWare.com

Public Relations Software is another way to think about all the on-line services you get with the Yearbook of Experts.

Mitchell P. Davis
Broadcast Interview Source, Inc.
Washington, DC USA
*Contact Phone:* 202-333-5000
**Click to Contact from Web Site**

**SMITH PUBLICITY**
Philadelphia, PA USA
www.smithpublicity.com

TCI-Smith Publicity provides comprehensive publicity, public relations, and creative communications services. Dan Smith, president of the firm, is a widely recognized expert on publicity and marketing and speaks regularly to groups and associations. TCI-Smith Publicity provides promotional services to a wide range of authors, companies, and non-profit organizations. Contact dan@smithpublicity.com or visit www.smithpublicity.com.

Dan Smith
Smith Publicity
Marlton, NJ USA
*Contact Phone:* 856-489-8654
**Click to Contact from Web Site**

"You cannot go wrong by starting with Debra."
–Jeff Cunningham, publisher at Forbes

Debra Benton is a leading expert in Executive Effectiveness Development, author of seven business books frequently highlighted in the Wall Street Journal, the Harvard Business Review, the New York Times and USA Today.

Organizations around the world have been seeking her advice for two decades – from Fortune 100 companies and the White House to the Crystal Cathedral as well as the U.S. Border Patrol.

Benton presents standards that exceptional leaders use to work differently and be different at work – standards that take you from promise to prominence.

She gives immediately applicable straightforward ideas with a fresh perspective and lively but humorous-in-the-right-places delivery.

## Debra Benton

Benton Management Resources, Inc.
521 Rattlesnake Road
Livermore, Colorado 80536

Please contact Mary Harrison
for booking information
at 800-416-7554.

www.debrabenton.com

debra@debrabenton.com

## ANNIE JENNINGS PR, AMERICA'S PUBLICITY FIRM
New York, NY USA
www.anniejenningspr.com

Annie Jennings PR provides book promotion and message marketing, internet marketing, publicity and book promotion services with high-quality, national exposure. Media placements include major media outlets such as top, high-listenership radio interviews, national TV, national major magazines and top newspapers. Annie Jennings PR has worked with thousands of book authors and experts and has booked THOUSANDS of high-exposure radio interviews, TV, print, magazine, newspaper and internet marketing book promotion articles. Annie's book authors & experts appear daily on the most prestigious, most sought-after TV, radio, magazine and newspaper and internet marketing media in the country. Our passion is to help you reach millions with your message! We would honored if you would join us!

Annie Jennings
Annie Jennings PR
Belle Mead, NJ USA
*Contact Phone:* 908-281-6201
**Click to Contact from Web Site**

## DR. MARILYN KERN FOXWORTH, APR, COMMUNICATIONS & MARKETING EXPERT
Washington, DC USA

Kern Foxworth International, LLC (KFI) is a marketing communications firm located in Silver Spring, Maryland. The company was founded by Dr. Marilyn Kern-Foxworth, APR, a leading marketing expert and noted research specialist for over 30 years.

Dr. Marilyn Kern Foxworth, APR
Kern Foxworth International, LLC
Silver Spring, MD USA
*Contact Phone:* 301-460-6004
*Cell:* 301-332-9748
**Click to Contact from Web Site**

## HOWARD LEVY — RED ROOSTER GROUP
Brooklyn, NY USA
http://www.RedRoosterGroup.com

Howard is an award-winning designer and an expert in branding for nonprofit organizations. He combines 15 years experience in branding, marketing, design and writing for a range of nonprofits and business services. He is dedicated to the cause of using design to promote causes and is a speaker at nonprofit conferences and president of networking groups. He is involved in many associatons including the marketing committee of Governance Matters and the Association of Fundraising Professionals.

Howard Levy
Red Rooster Group
Brooklyn, NY USA
*Contact Phone:* 718 636-1297
**Click to Contact from Web Site**

## LEVINE COMMUNICATIONS, INC.
Los Angeles, CA USA
http://www.levinepr.com

Levine Communications Office (LCO) is one of the nation's most prominent entertainment PR firms. Established in 1983, by Michael Levine, LCO has represented many hundreds of very well known celebrities including Barbra Streisand, Michael Jackson, Charlton Heston, Nancy Kerrigan, Demi Moore. Michael Levine as an author has written many books including the original best seller Guerrilla PR, now in a totally new edition for the computer age as: Guerrilla PR Wired: Waging A Successful Publicity Campaign Online, Offline, and Everywhere in Between.

Michael Levine
Levine Communications, Inc.
Los Angeles, CA USA
*Contact Phone:* 310-300-0950
**Click to Contact from Web Site**

## BERNSTEIN CRISIS MANAGEMENT
Los Angeles, CA USA
www.bernsteincrisismanagement.com

Jonathan Bernstein is an internationally renowned crisis management consultant, author and newsletter editor who can be counted on to provide golden nuggets on breaking news, on- or off-camera. He is a former investigative reporter who can speak about all aspects of crisis management — response, prevention and training.

Jonathan Bernstein
*President*
Bernstein Crisis Management
Monrovia, CA USA
*Contact Phone:* 626-305-9277
*Cell:* 626-825-3838
**Click to Contact from Web Site**

## PROOFREADNOW.COM —- PHIL JAMIESON, FOUNDER
Boston, MA USA
www.ProofreadNOW.com

ProofreadNOW is a zero-overhead, B2B copyediting service available 24/7. We bring fresh eyes to bear on important documents that are key to projecting your professional image. Securely upload your brochure, proposal, advertisement, contract, report, newsletter, Web pages, presentations, and other documents. We'll find grammar, spelling, punctuation, clarity, and style errors that would go unnoticed by you and others too close to the process. Your house style sheets are supported. We offer a 100% satisfaction guarantee.

Phil A. Jamieson
*President*
ProofreadNOW.com, Inc.
Topsfield, MA USA
*Contact Phone:* 978-887-6675
**Click to Contact from Web Site**

## LEVICK STRATEGIC COMMUNICATIONS
Washington, DC USA
www.Levick.com

Levick Strategic Communications is a global leader in high stakes communications. The firm directs communications programs on the highest-profile matters, from global banking disputes and the largest civil litigation arising out of the war in Iraq, to the ongoing dispute over prisoners currently being held in Guantanamo Bay and the Catholic Church controversy. Richard Levick was named by PR News as the Public Relations Professional of the Year for U.S. Agencies and was recently a finalist for the 2005 Ernst & Young Entrepreneur of the Year. With other members of the firm, he has written several books, including Stop the Press: The Litigation PR Desk Reference and 365 Marketing Meditations: Daily Lessons for Marketing & Communications Professionals.

Richard S. Levick. Esq.
*President/CEO*
Levick Strategic Communications
Washington, DC USA
*Contact Phone:* 202-973-1302
*Contact Main Phone:* 202.973.1300
**Click to Contact from Web Site**

## ANNE ALDRICH — ACROSS THE BOARD MARKETING, INC.
Chicago, IL USA
www.acrosstheboardmarketing.com

Need an expert source? ABM represents clients in myriad financial areas: Experts in stock, futures, options, fixed income, forex trading, Online investing/trading, Electronic brokerage firms, Professional traders, floor traders, Best-selling authors, Publishers of trading/investing information, Financial software providers. Most have extensive print and broadcast media experience and are frequently quoted in major international publications. Need publicity or marketing? We can help! Contact ABM@covad.net.

Anne Aldrich
Across The Board Marketing, Inc.
Chicago, IL USA
*Contact Phone:* 312-787-1642
**Click to Contact from Web Site**

## IUNIVERSE INC. BOOK PUBLISHER
Lincoln, NE USA
http://click.linksynergy.com/fs-bin/click?id=
PxVFzzh5Ruo&offerid=65159.
10000004&type=3&subid=0

We are experts in the publishing industry specifically print-on-demand self-publishing. Our unique approach to publishing books helps authors get quick industry exposure and helps them build a unique platform from which to effectively promote and sell books. Without iUniverse many talented authors may never get discovered!

Carol Ash
iUniverse Inc. Book Publisher
Lincoln, NE USA
*Contact Phone:* 402-323-7800
**Click to Contact from Web Site**

## PUBLISIDE PERSONAL PUBLICITY, GAIL SIDEMAN
Milwaukee, WI USA
www.publiside.com

PUBLISIDE Personal Publicity, a media savvy, information warehouse, is on a perpetual fast track to generate press coverage for athletes and athletics organizations, authors, and entrepreneurs. Its goal is to communicate what is most important to targeted audiences. Owner Gail Sideman is always on hand and proud of her diverse client roster which includes the Tim & Tom Gullikson Foundation, Barb Friedman and Organize IT (www.organizeitbiz.com), psychotherapist Betsy Collins (www.counselorbetsy.com) and Elite Fitness & Racquet Clubs (www.elite-clubs.com).

Gail Sideman
*Owner, Publicist, P.R. Director*
PUBLISIDE Personal Publicity
Milwaukee, WI USA
*Contact Phone:* 262-240-SIDE (7433)
**Click to Contact from Web Site**

## HARRIET LESSY - BUZZCOMMUNICATIONS
Philadelphia, PA USA
http://www.BuzzCommunications.biz

BuzzCommunications specializes in public relations and public affairs, local and state lobbying, issue advocacy, sports and event marketing, executive media training, leadership and presentation skills training, and Business-to-Business Communications. Recent successes include a grassroots campaign to ban soda from Philadelphia's public schools, groundbreaking, of the Ikea's first urban store, in South Philadelphia at Columbus Crossings and similar events for other major development projects in and around Philadelphia.

Harriet Lessy
*Founder*
BuzzCommunications LLC
PR Consultants
Philadelphia, PA USA
*Contact Phone:* 215-985-0660
*Contact Main Phone:* 215-985-2899
*Cell:* 215-816-6093
**Click to Contact from Web Site**

## SCOTT LORENZ, WESTWIND COMMUNICATIONS
Plymouth, MI USA
www.westwindcos.com

Westwind Communications excels at helping clients get all the publicity they deserve and more. We work with a wide variety of small to medium sized businesses including Doctors, Lawyers, Inventors, Authors and Entrepreneurs. The firm's extensive media contacts have produced volumes of clippings and hours of broadcast coverage including: Fox & Friends, Good Morning America, Today Show, Early Show, HBO, CNN, NPR, Voice of America, USA Today, Investors Business Daily and The Wall Street Journal.

Scott Lorenz
*President*
Westwind Communications
Plymouth, MI USA
*Contact Phone:* 734-667-2090
*Cell:* 248-705-2214
**Click to Contact from Web Site**

# BERNSTEIN CRISIS MANAGEMENT LLC

## CRISIS RESPONSE, PREVENTION, PLANNING & TRAINING

### CRISIS PREVENTION/RESPONSE

Immediate assistance with preventing or responding to serious reputation threats and/or business interruptions.

### CRISIS MANAGEMENT TRAINING/PRESENTATIONS

Identifying a crisis management expert who can conduct training or make a presentation — Jonathan Bernstein does both.

### CRISIS MANAGEMENT EDUCATION

Education in the field of Crisis Management public relations, in which case you are welcome to browse the more than 400 articles archived on our Web site and/or to sign up for the free Crisis Manager newsletter.

Jonathan L. Bernstein, president of Bernstein Crisis Management LLC, has more than 20 years experience in the design and conduct of public relations and strategic communications programs — with particular expertise in all aspects of crisis management: crisis response, vulnerability assessment, planning, training and simulations.

Before launching his own firm in 1994, Bernstein had international-level experience as senior vice president and director of the Crisis Communications Group for Ruder Finn, Inc., one of the world's largest public relations agencies.

Bernstein is publisher and editor of Crisis Manager, a first-of-its-kind e-mail newsletter, written for "those who are crisis managers whether they want to be or not," currently read in 75 countries, and author of "Keeping the Wolves at Bay: A Media Training Manual."

Bernstein has been quoted as an expert source by many media outlets, including the AP, BBC, Business 2.0, BusinessWeek, CBS, ESPN, Fox News, NPR, Reuters, The Christian Science Monitor, TheStreet.com, The Wall Street Journal, USA Today as well as many local and regional publications. In September 2004, he was one of 22 individuals nationwide identified as "people who should be on the speed dial in a crisis" in a PR Week feature, entitled "The Crunch-Time Counselors."

## Write to jonathan@bernsteincrisismanagement.com.

## Call Jonathan Bernstein — NOW — at 626-825-3838.

Jonathan Bernstein, President
Bernstein Crisis Management LLC
180 S. Mountain Trail   Sierra Madre, California  91024
Office: 626-825-3838 ■ Fax: 877-471-1573

## DEBRA HOLTZMAN, J.D., M.A. — CORPORATE SPOKESPERSON

Hollywood, FL USA

www.thesafetyexpert.com

Debra Smiley Holtzman brings integrity, technical expertise and experience to your media campaign. Many Fortune 500 corporations have enjoyed the benefits of Debra's endorsement.An internationally recognized safety and health expert and an award-winning parenting author, Debra is a respected spokesperson for high quality products and services that support children, motherhood and families. She has a law degree, an M.A. in occupational health and safety, a B.A. in communications, and is the mother of two children. Her books, The Panic-Proof Parent (McGraw-Hill, 2000) and The Safe Baby (Sentient Publications, 2005), have received rave reviews and endorsements by leading parenting authorities and safety and health organizations.

Debra Holtzman
Hollywood, FL USA
*Contact Phone:* 954-963-7702
**Click to Contact from Web Site**

## PUBLIC RELATIONS SOCIETY OF AMERICA

New York, NY USA

http://www.prsa.org

When Your Question is About Public Relations — call the pre-eminent organization that builds value, demand and global understanding for public relations. The World's Largest Organization for Public Relations Professionals — Consult the Top Experts in the World of Public Relations on Media Relations, Investor Relations, Corporate Communications, Crisis Communications — A Rich Legacy of the Best Public Relations Practices and Notable Individuals recognized by the Most Prestigious Awards in the Industry: Public Relations Professional of the Year, Bronze Anvils, Silver Anvils, Gold Anvil.

Catherine Bolton
*Chief Public Relations Officer*
Public Relations Society of America
New York, NY
*Contact Phone:* 212-460-1400
**Click to Contact from Web Site**

## T. J. WALKER — MEDIA TRAINER/ PRESENTATION COACH

New York, NY USA

http://www.mediatrainingworldwide.com

TJ Walker can provide expert analysis to your readers/listeners/viewers on the following topics: Media: how to communicate on TV, radio, and print, Presentations: effective speeches, sales pitches, panel discussions, crisis management, and presidential candidates/political leader communication skills. TJ and Media Training Worldwide conduct more then 50 different media/presentation training courses and publish more than 100 different books/DVDs/CDs. TJ has personally trained thousands of executives/companies over the last 20 years including Bank of America, Miss Universe, The Hartford, the Osmonds, Unilever, Amerada Hess, and Charles Schwab.

TJ Walker
*President*
Media Training Worldwide
New York, NY USA
*Contact Phone:* 212-764-4955
*Cell:* 917.204.9490
**Click to Contact from Web Site**

## THE NEWSLETTER ON NEWSLETTERS

Rhinebeck, NY USA

NewsletterBiz.com

The Newsletter on Newsletters offers an invaluable resource for marketing and promotion ideas, money-saving tips, editorial and design trends, and financial management strategies that improve the bottom line. We regularly provide informative and inspirational success stories about smaller firms and start-ups that continue to challenge larger publishers—often succeeding where the big publishers stumble. NL/NL also presents tips and case studies of online publishing and marketing. The internet and its impact on newsletters and specialized information publishing have also become a staple of our editorial fare.

Paul Swift
The Newsletter on Newsletters
Rhinebeck, NY USA
*Contact Phone:* 845-876-5222
**Click to Contact from Web Site**

## YEARBOOK SHOP WEB SITE

Washington, DC USA

www.YearbookShop.com

This is the Web Site where you can buy a copy of the printed Yearbook of Experts.

Mitchell Davis
Broadcast Interview Source, Inc.
Washington, DC USA
*Contact Phone:* 202-333-5000
**Click to Contact from Web Site**

## WALKER & CO. PUBLISHERS

New York, NY USA

www.WalkerBooks.com

When Sam Walker founded Walker & Company 45 years ago, in 1959, Sputnik had recently been launched. Dwight Eisenhower was president, and department stores were America's primary booksellers. As with almost everything, the publishing landscape today is utterly different than it was then; but Walker remains proudly independent at a time when independence throughout the book industry has never been more meaningful. From the start, Walker's list has reflected varied personal tastes and publishing opportunities. Sam Walker loved history, publishing over the years authors like the legendary journalist, Harrison Salisbury. In its many guises, history has remained a cornerstone of our program: In recent years, Dava Sobel's Longitude and Galileo's Daughter, and Ross King's Michelangelo & the Pope's Ceiling were New York Times bestsellers, while Mark Kurlansky's Cod and Salt, King's Brunelleschi's Dome, Diana Preston's The Boxer Rebellion and Lusitania, and Andro Linklater's Measuring America, among many others, have appeared in our catalogs.

Peter Miller
Walker Company
New York, NY USA
*Contact Phone:* 646-307-5579
**Click to Contact from Web Site**

## ROBERT X. LEEDS, AUTHOR/ PUBLISHER (EPIC PUBLISHING)
Las Vegas, NV USA
http://www.epicpublishing.com

Robert X. Leeds has been a Merchant Mariner, a wing walker, stunt pilot, a gun runner and diamond smuggler. He spent time in an African prison and faced a firing squad in China. He trained and commanded Israel's First Airborne Brigade in 1948. Leeds holds a Master's of Business Management and was a senior executive at GM. He has partnered in business with Ray Kroc and Orson Wells and is an accomplished author and publisher.

Stephanie Galloway
*PR Consultant*
Russ Fons Public Relations
Las Vegas, NV USA
*Contact Phone:* 617-820-7321
**Click to Contact from Web Site**

## BRIAN TAYLOR, PUBLISHING INDUSTRY CONSULTANT & BOOK MARKETER
Baltimore, MD USA
www.pneumabooks.com/bio.htm

Brian Taylor is a seasoned book publishing consultant who has assisted hundreds of book publishers over the last 15 years. Garnering 24 publishing awards for his clients in the last 4 years alone, he is the CEO and Creative Director for Pneuma Books, LLC. Brian is an expert strategist and helps publishers plan new product lines; develop commercially viable books; and market those books. Brian is a popular conference speaker on the issues of publishing.

Brian Taylor
*CEO / Creative Director / Publishing Consultant*
Pneuma Books, LLC
Elkton, MD USA
*Contact Phone:* 410-996-8900
*Cell:* 410-441-0333
**Click to Contact from Web Site**

**HOMER HICKAM**
Huntsville, AL USA
http://www.homerhickam.com

Homer Hickam is the author of Rocket Boys made into the movie October Sky. A Vietnam veteran, a scuba instructor, an expert wreck diver, and the recent discoverer of a juvenile T.Rex, Mr. Hickam has adventured around the world. He also had a long career with NASA, specializing in crew training and spacecraft design. He is one of the most popular authors in the world, his books translated into many languages.

Homer Hickam
Huntsville, AL USA
*Contact Phone:* 256-880-7527
**Click to Contact from Web Site**

## EXCEND HISPANIC CONSULTING
Salt Lake City, UT USA
http://www.excend.com

Hispanic - Latino Market Penetration. Excend Consulting Group assists leading businesses in penetrating the $700 billion Hispanic market within North America. Excend clients receive guidance on modifying their products and services to attract and retain Hispanic clientele. Clients throughout North America have used Excend's consulting services to make changes to their branding, marketing, merchandising, distribution, and personnel in order to successfully do business in the Hispanic market. Contact Excend at 1-877-860-8082.

Ryan Nichols
*Managing Consultant*
Excend Hispanic Consulting
Sandy, UT USA
*Contact Phone:* 801-569-1747
**Click to Contact from Web Site**

## LIVE THE JAMES BOND LIFESTYLE
Los Angeles, CA USA
http://www.bondlife.com

Live the JAMES BOND Lifestyle. A serious seminar and book. Subjects include: Appearance — Relationships — Car — Hotels — Casino Gambling — Upgrading Image — Avoiding Villains — The Ultimate Secret of Women.

Paul Kyriazi
Live the James Bond Lifestyle
Los Angeles, CA USA
*Contact Phone:* 310-826-0222
**Click to Contact from Web Site**

## EPM COMMUNICATIONS, INC. — ENTERTAINMENT MARKETING COMPANY
New York, NY USA
http://www.epmcom.com

EPM publishes newsletters and research studies about marketing, merchandising and consumer demographics. In addition to providing abstracts of research on consumer behavior covering women; youth; Black, Hispanic and Asian Americans; and others, EPM analyzes business and consumer trends. Among EPM's newsletters are Research Alert, Youth Markets Alert, Marketing To Women, Marketing to Emerging Majorities, Entertainment Marketing Letter and The Licensing Letter. EPM President Ira Mayer also speaks about business and consumer trends to corporate, association and non-profit groups.

Ira Mayer
*President and Publisher*
EPM Communications, Inc.
New York, NY
*Contact Phone:* 212-941-1633
*Contact Main Phone:* 212-941-0099
**Click to Contact from Web Site**

MEDIA TRAINING WORLDWIDE

# Media Training Worldwide

Specializing in media and presentation training for over 20 years.

## Media Trainer/Presentation Coach TJ Walker

TJ Walker can provide expert analysis to your readers/listeners/viewers on the following topics:

- Media: how to communicate on TV, radio, and print
- Presentations: effective speeches, sales pitches, panel discussions
- Crisis management
- Presidential candidates/political leader communication skills

TJ has appeared on or been quoted in the following: New York Times, Miami Herald, Fox News Channel, MSNBC, Court TV, Bloomberg TV, E! Entertainment, NPR, NBC Radio, and Montel Williams.

TJ and Media Training Worldwide conduct more then 50 media/presentation training courses including the following:

- "Prepare for the Media Major Leagues"
- "Secrets of the Media Mavens"
- "Lights, Camera, Act Natural!"
- "Talk Your Way to the Best-Seller List"
- "Life Raft" - Staying Afloat in a Sea of Media Crises"
- "Unleashing Your Inner Orator"
- "Present Pro™ Master Speaker"
- "10 Steps to Overcoming the FEAR of Public Speaking"
- "Attention Grabbing Financial Presentations –
  The story behind the numbers"
- "CEOTalk Become a Presenting Superstar"
- "Ka-Ching! $ales $peak, Improving your Sales Pitch"

*MEDIA TRAINING WORLDWIDE IS THE LARGEST PUBLISHER OF MEDIA TRAINING PRODUCTS IN THE WORLD!*

TJ is the author/producer/host of more than 100 books/DVDs/CDs including the following:

- It's Showtime!  Preparing for Your Next Television Appearance
- 1001 Ways to Wow the Media and Speaking Audiences
- Sizzling Sound Bites-Getting the Media to Use Your Quotes Every Time
- Not for Bedtime Stories-Making Your Presentations Come Alive Through Story Telling
- Space Age Interviews-How to Ace Your Next Satellite TV Interview

TJ has personally trained thousands of executives/companies over the last 20 years including Bank of America, Miss Universe, The Hartford, the Osmonds, Unilever, Amerada Hess, Charles Schwab and UCLA.

To Book TJ contact Media Training Worldwide 110 West 40th Street, Suite 203, New York, NY 10018. 212-764-4955 (0ffice)  917-204-9490 (cell) tj@mediatrainingworldwide.com. www.mediatrainingworldwide.com

110 West 40th St. • New York • New York • 10018 • Tel: 212/764.4955 • www.mediatrainingworldwide.com

## OAKHILL PRESS — BUSINESS AND SELF-HELP BOOKS
Winchester, VA USA
www.oakhillpress.com

Oakhill Press, an independent equity publisher, has been filling a unique niche providing publishing and distribution opportunities since 1988 for authors of quality business and self-help books targeted to specific markets and professionals that don't appeal to the large publishing houses. The Oakhill staff stays on the cutting edge of modern publishing technology and methods to produce high quality books and audio products. Ed Helvey presents seminars on publishing alternatives for both first time and veteran authors.

Ed Helvey
Oakhill Press
Winchester, VA USA
*Contact Phone:* 540-535-0744
**Click to Contact from Web Site**

## PUBCOM -- PUBLISHING COMMUNICATIONS GROUP
Washington, DC USA
http://www.pubcom.com

Cross-media publishing = produce content once and distribute via print, Web, and electronic technologies. PubCom is a leading consultancy, training firm, and design studio for Adobe Acrobat PDF, desktop publishing, XML, and Website development. The firm guides businesses, nonprofits, and government agencies to implement appropriate technologies for their communication goals. PubCom's founder, Bevi Chagnon, is a well-known teacher, as well as a conference speaker, contributing author to trade publications, and commentator in online industry forums.

Bevi Chagnon
*Principal, Founding Honcho*
PubCom -- Publishing Communications Group
Takoma Park, MD USA
*Contact Phone:* 301-585-8805
**Click to Contact from Web Site**

## RISING STAR PRESS
Central Oregon, OR USA
http://www.risingstarpress.com

Rising Star Press publishes books that cause the reader to think and be inspired to act in some positive and proactive way to improve their own life as well as the lives of those around them. Books are chosen, in part, based on a consistency between the author's words and life. Our authors include experts on brain injury, communication, cancer, child abuse, community trauma, activism, Christianity, and women's studies.

Donna Jacobsen
*Publisher*
Rising Star Press
Bend, CA USA
*Contact Phone:* 541-330-9119
*Contact Main Phone:* 888-777-2207
**Click to Contact from Web Site**

## SAFE GOODS PUBLISHING
Hartford, CT USA
http://www.safegoodspub.com

Safe Goods Publishing specializes in books on natural health, aviation, sports, science and metaphysics. We represent authors who have prominent recognition in their areas of expertise: Nina Anderson, S.P.N. (health, pets, aviation, metaphysics), Dr. Howard Peiper, N.D.,(health, Attention Deficit Disorder, virus immunity, sports), Roger Mason (health, prostate, cholesterol), Nova Hall (aviation history), Dr. Ogi Ressel, D.C. (health, chiropractic, children), Frances Meiser (health, brain, children), Michael Geiger, O.D. (health, eye), Walter Wainright (health, cancer).

Jessica L. Van Deusen
*Marketing Director & Author Liaison*
Safe Goods Publishing
Sheffield, MA USA
*Contact Main Phone:* 413-229-7935
**Click to Contact from Web Site**

## TRADE DIMENSIONS INTERNATIONAL, INC.
Wilton, CT USA
www.TradeDimensions.com

Trade Dimensions International, Inc. is a VNU company. Trade Dimensions has over 35 years of experience as an innovator in developing some of the most sophisticated, reliable and widely used retailer information products available. From print directories priced within reach of a startup enterprise to custom databases used by the largest consumer packaged goods manufacturers in the world - when it comes to retail, you've come to the right place.

Thomas Donato
Trade Dimensions
Wilton, CT USA
*Contact Phone:* 203-563-3041
**Click to Contact from Web Site**

## SUSAN FRIEDMAN, CSP — THE TRADESHOW COACH
Lake Placid, NY USA
http://www.TheTradeShowCoach.com

Susan Friedmann, Certified Speaking Professional (CSP), is a how to coach specializing in the tradeshow industry. * She works with organizations who want to boost their exhibiting results by attracting new business at tradeshows. * She designs and implements strategies for show organizers and exhibitors who want to retain and grow their customer base. * She also works one-on-one with exhibit managers and conducts national and international presentations and workshops.

Susan Friedman, CSP
The Tradeshow Coach
Lake Placid, NY USA
*Contact Phone:* 518-523-1320, X 10
**Click to Contact from Web Site**

## MY FIRST TRADESHOW
Miami Beach, FL USA
http://www.myfirsttradeshow.com

Linda Rodriguez is a tradeshow consultant with extensive experience providing business with training for exhibiting at tradeshows; from walking through the exhibitor manual, marketing planning, tools & templates, down to what supplies will be needed. Many years have been spent - in the trenches - to gain this experience; businesses that desire to exhibit at tradeshows, but have little or no previous experience will benefit greatly from learning these skills and implementing them.

Linda Rodriguez
*Founder and TradeShow Consultant*
My First TradeShow
Miami Beach, FL USA
*Contact Phone:* 786-866-7873
*Contact Main Phone:* 888-547-7410
**Click to Contact from Web Site**

## JULIA O'CONNOR —- TRADE SHOW MARKETING IDEAS
Richmond, VA USA
www.TradeShowTraining.com

Speaker. Author. Consultant. Funny. Smart. MBA. Julia O'Connor knows it takes more than a display and a handshake to sell at a trade show. Add psychology, sales, marketing and moxie.

Julia O'Connor
Trade Show Training, Inc.
Richmond, VA
*Contact Phone:* 800-355-3910
*Contact Main Phone:* 804-355-7800
**Click to Contact from Web Site**

## SPEAKING OF LEADERSHIP® - PHIL HOLBERTON, CPA, CMC
Boston, MA USA
www.holberton.com

Phil Holberton, CPA, CMC is an internationally recognized financial expert engaged by many to solve complex business and organizational problems. As a professor of leadership at Brandeis University and communications at Babson College, he has enjoyed a thriving practice of business advisory services that focuses on senior level business consulting and coaching to individuals and organizations and works with them to accelerate their development to the next level.

Phil Holberton, CPA, CMC
Speaking of Leadership®
Lincoln, MA USA
*Contact Phone:* 781-259-9719
**Click to Contact from Web Site**

## DIAN THOMAS — FREE PUBLICITY EXPERT
Salt Lake City, UT USA
www.milliondollarpr.com

There isn't any individual, business, or entrepreneur that couldn't benefit from free publicity. It's the best way to make the most of your marketing dollars. I can show you how to harness the power of publicity and get the word out about you or your product without spending a dime. I spent 30 years gaining my knowledge of publicity and how to get and I can show you how to effectively approach the media.

Dian Thomas
*President/CEO*
Holladay, UT USA
*Contact Phone:* 800-846-6355
**Click to Contact from Web Site**

## MICHAEL G. ZEY, PH.D. -- LONGEVITY TRENDS EXPERT.
Mt. Freedom, NJ USA
http://www.zey.com

Dr. Michael Zey, an internationally-recognized sociologist and future-trends/ longevity expert, is the author of The Future Factor (McGraw-Hill/ Transaction), Seizing the Future (Simon and Schuster), The Ageless Society (forthcoming, New Horizons/Kensington), and articles on social, economic and political trends. Dr. Zey has discussed topics such as longevity, energy, the media and communications, and the emerging space race on CNN, CNBC, and FoxNews and at conferences hosted by Sprint, Prudential, IBM and United Technologies.

Michael G. Zey, Ph.D.
Mount Freedom, NJ
*Contact Phone:* 973-538-8192
**Click to Contact from Web Site**

## ROHIT TALWAR — FAST FUTURE
London, United Kingdom
www.FastFuture.com

A futures and innovation consultancy formed in October 1999 to enable clients to create rich future oriented conversations within the organisation. Our approaches help generate fast insights into alternative futures and enable clients to use these insights to drive strategic change, innovation and new venture creation. Fast Future draws on an international network of partners who develop innovative, participative approaches to help clients engage with the future and develop powerful insights that lead to imaginative strategies and result in rapid change and demonstrable commercial returns.

Rohit Talwar
Fast Future
London, England
*Contact Phone:* +44 (0)20 7435 3570
**Click to Contact from Web Site**

## JONATHAN KOOMEY
Oakland, CA USA
http://www.koomey.com

Jon Koomey, Ph.D., teaches the art of critical thinking to business practitioners, students, and researchers. His latest solo book, Turning Numbers into Knowledge: Mastering the Art of Problem Solving, is a lively and entertaining guide to discerning what numbers really mean, in business and in life. Jon's insights help people beat information overload, hone their decision making skills, and achieve success in this information-glutted world. He is a staff scientist at Lawrence Berkeley National Laboratory and a Consulting Professor at Stanford University.

Jonathan G. Koomey
Analytics Press
Oakland, CA
*Contact Phone:* 510-547-7860
*Contact Main Phone:* 510-547-7860
**Click to Contact from Web Site**

## DR. JAY LEHR — TECHNOFUTURIST, ENVIRONMENTAL SCIENTIST
Columbus, OH USA
http://www.e3power.com/Lehr.htm

Princeton Scientist Dr. Jay Lehr helped write all major U.S. environmental regulations in the 1970s and 80s, testifying before congressional committees over three dozen times. He has authored or edited 18 textbooks on science, health and technology. Dr. Lehr's speaks and debates on subjects varying from genetics and biotechnology to nuclear energy, hydrogen fuel cells and global warming. His most recent release explains how satellite data can help us locate useful water supplies around the world.

Rich Tiller
*President*
The Tiller Group
Zionsville, IN USA
*Contact Phone:* 317-873-9797
**Click to Contact from Web Site**

## SPEAKER BANK — YOUR PROFESSIONAL KEYNOTE SPEAKER SOURCE
Washington, DC USA
speakerbank.com

Speaker Bank — Your Professional Keynote Speaker Source is the source for paid professional Keynote Speakers.

Mitchell P. Davis
Broadcast Interview Source, Inc.
Washington, DC USA
*Contact Phone:* 202-333-5000
**Click to Contact from Web Site**

## DU PLAIN ENTERPRISES, INC.
Washington, DC USA
http://www.duplain.com

Du Plain Enterprises, Inc., a Washington, DC corporation which began in 1997, & represents public relations; media & marketing; advertising & promotional campaigns; special programs; and event planning. In 1996, Du Plain International Speakers Bureau, LLC, opened its' doors bringing together our vast network of contacts in the worlds of diplomacy, journalism, entertainment, politics, advocacy, business and the arts. Our bureau offers speakers, trainers, consultants and entertainers for conferences, workshops, seminars and programs through our Web site located at www.duplain.com. CEO and President, Jan Du Plain, is a graduate of the School of Public Affairs and Government, American University.

Jan Du Plain
Du Plain Enterprises, Inc.
Fall Church, VA USA
*Contact Phone:* 1-866-DuPlain
*Contact Main Phone:* 703-992-0770
**Click to Contact from Web Site**

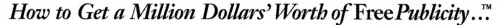

**THE HERMAN GROUP -- STRATEGIC BUSINESS FUTURISTS**
Greensboro, NC USA
http://www.hermangroup.com

High content thought leaders on workforce and workplace issues, trends, and employee retention. Available 24/7, highly responsive and deadline-sensitive. Articulate Certified Management Consultants, they demystify complicated issues. Upbeat about the future, with realistic focus on employee turnover, labor shortages, corporation of the future and similar current issues. Authors of recent books on management and near-term future, including 'Impending Crisis,' 'How to Become an Employer of Choice,' 'Keeping Good People,' 'Lean & Meaningful,' 'Signs of the Times,' and 'How to Choose Your Next Employer.' The Herman Group helps organizations and their leaders prepare for tomorrow.

Roger E. Herman
*Certified Speaking Professional & Management Consultant*
The Herman Group
Greensboro, NC
*Contact Phone:* 336-282-9370
*Cell:* 336-210-3548
**Click to Contact from Web Site**

**SPEAKERLEADS.COM**
Washington, DC USA
www.SpeakerLeads.com

SpeakerLeads.com is a free service of Broadcast Interview Sources' www.SpeakerBank.com web site. This site shows future events that are seeking speakers, MOSTLY FREE SPEAKERS for conventions or trade shows. These are designated as Speak4Miles opportunities, and are best suited for those seeking to network, enhance their business, or meet professional speaking goals of a given number of presentations before professional audiences. Paid Speaking Opportunities are distributed via the interactive lead program at www. SpeakerBank.com to paid members of the SpeakerBank community — plus paid members get advance notice of events to be posted to this page.

Mitchell P. Davis
Broadcast Interview Sources, Inc.
Washington, DC USA
*Contact Phone:* 202-333-5000
**Click to Contact from Web Site**

**THE CELEBRITY SOURCE**
Los Angeles, CA USA
http://www.CelebritySource.com

Rita Tateel, president of The Celebrity Source, has been matching celebrities with corporate and non-profit events and public relations campaigns for 20 years. Her international company has access to over 10,000 stars of film, television, music, sports and fashion. Ms. Tateel has been interviewed as a celebrity expert for countless media sources including CNN, Wall Street Journal, People Magazine, Playboy, LA Times, NY Times, E! Entertainment Television, Extra! and Entertainment Tonight, among many others.

Rita Tateel
*President*
The Celebrity Source
Los Angeles, CA
*Contact Phone:* 323-651-3300
**Click to Contact from Web Site**

**BLACK SPEAKERS ONLINE**
Los Angeles, CA USA
www.BlackSpeakers.Net

Black Speakers Online, a division of SPEAKERS ETCETERA, offers quality speakers from a wide range of topics, talents, geographic areas and fees. Our speakers share knowledge and information in original ways, offering lasting impressions that speak to the heart of the matter and get results. Our committed staff offers an effortless booking experience in locating the right speaker to fit your budget. SPEAKERS ETCETERA also offers coaching, seminars and products for speaker development.

Linda Walker
*P.R. Director*
Black Speakers Online
Inglewood, CA USA
*Contact Phone:* 310-671-7136
*Cell:* 323-712-4321
**Click to Contact from Web Site**

**HELLEN DAVIS, CLU, MASTER INFLUENCER**
Tampa, FL USA
http://www.21laws.com/

Hellen Davis, CLU, entrepreneur, self-made millionaire, and author of more than 12 books, including The 21 Laws of Influence, has been a corporate political strategist, executive consultant, management coach, and motivational speaker for over 20 years. Her clients include CEOs, executives and leaders from dozens of Fortune 100 corporations. She has been a guest on CNN, Dateline, EXTRA, etc., recently appeared on the cover of Main Line Today, and is frequently quoted in national publications.

Hellen Davis, CLU
*President & CEO*
Indaba, Inc.
The 21 Laws of Influence
Treasure Island, PA USA
*Contact Phone:* 727-360-0111
**Click to Contact from Web Site**

# Experts to Keep *You* Ahead of the Curve.

**Your Story Will Come Alive with the Details They Provide.**
Strategic Business Futurists and best-selling authors Roger Herman and Joyce Gioia (joy-yah) are the industry authorities in the future of the workforce and workplace. Joyce and Roger develop solid research, monitor the global business horizon, and forecast trends to keep you and your audience ahead of the curve. Give your audience the background to fully understand what's happening now and what will happen in the future.

**Your Resource for Workforce Stability & Employee Retention.**
For 25 years, they've offered advice and counsel to corporate leaders. Whether the problem is retaining top talent or designing a program to bring new hires on board so that they will stay, Joyce and Roger have the answers people are looking for.

**Provocative and Insightful Consultants with Answers.**
Through 11 books and a popular weekly e-advisory, Roger and Joyce convey vital information and insights. As Certified Management Consultants and active Professional Speakers, they operate at a research-supported, strategic level.

# The Herman Group

MANAGEMENT CONSULTANTS/SPEAKERS/FUTURISTS
**4057 Battleground Avenue, Greensboro, North Carolina 27410**
**336-282-9370 • FAX: 336-282-2003 • *www.hermangroup.com***

## MIKKI WILLIAMS UNLTD. * VISTAGE INTERNATIONAL * COACHING, ETC...
Chicago, IL USA
www.mikkiwilliams.com

Mikki Williams, CSP, is an experience. . . a one of a kind talent, eclectic, refreshing, and smart. She has a dynamic ability to communicate to an audience, delivering practical information in a down to earth style. A speaker, trainer, consultant, coach, author, radio & TV personality and entrepreneur extraordinaire, Vistage International speaker (the world's largest leadership organization of 11,000 CEO's) and Chair of her own Executive Forums in Chicago and coaching firm, Coaching, etc. . . SLIP 'EM A MIKKI! ™

Mikki Williams, CSP
Mikki Williams Unltd.
Chicago, IL USA
*Contact Phone:* 312-664-8447
**Click to Contact from Web Site**

## DOTTIE WALTERS — WALTERS SPEAKER SERVICES
Los Angeles, CA USA
www.SpeakandGrowRich.com

Dottie Walters' Speak and Grow Rich — Consulting Seminars, workshops and success products are the #1 source for total speaking success. For over 30 years Dottie Walters has been a leading force in the professional speaking industry delivering her magic to audiences around the globe. Her knowledge and How-To of the speaking business have helped launch thousands of successful speaking careers and are considered the most respected and complete information in speaking.

Dottie Walters
Walters Speaker Services
Glendora, CA
*Contact Phone:* 626-335-8069
**Click to Contact from Web Site**

## NATIONAL SPEAKERS ASSOCIATION
Tempe, AZ USA
http://www.nsaspeaker.org

Members are experts in a variety of fields and are ideal sources for expert commentary and interviews. NSA offers Who's Who in Professional Speaking® The Meeting Planner's Guide. This is one of the speaking industry's most comprehensive reference books. Call 480-968-2552 for your free copy. Click on the Find a Speaker section of NSA's website to search by keyword, name, location or topics. NSA's online press room offers quick links to events and news from the speaking profession.

Marsha Mardock
*Director of Communications*
National Speakers Association
Tempe, AZ
*Contact Phone:* 480-968-2552
**Click to Contact from Web Site**

## JUNE DAVIDSON, AMERICAN SEMINAR LEADERS ASSOCIATION
Pasadena, CA USA
www.asla.com

According to Readers Digest, April 2004, 'Seminar Leader is one of the hottest careers.' ASLA has trained over 5,000 international members from different professions and each becomes an expert in their fields. They become powerful seminar leaders, speakers and they are trained to enhance their professional skills, market their services and products with seminars. ASLA trains advanced techniques in Turbo Training for accelerated learning. ASLA also answers the training needs for the Corporations.

Alina Pogaceanu
American Seminar Leaders Association
Pasadena, CA USA
*Contact Phone:* 626-791-1211
**Click to Contact from Web Site**

**PAUL LAWRENCE VANN --
MOTIVATIONAL SPEAKER, AUTHOR,
TRAINER**
Washington, DC USA
http://www.paullawrencevann.com

Paul Lawrence Vann, Lieutenant Colonel, USAF (Ret) is Founder and President of Laurel Wreath Communications Inc and Laurel Wreath Publishing, located in the Washington, DC metropolitan area. He is a motivational keynote speaker and author. Paul Lawrence Vann is a highly decorated military officer with over twenty years of duty and more than twelve consecutive years in the Pentagon. He works with military, associations, and Fortune 500 companies on leadership, diversity, and peak performance solutions

Paul Lawrence Vann
*Author/Speaker*
Laurel Wreath Communications Inc.
Laurel Wreath Publishing
Fort Washington, MD USA
*Contact Phone:* (800) 476-8976
*Cell:* 240-476-8976
**Click to Contact from Web Site**

**GEELA PARISH, AUTHOR**
Los Angeles, CA USA
www.geela.com

Geela was born in a remote part of Iran and raised in a very small town in Israel. She is the author of the bestselling and highly praised book The American Dream, her remarkable true-life story of how she came to America as a young immigrant with nothing and no support system and overcame incredible obstacles including poverty, discrimination and abuse to achieve mega-success. She is also a columnist, a speaker, an accomplished singer (she sings in ten different languages), songwriter, composer and producer, with many albums and awards to her credit including the critically acclaimed album The Veil of Life, the creator of the acclaimed spiritually-based system for achieving success and total prosperity (everything from health to wealth) called Principles of Successful Living, and the founder of the nonprofit organization, One Spirit, One World. She lives in Westlake Village, California with her husband John and their daughter, Ashley.

Geela Parish
Global Vision Media
Westlake Village, CA USA
*Contact Phone:* 818-597-0574
**Click to Contact from Web Site**

**GAYLE LANTZ - ORGANIZATIONAL
DEVELOPMENT EXPERT**
Birmingham, AL USA
http://www.gaylelantz.com/

Gayle Lantz is on a mission to help people make the most of their work. She founded the business based on the belief that work is one of the most important parts of life. When individuals are fully engaged in their work, they expand possibilities for themselves and the organization. As an organizational development consultant, she helps organizations and individuals improve performance.

Gayle Lantz
Gayle Lantz, LLC
Birmingham, AL USA
*Contact Phone:* 205 879-8494
**Click to Contact from Web Site**

**TERRY WALL, CERTIFIED
MANAGEMENT CONSULTANT**
Washington Township, NJ USA
http://www.tgwall.com

Terry Wall is the extraordinary fusion of expertise and eloquence — an articulate, insightful commentator on today's business world, and on future management and workplace trends. He is a consultant who has achieved the coveted CMC (Certified Management Consultant) designation from the Institute of Management Consultants, USA. Also, he is a professional speaker and skilled facilitator who is a member of the National Speakers Association and a recognized expert on strategy, leadership, and productivity.

Terry Wall, CMC
T.G. Wall Management Consulting, LLC
Washington Township, NJ
*Contact Phone:* 856-218-7200
**Click to Contact from Web Site**

**CAROL DUNITZ, PH.D -- EFFECTIVE BUSINESS COMMUNICATION EXPERT**
Ann Arbor, MI USA
http://www.drcaroldunitz.com

Dr. Carol Dunitz, effective business communication expert, is a speaker, writer/author, producer and consultant. Her colorful presentations for which she dresses in costume and sings original songs include Leadership, Teambuilding and Communciation in the Workplace; and Surefire Sales & Negotiating. Dunitz' new communication book, 'Louder Than Thunder: A Contemporary Business Parable' has received rave reviews in national media. She is also a seasoned marketing professional who provides comprehensive creative services to business.

Carol Dunitz
*President*
The Last Word
Canterbury & Parkside, Publishers
Ann Arbor, MI USA
*Contact Phone:* 734-747-6266
**Click to Contact from Web Site**

**ANNMARIE KELLY - - SKILLBUILDER SYSTEMS**
Philadelphia, PA USA
http://www.victoriouswoman.com

Annmarie Kelly, author of Victorious Woman! Shaping Life's Challenges into Personal Victories is a speaker, trainer, and victory strategist. She is an expert on women's issues, specifically on topics involving success, overcoming challenges, goal achievement, life balance and the advancement of women in society. Her Victorious Woman strategies show women how to choose and develop fulfilling and more satisfying lifestyles, beginning with self-awareness and following up with specific actions that result in a victorious outcome.

Annmarie Kelly
SkillBuilder Systems
West Chester, PA USA
*Contact Phone:* 610-738-8225
**Click to Contact from Web Site**

**JEAN PALMER HECK -- EXECUTIVE SPEECH COACH**
Indianapolis, IN USA
real-impact.com

How can you CUT THROUGH INFORMATION OVERLOAD to reach your boss? Is TV NEWS revolutionizing how you communicate? What's your BABBLING QUOTIENT? Is your boss boring? International Communications Expert. Advisor to Fortune 100 presidents. Media critic. Author. Former TV anchor. Great interview on: -- Public speaking -- Success/failure stories about the workplace and home -- Analysis of newsworthy speeches -- Soundbites that promote you.

Jean Palmer Heck
Zionsville, IN USA
*Contact Phone:* 317-873-3772
**Click to Contact from Web Site**

## LUAN MITCHELL-HALTER — ENTREPRENEUR/AUTHOR/ MOTIVATIONAL SPEAKER
Los Angeles, CA USA
http://www.LuAnMitchell.com

LuAn Mitchell-Halter has led an inspiring life as an entrepreneur, author, and citizen. As a minority, she has ran her own company and defied stereotypes. She now mentors women all over the United States and shares her strategies to overcome diversity in her book Paper Doll: Lessons Learned From a Life in the Headlines. She has also established a scholarship and a trust fund helping others to fulfill dreams.

Mike Nason
Nason Group
Laguna Niguel, CA USA
*Contact Phone:* 949-661-6031
*Cell:* 949-500-1180
**Click to Contact from Web Site**

## THE VERGHIS GROUP
Boston, MA USA
http://www.verghisgroup.com

Founded by Phil Verghis, The Verghis Group works with motivated clients to get and keep profitable customers for life. Phil and his teams have won a number of international awards for excellence in people, process and technology innovations in the customer support arena. He has spoken to thousands of people in four continents on customer service and technical support issues, and is the author of 'The Ultimate Customer Support Executive', published by Silicon Press.

Phil Verghis
*President*
The Verghis Group, Inc.
Cambridge, MA USA
*Contact Phone:* +1 (617) 395 6613
**Click to Contact from Web Site**

## SHEILA KESSLER, PHD-- CUSTOMER SATISFACTION EXPERT & EXECUTIVE COACH
San Clemente, CA USA
http://www.CompetitiveEdge.com

Dr. Sheila Kessler, author of the best selling 'Measuring and Managing Customer Satisfaction' is an international expert on customer satisfaction. She has done over 1,000 keynote speeches, executive coaching, training and consulting projects for the Fortune 500 companies. Customer research, strategic planning, quality metrics and initiatives are all integral parts of the system to be the best. She uses the 'voice of the customer' to make Six Sigma, Lean Service/Manufacturing and Baldridge efforts successful.

Sheila Kessler, Ph.D.
*President*
Competitive Edge
San Clemente, CA USA
*Contact Phone:* 949-498-0122
**Click to Contact from Web Site**

# Phil Verghis

## Global Customer Support Expert

A pre-eminent authority on global service delivery, Phil Verghis is both an experienced practitioner and a knowledgeable observer. As an expert in people, processes and technology, Phil combines hands-on experience in the trenches with keen insights from his tenure in upper management to deliver innovative solutions that satisfy the needs of each. Call Center Magazine says he is "among the best minds in his field."

Heading the Verghis Group, he designs and implements world-class customer support strategies that enable organizations to delight their customers and enhance their bottom line.

In addition to serving clients internationally, Phil is the author of "The Ultimate Customer Support Executive" (Silicon Press, 2005), a ground-breaking book on how support executives can work with key teams within their organizations to help acquire and retain profitable customers for life.

Phil is the past chairperson of the Strategic Advisory Board of the HDI, the world's largest membership association for the service and support industry. Among his numerous industry accolades, Phil is the only two-time winner of the Service 25 award, presented to those who have made a significant impact in the field of service and support. He was also named a "Leader and Legend" of the support industry.

Before founding the Verghis Group, Phil was vice president of infrastructure & support at Akamai Technologies (an MIT spin-off) and a member of the senior executive operations group. Among his responsibilities, Phil managed all aspects the world's largest distributed IP network with 15,000 servers in more than 60 countries.

**Phil Verghis, President, The Verghis Group, Inc.**
Cambridge, Mass. USA --- phil@verghisgroup.com
(800) 494-9142          +1 (617) 395 6613

THE **VERGHIS** GROUP

## POWERHOUSE CONSULTING, INC.
Bedford, NH USA
http://www.powerhouse1.com

PowerHouse is a professional management and technology company providing expertise on applied telecommunications (voice/data/image/integration) and customer service (call centers/help desks) applications. Kathleen M. Peterson is CEO, Founder, and Chief Vision Officer. She is sought after by Customer Service, Call Center, and Help Desk operators in finance, insurance, government, retail, media, and utilities for advice, counsel, and recommendations regarding management, operations, staffing, and technology. Widely published, she is frequently requested as a keynote speaker or seminar leader to address diverse business audiences.

David M. Peterson
*President*
PowerHouse Consulting, Inc.
Bedford, NH
*Contact Phone:* 800-449-9904
**Click to Contact from Web Site**

## ROGER NUNLEY — CUSTOMER CARE INSTITUTE
Atlanta, GA USA
www.customercare.com

Roger H. Nunley is a Customer Care professional with 20+ years of global experience. A frequent speaker at industry conferences, Roger has gained a reputation as an effective communicator, a creative problem-solver and a leader in the field of Customer Care. He is recognized for his leading-edge Customer Care initiatives and strategies. The Customer Care Institute is an international resource organization that assists Customer Care professionals with improving the delivery of corporate Customer Care.

Roger Nunley
Customer Care Institute
Atlanta, GA USA
*Contact Phone:* 404-352-9291
**Click to Contact from Web Site**

## JEFF GEE, CUSTOMER SERVICE EXPERT
Chicago, IL USA
http://www.mjlearning.com

Jeff is author of several books: SuperService, The Customer Service Training Toolkit, and The Winner's Attitude published by McGraw-Hill. He has co-authored Mission Possible with Steven Covey and Brian Tracy, and Pillars of Success with Alexander Haig and Pat Summitt. FOX, CBS, ABC, and NBC networks have all aired a story featuring Jeff, which focused on the state of customer loyalty. Jeff tackles serious topics with humor and candor, teaching his audiences to look first at what they do to create change, rather than wait for the other guy to make a move.

Val Gorick
*Director of Development*
MJ Learning Corp.
Lake Zurich, IL USA
*Contact Phone:* 847.438.9366
**Click to Contact from Web Site**

## NANCY FRIEDMAN, TELEPHONE DOCTOR
St. Louis, MO USA
http://www.telephonedoctor.com

Hell hath no fury like a customer scorned. It seems as though everyone has a horror story of how they've been treated either on the phone or in person. Nancy Friedman, the Telephone Doctor, has the cure for these ailments. Whatever the medium, Nancy keeps her audience entertained, informed and ready for more.

Nancy Friedman
*President*
Telephone Doctor
St. Louis, MO USA
*Contact Phone:* 314-291-1012
**Click to Contact from Web Site**

# HELL HATH NO FURY
# LIKE A CUSTOMER SCORNED

## Nancy Friedman

Seems as though everyone has a pet peeve or horror story of how they've been treated. **Nancy Friedman**, the Telephone Doctor®, has the cure for these ailments.

Whatever the medium, Nancy keeps her audience entertained, informed and ready for more.

### Just ask the Doctor:

1.  What's the single biggest pet peeve committed on the telephone?

2.  What's the best way to make a complaint call?

3.  What about speakerphones, answering machines and music on hold?

4.  How do you escape from voice mail jail?

5.  What about cell phones, car phones and all this new equipment?

6.  How do I get more value out of every telephone call?

7.  What are the 6 touch points of communications?

**Selected as one of the top 25 most influential women in St. Louis**

## THE AUTHORITY

Nancy Friedman is internationally recognized as a leading expert on customer service and communications. Nancy delivers her message to conference attendees worldwide. Thousands more have been trained by her best-selling videos. No matter the audience, Nancy's common sense approach is changing the way corporate America does business for the better.

**Nancy often appears on *The Today Show, Oprah, Good Morning America, CBS This Morning, Crook & Chase,* CNN, WOR, WJR, KMOX, WCCO, KCMO, WSB, <u>USA Today</u>, <u>Wall Street Journal</u> and hundreds of other radio, TV and print outlets.**

The Telephone Doctor's® book, **<u>Customer Service Nightmares</u>**, is a great story for all media.

LIVELY, HUMOROUS *and* **ALWAYS ASKED BACK!**

**For an interview, call us in St. Louis at 314-291-1012.**

Nancy Friedman, The Telephone Doctor®
www.telephonedoctor.com
nancy@telephonedoctor.com

**BELL**SOUTH®

## BELLSOUTH CORPORATION
Washington, DC USA
http://www.bellsouthcorp.com
NYSE BLS

BellSouth Corporation is a Fortune 500 communications company headquartered in Atlanta which has joint control and 40 percent ownership of Cingular Wireless. Customers can bundle local and long distance service with Internet access, satellite television and Cingular® Wireless service. For businesses, BellSouth provides secure, reliable local and long distance voice and data networking. BellSouth offers online and directory advertising through BellSouth RealPages.com® and The Real Yellow Pages®. More information can be found at www.bellsouth.com.

Bill McCloskey
*Director of Media Relations*
BellSouth Corporation
Washington, DC USA
*Contact Phone:* 202-463-4129
*Pager:* 800-742-6803
**Click to Contact from Web Site**

## ROSANNE DAUSILIO, PH.D.--CUSTOMER SERVICE EXPERT
New York, NY USA
http://www.human-technologies.com

Rosanne D'Ausilio, Ph.D., industrial psychologist, President of Human Technologies Global, Inc., specializes in human performance management for contact centers, providing needs analyses, instructional design, and customized, live, world class customer service skills trainings. Also offered: agent/facilitator certification through Purdue University's Center for Customer Driven Quality. Known as 'the practical champion of the human,' she authors the best-sellers, Wake Up Your Call Center: Humanize Your Interaction Hub, 4th edition, Customer Service and The Human Experience and her latest Lay Your Cards On The Table: 52 Ways to Stack Your Personal Deck (which includes a 32 card deck of cards), as well as a 'tip's newsletter at www.HumanTechTips.com.

Rosanne Dausilio, Ph.D.
Human Technologies Global Inc
Carmel, NY USA
*Contact Phone:* 845/228-6165
*Contact Main Phone:* 866/228-1497
*Cell:* 845/222-2455
**Click to Contact from Web Site**

## GREGORY GIRARD -- TELECOM TECHNOLOGY EXPERT
Boston, MA USA
http://www.girardcp.com

Mr. Girard is a computer and network architectural specialist concentrating on voice, video, data and facsimile transmission systems for the telecommunications industry. Industrial R&D experience includes 19 years developing computer hardware and software systems for microprocessor platforms. Recent projects focused on emerging voice-over-packet telecommunications network architectures, enhanced services platforms and IP-based switching systems. Expertise extends to analysis of telecommunications intellectual property, including evaluation of patent claims, offering opinions on infringement and constructing new claims.

Gregory Girard
Girard Consulting Partners
Manchester, MA USA
*Contact Phone:* 978-764-5196
**Click to Contact from Web Site**

## THE INSIGHT RESEARCH CORPORATION
Boonton, NJ USA
http://www.insight-corp.com

Providing telecommunications market research and strategic analysis for major industry players, our perspective comes from over a decade of market research expertise. We will supply analysis of current and future trends, backing it up with five-year revenue forecasts, charts, and tables. Insight Research has been quoted in BusinessWeek, LA Times, Newsweek, USA Today, America's Network, InternetWeek, Network World, Telephony, and Telecommunications and has appeared on World News Tonight with Peter Jennings, ABC's 20/20, CNN, CNBC, Reuters Financial Television, Fox News Channel, and the BBC.

Robert Rosenberg
*President*
The Insight Research Corporation
Boonton, NJ
*Contact Phone:* 973-541-9600
**Click to Contact from Web Site**

## CREATEAWAY
Gilroy, CA USA
http://www.createaway.com

Elevate Your Opportunity — Doing more to promote yourself will lead to more opportunity for your Speaking and Coaching business. Are you aiming high, or flying below the radar?

Mike Rabbitts
*President & Co-Founder*
createaway
Gilroy, CA USA
*Contact Phone:* 877-273-8292
*Contact Main Phone:* 1-877-CRE8AWAY
**Click to Contact from Web Site**

## DENISE WAKEMAN — THE BLOG SQUAD
North Hollywood, CA USA
http://www.buildabetterblog.com

Specialty: Project management and implementation, internet marketing strategies, including business blogs, electronic newsletters, automated marketing systems and ecommerce solutions. Co-author: Build a Better Blog: The Ultimate Guide to Boosting Your Business with a Professional Blog Denise Wakeman is Chief Implementor of Next Level Partnership, a company dedicated to assisting you to take your business to the next level by partnering with you to realize your big ideas through strategy, support and implementation. Denise has more than 20 years experience in small business administration and management. She has specific experience in leveraging Internet marketing strategies to create awareness, build customer loyalty and increase the bottom line.

Denise Wakeman
The Blog Squad
North Hollywood, CA USA
*Contact Phone:* 213-820-5332
**Click to Contact from Web Site**

## BUSINESSOL - SEARCH ENGINE OPTIMIZATION EXPERTS
San Diego, CA USA
www.businessol.com

Since 1996, BusinessOnLine has been building Internet marketing solutions for companies of all sizes, with a focus on the following core market segments: manufacturers/distributors, associations, publishers and the Fortune 1000. BusinessOnLine's experience includes over 400 Web sites built. We start with Internet Strategy to monetize Web site properties for some of the largest B2B publishers and directories including Business. com, Thomas Register and Managing Automation. Additionally, our expertise includes Usability, Search Engine Optimization, and Analytic consulting with over 60 of the Fortune 500 including industry leaders such as Chevron, Cisco Systems, Thomas Register, Pitney-Bowes, Omron, Tyco, EDS, HSBC, Charlotte Pipe, NEC, Siemon and many more. Our team consists of subject matter experts in areas including Internet marketing, Web site usability, design, information architecture, search engine optimization, e-commerce and Web analytics (tracking). Our philosophy is to view each client relationship as a long-term partnership. Unlike many project-based Web development firms, our business model focuses on making every client successful on the Web. BusinessOnLinc's turnkey solutions drive quality traffic, convert casual visitors into leads or sales, and measure the overall Web site success. With a team of experts in specific disciplines, we deliver the best solution every time.

Aaron Kahlow
*VP of Sales and Marketing*
BusinessOL
San Diego, CA USA
*Contact Phone:* 619-699-0767
**Click to Contact from Web Site**

## JENNIFER BEEVER -- NEW INCITE MARKETING
Los Angeles, CA USA
http://www.NewIncite.com

Marketing Strategy - Online Marketing - Search Engine Optimization - Specialization in Software, High Tech, and Medical Industries. Marketing Consultant Jennifer Beever works with small to mid-sized businesses that are "selling in spite of themselves" to find new opportunities, plan new marketing programs, execute marketing and set up results-tracking to measure return on marketing investment. She believes that websites and the Internet are central to B2B marketing, and welcomes interviews and queries on the subject.

Jennifer Beever, CMC
New Incite
Woodland Hills, CA USA
*Contact Phone:* 818-347-4248
**Click to Contact from Web Site**

## JILL TANENBAUM — WASHINGTON DC GRAPHIC DESIGN
Bethesda, MD USA
www.jtdesign.com

The almost quarter-century success of Jill Tanenbaum Graphic Design & Advertising Inc. (JTGD&A) stems from a business philosophy that is very different from other agencies. Our studio integrates marketing skills, innovative design, and the most advanced technologies to efficiently achieve each client's communication goals. We rely on a select group of professionals with a combined 125 years of experience, and supplement our core staff with strategic partners. This practice enables clients to access the highest-quality services, while avoiding the higher overhead of larger companies that retain personnel not related to a client's project.

Jill Tanenbaum
Jill Tanenbaum Graphic Design & Advertising Inc.
Bethesda, MD USA
*Contact Phone:* 301-229-1135
**Click to Contact from Web Site**

## PHILIPPA GAMSE, WEB STRATEGY SPEAKER
San Jose, CA USA
http://www.CyberSpeaker.com

Philippa Gamse is an eBusiness and Web strategy consultant. She helps companies and nonprofit organizations maximize their return on investment in their Internet presence. Her innovative thinking has created key improvements in her clients' Websites by significantly increasing levels and quality of leads, sales and customer relationships. Philippa is regularly contacted by media for her expertise on subjects including eBusiness strategy best practices, creating Websites that produce results, and small business online techniques and solutions.

Philippa Gamse, CMC
*President*
Total 'Net Value, Inc.
Santa Cruz, CA USA
*Contact Phone:* 831-465-0317
**Click to Contact from Web Site**

## CITYCAST MEDIA — PODCASTS, WEBCASTS, BLOGS, & RSS TECHNOLOGIES
New York, NY USA
citycastmedia.com

CityCast Media specializes in helping organizations develop Web 2.0 outreach strategies. In addition to traditional PR and marketing tools, CityCast specializes in integrating and developing Direct Mediacasting (DMC) solutions for our clients. CityCast develops, creates, implements, and integrates a variety of DMC solutions including: Audio and Video Podcasts, Webcasts, Blogs, RSS feeds, E-newsletters and Wiki systems. All of the DMC solutions marry the idea of broadcasting, narrowcasting, and subscription/on-demand media.

Jason Cohen
CityCast Media
New York, NY USA
*Contact Phone:* 212-931-4866
**Click to Contact from Web Site**

## TOM NARDONE — ONLINE PRIVACY EXPERT
Detroit, MI USA
http://www.IsderaCorp.com

Tom Nardone invented a unique business that allows people to shop in private for embarrassing products. His company now operates 9 retail websites that sell interesting personal items. Over 250,000 customers in more than 70 countries trust him with their deepest secrets. Some customers shop in private to cure hemorrhoids, bad breath, acne, incontinence, and even sexual dysfunction. Others want to keep information about their personal and sex lives private. Isdera Corp. holds everyone's information in the strictest of confidence.

Tom Nardone
*President*
IsderaCorp.com
Isdera Corporation
Hazel Park, MI USA
*Contact Phone:* 248-744-3580
*Contact Main Phone:* 248-744-3580
**Click to Contact from Web Site**

## TOM ANTION -- INTERNET MARKETING EXPERT
Virginia Beach, VA USA
http://www.GreatInternetMarketing.com

Tom Antion, Internet Marketing Expert, will show your audience how to keep from bludgeoning, kicking, cursing, shooting, slapping, spitting on and generally wanting to dismember the people who are supposed to be helping them with their websites. Tom is an internationally acclaimed expert in Internet Marketing for small business who actually makes large sums of money on the Internet. He's not giving book reports, theories or untested ideas like most of the other media hounds who never made a nickel selling anything on the Internet.

Tom Antion
Antion & Associates
Virginia Beach, VA USA
*Contact Phone:* 757-431-1366
**Click to Contact from Web Site**

## CREATION CHAMBER
Denver, CO USA
http://www.creationchamber.com

Our end-to-end website design solutions include: Analysis of your unique needs, Identification of key success factors New domain registration, Interface design, Information architecture and site layout, Brand integration / corporate identity development, Flash animation, Shopping carts, Traffic analysis, Secure server Credit card Processing, Custom applications and extended web solutions Marketing and distribution campaigns, High-availability website and e-mail hosting services, and Ongoing quality assurance.

Stefanie Jones
P.R.
Denver, CO USA
*Contact Phone:* 303-388-8460
*Cell:* 303-324-0857
**Click to Contact from Web Site**

## PROF. WILLIAM CROSSMAN - FUTURIST & TALKING COMPUTERS EXPERTTALKING COMPUTERS EXPERT
San Francisco, CA USA
www.CompSpeak2050.org

William Crossman is a talking computers expert. He says: Voice-in/voice-out (VIVO) talking computers using voice-recognition technology are going to erase the "digital divide" and democratize the flow of information worldwide. Text/written language is an ancient technology for storing and retrieving information. VIVOs will do the same job more quickly, efficiently, and universally, making text obsolete, replacing all writing and reading with speech and graphics/video, and recreating an oral culture by 2050. By enabling a true "global conversation," VIVOs will completely reshape international relations, education, global business, the arts, and human consciousness itself. Author, new book: VIVO [Voice-In/Voice-Out]: The Coming Age of Talking Computers.

Prof. William Crossman
*Founder/Director*
CompSpeak 2050 Institute
San Francisco, CA USA
*Contact Phone:* 510-839-5691
**Click to Contact from Web Site**

## MEQUODA GROUP — HELPING PUBLISHERS HARNESS THE INTERNET
Boston, MA USA
http://www.Mequoda.com

Don Nicholas is the editor and publisher of the weekly Mequoda Media Advisor and Mequoda Research Update. He and his Mequoda research team have authored 9 books on media management including Internet Strategy for Publishers and Authors, Internet Marketing Strategy for Publishers and Authors, Website Design and Usability for Publishers and Authors and Creating Landing Pages that Sell. A comprehensive collection of their work is available at the Mequoda Library.

Don Nicholas
Mequoda Group
Sudbury, MA USA
*Contact Phone:* 978-440-8037
**Click to Contact from Web Site**

## CHRISTOPHER FAULKNER, C I HOST
Dallas, TX USA
http://www.CIHOST.com

C I Host (www.cihost.com), based in the Dallas/Fort Worth market, is a global Web hosting company, Internet solutions provider and software developer, serving 205,000 clients in 182 countries. C I Host is headquartered from its main facility and Network Operations Center in Bedford, Texas, and it operates additional diverse data centers in Los Angeles and Chicago with a grand opening in London scheduled for 2004. C I Host is the largest privately held hosting company.

Christopher Faulkner
C I Host
Bedford, TX USA
*Contact Phone:* 817-868-6999
*Contact Main Phone:* 817-868-9931
**Click to Contact from Web Site**

## MARC HARTY -- PRTRAFFIC.COM
Dallas, TX USA
www.PRTraffic.com

Ninety per-cent of small businesses today do no search marketing. Marc Harty, Internet Marketing Strategist and 25-year marketing veteran, is changing that. Marc's proven, step-by-step methods help anyone generate targeted web traffic. Marc's www.PRTraffic.com course introduced the world's first Press Release Optimization System™, integrating all four key marketing disciplines: PR, Publicity, Web Traffic Creation and Web Traffic Conversion. Marc has spoken to millions globally about Web PR, Internet Marketing, and Web Site Traffic.

Marc Harty
PRTraffic.com
Dallas, TX USA
*Contact Phone:* 214-528-8300
**Click to Contact from Web Site**

## MINUTEPAGE.COM BRAND HOMEPAGE CREATOR
Washington, DC USA
pages.zdnet.com/biswire/

MinutePage.com is the United States Trademark for the Broadcast Interview Source's HomePage Creator software. This is the code that runs the back-end of the ExpertClick system.

Mitchell Davis
Broadcast Interview Source, Inc.
Washington, DC USA
*Contact Phone:* 202-333-5000
**Click to Contact from Web Site**

## TAMPA BAY TECHNOLOGY FORUM
Tampa, FL USA
tbtf.org

The Tampa Bay Technology Forum (TBTF) is a group of people united to make Tampa Bay a place where technology-based business and innovation thrives. TBTF is a professional association of technology and business leaders, investors, government, researchers and educators dedicated to growing and promoting Tampa Bay's technology eco-system. TBTF supports this purpose through networking, educational programs, awareness campaigns, and advocacy for our members. Our members are technology professionals, technology companies, entrepreneurs, capital sources to fund technology, support firms, universities, government and economic development representatives.

Andy Hafer
Tampa Bay Technology Forum
Tampa, FL USA
*Contact Phone:* 813 610-5774
**Click to Contact from Web Site**

## technolytics

## TECHNOLYTICS -- KEVIN G. COLEMAN
Pittsburgh, PA USA
http://www.technolytics.com

The Technolytics Institute (Technolytics) was established in 2000 as an independent executive think-tank. Our primary purpose is to undertake original research and develop substantive points of view on strategic issues facing executives in businesses, government and industry around the world. Our strategic goals focus on improving business performance, creating sustainable competitive advantage, delivering innovation and technology, and managing security and risk. We operate three centers: [Business & Commerce] - [Security & Intelligence] and [Science & Technology].

Kevin G. Coleman
*Senior Fellow/Chief Strategist*
Technolytics
McMurray, PA
*Contact Phone:* 412-818-7656
*Contact Main Phone:* 888-650-0800
**Click to Contact from Web Site**

# Tom Antion

## Internet Money-Making Expert

Tom Antion will show your audience members how to keep from bludgeoning, kicking, cursing, shooting, slapping, spitting on and generally wanting to dismember the people who are supposed to be helping them with their Web sites.

Tom is an internationally acclaimed expert in Internet marketing for small business who actually makes large sums of money on the Internet. He's not giving book reports, theories or untested ideas like most of the other media hounds who never made a nickel selling anything on the Internet.

Big business owners and CEOs aren't too thrilled with Tom when he tells them what morons they are for spending millions of dollars on things that can be done for a few hundred. They really hate it when they find out that Tom got "Best-of-the-Web" in INC. magazine on a site that cost only $650 to create. This site beat out three others that cost more than one million dollars each to create.

Tom has been featured on major news media worldwide, including the Canadian Broadcast Network, the Australian Broadcast Network, Associated Press, the Tokyo Today Show and hundreds of radio, television and print outlets across the United States, including four feature articles in the Washington Post.

Whether in a print or broadcast medium Tom is totally focused on your audience and he knows his job is to give them great tips that will help them succeed, while making you look great for interviewing him. He was media trained by Joel Roberts.

Tom was also the chief spokesperson for CBS-owned Switchboard.com in their "Main Streets Online" outreach program for small business. Switchboard is one of the largest and most heavily visited Web sites on the Internet. Tom beat out thousands of book-learned Ph.D.'s and other pseudo experts for the job.

Tom consistently makes large sums of money while sitting in front of his computer which gave him the idea for his infamous "Butt Camp" Seminars where you learn to make more money sitting on your rear end than going out and working for a living.

## CONSUMER ELECTRONICS ASSOCIATION (CEA)
Arlington, VA USA
http://www.ce.org

The Consumer Electronics Association (CEA) is the preeminent trade association promoting growth in the consumer technology industry through technology policy, events, research, promotion and the fostering of business and strategic relationships. CEA represents more than 2,000 corporate members involved in the design, development, manufacturing, distribution and integration of audio, video, mobile electronics, wireless and landline communications, information technology, home networking, multimedia and accessory products, as well as related services that are sold through consumer channels. Combined, CEA's members account for more than $122 billion in annual sales. CEA's resources are available online at www.CE.org, the definitive source for information about the consumer electronics industry. CEA also sponsors and manages the International CES - Defining Tomorrow's Technology. All profits from CES are reinvested into industry services, including technical training and education, industry promotion, engineering standards development, market research and legislative advocacy. Additional contacts: Gary Shapiro - President & CEO 703 907 7610, Michael Petricone - VP Technology Policy, Government and Legal Affairs mpetricone@ce.org and Sean Wargo - Market Research and Senior Economist swargo@ce.org.

Jeff Joseph
*VP, Comm. & Strategic Rel.*
Consumer Electronics Association (CEA)
Arlington, VA
*Contact Phone:* 703-907-7664
**Click to Contact from Web Site**

## C. CRANE COMPANY — CONUSMER RADIO EXPERTS
Fortuna, CA USA
www.ccrane.com

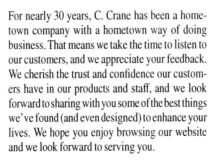

For nearly 30 years, C. Crane has been a hometown company with a hometown way of doing business. That means we take the time to listen to our customers, and we appreciate your feedback. We cherish the trust and confidence our customers have in our products and staff, and we look forward to sharing with you some of the best things we've found (and even designed) to enhance your lives. We hope you enjoy browsing our website and we look forward to serving you.

Robert C. Crane
C. Crane Company
Fortuna, CA USA
*Contact Phone:* 707-725-9000
**Click to Contact from Web Site**

## BILL JELEN — EXCEL CONSULTANT — MREXCEL.COM
Akron, OH USA
http://www.MrExcel.com/

Microsoft Office is undergoing dramatic changes. Despite amazing new features, corporations face phenomenal retraining costs. As MrExcel, Jelen is the go-to guy for Office problems. His MrExcel.com website features 150,000 Excel solutions, a top-ranked daily video-podcast, and a community of 20K+ Excel fans. An internationally recognized speaker/consultant on spreadsheets, he is author of eleven books. As a Microsoft MVP, he's been alpha & beta testing Office 2007 since 2005. Experience includes 40+ TV appearances.

Bill Jelen
*Publisher*
MrExcel.com
Uniontown, OH USA
*Contact Phone:* 330-715-2875
**Click to Contact from Web Site**

## JEANETTE S. CATES, PHD - THE TECHNOLOGY TAMER ™
Austin, TX USA
http://www.techtamers.com

Why do some companies spend thousands of dollars for technology that still doesn't solve their problem? Why do organizations launch a winning initiative, then watch it fail? Why do some people have a knack for using technology and others don't? Dr. Jeanette Cates, a Technology Implementation Expert, has helped launch successful technology programs for multinational corporations and solo entrepreneurs. Ask about ways to increase your productivity and effectiveness. Dr. Cates has studied and implemented programs for more than 30 years.

Jeanette S. Cates, Ph.D.
The Technology Tamer ™
Austin, TX
*Contact Phone:* 512-219-5653
**Click to Contact from Web Site**

## SIIA
Washington, DC USA
http://www.siia.net

The Software & Information Industry Association is the principal trade association for the software and digital content industry. SIIA provides global services in government relations, business development, corporate education and intellectual property protection to the leading companies that are setting the pace for the digital age.

David Williams
Washington, DC United States
*Contact Phone:* 202.789.4473
**Click to Contact from Web Site**

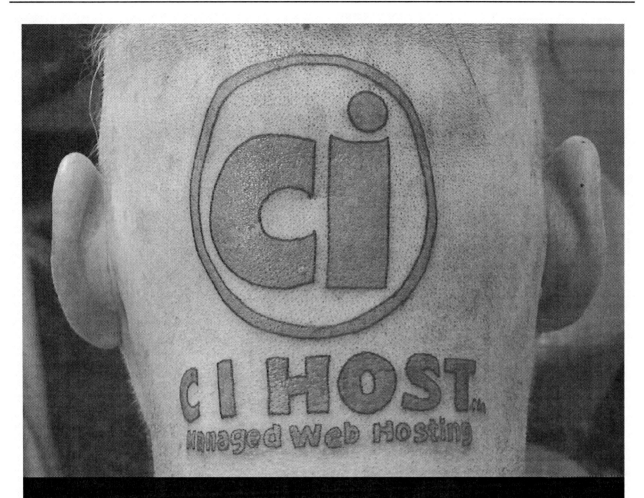

### TIME WARNER TELECOM, INC.
Denver, CO USA
www.twtelecom.com

Time Warner Telecom, headquartered in Littleton, CO, is a leading provider of managed networking solutions to a wide array of businesses and organizations in 22 states and 44 U.S. metropolitan areas. As one of the country's premier competitive service providers, Time Warner Telecom integrates data, dedicated Internet access, and local and long distance voice services for long distance carriers, wireless communications companies, incumbent local exchange carriers, and enterprise organizations in healthcare, finance, higher education, manufacturing, and hospitality industries, as well as for military, state and local government.

Bob Meldrum
*Senior Director of Marketing*
Time Warner Telecom, Inc.
Littleton, CO USA
*Contact Phone:* 303-566-1354
**Click to Contact from Web Site**

### ADTRAN, INC.
Huntsville, AL USA
http://www.adtran.com
NASDQ ADTN

ADTRAN, Inc. supplies innovative network access products that enable today's widespread digital telecommunications applications, including Internet access, telecommuting, corporate connectivity, distance learning, videoconferencing, and teleradiology. Used extensively in the networks of incumbent local exchange carriers, independent carriers, competitive service providers, interexchange carriers, Internet service providers, and private and public enterprises worldwide, ADTRAN products consistently reduce operating costs and improve network performance. ADTRAN also provides custom-designed products for many well-known Original Equipment Manufacturers (OEMs).

Michael Becce
MRB Public Relations, Inc.
Red Bank, NJ USA
*Contact Phone:* 732-758-1100
**Click to Contact from Web Site**

### MAQ SOFTWARE
Seattle, WA USA
http://www.MAQSoftware.com

As the founder and the managing consultant of MAQ Software, Rajeev works with customers to plan and develop innovative applications on various technology platforms. Prior to founding MAQ Software, Rajeev worked at Microsoft® Corporation, where he held product management responsibilities for several products including Visual C++, Windows and Exchange Server. Furthermore at Microsoft Corporation, his responsibilities included product planning, marketing strategy and advertising for products ranging in annual revenue from $50 million to $5 billion.

Rajeev Agarwal
*Founder and Managing Consultant*
MAQ Software
Redmond, WA USA
*Contact Phone:* 425-558-7775
*Cell:* 425-444-8808
**Click to Contact from Web Site**

### SEARCH OPTIMIZATION NEWS
Washington, DC USA
search-optimization-news.com

Search Optimization News is written for Yearbook of Experts' members.

Mitchell P. Davis
Broadcast Interview Source, Inc.
Washington, DC USA
*Contact Phone:* 202-333-5000
**Click to Contact from Web Site**

### JUDY COLBERT -- WEB USABILITY SPEAKER
Washington, DC USA
http://www.JudyColbert.com

Web design usability is a key part of any marketing plan and an area where Judy Colbert, co-author of 'Big Bang Marketing for Spas' and the forthcoming 'Hotel and Resort Marketing Ideas' and 'Destination Marketing Ideas. She has specific knowledge about Web site usability, From domain names to taglines to search buttons, she reviews Web sites for their ease of use by site visitors. She is available for interviews, consulting, and speaking engagements.

Judy Colbert
TUII Turtle Publishing, LLC
Crofton, MD United States
*Contact Phone:* (301) 858-0196
*Cell:* 301 257 0196
**Click to Contact from Web Site**

# ExpertClick.com's
## *Search Optimization News*

### Look No Further:
**ONE OF THE BEST NEWSLETTERS ON SEARCH ENGINE SAVVY IS AVAILABLE WITH YOUR EXPERTCLICK MEMBERSHIP.**

- Visit SearchOptimizationNews.com to get the current and all past issues of this up-to-date, very useful newsletter, another service from ExpertClick.com.

- Subscribe now by simply visiting SearchOptimizationNews.com.

- Or, if you wish, pick up the phone, and call 202-333-5000.

**DAVID MEERMAN SCOTT --
STRATEGIC INTERNET MARKETING
CONSULTANT**
Boston, MA USA
http://www.davidmeermanscott.com

Web marketing expert David Meerman Scott, author of 'Cashing In With Content: How Innovative Marketers Use Digital Information to Turn Browsers Into Buyers,' focuses on using online content to market and sell products and services to demanding customers worldwide. He is also an expert on business blogs and blogging. David has lived in New York, Tokyo, Boston, and Hong Kong, and has presented at conferences and events in over twenty countries on four continents.

David Meerman Scott
Lexington, MA USA
*Contact Phone:* 617-513-9548
**Click to Contact from Web Site**

**KEVIN SAVETZ**
Blue Lake, CA USA
http://www.savetzpublishing.com

Kevin Savetz is owner of Savetz Publishing, a company that creates high-quality, content-driven web sites. His more than 40 sites include FreePrintable.net, which offers free business cards, certificates, and other printable documents; FreeAfterRebate.info, which points buyers to free-after-rebate deals at online merchants; and FaxZero.com, a service that lets users send free faxes throughout the U.S. and Canada.

Kevin Savetz
Blue Lake, CA United States
**Click to Contact from Web Site**

**MIKE STEWART — INTERNET AUDIO GUY**
Atlanta, GA USA
www.internetaudioguy.com/

Who else wants to learn the secrets to making digital audio products to sell? Now you can easily do it with our packages & DVD tutorials that no else has!

Mike Stewart
Lawrenceville, GA USA
*Contact Phone:* 770-932-9567
**Click to Contact from Web Site**

**VERTICAL SEARCH ENGINE**
Washington, DC USA
www.verticalsearch.com

VerticalSearch.com's mission is to provide the B2B community with the best search experience on the web. We accomplish this first by focusing our search engine on the most relevant web sites for the B2B user. To begin with, we have indexed over 4,000 of the B2B trade press sites, including many online -only publishers of B2B information. These sites offer a wealth of content and editorial expertise in the whole range of B2B verticals, from Agriculture to Mining, Construction to Transportation. Soon we will be adding tens of thousands of B2B company sites to augment the B2B trade press sites. And, as VerticalSearch.com evolves, watch for useful community tools and features that will allow each vertical B2B community to share domain expertise, product offerings, and business and job opportunities by sector.

Jeffrey Dearth
Vertical Search
Washington, DC USA
*Contact Phone:* 202 338 5790
**Click to Contact from Web Site**

**JOHN PAUL MENDOCHA - POD CASTING PROFITS**
Grand Terrace, CA USA
www.podcasting-profits.com

Cutting edge, up to the minute information on Podcasting, the technology behind Podcasting and regular lessons on creating a Podcast Strategy for your business!

John Paul Mendocha
Pod Casting Profits
Grand Terrace, CA USA
*Contact Phone:* 909-783-2000
**Click to Contact from Web Site**

- **Internet Consulting**
- **Website Design**
- **Hosting**
- **Ecommerce**
- **Database Integration**
- **Since 1995**

PlanetLink CEO, Steve Lillo

**STEVE LILLO, PLANETLINK:
INTERNET SOLUTIONS FOR BUSINESS**
San Francisco, CA USA
www.PlanetLink.com

We work with businesses that want to have an Internet game plan and a website that works. If you're not successful, we're not successful. Expertise: PlanetLink is a mature and well-rounded website design firm. Since 1995 we have been working with our clients to create and maintain their websites Each project is created specifically to the needs of each client from three perspectives: 1. Marketing (intention, fulfillment, needs), 2. Technology (what technologies are required to achieve the desired results), and 3. Design (what should the site look like, how should the business be presented visually and what are the expectations of the visitors).

Steve Lillo
*Contact Phone:* 415-884-2022
**Click to Contact from Web Site**

## INFOCOMMERCE REPORT
Philadelphia, PA USA
www.infocommercegroup.com/

InfoCommerce Report, the flagship product of Infocommerce Group, is a continuous information service designed to meet a single goal: to satisfy our subscribing clients ever-changing needs for cutting edge information on the database and directory industry. Instead of merely providing news, ICR's unique ingredient is insight. ICR couples a keen understanding of the industry's dynamics with access to the people who drive it. The benefits to you are the ideas, contacts, strategies and intelligence that can help you be more successful.

Russell Perkins
InfoCommerce Report
*Contact Phone:* 610.649.1200, ext. 2
**Click to Contact from Web Site**

## THINK TANK DIRECTORY
Topeka, KS USA
www.ThinkTankDirectory.com

Founded in 1978, Government Research Service publishes several political reference books. The company's primary publications are the Think Tank Directory and the State Legislative Sourcebook. The State Legislative Sourcebook is an annual resource guide to legislative information in each of the fifty states. Choice magazine said that the Sourcebook provides useful legislative information sources and data for those studying or attempting to influence state legislatures. In addition to editing the Think Tank Directory and the State Legislative Sourcebook, publisher Lynn Hellebust is the author of How to Lobby Your State Legislature and the Kansas Legislative Handbook.

Lynn Hellebust
Government Research Service
Topeka, KS USA
*Contact Phone:* 785-232-1615
**Click to Contact from Web Site**

## DEBBIE WEIL-- CORPORATE BLOGGING EXPERT
Washington, DC USA
http://www.BlogWriteForCEOs.com

Wondering what in heck the blogging buzz is about? Ask Debbie Weil. She is an online marketing and corporate blogging consultant to clients such as HP and Wells Fargo. She is currently writing a book about corporate blogging for Penguin Portfolio. She blogs at www.BlogWriteForCEOs.com and www.BlogSmartCompanies.com.

Debbie Weil
WordBiz.com, Inc.
Washington, DC USA
*Contact Phone:* 202-364-5705
*Cell:* 202.255.1467
**Click to Contact from Web Site**

## PIXELPAGESPLUS.COM (SM)
New Orleans, LA USA
http://www.pixelpagesplus.com

PixelPagesPlus.com (sm) is the first and only pixel pages (sm) tourist related web site targeting specific cities around the world where people want to visit. As an advertiser, you pick your level of advertising to target your advertising dollars. Both businesses and individuals can stake their claim on the stylized map of the city. PixelPagesPlus.com (sm) believes that advertising is for where you are physically located, where you would like a presence and where visitors want to visit.

Irv Schwary
PixelPagesPlus.com (sm)
Metairie, LA
*Contact Phone:* 504-837-4025
**Click to Contact from Web Site**

## CYNTHIA BERCOWETZ, IDENTITY THEFT EXPERT
Hartford, CT USA
www.deargeorge.org

Cynthia Bercowetz is a graduate of American International College. She has been a consumer writer for the Hartford Courant. She wrote the Get Help! Tell It to George column for the Journal Inquirer. Her career started at the Hartford Times where the Dear George column originated. Her column received a national award from the Major Appliance Consumer Action Panel for consumer education. She has spoken to many groups on How to Be A Smart Consumer.

Cynthia Bercowetz
Bloomfield, CT USA
*Contact Phone:* 860-243-2208
**Click to Contact from Web Site**

## SHAWN COLLINS — AFFILIATE PROGRAM EXPERT
Berkeley Heights, NJ USA
http://www.shawncollinsconsulting.com

Shawn Collins is CEO of Shawn Collins Consulting (www.ShawnCollinsConsulting.com), an agency that manages affiliate programs for clients such as Payless ShoeSource and Snapfish, a division of Hewlett-Packard. He is also a co-founder of the Affiliate Summit conference (www.affiliatesummit.com). Shawn authored the book, Successful Affiliate Marketing for Merchants, and the AffStat (www.affstat.com) affiliate marketing benchmark reports. Additionally, he runs the Affiliate Tip directory (www.affiliatetip.com) and regularly blogs on the state of the affiliate marketing space.

Shawn Collins
Berkeley Heights, NJ United States
*Contact Phone:* 908-771-5574
*Cell:* 973-568-8172
**Click to Contact from Web Site**

## PANTHEON SOFTWARE — WEB SITE DESIGN DEVELOPMENT EXPERTS

Arlington, VA USA

www.pantheonsoftware.com

Pantheon Software, Inc. — Web Site Design Development Experts— offers services and software which fit the needs of almost any Internet project, large or small. Since 1994, Pantheon's outstanding team of account representatives, project managers, designers and programmers has taken great pride in providing our valued clients with the highest quality services in the industry.

Mark Tobias
*President*
Pantheon Software
Arlington, VA United State
*Contact Phone:* 703-387-4000
**Click to Contact from Web Site**

## STAN CRAIG — PERFORMANCE LEADERSHIP SPEAKER

Southport, NC USA

www.StanCraig.com

More than 25 years of experience and expertise are evident in all of Stan Craig's presentations. Whether the topic is marketing, client service, client retention or understanding how money works, few offer as much original insight into the topic or present it with such enthusiasm and passion as Stan does. From Wall Street and the World Financial Center to Main Street and your boardroom or meeting room, audiences participate in a meaningful experience every time Stan steps up to speak. Stan is a recognized authority in the financial services industry, appearing on CNBC and quoted in the Wall Street Journal, Business Week, Barron's, and Money Magazine. And the response is always positive.

Stanley L. Craig
Southport, NC USA
*Contact Phone:* 910-540-1447
**Click to Contact from Web Site**

## KIM SNIDER - RETIREMENT INCOME EXPERT

Dallas, TX USA

http://www.kimsnider.com/

For investors needing a consistent income, The Snider Investment Method generates a consistent cash flow with risk similar to a diversified bond portfolio. For growth investors, the method's consistent return can be reinvested to grow your portfolio faster than traditional stock market investments. The Snider Investment Method is tops among innovative new investment alternatives for meeting both growth and income objectives. Find out everything you need to know about how you can put the Snider Investment Method to work for you at themethod.kimsnider.com

David Drewitz
Guru Partners
Irving, TX USA
*Contact Phone:* 972-248-8600
**Click to Contact from Web Site**

## WILLIAM E. DONOGHUE -- THE FATHER OF SAFE MONEY INVESTING

Boston, MA USA

http://www.donoghue.com

Registered Investment Advisors, proactive mutual fund investment advisors, retirement savings strategists, tax-managed accounts, mutual fund separate accounts, variable annuities and insurance.

William E. Donoghue
*Chairman*
W. E. Donoghue Co., Inc.
Natick, MA USA
*Contact Phone:* 800-642-4276
*Cell:* 206-954-4762
**Click to Contact from Web Site**

## HAROLD LUSTIG — ACHIEVE FINANCIAL SECURITY

San Francsico, CA USA

www.FourSteps.com

Harold Lustig is a financial planner and advisor, specializing in financial and estate planning for the gay and lesbian community. Lustig's clients include professionals, business owners, retirees, singles and couples. He is a Chartered Life Underwriter, Chartered Financial Consultant and holds an MBA from Drexel University. He has an independent financial planning practice in San Francisco and is an Associate Registered Investment Advisor and Registered Representative with Multi-Financial Securities of Denver, Colorado.

Harold Lustig, CLU, ChFC
San Rafael, CA USA
*Contact Phone:* 415-472-1396
**Click to Contact from Web Site**

# 76 MILLION BABY BOOMERS WILL BEGIN RETIRING IN 2008. ARE THEY PREPARED?

## KIM SNIDER KNOWS THE ANSWER!

Kim Snider, the Founder and President of Kim Snider Financial Communications is attacking a problem that will affect our entire nation – the looming crisis of baby boomers retiring without the financial resources required to live out their retirement, free from financial worry.

Kim Snider knows and understands the responsibility for providing retirement income is shifting away from our employers and the government – and on to individuals. This shift demands a shift in the way retirement portfolios are managed. A shift which Kim Snider knows well and is passionate about.

According to a survey, more than eight in ten near-retirees say a guaranteed stream of income during retirement is their number-one financial goal, but the vast majority have no idea how to convert their nest egg into "a retirement paycheck." Kim Snider is helping these pre-retirees using a one-of-kind investment method she developed herself. The Snider Investment Method™ is unique, successful and helps ill-prepared, pre-retirees enter retirement with a steady stream of income.

If you want a story that resonates with a potential audience of 76 million interested readers, you won't find a more dynamic and informative interview than Kim Snider.

KIM SNIDER
214-965-9950
1-866-952-0100
KIM@KIMSNIDER.COM

## KIMSNIDER.COM

## DAN COUGHLIN, THE CORPORATE CATALYST
St. Louis, MO USA
www.thecoughlincompany.com

Dan Coughlin is a leading authority on business acceleration. Dan's clients include McDonald's, Coca-Cola, and Marriott. His new book, Corporate Catalysts, provides enormously pragmatic approaches to effective leadership, management, and branding. Dan has provided over 500 presentations on business acceleration, and more than 1,000 Executive Coaching sessions for executives in Fortune 500 Companies. He has spent over 3,000 hours on-site observing executives and managers deal with real-life business situations in more than 20 different industries.

Dan Coughlin
*President*
The Coughlin Co., Inc.
Fenton, MO USA
*Contact Phone:* 636-825-6611
*Cell:* 314-614-8622
**Click to Contact from Web Site**

## ANTHONY HSIEH - LOANS AND PERSONAL FINANCE EXPERT
Atlanta, GA USA
http://www.LendingTree.com/

Anthony Hsieh, president of LendingTree.com, has nearly two decades of mortgage industry experience and is widely recognized for his critical role in the development and shaping of the online lending category. Mr. Hsieh is a nationally recognized mortgage industry expert and frequent media commentator who has appeared regularly on CNNfn, CNBC, and the Fox News Channel, and in publications such as the Los Angeles Times, Orange County Register, CBSMarketWatch and Money magazine.

Yona A. Benstock
Edelman
Atlanta, GA USA
*Contact Phone:* 404-460-1491
**Click to Contact from Web Site**

## SILVER-INVESTOR.COM — ANALYSIS FOR SERIOUS INVESTORS
Spokane, WA USA
www.Silver-Investor.com

David Morgan is a private metals analyst. His background in engineering with an advanced degree in Economics/Finance gives a unique perspective to the financial markets. Mr. Morgan has been published in over seventy-five publications. He hosts a weekly radio show called the Morgan Report on the metals markets, and a weekly eTV show on the FreeMarketNews.com website. He is sought as a speaker on the economy and precious metals all over the world.

David Morgan
Stone Investment Group
Colberg, WA USA
*Contact Phone:* 509-464-1651
**Click to Contact from Web Site**

## RIC EDELMAN - RADIO/TV/AUTHOR/ COLUMNIST
Fairfax, VA USA
http://www.ricedelman.com

Ric Edelman, CFS, CMFC, RFC, CRC, QFP, BCM, EIEIO is unlike any other financial advisor because his main focus is educating consumers about personal finance. He is an entertaining speaker who can give you the sound bite you need, and he is equally at home before a live audience on both TV and radio. Turn to Ric for any financial topic, including investments, insurance, taxes, real estate, retirement planning, wills and trusts, college planning, and much more.

William Casserly
*Director, Communications Dept.*
Edelman Financial Services Inc.
Fairfax, VA
*Contact Phone:* 703-251-0110
*Contact Main Phone:* 703-818-0800
**Click to Contact from Web Site**

## JEFFREY B. HARRIS, CHFC, INDEPENDENT WEALTH MANAGEMENT CONSULTANT
Harrisonburg, VA USA
www.retirerich-online.com

Jeff Harris is the creator of Whole-Brain Wealth Management™, (WBWM). This unique client-centered approach to financial planning blends the left-brain technical expertise, strategies and tactics of CPA's, attorneys and investment consultants with the client's right-brain goals, dreams and ideal lifestyle. The result is financial peace-of-mind which enables the client to live their ideal lifestyle without worrying about money. Mr. Harris is a Chartered Financial Consultant (ChFC) and is the author of Retire Rich and Happy.

Jeffrey B. Harris, ChFC
*President*
Jeff Harris & Associates. Inc.
Harrisonburg, VA USA
*Contact Phone:* 800-296-2680
*Cell:* 803-487-7103
**Click to Contact from Web Site**

# William E. Donoghue

## "Proactive Fund Investing Guru"

### *Proactive Fund Investing Advocate Manager*

Today's volatile markets demonstrate that traditional "Buy and Hold" strategies alone are unlikely to be effective. Donoghue's proactive investing strategies seek to earn high-return, low-risk returns by avoiding known risks and diversifying to reduce unknown risks.

A mutual fund expert for 43 years, an asset manager for 20 years and a proactive sector fund and ETF portfolio manager for 10 years, Donoghue offers innovative portfolios using Sector Rotation, Long/Short Investing, Power Income and Tactical Growth strategies in taxable, potentially tax-free and tax-deferred accounts.

William E. Donoghue
Chairman, W. E. Donoghue & Co., Inc.
Registered Investment Advisors
260 N. Main Street
Natick Massachusetts 01760
800-642-4276

Chairman's Office: 206-281-8188
(Seattle)
or 206-954-4762 (Cell)

www.donoghue.com
guru@donoghue.com

MANAGING THE INVESTMENT OPPORTUNITIES OF YOUR LIFETIME

**W.E. DONOGHUE & CO., INC.**

*Registered Investment Advisors*

## JIM LORENZEN, CFP®, AIF® - THE INDEPENDENT FINANCIAL GROUP
Thousand Oaks, CA USA
www.indfin.com

Jim Lorenzen, Cfp®, AIF® is an independent fee-only consultant on retirement and retirement plan investing: Does not sell investment products and receives no commissions. 15 years' experience. Entrepreneur: Founded, built, and sold five successful businesses in publishing before entering management consulting 23 years ago. Headline speaker: More than 500 national and international conventions throughout U.S., Canada, and the U.K. Writer: Multiple appearances in more than 25 national trade publications. Interviewed on American Airlines' Sky Radio. Credentials: Certified Financial Planner, CFP Board of Standards through The American College. Accredited Investment Fiduciary, Center for Fiduciary Studies in association with Katz Graduate School of Business, University of Pittsburgh. Professional Affiliations: Financial Planning Association (FPA), American Association of Pension Professionals and Actuaries (ASPPA), Profit Sharing Council of America (PSCA), Center for Due Diligence, Foundation for Fiduciary Studies, Society for Human Resources Management (SHRM), Professionals in Human Resources Association (PI-HRA).

Jim Lorenzen
The Independent Financial Group
Thousand Oaks, CA USA
*Contact Phone:* 805-374-8695
*Contact Main Phone:* 800-257-6659
**Click to Contact from Web Site**

## JORDAN E. GOODMAN - AMERICA'S MONEY ANSWERS MAN
Scarsdale, NY USA
http://www.moneyanswers.com

Jordan E. Goodman is 'America's Money Answers Man' and a nationally-recognized expert on personal finance. He is a regular contributor to Public Radio International's The Marketplace Morning Report and is a daily guest on radio and television call-in shows across the country, answering questions on personal financial topics. He appears frequently on NBC's The Today Show, PBS, MSNBC, CNN, CNBC, and Nightline. For 18 years, Mr. Goodman was on the editorial staff of Money magazine, where he served as Wall Street correspondent. While at Money, Mr. Goodman reported and wrote on virtually every aspect of personal finance. In addition, he served as weekly financial analyst on NBC News at Sunrise for 9 years. He has written 11 books on personal finance, including Everyone's Money Book, and Master Your Money Type.

Jordan E. Goodman
MoneyAnswers.com
Scarsdale, NY USA
*Contact Phone:* 914-722-0032
**Click to Contact from Web Site**

## THE FINANCIAL SERVICES ROUNDTABLE
Washington, DC USA
http://www.fsround.org

Based in Washington, D.C., The Financial Services Roundtable is a CEO-driven trade association representing 100 of the largest integrated financial services companies in the United States. The mission of The Financial Services Roundtable is to advocate policies in Congress and among regulators that are good for the financial industry and its customers and to prevent enactment of harmful rules and legislation.

Shannon Finney
*Communications Manager*
The Financial Services Roundtable
Washington, DC USA
*Contact Phone:* 202-289-4322
**Click to Contact from Web Site**

## JANET TAVAKOLI - PRESIDENT, TAVAKOLI STRUCTURED FINANCE, INC.
Chicago, IL USA
http://www.tavakolistructuredfinance.com/janettavakoli.html

Janet Tavakoli is a dynamic expert in finance and derivatives with over 22 years of Wall Street experience. She is a former adjunct professor University of Chicago Graduate School of Business where she taught derivatives. Author of the global bestsellers: Credit Derivatives and Collateralized Debt Obligations and Structured Finance. Radio/TV interviews welcomed.

Janet Tavakoli
*President*
Tavakoli Structured Finance, Inc.
Chicago, IL USA
*Contact Phone:* 312-540-0243
**Click to Contact from Web Site**

## JK HARRIS & COMPANY
North Charleston, SC USA
www.jkharris.com

JK Harris & Company, based in North Charleston, S.C., is the nation's largest tax resolution company and can meet with customers, by appointment only, in over 450 locations nationwide. JK Harris also provides services for credit card debt, student loan debt, victims of investment fraud, financial planning, tax return preparation, and audit representation.

Josh Baker
*Director of Corporate Communications*
JK Harris & Company
North Charleston, SC USA
*Contact Phone:* 843-576-2255
*Contact Main Phone:* 843-576-2255
*Cell:* 843-991-1686
**Click to Contact from Web Site**

## When your topic is personal finance, turn to

# Ric Edelman

### *Highly-Acclaimed Financial Advisor*

Ric Edelman, CFS, CMFC, RFC, CRC, QFP, BCM is one of the nation's most entertaining speakers, equally at home before a live audience or appearing on radio or television. Turn to Ric for any financial topic, including investments, insurance, taxes, real estate, retirement planning, wills and trusts, college planning, and much more.

**#1 *New York Times* Bestselling Author of *Ordinary People, Extraordinary Wealth***

### Highly Regarded Financial Advisor

- Dow Jones: "One of the nation's most successful advisors"
- CBS News: "a guru"
- CNBC: "One of the most engaging communicators of our time"

### Award-Winning Entrepreneur

- 2001 Washington D.C. "Entrepreneur of the Year"
- Ranked by *Bloomberg Wealth Manager* among the largest planning firms in the nation
- Ranked by *Research Magazine* as #1 advisor in nation for "focus on individual client"
- Ranked 3 times on the *Inc. 500*

### Renowned Educator

- Taught personal finance at Georgetown University for 9 years
- AICPA-approved continuing ed instructor and member NASD board of arbitrators

### Bestselling Author

- *The Truth About Money,* 1997 Book of the Year
- *The New Rules of Money,* *New York Times* Bestseller
- *Ordinary People, Extraordinary Wealth* — #1 *New York Times* Bestseller
- *Discover the Wealth Within You*
- *What You Need to Do Now*

### Syndicated Columnist and Newsletter Publisher

- Nationally Syndicated Newspaper Columnist
- *Inside Personal Finance,* 12-page monthly newsletter. < call for free sample >

### RicEdelman.com Online

- One of the most complete financial education sites on the web
- Free email advisor newsletter

### Award-Winning Radio and TV Talk Show Host

- Heard in Washington D.C. on WMAL 630AM
- Winner of A.I.R. Award for "Best Talk Show Host"
- Host of live weekly show on Newschannel 8
- 15 years of broadcast journalism experience

### Nationally-Recognized Financial Advisor

- Financial Advisor Hall of Fame
- Three times ranked by *Barron's* as one of America's top 100 financial advisors
- Hundreds of interviews with TV, radio, newspapers and magazines coast to coast: *The CBS Evening News, CNN, The Oprah Winfrey Show, Fox Morning News, The Today Show, CNBC* and more
- Has testified before Congress and provided services to many agencies within the federal government

**For commentary or quotes on personal finance issues, or to schedule an interview contact:**
**Will Casserly at 703-251-0110 or wcasserly@RicEdelman.com**

Edelman Financial Services LLC, 4000 Legato Road, 9th Floor, Fairfax, Virginia 22033-4055, 888-PLAN-RIC or visit RicEdelman.com

Ric Edelman is also separately a registered representative of and offers securities through Sanders Morris Harris Inc., Member NASD, SIPC.
Investment Advisory Services are offered through Edelman Financial Services LLC, a registered investment advisor.

081406

## ASSOCIATION OF DIVORCE FINANCIAL PLANNERS

New Haven, CT USA
divorceandfinance.com

The mission of the ADFP is to heighten awareness of the benefits of divorce financial planning so it will become an integral part of the divorce process. Divorce Financial Planners are experts who are trained and experienced in researching and analyzing personal, business and tax issues related to divorce. We help individuals, couples, matrimonial attorneys and divorce mediators to achieve fair and workable agreements. We use special divorce financial software to produce powerful graphs and charts that demonstrate the financial consequences of settlement proposals for the long term and to recommend alternatives. Members of the Association of Divorce Financial Planners work closely with clients both during and after divorce.

Lili A. Vasileff, CFP
Association of Divorce Financial Planners
Woodbridge, CT USA
*Contact Phone:* 203 393-7200
**Click to Contact from Web Site**

## ESTHER M. BERGER -- THE MONEYSMART EXPERT

Los Angeles, CA USA
www.bergerassoc.com

Esther M. Berger is a Certified Financial Planner and former Managing Director of the registered investment advisory firm Berger & Associates LLC in Beverly Hills and First Vice President of PaineWebber, Inc. The author of MoneySmart and MoneySmart Divorce (Simon & Schuster), she has also served as financial expert for Hearst Magazines' Money Minded website, and as a contributor to Town & Country magazine. A frequent speaker to business and investor groups, Esther was invited by the Pentagon to address its Senior Professional Women's Association, which meets under the auspices of the Secretary of Defense. She was also a keynote speaker at the Smithsonian Institution lecture series. Esther has been published in Newsweek's My Turn and has been interviewed by Good Morning America, Oprah, CNN, PBS, The Wall Street Journal, USA Today, The New York Times, Los Angeles Times, The Financial Times, National Public Radio, Forbes, Business Week, Money, Working Woman, Cosmopolitan, Ladies' Home Journal, and News Limited Australia.

Esther M. Berger
*Managing Director*
Berger Consulting Group LLC
Los Angeles, CA USA
*Contact Phone:* 310-663-5770
*Contact Main Phone:* 310-246-5770
**Click to Contact from Web Site**

## PAM LITTLE — EDITOR - WOMENSWALLSTREET.COM

New York, NY USA
WomensWallStreet.com

WomensWallStreet.com is designed to help women research, compare and manage their personal finances using comprehensive, targeted financial information and advice.

Tricia Whittemore
Porter Novelli
San Diego, CA USA
*Contact Phone:* (619) 687-7018
*Cell:* (603) 219-6088
**Click to Contact from Web Site**

## JOSEPH F. DUNPHY, M.B.A.

Clifton, NJ USA
www.jfdunphymba.com

Joseph F. Dunphy, M.B.A., is a financial planner and author of Financial Planning for Senior Executives Executive M.B.A. Seminar. Securities offered through Prime Capital (Poughkeepsie, NY).

Joseph F. Dunphy, M.B.A.
*Registered Representative*
Clifton, NJ
*Contact Phone:* 1-973-773-7867
**Click to Contact from Web Site**

 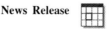

# James Lorenzen, CFP®
ACCREDITED INVESTMENT FIDUCIARY™

**The Independent Financial Group**
Registered Investment Advisor
www.indfin.com
Independent Fee-Only Consulting
86 Long Court, Suite C
Thousand Oaks, CA 91360

**Phone: 805.374.8695**
**E-mail: jiml@indfin.com**

*Fiduciary Myths:*
*"Very few people on the corporate board or in HR know they may be plan fiduciaries. This is serious because fiduciary liability is personal, not corporate."*

*401(k) Myths:*
*"It's amazing how many plan sponsors think they have 'safe harbor' protection while, in truth, they have little protection at all."*

*-James Lorenzen*

**Headline Speaker**
Over 500 Conventions
throughout U.S., Canada,
and the U.K.

**Entrepreneur**
Successfully founded, built,
and sold five businesses

# Retirement Plan & Fiduciary Consulting

Retirement and
ERISA Plan
Consulting

Board &
Committee
ERISA
Fiduciary
Education

100% Fee-Only
No Product Sales

**James Lorenzen** founded, built, and sold five successful businesses before beginning his management consulting career in strategic management and organization development more than twenty-five years ago. Since then he has been the headline speaker at more than 500 national and international conventions and conferences and has contributed to numerous publications as well as being interviewed for American Airlines' Sky Radio®. For the past fifteen years, his independent consultancy has been focused on retirement issues facing individuals... and now retirement plan sponsors.

Jim is a certified financial planner and also became an accredited investment fiduciary through the Foundation for Fiduciary Studies and the Katz Graduate School of Business at the University of Pittsburgh.

Professional memberships include The Financial Planning Association, American Association of Pension Professionals and Actuaries, Profit Sharing Council of America, Center for Due-Diligence, Center for Fiduciary Studies, Society for Human Resource Management, and Professionals in Human Resources.

**100% Independent Fee-Only Consulting**

**For Company Retirement Plan Sponsors**
Investment Advisory • Searches/Monitoring/Reviews
Corporate Board/Investment Committee Education
**For Business Owners, Senior Executives, Individual Investors**
Retirement Planning & Investment Management Consulting

**www.indfin.com**

**ALTON J. JONES -- HOW TO GET GOOD CREDIT EXPERT**
Phoenix, AZ USA
http://howtogetgoodcredit.blogspot.com/

Author of the book, 'Evil Money Evil Credit', Alton J. Jones, from his own experience, delivers clear and concise guidelines which tell people the importance of building and maintaining good credit and the perils of personal financial misman- agement. Jones lives in Phoenix, Arizona. He re- ceived his A.A. degree from New Mexico Mili- tary Institute, his B.S. in Aviation Business Administration from Embry-Riddle Aeronautical University and M.S. in Management Science from the University of Central Texas.

ALTON J. JONES
*AUTHOR AND HOW TO GET GOOD*
*CREDIT EXPERT*
HIGH TOWER BOOKS
PHOENIX, AZ USA
*Contact Phone:* 623.205.2415
*Cell:* 623.205.2415
**Click to Contact from Web Site**

**IVAN GELFAND -- AMERICA'S MONEY MAN; FINANCIAL STRATEGIST**
Pepper Pike, OH USA
http://www.ivangelfand.com

Recognized expert in corporate/personal finance and business forecasting. Nationally recognized as an expert on: Money Management, Bond Mar- kets, Corporate Cash Management, Business Eco- nomics, Bond Portfolio Management. Radio talk show host, 'Financial Week In Review' ™ -- Pub- lic speaker -- Frequent television and radio guest -- Radio and television station financial analyst -- Frequent newspaper and magazine subject -- Pro- ducer of internationally distributed educational video tape, 'Inside Investing.' Chairman of Maxus Investment Group. Producer and anchor of televi- sion financial inserts, 'Your Money, Your Future.'

Ivan Gelfand
*America's Money Man*
Ivan Gelfand
Pepper Pike, OH
*Contact Phone:* 888-886-1960
*Contact Main Phone:* 888-886-1960
**Click to Contact from Web Site**

**MICHAEL MENDELSOHN - INHERITANCE PLANNING OF ART ASSETS**
New York, NY USA
http://www.BriddgeArtStrategies.com/

Michael Mendelsohn is Founder and President of Briddge Art Strategies Ltd., the premier art suc- cession planning firm in the country. He is a noted art collector, philanthropist, and lecturer, and his innovative inheritance planning strategies for art and antiques assets have won him wide acclaim in the art community. His new book Life is Short, Art is Long - Maximizing Estate Planning Strate- gies for Collectors of Art, Antiques and Col- lectibles is due to be published this fall.

Paige Stover Hague
*Senior VP of Marketing & Media*
Briddge Art Strategies Ltd.
Boston, MA USA
*Contact Phone:* 617-230-2167
*Cell:* 508-577-0271
**Click to Contact from Web Site**

**CREDIT UNION EXECUTIVES SOCIETY (CUES)**
Madison, WI USA
http://cues.org

The Credit Union Executives Society (CUES) is a Madison, Wisconsin-based independent member- ship association advancing the professional devel- opment of credit union CEOs, senior manage- ment and directors. Opportunities for professional growth abound through our conferences, insti- tutes, seminars, publications, products and ser- vices.

Teri Schacker
Credit Union Executives Society (CUES)
Madison, WI
*Contact Phone:* 800-252-2664
**Click to Contact from Web Site**

## CONSUMER DATA INDUSTRY ASSOCIATION
Washington, DC USA
http://www.acb-credit.com

The only source for credit reporting industry information. Consumer Data Industry Association is an international trade association representing the consumer credit, mortgage reporting, collection service, resident screening and employment reporting industries. Involved in government affairs, public relations and education, members provide one billion credit reports annually to retailers, banks and other lenders. Call Norm Magnuson at (202) 408-7406 if you have any questions about credit reports or credit reporting.

Norm Magnuson
*V.P. Public Affairs*
Consumer Data Industry Association
Washington, DC
*Contact Phone:* 202-408-7406
**Click to Contact from Web Site**

## THE CONSUMMATE CONSUMER
Atlanta, GA USA
http://www.tcconsumer.com

Noted consumer advocate Marti Ann Schwartz, the nationally renowned author of Lessons Learned From Cancer and Listen to Me Doctor explains it all. You've seen her on CBS Evening News. You've read about her in The Wall Street Journal, The Washington Post, The New York Times and Good Housekeeping relating to: alternative and conventional health care, schools/education, fundraising and employer/employee relations.

Marti Ann Schwartz
*President*
The Consummate Consumer
Atlanta, GA
*Contact Phone:* 770-955-0330
**Click to Contact from Web Site**

## FINANCIAL FREEDOM INTERNATIONAL, INC.
Orem, UT USA
www.financialfree.com

The company has created a unique financial education program that is being used by thousands of people throughout the nation. The program is internet accessible. The mission of the company is to help people become financially fit by eliminating debt and mastering the use of their money.

Kelly Shelton
*Vice President*
Financial Freedom International, Inc.
Orem, UT
*Contact Phone:* 801-431-3800
*Contact Main Phone:* 800-669-8815
**Click to Contact from Web Site**

## CONSUMER BANKERS ASSOCIATION
Arlington, VA USA
http://www.cbanet.org

The recognized voice on retail banking issues in the nation's capital. Member institutions are the leaders in consumer finance (auto, home equity and education), electronic retail delivery systems, bank sales of investment products, small business services and community development. Founded in 1919 and providing leadership and representation on retail banking issues such as privacy, fair lending, and consumer protection legislation/regulation. CBA members include 85% of the nation's largest 50 bank holding companies.

Fritz Elmendorf
Vice President of Communications
Arlington, VA
*Contact Main Phone:* 703-276-1750
**Click to Contact from Web Site**

## VERNON JACOBS, CPA -- PRESIDENT, OFFSHORE PRESS, INC.
Kansas City, KS USA
http://www.offshorepress.com

International Tax Law: How to Go Offshore Without Getting in Trouble with the IRS. Foreign trusts, foreign corporations, foreign partnerships and foreign investments. Vernon Jacobs is a CPA and author with a focus on international tax law.

Vernon K. Jacobs, CPA
*President*
Offshore Press, Inc.
Prairie Village, KS USA
*Contact Phone:* 913-362-9667
*Contact Main Phone:* 913-362-9667
*Cell:* 913-481-3480
**Click to Contact from Web Site**

## STEPHANIE BREEDLOVE - HOUSEHOLD EMPLOYMENT TAX EXPERT

Austin, TX USA
http://www.breedlove-online.com

When it comes to tax & labor law for household employers, it's nice to know a know-it-all. Breedlove & Associates was formed in 1992 by Stephanie Breedlove. Having hired a nanny for her two young children, she found that tax and legal obligations for household employers (anyone who hires a nanny, nurse, chef, personal assistant, gardener, household manager, etc.) were overwhelmingly complex and time-consuming — and so specialized that it had been largely unserved by tax professionals. Stephanie left her consulting job at Andersen Consulting to focus on serving household employers with comprehensive tax payroll and HR services — she's now considered the country's foremost expert on household employment. Stephanie regularly speaks on topics, such as: * Federal, state and local tax *Compliance * Unemployment taxes and benefits * Overtime law * Independent Contractor law * Tax law for temporary workers * Tax law for illegal workers * Why household employees cannot be run through the company payroll Having served more than 10,000 families and processed more than $1 billion in payroll since 1992, Breedlove & Associates is the largest tax and payroll company in the U.S. that specializes in household employment.

Tom Breedlove
Breedlove & Associates
Austin, TX USA
*Contact Phone:* 1-888-273-3356
**Click to Contact from Web Site**

National Association
of Tax Professionals

## NATIONAL ASSOCIATION OF TAX PROFESSIONALS (NATP)

Appleton, WI USA
http://www.natptax.com

NATP, founded in 1979, is a nonprofit professional association dedicated to excellence in taxation and related financial services. It fosters the lifelong development and ethical practices of over 17,500 professionals (members) who provide tax and related financial services to nearly 8 million taxpayers. NATP members cover a broad spectrum of the tax profession, including individual tax preparers, enrolled agents, certified public accountants, accountants, attorneys, and financial planners.

Char De Coster
*Copywriter / Communications Editor*
National Association of Tax Professionals (NATP)
Appleton, WI U.S.A.
*Contact Phone:* 800.558.3402
*Contact Main Phone:* 800.558.3402
**Click to Contact from Web Site**

## RONALD GEORGE VANCE — COST SEGREGATION EXPERT

Charlotte, NC USA
http://costsegvfg.com

Ronald G. Vance is a national speaker on Cost Segregation Studies. His company has recovered more than $23 million so far —-but, all for small business owners, rather than global corporations. Mr. Vance, a CPA with more than 32 years' experience, who is licensed in seven states, has recovered $35,000 - $2.8 million per client through a complex engineering/accounting analysis, which reclassifies numerous items used to construct or improve buildings as 'personal property', reducing the depreciation period from 27.5 or 39 years to 5-15 years. Mr. Vance is a recognized professional in the field of Cost Segregation Studies, which evolved from the U.S. Tax Court ruling in the 1997 case HCA (Hospital Corp. of America) v. Commissioner. Formerly a well-kept secret, Cost Segregation Studies were done primarily for hundred-million dollar properties. But, Mr. Vance has exclusively serviced medium-sized business owners, performing 200+ studies nationwide.

Ronald George Vance
VFG Associates, Inc.
Charlotte, NC
*Contact Phone:* 866-924-7500
**Click to Contact from Web Site**

## NEW YORK STATE SOCIETY OF CPAS

New York, NY USA
http://www.nysscpa.org

The New York State Society of Certified Public Accountants (NYSSCPA) is the largest state accounting organization in the nation and currently has 30,000 members. It was incorporated in 1897 to cultivate, promote, and disseminate knowledge and information concerning certified public accountants and to establish and maintain high standards of integrity, honor, and character among certified public accountants. The Society furnishes information regarding accountancy and the practice and methods thereof to its members and the general public. Its goal is to protect the interests of its members and the general public with respect to the practice of accountancy.

Lois Whitehead
*Public Relation Manager*
New York State Society of CPAs
New York, NY USA
*Contact Phone:* 212-719-8405
*Contact Main Phone:* 212-719-8300
**Click to Contact from Web Site**

## DAN BORGE — RISK CONSULTANT

New York, NY USA
http://www.amazon.com/exec/obidos/ASIN/
0471323780/qid=1117122032/sr=2-1/ref=pd_
bbs_b_2_1/104-0798303-8858321

Dan Borge is a recognized leader in risk management, having designed and implemented the world's first enterprise risk management system. RAROC (Risk Adjusted Return on Capital) has since become the standard for measuring and managing risks in companies around the world. He is the author of The Book of Risk (John Wiley & Sons), an accessible introduction to the basics of risk management that has been translated into Spanish, German and Japanese (forthcoming).

Dan Borge
Clinton Corners, NY USA
*Contact Phone:* 845-266-8295
**Click to Contact from Web Site**

## SUSAN M. MANGIERO, PH.D. AVA, CFA, FRM -- BUSINESS CONSULTANT

Trumbull, CT USA
http://www.bvallc.com

Dr. Mangiero is a managing member of BVA, LLC, an independent valuation, risk analysis, and litigation support firm. She is also the founder of Pension Governance, LLC. A Chartered Financial Analyst, Accredited Valuation Analyst and certified Financial Risk Manager, Dr. Mangiero has over twenty years of experience in the areas of valuation, risk measurement and control, financial trading, and global capital markets. Her new book, 'Risk Management for Pensions, Endowments, and Foundations', adds to a long list of publications about risk, valuation, and governance.

Susan M. Mangiero
BVA, LLC
Trumbull, CT United States
*Contact Phone:* 203-261-5519
**Click to Contact from Web Site**

## CONSUMER CREDIT INSURANCE ASSOCIATION

Chicago, IL USA
http://www.cciaonline.com

CCIA is a national organization of 150 insurance companies providing life, disability, unemployment, and property coverage in connection with consumer credit transactions. CCIA is dedicated to preserving and enhancing the availability, utility, and integrity of insurance and insurance-related products delivered through financial institutions or in conjunction with financial transactions.

William Burfeind
*Executive Vice President*
Consumer Credit Insurance Association
Chicago, IL
*Contact Phone:* 312-939-2242
**Click to Contact from Web Site**

## NATIONAL ASSOCIATION OF PROFESSIONAL INSURANCE AGENTS

Alexandria, VA USA
http://www.pianet.com

The National Association of Professional Insurance Agents represents independent insurance agency owners and their employees — insurance professionals who handle all kinds of insurance but specialize in coverage of autos, homes and businesses. PIA members not only sell insurance but provide advice to consumers about ways to reduce their risks and limit losses. Because professional agents own their businesses and represent multiple insurance companies, they provide consumers greater choice in finding the best insurance value.

Ted Besesparis
*Vice President, Communications*
National Association of Professional Insurance Agents
Alexandria, VA
*Contact Phone:* 703-518-1352
**Click to Contact from Web Site**

## SCOTT SIMMONDS — INSURANCE EXPERT

Portland, ME USA
http://www.InsuranceFixer.com

Insurance Expert - A fee-only provider of insurance advice and counsel. I don't sell insurance. Unbiased insurance advice and information. Property insurance, life insurance, liability insurance, workers' compensation, auto insurance, personal and business coverage. Disability, health, and long term care insurance. Directors and officers insurance, crime insurance, professional liability insurance.

Scott Simmonds, CPCU, ARM
Saco, ME United States
*Contact Phone:* 207-284-0085
**Click to Contact from Web Site**

## AMERICAN COUNCIL OF LIFE INSURERS

Washington, DC USA
www.acli.com

The American Council of Life Insurers (ACLI) is a unified voice on issues from financial and retirement security to international trade. Led by President & CEO Frank Keating, we are backed by an industry with 250 years of experience protecting American families and businesses. ACLI shapes public debate, stays ahead of trends, and helps its members compete in changing times. ACLI expands awareness of how the products offered by life insurers—life insurance; annuities; disability income and long-term care insurance; pensions, 401(k), 403(b), 457 plans; and IRAs—help Americans plan for and achieve financial and retirement security.

Jack Dolan
American Council of Life Insurers
Washington, DC USA
*Contact Phone:* 202-624-2418
**Click to Contact from Web Site**

# Ronald George Vance,
## *National Director of Cost Segregation Studies*

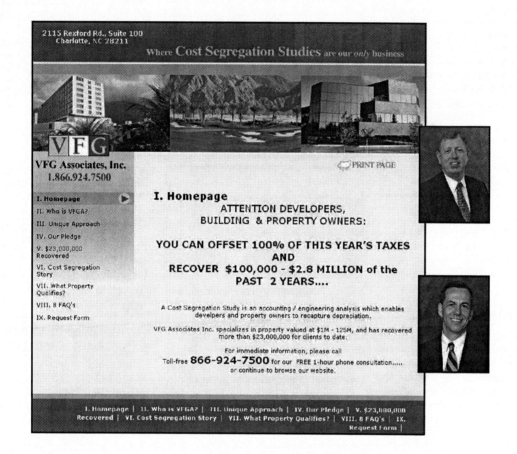

**Ronald George Vance**
**VFG Associates, Inc.**
**Charlotte, N.C.**
**Contact Phone: 866-924-7500**

# http://costsegvfg.com

## GERALD (GERRY) KATZ, MSPA, RHU, ALHC, DABFE
Weston, FL USA
http://www.disabilityconcepts.com

Services as a Disability Claims Consultant or Expert Witness throughout the US. Consultation and advice to potential and current disabled insured's and/or their attorneys on the entire claims process. Instructor and Provider of qualified Continuing Education courses on disability insurance topics. Over 38 years marketing and designing disability insurance products. Helped produce $10 million of individual disability insurance premiums during sales career. Was industry's 1997 Health Insurance Person of the Year.

Gerald Katz
*President & Founder*
Weston, FL
*Contact Phone:* 954-217-8260
**Click to Contact from Web Site**

## AMERICANS FOR FREE CHOICE IN MEDICINE
Los Angeles, CA USA
www.afcm.org

Americans for Free Choice in Medicine (AFCM) is a national non-profit, non-partisan educational organization. AFCM promotes the philosophy of individual rights, personal responsibility and free market economics in the health care industry. AFCM advocates a full, free market health care system by promoting health savings accounts (HSAs), tax equity for the individual, and AFCM teaches the history of HMOs, which were instituted by a long, incremental process of government intervention. AFCM sponsors educational programs, lectures and town hall meetings for the public. Membership grades begin at $40 per year and may be tax-deductible. Members include patients, Medicare recipients, physicians, nurses and health care professionals, insurance industry professionals, including agents, pharmacists and pharmaceutical industry professionals, financial services professionals, businessmen, employee benefits professionals and hospital staff. AFCM was founded in 1993

Richard E. Ralston
Americans for Free Choice in Medicine
Newport Beach, CA USA
*Contact Phone:* 949-500-6829
**Click to Contact from Web Site**

## FARMERS INSURANCE GROUP
Los Angeles, CA USA
http://www.farmers.com

As the nation's third-largest insurer of homes and autos, Farmers Insurance Group has qualified experts to answer your insurance questions. We're leaders in life and business insurance, too. Whether you need a comment for your state or want a national perspective, call Farmers for information on auto safety, teen driving safety, fraud, insurance rates, indentity theft coverage, catastrophes and personal financial solutions.

Mary Flynn
*Media Relations Manager*
Farmers Insurance Group
Los Angeles, CA
*Contact Phone:* 323-932-3662
**Click to Contact from Web Site**

## NETQUOTE — INSURANCE EXPERTS
Denver, CO USA
http://www.netquote.com

Discover How Easy Shopping Can Be — Since 1989, NetQuote® has provided consumers with a free, simple, and effective way to fulfill their insurance shopping needs. Free Quotes Available in All 50 States — NetQuote® works with hundreds of partner companies that provide insurance quotes based on information that you supply.

Scott Striegel
NetQuote Inc.
Denver, CO USA
*Contact Phone:* (303) 291-1991
*Contact Main Phone:* (720) 931-1000
**Click to Contact from Web Site**

## CHALLENGER, GRAY & CHRISTMAS, INC.
Chicago, IL USA
www.challengergray.com/

An international outplacement firm providing immediate response on any workplace issue. Areas of expert commentary include, but are not exclusive to, job searching, downsizing, retirement, benefits, compensation, future workplace trends, mergers, effects of demographic shifts, entrepreneurism, termination policies and corporate restructuring. Challenger, Gray & Christmas also tracks job-cut announcements daily and publishes the only comprehensive record of workforce reductions nationwide.

James Pedderson
*Director of Public Relations*
Chicago, IL
*Contact Phone:* 312-332-5790
**Click to Contact from Web Site**

## OVERCOMING JOB BURNOUT
Berkeley, CA USA
http://www.docpotter.com/index_useful.html#Overcome_Job_Burnout

When work goes bad, life is hell. Find out how to beat job burnout from Dr. Beverly Potter, author of Overcoming Job Burnout: How To Renew Enthusiasm for work and Get Peak Performance Every Day: How to Manage Like a Coach. What is the Burnout Potential of Your Job? and Am I Burning Out? quizzes free to audiences. Go to docpotter's site (docpotter.com) for many articles and other useful content.

Dr. Beverly Potter
*Author*
Overcoming Job Burnout
Oakland, CA
*Contact Phone:* 510-420-3669
**Click to Contact from Web Site**

## "Simplifying the Complex"

# SUSAN M. MANGIERO
### PH.D., AVA, CFA, FRM

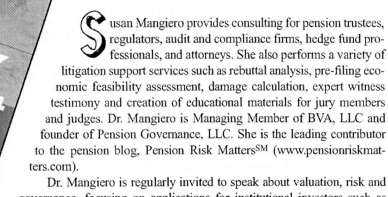

usan Mangiero provides consulting for pension trustees, regulators, audit and compliance firms, hedge fund professionals, and attorneys. She also performs a variety of litigation support services such as rebuttal analysis, pre-filing economic feasibility assessment, damage calculation, expert witness testimony and creation of educational materials for jury members and judges. Dr. Mangiero is Managing Member of BVA, LLC and founder of Pension Governance, LLC. She is the leading contributor to the pension blog, Pension Risk Matters[SM] (www.pensionriskmatters.com).

Dr. Mangiero is regularly invited to speak about valuation, risk and governance, focusing on applications for institutional investors such as pension funds. Audiences include the New York State Department of Insurance, Merrill Lynch, Association of Public Pension Fund Auditors, Association of Forensic Economics, New England Public Employee Retirement Systems Forum, Global Association of Risk Professionals, American Society of Appraisers, Connecticut State Department of Banking, North American Securities Administrators Association, Canadian Investment Review and the U.S. Department of Labor.

Her book, "Risk Management for Pensions, Endowments, and Foundations" (John Wiley & Sons, 2005), looks at risk management and valuation issues, with an emphasis on fiduciary responsibility and best practices. Her articles have appeared in Hedge Fund Review, Investment Lawyer, Valuation Strategies, RISK Magazine, Financial Services Review, Family Foundation Advisor, Hedgeco.net, Expert Evidence Report, and Bankers Magazine.

## *$10-Trillion Pension Promise: Will It Be Broken?*

### Susan M. Mangiero:
Author, Speaker and Consultant

**BVA, LLC**
Valuation, Risk Analysis & Litigation Support for Attorneys and Their Institutional Investor and Business Owner Clients

4 Daniels Farm Road
Trumbull, Conn. 06611-3938

Tel: 203-261-5519 Fax: 203-261-5520

smm@bvallc.com -- www.bvallc.com

## 100 JOBS FOR KIDS & YOUNG ADULTS—A SELF-EMPOWERMENT TOOL
Chicago, IL USA
www.wisechildpress.com

 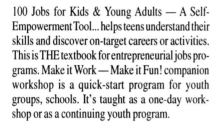

100 Jobs for Kids & Young Adults — A Self-Empowerment Tool... helps teens understand their skills and discover on-target careers or activities. This is THE textbook for entrepreneurial jobs programs. Make it Work — Make it Fun! companion workshop is a quick-start program for youth groups, schools. It's taught as a one-day workshop or as a continuing youth program.

Eva Marques
*Author/Instructor*
100 Jobs For Kids & Young Adults—A Self-Empowerment Tool
*Contact Phone:* 773-805-2375
**Click to Contact from Web Site**

**EXPRESS PERSONNEL SERVICES**
Oklahoma City, OK USA
http://www.expresspersonnel.com

Linda C. Haneborg is the spokesperson for Express Personnel Services. They place thousands of people in full-time and temporary positions from industrial workers to corporate presidents. Ranked by Inc. Magazine three times in succession in the top 500 fastest growing privately held companies and the number one personnel franchisor by SUCCESS Magazine and Entrepreneur Magazine, Express has more than 500 offices in the U.S. and six foreign countries. Spokespersons have expertise in employment trends, the staffing industry and extensive knowledge of franchising.

Linda C. Haneborg
*Sr VP, Communications/Public Relations*
Express Personnel Services
Oklahoma City, OK
*Contact Phone:* 800-652-6400
**Click to Contact from Web Site**

**CAREER COACH INSTITUTE**
Lake Havasu City, AZ USA
http://www.careercoachinstitute.com/media-and-events.htm

Career Coach Institute provides niche-specific training in the most stable coaching niche of all: career coaching. Whether you want to help people change jobs or simply enjoy the one they have, you can become trained and certified as a career coach in just 6 months. Work from home or add coaching to your corporate function. Our blended learning approach combines teleclasses, training kits, and internet-based resources to offer a flexible, affordable coach training program.

Marcia Bench, MCCC
*Founder/Director*
Career Coach Institute
Lake Havasu City, AZ USA
*Contact Phone:* 1-866-226-2244
*Contact Main Phone:* 1-866-CCOACH-4
**Click to Contact from Web Site**

# NetQuote,
## *Insurance Shopper*

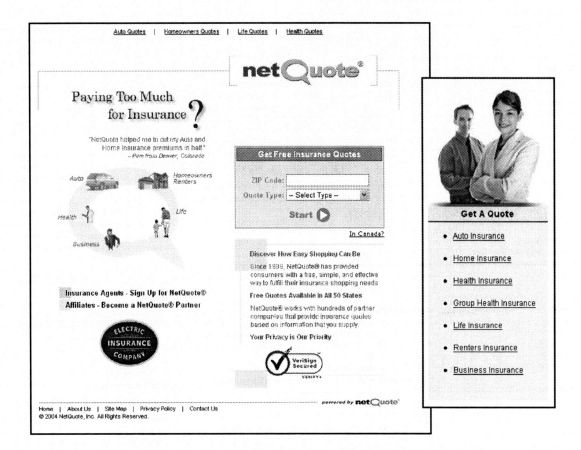

## Scott Striegel
## NetQuote, Inc.
## Denver, Colo. -- U.S.A.
## Contact Phone: (720) 931-1000 ext. 106
## Cell: (303) 817-8281

# www.netquote.com

## VERITAS INSTITUTE, INC.
Nashville, TN USA
http://veritasinstitute.org

Veritas (Ver-i-tas: Latin for truth, the true or real nature of reality — to enlarge and enhance our view of true life together). Founded in 2003, the Veritas Institute, Inc. is dedicated to bringing together and fostering open dialogue and understanding among people of different races and ethnicities, social classes, faith traditions, and nations. We provide forums where opponents on controversial public policy issues can thrash out their differences. We also solicit opinions and try to give voice to the concerns of ordinary people whose ideas are not regularly heard at the national and international levels.

Carol M. Swain, Ph.D
*Founding Director and Professor of Political Science and Law*
Veritas Institute, Inc.
Nashville, TN USA
*Contact Phone:* 615-310-6086
*Contact Main Phone:* 615 322-1001
*Cell:* 615 310-8617
**Click to Contact from Web Site**

## AL VIVIAN, BASIC DIVERSITY, INC.
Atlanta, GA USA
www.basicdiversity.com

Al Vivian is Pres & CEO of BASIC Diversity which has been operating nationally for over 30 years. Al has provided diversity counsel from CEO level to sanitation workers; and has provided commentary to CNN, FOX, NBC and PBS. Clients include Coca-Cola, Ford Motor, McDonald's, and The U.S. Army. BASIC is best known for conducting the most effective race relations seminar in the country; which was the sole feature for two consecutive days on 'The Oprah Winfrey Show'.

Al Vivian
Fayetteville, GA USA
*Contact Phone:* 770-716-0505
**Click to Contact from Web Site**

## BRENDA CAMPBELL — MANAGEMENT CONSULTING AND INFORMATION TECHNOLOGY
Washington, DC USA
http://www.ussmc.com

Campbell combines expertise in strategic counseling and business, military logistics and security to make her (15-year woman-owned, 8A/SDB, veteran million-dollar company, USSMC) a multi-dimensional powerhouse in organizational reengineering, business training, telework, and harnessing technology to achieve results. An inspiring trainer, consultant, and visionary, Campbell harnesses motivational business and spiritual principles to empower team-members and customers to excel. USSMC integrates technology, people-focused POSCORBE systems to reinvent client organizations through BETTER Planning, Organization, Staffing, Coordination, Ordering, Reporting, Budgeting, and Evaluation. Ms. Campbell looks forward to developing more Business Executives this year all over the United States.

Brenda Campbell
*President & CEO*
USSMC Inc. & USSMC Training
Management Consulting & Information
Largo, MD USA
*Contact Phone:* 301-322-2247
**Click to Contact from Web Site**

## DENISE MICHAELS — TESTOSTERONE-FREE MARKETING
Las Vegas, NV USA
http://www.MarketingForHer.com

'Marketing for Her' is for women entrepreneurs and women who want to be entrepreneurs. It's a one stop portal resource for 'Testosterone Free Marketing' ideas, strategies tips and much more that work with your personality as a woman. Leave the guns and cannons behind. 'Marketing for Her' is your definitive source of tips, advice, and tools for women entrepreneurs who love their business but hate getting the word out. If the thought of marketing your business drives you to chocolate, you're in the right place.

Ernie Martin
*Assistant*
Las Vegas, USA
*Contact Phone:* 702-647-1811
*Cell:* 702-401-6906
**Click to Contact from Web Site**

## JOEL WARADY - BRANDING & MARKETING EXPERT
Wilmette, IL USA
http://www.joelwarady.com

Joel Warady is well versed in all facets of marketing, branding, and growing businesses. He has extensive experience in developing marketing and brand strategy plans for small and mid-sized companies, and currently maintains ownership in a variety of product and service companies. Because Joel is involved with marketing and business growth in his own companies, he is able to utilize this experience to assist other companies in reaching their goals. Unlike many other consultants, he not only can tell you what to do to reach your goals, he actually heeds his own advice everyday of the week. He understands your needs.

Joel Warady
*Principal*
Joel Warady Group
Wilmette, IL USA
*Contact Phone:* 847-256-3915
**Click to Contact from Web Site**

## VOSS W. GRAHAM — INNERACTIVE CONSULTING
Memphis, TN USA
http://www.inneractiveconsulting.com

Expertise getting people to the next level of performance. Expertise in executive, manager and fast-tracker coaching. Provide insight for effective communication for individuals and teams. Experienced in Major Account Selling - moving sales teams and management from transactional to key account selling. Guide selection process using assessments and the interpretation of assessments to get the right people for the right jobs. Aligning performance with strategic objectives for accelerating growth. Author - Three Games of Selling.

Voss W. Graham
*CEO / Sr. Business Advisor*
InnerActive Consulting Group, Inc.
Cordova, TN USA
*Contact Phone:* 901-757-4434
*Cell:* 901-230-4036
**Click to Contact from Web Site**

## PATTI FRALIX — SPEAKER, CONSULTANT, COACH
Raleigh, NC USA
http://www.fralixgroup.com

The mission of Patti Fralix and the company she founded in 1992 is to enhance individual, team and organizational leadership excellence. The focus is leadership by behavior, not position. To be successful today, and even more so in the future, requires independent and interdependent people who effectively manage the many opportunities and challenges of an ever changing global marketplace. With 25 years of leadership and management experience in complex organizations, Fralix inspires personal and team excellence that results in increased productivity and profitability. High content is provided in an informative and entertaining manner for management or staff retreats, association meetings or conventions, or individual and team coaching sessions. Areas of focus include leadership, management and staff development, team building, communication, and customer service. Resources are available, such as audiotapes and How to Thrive in Spite of Mess, Stress and Less!, a book by Patti Fralix.

Patti Fralix
The Fralix Group, Inc.
Raleigh, NC USA
*Contact Phone:* 919-847-3440
**Click to Contact from Web Site**

## JILL KONRATH -- SELLING TO BIG COMPANIES
Minneapolis, MN USA
http://www.SellingtoBigCompanies.com

Jill Konrath, author of Selling to Big Companies, is a recognized expert in selling into the business-to-business marketplace. She helps her clients crack into corporate accounts, speed up their sales cycle, create demand and achieve their revenue growth goals. Jill publishes a leading online blog and writes an e-newsletter read by nearly 15,000 in 88 countries. She's also created the Winning More Sales manual and Getting Into Big Companies audio program. Most recently Jill has been featured in Selling Power, Sales Rep Radio, Entrepreneur, New York Times, Business Journal, Sales & Marketing Management, WSJ's Start-Up Journal, Sales & Marketing Excellence, Journal of Marketing, Business Advisor and countless online publications.

Jill Konrath
St. Paul, MN USA
*Contact Phone:* 651-429-1922
**Click to Contact from Web Site**

## AMERICAN ASSOCIATION FOR CAREER EDUCATION (AACE)
Hermosa Beach, CA USA
Connects education, work, and careers through Career Education for all ages. Promotes employability skills; career awareness, exploration, and decision-making; school-to-work transitions; productive, satisfying paid/nonpaid work; economic development; collaboration and partnerships. Bestows awards. National/international individual and organizational members from business, industry, education, government, labor, citizens, parents, students, and community. Newsletter, forum, registry, networks, resources, bonus briefs, distinguished member series, consulting.

Dr. Pat Nellor Wickwire
*President*
American Association for Career Education (AACE)
Hermosa Beach, CA
*Contact Phone:* 310-376-7378
**Click to Contact from Web Site**

## JAMES D. FELDMAN, CITE, CPT, MIP
Chicago, IL USA
www.ShiftHappens.com

Jim Feldman delivers ideas and sound bites for your pressing problems and issues. He adds value to your story. You'll get an INNOVATIVE interview that is Transformational, not transactional. Jim asks WHAT IF. . .? . . . You reevaluated your 'for sures' and started asking What IF? . . . You unleashed the unlimited opinions of an innovative problem solver? . . . You became a serial producer of great ideas using Jim's entrepreneurial expertise? . . . You called Jim @ 312 527-1111

James Feldman
Shift Happens, A Div of JfA, Inc.
Chicago, IL USA
*Contact Phone:* 312-527-1111
*Cell:* 312-909-9700
**Click to Contact from Web Site**

**EDWARD E. MORLER - MANAGEMENT CONSULTANT, EXECUTIVE COACH, AUTHOR**
Sonoma, CA USA
http://www.morler.com/

Dr. Morler is the award-winning author of The Integrity Leadership Challenge. He is a highly regarded consultant, speaker and guest lecturer on issues of integrity, emotional maturity, effective communication, leadership, ethics, negotiation skills and organizational change to revitalize organizations. Dr. Morler is the C.E.O. of Morler International, Inc., an international management training and consulting firm specializing in interpersonal and organizational effectiveness.

Edward E. Morler
*CEO*
Morler International
Sonoma, CA USA
*Contact Phone:* 707-935-7798
**Click to Contact from Web Site**

**DAVE JENSEN, MS - SALES & PRODUCTIVITY EXPERT**
Los Angeles, CA USA
http://www.davejensens3.com

Dave Jensen, M.S., runs a company that helps organizations improve their sales and productivity by integrating the latest scientific research with the timeless principles of the soul. He is the expert who wrote the book, 'Selling with Science & Soul.' As a recognized authority in helping others meet their goals, Dave's innovative research and dynamic programs have led to interviews with 48Hours, Time, The Washington Post, Modern Healthcare, Selling Magazine... (AND his niece's neighborhood newsletter).

Dave Jensen, MS
*President*
S3, Inc.
Los Angeles, CA USA
*Contact Phone:* 310-397-6686
**Click to Contact from Web Site**

**RICHARD GOTTLIEB - TOY INDUSTRY EXPERT**
New York, NY USA
http://www.richardgottliebassoc.com/strategic.htm

Richard Gottlieb, an expert on sales management, is the author of the Quality of Sales Survey which measures buyer and manufacturer satisfaction with the sales profession. Richard is a Contributing Editor for Playthings and Gifts & Decorative Accessories magazines in the United States and Toys 'n Playthings in the UK. He writes monthly columns in which he explores provocative sales and business issues like what to do about the abusive buyer and markdown money.

Richard Gottlieb
*President*
Richard Gottlieb & Associates, LLC
New York, NY USA
*Contact Phone:* 314-276-5144
*Cell:* 314-276-5144
**Click to Contact from Web Site**

 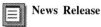

**Marketing Authority**    **Change Consultant**    **Customer Service Expert**

# James D. Feldman:

### Real-world expertise built on real-world experience.

As the owner of a group of thriving companies, James Feldman knows the challenges of today's marketplace, and will share real-world insights into marketing, customer service, problem solving, team building and leadership.

As a highly in-demand speaker, audiences from organizations ranging from Fortune 1000 companies to small organizations on the road to becoming larger ones all attest to his ability to "speak" their language on topics that include:

**James D. Feldman**
**A Practitioner Who Speaks**

### Interviews in:

Entrepreneur Magazine
Inc. Magazine
Investor's Business Daily
Marketing Business
Meetings News Mag.
Practice Pay Solutions
Profile Magazine
Rolling Stone
Successful Meetings
Wall Street Journal

### Articles
#### published in:

Advertising Age
AdWeek
Corporate Incentive Trvl.
Design/Build Business
Incentive Marketing
Inside Business
Key Notes
Leadership Magazine
Marketing Comm.
Marketing Insights
Meeting News
Nation's Business
Opportunity World
Prof. Insurance Agents
Sales & Marketing Mgt.
Sales Promotion Monitor
Scotsman
Selling Magazine
Small Business Opt.
Strategies & News Mag.
Successful Meetings
Transaction World Mag.
In Organizations

- ✓ Innovative Marketing
- ✓ Customer Service
- ✓ Change Management
- ✓ Leadership Skills
- ✓ Incentive Programs
- ✓ Motivation Programs
- ✓ Building Effective Teams
- ✓ Continuous Improvement

*"Build what your customer wants, not what the company makes."*
*Jim quoted in Investor's Business Daily*

## Clients:

James Feldman Associates, Inc., a performance improvement and incentive marketing agency, providing sweepstakes, contests, games, and give-aways for some of the biggest organizations in the world, including:

| | | | |
|---|---|---|---|
| ✓Toyota | ✓Del Monte | ✓Southern Bell | ✓Disney |
| ✓Helene Curtis | ✓McDonald's | ✓Lexus | ✓Mary Kay |
| ✓Neutrogena | ✓GE | ✓Xerox | ✓Lucent |
| ✓Apple | ✓Microsoft | ✓Avon | ✓Hyatt Corporation |
| ✓Kellogg's | ✓K-Mart | ✓NBC | ✓Hewlett-Packard |

*"Jim Feldman is a master trainer, presenter and developer... engaging, entertaining, thought-provoking and down-to-earth."*
**Karen Smith-Pilkington**
**President**
**Kodak Professional Division**

### eBooks
#### written by Jim:

- ✓ D•A•T•I•N•G Your Customer
- ✓ Over 100 Shifts to Exceed Customer Expectations
- ✓ Shift Happens!®

### Books
#### written by Jim:

- ✓ Celebrate Customer Service: Insider Secrets
- ✓ Doctor Travel's Cure for the Common Trip
- ✓ Thriving On Change

**MEMBER**
**NSA**
NATIONAL SPEAKERS ASSOCIATION

## James Feldman Associates, Inc.

505 N. Lake Shore Drive, Suite 6601 • Chicago, IL 60611 • ph.312/527.1111
fx.312/527-1116 • inquiries@jfainc.com • www.jfainc.com

## M. SEAN AGNEW ENTERPRISES LLC
Chicago, IL USA
http://www.bluemetallic.com

I think many of us have wondered how some in our industry get so much more out of there careers and experiences than others. Our subject, M. Sean Agnew, has been dealing with and advising thousands of others on the answers to that and many other questions during his 21 year career. He has blended many different life paths during his journey which have led him to being one of the business communities most relied on consultants and the conference worlds most sought after speakers. Sean has toured and consulted with recording artists such as Public Enemy, Tupac, De la Soul and Arrested Development, He served as a management executive for Karma records. He later became National Executive Director to Las Vegas based training powerhouse Advanced Marketing Seminars. Sean helped produce and personally conduct hundreds of trainings and events that included movie and television stars such as Arnold Schwarzenegger, Ted Danson, Christopher Reeves, Louie Anderson and many more.

M. Sean Agnew
*Executive Managing Director/CEO*
M. Sean Agnew Enterprises LLC
Blue Metallic Entertainment Group
Naperville, IL USA
*Contact Phone:* 888.300.0970
*Contact Main Phone:* 888.300.0970
*Cell:* 630.781.2908
**Click to Contact from Web Site**

## AL LAUTENSLAGER -- CERTIFIED GUERRILLA MARKETING COACH
Chicago, IL USA
www.market-for-profits.com/

Al Lautenslager is a marketing/PR consultant, speaker, author, entrepreneur and business owner. He is the best-selling, co-author of Guerrilla Marketing in 30 Days and a featured business coach on Entrepreneur.com. He is the principal of Market for Profits, a Chicago-based marketing consulting firm and president of a commercial printing and mailing company in Wheaton, IL. Recently Al joined forces with Donald Trump and former Apprentice Television show contestants in the Apprentice Legend Millionaire Forum.

Al Lautenslager
*Author, Speaker, Entrepreneur, Business Owner,*
Certified Guerrilla Marketing Coach
Naperville, IL USA
*Contact Phone:* 630-871-0085
**Click to Contact from Web Site**

## MARGO BERMAN - CREATIVE MARKETING EXPERT
Miami, FL USA
http://www.unlocktheblock.com/

Margo Berman -- Marketer, Professor, Author, Inventor, Corporate/Life Coach Margo is the creativity and marketing expert with more than 20 years as an award-winning creative director and advertising professor. She founded her own ad agency, Global Impact, handling American Express, Alamo Rent A Car and Banana Boat. Margo also hosted an interview talk show in Miami: Artists About Themselves.She just finished a new book: Creativity Caffeine: To Stir Up Ideas With a Buzz and is the inventor of tactikPAK®, a patented system of learning. Margo has co-authored three books on spirituality. In addition, she has written articles for national trade journals and eference publications including the Encyclopedia of Advertising.A keynote speaker and member of the National Speakers Association, Margo is a corporate trainer of creative, hands-on seminars such as Creativity to Shatter The Gray Matter®, Wow 'Em With Ads That Sell, Killer Copy and Mental Peanut Butter®. She has been honored with numerous advertising and teaching awards. She was named the 2001 Woman of the Year in Communications Education and is a 2005 Kauffman Faculty Scholar.

Margo Berman
Creative Catalyst Unlock The Block
North Miami, FL USA
*Contact Phone:* 305-949-7711
**Click to Contact from Web Site**

## JAY BLOCK — LEADERSHIP TRAINING COACH

Palm Beach, FL USA
http://www.jayblock.com

Business Training Coach, Jay Block, best-selling author, leading empowerment and success coach is recognized for high-impact/energy programs facilitating positive change quickly and effectively. Growing up in the Boston area, he watched the Celtics win 11 World Championships. He brings that same powerful winning philosophy to the corporate world inspiring individual excellence in pursuit of stringent corporate goals. Author of 11 books, 6 best sellers by McGraw-Hill, and 2 new blockbuster CD programs on emotional management and life balance.

Ellen Block
The Jay Block Companies
West Palm, FL USA
*Contact Phone:* 561-687-0888
**Click to Contact from Web Site**

## BRAD KENT -- SMARTLEADSUSA, LLC

Palm Harbor, FL USA
http://www.smartleadsusa.com

A sought after marketing expert, Brad Kent has performed live presentations in front of more than 11,000 business professionals on the topic of direct marketing. He has also written articles on the topic of neighborhood marketing for Entrepreneur. com. Brad is an expert in the field of home services, hospitality and mortgage related marketing. He has created market-changing programs and strategies built on the foundation of neighborhood marketing principals. You will be enlightened not only by the presentation of strategies, but also the tools that are offered to effectively execute the strategies that Brad presents. As President and CEO of SmartleadsUSA, LLC, a niche direct mal marketing company, Brad and his team have pioneered patent pending technology that has revolutionized the fulfillment of neighborhood marketing techniques. He has been personally involved in the creative and deployment of more than 280 million pieces of direct mail for his clients. What were once only great ideas, but nearly impossible to execute can now be done with a few clicks of the mouse thanks to the inventions of SmartleadsUSA.

Brad Kent
SmartleadsUSA, LLC
Palm Harbor, FL USA
*Contact Phone:* 727-785-0766
**Click to Contact from Web Site**

## HOMEWORKINGMOM.COM

East Meadow, NY USA
http://www.homeworkingmom.com

Mothers' Home Business Network is the first and largest national organization providing ideas, inspiration and support for mothers who choose to work at home. We have been helping mothers become homeworking mothers since 1984. We are proud to introduce homeworkingmom.com, the new online service of Mothers' Home Business Network.

Georganne Fiumara
HomeWorkingMom.com
East Meadow, NY USA
*Contact Phone:* 516-997-7394
**Click to Contact from Web Site**

## ABBOTT, LANGER & ASSOCIATES, INC. — SALARY AND BENEFITS SURVEY EXPERTS

Chicago, IL USA
http://www.abbott-langer.com

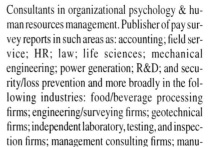

Consultants in organizational psychology & human resources management. Publisher of pay survey reports in such areas as: accounting; field service; HR; law; life sciences; mechanical engineering; power generation; R&D; and security/loss prevention and more broadly in the following industries: food/beverage processing firms; engineering/surveying firms; geotechnical firms; independent laboratory, testing, and inspection firms; management consulting firms; manufacturing firms; non-profits organizations; and publishers.

Dr. Steven Langer
*President*
Abbott, Langer & Associates, Inc.
Crete, IL USA
*Contact Phone:* 708/672-4200
**Click to Contact from Web Site**

### KARYL INNIS -- CAREER SUCCESS EXPERT
Dallas, TX USA
http://www.inniscompany.com

We are experts in career trends and issues. We utilize our knowledge to create programs for our corporate customers to help them address the career issues of their employees. Since 1987 hundreds of organizations nationwide from members of the Fortune 500 to smaller, local firms and not-for-profit organizations have turned to the experts at THE INNIS COMPANY for thoughtful, strategic, creative solutions to help their employees achieve successful careers.

Karyl Innis
*Chairman & CEO*
The Innis Company
Dallas, TX USA
*Contact Phone:* 9727029484
**Click to Contact from Web Site**

### CONTENTED COW PARTNERS, LLC
Jacksonville, FL USA
http://www.contentedcows.com

When it comes to the impact of employee motivation and morale on a company's bottom line, we wrote the book...literally. Based on years of research on the leadership and employee relations practices of some of America's best managed companies, coupled with 30 years of combined management experience, we address and can comment knowledgeably on: employee relations, turnover, morale, leadership, employee retention, recruitment, HR best practices, and workplace issues.

Richard Hadden
*Partner*
Contented Cow Partners, LLC
Jacksonville, FL
*Contact Phone:* 904-720-0870
*Cell:* 904-813-4322
**Click to Contact from Web Site**

### GREG SMITH -- CHART YOUR COURSE INTERNATIONAL
Atlanta, GA USA
www.ChartCourse.com

Greg Smith is the President of Chart Your Course International, a management-consulting firm located in Atlanta, Georgia. He shows business how to attract, keep, and motivate the workforce. He has consulted with some of the Best Companies to Work For in America. Greg serves on the Board of Examiners for the Malcolm Baldrige National Quality Award. He has written five books and was selected as one of the nation's Top-Ten Rising Stars in Human Resource Management.

Greg Smith
*President*
Chart Your Course International
Conyers, GA USA
*Contact Phone:* 770-860-9464
**Click to Contact from Web Site**

# Jay Block,
## *Leadership Training Coach*

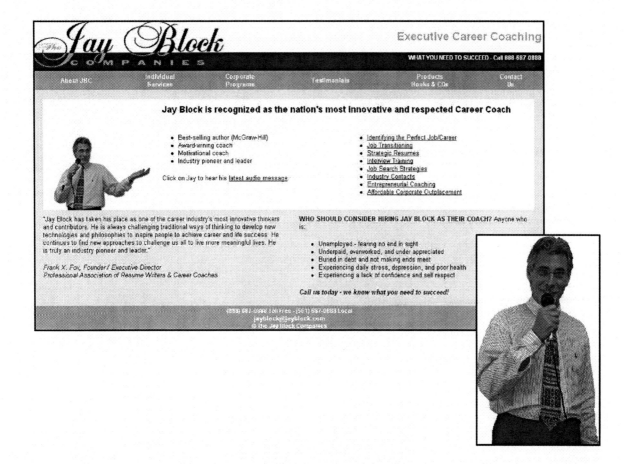

**Ellen Block**
**The Jay Block Companies**
**West Palm, Fla. -- U.S.A.**
**Contact Phone: 561-687-0888**

# www.jayblock.com

### KAREN SUSMAN — KAREN SUSMAN & ASSOCIATES
Denver, CO USA
www.karensusman.com

Karen's an expert on Humor, Life Balance, Stress, Presentation Skills, Networking and Building Community/Association Involvement. Since 1983, she's spoken internationally to organizations like INC Magazine, NBC, Marriott, American Society of Association Executives and National League of Cities. Her guidebooks on Networking, Time Management, Community Involvement and Humor at Work are crammed with doable ideas. $5 each. If you're looking for content plus mirth for interviews, articles and presentations, contact Karen. You'll like what you hear.

Karen Susman
*President*
Karen Susman and Associates
Denver, CO
*Contact Phone:* 1-888-678-8818
*Contact Main Phone:* 303-756-6939
**Click to Contact from Web Site**

### DR. MAYNARD BRUSMAN - WORKPLACE EXPERT
San Francisco, CA USA
http://www.workingresources.com

Dr. Maynard Brusman is a workplace psychologist and the president of Working Resources. We help companies assess, select, coach, and retain top talent. Maynard is a recognized expert in leadership coaching, leadership development, career coaching, coaching attorneys, succession planning, executive selection, pre-employment selection and assessment of emotionally intelligent people, and employee retention. He facilitates leadership retreats nationally and in Costa Rica. He has appeared in a variety of media including the Wall Street Journal, USA Today, San Francisco Chronicle, NBC, and Fast Company. The Society for Advancement of Consulting (SAC) has awarded Dr. Maynard Brusman two rare "Board Approvals" in the specialties of Executive/Leadership Coaching and Trusted Advisor to Attorneys and Law Firms.

Dr. Maynard Brusman
*Consulting Psychologist and Executive Coach*
Working Resources
San Anselmo, CA USA
*Contact Phone:* 415-546-1252
**Click to Contact from Web Site**

### MICHAEL MERCER, PH.D., EXPERT ON HIRING, LEADERSHIP, HR, & MANAGEMENT
Barrington, IL USA
http://www.drmercer.com

Dr. Mercer is a media personality, delivering print, TV and radio interviews on hiring, leadership, and management. He authored 5 books, including "Hire the Best — & Avoid the Rest" and "Absolutely Fabulous Organizational Change." Dr Mercer appeared on over 400 radio and TV talk shows - including Oprah and Today Show. Wall Street Journal, Forbes, Fortune, AP and other publications often quote him. Dr. Mercer developed 2 pre-employment tests used by companies to hire successful employees.

Michael Mercer, Ph.D.
Barrington, IL USA
*Contact Phone:* 847-382-0690
**Click to Contact from Web Site**

### CORBIN BALL, CSP, CMP, MS - MEETINGS & EVENTS TECHNOLOGY EXPERT
Bellingham, WA USA
http://www.corbinball.com/

Corbin Ball, CSP, CMP, MS is an international speaker, consultant and writer helping clients worldwide use technology to save time and improve productivity. With 20 years of experience running international technology meetings, he now is a highly acclaimed speaker with the ability to make complex subjects understandable and fun. His articles have appeared in hundreds of national and international publications and he has been quoted in the Wall Street Journal, the New York Times, Fast Company, PC Magazine and others. Corbin serves or has served on numerous hotel, corporate, convention bureau and association boards. He is Meeting Professionals International's 2002 International Supplier of the Year, MPI's 1997 International Chapter Leader of the Year, MPI's 1994 Meeting Planner of the Year (Washington State Chapter) and one of seven MPI Founding Global Chancellors. Corbin has been named for years 2000, 2001, 2002, and 2003 as one of The 25 Most Influential People in the Meetings Industry by MeetingNews Magazine.

Corbin Ball, CSP, CMP, MS
Corbin Ball Associates
Bellingham, WA USA
*Contact Phone:* 360-734-8756
**Click to Contact from Web Site**

### GERMANY-USA CAREER CENTER
Boston, MA USA
www.germany-usa.com

The Germany-USA Career Center is the premier recruiting source for business and trade between the U.S. and Germany. It provides professional search and staffing services for companies active in both markets. Co-founder Gerd Meissner is considered an excellent resource and interview partner on business with Germany in general and niche-focused Internet recruiting in particular. He has authored articles for many leading publications and the international business best-seller 'SAP - Inside the Secret Software Power' (McGraw-Hill).

Rob Delton
*Marketing Director*
Germany-USA Career Center
East Falmouth, U.S.A.
*Contact Main Phone:* +1 (508) 593-4246
**Click to Contact from Web Site**

### INSTITUTE FOR BUSINESS TECHNOLOGY --IBT-USA
San Diego, CA USA
www.ibt-pep.com

Everybody's stressed at work -- paper, email, voice mail, faxes, cell phones, cellular communications, meetings, interruptions, instant messaging. Downsizing and home offices guarantee the work never stops. However, overload doesn't equal productivity, quality, or excellent service. In order to work smarter, people need information-age work habits and systems. Our proven methodology helps corporate staff worldwide develop information-age survival techniques which improve productivity, effectiveness, customer service, and work/life balance.

Bary Sherman
Institute for Business Technology --IBT-USA
Fallbrook, CA USA
*Contact Phone:* 760-731-1400
**Click to Contact from Web Site**

## SOLUTIONS FOR HIRING
Phoenix, AZ USA
http://www.solutionsforhiring.com

We understand Superior Performance in ways no other organization does. Our research on the topic has helped people all over the world find the right job that fulfills their passions. Our solutions have also cut turnover, increased retention and improved results at thousands of companies worldwide.

Ashley Parks
*Public Relations Director*
Solutions For Hiring
Phoenix, USA
*Contact Main Phone:* 877-434-8010
**Click to Contact from Web Site**

## NATURALITY.NET, LLC
Toronto, Ontario Canada
www.naturality.net

We are a one-of-a-kind, specialized, career management and human capital maximization company with proprietary people technologies and processes. We are an international provider of customized people development through distance learning, action learning, leadership, consulting, implementation management, peer brainstorming, and, most importantly, through integrating evolution strategy, career strategy, and business strategy.

Lauren L. Holmes
*President*
Naturality.Net, LLC
Toronto, Ontario Canada
*Contact Phone:* 888-288-5895
**Click to Contact from Web Site**

## ACCORD MANAGEMENT SYSTEMS
Los Angeles, CA USA
www.accordsyst.com

Accord Management Systems provides clients with the necessary tools to assess, engage, and retain the most valuable asset in any organization, its people. Our clients utilize a series of surveys & assessments that allow them to scope job requirements, evaluate how potential employees fit into those jobs, and identify changes that will keep employees engaged at their jobs, which are all keys to improving productivity in today's business environment. In addition, we also offer an Employee Compliance Hotline, which protects employers and employees by providing an independent, third-party vehicle to report harassment and other workplace violations.

Bill Martin
Accord Management Systems
Westlake Village, CA USA
*Contact Phone:* 818-889-5600
**Click to Contact from Web Site**

## HUMAN RESOURCES ASSOCIATION OF NEW YORK
New York, NY USA
http://www.hrny.org

We like to call ourselves, the premier professional association for Human Resources professionals living or working in the five boroughs of New York City. As the largest member chapter of the Society for Human Resources Management (SHRM), the largest professional association for HR professionals in the world, we share the mission of focusing our efforts to serve the HR professional and advance the HR profession.

Heather Evans
*Executive Director*
Human Resources Association of New York
Trenton, NJ USA
*Contact Phone:* 877-625-4769
**Click to Contact from Web Site**

## DALE IRVIN — VERY FUNNY SPEAKER
Chicago, IL USA
www.DaleIrvin.com

Professional Summarizer — Dale Irvin is the World's only Professional Summarizer. He attends your meeting, paying attention to every word spoken by every speaker and noticing every detail of the event. Then, throughout the day, he will summarize the event with a comedy monologue written on the spot. One of his clients best described his performance when she said; What Billy Crystal brings to the Academy Awards, you brought to our meeting.

Dale Irvin
Downers Grove, IL USA
*Contact Phone:* 630-852-7695
**Click to Contact from Web Site**

## NATIONAL SPEAKERS ASSOCIATION, WASHINGTON D.C. AREA CHAPTER
Washington, DC USA
www.nsadc.org

Washington, D.C. Area Chapter of the National Speakers Association the recognized community for developing the content expertise, platform excellence, and business knowledge of those who speak professionally. Founded in 1980, our membership is compriced of speakers, trainers, consultants and authors who live in Washington, D.C., Maryland, Virginia, Pennsylvania and Delaware. We offer business development and networking to our members and guests through our monthly chapter programs, this website and other special events.

Sheila Summers
Washington, DC USA
*Contact Phone:* 202-363-5443
**Click to Contact from Web Site**

## ANN FRY --- HUMORU.COM
Austin, TX USA
www.HumorU.com

Humor University is committed to eradicating terminal seriousness from the world, especially the world of work. The magic keys to the kingdom of work are the keys that open the doors to laughter, lightheartedness and happiness at work. Our motto is: The company that plays together, stays together. We will definitely help you attract and retain the best employees, boost productivity and create profit.

Ann Fry
Austin, TX USA
*Contact Phone:* 512-342-1077
**Click to Contact from Web Site**

## DR. KATHLEEN HALL, STRESS MANAGEMENT AND WORK-LIFE BALANCE EXPERT
Atlanta, GA USA
http://www.drkathleenhall.com

Stress management and work-life balance authority, Dr. Kathleen Hall is founder of The Stress Institute, Founder and CEO of Alter Your Life, a Fellow of the American Institute of Stress, and author of A Life in Balance: Nourishing the Four Roots of True Happiness (Amacom Publication January 2006) and Alter Your Life: Overbooked? Overworked? Overwhelmed? (Oak Haven Press April 2005). These books offer simple methods and guided journeys for living an intentional life of mental, physical and spiritual health. Dr. Hall studied under some of the world's experts in spirituality and medicine, including President Jimmy Carter, the Dalai Lama, Dr. Herbert Benson, and Dr. Dean Ornish. Her media credits include The Today Show, CNN, The Wall Street Journal, Associated Press, Cosmopolitan, and corporate presentations to Proctor and Gamble, Home Depot, Turner Broadcasting and Office Depot.

Darlene Wyant
*Media Relations*
Dr. Kathleen Hall
The Stress Institute
Clarkesville,
*Contact Phone:* 706-947-1815
**Click to Contact from Web Site**

## AMERICAN PAYROLL ASSOCIATION
San Antonio, TX USA
http://www.americanpayroll.org

The American Payroll Association (APA) is the nation's leader in payroll education, publications and training. The nonprofit association conducts more than 300 payroll training conferences and seminars each year and publishes a library of resource texts and newsletters. National Payroll Week, APA's celebration of synergy between America's workers and payroll professionals, aims at educating the public about the payroll function. APA's Executive Director, Dan Maddux, has made numerous television and radio appearances. APA is the industry's collective voice in Washington, D.C.

Mark Coindreau
*Public Relations Coordinator*
American Payroll Association
San Antonio, TX USA
*Contact Phone:* 210-226-4600
**Click to Contact from Web Site**

## JINSOO TERRY: BUILDING SELF-CONFIDENCE IN THE MULTI-CULTURAL WORKFORCE
San Francisco, CA USA
http://www.jinsooterry.com

Jinsoo Terry, a Korean immigrant to the United States, has inspired thousands of people with her remarkable path to success in the world of international business. She is renowned for her ability to seamlessly bridge cultural differences by cultivating effective global business practices. Terry spoke before millions of viewers on Korean national television (SBS TV), and she has books slated to be published in both Korea and the United States in the near future.

Jinsoo Terry
ADVANCED GLOBAL CONNECTIONS
Berkeley, CA USA
*Contact Phone:* 415-240-5001
**Click to Contact from Web Site**

# Solutions for Hiring,
## *Talent Management Plus*

**Jeb Brooks,**
**Public Relations Director**
**Solutions For Hiring**
**Phoenix, Arizona -- U.S.A .**
**Main Phone: 877-434-8010**

# www.solutionsforhiring.com

## LOLA GILLEBAARD - HUMORIST & MOTIVATIONAL SPEAKER
South Laguna Beach, CA USA
http://laughandlearn.org/index.htm

Lola Gillebaard is an exceptional entertainer with southern charm and gutsy style. Lola inspires audiences all over the world using clean real-life humor with a heart-felt message. Lola will make you laugh until you cry, only to make you laugh all over again. Featured clean comedian of the Improv, regular humorist for Crystal Cruises, and hot charity fundraiser for community events, Lola captivates your guests with her personal humor magic... From Conventions to Workshops, from Women's Conferences to Teacher In Service Days, Hospital Nursing Seminars to Corporate Retreats, Lola is at home with people of all ages and all walks of life.

Lola Gillebaard
LaughandLearn.org
South Laguna Beach, CA USA
*Contact Phone:* 1-800-557-LOLA
*Contact Main Phone:* 1-800-557-5652
**Click to Contact from Web Site**

## PETER J. FOGEL - REINVENTION & COMMUNICATIONS EXPERT
Sunrise, FL USA
http://www.reinventyourselfnow.com

Mid-Life Career Crisis Expert, Communications Specialist, and noted Humorist, Peter "The Humorator" Fogel has been making people laugh and think for over 25 years. The former late night television comedian has worked on such shows as Married With Children, Evening At The Improv, and HBO's Comedy Central. . . Switching careers after 40 he became an in demand advertising copywriter and speaker who helps other people find their passion in new careers while using humor to help them overcome life's obstacles.

Peter J. Fogel
*Pres.*
Fortune 500 Comedy Communications
Sunrise, FL USA
*Contact Phone:* 954-742-4847
*Cell:* 917-519-2749
**Click to Contact from Web Site**

## JOEL EISENBERG — HOW TO SURVIVE A DAY JOB
Los Angeles, CA USA
www.toposbooks.com

Filmmaker, author, motivational speaker and entrepreneur Joel Eisenberg has channeled his experiences as a professional wage slave to become a tactical expert in the field of fulfilling creative passions. As President of Eisenberg Media Group and specialty publishing firm Topos Books, Joel now shares his expertise via the first volume of a new inspirational brand, Aunt Bessie's How to Survive a Day Job While Pursuing the Creative Life, along with an all-star cast of celebrity contributors.

Joel Eisenberg
Topos Books
Northridge, CA USA
*Contact Phone:* 818-891-2223
**Click to Contact from Web Site**

## CHRISTOPHER L. HANSEN, HOME-BASED BUSINESS EXPERT
New York, NY USA
www.clhassociates.com

Chris Hansen knows what's happening in the small business world. With experience in corporations, non-profits, the public sector, and entrepreneurship he has generated millions in profits, saved millions of tax dollars, formed businesses, created public/private partnerships and coalitions, and organized an international membership association. He was named the U.S. Small Business Administration's the National Home-based Business Advocate. He addresses the subject of job creation, self-employment, change, and opportunity creation to audiences of all sizes.

Christopher L. Hansen
*President*
The Home Based Business Council
Neptune City, NJ USA
*Contact Phone:* 732-776-6496
*Cell:* 732-513-9337
**Click to Contact from Web Site**

• SUCCESS IN THE 21 ST CENTURY WILL REQUIRE MULTI-CULTURAL UNDERSTANDING AND A GLOBAL PERSPECTIVE •

"CONFIDENT IN THE WORLD"

# Jinsoo Terry:
## Building Self-Confidence in the Multi-Cultural Workforce

### Learn -- And Have Fun -- With The Jinsoo Terry Experience

Jinsoo Terry, a Korean immigrant to the United States, has inspired thousands of people with her remarkable path to success in the world of international business. As an expert in Asian culture, she is a sought after speaker to American as well as to Asian audiences. In business, building self-confidence and understanding and appreciating the differences of your multi-cultural workforce is essential for increased productivity, quality implementation and team building. You will immediately put to practice what you learn.

### Speaker Topics:

- Self-Confidence: The Secret Ingredient to Success
- The ABCs of Doing Business in Asia
- How to Overcome Language Barriers to Create a Productive Workforce
- How to Successfully Do Business in Korea
- How to Maximize Your Diverse Workforce
- How to Close Cultural Gaps and Make the Best Teams Motivating a Multi-Cultural Workforce
- How to Cultivate True Leaders in a Multi-Cultural Environment
- How to Prepare Your Manufacturing Workforce for the Global Marketplace

Jinsoo Terry
ADVANCED GLOBAL CONNECTIONS
Berkeley, California, USA
415-240-5001
**JinsooTerry.com**

## JOHN PATRICK DOLAN - NEGOTIATE LIKE THE PROS
La Quinta, CA USA
http://www.negotiatelikethepros.com

John Patrick Dolan delivers entertaining presentations on the strategy and tactics of negotiation using more humor, theatrics and energy than you might think the subject of negotiation could inspire. John Patrick Dolan is a radio broadcaster and television legal news analyst appearing frequently on Fox News Channel, MSNBC, and Court TV. He has also been honored by the National Speakers Association as a member of the Professional Speakers Hall of Fame.

George L. Graham II
*Marketing Director*
Negotiate like the Pros
La Quinta, CA USA
*Contact Phone:* 760-771-5490
*Contact Main Phone:* 760-771-5490
*Cell:* 562-824-4007
**Click to Contact from Web Site**

## DR. GAYLE CARSON, CSP, CMC -- AUTHOR OF WINNING WAYS
Miami, FL USA
www.GayleCarson.com

Dr. Gayle Carson, also known as the Wiz of Biz has written a new book especially for women over 50. It teaches the nine strategies for living a life free of regret and offers 13 key tips to living a more productive and fulfilled life. The book is called How to Be an S.O.B.--A Spunky Old Broad Who Kicks Butt. Gayle offers short, easy to follow advice to achieve health and fitness, open your own business, invest in real estate or whatever else your SOB heart desires.

Dr. Gayle Carson
Carson Research Center
Miami Beach, FL USA
*Contact Phone:* 305-534-8846
**Click to Contact from Web Site**

## KAREN MCCULLOUGH, CSP - EXECUTIVE PRESENTATION COACH
Houston, TX USA
http://www.karenmccullough.com/

Karen McCullough tells it like it is. Karen is the perfect speaker to kick off your next event. Karen does her homework; the extra research behind the scenes allows her to customize her message to your audience. Karen McCullough has been inspiring lives as a highly successful entrepreneur for over 20 years and is passionate about helping people achieve the success they deserve.

Karen McCullough, CSP
Karen McCullough & Co.
Houston, TX USA
*Contact Phone:* (713) 880-8784
**Click to Contact from Web Site**

## ASTD
Alexandria, VA USA
http://www.astd.org

Your Source for Information on Workplace Learning and Performance for more than 50 years, ASTD has been the leading resource on workplace learning and performance issues, providing information, research, analysis, and practical information derived from its own research, the knowledge and experience of its members, its conferences and publications, and the partnerships it has built through research and public policy work.

Jennifer Homer
*Director of PR*
ASTD
Alexandria, VA
*Contact Phone:* 703-683-8123
**Click to Contact from Web Site**

## STEVE GILLILAND -- TRAINING & MOTIVATING TODAY'S PROFESSIONALS
Pittsburgh, PA USA
http://www.PerformancePlus1.com

If you develop your people, the business will follow. Whether it is improved time management, better teamwork, or a wider range of skills being used to solve a wider range of problems, training is the key to adding measurability to the bottom line. We invite you to see why companies, organizations, and associations, both large and small, representing every industry, have hired Performance Plus Professional Development to make a difference.

Steve Gilliland, CSP
Performance Plus Professional Development
Pittsburgh, PA USA
*Contact Phone:* 412-766-0806
**Click to Contact from Web Site**

## GREGG GREGORY, CSP — AMERICA'S BUSINESS NAVIGATOR

Washington, DC USA
http://www.GreggSpeaks.com

Gregg Gregory Certified Speaking Professional (CSP) focuses his work on the WHY to be a team member, as opposed to just the HOW to be a team member. Gregg works with and speaks to organizations and their leaders about why being a team member is vital to the organization's success. While those who know how are important and they will most assuredly have a job, they will most likely be working for those who know why.

Gregg Gregory, CSP
*America's Business Navigator*
Kensington, MD USA
*Contact Phone:* 301-564-0908
*Cell:* 301-252-1347
**Click to Contact from Web Site**

## GOT GAME CONSULTING

Phoenix, AZ USA
www.gotgameconsulting.com

The creator of 'Got Game! Theory'. Helping organizations maximize change through the revolutionary use of Game Theory. Got Game Consulting provides a unique business platform for establishing strategic and tactical planning objectives through the practice of Game Theory. Got Game Theory will place you and your organization in a position of strength and advantage.

Zogby, Douglas J.
Got Game Consulting
Phoenix, AZ USA
*Contact Phone:* 480-272-7640
*Cell:* 480-215-9518
**Click to Contact from Web Site**

## KEVIN JOYCE, MANAGEMENT CONSULTANT AND ORGANIZATIONAL CHANGE EXPERT

Toledo, OH USA
http://www.e-quantumgroup.com

Make a Quantum Leap! Kevin Joyce, J.D., M.O.D., SPHR, is a management consultant, employment lawyer, business college instructor, researcher and author. He is the principal of The Quantum Group, LLC, which collaborates with clients to achieve performance improvements through services including strategic planning, HR management, organizational diagnosis, leadership development and change management. Kevin has written for many business publications, including Building Profits, Group Practice Journal, Law Practice Management, and Business Horizons.

Kevin Joyce
*Principal*
The Quantum Group, LLC
Sylvania, OH USA
*Contact Phone:* 419-340-8115
**Click to Contact from Web Site**

## DR. BILL CRAWFORD — PERFORMANCE TRAINING EXPERT

Houston, TX USA
www.billcrawfordphd.com/

In addition to holding a Ph.D. in psychology from the University of Houston, Dr. Crawford is a licensed psychologist, organizational consultant, executive coach, and professional speaker. In the past 20 years, he has created over 3000 successful presentations for organizations such as Shell, J.P. Morgan/Chase, Sprint, IBM, the Texas Medical Center, as well as many state and national professional associations. As a presenter, he shares his perspective on Life from the Top of the Mind with such humor and energy that he is constantly referred to as the Steve Martin of corporate America. In addition, his two PBS specials have been seen by over 15 million people nationwide and he has been quoted as an expert in such diverse publications as: The New York Times, Entrepreneur, The Chicago Tribune, Investor's Business Daily, Cosmopolitan, The Dallas Morning News, Self Magazine, NBCi.com, Working Mother Magazine, Office.com, Forbes Small Business, CBS MarketWatch, MSN.com, DrKoop.com.

Dr. Bill Crawford
Crawford Performance Training
*Contact Phone:* 832-772-6147
**Click to Contact from Web Site**

## ACHIEVEMENTORS, INC., LESLIE FURLOW, RN, PH.D.

Dallas, TX USA
www.AchieveMentors.com

AchieveMentors, consulting, presentations, and performance improvement company specializes in healthcare and information management. Providing coaching, mentoring and increasing personal hardiness, Leslie Furlow, PhD assists in improving overall performance. Operations and management consulting services includes increasing productivity, performance improvement and maximizing human resources and relationships. Educational & Keynote presentations are available for many topics. In conjunction with Unified ConneXions, Inc., AchieveMentors, offers information management services for education and healthcare organizations, including network and data management solutions.

Leslie Furlow, RN, Ph.D.
Cleburne, TX USA
*Contact Phone:* 877-331-4321
*Cell:* 817-291-6303
**Click to Contact from Web Site**

# GAYLE CARSON

## *The Go-To Source for Women Over 50*

Dr. Gayle Carson, also known as the "Wiz of Biz" has written a new book especially for women over 50.

"How to Be an S.O.B.: A Spunky Old Broad Who Kicks Butt" teaches the nine secrets of a regret-free life and offers 13 key tips to living a more productive and fulfilled life. Gayle offers short, easy-to-follow advice to achieve health and fitness, open your own business, invest in real estate or do whatever else your SOB heart desires.

Celebrating more than 47 years in business, the "Wiz of Biz" heads up a radio show for Entrepreneur Magazine -- "Women in Business" – which celebrates women who embody success in many different ways, giving its audience valuable life lessons.

An expert advisor and coach to CEOs and entrepreneurs, Gayle is also a CSP (certified speaking professional) and CMC (certified management consultant), who has been named to many "Who's Who" books, and whose media exposure ranges from USA Today to the Larry King Radio Show.

Carson Research Center
2957 Flamingo Drive
Miami Beach, Florida 33140-3916
305-534-8846 Phone
305-532-8826 Fax
gayle@gaylecarson.com

*The Master of "Staying at The Top"*

## IN THE MOMENT PRODUCTIONS, INC.
Austin, TX USA
http://www.inthemoment.com

In The Moment Productions entertains, equips, and inspires through customized training, interactive keynotes, and comedy programs. We make training stick, corporate meetings sizzle, and leave audiences laughing. We are a unique combination of top flight educators and talented entertainers. We create original entertainment, captivating keynotes, and activity-filled training using humor for all types of organizations. We have the experience and data to help you unleash your human capital in ways that promote sustainable growth.

Terrill Fischer
*CEO (Chief Entertainment Officer)*
In the Moment Productions, Inc.
Austin, TX USA
*Contact Phone:* 512-476-9457
*Cell:* 512-771-4320
**Click to Contact from Web Site**

# ASTRON
## SOLUTIONS
www.astronsolutions.com

## ASTRON SOLUTIONS - HUMAN RESOURCE CONSULTING
New York, NY USA
www.astronsolutions.com

Since 1999, Astron Solutions has met the Human Resource needs of cost-conscious organizations nationwide. We develop and implement HR programs impacting an organization's two most important HR concerns: rising costs and retaining qualified staff. Our work supports organizations' strategic directions by creating a positive employee relations environment. National Directors Jennifer Loftus and Michael Maciekowich present highly-rated sessions on a variety of compensation and employee retention topics and are available to share their knowledge with you.

Sharon M. Terry
*Writer / Marketing Specialist*
Astron Solutions
New York, NY USA
*Contact Phone:* 800-520-3889
**Click to Contact from Web Site**

## NELSON MOTIVATION, INC.
San Diego, CA USA
http://www.nelson-motivation.com

Dr. Bob Nelson is recognized around the world as one of the leading authorities on motivating, energizing, and inspiring employees to new peaks of performance. With more than 2.5 million books in print, he has his pulse on the changing needs and trends in today's workplace. He has appeared in: The New York Times, The Wall Street Journal, The Washington Post. He has appeared on: CNN, CNBC, PBS, and MSNBC and many others.

Bob Nelson
*President*
Nelson Motivation, Inc.
San Diego, CA
*Contact Phone:* 858-673-0690
**Click to Contact from Web Site**

## ROBIN L. GRAHAM, INNERACTIVE CONSULTING GROUP INC.
Memphis, TN USA
www.inneractiveconsulting.com

Specialist in bridging the knowing-doing gap. Rather than spending additional time, effort and dollars on standard Sales, Leadership, Team work, Wellness and other initiatives - redirect the focus to where success ultimately resides. The inner mind-set, thoughts and beliefs of the individuals involved. Knowing what to do, how to do it and why it is important is not enough. Achieve sustainable success by accessing and aligning subconscious thoughts, decisions, and actions with external goals.

Robin L. Graham
*President*
InnerActive Consulting Group Inc.
Cordova, TN USA
*Contact Phone:* 901-757-4434
**Click to Contact from Web Site**

"ACHIEVING SUCCESS THROUGH MENTORING EXCELLENCE"

AchieveMentors, a consulting, presentations and performance-improvement company, specializes in healthcare and information management.

Providing coaching, mentoring and increasing personal hardiness, Leslie Furlow, Ph.D., assists in improving overall performance. Operations and management consulting services includes increasing productivity, performance improvement and maximizing human resources and relationships.

Educational and keynote presentations are available for many topics. In conjunction with Unified ConneXions, Inc., AchieveMentors, offers information management services for education and healthcare organizations, including network and data management solutions.

**AchieveMentors, Inc.,
Leslie Furlow, RN, Ph.D.**

P.O. Box 38
Cleburne, Texas 76033

Toll-free: 877-331-4321
Cell: 817-291-6303
Fax: 1-866-203-0622

Email:
info@achievementors.com

Leslie Furlow, the president of AchieveMentors, Inc., has a breadth of "healthcare, municipal and industrial experience," including work with the petrochemical, insurance, municipal utilities, retail, food services and manufacturing organizations. This broad base of experience has enabled her to help her clients improve effectiveness and outcomes, increase staff contribution and develop new products and service lines. Throughout her career, Leslie has assisted individuals and companies in their quest to define visions, clarify mission statements, identify and solve issues as well as develop personal and corporate goals.

## BEN B. GRAHAM -- BUSINESS PROCESS MAPPING SOFTWARE EXPERT
TIpp City, OH USA
http://www.worksimp.com

Ben is President of The Ben Graham Corporation and author of the book 'Detail Process Charting: Speaking the Language of Process' published by John Wiley Publishers. His company pioneered the field of business process improvement, and has provided process improvement consulting, coaching and education services to organizations across North America since 1953. Ben has worked with many organizations to build libraries of business process maps and develop effective, process-focused, continuous improvement programs.

Ben B Graham
Tipp City, OH United States
*Contact Phone:* 937-667-1032
**Click to Contact from Web Site**

## DR. LIZ BERNEY — TRAINING & ORGANIZATIONAL DEVELOPMENT
Washington, DC USA
www.berneyassoc.com

Dr. Liz Berney provides services in staff/management training; retreat/meeting facilitation; organizational consulting and, motivational speaking. Clients include Coca Cola, Tropicana, Raytheon, AT & T, U.S. House of Representatives, J.F. Kennedy Center for Performing Arts, Baldrige National Quality Program, Bill & Melinda Gates Foundation. She specializes in change and conflict management, dealing with difficult personalities, leadership skills, and team development. High energy and dynamic, she takes a hands-on, strategic approach to enhancing individual and team performance.

Dr. Liz Berney
Berney Associates, Training & Organization Development
Rockville, MD USA
*Contact Phone:* 301-424-4633
*Contact Main Phone:* 301-424-4633
**Click to Contact from Web Site**

## ROBERT STACK, CLC, APR, FELLOW PRSA - THE COMEBACK COACH
Palm Beach Gardens, FL USA
http://www.comebackcoach.com/

Robert Stack is a credentialed executive life coach with an unusual and deeply personal specialty. Robert's mission (born from tough experience and keen observation) has been to create The Course in Comeback (sm). Using heartfelt presentations, Comeback Circles (sm), and one-on-one coaching, Robert empowers individuals in the grip of adversity to take ownership of their lives and discover that within their challenges lie the seeds of opportunity for healing and personal growth.

Robert Stack
Palm Beach Gardens, FL USA
*Contact Phone:* 561-776-0101
**Click to Contact from Web Site**

## ROBERT S. GROSSMAN — BUSINESS PERFORMANCE EXPERT
Los Angeles, CA USA
www.focuscreative.com

Robert Grossman delivers leadership and employee development programs that achieve higher performing individuals, teams and organizations. Robert is a creative solution generator that comes only with his unique package of training, executive coaching; keynote speaking, video and event production and multimedia communications. In addition, Robert is the co-founder and President of Production for a new dynamic marketing and education media company called Waiting Room Theater, Inc.

Robert S. Grossman
*Founder & President*
Focus Creative Group
Tarzana, CA USA
*Contact Phone:* 1-800-560-4649
**Click to Contact from Web Site**

## CAROLYN STEIN -- THE TRAINING EXPRESS
Miami, FL USA
www.carolynstein.com

Carolyn Kerner Stein, Author, Coach, Keynoter, Trainer. International Speaker Expertise: Delivering Powerful Speeches, Public Speaking, Mingle Management (people skills), Professional & Personal Development. Self Esteem Coach, CEO of The Training Express A fast track to executive and employee training on leadership and customer service featuring a portable employee training kit. Workshops include: Executive Image, Working with Difficult People, Networking Skills, Leadership and Business Etiquette.

Carolyn Stein
*Author*
Carolyn Stein & Associates
Miami, FL USA
*Contact Phone:* 305-931-3237
**Click to Contact from Web Site**

"Bob Nelson helps managers take rewards and mold them into new management styles at their companies."
- *The New York Times*

"Better than money: Praise and personal gestures motivate workers. Things that don't cost money are ironically the most effective."
- *The Wall Street Journal*

# THE EXPERT ON EMPLOYEE MOTIVATION & MANAGEMENT

## BOB NELSON, PH. D.
### BEST-SELLING AUTHOR AND RECOGNITION EXPERT

Bob Nelson is recognized around the world as one of the leading authorities on motivating, energizing, and inspiring employees to new peaks of performance. With more than 2.5 million books in print, he has his pulse on the changing needs and trends in today's workplace.

## BOB'S TOPICS OF EXPERTISE:

- Employee Recognition and Motivation
- Hiring and Retaining Today's Workers
- Enhancing Initiative and Performance

Bob is a seasoned media source perfect for interviews, quotes, examples, best practices and original research. Best of all he is responsive to all media requests.

## HE HAS APPEARED IN:

*The New York Times, The Wall Street Journal, The Washington Post, The Chicago Tribune, Fortune, BusinessWeek & Inc.* magazines. He has appeared on: CNN, CNBC, PBS, and MSNBC; NPR, USA Radio Network, Business News Network, and Bloomberg Media, among others.

## TO CONTACT BOB:
bobrewards@aol.com
858-673-0690 (direct line) or 800-575-5521
www.nelson-motivation.com
- **Guaranteed Responsiveness**
- **Extensive Examples**
- **Original Research**

## KATE ZABRISKIE - TRAINING SEMINARS, WORKSHOPS, AND KEYNOTES
Washington, DC USA
www.businesstrainingworks.com

Business Training Works - Onsite training provider answers your questions about soft-skills: customer service, communication skills, business etiquette, business writing, time management, presentation skills, train the trainer, creativity and critical thinking, negotiation, supervision skills, and the other basics that people need to be successful at work. Founder, Kate Zabriskie and her team of trainers work with the Fortune 500, government, and small businesses to improve business results. Are you wondering which fork to use? We can help. Do you need to know how to write clear sentences that get results? We can help. Are you trying to improve customer service? We can help. THE BOTTOM LINE: WE CAN ANSWER HARD QUESTIONS ABOUT SOFT SKILLS Our clients include: Earthlink, Microsoft, Boeing, United States Government, Toyota, The University of Maryland, Georgetown University, and hundreds of other organizations. From communication skills to getting organized and staying that way, we're happy to tell you what we know. You ask the question. We'll answer it or recommend someone who can.

Kate Zabriskie
*Owner*
Business Training Works, Inc.
Port Tobacco, MD USA
*Contact Phone:* 301.934.3250
*Contact Main Phone:* 800.934.4825
*Cell:* 240.412.3955
**Click to Contact from Web Site**

## NATIONAL BORDER PATROL COUNCIL
Campo, CA USA
http://www.nbpc.net

The National Border Patrol Council is the labor organization that represents the more than 10,000 front-line Border Patrol employees responsible for enforcing U.S. immigration laws. It strongly advocates for secure borders and fair treatment of the dedicated men and women who patrol them. In order to achieve these goals, the Council lobbies Congress, negotiates with DHS, represents employees in various proceedings, and provides the news media with reliable and candid information from a front-line perspective.

T.J. Bonner
*President*
National Border Patrol Council
Campo, CA
*Contact Phone:* 619-478-5145
**Click to Contact from Web Site**

## EMPLOYEE RETENTION SURVEY
Greensboro, NC USA
www.employee-retention-news-survey.com

A new employee retention survey will support human resource professionals and corporate executives concerned about the impact of employee turnover. The Herman Group, the pioneers in the field of workforce stability strategies and education, has developed a web-based research service for employee retention. The database is the most robust resource on the internet for staying current with what is happening in the field of employee retention.

Roger Herman
The Herman Group
Greensboro, NC USA
*Contact Phone:* 336-282-9370
**Click to Contact from Web Site**

# Get the answers to the hard questions about soft skills.

Onsite training provider can answer your questions about soft skills: customer service, communication, business etiquette, business writing, time management, presentation skills, train the trainer, change management, military writing, creativity and critical thinking, cross-cultural management, negotiation, supervision skills, and the other basics that people need to be successful at work.

Are you wondering which fork to use?
We can help.

Do you need to know how to
write clear sentences that get results?
We can help.

Are you trying to
improve customer service?
We can help.

From communication skills to getting organized and staying that way, we're happy to tell you what we know.  You ask the questions. We'll answer them or recommend someone who can.

Our clients include: Earthlink, Microsoft, Boeing, United States Government, Toyota, The University of Maryland, Georgetown University, Northrop Grumman, and hundreds of other organizations.

## ALL CALLS ANSWERED
## (301) 934.3250 | info@businesstrainingworks.com

## TIM KERN, ECONOMIC INSIGHT
Winter Haven, FL USA
www.timkern.com

Expert in explaining the economic reasons behind macro moves in economic sectors, and in politics. Ties political and economic thought, to explain political moves. Why does health insurance cost so much? Where are the jobs? What happened to manufacturing in the US? Why do terrorists target innocent civilians? Believe it or not, the answers to these questions are simple. when you understand economics and step away from political correctness. Ask Tim - he will explain.

Tim Kern
*Director*
TimKern.com
Winter Haven, FL USA
*Contact Phone:* 863-651-6095
**Click to Contact from Web Site**

## DR. VALERIE KIRKGAARD — GETTING THE BEST OUT OF PEOPLE
Pacific Palisades, CA USA
www.doctorvalerie.com

Dr. Valerie Kirkgaard, PhD, creator of the Kirkgaard Method, works in the electromagnetic body field neutralizing past traumatic charges. The result, you become responsive, rather than reactive. A retired MFCT Therapist, she works with artists, celebrities and professionals in reaching peak performance and personal peace. She loves to help people get married and stay married. Dr. Kirkgaard is the veteran radio talk show host of Waking Up in America. She can be heard at voiceamerica.com, KTBL in Albuquerque, NM, WMNY and WHLD in Buffalo, NY.

Dr. Valerie Anne Kirkgaard
Topanga, CA USA
*Contact Phone:* 310-455-8623
**Click to Contact from Web Site**

## DOUGLAS M. MCCABE, PH.D. — EMPLOYEE RELATIONS EXPERT
Washington, DC USA

Dr. Douglas M. McCabe is Professor of Labor Relations, Human Resource Management, and Organizational Behavior at Georgetown University's School of Business in Washington, DC. He is the author of more than 200 articles, papers, monographs and speeches presented at professional and scholarly meetings in the field of employee relations. He is also an active domestic and international management consultant. Dr. McCabe has appeared more than 200 times on television and radio.

Douglas M. McCabe, Ph.D.
*Professor of Management*
Georgetown University
Washington, DC
*Contact Phone:* 202-687-3778
**Click to Contact from Web Site**

## NATIONAL ASSOCIATION OF LETTER CARRIERS(AFL-CIO)
Washington, DC USA
http://www.nalc.org

The 300,000-member National Association of Letter Carriers union represents city delivery letter carriers employed by the U.S. Postal Service in all 50 states and U.S. jurisdictions. NALC President William H. Young was elected to the union's top leadership position in 2002 after serving as the union's Executive Vice President for the previous four years. He is a available to provide insight and information regarding: Postal Reform, Organized Labor, Politics, Legislation, Grievance and Arbitration Procedures, and Hunger.

Drew Von Bergen
*Director of Public Relations*
National Association of Letter
Carriers(AFL-CIO)
Washington, DC
*Contact Phone:* 202-662-2489
*Contact Main Phone:* 202-393-4695
**Click to Contact from Web Site**

# EMPLOYEE RELATIONS ANALYSIS— TELEVISION, RADIO & PRINT MEDIA

DOUGLAS M. MCCABE, PH.D.
GEORGETOWN UNIVERSITY
The McDonough School of Business

OLD NORTH, 315
37TH AND O STREETS, NW
WASHINGTON, DC 20057
202-687-3778

E-MAIL: mccabed@georgetown.edu

**DR. DOUGLAS M. MCCABE**

Dr. Douglas M. McCabe is Professor of Labor Relations, Human Resource Management, and Organizational Behavior at Georgetown University's School of Business, Washington, D.C. He is the author of more than 200 articles, papers, monographs, and speeches presented at professional and scholarly meetings in the field of employee relations. He is also an active domestic and international management consultant.

Considered by the media to be an expert in his field, Dr. McCabe has appeared more than 200 times on international, national, and local television and radio as the networks have sought his views on critical issues in employee relations.

His television credits include being interviewed on "ABC World News Tonight with Peter Jennings"; "NBC Nightly News with Tom Brokaw"; "CBS Evening News with Dan Rather"; "Newshour with Jim Lehrer"; and CNN's "Crossfire" and "Inside Politics."

His print media credits include being quoted in *Business Week, U.S. News & World Report, USA Today, The Washington Post, Los Angeles Times, The New York Times, Chicago Sun-times, Chicago Tribune, The Milwaukee Journal, and The Detroit News.*

Furthermore, Dr. McCabe is a premier executive education professor. He has conducted more than 250 management development programs on the area of employee relations. Also, he is a member of the American Arbitration Association. He holds a Ph.D. from Cornell University and is a member of Phi Beta Kappa.

**Analysis provided on the following topics:**

Labor-Management Relations

Human Resources Management

Organizational Behavior

Employee Relations

International Industrial Relations

Management Consulting Practices

Global Employment Trends

Ethical Issues in Management

Negotiation

Mediation

Arbitration

International Business Negotiation

Executive Leadership

## JOE RODRIGUEZ, GLOBAL INNOVATION LEADERSHIP, INC.
Miami, FL USA
www.joe-rodriguez.com

Joe can help explain Lean Management and New Product topics in a simple, clear and interesting way. He has the expertise you need to call on when you want your questions answered about Manufacturing, New Products and Latin American cultural issues. He works with leaders who want their organizations LEAN and their new products Fast to Market. Joe provides consulting, seminars, workshops, keynotes and facilitation to clients. He is the "Innovative Lean Manufacturing Management" Expert.

Joe Rodriguez
Global Innovation Leadership, Inc.
Miami, FL USA
*Contact Phone:* 305-790-3303
**Click to Contact from Web Site**

## STEPHEN VISCUSI - WORKPLACE EXPERT , LIFE COACH , CAREER COACH & HEADHUNTER
New York, NY USA
http://www.viscusigroup.com/

Stephen Viscusi is the author of On the Job: How to Make It in the Real World of Work (Random House). Known as America's workplace guru, Viscusi combines education, experience, common sense, along with intuition help to answer caller and viewers questions. His syndicated radio show, "On the Job" was heard in over 65 markets. Viscusi also writes a national column with the same title, published in U.25 magazine (circulation of 600,000). Viscusi lectures nationally as an America's Headhunter. Viscusi is the CEO of The Viscusi Group, a retainer based search practice based in New York City that has been servicing the interior furnishings industry for over 20 years.

Stephen P. Viscusi
*Workplace Expert*
The Viscusi Group
New York, NY
*Contact Main Phone:* (212) 979-5700
**Click to Contact from Web Site**

## MICHAEL E. BRIZZ, CMC, REFERRALMASTERY.COM
Chagrin Falls, OH USA
www.referralmastery.com

The Center for Professional Achievement, Inc. is a leading authority in helping companies secure new clients more quickly and at lower costs, raise sales force productivity, strengthen client loyalty, and utilize teams to raise service quality. We created the widely-used Referral Mastery System and How to Easily Host Referral Events training programs.

Michael E. Brizz
Center for Professional Achievement
Chagrin Falls, OH USA
*Contact Phone:* 800-865-2867
*Contact Main Phone:* 440-543-2867
**Click to Contact from Web Site**

## BERNHOFF A. DAHL, M.D. - TRIONICS INTERNATIONAL, INC.
Bangor, ME USA
http://www.TrionicsUSA.com

Since 1975, Dr. Dahl has produced over 3,500 professional seminars on a nationwide basis, for a wide range of organizations and associations. His presentations are motivational and inspirational, spiritual yet ecumenical, entertaining and interactive, and adaptable to a wide range of audiences. During his 25 years of medical practice, he co-founded a wide range of leadership and strategic planning businesses. He is also the author of four books and workbooks on leadership and strategic planning.

Bernhoff A. Dahl, M.D.
*President*
Trionics International, Inc.
Winterport, ME
*Contact Phone:* 207-223-9998
*Cell:* 207-745-7272
**Click to Contact from Web Site**

## JOE KENNEDY — THE SMALL BUSINESS OWNERS MANUAL
Los Angeles, CA USA
http://www.thesmallbusinessownersmanual.com

A popular speaker with an MBA from the Pennsylvania State University, Joe Kennedy's new book is The Small Business Owner's Manual (Career Press). The book is garnered from his 25+ years of real-world experience as owner, officer, director, vendor, customer, manager and consultant to hundreds of small businesses. Kennedy is also the entrepreneur and president of ANT in Los Angeles (www.anti91.com) providing IT products and services to some of the largest - and smallest - organizations in the world.

Joe Kennedy
The Small Business Owners Manual
Los Angeles, CA USA
*Contact Phone:* 888 394 3571
*Contact Main Phone:* 310 207 4080
*Cell:* 310 259 2403
**Click to Contact from Web Site**

## LAURA STACK, MBA, CSP, THE PRODUCTIVITY PRO
Denver, CO USA
www.TheProductivityPro.com

Laura Stack is the media's go-to expert on personal productivity and workplace issues. You may have seen her featured on CNN, NBC-TV, NPR, Bloomberg, the New York Times, the WashingtonPost.com, and other news and business media outlets. As 'The Productivity PRO,' Laura helps people leave the office earlier, with less stress, and more to show for it. She is the president of a time management consulting firm in Denver, Colorado, that caters to high-stress industries. Since 1987, Ms. Stack has presented keynotes and seminars to associations and Fortune 500 corporations on reducing information overload, managing multiple priorities, balancing work and family, getting organized, and reducing stress.

John Stack
*Chief Operations Officer*
The Productivity Pro, Inc.
Highlands Ranch, CO
*Contact Phone:* 303-471-7401
*Contact Main Phone:* 303-471-7401
**Click to Contact from Web Site**

## LISA ALDISERT — PHAROS ALLIANCE, INC.
New York, NY USA
http://www.businessgrowthcenter.com

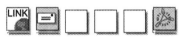

Lisa Aldisert is president of Pharos Alliance, a management consulting firm specializing in business growth strategies and leadership development. A workplace trends expert, consultant, and speaker, she provides solutions for business growth and development, leadership development, and personal performance. Lisa Aldisert is available to comment on workplace trends, business growth strategies and leadership development. She is the author of 'Valuing People: How Human Capital Can Be Your Strongest Asset-'(Dearborn, June 2002).

Aja Richmond
Pharos Alliance, Inc.
New York, NY
*Contact Phone:* 212-332-3241
**Click to Contact from Web Site**

## SUPERB SPEAKERS AND CONSULTANTS BUREAU - JOYCE SCOTT, CEO
Austin, TX USA
http://www.joycescott.com

Joyce Scott, Fortune 500 record breaker who balanced work and Family Life, is a nationally featured speaker, media expert, author, and success coach with the Superb Speakers and Consultants Bureau. Joyce hosts a television show in Austin, Texas named the Texas Strategist, which features career and business success. She is certified in HRD Design/Training, and Career Consulting. She handles topics such as sales, women in the workplace, workplace trends, and job performance improvement.

Joyce Scott
*Performance Improvement Consultant*
Superb Speakers and Consultants Bureau
CEO
Austin, TX USA
*Contact Phone:* 800.795.0493
*Contact Main Phone:* 512.445.8380
**Click to Contact from Web Site**

## CHANGE MASTERS INCORPORATED
Minnetonka, MN USA
http://www.changemasters.com

Change Masters Incorporated coaches individual executives and technology teams. They learn to master effective communications in their rapidly changing organizations. Change Masters' staff has worked with over 2,000 individual clients from over 100 companies. Tom Mungavan has 30 years of corporate experience. He has been featured in major newspapers, conducted radio interviews and is a professional member of the National Speakers Association.

Thomas Mungavan, MBA, CSP
*President*
Change Masters Incorporated
Minnetonka, MN
*Contact Phone:* 800-242-6431
**Click to Contact from Web Site**

## JAMES E. WHITE — HONEST INVENTOR HELP
Lansing, MI USA
http://www.willitsell.com

Inventor, marker, and author of 'Will It Sell?...,' James White knows the stories: Why few inventors succeed but expect they should. How 3,000 worthless patents issue weekly. Who besides Jamie Lee Curtis and Abraham Lincoln are among the famous with worthless patents. Why patent holders such as Thomas Edison and Samuel Colt are wrongly credited with originating the idea behind their inventions. How scams fleece inventors for $1.5-2 billion annually. Access to many inventor/inventing experts.

James E. White
Okemos, MI
*Contact Phone:* (517)347-0190
**Click to Contact from Web Site**

*Home of The Standing O®*

## OVATIONS INTERNATIONAL INC. -- MATTHEW COSSOLOTTO
New York, NY USA
www.Ovations.com

Matthew Cossolotto is the author of HabitForce! - The User's Guide for your Personal Operating System. His career includes eight years as a congressional aide followed by senior-level speechwriting and executive communications positions at MCI, GTE and Pepsi-Cola International. In 1996, Mr. Cossolotto formed Ovations International -- Home of the Standing O® -- providing speechwriting, speech coaching and training services. He speaks to audiences about Podium Power and HabitForce! May the HabitForce be with you! www.ovations.com.

Matthew Cossolotto
*President/Author-HabitForce!*
Ovations International, Inc.
Home of the Standing O
Yorktown Heights, NY USA
*Contact Phone:* 914-245-9721
**Click to Contact from Web Site**

## KRISTIN J. ARNOLD, CMC, CPF, CSP
Washington, DC USA
http://www.qpcteam.com

Kristin J. Arnold, CMC, CPF, CSP helps corporations, government and non-profit organizations achieve extraordinary results. With years of team-building and facilitation experience, Kristin specializes in coaching executives and their leadership, management and employee teams, particularly in the areas of strategic, business and project planning, process improvement, decision-making, and collaborative problem-solving. As a master facilitator, Kristin also trains other facilitators. 'I train your people to do what I do—facilitate teams to higher levels of performance.'

Kristin J. Arnold
*President*
Quality Process Consultants, Inc.
Alexandria, VA USA
*Contact Phone:* 703-256-8326
**Click to Contact from Web Site**

# Bernhoff A. Dahl, M.D.

● **Physician**  ● **Keynote Speaker**  ● **Consultant**  ● **Mountaineer**  ● **Author**

Expert in *Personal* and *Organizational* Strategic Thinking and Planning (STP)

Since 1975, Dr. Dahl has produced more than 3,500 professional seminars on a nationwide basis for a wide range of organizations and associations. His presentations are motivational and inspirational, spiritual yet ecumenical, entertaining and interactive, and adaptable to a wide range of audiences.

A graduate of Wheaton College (Ill.) with degrees in Chemistry and Bible, he earned an M.D. from Cornell University and completed residency in Pathology at University of Vermont. After serving as an Epidemic Intelligence Officer with the CDC, he was named Chief of Pathology at a New England Medical Center.

During his 25 years of medical practice, he founded and managed a wide range of successful ventures, based on his mastery of the principles of Organizational Design and Dynamics, Leadership and Strategic Planning. He has written four books on these subjects.

**Dr. Dahl's topics include:**

*Optimize Your Life!*      **Suddenly You are the Leader – Now What?**
*Values-driven* **Leadership**      *Values-driven* **Strategic Planning**

**Signature keynote:**
Rescued from "near death," Dr. lives to share
**"Lessons for Living from a Mt. Washington Misadventure"**

---

*Optimize Your Life!* synergistically merges *personal* and *organizational* **Strategic Thinking and Planning.** This book provides step-by-step text and user-friendly worksheets for addressing the major questions of one's life, starting with:

| | |
|---|---|
| Who am I? | What is a "successful" life? |
| What am I doing now? | What toxic forces are in my life? |
| What do I value? | What do I want to have/do/be in life? |
| What am I good at? | What is my risk tolerance? |
| What are my passions? | How can I "clean up" my life? |

These questions lead to other questions, answered so as to produce a personal inventory as well as Mission, Vison, and Values Statements and Goals. The unique concept is to reduce each Goal to component Projects, and then into a series of Tasks, each one assigned a *One-page* **Strategic Plan** sheet for its completion.

*Optimize Your Life!* is a self-development system that features a program for readers to define, improve, and accept themselves and then to apply the same concepts to their organization.

---

*Optimize Your Life!*, our **International Bestseller**, has been licensed for editions in Korea, Japan, Mainland China, India (Tata McGraw-Hill) and a worldwide Spanish edition (Random House).

**CONTACT: DrBDahl@aol.com      207-223-9998      www.TrionicsUSA.com**

**www.Path-Quest.com      www.DrBDahl.com      www.MtWashingtonMisadvenure.com**

**Apellicon-Pearson Press   66 Upper Oak Point, Winterport, Maine 04496 U.S.A.**

## KELLEY CONNORS MPH - WOMEN'S HEALTH & WELLNESS MARKETING EXPERT
Norwalk, CT USA
http://www.kchealthcarecommunications.com/

Kelley Connors is a highly effective strategic integrated marketing professional with expertise in helping companies leverage the power of women as consumers, caregivers, careerists and community leaders to advance healthy living. A strong foundation of experience beginning in 1989 makes Ms. Connors a seasoned expert in integrating health care public relations and advertising initiatives. She is currently developing a community-based network of women as consumers, caregivers, careerist and community leaders for the dynamic exchange of information and health care experience. Her personal passion is to foster greater dialogue between healthcare professionals and patients to advance healthy living. Ms. Connors is co-chair of the marketing committee for the Healthcare Businesswomen's Association, and has been on the advisory board for the National Health, Wellness and Prevention Congress, a driving force in consumer-directed health care. She was a speaker on the topic of Marketing to Women as Health Care Consumers and Effective Launch and Marketing Strategies for health care payors and providers. Ms. Connors received a Masters in Public Health from Boston University School of Public Health with a Certificate in Public Communication from BU's School of Public Communication.

Kelley Connors MPH
K.C. Healthcare Communications LLC
Norwalk, CT USA
*Contact Phone:* 203-856-3732
**Click to Contact from Web Site**

## GREGG WARD, CMC — WORKPLACE DIVERSITY EXPERT
San Diego, CA USA
diversityguy.blogs.com

What are the direct links between diversity and the corporate bottom line? What are the warning signs of workplace diversity tension? Isn't diversity just affirmative action with a fancier name? Why should CEO's care about diversity? Which diverse markets are hot? GREGG WARD, CMC - expert consultant, trainer, speaker and author on diversity, harassment, leadership, ethics and teamwork - can answer these important questions. Clients include American Express, Bristol-Myers Squibb, Ford, Harley-Davidson and Warner Bros Studios.

Gregg Ward, CMC
*President*
Orlando-Ward & Associates, Inc.
Fletcher Hills, CA USA
*Contact Phone:* 619-461-6777
**Click to Contact from Web Site**

## AMY S. TOLBERT, PH.D., CSP, DIVERSITY CONSULTANT
Minneapolis, MN USA
www.eccointernational.com

Amy S. Tolbert, Ph.D., CSP, principal of ECCO International, develops multicultural and global competencies within today's diverse workforce. Expertise includes developing multicultural and diversity initiatives, leadership competency development, managing to style, and creating breakthrough teams. An international speaker and author of several best-selling books and assessment tools, Dr. Tolbert has also written Reversing the Ostrich Approach to Diversity: Pulling your head out of the sand. Dr. Tolbert holds her Ph.D. and Certified Speaking Professional designation.

Amy S. Tolbert, Ph.D., CSP
*Principal*
Ecco International
St. Paul, MN USA
*Contact Phone:* 651-636-0838
**Click to Contact from Web Site**

## JILL LUBLIN -- NETWORKING EXPERT
San Francisco, CA USA
www.JillLublin.com

Jill Lublin is the author of two national best selling books, Guerrilla Publicity (which is often considered the PR bible and is used in university publicity courses) and Networking Magic (which went to #1 at Barnes and Noble). Jill is the founder of GoodNews Media, Inc. and host of the nationally syndicated radio show, Do the Dream and TV pilot, GoodNews TV.

Jill Lublin
Promising Promotion
Novato, CA USA
*Contact Phone:* 415-883-5455
**Click to Contact from Web Site**

## COACHING MAKES A DIFFERENCE
Seattle, WA USA
http://www.coachingmakesadifference.com

Coaching Makes a Difference is a network of professional coaches dedicated to helping communities, businesses, families and individuals rebuild in the aftermath of catastrophe. We offer tools and resources as well as an online directory of coaches who provide pro bono services in a wide variety of specialties, including career transition, relationships, job performance, and life and business coaching. CMD also provides outreach services and information about coaching to relief organizations and community centers.

Kathleen Mallary
Coaching Makes a Difference
Kenmore, WA United States
*Contact Phone:* 425-821-9150
**Click to Contact from Web Site**

# Lisa Aldisert

♦ **Workplace Trends**

♦ **Business Growth Strategies**

♦ **Leadership Development**

Lisa Aldisert is president of Pharos Alliance, a management consulting firm specializing in business growth strategies and leadership development. Lisa works with companies that want to profitably grow their businesses by offering them a unique blend of financial acumen, trend analysis, and leadership insight. A workplace trends expert, consultant, and speaker, she provides solutions for business growth and development, leadership development, and personal performance.

Ideas for interview topics include:
- Workplace trends
- Growing a business smartly
- Increasing profitability
- Building a company vs. a practice
- Succession and exit strategies
- Small business growth strategies
- Managing generational issues
- Challenges in executive transitions
- How to attract, retain, and motivate top performers
- The use of assessments for hiring and performance management
- Developing leadership or managerial skills
- Strategic human capital matters

Lisa has been featured in articles in *The Wall Street Journal, the Associated Press, Gannett News Service, the Chicago Tribune,* and *the Atlanta Journal Constitution* among others, as well as numerous trade and professional journals.

To interview Lisa Aldisert, contact Aja Jayne Richmond at (212) 332-3241 or by e-mail at Aja@businessgrowthcenter.com.

**Lisa is the author of *Valuing People: How Human Capital Can Be Your Strongest Asset* (Dearborn 2002), and she co-authored *The Small Business Money Guide: How to Get It, Use It, Keep It* (Wiley 1999).**

### SCOTT LOVE — LEADERSHIP EXPERT, AUTHOR, SYNDICATED COLUMNIST
Charlotte, NC USA
http://www.scottlove.com

Internationally recognized expert on leadership and employee motivation; empirical research includes over 16,000 interviews with managers on job satisfaction and employee loyalty; U.S. Naval Academy graduate; former naval officer and leadership trainer; owned four companies; consulted to companies in every major city in the US; quoted weekly including Wall Street Journal, Business Journals, and major city dailies. Published author; sought-after (funny with content) keynote speaker to association and corporate events; executive advisor and leadership consultant.

Scott T. Love
Scott Love Associates, Inc.
Fairview, NC USA
*Contact Phone:* 828-225-7700
*Cell:* 480-650-0230
**Click to Contact from Web Site**

### BOB BLOCH — FACILITATION EXPERT
Albany, NY USA
Who knows more about your business? You or I? Since it must be you, I can help you find answers to your most pressing situations by giving you the ability to find your own answers. The obvious answers that you are unwilling to face are the answers you are seeking. My expertise is to help you find these answers in your own knowledge.

Bob Bloch
Cavalier Enterprises
Lenox, MA USA
*Contact Phone:* 413-637-0958
**Click to Contact from Web Site**

### S. G. HART & ASSOCIATES, LLC
Ridgefield, CT USA
www.sghartassociates.com

S. G. Hart & Associates, The Brand Equity Protection Company, is a supply chain security consulting company. S. G. Hart & Associates helps firms realize their full brand equity potential by supporting its clients in the development and implementation of strategies that protect global supply chains from disruptions caused by product diversion, counterfeiting, theft and tampering. For answers to questions about brand equity protection, please contact Mr. Stanley G. Hart, President & CEO.

Stanley G. Hart
*President & CEO*
S. G. Hart & Associates, LLC
Ridgefield, USA
*Contact Main Phone:* 203-438-4300
**Click to Contact from Web Site**

### MILESTONE CONSULTING
Dedham, MA USA
http://www.milestoneideas.com

Bob Taraschi a facilitator, conciliator and business marketing consultant who works on both the human and business side of the enterprise - what is known and attended to, and what is below the surface. He can open up fresh and sometimes unexpected avenues for decision and action, creating and managing new ideas, handling conflict, rethinking business or crafting strategy.

Bob Taraschi
*Founder*
Milestone Consulting
Dedham, MA
*Contact Phone:* 781-467-1200
**Click to Contact from Web Site**

### KATHY LOVELESS — BUSINESS PRODUCTIVITY EXPERT
Salt Lake City, UT USA
www.lovelessenterprises.com

We've got answers, new ideas and a desire to help you. You will benefit from our extensive experience in designing customized training programs, keynote speeches, management and executive consulting, and succession planning. We can help you increase the profitability and productivity of your organization. We have worked with groups across the globe on such issues as: improving management practices, involving the public in decision making, creating processes and systems that work, building teams, sharpening communication skills and much more

Kathy Loveless
Loveless Enterprises, Inc.
Salt Lake City, UT USA
*Contact Phone:* 801-363-1807
**Click to Contact from Web Site**

### COACHING INSIDER
Scottsdale, AZ USA
http://www.coachinginsider.com

Coaching Insider is an independent, twice-monthly, web-delivered newsmagazine covering the personal, business and executive coaching industry.

Susan Austin
Coaching Insider
Scottsdale, AZ USA
*Contact Phone:* 480.424.7545
**Click to Contact from Web Site**

## Matthew Cossolotto

**EXECUTIVE COMMUNICATIONS EXPERT**
GUEST SPEAKER, WORKSHOPS, SPEECHWRITING, COACHING

# LOWER THE PUBLIC SPEAKING TERROR ALERT.

Public speaking is a widely recognized leadership and success skill.  And yet many people... even those in leadership positions... are hampered by some degree of anxiety, trepidation, or outright fear.  As **The Podium Pro**,™ Matthew Cossolotto is on a one-man mission to banish the fear of speaking to audiences. He helps clients make the shift from *stage fright* to *stage delight...* and gives their careers a boost in the process.

Matthew spent eight years as a congressional aide, followed by senior-level speechwriting and executive communications positions at MCI, GTE, and Pepsi-Cola International. He formed Ovations International in 1996.

In his programs and forthcoming book – *There's No Such Thing As Public Speaking!* – Matthew addresses the "Presentation Paradox," the need to strike a balance between "preparation" and "presence."  He identifies five essential "mindset shifts" needed for fear-free speaking and explains how to leverage **The Power of S.P.E.E.C.H.** and the secrets of **Whole-Brain Speaking**.

*"Success is an inside job... on and off the podium!"*

As **The Empowerment Pro**™ and author of *HabitForce!*, Matthew works with individuals and organizations who want to change self-defeating habits and mindsets so they can reach their goals and achieve their potential.

User's Guide
For Your Personal
Operating System!™

## Matthew Cossolotto

**OVATIONS INTERNATIONAL INC.**
*Home of the Standing O®*

914.245.9721
standingo@ovations.com
www.ovations.com

## DAN STOCKDALE — BUSINESS RELATIONSHIP EXPERT
Knoxville, TN USA
www.AdventuresInLeadership.com

BUSINESS RELATIONSHIP EXPERT — From Tiger Stripes to Pin Stripes, Dan Stockdale Explains the Seven Deadly Sins That Kill Businesses and Maul Managers —GREED/MISTRUST — Corporate scandals? Dan teaches organizations how to achieve high growth and phenomenal credibility — ENVY/RESENTMENT—Train employees to achieve team work, even when they compete for sales — ANGER/NEGATIVITY—Turn negativity into profitability by redirecting the naysayer's destructive energy — PRIDE/ARROGANCE — Learn techniques to tame condescending bosses and disrespectful co-workers — LUST/SELF-INDULGENCE—Focus employees on productivity, not inter-office foreplay — EXCESS/AGGRESSION — Turn backstabbing into backslapping support — LAZINESS/RUDENESS — Discharge employees who infuriate customers before they destroy your revenues

Dan Stockdale
Adventures in Leadership, Inc.
Knoxville, TN USA
*Contact Phone:* 877.3.JUNGLE
**Click to Contact from Web Site**

## DREAM MERCHANT NEW PRODUCT GUIDANCE
Los Angeles, CA USA
www.DreamMerchant.net

For over a decade. The Dream Merchant has provided an informative, motivational and entertaining website, free of charge. Our contributing editors have provided hundreds of articles on new product development, patents, trademarks, licensing, marketing, internet promotion and small business ownership. We have featured famous inventions in our Inventors Hall Of Fame section, while helping children start their own business in our Kids Kreative Korner. Turn your Dreams Into Reality. Visit: www.dreammerchant.net

John K. Moreland
Dream Merchant New Product Guidance
Torrance, CA USA
*Contact Phone:* 310-328-1925
**Click to Contact from Web Site**

## NATHAN GREENO, DRAWING BOARD CONSULTING GROUP
Washington, DC USA
http://www.fromrisk2return.com

Transforming human capital Risk into dramatic Returns is Nathan's focus as an organizational learning expert, strategic process consultant, author and speaker. With over a decade of experience as a national consultant, his clients range from companies such as Verizon and Mobil Oil to The U.S. Department of Education, bridging the gaps between training, learning and organizational strategy - creating business return on investment. His most recent book, Corporate Learning Strategies (2006), received the accolade of being named The American Society of Training and Development's Spotlight Book for 2006. His speaking engagements continue at a record rate as he focuses on the strategic transformation of training to learning — leading to reduced risk and increased rates of personal and organizational return. His educational credentials include a bachelor's degree in psychology from Roberts Wesleyan College; a master's degree in educational administration and organizational behavior from Michigan State University; extensive post graduate work totaling over 40 doctoral credits in social psychology and organizational development at Bowling Green State University; and a doctoral degree (honoris causa) in commercial science from John Dewey University, awarded to Greeno for his significant advancement of the business learning field.

Nathan Greeno
*President*
Drawing Board Consulting Group
Centreville, VA USA
*Contact Phone:* 703-815-1924
**Click to Contact from Web Site**

## JOHN CARROLL, AUTHOR AND CONSULTANT
Charleston, SC USA
http://www.JohnCarroll.com

With more than 23 years of marketing and business experience, John Carroll applies a wealth of knowledge and ideas to client challenges. His work in organizational development spans a wide range of industries and covers many phases of those businesses. John is president of Unlimited Performance, a Mount Pleasant, South Carolina, firm specializing in organizational and individual performance improvement. He has trained hundreds of sales professionals and facilitated strategic planning, annual retreats and leadership development for dozens of organizations, large and small, business and not-for-profit.

John Carroll
Unlimited Performance, Inc.
Mount Pleasant, SC USA
*Contact Phone:* 843-881-8815
*Cell:* 843-224-8815
**Click to Contact from Web Site**

## COACH AND GROW R.I.C.H.

Oakland, CA USA
http://www.coachandgrowrich.com/

A veteran coach and sales and marketing expert, Michelle Schubnel is the President and owner of Coach & Grow R.I.C.H. — the premier business-building company for professional life, business and executive coaches. Since the year 2000 thousands of coaches worldwide have successfully implemented the proven, step-by-step Coach & Grow R.I.C.H. system for securing more clients and building a thriving, rewarding and profitable coaching business. Michelle was a featured presenter at the 2005 International Coach Federation Annual Conference, delivering How to Thrive Your First Year in Business as a Professional Coach.

Michelle Schubnel
*President*
Coach and Grow R.I.C.H.
Oakland, CA USA
*Contact Phone:* 510-530-3576
**Click to Contact from Web Site**

## GREG MACIOLEK - SPEAKER, AUTHOR, BUSINESS CONSULTANT

Knoxville, TN USA
http://www.integratedmanagementresources.com

Speaker, author, consultant and session facilitator, Greg Maciolek focuses on the loss of productivity of workers through their mismanagement by owners and managers. He promotes the use of assessments for hiring and developing all employees. His insights into leadership, management, communications, performance feedback and hiring the right person for the job all combine into making Greg a top consultant to businesses. He is published in six books. He is a former Air Force fighter pilot.

Gregory Maciolek
*President*
Integrated Management Resources, Inc.
Knoxville, TN USA
*Contact Phone:* 800-262-6403
**Click to Contact from Web Site**

## KARMA BROWN, THE STRATEGIC COACH

Chicago, IL USA
http://www.strategiccoach.com

The Strategic Coach, a Toronto-based firm with over 3,000 clients from around the world, offers a highly acclaimed workshop program, and publications, that help established, successful entrepreneurs to continuously improve their quality of life while also dramatically increasing their business profits.

Karma Brown
Strategic Coach
Toronto, Ontario Canada
*Contact Phone:* 416-531-7399 ex 236
**Click to Contact from Web Site**

## PATRICIA R. ADSON, PH.D., ADSON COACHING AND CONSULTING

Rochester, MN USA

Patricia R. Adson, Ph.D.
Patricia R. Adson, Ph.D. Adson Coaching and Consulting
Rochester, MN USA
*Contact Phone:* 507-287-0838
**Click to Contact from Web Site**

## MULTIPLE STREAMS OF COACHING INCOME

Calgary, Alberta Canada
http://www.multiplestreamsofcoachingincome.com/

Multiple Streams of Coaching Income not only separates the myths from truth, but provides new truths which, if followed, will lead many frustrated coaches to the success they desire. A must-read!

Andrea J. Lee
*Speaker, Coach & Author*
Multiple Streams of Coaching Income
Calgary, AB-, Canada
*Contact Phone:* 403-615-1237
**Click to Contact from Web Site**

## MARIPOSA LEADERSHIP
San Francisco, CA USA
http://www.mariposaleadership.com/

MARIPOSA LEADERSHIP, INC. offers leadership coaching and consulting that get results quickly. We match the best coach with each client, we base our work on a cutting-edge model, Corporate Sage Leadership Framework, and we offer a clear and consistent approach to track results.

Susan J. Bethanis, Ed.D.
*President*
San Francisco, CA USA
*Contact Phone:* 415-861-5900
**Click to Contact from Web Site**

## RESOURCE REALIZATIONS
Healdsburg, CA USA
http://www.resourcerealizations.com/

A training company founded by David Gilcrease in 1986, committed to shaping a partnership of shared purpose with people and organizations to take on growth and change. We provide the resources for individuals to learn, to grow, and to make changes so that they are able to realize their dreams.

Barbara Fagan
*President*
Resource Realizations
Healdsburg, CA USA
*Contact Phone:* 707-431-1911
**Click to Contact from Web Site**

## STROZZI INSTITUTE
Petaluma, CA USA
http://www.strozziinstitute.com/

Strozzi Institute is the premier training institute for Embodied Leadership. We offer public and private programs for corporations, small businesses and individuals interested in developing their leadership presence and effectiveness. In addition, we offer a unique coaching certification program that teaches the relevance of the body in coaching.

Kathleen McCauley Anast
*Director Business Development*
Strozzi Institute
Petaluma, CA USA
*Contact Phone:* 707-778-6505
**Click to Contact from Web Site**

## INTERNATIONAL COACH FEDERATION
Lexington, KY USA
www.coachfederation.org

The International Coach Federation is the professional association of personal and business coaches that seeks to preserve the integrity of coaching around the globe. The mission of the ICF is to be the global forum for the art and science of coaching, where we inspire transformational conversations, advocate excellence and expand awareness of the contribution coaching is making to the future of humankind. ICF helps people find the coach most suitable for their needs. It supports and fosters development of the coaching profession, has programs to maintain and upgrade the standards of the profession, conducts a certification program that is the gold standard for coaches worldwide, and conducts the world's premier conference and other educational events for coaches. ICF is the largest non-profit professional association worldwide of personal and business coaches with 8,366 members and more than 132 chapters in 34 countries.

Kim Livesay
International Coach Federation
Lexington, KY USA
*Contact Phone:* 859.219.3581
**Click to Contact from Web Site**

## MARSHA EGAN, SUCCESS & EXECUTIVE COACH
Reading, PA USA
http://www.marshaegan.com

Celebrated speaker, facilitator, ICF-certified executive coach and author, Marsha Egan has coached CEOs and leaders from some of the country's top companies and built a thriving coaching practice. She brings over twenty-five years of outstanding corporate and volunteer experience to her success coaching firm, The Egan Group, Inc. Marsha orignated and shares with her clients the eight Silent Signals of Success, actions and attitudes every successful person communicates, often unknowingly, to those around them.

Marsha Egan
*President and CEO*
The Egan Group, Inc.
Reading, PA USA
*Contact Phone:* 610-777-3795
*Cell:* 610-780-1640
**Click to Contact from Web Site**

## DR. ALDEN M. CASS, PRESIDENT OF CATALYST STRATEGIES GROUP
New York, NY USA
http://www.catsg.com

Dr. Alden M. Cass, licensed clinical psychologist, is president at Catalyst Strategies Group (CSG), New York City. Dr. Cass helps senior financial services executives achieve corporate and personal goals through his 'Bullish Thinking' system of total emotional discipline. His research presentations include national and international conferences (A.P.A., ICPP). Media placements include: Businessweek, Barrons, Wall Street Journal, CNN, CNBC London, New York Times, Financial Times, London Financial Weekly, NY Newsday, BBC Radio, Reuter's Business Newswire.

Dr. Alden M. Cass
*President*
Catalyst Strategies Group
New York, NY USA
*Contact Phone:* 212-576-1410
*Contact Main Phone:* 212-576-1410
*Cell:* 914-774-1319
**Click to Contact from Web Site**

## JEFF KORHAN -- GROW FROM WHAT YOU KNOW
Chicago, IL USA
www.truenature.com

Jeff Korhan is a nationally recognized entrepreneur and principal of True Nature®, a speaking and coaching company that helps leaders transform their businesses and industries. He is also the president and owner of Treemendous Landscape Company®, an award winning design-build company in suburban Chicago. Jeff's extraordinary business and life experiences have shaped his unique approach, which is the The True Nature System™. Jeff speaks to audiences that want to grow their businesses by inspiring their people.

Jeff Korhan
*Author, Speaker, Entrepreneur, Business Owner*
Naperville, IL USA
*Contact Phone:* 630-774-8350
**Click to Contact from Web Site**

## MIKE JAY -- WORLD'S MOST INNOVATIVE COACH
Mitchell, NE USA
www.mikejay.com

Meet the World's Most Innovative Coach. Mike stopped counting at 10,000 coaching sessions and has worked with more than 1500 clients spanning fields as diverse as athletics, agriculture, medicine and hospitality over more than 25 years in his professional career as a entrepreneur, manager, consultant, leader and coach. Mike has written 100s of articles, books and papers on a variety of subjects in almost every known aspect of coaching.

Mike Jay
B©oach Systems, LLC
Mitchell, NE USA
**Click to Contact from Web Site**

# International Coach Federation

The International Coach Federation currently has more than 9,000 members worldwide. Members include personal and business coaches. ICF sets the industry standard of excellence and integrity for professional coaching worldwide. ICF also developed the only worldwide recognized independent credential in the industry to ensure the professionalism of coaches.

ICF provides expert spokespeople for virtually any aspect of the coaching industry, including:

What is a coach?

What can I expect from coaching?

What is a life coach?

What is a business coach?

What is an internal coach?

How do I choose a coach?

Why should I choose a credentialed coach?

To connect with an expert spokesperson, contact ICF at 859.219.3581.

**International Coach Federation**

2365 Harrodsburg Rd., Suite A325
Lexington, KY 40504-3335
859.219.3580 • 888.423.3131 (toll free)
www.coachfederation.org

**MICHAEL YORK -- THE MICHAEL YORK LEARNING CENTER INC.**
Charlotte, NC USA
www.michaelyork.com

Michael York is a consultant and author who wrote the book on 'Becoming Uncommon' for individuals and organizations. His expertise revolves around four P's: Purpose - the mission and vision for the group or individual. Performance - How 'The Show' looks from the customer's perspective. Plan - The Goal: What's yours and where are you headed. Passion - How you approach your life and work. His upcoming books are 'The Ten Commitments' and 'The NOW Economy.'

Michael York
The Michael York Learning Center, Inc.
Charlotte, NC USA
*Contact Phone:* 704-622-2400
**Click to Contact from Web Site**

**MICHAEL R. MARTORELLA, EXECUTIVE COACH & ADVISOR — MMI COMMUNICATION**
Bedminster, NJ USA
http://www.mmicom.com

Mike Martorella, CEO of MMI Communication of Bedminster, New Jersey, is an executive coach and management advisor who works one-on-one with senior level leaders. Mike's clients benefit from his insights derived from his background as CEO of a global advertising agency. He is known for asking provocative questions that help leaders frame the issues and "tune in" to audiences. As a result, his clients become effective communicators who build success for themselves, their people and their organizations. His client list includes Aventis Pharmaceuticals, Bayer, Bunge, General Motors, IBM, JPMorgan Chase, Lucent, MCI, Pitney Bowes, and Vivendi.

Loraine Kasprzak
MMI Communication
Bedminster, NJ USA
*Contact Phone:* 908-233-6265
**Click to Contact from Web Site**

**TERRI LEVINE, CEO OF COMPREHENSIVE COACHING U. INC.**
North Wales, PA USA
www.terrilevine.com

Terri Levine, MCC, made the transition from senior executive to become one of the top professional coaches in the industry, founded 2 leading coach training programs and developed world renowned home study coaching kits. She has worked with clients from every walk of life. Terri is a Master Certified Coach. She is also Founder and President of Comprehensive Coaching U and The Coaching Institute which train and certify coaches internationally and are highly regarded.

Terri Levine
Comprehensive Coaching U
North Wales, PA USA
*Contact Phone:* 215-699-4949
**Click to Contact from Web Site**

# Michael York:
## Beyond Amazing . . .
## Committed and
## Uncommon

Author, businessman, consultant and professional speaker Michael York wrote the book on "Becoming Uncommon!" and is the author of the new book, "The 10 Commitments."

He has been called "a unique and entertaining teacher who makes learning fun, beats boring training and helps individuals and organizations to become more powerful than the status quo."

As a consultant, he is the "Chief Learning Officer" for many different companies and organizations on thinking differently and creating radical results.

As a businessman, he is the founder and CEO of The Michael York Company, Inc., in Charlotte, North Carolina as well as head of COOL $chool, which provides cutting-edge, continuing education for business owners and salespersons. He has more than 25 years of sales, marketing and management experience.

Michael Yorks addresses groups around the nation and the world on subjects, ranging from personal development to powerful communication to winning in the NOW economy.

*The Michael York Company, Inc.*
*4801 E Independence Blvd, Suite 1000*
*Charlotte, North Carolina 28212*

**Phone: 704-622-2400**
**Fax: 704-227-1228**

**E-mail: leader@michaelyork.com**
**www.michaelyork.com**

MEMBER
**NSA**
NATIONAL SPEAKERS ASSOCIATION

*"Michael York is one of the best speakers in the country...period!"*
*-- Carroll Gray,*
*President,*
*Charlotte*
*Chamber of Commerce*

## GARY GRIFFIN - ON TURNAROUND MANAGEMENT
New Brunswick, NJ USA
www.ren-consultants.net

Gary Griffin, Managing Director of On Turnaround Management & Corporate Renewal, has over 25 years of operational experience in the management of businesses in crisis at the CEO and COO level. Gary's functional expertise includes recovery strategy and planning, cash management and financial control, manufacturing reorganization, mergers and acquisitions, capital acquisition, and strategic alliances. Gary has lectured to the Commercial Finance Association, the Harvard Business Club, the New Jersey Entrepreneurial Network, and various other associations.

Gary Griffin
*Chairman & CEO*
Renaissance Research Group, Ltd
New Brunswick, NJ
*Contact Phone:* 732-828-4901
**Click to Contact from Web Site**

## STRATEGIC MANAGEMENT PARTNERS, INC. - TURNAROUND MANAGEMENT & EQUITY INVESTING EXPERTS
Annapolis, MD USA
www.strategist.ws

Our principal has been advisor to Presidents Bush (41&43), Clinton and Yeltsin, World Bank, European Bank for Reconstruction and Development, on turnaround management and equity capital investing techniques. A leading turnaround management firm specializing in interim executive leadership, corporate governance and renewal, valuation enhancement, asset recovery, M&A, equity investing in underperforming companies. We serve as CEO, or advisor to private equity investment funds, start-up and middle market companies representing the venture, investment, manufacturing, defense, electronics, engineering services, computer, telecommunications, printing, and marine industries.

John M. Collard
*Chairman*
Strategic Management Partners, Inc.
Annapolis, MD
*Contact Phone:* 410-263-9100
**Click to Contact from Web Site**

## BILL SHIRLEY, EXECUTIVE LEADERSHIP COACH, INSEARCHOFEAGLES.COM
Portland, OR USA
www.billshirleyonline.com

Bill Shirley, the founder of ISOE, brings a unique perspective and over 40 years of practical experience to the challenges of guiding organizations toward success in the global economy. His focus on the selection, leadership development and retention of key employees in tight labor markets creates loyal customers and long term sustainable growth. He shows his clients how to navigate isolation, frustration and overwhelm to create a meaningful, balanced life of their own design.

Elge Peremeau
E-Marketing Strategist
Portland, OR USA
*Contact Phone:* 503-284-2888
**Click to Contact from Web Site**

## SOCIETY FOR ADVANCEMENT OF CONSULTING, LLC
Boston, MA USA
http://www.consultingsociety.com

Society for Advancement of ConsultingSM LLC is dedicated to the advancement of independent consultants and solo practitioners. Our mission is to build the business, competencies, and 'voice' of consultants in the business community and within the organizational world.

Alan Weiss
Society for Advancement of Consulting
East Greenwich, RI USA
*Contact Phone:* 401-886-4097
**Click to Contact from Web Site**

## ABHAY PADGAONKAR
Phoenix, AZ USA
http://www.innovativesolutions.org

Abhay Padgaonkar is a highly regarded independent consultant. He is an expert in improving organizational and individual performance by making the complex simple and making the simple work. He advises marquee clients such as American Express on turning strategy into action. His clients have profited from his advice by uncovering and capitalizing on various opportunities. He has authored articles and presented on a variety of topics including leadership, strategy formulation, strategy execution, project management, customer loyalty, employee engagement, demographics, and sales effectiveness. He is a current professional member and past president of Institute of Management Consultants USA (IMC) - Arizona chapter. He is also a member of the Society for Human Resource Management (SHRM). More information about his unique approach, broad experience, value creation, and strong testimonials can be found on the website at: http://www.innovativesolutions.org. Find out why he is a sought-after leadership and management expert.

Abhay Padgaonkar
*President*
Innovative Solutions Consulting, LLC
Phoenix, AZ United States
*Contact Phone:* 602-628-1234
*Contact Main Phone:* 602-628-1234
**Click to Contact from Web Site**

## BOB BROWN, CONSULTING INTELLIGENCE, LLC
Tampa, FL USA
www.consultingintelligence.com

A consultant on consultants? Yes! Bob Brown is a sought after authority on the business of consulting, the consulting profession and on relations - both good and bad -- between consultants and their clients. Prior to retiring and founding Consulting Intelligence, Bob was a senior consultant with IBM Business Consulting Services, where he developed and taught consulting methods and practices. In addition to helping clients resolve troubled projects and deal with other consultant-related problems, Consulting Intelligence specializes in consulting firm evaluations; contract negotiation assistance; capability and competence assessments; staff education and training; project management oversight; and mediation and arbitration. Bob is a member of the Institute of Management Consultants, The Project Management Institute, The American College of Forensic Examiners and the National Speakers Association. He is the author of the upcoming book: 'Who's Managing the Consultants? A client's guide to managing - and maximizing the return from - their consulting resources.'

Bob Brown
*Managing Director*
Consulting Intelligence, LLC
Tampa, FL USA
*Contact Phone:* 727-579-7900
**Click to Contact from Web Site**

## SUMMIT CONSULTING GROUP, INC. -- ALAN WEISS, PH.D.
East Greenwich, RI USA
http://www.summitconsulting.com

Alan Weiss, Ph.D., is one of the most highly regarded independent consultants in the country, according to the New York Post. He is the author of Million Dollar Consulting (McGraw-Hill, 1992, 1998, 2002), as well as Making It Work (on strategy), Managing for Peak Performance (on behavior), and The Unofficial Guide to Power Management. His books have been major book club selections and translated into German, Spanish, Chinese and Italian, generating interviews in media worldwide.

Crysta Ames
*Office Manager*
Summit Consulting Group, Inc.
East Greenwich, RI
*Contact Phone:* 401-884-2778
**Click to Contact from Web Site**

## INSTITUTE OF MANAGEMENT CONSULTANTS USA, INC.
Washington, DC USA
http://www.imcusa.org

Get a fresh perspective on management and business. Members of the Institute of Management Consultants (IMC USA) bring independence and objectivity to topics and trends in business and management. To find an expert member or Certified Management Consultant (CMC®), contact Megan Renner at 800-221-2557 or experts@imcusa.org.. Search our member roster by key word, area of expertise or industry at www.imcusa.org. Founded in 1968, IMC USA is the premier professional association and sole certifying body for management consultants in the United States.

Siobhan Walker
Institute of Management Consultants USA, Inc.
Washington, DC
*Contact Phone:* 800-221-2557
*Contact Main Phone:* 202-367-1134
**Click to Contact from Web Site**

## KEITH E. NABE - MANAGEMENT CONSULTANT/PUBLIC SPEAKER
Crestview, FL USA

The Message is simple! Keith Nabe delivers value, realizing our clients full business potential by providing the implementation support necessary to achieve measurable and sustainable performance improvement. We also Buy Secured Real Estate & Business Notes for CASH!

Keith E. Nabe
*Management Consultant/Public Speaker*
Accelerated Relief LLC
Crestview, FL USA
*Contact Phone:* 850 682 1213
*Cell:* 850-685-3719
**Click to Contact from Web Site**

## GENE C. MAGE
Rochester, NY USA
http://makingitwork.com

Leadership development expert Gene C. Mage provides media interviews and resources on workplace issues including: coaching employees; dealing with a difficult boss; and creating a positive work environment. Author of the book, Managing for High Performance (Amazon.com), Gene's syndicated newspaper column reaches 400,000 readers weekly. He has published over 150 articles, many appearing in national publications such as HR Magazine. Gene's clients include Corning Incorporated, The Adventist Health Care System, and Gannett Newspapers.

Gene C. Mage
*President*
Makingitwork.com
Horseheads, NY USA
*Contact Phone:* 866-290-1404
*Cell:* 607-738-7345
**Click to Contact from Web Site**

## DEBRA J. SCHMIDT, MS, APR--'THE LOYALTY LEADER'®
Milwaukee, WI USA
http://www.TheLoyaltyLeader.com

Debra J. Schmidt, a.k.a. 'The Loyalty Leader'™, is the owner of Spectrum Consulting Group Inc. With 25 years of business management experience, she helps companies boost profits by leading them to greater customer and employee loyalty. Emmy nominee, television personality and marketing award winner, Debra's one of the nation's top business speakers and trainers. She's the author of '101 Ways to Build Customer Loyalty' and 'The Extra Mile: 15 True Stories of Exceptional Customer Service'.

Debra J. Schmidt, MS, APR
*The Loyalty Leader*
The Loyalty Leader
Milwaukee, WI
*Contact Phone:* 414-964-3872
**Click to Contact from Web Site**

## JIM THOMAS, NEGOTIATE TO WIN
McLean, VA USA
www.jimthomas.info

Jim Thomas is the choice of U.S. presidents and their staffs for negotiating coaching and advice. Based in Washington, DC, Jim is a world-renowned consultant to billion-dollar-plus corporations and an undisputed master of high-performance negotiating. When Fortune 100 companies demand that their people learn negotiation skills from only the best, they unhesitatingly pick Jim. His presentations on negotiating have been enthusiastically received by tens of thousands in the United States and abroad. Jim is the author of Negotiate to Win, published by HarperCollins. Jim founded Common Ground, a leading producer of tailored, in-house negotiation workshops in the U.S. Common Ground's instructors - well-known domestic and international negotiators - are involved in the resolution of many of the country's most dramatic disputes. Call Jim Thomas when you need world-class expertise, advice, or penetrating, practical commentary on issues involving negotiating, dispute resolution, or conflict management.

James C. Thomas, Jr.
*Founder and Principal*
Common Ground
McLean, VA USA
*Contact Phone:* 703-287-8753
*Contact Main Phone:* 703-287-8752
*Cell:* 703-795-3578
**Click to Contact from Web Site**

# CONSULTING intelligence SM

"The Consultant Resource Management Specialists" SM

> **THE Consultant on Consultants: Bob Brown, Consulting Intelligence, LLC**

A consultant on consultants? Yes! Bob Brown is a sought-after authority on the business of consulting, the consulting profession and on relations – both good and bad – between consultants and their clients.

Before retiring and founding Consulting Intelligence, Bob was a senior consultant with IBM Business Consulting Services, where he developed and taught consulting methods and practices.

In addition to helping clients resolve troubled projects and deal with other consultant-related problems, Consulting Intelligence specializes in consulting firm evaluations; contract negotiation assistance; capability and competence assessments; staff education and training; project management oversight; and mediation and arbitration.

Bob is a member of the Institute of Management Consultants, the Project Management Institute, the American College of Forensic Examiners and the National Speakers Association. He is the author of the upcoming book: **"Who's Managing the Consultants? A client's guide to managing – and maximizing the return from – their consulting resources."**

*For an insightful analysis of consultants and consultant-related issues, contact Bob Brown of Consulting Intelligence – www.consultingintelligence.com.*

*Bob Brown, Managing Director*
*Consulting Intelligence, LLC*

P.O. Box 20007      Tampa, Fla. 33622

Phone: 727-579-7900  Cell: 727-560-2233  Fax: 810-222-2201

E-mail: alohabob@consultingintelligence.com

MEDIA CONTACT:
*Michelle Bauer*
*Sextant Marketing Group*
Phone: 727-510-2524
E-mail: mbauer@smgflorida.com

## GARY PATTERSON — FISCAL DOCTOR
Boston, MA USA
http://www.FiscalDoctor.com

Gary Patterson has over 30 years senior management experience with high growth technology, manufacturing and service companies. He has worked with over 92 companies — from start-ups to Inc 500 to Fortune 500 — providing high level strategic guidance and expertise, helping them successfully navigate that often murky pathway to exceptional growth and profitability. Gary's extraordinary track record includes building two start-ups (each achieving $10 million revenue their first year), diagnosing company oversights to save $150K to $3 million annually; guiding a young company through a liquidity search resulting in $25 million in financing, and; helping a company broaden its client base 525%, increasing revenue from $16 million to $100 million. His international experience includes serving as European coordinator for the global enterprise-wide application software pilot program for a Fortune 500 company. Gary holds an MBA in Finance and Operations from Stanford, a BA in Accounting from the University of Mississippi, and a CPA.

Gary Patterson
*Trusted Advisor*
FiscalDoctor Inc.
Wellesley, MA USA
*Contact Phone:* 781-237-3637
**Click to Contact from Web Site**

## PAUL BASILE — I TO I LLC
New York, NY USA
http://www.seeingitoi.com

I to I helps professional services firms develop relationships. We create marketing and business development strategies and approaches that work. We develop marketing strategies, design marketing plans and budgets, create capabilities, increase brand value, and build the relationships that generate leads and new business. We manage marketing and business development for clients. Paul Basile acts as outsourced Chief Marketing Officer, with responsibility and accountability for the full scope of the marketing and business development function. This includes directing, guiding, setting strategy, managing operations, controlling budgets, and ensuring effectiveness.

Paul Basile
I to I LLC
New York, NY USA
*Contact Phone:* 212 982 6479
**Click to Contact from Web Site**

## GREGG FRALEY
Chicago, IL USA
www.greggfraley.com

Gregg Fraley speaks on the subject of creativity, innovation, and applied imagination. He consults with Fortune 500 companies on new product development and conducts ideation/brainstorming sessions that produce breakthrough new product ideas. He does public speaking and workshops on creative thinking and problem solving. Fraley believes that enhanced creative thinking is the foundation for continuous innovation, better problem solving, and wise decision making. He thinks that creative technique can be taught and everyone can improve their innovative capacity.

Gregg Fraley
D.S. Fraley Associates
Chicago, IL USA
*Contact Phone:* 773-764-6499
**Click to Contact from Web Site**

## THREE DIMENSIONAL DEVELOPMENT, LLC
Corpus Christi, TX USA
3ddresults.com

Business schools work diligently to develop academic solutions to the questions of how to build high performance teams. Through real world systems used at Three Dimensional Development L.L.C., companies transform their results by gaining "Insights" into the "color of communication," developing life skills to compliment traditional business skills (financial, human resources, customer relations), embracing high performance principles, and knowing how to effectively communicate to internal/external stakeholders.

Debbie Lindsey-Opel
Three Dimensional Development, LLC
Corpus Christi, TX USA
*Contact Phone:* 361-728-1459
**Click to Contact from Web Site**

## LINDA POPKY - L2M ASSOCIATES, INC.
San Francisco Bay Area, CA USA
http://www.L2MAssociates.com

Linda Popky, President of L2M Associates, Inc. is a senior marketing professional who helps clients improve their bottom line by more effectively leveraging their marketing programs, processes and people. She has over 20 years of proven performance in technology and B2B marketing, including experience with Sun Microsystems and Cisco Systems.

Linda Popky
L2M Associates Inc.
Redwood City, CA USA
*Contact Phone:* 650 281-4854
**Click to Contact from Web Site**

## CINDY LAFRANCE - STRATEGY AND TACTICS FOR REVENUE GROWTH
Austin, TX USA
http://www.cindylafrance.com

Lafrance International is the strategic marketing firm dedicated to assisting companies with emerging technology discover and articulate their compelling advantage and drive revenue. We focus on understanding your product and technology through hands-on product test drives. We get inside the mind of your potential prospects through in-depth interviews. We can help you discover the critical wedge issues that will drive prospects to purchase your product or service. We have the business and technical experience to comprehend the underlying technology and can match your product advantages to prospect needs. We deliver customized services designed to answer the specific questions that make a difference to your business today.

Cindy Lafrance
Austin, TX USA
*Contact Phone:* 512-328-5165
**Click to Contact from Web Site**

## SVEN RINGLING — IPROCON GMBH

Koenigswinter, Germany

http://www.iprocon.com

I am founder and managing director of iProCon - a Germany-based consulting company specialized in mySAP HR software and process management in Human Resources. As a consultant I work in these areas since 1996. Besides some articles and speeches, I am author of two books published in Germany with SAPPRESS about Personnel Administration with mySAP HR?and Personnel Planning and Development with mySAP HR? The latter will be published in English by SAPPRESS America in 2004.

Sven Ringling

*Managing Director*

iProCon GmbH

Member of AdManus Network

Koenigswinter, Germany

*Contact Phone:* +49 2223 909680

*Cell:* +49 171 4775591

**Click to Contact from Web Site**

## THE INSTITUTE FOR EFFECTIVE INNOVATION

Los Angeles, CA USA

http://www.InnovatorsWay.com

We have our fingers on the pulse of innovation as it's happening worldwide. Innovation has been the driver of progress since the beginning of time. It should be easy, but it isn't. We'll provide you with valuable insights. Creating innovative solutions is a people process and MUST be embraced as a fundamental business basic. If not, kiss your organization goodbye. David Markovitz and Lynda Curtin, Founders of the Institute for Effective Innovation, are your leading Resource on making innovation happen. Their real-world experience guides corporate leaders to innovative solutions - since 1975. They demystify the innovation process and speak in plain language. Authors - The Innovation Resource Handbook. Creators - Innovation Boot Camp. Clients include Pfizer, HP, Nestle, Zenith Insurance, Volunteers of America, Caltech, GE Healthcare, and a host of others. In-demand keynote speakers at conferences globally, Lynda and David frequently appear in newspapers, magazines, radio, and on television.

David Markovitz

The Institute for Effective Innovation

Los Angeles, CA USA

*Contact Phone:* 714-289-1233

**Click to Contact from Web Site**

## UPLEVEL STRATEGIES

Los Gatos, CA USA

http://www.uplevelstrategies.com/about.asp

UpLevel Strategies is a company run by entrepreneurs, for entrepreneurs. Founded by Kelly O'Neil in 2001, UpLevel Strategies mission is to support entrepreneurs in transforming their businesses to achieve greater income, focus, ease, joy, and ultimately freedom to enjoy the fruits of their labor. I believe in the freedom that is possible with a successful entrepreneurial venture. I have also seen the very freedom entrepreneurs are chasing taken away by the business they are creating. It is my mission to help them create a profitable venture that brings freedom to their life. Kelly O'Neil, founder

Kelly K. O'Neil

*Chief Strategy Officer*

UpLevel Strategies

Los Gatos, CA USA

*Contact Phone:* 408-615-8150

**Click to Contact from Web Site**

## JAMES A. ZIEGLER — FINANCIAL PROSPERITY SPEAKER

Atlanta, GA USA

http://www.zieglerdynamics.com

James A. Ziegler is a dynamic keynote speaker and seminar producer who specializes in business networking, sales and prosperity seminars. Through his programs, Jim assists companies and organizations that desire to improve the moral and overall attitude of their members and employees. Attendees learn how to leverage relationships for increased sales and profits. He is the consummate executive management trainer. Not just a motivational speaker, Jim is a nationally recognized authority on entrepreneurial business, sales and marketing.

James A. Ziegler

Ziegler Dynamics, Inc.

Duluth, GA USA

*Contact Phone:* 770-921-4440

**Click to Contact from Web Site**

**Gary Patterson**

# FiscalDoctor™
*Enhancing Growth & Profitability*

Gary Patterson has more than 30 years of senior management experience with high-growth technology, manufacturing and service companies. He has worked with more than 92 companies — from start-ups to Inc 500 to Fortune 500 — providing high-level strategic guidance and expertise, helping them successfully navigate that often murky pathway to exceptional growth and profitability.

As a trusted advisor, Patterson's FiscalDoctor™ helps CEOs, board members, executive teams, private equity investors and owners achieve fiscal health. From a quick financial assessment to a comprehensive financial management review, Fiscal Doctor™ will heal what ails you.

Patterson's extraordinary track record includes building two start-ups (each achieving $10 million revenue their first year), diagnosing company oversights to save $150K to $3 million annually; guiding a young company through a liquidity search, resulting in $25 million in financing, and; helping a company broaden its client base 525 percent, increasing revenue from $16 million to $100 million.

His international experience includes serving as European coordinator for the global enterprise-wide application software pilot program for a Fortune 500 company.

Patterson holds an MBA in Finance and Operations from Stanford University, a BA in Accounting from the University of Mississippi and a CPA.

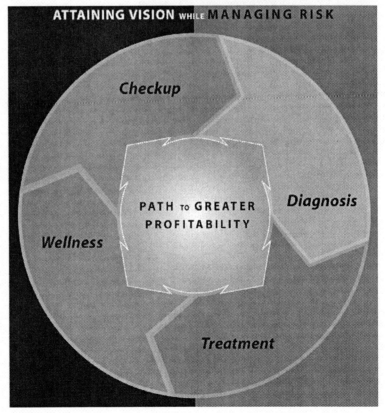

**ATTAINING VISION** WHILE **MANAGING RISK**

Checkup

Diagnosis

**PATH** TO **GREATER PROFITABILITY**

Wellness

Treatment

---

## Gary W. Patterson
21 Westerly Street, Suite 7, Wellesley, Massachusetts 02482
**781.237.3637**
gary@FiscalDoctor.com ■ www.FiscalDoctor.com

## PAM NEWMAN
Kansas City, MO USA
http://PamNewmanNow.com

Pam Newman is an Entrepreneur, Accountant, Weekly Radio Show Host, Speaker, and Author. Her passion is helping small business owners manage their business more effectively through a basic understanding of their financial information. Pam provides a variety of tools for business owners to help them utilize their financials to make better decisions. Pam is available for full or half day workshops, keynotes, break out sessions, panels and consultations.

Pam Newman, CMA, CFM, MBA
Blue Springs, MO USA
*Contact Phone:* 816.304.4398
**Click to Contact from Web Site**

## POSSIBILITIES AT WORK
Peabody, MA USA
http://www.possibilities-at-work.com/

Ellen Kaplan, advisor to CEOs of small companies, improves client's ability to grow business. Ellen focuses on the whole business rather than one function. Her work centers on integrating interpersonal with business issues. Also, Possibilities@Work eases family business's transition from one generation to the next while leaving the family unit intact. Coming from a family business, Ellen understands the challenges of family firms. Growing Possibilities e-zine, http://www.possibilities-at-work.com/newsletter/index.html, addresses classic small business issues with practical solutions.

Ellen Kaplan
*President*
Possibilities@Work
Peabody, MA USA
*Contact Phone:* 978-535-7150
**Click to Contact from Web Site**

## WILLIAM R. O'CONNELL — BUSINESS CONSULTANT
Head of the Harbor, NY USA
www.wroconnellconsulting.com

75% of small to medium sized businesses fail in any 10 year period. Do you know why? Entrepreneurs usually start a business because they are good at something. They may be inventors, manufacturers, software developers, etc. Few entrepreneurs go into business because they first know how to run a business and then figure out what their business will sell later, and what they don't know can kill the business. We help them survive and thrive.

William R. O'Connell
*Principal*
W.R. O'Connell Consulting, L.L.C.
Head of the Harbor, NY USA
*Contact Phone:* 631-366-3313
*Cell:* 516-849-3472
**Click to Contact from Web Site**

## MAURER & ASSOCIATES
Arlington, VA USA
www.beyondresistance.com

Leading change. Two-thirds of major changes in organizations fail. That's a lot of wasted money, time and opportunities. Resistance is the primary reason these initiatives fail - and Rick Maurer wrote the book on resistance. (Beyond the Wall of Resistance) He advises leaders of organizations on change. His opinion is sought by major media. Learn why his Change without Migraines approach is so popular - and practical. He can address why mergers and other new projects fail - and offer proven strategies to avoid the pitfalls.

Rick Maurer
Maurer & Associates
Arlington, VA
*Contact Main Phone:* 703-525-7074
**Click to Contact from Web Site**

## CARMEN DAY -- WEALTH4U IN SPIRIT
Los Angeles, CA USA
http://www.wealth4u.tv

'Carmen J. Day is a breath of fresh air' - 'she is right on target, as if she can see right through to the source of my concerns'. Carmen has been gifted with a laser-beam intuitive radar that hits her audience right at the core, giving each person exactly what is needed to pursue goals and dreams. These are just a few comments about Carmen J. Day, the speaker with an intensed desire to serve. Day should be on your schedule for your next event. Call Day today!

Carmen J Day
*P.R.*
Wealth4u In Spirit
Winnetka, CA USA
*Contact Phone:* 310-924-9216
*Cell:* 310-924-9216
**Click to Contact from Web Site**

# INNOVATE *or* EVAPORATE

> *Innovation will be the single most important factor in determining America's success through the 21st century.*
>
> National Innovation Initiative Report
> Council on Competitiveness
>
> December 2004

## To Survive and Thrive in Today's World, Organizations
## MUST:

- Embrace innovation as a fundamental business basic
- Cultivate their Innovation Instinct™ to succeed
- Use thinking power as their invisible competitive advantage
- Be skilled at sculpting ideas into masterpieces of innovation
- Break the Idea Killer habit that shuts down the creative process

## David Markovitz and Lynda Curtin

are your Resource to show you how – using compelling stories and proven tools drawn from their real-world experience guiding corporate leaders to valuable innovative solutions – since 1975.

*Authors of*
**The Innovation Resource Handbook:**
A Practical Blueprint for Leaders in
Business, Industry, Government, and Education

*Creators of*
**The Innovation Boot Camp:**
The Innovators Way™
to Succeeding in the 21st Century

Clients: **Pfizer, H.P., Nestle, Zenith Insurance, OSHA, VOA, Caltech**

## INSTITUTE FOR EFFECTIVE INNOVATION

4802 East Blue Jay Avenue • Orange, California 92869-1923
Phone: 714-289-1233 or 818-507-6055 • Fax: 714-289-0190
Info@TheInnovatorsWay.com • www.TheInnovatorsWay.com
www.deBonoForBusiness.com • www.GMPTrainingSystems.com

## LEADERS AT MAKING INNOVATION HAPPEN

MEMBER
NSA
NATIONAL SPEAKERS ASSOCIATION

## LIZ TAHIR
New Orleans, LA USA
www.LizTahir.com

Liz Tahir is a marketing expert, writer, independent consultant, and professional speaker. A former retailing executive, she works internationally with companies and associations, providing practical analysis and information in helping businesses grow and prosper. Liz, using her own experience, has given workshops on Negotiating Skills, Merchandising, Positioning, Customer Service, around the globe. Experienced media subject, she has been quoted or written about in numerous publications, including the Wall Street Journal, Advertising Age, Women's Wear Daily. Co-author: Sizzling Customer Service.

Liz Tahir
Tahir & Associates
New Orleans, LA USA
*Contact Phone:* 504-569-1670
*Contact Main Phone:* 800-506-1670
**Click to Contact from Web Site**

## WENDY BARLIN CPA
Chicago, IL USA
http://www.wbarlincpa.com

Wendy Barlin is more than an accountant. She is a Personal Business Manager and financial confidante. Her specialty is taking all the tedious financial chores off the shoulders of busy professionals and business owners so that they can focus on the areas where they excel. She and her team provide a full range of accounting, bookkeeping and income.

Wendy Barlin
Edwardsburg, MI USA
*Contact Phone:* 269-978-8967
**Click to Contact from Web Site**

## DEBORAH C. MILLER — STRATEGY AND PROCESS DEVELOPMENT SERVICES
Fort Wayne, IN USA
http://www.springboardthinking.com

Deborah Miller, co-founder of Springboard Thinking Group, Inc. assists businesses find increased success by providing innovative strategic planning and organizational development - partnering with leaders to achieve results that matter. We have found that organizations with goal-directed, results-based corporate cultures have distinct competitive advantages. Productive behaviors and attitudes can be developed through a continuous, practical, common-sense process. Please contact us to discuss how we can help you reach your goals.

Deborah C. Miller
*President*
Springboard Thinking Group, Inc.
Fort Wayne, IN United States
*Contact Phone:* 260-436-5064
**Click to Contact from Web Site**

## DAVID KRUEGER MD
Houston, TX USA
http://www.MentorPath.com

MentorPath™ is a unique system for success honed by twenty five years of helping exceptional people create strategies to master change and achieve uncharted dimensions of purpose, passion, and profit. Exploring new territory. . . To write the next chapter of your Life Story — To write the next chapter of your Business Story Departure from the familiar causes uncertainty. In the old story, anxiety warned of danger, prompting a retreat to safety. Yet if you pause to interpret the apprehension as validation of being in new, unfamiliar territory, you can see it as a signpost of progress. It becomes your signal to proceed. Success involves creating a new story inside and outside: an evolving internal model combined with new experiences. I help my clients write the next chapters in their life and business stories. As executives and self employed business people develop their success skills, they come to know themselves and others better. They apply human dynamics to strategic growth and personal fulfillment. Are you doing what you are passionate about? Have you fully developed your talents? And do those two go together?

David Krueger MD
MentorPath
Houston, TX USA
*Contact Phone:* 281.397.9001
**Click to Contact from Web Site**

# Carmen Day,
## Wealth4u In Spirit:
### Inspirational Speaker/Prosperity Coach

Carmen Day is a professional speaker and trainer with an assignment: Effectively transform the quality of lives for each individual with whom she connects. As a former flight attendant and manager for United Airlines as well as a professional mortgage broker, Day speaks about "Soaring through Fear," "Destiny of a Woman" and "Paradigm Shifts for Optimum Performance."

A national speaker and trainer, Day's clients agree that she is dynamic, energetic, passionate, articulate, sincere, and her life experiences connect with her audiences with precision. Day is a trainer for Rockhurst University and a professional facilitator for the American School of Mortgage Banking, where she trains others in mortgage finance and loan processing.

Day is an expert in creating wealth spiritually and strategically. She has produced and hosted a television show, "Destiny of a Woman," and now hosts a talk show of a popular international Internet radio show, "Wealth4u in Spirit" for World Talk Radio.

Day speaks on Universal Laws and principles that create successful results in any area of the lives of those who apply the information. She believes that school is never out for the pros, and this philosophy compels her to continue learning and teaching the divine discoveries along the way.

Along with Stephen Covey and Brian Tracy, Day co-authored "Mission Possible," as well as being the author of "Divine Brain Snippets of the Wealthy."

As an ordained minister, a clinical and medical hypnotist and a certified life coach, Day engages these different modalities successfully to effectively shift paradigms of each of those who hear her speak and attend her seminars.

## Some "Day-enlightened" topics include:

■ *Putting Fear in Its Place (F.E.A.R. = false evidence appearing real)*

■ *Destiny of a Woman: Waking up to the call*

■ *Your Intuition Needs Dusting Off: Allow your sixth sense to lead you*

■ *Effective Leadership: When a woman is in charge*

■ *Universal Law of Attraction: Prosperity is yours*

■ *What Women Need to Know About Finance*

**Carmen J. Day,**
CEO & President
Venus Investments
& Mortgage

*www.
venusinvestmentcorp.com*

**Public Speaker & Trainer**
**Expert in Creating Wealth**

310-924-9216
*www.wealth4u.tv*
*wealth4u@sbcglobal.net*

## MICHAEL CLARK -- BUSINESS AND BEYOND
San Francisco, CA USA
http://www.biznbeyond.com

Business consultant and professional speaker Michael Clark has been helping businesses including Fortune 500 companies including IBM and Cellular One succeed for over 20 years. Michael is a serial entrepreneur having opened multiple successful businesses over the last decade. Before that he built a successful career in finance and accounting for large corporations. He has been interviewed on radio, tv, and in print, and is a featured speaker at The Learning Annex, Rotary, and other business and professional groups.

Michael Clark
*Visionary Consultant*
Business and Beyond
Greenbrae, CA USA
*Contact Phone:* 415-461-3520
*Cell:* 415-686-1826
**Click to Contact from Web Site**

## MELVIN J. GRAVELY, II, PH.D. - INSTITUTE FOR ENTREPRENEURIAL THINKING, LTD.
Cincinnati, OH USA
http://www.entrethinking.com

If you own a business, you will want to know this guy! He is the Entrepreneurial Coach Mel Gravely is a recognized expert, author and national speaker on the subjects of entrepreneurship and small business development. As the founder of the Institute For Entrepreneurial Thinking, Mel has helped thousands of entrepreneurs get the results they expect. Entrepreneurs: He is one, he's coached them & no one knows them better. Entrepreneurs: He is one, he's coached them & no one knows them better. What are the four principles every entrepreneur better know? What are the three moves guaranteed to improve your business? Why marketing never works & how you can get customers anyway. What are the two things you must know about getting capital? How has the new economy ruined entrepreneurship? How can you grow a solo business and still keep it solo? What is the one, overwhelming reason businesses fail and how you can avoid it?

Robin Bischoff
*Program Manager*
Institute For Entrepreneurial Thinking, LTD.
Cincinnati, OH
*Contact Phone:* 513-469 6772
**Click to Contact from Web Site**

## LYNDA MCDERMOTT, AUTHOR, EXPERT ON LEADERSHIP & TEAMS
New York, NY USA
www.equipoint.com

Lynda McDermott is President of EquiPro International and an expert on leadership, team-performance, and culture change. She has 30 years of consulting experience, working for AT&T, Ernst & Young, and KPMG, and is the author of two best-selling books, World-Class Teams and Caught In The Middle: How To Survive and Thrive In Today's Management Squeeze. Lynda has been on the adjunct faculty for the New School for Social Research and for INSEAD, in Fontainebleau, France.

Lynda McDermott
EquiPro International, Ltd.
New York, NY USA
*Contact Phone:* 212-573-9046
**Click to Contact from Web Site**

## RUTH KING - BUSINESSTVCHANNEL.COM
Norcross, GA USA
http://www.businesstvchannel.com/

Ruth King coaches, speaks, and helps small businesses reach their goals. Her greatest achievement was helping an owner climb out of a negative $400,000 net worth hole. She founded HVACChannel.tv and BusinessTVChannel.com, Internet television stations currently serving businesses worldwide. Ruth holds BSChE and MSE Degrees from Tufts University and University of Pennsylvania, and an MBA from Georgia State University. Her book, The Ugly Truth About Small Business (SourceBooks) was a 2006 Independent Publisher Awards finalist.

Ruth King
*CEO*
BusinessTVChannel.com
Duluth, GA USA
*Contact Phone:* 770-729-1004
*Contact Main Phone:* 1-800-511-6844
**Click to Contact from Web Site**

# Melvin J. Gravely II, Ph.D.
## Author of
# *When Black & White Make Green*

## Expert on Minority Business Development

Dr. Melvin Gravely is professionally dedicated to developing capacity and opportunity for minority entrepreneurs. Dr. Gravely is a sought-after keynote speaker and respected advisor to major corporations, chambers of commerce executives, urban city leaders and NMSDC affiliates.

Dr. Gravely is a frequent guest on radio stations and has been featured in many national publications. After ten successful years working for a large corporation, he co-founded a civil engineering firm and grew it to a multimillion-dollar company. He is the author of five other books, including "The Lost Art of Entrepreneurship."

## Leading the Next Evolution of Business & Race

As founder of the Institute for Entrepreneurial Thinking, Dr. Gravely's mission is to help clients improve the outcomes of minority business development initiatives.

He is the leading authority on issues related to minority business development.

Clients look to Dr. Gravely to assist them in overcoming the legacy of missed expectations and in creating strategies that produce tangible outcomes.

## Core Principles That Highlight His Approach
- Professional Interactions
- Balanced Perspective
- Practical Approach
- Market Driven Solutions

## Frequently Requested Topics
- Economic Inclusion
- Partnering to Prosper
- Minority Business Development
- Supplier Diversity
- The Power of Entrepreneurial Thinking
- The Lost Art of Entrepreneurship

"Mel Gravely has spoken several times to the members of the American Chamber of Commerce Executives (ACCE) and has consulted for several chambers. He brings lively, important and original perspective to the key topic of minority and small business development. Chamber executives appreciate his practical approach."

*-- Mick Fleming, President and CEO*
*American Chamber of Commerce Executives*

## The Institute for Entrepreneurial Thinking, Ltd.

P.O. Box 621170
Cincinnati, Ohio 45262-1170
Telephone: 513-469-6772
Fax: 513-793-6776

Melvin Gravely II, Ph.D.
Managing Director
513-469-6772, ext. 12
Email: Mel@entrethinking.com

**VISTAGE INTERNATIONAL
(FORMERLY TEC INTERNATIONAL)**
San Diego, CA USA
http://www.VistageInternational.com

Vistage International, the world's largest CEO membership organization, provides business leaders with the tools to outperform. Vistage member companies grow, on average, 250% faster than non-member companies. Having annual sales between $1 million and $1 billion, Vistage member companies in the U.S. represent the small-to mid-sized business sector creating 75% of all new jobs and generating 50% of all revenue. The Vistage Confidence Index survey provides a quarterly snapshot of current economic, market, and industry trends.

Tony Vignieri
*Director of Corporate Communications*
Vistage International
San Diego, CA USA
*Contact Phone:* 858-509-5882
*Cell:* 858-208-7501
**Click to Contact from Web Site**

**PETER RESSLER & MONIKA MITCHELL RESSLER**
New York, NY USA
http://www.spiritualcapitalism.com

Dynamic and inspirational... -- That's what people say about the Resslers. High-powered Wall Street executives, Peter Ressler and Monika Mitchell Ressler have emerged as the new leaders of a spiritual revolution in business. Using the principles from their groundbreaking book, Spiritual Capitalism: What the FDNY Taught Wall Street About Money, authors Peter and Monika are guaranteed to reshape your view of business. In their compelling style, they blow apart myths like it's not personal, it's business.

Ron Davison
Chilmark Books
New York, NY USA
*Contact Phone:* 212-741-1748
**Click to Contact from Web Site**

**JIM JACOBUS — HUMAN PERFORMANCE IMPROVEMENT EXPERT**
Sugarland, TX USA
http://www.dealerexecs.com/ourteam.html

For over a decade Jim Jacobus has shared that message with his audiences around the world. For at least one brief moment each of us has experienced the incredible potential that lies inside. Some experience it more often than others and some for longer periods of time. But every one of us has experienced it and long to make it an every day occurrence. Jacobus is an international expert on extraordinary performance or what it would take for us individually and collectively, personally or professionally, to experience our immense potential. He is a trusted resource for organizations looking to get maximum personnel results in today's competitive environment.

Jim Jacobus
Sugarland, TX USA
*Contact Phone:* 281-937-9911
**Click to Contact from Web Site**

**BARTON GOLDSMITH, PH.D.**
Westlake Village, CA USA
http://www.BartonGoldsmith.com

Leadership & business expert Barton Goldsmith, Ph.D.: For more than two decades Fortune 500 companies, and over 400 other organizations and CEOs world-wide have relied on Dr. Goldsmith to help them develop creative and balanced leadership. He is the author of 'Passionate Leadership, Thinking Outside the Box,' and 'The Olympic Formula for Success.' Discover why clients like Southern California Edison, Williams Worldwide Television and YPO call him 'The Best Ever!'

Barton Goldsmith, Ph.D.
*CEO*
Goldsmith Consulting
Westlake Village, CA USA
*Contact Phone:* 866-522-7866
**Click to Contact from Web Site**

## JONATHAN COWAN — PEAK ACHIEVEMENT TRAINING
Goshen, KY USA
http://www.peakachievement.com

Peak Achievement Training enhances personal performance while decreasing stress. The Peak Achievement Trainer analyzes brainwaves and shows how well you are focusing and how alert you are. Helps improve concentration, learning, visualization and relaxation. This complete PC-based training package requires no specialized knowledge. Developer Jonathan Cowan, Ph.D., will explain how executives, athletes, and students can improve performance and simultaneously decrease stress, by discussing the successful application of this Training at Fortune 500 companies and elsewhere.

Jonathan D. Cowan, Ph.D, BCIAC
Peak Achievement Training; President,
Chairman, and CTO
Goshen, KY USA
*Contact Phone:* 800-886-4228
**Click to Contact from Web Site**

## MINORITY BUSINESS DEVELOPMENT AGENCY
Washington, DC USA
http://www.mbda.gov

MBDA's mission is to achieve entrepreneurial parity for MBEs by actively promoting their ability to grow and compete in the global economy. MBDA is addressing challenges faced by MBEs by developing programs that provide the keys to entrepreneurial success: 1. Access to Financing, 2. Access to the Marketplace, 3. Access to Education. 4. Access to Technology.
*Contact Main Phone:* 888-324-1551
**Click to Contact from Web Site**

## TRIANGLE PERFORMANCE, LLC
Houston, TX USA
www.triangleperformance.com

Kevin Berchelmann is a management, leadership, and strategy expert specializing in organizational development and value-added human capital strategies. With 20+ years of senior executive experience before starting his successful consulting firm, Triangle Performance, LLC. From executive compensation and teambuilding, strategy development and planning, to individualized coaching, performance improvement and search. Triangle Performance, LLC is a solutions-focused management consultancy specializing in creating measurable financial success through deliberate, creative, and effective human capital strategies.

D. Kevin Berchelmann
*President & Founder*
Triangle Performance, LLC
Bellaire, USA
*Contact Phone:* 713-723-2500
**Click to Contact from Web Site**

## WORLD BUSINESS EXCHANGE NETWORK/GLOBAL INTERNET TRADE COURSE
Los Angeles, CA USA
http://www.wbe.net

Entrepreneur Roosevelt Roby, Founder and CEO of the World Business Exchange Network [www.wbe.net] a global trade association on the Internet, is the leading expert on International Import/Export trade. As seen on CBS, MSNBC, Bloomberg, CNN and in the Los Angeles Times, Roby has offered solutions to millions of Americans looking to get involved in International Trade.

Tonie Moses
*Vice-President, Public Relations*
World Business Exchange Network
Global Internet Trade Course
Los Angeles, CA
*Contact Phone:* 310-670-5302
*Contact Main Phone:* 800-537-7347
*Cell:* 323-228-3127
**Click to Contact from Web Site**

# Human Performance Improvement Expert

"Inside every human being a CHAMPION heart beats!"

Jim Jacobus   The Real World Champion

For more than a decade, Jim Jacobus has shared that message with his audiences around the world. For at least one brief moment, each of us has experienced the incredible potential that lies inside. Some experience it more often than others and some for longer periods of time. But every one of us has experienced it and long to make it an everyday occurrence.

Jacobus is an international expert on extraordinary performance or what it would take for us individually and collectively, personally or professionally, to experience our immense potential.

He is a trusted resource for organizations looking to get maximum "personnel results" in today's competitive environment.

Professionally, Jacobus he has more than 20 years of research and application in human behavior and performance -- as well as 16 years in sales and sales management with America's elite sales organizations where he earned the honors of salesperson of the year and manager of the year many times. He has been the #1 trainer worldwide with America's largest seminar company.

Along with his champion experience on sports teams, he has held civic and community service board positions and is the current president of the National Speakers Association, Houston Chapter.

As a keynoter, he is compelling, dynamic and witty. As a trainer, he is insightful, powerful and gets results. You need look no further than the names on his client list to know he is dependable and proven. IBM, Xerox, Siemens, Southwest Airlines, Bell Atlantic, The National Automobile Dealers Association, The PGA of America, The National Aeronautics and Space Administration (NASA), Wells Fargo and many more regularly rely on Jacobus and Champion Education Resources to take them to new heights.

The Real World
CHAMPION
JimJacobus!
Real World People ... World Class Results

**Toll Free: 1-800-688-2387**
**Phone: 281-937-9911**
**Fax: 281-545-2512**
**Email: Info@dealerexecs.com**

17424 W. Grand Parkway S., Suite 403
Sugarland, Texas 77479

## GLOBAL TRAINING SYSTEMS
Hillsborough, NJ USA
www.globaltrainingsystems.com

Dr. Neil S. Orkin is a professional speaker and international management consultant who teaches organizations how to succeed doing business abroad. Contact Global Training Systems when you need information on: Doing Business Globally, Building a Global Workforce, Key Steps to Learning a Foreign Language, Repatriate Retention Strategies, Repatriate Training.

Dr. Neil S. Orkin
*Principal*
Global Training Systems
Hillsborough, NJ
*Contact Phone:* 908-281-9563
**Click to Contact from Web Site**

## PROJECTIZE GROUP
Hartford, CT USA
http://www.projectize.com

Global Project and Program Management specialists providing consulting, training and tools to leading companies worldwide with an emphasis on Next Generation techniques and emerging trends - From PMO, Portfolio Management, Business Process Management, Strategic Risk Assessments and Measurement Scorecards to applications like Forecasting, Estimation, Methodology, Standards, Transition Management and IT Governance. Recognized experts in Global Sourcing issues - Outsourcing vs Insourcing; Vendor Relationship Management; Global Project Management; IT Outsourcing challenges; Value Management and Benefits Realization.

Jack Duggal
*Managing Principal*
Projectize Group
Avon, CT USA
*Contact Phone:* 860-675-1010
*Cell:* 860-508-6622
**Click to Contact from Web Site**

## DOMINIC A. CINGORANELLI, CPA, CMC -- SPECIALIST IN GROWTH, STRATEGY AND PERFORMANCE ISSUES
Denver, CO USA
http://www.wdgconsulting.net

Dom Cingoranelli specializes in growth, strategy and performance issues. He assists leaders in articulating their organizational visions, and helps them develop strategies and plans to realize their visions and goals, using process consulting, as well as traditional management consulting services dealing with performance management and measurement. Services include assistance with strategy development, planning facilitation, succession management, performance management, profitability improvement, partnering, team building and executive coaching and development, organizational and leadership assessments and organization design and structure.

Dominic A. Cingoranelli, CPA, CMC
Wilson Downing Group, LLC
Wheat Ridge, CO USA
*Contact Phone:* 719 544-1047
*Contact Main Phone:* 877.544.1047
**Click to Contact from Web Site**

## GLOBAL SYSTEM SERVICES CORPORATION
Silicon Valley, CA USA
http://www.gssnet.com

Ron Herardian is a leading expert in IT infrastructure for e-mail and collaboration with broad experience in e-mail and messaging, directory services and metadirectories, calendaring, groupware and workflow, as well as mobile technology for enterprises such as wireless e-mail and messaging. Mr. Herardian has served as Chief Systems Architect for Global System Services Corporation (GSS) since 1995 when he founded the company in order to bridge the gaps between vendors, top industry experts, and mainstream IT customers.

Ron Herardian
Global System Services Corporation
Mountain View, CA United States
*Contact Phone:* 1 (650) 965-8669
**Click to Contact from Web Site**

## CHIN-NING CHU — ASIAN MARKETING CONSULTANTS
San Francisco, CA USA
www.chin-ningchu.com

Chin-Ning Chu is an international best-selling author and speaker with readers/clients in forty countries. Chin-Ning is the foremost authority on the application of Sun Tzu's Art of War strategies. Chin-Ning's books include Do Less, Achieve More; Thick Face, Black Heart and The Asian Mind Game. Her work is frequently praised by such diverse global media as CNN, Financial Times, USA Today and Asian Wall Street Journal.

Chin-Ning Chu
Asian Marketing Consultants, Inc
Antioch, CA USA
*Contact Phone:* 1-925-777-1888
**Click to Contact from Web Site**

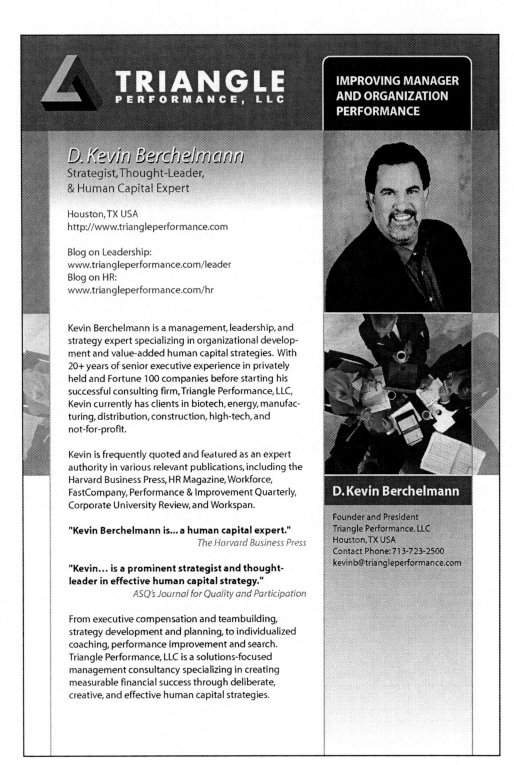

# TRIANGLE
## PERFORMANCE, LLC

**IMPROVING MANAGER AND ORGANIZATION PERFORMANCE**

### D. Kevin Berchelmann
Strategist, Thought-Leader, & Human Capital Expert

Houston, TX USA
http://www.triangleperformance.com

Blog on Leadership:
www.triangleperformance.com/leader
Blog on HR:
www.triangleperformance.com/hr

Kevin Berchelmann is a management, leadership, and strategy expert specializing in organizational development and value-added human capital strategies. With 20+ years of senior executive experience in privately held and Fortune 100 companies before starting his successful consulting firm, Triangle Performance, LLC, Kevin currently has clients in biotech, energy, manufacturing, distribution, construction, high-tech, and not-for-profit.

Kevin is frequently quoted and featured as an expert authority in various relevant publications, including the Harvard Business Press, HR Magazine, Workforce, FastCompany, Performance & Improvement Quarterly, Corporate University Review, and Workspan.

**"Kevin Berchelmann is... a human capital expert."**
*The Harvard Business Press*

**"Kevin... is a prominent strategist and thought-leader in effective human capital strategy."**
*ASQ's Journal for Quality and Participation*

From executive compensation and teambuilding, strategy development and planning, to individualized coaching, performance improvement and search. Triangle Performance, LLC is a solutions-focused management consultancy specializing in creating measurable financial success through deliberate, creative, and effective human capital strategies.

**D. Kevin Berchelmann**

Founder and President
Triangle Performance, LLC
Houston, TX USA
Contact Phone: 713-723-2500
kevinb@triangleperformance.com

**DR. AUDREY GUSKEY**
Pittsburgh, PA USA
http://www.bus.duq.edu/faculty/guskey/

America's leading marketing expert, Dr. Audrey Guskey has appeared in over 1,200 interviews: CNN, MSNBC, CBS, Fox, Montel Williams, USA Today, Wall Street Journal, Fortune, Time, Newsweek. She is a professor of Marketing at Duquesne University and consultant to FedEx, GM, Kodak, United Way, and Dick's Sporting Goods. Her passion for marketing has driven her to research consumer trends for over 25 years. Host of a daily TV segment, At Your Service, and author of Service Rules, Dr. Guskey advises consumers how to get better service, save time and money and be treated as every company's favorite customer. She will WOW you and your audience!

Dr. Audrey Guskey
Duquesne University, School of Business
Pittsburgh, PA
*Contact Phone:* 412-396-5842
**Click to Contact from Web Site**

**FINANCIAL VOYAGES, LLC.**
Atlanta, GA USA
http://www.TeamFV.com

Financial Voyages, LLC. is a CFO solutions company specializing in business analysis and decision support. We provide competency-based training solutions and performance consulting in four core knowledge areas: Business Analysis, Enterprise Risk & Management Control, Program/ Project Management and Human Capital Performance. We work with companies and government entities to develop leaders with strong technical skills and behavioral competencies to add value to the decision making process.

Pamela Robinson, MBA, CDFM, CPBA
*CEO and Founder*
Financial Voyages. LLC.
Atlanta, GA USA
*Contact Phone:* 770-541-0111
**Click to Contact from Web Site**

**CATHY STUCKER — THE IDEA LADY**
Houston, TX USA
http://www.IdeaLady.com/

Cathy Stucker is an author, speaker, consultant and newspaper columnist. She has written books on publishing, marketing and mystery shopping, and frequently speaks on these topics. Her Web sites, including http://www.IdeaLady.com/, http://www.SellingBooks.com/ and http://www.MysteryShoppersManual.com/ provide free information on topics of interest to authors, professionals, consultants, coaches, mystery shoppers and others. Recent projects include a multimedia program on profiting from content, online and offline. Cathy is available for media interviews and speaking engagements.

Cathy Stucker
Sugar Land, USA
*Contact Phone:* 281-265-7342
*Cell:* 281-451-4116
**Click to Contact from Web Site**

**MYSTERY SHOP LINK, LLC**
Ventura, CA USA
www.MysteryShopLink.com

Mystery Shop Link is America's leading mystery shopping company. Mystery shoppers file observational reports to companies to help them perform better and stay in compliance with their policies and regulatory requirements.

George Ortiz
Mystery Shop Link, LLC
Ventura, CA USA
*Contact Phone:* 866-805-7467
*Cell:* 805-403-6861
**Click to Contact from Web Site**

**ROBERTA GUISE — SMALL BUSINESS MARKETING EXPERT**
San Francisco, CA USA
www.GuiseMarketing.com

Roberta Guise who - according to her clients, kicks butt! - works with small business owners and professionals who want to build a profitable stable of customers, save money on ineffective promotions, and get known through branding, precision marketing and public relations. Roberta coaches and consults clients one-one one, and writes and speaks on how to get a distinctive marketing edge and be extraordinarily visible. For a lively mix of her ideas and opinions, read her articles at www.guisemarketing.com.

Roberta Guise, MBA
Guise Marketing & PR
San Francisco, CA USA
*Contact Phone:* 415-979-0611
**Click to Contact from Web Site**

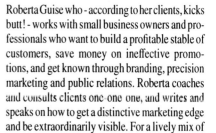

# ◈ Projectize·Group

Projectize Group is a leading Organizational Project Management (OPM) firm focusing on project, program and portfolio management and program management office (PMO) solutions.

We specialize in improving the execution capability of organizations by bridging strategy with tactics and focusing on process innovation and project management discipline.

Projectize Group solutions are provided by the top thinkers and practitioners with decades of experience in various industry sectors highly skilled in their area of expertise. We have a distinguished group of internationally recognized experts committed to providing the highest, critical, objective expertise.

*Projectize Group provides next generation consulting, training, tools and processes in:*

- Program Management Office (PMO) design and implementation

- Organizational Project Management training and certification

- PMO-in-a-Box – project and process management framework

- Organizational Project Management Maturity Assessments (OPM3)

- Business Process Management

- Governance and Performance management tools and consulting

- Measurement and Metrics Scorecard

- Strategic Risk Assessments

- Project Health Checks and Reviews

- Sourcing effectiveness - Global Project Management and Relationship management

- Cultural Intelligence (CQ) training and consulting

- Benefits realization and Value Management

**Projectize Group LLC**
14 Brian Lane
Avon, Connecticut
06001

Phone: 860.675.1010
Fax: 860.760.6251
Email:
info@projectize.com

Jack Duggal,
Managing Principal
Cell: 860.508.6622

## JOANN HINES - THE PACKAGING DIVA
Kennesaw, GA USA
http://www.packaginguniversity.com/

As the leading online career expert for the packaging industry and creator of multiple packaging web portals, JoAnn R. Hines combines an active career plan and the development process with a targeted approach toward professional advancement. When Hines organized the women in a male-dominated industry by founding Women in Packaging, Inc. in 1993, she essentially became the change agent for an industry of women in a state of flux. The number of women in the world's third largest industry grew 20 percent under her direction. Today, the packaging industry employs one million people of which 25 percent are women.

JoAnn R. Hines
PackagingUniversity.com
Kennesaw, GA USA
*Contact Phone:* 678-594-6872
**Click to Contact from Web Site**

## WOMEN IN PACKAGING, INC. — CONSUMER PRODUCT PACKAGING EXPERT
Kennesaw, GA USA
http://www.WomeninPackaging.org

Packaging Experts, Packaging Consultants, Packaging Speakers: The Public Relations Department at Packaging University connects you with the country's top leaders, experts, consultants and speakers, in packaging. Our experts work in all facets of packaging and they will speak with you about new innovations, trends, legislation, technology, and other packaging news. Contact us if you need experts to interview, article ideas, news, hot topics, or quotes, opinions, and insights from prestigious sources.

JoAnn R. Hines
*Packaging Diva*
Women in Packaging, Inc.
Kennesaw, GA
*Contact Phone:* 678-594-6872
**Click to Contact from Web Site**

## JENNIFER VESSELS
San Francisco, CA USA
http://www.nextstepgrowth.com

Jennifer Vessels' practical, proven methods for increasing sales results, return on marketing investments, and company profitability have maximized results for technology companies ranging from Cisco Systems and Palm, to SonicWall and other emerging companies. Jennifer's team at Next Step have provided employee recruitment, retention and development programs for Goodwill Industries, Wilson Sonsini, and other manufacturing and service firms. Having worked extensively in Europe, Jennifer has also launched European technology companies including Tandberg Telecom and TiFiC.

Jennifer Vessels
Next Step
Redwood City, CA USA
*Contact Phone:* 650 361 1902
**Click to Contact from Web Site**

## VISION STRATEGIC MARKETING & COMMUNICATIONS
Washington, DC USA
www.visionsmc.com

At Vision, we believe that strategy is essential to success. Vision Strategic Marketing & Communications works with select companies with high growth potential to reach their business goals through marketing strategies. Molly Hughes Wilmer is a strategist with a marketing focus. With a well-rounded background in non-profits, public and private businesses, she brings a holistic understanding of organizational growth strategies and out-of-the-box thinking. As a strategist, she is able to stay focused on the big picture while understanding the importance of details and the balance between all components of marketing—product, price, promotion and placement. With experience in international relations, she is sensitive to the nuances of interpersonal and organizational communications, and the dynamics of organizational cultures. Molly Hughes Wilmer is a dynamic public speaker and a teaching-oriented workshop leader and group facilitator.

Molly Hughes Wilmer
Vision Strategic Marketing & Commmunications
Annapolis, MD USA
*Contact Phone:* 410-849-8095
**Click to Contact from Web Site**

# Dominic A. Cingoranelli, CPA, CMC
## Strategic Management Expert

Dom Cingoranelli assists organizations with growth, strategy and performance improvement. He helps clients develop strategies and plans to realize their visions and goals, using participative process consulting, as well as traditional management consulting services dealing with performance management and measurement.

He also conducts other management consulting, training and development for general managers, professionals and technical specialists through his work in organization development. Dom earned his MBA with honors from Regis University. He is a Certified Management Consultant and a member of the Institute of Management Consultants and the Society for the Advancement of Consulting. He is a member of the Society for Human Resource Professionals, as well as the American Institute of CPAs, and the Colorado Society of CPAs.

He has performed strategy consulting and planning, process improvement studies, management consulting, training and development, team building, coaching and group process facilitation for a variety of groups. His clients include professional and trade associations, project managers and executives on large, complex projects for major manufacturers, midsize to very large businesses, and other organizations dealing with change, performance and leadership issues.

Dom and his firm, Wilson Downing Group, LLC assist a wide variety of organizations with improvement strategies and implementation. They maintain an industry concentration in the design and construction industry, and in construction-related businesses. As part of his work with the construction industry, Dom provides partnering facilitation and assistance for project management teams on projects ranging from $1 million to over $300 million in size. In addition to partnering charter sessions, he also provides assistance to teams on troubled projects through practical, behavior-based conflict resolution and work outs that result in effective teamwork for the balance of the project

COLLOQUY®
The Voice of the Loyalty Marketing Industry Since 1990

**COLLOQUY**
Cincinnati, OH USA
www.colloquy.com

The voice of the loyalty marketing industry since 1990, COLLOQUY (www.colloquy.com) provides editorial, educational and research services on a global basis. COLLOQUY and colloquy.com present commentary, analysis, breaking news, research libraries and article and program archives to qualified subscribers. COLLOQUY subscriptions are available at no cost at www.colloquy.com/register.asp or by calling 513/248-5918. Reader participation is invited at info@colloquy.com.

Jill McBride
*Public Relations*
COLLOQUY
Milford, OH
*Contact Phone:* 513-231-5115
**Click to Contact from Web Site**

**BILL BROOKS -- THE BROOKS GROUP**
Greensboro, NC USA
http://www.brooksgroup.com

CEO of The Brooks Group, a consulting firm based in North Carolina, Bill Brooks is a world-renowned expert on sales and sales management screening, development and retention systems. He is a thought leader on these topics and is the author of 14 acclaimed books. Interviewed regularly by leading publications for his insightful and relevant points of view, he also delivers keynote and informational sessions nearly 100 times per year at organizations, associations, and groups worldwide.

Corrie Lisk-Hurst
*Director of Marketing*
The Brooks Group
Greensboro, NC USA
*Contact Phone:* 336-282-6303
*Contact Main Phone:* 800-633-7762
**Click to Contact from Web Site**

**RANDY GAGE**
Miami, FL USA
http://www.RandyGage.com

Randy Gage has been called the Millionaire Messiah because he believes that you are meant to be rich, and it is a sin to be poor! His Deepak Chopra meets Dennis Miller style is bold, brash, but right on target if your audience wants to know the secrets of success and making money. A former high school dropout, Randy rose from a dishwasher in a pancake house to become a multi-millionaire. Today Randy is recognized as one of the world's preeminent experts on prosperity, creating wealth, and success. Randy is the author of Why You're Dumb Sick and Broke. . .and How to get Smart, Healthy and Rich! as well as 40 other books, CDs and DVDs. His materials have been translated into more than 14 languages.

Meryl
*Media Relations*
Meryl L. Moss Media Relations, Inc.
Westport, CT USA
*Contact Main Phone:* (203) 226-0199
**Click to Contact from Web Site**

**STEVE YASTROW — YASTOW MARKETING**
Chicago, IL USA
www.yastrow.com

Steve Yastrow, President of Yastrow Marketing, recently authored Brand Harmony: Achieving Dynamic Results by Orchestrating your Customer's Total Experience; a book Tom Peters called "clear, compelling and powerful." Yastrow is a sought after speaker, writer and consultant, known for his revolutionary marketing systems that yield major profit breakthroughs. Yastrow Marketing clients include Tom Peters Company, The Cayman Islands Department of Tourism, McDonald's Corporation, White Castle, Jenny Craig, Agilent Technologies, and Great Clips for Hair, among others.

Steve Yastrow
Yastow Marketing
Deerfield, IL USA
*Contact Phone:* 847-686-0400
*Contact Main Phone:* 847-686-0400
**Click to Contact from Web Site**

# Dr. Audrey Guskey
## *America's Leading Marketing Expert*
### *... At Your Service!*

# What Consumer Trends Will Rule in 2007?

Dr. Audrey Guskey has been researching consumer trends and customer service for more than 25 years. Her passion for marketing has driven her to become a leading expert in the field of marketing. Host of her own daily television evening news segment, "At Your Service," Dr. Guskey advises consumers how to get better service and save time and money. In her upcoming book, "Service Rules," she demonstrates how to be treated as every company's favorite customer.

*Her areas of expertise include:*
- ■ **Customer Satisfaction**
- ■ **Customer Service**
- ■ **Demographic Trends**
- ■ **E-commerce**
- ■ **Advertising**
- ■ **Retailing**

*At Your Service!*

America's leading marketing expert, Dr. Audrey Guskey, has appeared in more than 1,000 TV and radio interviews: CNN, MSNBC, CBS, Fox News Channel, Montel Williams Show, CBS Radio, ABC Radio, NPR, and in than 400 news articles: *USA Today, the Wall Street Journal, Fortune, Time, Newsweek, U.S.News & World Report, Money Magazine, Reader's Digest, the New York Times* and *Cosmopolitan.*

Dr. Audrey Guskey is professor of marketing at Duquesne University and a consultant to GM, Kodak, United Way, Ramada Inn and Blue Cross.

---

She will WOW you and your audience!

## Dr. Audrey Guskey

**Professor of Marketing
Duquesne University,
Pittsburgh, Pennsylvania 15282**

(412) 396-5842

guskey@duq.edu

www.bus.duq.edu/faculty/guskey

## AD COLLEGE - BDNI
Kenilworth, IL USA
http://www.adcollege.com

Richard Czerniawski and Michael Maloney, experts in the fields of advertising, brand marketing, positioning and creating brand loyalty, have authored numerous articles on marketing management and have served as guest lecturers for a wide variety of business and management schools. Richard and Mike are both principals with Business Development Network, Inc., a marketing consulting firm that develops strategies and initiatives that create brand loyalty and grow business. Mr. Czerniawski and Mr. Maloney are the authors of Creating Brand Loyalty: The Management of Power Positioning and Really Great Advertising.

Lori Vandervoort
*Director of Operations*
Brand Development Network, International
Chanute, KS
*Contact Phone:* 800-255-9831
*Contact Main Phone:* 620-431-0780
**Click to Contact from Web Site**

## ALLAN GORMAN — BRAND MARKETING CONSULTANT
New York, NY USA
www.brandspa.net

Allan Gorman is a market leadership advisor and a proponent of Brand Delight — those gratifying experiences that are the true path to brand distinction. Director of Brandspa, LLC and author of the book, 'Briefs for Building Better Brands', Gorman helps company leaders find, tell, and live more effective stories. Download his eye-opening paper, 'Ten Marketing Secrets for Building a Sexier Brand' at http://www.brandspa.net. Mr. Gorman is available for interviews and speaking engagements.

Allan Gorman
*Director*
Brandspa LLC
New York, NY USA
*Contact Phone:* 973-509-2728
**Click to Contact from Web Site**

## ROBERT RADI — PRODUCT DESIGNER
Beverly Hills, CA USA
http://www.Radidesign.com

As a third generation designer Robert Radi takes his role in design very seriously. In 1993, Mr. Radi established his design studio in Beverly Hills, California. Since then his unique design signature has been recognized by several US and International brands, that have constantly engaged his talent to give that unique edge to everyday products. Educated in Italy and the USA Mr. Radi has served as a professor at Otis College teaching Product Design.

Robert Radi
Radi Design Inc.
Beverly Hills, CA USA
*Contact Phone:* 310-385-8411
**Click to Contact from Web Site**

## ROOM 214, INC. - SOCIAL MEDIA EXPERTS
Boulder, CO USA
http://www.capturetheconversation.com

ROOM 214, INC Boulder, Colorado USA www.Room214.com www.CapturetheConversation.com Room 214 is a social media and search marketing agency focused on delivering integrated online communications and word of mouth marketing campaigns. Our services include social media strategy and training, blogging, podcasting, search engine optimization, pay per click, article marketing, optimized press releases, syndicating press rooms, RSS marketing and customized online reputation monitoring.

James Clark
Room 214, INC
Capture the Conversation
Boulder, CO USA
*Contact Phone:* 303-444-9214
*Cell:* 303-886-4259
**Click to Contact from Web Site**

## DON CROWTHER -- MARKETING & INTERNET MARKETING EXPERT
Chicago, IL USA
www.101PublicRelations.com

Don Crowther helps companies make money online and through traditional marketing. Don lives and works on the cutting edge of Internet and traditional marketing and is known for providing powerful insights, opinions, leads and examples that add life to stories and media reports. Don is regularly quoted by media in the areas of Internet marketing, pay-per-click advertising, business blogging, search engines, internet success stories, marketing, public relations, branding, positioning, and advertising. Call Don, he'll help!

Don Crowther
*President*
Breakthrough Consulting Inc.
101PublicRelations.com
Racine, WI USA
*Contact Phone:* 262-639-2270
*Contact Main Phone:* 262-639-2270
*Cell:* 262-880-1362
**Click to Contact from Web Site**

# Rock-solid marketing advice for small business owners.

Roberta Guise

More and more, readers, viewers and listeners are thinking about starting a small business or already have one. According to the U.S. government, nearly 75% of all business owners are self-employed. To get up and running and stay on top of their game, these entrepreneurs seek ideas they can quickly put to good use.

Roberta Guise has the answers small business owners need to succeed, and offers advice about how to avoid the pitfalls along the way. With her *Top Seven Keys to Marketing Success*™, she answers questions about

- How to compete, get known and be visible in a noisy, competitive marketplace
- How to know what customers really want and value
- Marketing pitfalls—what to do to avoid them and save a ton of money
- Planning for the wild and wooly ride of owning a small business
- Knowing one's best customers, and why they are the best (it's not that obvious)
- Caring about customers to the point of obsession
- How to know when marketing is—or isn't—working

Decide for yourself—Roberta will captivate your audiences and keep them wanting more.

**To interview Roberta:**

415-979-0611
roberta@guisemarketing.com

Be

Visible!

Guise Marketing & PR
401 Terry Francois, Suite 220
San Francisco, CA 94158
415-979-0611
www.guisemarketing.com

## WONDERGROUP YOUTH MARKETING AND ADVERTISING
Cincinnati, OH USA
http://www.wondergroup.com

Where in the world do you learn about today's youth? Call WonderGroup for fast, reliable information on today's kids, tweens and teens. We're a full-service youth marketing resource that helps companies better understand and market to the next generation. WonderGroup founders (Tim Coffey, Dave Siegel and Greg Livingston) have even written about some of their experiences in The Great Tween Buying Machine: Marketing to Tweens.

Dave Siegel
*President*
WonderGroup Youth Marketing and
Advertising
Cincinnati, OH
*Contact Phone:* 513-357-2950
**Click to Contact from Web Site**

## DR JANELLE BARLOW SAYS: 'GOOD CUSTOMER SERVICE IS NO LONGER ENOUGH!'
Las Vegas, NV USA
www.brandedservice.com

A brand is more than a name, a logo and a marketing campaign. A brand is a unique identity and a reputation that needs to be reflected everywhere in an organization, especially in the service staff delivers. When branding is seen as a quality process to ensure all customer experiences are aligned to the expectations created by brand images, it provides a road-map to build a brand from the inside-out and transform an organization.

Jeffrey Mishlove
Branded Customer Service
Las Vegas, NV USA
*Contact Phone:* 702-378-0348
**Click to Contact from Web Site**

## SCOT KENKEL - SALES COACHING EXPERT
Clinton, TN USA
http://www.successlearninginstitute.com/

Scot's products or services may result in serious side effects, such as a bulging bank account, persistent peer envy, or the uncontrollable urge to purchase that fourth BMW. If you experience any or all of these symptoms, we have only one thing to say - you're welcome, very very welcome!! Before we begin, let's get something straight; I'm only here to accomplish one thing - to help you make serious money in the real estate business. Seriously! Regardless of whether you're a real estate virgin or a real estate veteran, I can show you how to start earning tons of cold, hard cash (yes, I said hard) today. Bread. Lettuce. Dough. Moolah. Greenbacks. Bucks. Big Ones. Bacon. Cabbage. Kale. Folding Green. Long Green. Jackpot. Vig. Rhino. Plaster. Scratch. Fish. Rock. Big One. Smacker. Macaroni. Yellowback. Brass. Carpet. Notes. Bills.

Scot Kenkel
Clinton, TN USA
*Contact Phone:* 1-888-831-5945
**Click to Contact from Web Site**

## DEBBIE ALLEN — MOTIVATIONAL SPEAKER FOR BUSINESS
Phoenix, AZ USA
www.DebbieAllen.com

Debbie Allen has built and sold numerous companies, taken a business from disaster to success and even lived to tell about it. Debbie's acute business sense, contagious enthusiasm, positive energy and fun sense of humor make her a dynamic presenter. Debbie has been a member of National Speakers Association since 1995, and has achieved the level of Certified Speaking Professional (CSP) for her professional platform skills, an honor achieved by less than 10 percent of all professional members and only 160 women worldwide. Debbie is the recipient of the National Chamber of Commerce Blue Chip Enterprise Award for overcoming business obstacles and achieving fast business growth. She is the author of six books including Confessions of Shameless Self Promoters, and Skyrocketing Sales. Debbie is a frequent guest on dozens of syndicated radio talk shows throughout the U.S. and Canada. Her sales and marketing expertise has been featured in dozens of national and international publications, including Entrepreneur, Selling Power, Sales & Marketing Excellence and Franchising Magazine.

Debbie Allen, CSP
*Motivational Speaker for Business*
Allen & Associates Consulting, Inc.
Scottsdale, AZ USA
*Contact Phone:* 480-634-7691
*Contact Main Phone:* 800-359-4544
*Cell:* 602-791-9390
**Click to Contact from Web Site**

# Shocking.
# Controversial.
# Brilliant.

Randy Gage has been called "the Millionaire Messiah" because he believes that you are meant to be rich, and it is a sin to be poor!

His "Deepak Chopra meets Dennis Miller" style is bold, brash but right on target. If your audience wants to know the secrets of success and making money. A former high school dropout, Randy rose from a dishwasher in a pancake house to become a multi-millionaire. Today, Randy is recognized as one of the world's pre-eminent experts on prosperity, creating wealth and success.

Randy is the author of *Why You're Dumb Sick and Broke ... And How to Get Smart, Healthy and Rich!* as well as 40 other books, CDs and DVDs. His materials have been translated into Spanish, Chinese, Norwegian, Korean, German, Russian, Czech, Indian, Portuguese, Slovene, Macedonian, Croatian, Indonesian and Dutch. In addition to his books, he has written dozens of published articles on the subject.

If you are looking for an engaging media guest, Randy is your guy! He has appeared on dozens of radio and TV shows and been interviewed or featured in hundreds of print and online publications, including *SUCCESS* magazine. Prosperity and wealth building are perennial favorite topics for all audiences.

---

*To book Randy for an interview,*
*call Meryl Moss from Muscle Media at 203-226-0199.*

**DIANA VOLLMER -- ASCEND CONSULTING GROUP**
San Francisco, CA USA
http://www.mfmi.com

Helps organizations maximize value by increasing revenues and profits simultaneously through effectiveness and efficiency of marketing, competitive analysis, market research, positioning and leveraging a unique selling proposition (USP). Served the business community both domestically and internationally with a career spanning retailing, real estate, and financial services in line management, consulting, sales management and marketing. Lead two companies from inception to buy-out/merger with international firm. First hand experience of challenges and rewards of small business ownership.

Diana Vollmer
Ascend Consulting Group
San Francisco, CA USA
*Contact Phone:* 415-563-9688
*Contact Main Phone:* 415.563-2227
*Cell:* 415-577-6544
**Click to Contact from Web Site**

## ERIC WOOLF — MAILING LIST EXPERT
New York, NY USA
cml-llc.com

Complete Mailing Lists has brought together the knowledge of 4 industry veterans, each with a minimum of 10 years of experience. The goal of the company is to be a premier compiler of specialty data, taking the data to a new level of compiled and having the data mirror response data by adding enhancements that will ultimately improve results - blurring the line between compiled and response lists.

Eric Woolf
Complete Mailing Lists, LLC
Bronxville, NY USA
*Contact Phone:* 914-771-6640
**Click to Contact from Web Site**

**BRIAN CARROLL, CEO OF INTOUCH, INC., AUTHOR, SPEAKER**
Minneapolis, MN USA
http://www.startwithalead.com

Brian J. Carroll is founder and CEO of InTouch Inc., one of the first companies to provide lead generation solutions for the complex sale and recognized by Inc. Magazine as one of America's fastest growing companies. He speaks to 20,000 people a year on improving sales effectiveness and lead generation strategies. Carroll has been featured in publications including The Wall Street Transcript, Sales and Marketing Management, and Inc. His blog, http://blog.startwithalead.com, is read by thousands.

Brian Carroll
*CEO*
InTouch, Inc.
Arden Hills, MN USA
*Contact Phone:* 651-255-7600
*Contact Main Phone:* 651-255-7600
*Cell:* 651-226-4516
**Click to Contact from Web Site**

## DENNY HATCH — DIRECT MAIL EXPERT
Philadelphia, PA USA
www.dennyhatch.com

Denny Hatch, Direct Mail Expert & founder of the newsletter, Who's Mailing What! (now titled InsideDirectMail) has analyzed thousands of direct mailings in more than 200 categories in the past 25 years. He is a freelance writer, designer and consultant on direct mail/direct marketing and the author of four books on marketing and business as well as four novels. His new veutre is the e-newsletter, www.businesscommonsense.com.

Denny Hatch
Denny Hatch Associates, Inc.
Philadelphia, PA
*Contact Phone:* 215-627-9103
**Click to Contact from Web Site**

## MICHAEL CANNON -- SALES CONSULTANT
San Francisco, CA USA
http://www.silverbulletgroup.com

Michael Cannon is an internationally renowned sales and marketing expert, a dynamic speaker and a best selling author with business gurus Brian Tracy, et. al., of "Create the Business Breakthrough You Want." He has over 20 years of sales and management experience and has held positions ranging from Account Executive to VP of Sales to CEO. Michael has made guest appearances on shows like "Entrepreneur Magazine Radio" and the American Marketing Association's "Marketing Matters LIVE!"

Michael Cannon
*CEO*
Silver Bullet Group, Inc.
Walnut Creek, CA United States
*Contact Phone:* 925.930.9436
**Click to Contact from Web Site**

## SIGN*A*RAMA — START-UP YOUR OWN BUSINESS
West Palm Beach, FL USA
www.signarama.com

SIGN*A*RAMA is the "World's Largest Sign Franchise" with over 700 outlets in 34 countries. As the leading authority on visual impact product and services, SIGN*A*RAMA creates and installs vehicle-boat-aircraft lettering, window graphics, digital printing, building lettering, banners, and many other diverse and creative signs and advertising services. With over 19 years of franchising experiencing, SIGN*A*RAMA can offer you an incredible turn-key opportunity with 5 weeks of training, financing available, mass-purchasing power, and on-going local support.

John Pugsley
SIGN*A*RAMA
West Palm Beach, FL USA
*Contact Phone:* 561-640-5570
**Click to Contact from Web Site**

# Don Crowther -- Marketing and Internet Marketing Expert

D on Crowther helps companies make money on-line and through traditional marketing. Don lives and works on the cutting edge of Internet and traditional marketing, and he is known for providing powerful insights, opinions, leads and examples that add life to stories and media reports.

*Don Crowther is regularly quoted by media in the areas of:*

**Internet Marketing**          **Marketing**
**Pay Per Click Advertising**   **Public Relations**
**Blogging**                    **Branding and Positioning**
**Search Engines**              **Advertising**
**Internet Success Stories**

*What Don brings to the table:*

■ 25 years of marketing experience (10 of that online), working with companies -- ranging from packaged goods companies to manufacturers, Fortune-100 companies to Internet start-ups, the Federal government to one-person companies;

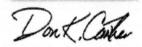

■ His own sites and those of his top five clients generate more than 40 million visitors and millions of dollars in on-line sales every month;

■ Managed several of the world's top brands and introduced dozens of new products, resulting in incremental sales of more than $800 million;

■ Author of more than 10 books, including the bible for the pay-per-click advertising world, "Pay Per Click Money Machine," as well as "Creating Powerful Press Releases," "Crisis Communication Planning" and the "GreatPR Newsletter."

*For more information on Don and his services,*
*visit 101PublicRelations.com, PayPerClickMoneyMachine.com and GreatResults.com.*

Don Crowther, president, Breakthrough Consulting, Inc.
Racine, Wisconsin, U.S.A.
Main Phone: 262-639-2270
Contact Phone: 262-639-2270  Cell: 262-880-1362

**MARKETING SOLUTIONS**
Fairfax, VA USA
www.mktgsols.com

Specialists in the professional business of beauty!
The leading marketing, advertising, public relations and consulting services agency in the salon and beautycare industries. Nationally recognized experts and spokespersons on: professional haircare, beautycare, nailcare & skincare, total hair & beauty makeovers, hair fashion trends, salon & day salons, salon & spa services, medical spas & plastic surgery, salon & medical retail products, and anti-aging. They have salons, dayspas, medical services, national and international haircare and beautycare companies as clients.

Larry H. Oskin
*President*
Marketing Solutions
Fairfax, VA
*Contact Phone:* 703-359-6000
**Click to Contact from Web Site**

**WIEST & ASSOCIATES INC.,THE CUSTOMER ACQUISITION AND RETENTION COMPANY™**
Toronto, Ontario Canada
http://www.wiest.ca

Dan Wiest is a direct marketing and online consultant and is a major industry contributor. He is currently Chairman, The Canadian Marketing Association's Annual Conference; Executive Member, e-Marketing Council; Co-Chair, Search Engine Marketing Committee; Past Chairman, Digital Marketing Conference. His specialty is direct marketing as it applies to both traditional (mail & print) and online media. His research appears in the CMA 2005 Fact Book. Dan is in demand as a speaker for his humor and ability to make tough concepts understandable. He has a long history of successful speaking appearances, including many one-day seminars and workshops. He is the longest tenured instructor for the Canadian Marketing Association's Direct Marketing Certification Program, the program that defines direct marketing expertise in Canada.

Daniel G. Wiest
Wiest & Associates Inc.
Caledon, Ontario Canada
*Contact Phone:* 905-873-6000
**Click to Contact from Web Site**

**SUGGESTIONBANK.COM FOCUS GROUP SERVICES**
Washington, DC USA
www.SuggestionBank.com

SuggestionBank.com is the Focus Group Marketing Service of the Universal Coupon Corporation.

Mitchell P. Davis
Universal Coupon Corporation
Washington, DC USA
*Contact Phone:* 202-333-5000
**Click to Contact from Web Site**

**THE RESEARCH DEPARTMENT**
New York, NY USA

Alexa Smith is a leading expert on consumer attitudes and behavior. As a focus group moderator and market research practitioner for over 20 years, Ms. Smith has been quoted in many publications, has written byline articles and is a frequent speaker and lecturer on consumer trends, attitudes and habits.

Alexa Smith
*President*
The Research Department
New York, NY
*Contact Phone:* 212-717-6087
**Click to Contact from Web Site**

**ANDREW SOBEL**
Santa Fe, NM USA
www.andrewsobel.com

The Leading Authority on Client Relationships and Loyalty. Andrew Sobel is the leading authority on client relationships and the skills and strategies required to earn enduring client loyalty. His best-selling book, Clients for Life (Simon & Schuster), is considered the definitive work on how professionals become extraordinary advisors to their clients and customers. A sought-after speaker on building long-term business relationships, he lived abroad for 13 years and has served as a strategy advisor to top executives in over 25 countries.

Andrew Sobel
*President*
Andrew Sobel Advisors, Inc.
Santa Fe, NM
*Contact Phone:* 505-982-0211
**Click to Contact from Web Site**

## KRISTIN ZHIVAGO, REVENUE COACH
Jamestown, RI USA
http://www.Zhivago.com

Kristin Zhivago is an expert on how customers make buying decisions. She has interviewed thousands of customers for hundreds of clients in dozens of industries over the past 35 years. She is the author of 'Rivers of Revenue,' and the editor of the Revenue Journal, an online newsletter/blog. She founded her own high-tech marketing consulting firm in Silicon Valley in 1979, and now serves clients in all industries, worldwide.

Kristin Zhivago
*President*
Zhivago Marketing Partners, Inc.
Revenue Journal
Jamestown, RI USA
*Contact Phone:* 401-423-2400
**Click to Contact from Web Site**

## RON KARR — KARR ASSOCIATES, INC.
New York, NY USA
http://www.ronkarr.com

THE TITAN PRINCIPLE Sales — Negotiations — Customer Service — The Key to Market Domination — Call today and find out how the TITAN PRINCIPLE will help your audience: Increase Client $ Value — Differentiate from the Competition — Gain Customers — Increase Market Share — Position Themselves as a Valued Resource Sell on Value — Partner for Influence — Increase Profits.

Ronald Karr
*President*
Karr Associates, Inc.
Westwood, NJ
*Contact Phone:* 800-423-5277
**Click to Contact from Web Site**

## BETH TERRY - PHOENIX LIFE COACH
Phoenix, AZ USA
http://www.bethterry.com/

Are you looking to find balance in a tough world? Tired of programs that don't work? Need to find a common sense approach that helps you make real changes … in your life, your work, and your community? Beth is real and she delivers substance that works. The words above are not ours. These are comments taken right from audience members about motivational keynote speaker, Beth Terry. Since 1989 Beth Terry has presented keynotes and workshops to thousands of people in 6 countries. She is well known for her dynamic, personable style and for her uplifting, motivational and inspirational stories. Beth draws from her experience as a successful businesswoman, consultant, professional speaker, parent and author. Her common sense and focused approach appeal to Management as well as to the front line and to anyone wrestling with day to day challenges.

Beth Terry
Beth Terry's Overwhelm Solutions
Phoenix, AZ USA
*Contact Phone:* 877-672-5008
**Click to Contact from Web Site**

## LAURA BERMAN FORTGANG - THE LIFE BLUEPRINT INSTITUTE
Montclair, NJ USA
http://www.laurabermanfortgang.com/

Laura Berman Fortgang is internationally recognized as a pioneer in the personal coaching field and is known for her no-nonsense, entertaining writing and speaking style. She is the best-selling author of Now What? 90 Days to a New Life Direction, Living Your Best Life and Take Yourself to the Top. Laura was the first personal coach to be featured on national television as well as in international print and digital media. Her appearances on Oprah, The CBS Early Show, NBC's Weekend Today, MSNBC, CNBC, CNN and many others, combined with print media such as USA Today, Fast Company, MONEY and many national and international newspapers have paved the way for most of the successful coaches in the industry today. Laura's books are published in 11 languages and distributed around the world. She is currently a contributing editor for REDBOOK magazine and has been seen most recently on the Jane Pauley show and Weekend Today. Through her coaching company, LBF*InterCoach, Inc. and her seminar company, The Life Blueprint ® Institute, Laura has provided coaching to diverse clients ranging from homemakers, celebrities and Fortune 500 companies to NASA and the Army Corps of Engineers.

Laura Berman Fortgang
The Life Blueprint Institute
Montclair, NJ USA
*Contact Phone:* 973-857-8180
**Click to Contact from Web Site**

# Ron Karr

## Dedicated to Developing High Performing Sales Cultures...
## Sell More In Less Time At Higher Profits

**Sales**

**Negotiations**

**Customer Service**

**Specializing in:**
- Media Interviews
- Author
- Keynote & Seminars
- Consulting
- Executive Coaching

**Call today and find out how the TITAN PRINCIPLE® will help your audience:**

- Sell more in less time
- Increase profit
- Increase market share
- Differentiate from the competition
- Achieve maximum potential

**What do the following organizations have in common?**

- Hertz
- Met Life
- Mutual of Omaha
- Marriott Hotels
- Wright Medical
- Southwestern Bell Yellow Pages
- Morgan Stanley
- Agfa Medical
- Cognis
- Sprint
- UPS

**They have realized significant results from implementing the TITAN PRINCIPLE®**

*The Key to Market Domination*

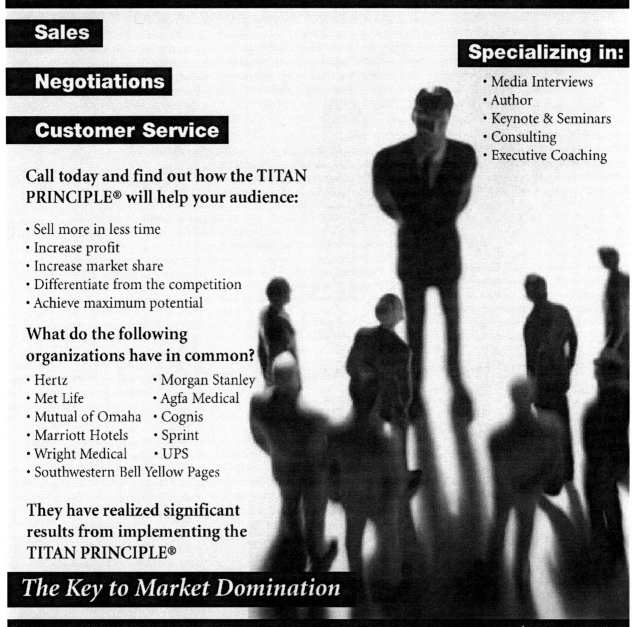

**Call now** and help your audience members become **TITANS IN THEIR INDUSTRY. LATEST BOOKS:**

*The Titan Principle®: The Number One Secret to Sales Success*
*The Complete Idiot's Guide to Great Customer Service*

*Ron Karr*

**Karr Associates, Inc.** Westwood, New Jersey
1-800-423-5277 or e-mail: ron@ronkarr.com
visit our website at: www.ronkarr.com

## TERRY L. ANNA CDMP - PROFESSIONAL BUSINESS & LIFE JOURNEY COACH

Loveland, CO USA
http://www.nccoaches.org/Coaches/Anna_T.htm

With 34 years of experience in corporate America, the high-tech industry and a sole proprietor business, I understand the unique challenges of working in a rapidly changing, fast paced and highly competitive environment. I especially like working with professionals and small business owners who want to excel in their profession while balancing work and family. My business coaching reflects my team experience, marketing and mentoring experience. My mission is to help teams excel at what they do by coaching managers and individual contributors to work from their strengths and personal values. Using my philosophy of great coaching equals great teams, I work with managers to have them use the coach approach style of management to develop high impact teams. As a Life Journey coach, I especially enjoy working with people who are in a career transition, seeking work/life balance, seeking fulfilling relationships or greater spirituality. People who desire a more fulfilling life and want to know and live their God-given heart values. My mission is to profoundly impact the lives of those I coach so they live the life they love.

Terry L. Anna CDMP
ROL Resources, LLC
Loveland, CO USA
*Contact Phone:* 970-613-8398
**Click to Contact from Web Site**

## DAVE GERBER — INNOVATIVE ORGANIZATIONAL SOLUTIONS

Washington, DC USA
www.SynergyDT.com

David Gerber is an expert and an specialist in the areas of training, education, facilitation, coaching, mediation and conflict. His passion and focus is helping businesses, schools and the government to increase employee professional and personal potential. In addition, he has been developing strategic and customized curriculum for more than 12 years, developed conflict and violence prevention organizations, participated in local and international conferences on conflict, violence and prevention, guest lectured at Ithaca College, Drexel and Temple Universities and more. As an education, training, facilitation and coaching specialist, Dave Gerber is the president of Synergy Development & Training, LLC.

Dave Gerber
Synergy Development & Training, LLC
Springfield, VA USA
*Contact Phone:* 703-752-7588
**Click to Contact from Web Site**

## DON BENTON — YELLOW PAGES EXPERT

Portland, WA USA
http://www.thebentongroup.net

Don Benton is a Yellow Pages Expert. He presents: Developing the consulting relationship with your sales force and potential clients. How to make cold calls and feel comfortable doing it. Self Management: Using personal assessments to improve your life. How to teach your people to become more alert and anticipate problems before they arise. A new approach to goal setting and achieving those goals. Proper marketing makes you number one in the customer's eye. How to get more from your newspaper and Yellow Pages advertising. Learn to apply Og Mandino's Success System ™ for a better life.

Don Benton
*CEO*
The Benton Group
Vancouver, WA USA
*Contact Phone:* 360-574-7369
**Click to Contact from Web Site**

## GIANT LEAP CONSULTING

Atlanta, GA USA
www.giantleapconsulting.com

Bill Treasurer is dedicated to helping people reach their professional potential by taking smart risks. A former member of the U.S. High Diving Team, he performed over 1500 dives from up to 100 feet. His new book, 'Right Risk' helps people take whatever High Dives they may be facing, and was endorsed by Dr. Stephen Cover & Ken Blanchard. Bill's risk-taking insights have been featured in over 100 major publications, including: The Washington Post, Investor's Business Daily, Chicago Tribune, NY Daily News, and Women's Day, among others.

Patti Danos
Chicago, IL USA
*Contact Phone:* 312-335-1464
**Click to Contact from Web Site**

## DR. PAMELA BRILL, PEAK PERFORMANCE CONSULTANT

Boston, MA USA
http://www.inthezoneinc.com

Dr. Pam Brill, licensed psychologist, is an expert at building performance, leadership and team membership for individuals and organizations. For over two decades, Dr. Brill has taken psychology to the wide worlds of sport, work, and life to enable thousands to improve bottom-line results and recapture purpose, values, and joy in the process. Dr. Brill has provided consulting, coaching, seminars and keynotes to a client roster that crosses industries including Fortune 500 members, athletes, and competitors on Capitol Hill.

Dr. Pamela Brill
*President*
In The Zone, Inc. Peak Performance Consulting
Bedford, NH USA
*Contact Phone:* 603.494.0977
**Click to Contact from Web Site**

**THERESA M. SZCZUREK, PH.D.,
LEADERSHIP DEVELOPMENT
CONSULTANT**
Boulder, CO USA
http://www.TMSworld.com

Theresa Szczurek helps organizations and individuals achieve the meaning, peak performance, financial gain, and professional results they want. Offering success strategies used in taking her company to over $40 million in six years, she is an award-winning business leader and enthusiastic media veteran specializing in sales/marketing, strategic planning, organization development, and life balance. Her newest book, Pursuit of Passionate Purpose (Wiley 2005), is an Amazon Bestseller which uplifts spirit in life and productivity at work.

Theresa M. Szczurek, Ph.D.
*CEO, Consultant, Speaker, and Author*
Technology and Management Solutions, llc
Boulder, CO
*Contact Phone:* 800-505-8674
**Click to Contact from Web Site**

**TIM WRIGHT - LEADERSHIP TRAINING
EXPERT**
Austin, TX USA
http://www.WrightResults.com/

A business improves when its people improve their performance, says Tim Wright, MBA and performance improvement expert. Tim's helps leaders, managers and personnel build Performance Improvement cultures that work. Tim's training programs, keynote speeches, books and articles relate performance improvement to business results. President/CEO of Wright Results, Inc., Tim has served more than 200 healthcare clients, as well as people and companies in nutrition, financial, staffing, administrative, telecommunication, and education. Tim authored Batteries Included: How to Charge and Recharge Your Creative Cells and KAPOW! 64 Blasts to Blow the Lid Off Your Job Performance. Tim draws upon his poly-experiences: teacher, manager, executive, entrepreneur and older brother. He has researched and articulated concepts and principles key to performance improvement at all levels and in most industries. While much of Tim's work since 2000 has been with healthcare organizations, he has demonstrated how performance ownership is relevant everywhere, to everyone. Tim conveys his performance improvement expertise through keynote presentations, creative workshops, team coaching, executive consulting, and performance assessment tools.

Tim Wright
Wright Results
Austin, TX USA
*Contact Phone:* (512)372-9933
**Click to Contact from Web Site**

**BARRY DEMP COACHING, LLC —
DETROIT LIFE COACH**
Detroit, MI USA
http://www.dempcoaching.com/

Barry Demp is a highly successful business and executive coach. As president of the International Coach Federation of Michigan, Barry spends much of his time helping individuals and organizations master the leadership, management and communication skills needed in today's world. He offers all who register a free assessment instrument of individual networking skills.

Barry Demp
Barry Demp Coaching, LLC
Troy, MI USA
*Contact Phone:* 248-740-3231
**Click to Contact from Web Site**

**STEPHEN FAIRLEY, M.A., RCC, --
TODAY'S LEADERSHIP COACHING**
Gilbert, AZ USA
www.todaysleadershipcoaching.com

At Today's Leadership Coaching, our mission is to provide the highest quality coaching, executive leadership development, management training and speaking services possible that deeply impact individuals, transform organizations, and produce significant and lasting results. We will do this by being a company that acts with integrity, honesty, confidentiality and provides services only when we are confident we can truly add considerable value to our clients.

Stephen Fairly, M.A., RCC
TLC
Gilbert, IL USA
*Contact Phone:* 480-659-9700
**Click to Contact from Web Site**

## PETE SILVER — MARKETING COMMUNICATIONS WRITER
Ft. Lauderdate, FL USA
http://www.petesilver.com

Pete Silver is a proven media resource, interviewed by CBS Evening News, USA Today, New York Times, and hundreds of radio talk shows. A former journalist and photojournalist (Time, National Geographic, Newsweek), Silver analyzes topics for businesses and non-profits. Topics: New opportunities for fundraisers and marketers after the Do Not Call phenomenon; The telecom meltdown; New ways politicians target voters; Grassroots tactics impacting public policy; New trends in personal networking for employment and small business marketing.

Pete Silver
The Marketing Communications Report
Ft. Lauderdate, FL
*Contact Main Phone:* 561-674-3344
**Click to Contact from Web Site**

## DR. ALAN ZIMMERMAN - AUTHOR, PROFESSIONAL SPEAKER, BUSINESS CONSULTANT
Minneapolis, MN USA
http://www.DrZimmerman.com

Attitude, motivation, and communication expert. Author of "Up Your Attitude." One of only nine people in the world to have a Ph.D., be a Certified Speaking Professional, and be inducted into the Speaker Hall of Fame. Has delivered more than 3000 keynote and educational sessions to organizations across the world in the last 20 years. Known for his ability to cut through all the theory and focus on the skills that really work on and off the job.

Dr. Alan Zimmerman, CSP, CPAE
*President*
Zimmerman Communi-Care Network, Inc.
Minneapolis, MN USA
*Contact Phone:* 952-492-3888
**Click to Contact from Web Site**

## TANGIBLEFUTURE, INC. — RICHARD G. CARO
San Francisco, CA USA
http://www.tangiblefuture.com

Richard Caro is CEO and founder of TangibleFuture, Inc., where he helps entrepreneurs and managers create and grow high technology businesses. Richard has particular expertise in turning science projects into profitable businesses; and in managing innovation. Recent work has been in fields such as the convergence of communications, computing and content; the intersection of nanotechnology and life sciences; and in the medical device and telecommunications industries.

Dr. Richard G. Caro
*Founder & CEO*
TangibleFuture, Inc
San Francisco, CA United States
*Contact Phone:* 415 344 0140
**Click to Contact from Web Site**

## MICHAEL LEVIN, HOW TO TAKE A PRODUCT TO MARKET
San Francisco, CA USA
www.Neuantiaging.com

Michael Levin shares his knowledge with desirous entrepreneurs about 'How To Take A Product To Market'. His personal experiences as an entrepreneur launching national cosmetic and anti-aging lines gives him tremendous insights about what to do and not to do. His '7 Keys To Entrepreneurial Success' help entrepreneurs put together their business and personal game plan.

Michael Levin
*President*
Neu Technologies, Inc.
Danville, CA USA
*Contact Phone:* 925-837-4324
**Click to Contact from Web Site**

## CERULEAN ASSOCIATES LLC
Williamsburg, VA USA
www.ceruleanllc.com

At Cerulean Associates LLC, we help executives who face challenges with IT, strategy, regulatory compliance and new product development. You get more innovation, faster time-to-market, cost-effective compliance and better results. You improve your bottom-line and grow your global competitiveness. To learn more, visit our website at http://www.ceruleanllc.com or contact us directly to discuss working together.

John Avellanet
*Managing Director*
Cerulean Associates LLC
Williamsburg, VA USA
*Contact Phone:* 757-645-2864
**Click to Contact from Web Site**

## BILL THOMPSON — TV, INC. — INFOMERCIAL PRODUCTION COMPANY
Los Angeles, CA USA
www.tvinc.com

Infomercial Production Expert — Bill Thompson from TV Inc., is a major force in the marketing of products, services, political agendas, cause marketing and image development. For over 30 years, we have provided our clients immediate access to the marketplace using strategies that are both effective and economical. We are available: On a fee basis; As your Joint Venture partner; As the Underwriter, Manager & Implementer. With offices in California, Florida and New York City we are available to serve your needs worldwide.

Bill Thompson
TV, Inc.
Largo, FL USA
*Contact Phone:* 800-326-5661
*Contact Main Phone:* 310-985-1229
*Cell:* 310.985.1229
**Click to Contact from Web Site**

*Best-selling Business Author · Professional Speaker · Master Business Coach*

# Stephen Fairley, M.A., RCC

## Are you looking for a proven expert on:

- **Marketing for professional service firms** (attorneys, accountants and consultants)
- **Strategies for small business growth**
- **Future business trends** for consulting, coaching, training and speaking
- **Psychological insights into small business owners** and family run businesses
- **Building and running a SOHO and challenges of being an Entrepreneur**

## Who is Stephen Fairley?

**Stephen Fairley is the best-selling author of 9 books and 5 audio programs, including:**

*Practice Made Perfect for Lawyers (2005)*     *Becoming A Rainmaker for Lawyers (2005)*
*Top 10 Marketing Mistakes Business Owners Make (2005)*     *How To Create An Info Product in 30 Days (2004)*
*7 Proven Strategies For Finding New Clients Now (2004)*     *Plan, Promote, and Profit From Your Business (2004)*
*Lead With Purpose, Live With Passion (2004)*     *Critical Communication Skills for Clients (2004)*
*Rich Integration: Build a Million Dollar Practice (2004)*     *6 Secrets of Highly Successful Entrepreneurs (2003)*
*6 Keys for Successful Leaders (2003)*     *Practice Made Perfect: Marketing Your Services (2002)*
*Getting Started in Personal and Executive Coaching (Wiley, 2003) – the #1 best-selling book in the field of professional coaching*

**In 2004, Stephen was named "America's Top Marketing Coach"** by CoachVille, the world's largest professional coaching association and given their top industry award. He has appeared in Entrepreneur, Inc, Fortune Small Business, Harvard Management Update, Business Advisor, the Chicago Tribune, Crain's Chicago Business, and on the front covers of AdvantEdge and Choice magazines. He has received international attention for his advanced coaching strategies for professional service companies. Stephen regularly speaks to state and local bar associations on "Becoming a Rainmaker," with over 20 seminars given last year alone.

Stephen is the **President of Today's Leadership Coaching**, one of Chicago's premier business coaching companies. He has coached, trained, consulting with and counseled thousands of professionals from hundreds of firms and small businesses. He has also worked with executives, managers and professionals from more than 22 Fortune 500 companies.

As the **CEO of the Business Building Center**, Stephen assists thousands of solo-preneurs, consultants, coaches, speakers and trainers to break the 6-figure revenue barrier using low-cost, high-impact marketing and sales strategies.

Contact Information:

**Stephen Fairley, M.A., RCC**
President of Today's Leadership Coaching
(www.TodaysLeadership.com)
CEO of the Business Building Center
(www.BusinessBuildingCenter.com)
For more info: www.SFairley.com www.YourPMP.com
www.RMGym.com
Email:       Stephen@TodaysLeadership.com
Work:        888-588-5891
Direct:       480-659-9700

## WAYNE MESSICK
New York, NY USA
http://www.FamilyBusinessStrategies.com

For the past 25 years Wayne Messick has immersed himself in the fears, concerns, and motivations of America's family business owner, and he shares his insights by his presentations and consultations with family businesses, and professionals who provide services to them.

Wayne Messick
Family Business Strategies
Bronxville, NY
*Contact Phone:* 212-501-4912
**Click to Contact from Web Site**

## CAROL M. OLMSTEAD -- FENG SHUI FOR REAL LIFE
Washington, DC USA
http://www.FengShuiForRealLife.com

Practicle, Real-World, Sensible FENG SHUI. Carol M. Olmstead, Certified Feng Shui Practitioner -- The Feng Shui Maven! National-recognized consultant, speaker, author. Specialties include: clutter-clearing, workplace, home-based businesses, children's rooms, bedrooms, real estate. Quoted in: Cosmopolitan, Washington Post, Washingtonian Magazine, Bethesda Magazine, Baltimore Magazine, The Hill, Prevention Books, The Scientist Magazine, Telecommuting for Dummies, Fox 5 Morning News; Resident Expert on Feng Shui for the ww.ByForAndAboutWomen.com Internet radio website. Author of the Feng Shui Quick Guide.

Carol M. Olmstead
*Certified Feng Shui Practitioner*
Feng Shui For Real Life
*Contact Phone:* 301-922-0320
**Click to Contact from Web Site**

## ANGI MA WONG
Palos Verdes Estates, CA USA
http://www.wind-water.com

Angi Ma Wong, the Feng Shui Lady, an award-winning entrepreneur and author, has been a guest on Oprah, CBS Sunday Morning, CNN Headline News, Learning & Discovery Channels She has been featured in TIME, N.Y. Times, L.A. Times, fastcompany.com, cnnfn.com, The Wall Street Journal, Seattle Times, USA Today, The Atlantic, Chicago Tribune, FOX, CBS Morning Show, ABC News, and Asian Week. Author of bestsellers on Feng Shui, she has been an award winner for TARGET: The U.S. Asian Market, A Practical Guide to Doing Business.

Betty Rombro
*Media Relations*
Angi Ma Wong
Palos Verdes Estates, CA
*Contact Phone:* 310-541-8818
*Cell:* 310-213-2898
**Click to Contact from Web Site**

## EVANA MAGGIORE -- FASHION FENG SHUI INTERNATIONAL
Boston, MA USA
http://www.fashionfengshui.com

Evana Maggiore, AICI, CIP, President of Fashion Feng Shui International, is an award winning professional image consultant, internationally-recognized feng shui practitioner and environmental healer. The world's foremost expert on the feng shui of personal appearance; she is a pioneer of the holistic lifestyle movement. Feng Shui is a three thousand year old body of knowledge that links environment with empowerment. Evana's ground-breaking concept of Fashion Feng Shui™ teaches that clothing is the body's most intimate environment, and therefore, as influential on the wearer's life as feng shui purports one's home and business decors to be.

Evana Maggiore
*President*
Fashion Feng Shui International
Woburn, MA United States
*Contact Phone:* 781 569-0599
*Cell:* 781 718 2003
**Click to Contact from Web Site**

## MARKETING INTELLIGENCE SERVICE LTD./DATAMONITOR NAPLES
Naples, NY USA
http://www.productscan.com

Frequently quoted in The Wall Street Journal and USA Today, we are recognized as the industry's authority on new products and innovations. Publishers of Product Alert and Productscan Online, we've been reporting on new foods, beverages, health & beauty aids, and household and pet products since 1968. We'll give you views, statistics and trend analysis to enhance your report.

Tom Vierhile
*Executive Editor, Productscan Online*
Marketing Intelligence Service Ltd./
Datamonitor Naples
Naples, NY
*Contact Phone:* 800-836-5710
*Contact Main Phone:* 585-374-6326
**Click to Contact from Web Site**

## GLORIA STARR
Charlotte, NC USA
http://www.gloriastarr.com

For more than twenty years, Gloria Starr has been an indispensable resource in helping people dramatically increase their visual presence, maximize their communication skills and improve their levels of performance. Gloria Starr is the leading provider of Impression Management and Etiquette seminars and training programs. Ms. Starr has worked in more than 30 countries worldwide. Her experience, insight and vision make her a highly sought after resource in today's global marketplace.

Gloria Starr
Charlotte, FL USA
*Contact Phone:* 704-596-9866
**Click to Contact from Web Site**

## ETIQUETTE INTERNATIONAL
New York, NY USA
http://www.etiquetteinternational.com

For greater effectiveness and impact at home and abroad, when you want 'eminently quotable' comments on what's hot and what's not in the global marketplace, get an expert perspective from an expert resource, Hilka Klinkenberg, founder and director of Etiquette International and author of At Ease... Professionally. Executives and professionals turn to Hilka to coach them individually, in groups, and at national conferences and conventions in the etiquette and protocol skills they need to be more effective and have greater impact.

Hilka Klinkenberg
*Managing Director*
Etiquette International
New York, NY
*Contact Phone:* 212-628-7209
**Click to Contact from Web Site**

## STEVE WILSON
Las Vegas, NV USA
http://www.barrymaher.com

Steve Wilson is an experienced, highly-regarded speaker and a trainer. He is an associate of Barry Maher, presenting workshops and keynotes on many of the same topics. His expertise includes communication, leadership, motivation, management, productivity, work/life balance, sales and sales management. Steve is based in Las Vegas, Nevada & San Diego, California.

Steve Wilson
Helendale, CA USA
*Contact Phone:* 760-962-9872
**Click to Contact from Web Site**

## BARRY MAHER - BARRY MAHER & ASSOCIATES
Las Vegas, NV USA
www.barrymaher.com

Barry Maher speaks and writes on communication, leadership, motivation, management, sales. Clients include ABC, AT&T, Blue Cross and Johnson and Johnson. He's been featured on the Today Show, NBC Nightly News, CNBC, in USA Today, the New York Times and the Wall Street Journal. Today's Librarian honored his book, Filling the Glass as '[One of] The Seven Essential Popular Business Books.' And for sales, Selling Power says: 'simply the best sales trainer in the business.'

Barry Maher
*President*
Barry Maher, Barry Maher & Associates
Helendale, CA
*Contact Phone:* 760-962-9872
**Click to Contact from Web Site**

## BARBARA PACHTER, COMMUNICATIONS EXPERT
Cherry Hill, NJ USA
www.pachter.com

Barbara Pachter is a versatile speaker, trainer and author of 7 books, including When The Little Things Count and The Jerk With The Cell Phone. She can provide insightful and entertaining commentary on a variety of business etiquette, assertiveness and conflict issues, including: 8 Business Meal Blunders That Can Hurt Your Career, The 6 Essential Steps To Positive Confrontation, Preventing The Passive Pattern for Women.

Barbara Pachter
*President*
Pachter and Associates
Cherry Hill, NJ
*Contact Phone:* 856-751-6141
Click to Contact from Web Site

## CAROL GRACE ANDERSON, M.A.
Nashville, TN USA
http://www.getfiredup.com

From 18 foot trailer to the star studded stage, Mega Motivator® Carol Grace Anderson knows first-hand how to turn struggle into strength and road-blocks into pathways. She inspires audiences to get fired up! Learn how to reach, risk and refuel your way to the top. Carol is a former psychology teacher, an author of five books, including Get Fired Up Without Burning Out!® and has contributed to the mega-bestseller Chicken Soup for the College Soul.

Carol Grace Anderson
Anderson Programs Inc.
Nashville, TN USA
*Contact Phone:* 800-758-2964
**Click to Contact from Web Site**

## ROBERT PAISOLA'S WESTERN CAPITAL CORPORATE TRAINING SERVICES
Salt Lake City, UT USA
http://www.mywesterncapital.com/media.html

Robert Paisola, International Author and Motivational Keynote Speaker who is known as The Collector's Collector has shared his unusual methods of debt collection with audiences throughout the world and would love nothing more than to sit down with your audience! His motto is People Pay Their Friends, Not Their Enemies. His friendly debt collection techniques have gained the attention of the nations largest companies, media and collection agencies. Robert is a speaker who trains groups on Sales Training, Time Share Sales, Real Estate Investments and The Business of The Seminar Industry. Robert Paisola shows his audience how to be the best of the best!

Robert Paisola
*CEO*
Robert Paisola's Western Capital Training Services
The Success Training Networks
Sandy, UT USA
*Contact Phone:* 801-671-7843
*Contact Main Phone:* 1-877-517-9555
*Cell:* 801-671-7843
**Click to Contact from Web Site**

## JEFFREY HANSLER, CSP
Los Angeles, CA USA
www.oxfordco.com

Jeffrey Hansler, CSP, author of Sell Little Red Hen! Sell! is an expert trainer, motivator and educator with over 100 articles published. A specialist in sales, negotiation, influence, and persuasion, he focuses on the dynamics and interaction in business while inspiring audiences with his unique ability to translate organizational objectives into entertaining, absorbable and memorable programs. He is eager to serve those who are excited about their future, and what they have learned.

Jeffrey Hansler, CSP
*Speaker, Trainer, Author, Consultant*
Oxford Company
Huntington Beach, CA USA
*Contact Phone:* 714-960-7461
*Contact Main Phone:* 714-960-7461
*Cell:* 714-225-7461
**Click to Contact from Web Site**

## INTERNATIONAL SOCIETY OF PROTOCOL & ETIQUETTE PROFESSIONALS
Washington, DC USA
www.ispep.org

International Society of Protocol & Etiquette Professionals is the professional association for protocol, etiquette and communications consultants and trainers serving business and community.

Cynthia W. Lett
ISPEP
Silver Spring, MD USA
*Contact Phone:* 301-946-5265
**Click to Contact from Web Site**

## THE LETT GROUP
Silver Spring, MD USA
http://www.lettgroup.com

Cynthia Lett is respected worldwide for her knowledge of American and international etiquette and protocol. Clients include executives and professionals at all levels. Quoted in Entrepreneur, Robb Report, Success, Washington Post, Washington Business Journal, CFO, CIO, TellerVision, Esquire and dozens more print and broadcast sources, Cynthia hosts a weekly one-hour talk show called It's Apropos! on the Success Talk Channel on Internet. The show covers a different etiquette topic each week and provides in-depth information about doing business in a particular country.

Cynthia Lett
*Director*
The Lett Group
ISPEP
Silver Spring, MD USA
*Contact Phone:* 301-946-8208
*Contact Main Phone:* 301-946-8208
**Click to Contact from Web Site**

## GESTECH, INC.
Nesconset, NY USA
http://www.gestech.biz

Profit from Ray McGraime's 20 years of experience in Non-Verbal Communication. Discover where the power seats are at meetings, in restaurants, and in social arenas. Develop strength and confidence through gestures. Recognize the signs of deception or doubt. Use subconscious channels of non-verbal communication to improve negotiations, insure managerial success, facilitate sales, and take the guess-work out of the interview process. Learn how to modify the behavioral architecture of offices, conference rooms, catering facilities, and other business environments to maximize success.

Raymond C. McGraime
*President*
Gestech, Inc.
Nesconset, NY
*Contact Phone:* 631-724-5127
**Click to Contact from Web Site**

## JOYCE KNUDSEN, PH.D., AICI, CIM, IMAGE & ASSESSMENTS
Nashville, TN USA
www.imagemaker1.com

Joyce M. Knudsen, Ph.D. is the first image professional to be awarded Certified Image Master status within the Image Industry, has been awarded both the IMMIE Award and The Award of Excellence for Education from AICI. Dr. Knudsen co-founded and funded the first international research study about the power of image in 2004 with Central Michigan University. (See www.imagemaker1.com under Image Study). Dr. Knudsen created the first complete home study program for image consultants in 1990 and has clients worldwide who she has certified. As an assessment counselor, she makes that difference between motivating short-term or changing an entire culture.

Dr. Joyce Knudsen
The ImageMaker, Inc.
Nashville, TN USA
*Contact Phone:* 1-888-845-5600
**Click to Contact from Web Site**

## LINDA TALLEY, CSP -- TEXAS LEADERSHIP COACH
Houston, TX USA
www.LindaTalley.com

Linda Talley is a speaker, author and executive coach from Houston, TX. She speaks more than 60 times a year to people who want to enhance their performance in business by giving them key ideas to act on in the area of relationship selling, marketing, staff motivation, conflict, customer care and leadership. She gives people specific steps to take to create the difference between someone who's excellent and someone who's mediocre in their business arena. Her thought-provoking presentations on verbal and non-verbal communication have captured the attention of business and association audiences across America for well over a decade. She is the author of Business Finesse: Dealing With Sticky Situations in the Workplace and The Daily Win and has both authored and been featured in numerous magazine articles. Linda takes pride in being known as a coach and speaker who gives people something to talk about! Her common sense, humor and enthusiasm gives you take home ideas to implement immediately in your business and personal life.

Linda Talley
Houston, TX USA
*Contact Phone:* 713-668-9659
**Click to Contact from Web Site**

**MARJORIE BRODY, CSP, CPAE**
**SPEAKER HALL OF FAME, PCC**
Jenkintown, PA USA
http://www.MarjorieBrody.com

Workplace/career expert, executive coach & professional speaker Marjorie Brody, CSP, CPAE Speaker Hall of Fame, CMC, PCC, has been contacted by CNBC, FOX-TV News, Fox News Channel, Oxygen Network, ABCNews.com, CNN.com, CBS.com, ABC 'World News Tonight' Webcast, FoxNews.com, The Wall Street Journal, USA Today, The Washington Post, Chicago Tribune, Christian Science Monitor, Fortune, BusinessWeek, People, and other national media outlets. She is author of more than 18 books, including 'Career MAGIC: A Woman's Guide to Reward & Recognition' & '21st Century Pocket Guide to Proper Business Protocol.' Marjorie has contributed business etiquette columns on the BusinessWeek Online web site.

Marjorie Brody, CSP, CPAE, PCC
*Founder & Fearless Leader*
Brody Communications Ltd.
Jenkintown, PA
*Contact Phone:* 215-376-5082
*Contact Main Phone:* 215-886-1688
**Click to Contact from Web Site**

## LOOK CONSULTING INTERNATIONAL
New York, NY USA

As a pioneer in the field of image consulting, Jennifer Maxwell Parkinson has helped clients — individuals and corporations — fine-tune their public personas. Because of the results she has delivered, she has been invited by many major corporations to speak to their employees about how they can use the same principles. As founding president of the Association of Image Consultants International (AICI), she helped put image consulting on the professional map.

Jennifer Maxwell Parkinson
*President*
Look Consulting International NY
*Contact Phone:* 914-629-9180
**Click to Contact from Web Site**

## 7FIGUREBUSINESS
Nacogdoches, TX USA
www.7figurebusiness.com/default.html

Through our proven 7 Step process, we teach entrepreneurs skills and systems required to develop their own 7FigureBusiness. We teach business development and simple planning and advancement tools for entrepreneurs. Our teachings include creating wealth and financial freedom and security in order to generously give at least 10% of our wealth, time and talents to worthwhile charitable causes, groups and organizations. Our products and services will benefit entrepreneurs who in turn will benefit their communities. 10% of profits from Enlightened Group, Inc. dba 7FigureBusiness™ will be donated to women business organizations.

Teresa Luquette
Nacogdoches, TX USA
*Contact Phone:* 936-559-0500
**Click to Contact from Web Site**

## STU NEEDEL
Baltimore, MD USA
http://www.StuartNeedel.com

Stu Needel is the Technology Teddy-Bear and President of Stu Needel Communications, LLC of Baltimore, MD., specializing in "Making the World a Small Village." As a speaker, trainer, consultant, coach, entertainer, and author, he assists organizations in effectively communicating in many ways and helps clients implement information technology and telecommunications, while keeping people the higher priority. He provides seminars and coaching in customer care, communications and presentation skills, product and conceptual knowledge, and problem-solving abilities. Stu works with people to discover how truly connected we all are, how much of a difference we each make, and how important honest and expressive communication is. As a trainer, Stu makes ordinary classes feel like major events, transforms boring topics into exciting journeys, and makes even the most complicated technology and concepts understandable, useful, powerful, and fun. Stu Needel is also a professional drummer, percussionist, and drum circle facilitator and conducts events in both corporate and community settings, to allow groups, large and small, to experience the many connections between human beings that rhythm and playing drums and music together provides.

Stu Needel
*President*
Stu Needel Communications, LLC
Baltimore, MD USA
*Contact Phone:* 866-688-8788
*Cell:* 443-845-1715
**Click to Contact from Web Site**

# Dr. Joyce Knudsen
## *The ImageMaker, Inc.*

## Do you want to make a difference in the work culture that lasts more than a day?

The ImageMaker, Inc. assists businesses with groundbreaking knowledge that's designed to maximize your company's investment in current employees, assist in the hiring process, and improve the bottom line. Ask her about the 5 Step Process that will change the culture of a business by making your employees want to come to work!

**Dr. Joyce Knudsen established The ImageMaker, Inc. 20 years ago to help people achieve their full potential.**

## Do you understand yourself?

Research shows that the most effective people are those who know and understand themselves. And Dr. Joyce Knudsen should know. In 2004, at the request of the Director of the image study, she was invited to be on a Task Force for Image and Self-esteem. Dr. Knudsen negotiated with her Alma Mater (Central Michigan University) and with the help of her staff, administered the Hartman Instruments to participants. This is how much she believed that self-esteem is attained through Image Enhancement.

Now, there is scientific proof!

Dr. Knudsen has spent countless hours of one-on-one time with clients. She received the highest honor in the Image Industry when she was awarded the first CIM (Certified Image Master) through AICI. In 2001, she received the IMMIE (Image Makers Merit of Industry Excellence) award and most recently she was recognized with the 2004 Award of Excellence for Education.

## Her work is crossing borders too.

The 2005 release *From Head to Soul, International* finds Dr. Joyce collaborating with Hong Kong Image Consultant Desmond Chan.

*The book offers useful and easy to comprehend guidelines for those who want to enhance their image. A must for those who are looking for a holistic approach to image enhancement.*

*-- Lesley Watt,*
*Training Consultant, Vocational Training Council, Hong Kong.*

### Call Today at 1-888-845-5600 or 615-309-9168

www.imagemaker1.com          www.testingforexcellence.com          www.body-styles.com

## DONNA FISHER, AUTHOR OF POWER NETWORKING
Houston, TX USA
http://www.donnafisher.com

Donna Fisher, CSP is a marketing consultant, author and expert on people and how people can best communicate and connect with one another to create opportunities. Her programs are ideal for people who want to increase their business by mastering their people skills and building strong alliances with others. She is the president of both Donna Fisher Presents, a provider of keynotes and trainings for corporate meetings, conferences and conventions, and HiHat Inc., a manufacturing and retail business for drums and percussion instruments.

Donna Fisher, CSP
Houston, TX
*Contact Phone:* 800-934-9675
*Contact Main Phone:* 713-789-2484
**Click to Contact from Web Site**

## DAVID NOUR -- RELATIONSHIP ECONOMICS EXPERT
Atlanta, GA USA
www.relationshipeconomics.NET

David Nour is considered by many as one of the foremost thought leaders on the quantifiable value of relationships. A native of Iran, David came to the U.S. with limited family ties and no fluency in English! Fast forward twenty five years and he has become an author, a senior management advisor, and a featured keynote speaker sharing his knowledge and experience as a leading change agent and visionary for RelationshipEconomics™ - the art & science of relationships.

David Nour
*Managing Partner*
The Nour Group, Inc.
Atlanta, GA USA
*Contact Phone:* 404-419-2115
*Cell:* 404-683-0140
**Click to Contact from Web Site**

## HARMONY TENNEY, SALES PERFORMANCE CONSULTANT
Richmond, VA USA
www.businessempowerment.com

International Business Empowerment Consultants, Inc. www.BusinessEmpowerment.com What if your organization could have sales certainty, rather than 'guess your best' ?? What if your marketing was actually a profitable investment, rather than 'hope we get some calls' ?? IBEC, Inc brings performance to the equation, catalyzing desired outcomes and benchmarks. It brings concrete experience to each team member for maximum value contribution, and accountability for continued achievement. Harmony Tenney IBEC, Inc.

Harmony Tenney
International Business Empowerment
Consultants, Inc.
Staunton, VA USA
*Contact Phone:* 540-255-5686
**Click to Contact from Web Site**

# Linda Talley, CSP
## Texas Leadership Coach

Linda Talley is a speaker, author and executive coach from Houston, Texas. She speaks more than 60 times a year to people who want to enhance their performance in business by giving them key ideas to act on in the area of relationship selling, marketing, staff motivation, conflict, customer care and leadership.

She gives people specific steps to take to create the difference between someone who is excellent and someone who is mediocre in their business arena. Her thought-provoking presentations on verbal and non-verbal communication have captured the attention of business and association audiences across America for well over a decade.

She is the author of "Business Finesse: Dealing With Sticky Situations in the Workplace" and "The Daily Win" and has both authored and been featured in numerous magazine articles. Linda takes pride in being known as a coach and speaker who gives people something to talk about! Her common sense, humor and enthusiasm gives you "take-home" ideas to implement immediately in your business and personal life.

*"A good coach decorates a person's soul."*

**Linda Talley**
P.O. Box 271488
Houston, Texas 77277
Toll Free: 800.856.6607
Houston Area: 713.668.9659
Fax : 713.668.9610
Email : linda@lindatalley.com
**www.lindatalley.com**

## RHONDA L. SHER — TWO MINUTE NETWORKER
Thousand Oaks, CA USA
http://www.2minutenetworker.com

Rhonda Sher is a recognized expert on how to create a powerful 30 second marketing message, identify your target market, the secrets to developing strategic alliances and networking at tradeshows to get solid leads and a high return on your investment. Rhonda's programs are ideal for corporate meetings, conferences, conventions as well as chambers of commerce, and associations. Rhonda provides innovative ideas for taking any business to the next level using the power of networking.

Rhonda L. Sher
Thousand Oaks, CA USA
*Contact Phone:* 805-241-1800
**Click to Contact from Web Site**

## BROADCAST INTERVIEW SOURCE, INC. — PUBLISHER OF THE YEARBOOK OF EXPERTS
Washington, DC USA
www.ExpertClick.com

Broadcast Interview Source, Inc., was started in 1984 by Mitchell P. Davis, a recent Georgetown University graduate. His e-mail is Davis@Yearbook.com. The Yearbook has been reviewed in The Sunday New York Times Magazine.

Mitchell P. Davis
*Editor*
Broadcast Interview Source, Inc.
Washington, DC
*Contact Phone:* 202-333-4904
*Contact Main Phone:* 202-333-5000
**Click to Contact from Web Site**

## JIM MEISENHEIMER — CREATOR OF NO-BRAINER SELLING SKILLS
Tampa, FL USA
www.Meisenheimer.com

Jim Meisenheimer shows sales managers and their salespeople how to increase sales, earn more money, have more fun, and how to do it all in less time. Jim's a former U.S. Army Officer, who served in Germany and Vietnam, and a former Vice President of Sales and Marketing for Baxter Healthcare. Jim's focus is on practical ideas that get immediate results. The centerpeice for his work is No-Brainer Selling Skills.

Jim Meisenheimer
Lakewood Ranch, FL USA
*Contact Phone:* 800-266-1268
**Click to Contact from Web Site**

## STEVE WATERHOUSE
Jacksonville, FL USA
http://www.waterhousegroup.com

Steve speaks from experience. He increased sales by 300% in under 24 months and set sales records throughout his career. He designed parts of the Patriot Missile. He built a successful chain of community newspapers and authored, 'The Team Selling Solution' (McGraw-Hill, 2004) and 'Ending The Blame Game'. He has trained tens of thousands of professionals world-wide. His clients include AT&T, Lucent, United Airlines, Monsanto, Smith & Wesson, and Countrywide Home Loan. He has been interviewed, published and quoted by business, sales and technology publications and media.

Gina Shanahan
*Director of Marketing*
Waterhouse Group
Orange Park, FL USA
*Contact Phone:* 904-269-2299
**Click to Contact from Web Site**

## LOREN EKROTH - CONVERSATION & COMMUNICATIONS EXPERT
Las Vegas, NV USA
http://www.conversation-matters.com/codetest/index.php

Your source for conversation skills, insights, coaching, and seminars. Browse our rich resources to help you to better your talk. Inside you'll find free articles, tips, quotes, booklets, kits, and Q&A about speaking

Loren Ekroth
Conversation-Matters.com
Las Vegas, NV USA
*Contact Phone:* 702-214-6782
**Click to Contact from Web Site**

## OLIVIA FOX CABANE - COMMUNICATIONS EXPERT & NETWORKING EXPERT
New York, NY USA
http://www.spitfireteam.com

Author of 'The Pocket Guide To Becoming a Superstar In Your Field', Olivia has lectured on networking at Harvard, Yale, MIT and the United Nations on the topics of networking, business development, and communication skills. She is often interviewed as the current networking expert on both television (such as Bloomberg or KTLA) and radio. Olivia has lived and worked in 7 countries and is fluent in 4 languages; her education includes three Master's degrees from the universities of Paris and Munich.

Olivia Fox Cabane
Spitfire Communications
New York, NY USA
*Contact Phone:* 212-561-9146
*Cell:* 917 723 4181
**Click to Contact from Web Site**

# Business Blunders Can Cost You a Client, a Colleague or a Career

*The nation's news media turns to Marjorie Brody, CSP,
CPAE Speaker Hall of Fame, PCC, for her expertise on*
● *Corporate Etiquette* ● *Business Blunders* ● *Professional Presence*
● *Presentation Skills* ● *Career Enhancement*

# Marjorie Brody
a professional helping develop professionals

*Marjorie has been featured on:*

CNBC, Fox-TV News,
Fox News Channel,
ABC "World News
Tonight" webcast,
Oxygen Network,
ABCNews.com, CBS.com, CNN.com.

Also featured in the
Wall Street Journal,
Washington Post,
Chicago
Tribune,
Christian
Science Monitor,
USA Today,
Fortune, BusinessWeek,
Glamour, People

**M**arjorie Brody, your "go-to" source for information on workplace/career trends and issues, is an internationally recognized expert on professional presence, corporate etiquette, career enhancement, and presentation skills. She knows business manners affect the bottom line, and that it's all about connecting — with customers and coworkers.

● Etiquette & Workplace Expert
● Professional Speaker
● Business Trainer
● Executive Coach
● Entrepreneur
● Author

Marjorie Brody, CSP, CPAE, PCC
CEO, BRODY
815 Greenwood Avenue, Suite 8
Jenkintown, Pennsylvania 19046

www.MarjorieBrody.com

(800)726-7936 toll-free
(215)886-1688 phone
(215)886-1699 fax
*Contact Miryam S. Roddy for
booking/interview details:*
mroddy@brodycommunications.com

**COMMUNICARD**
Austin, TX USA
http://www.thecommunicard.com

CommuniCard™ pocket-guides and card sets use illustrated drawings for English and Spanish speakers to communicate contractor and housecleaning tasks without speaking. The fold-out guides are easy to use, and fit in a front or back pocket. Card sets for housecleaning are also available to leave behind instructions when your house cleaner visits. CommuniCard™ products are available for worker tasks such as lawn care, painting, demolition, drywall, irrigation and housecleaning service. Illustrations are included for supplies, tasks, pay per hour, work experience and a variety of general instructions. CommuniCard™ LLC can also create customized products for your business. The English and Spanish is included on the drawing for those who wish to speak. Both employers and workers who use CommuniCard™ can be confident that their instructions are understood to get the job done right the first time. CommuniCard™, improves efficiency and reduces misunderstandings by removing language as a barrier. No need to speak. The pictures do the talking. ®

Sylvia Acevedo
Austin, TX USA
*Contact Phone:* 512-560-6385
**Click to Contact from Web Site**

**ALDONNA R. AMBLER, CMC, CSP**
Hammonton, NJ USA
http://www.TheGrowthStrategist.com

The Growth Strategist™, Aldonna R. Ambler, CMC, CSP helps professional service firms, technology/telecommunication companies, and construction-related/distribution companies reach their goal of Achieving Accelerated Growth With Sustained Profitability® through a combination of speaking, consulting, executive coaching, authorship, and growth financing. Her clients seek a minimum of 50% growth/year, with the majority achieving between 100-200%. Her clients include 16 of the major telecommunication corporations including Nortel, AT&T, and SBC, international service firms like H&R Block, and award winning distributorships like CLS and Granite City Electric Supply. She has executed an ESOP, grown multiple international businesses, won just about every major award an entrepreneur can win, provided expert testimony on economic growth at over 30 legislative hearings, conferred with four different Presidents in the Oval Office, and published two books and over 100 articles. Aldonna was named the national (USA) 'Woman Business Owner of the Year' for 2000. Aldonna Ambler is the host of a weekly Internet radio show on VoiceAmerica Business (www.business.voiceamerica.com) that focuses on Aldonna's list of Growth Strategies.

Aldonna R. Ambler, CMC, CSP
*President/CEO*
AMBLER Growth Strategy Consultants, Inc.
Hammonton, NJ USA
*Contact Phone:* 609-567-9669
*Contact Main Phone:* 888-253-6662
**Click to Contact from Web Site**

**JON PETZ - OHIO MOTIVATIONAL SPEAKER**
Powell, OH USA
www.jonpetz.com

Jon Petz is one of the top motivational speakers and corporate entertainers (corporate magician) in America. His talents stem from his high energy and engaging personality mixed with his unique ability to creatively combine a business or inspirational message with an entertainment twist. This energy and new approach is refreshing and exciting and gets people actively engaged in the presentation rather than simply sitting back and watching. "This leads to retention of the message and an increased rate of sustained initiative on part of your organization" Jon states.

Jon Petz
Magical Experiences LLC
Powell, OH USA
*Contact Phone:* 877-457-3981
**Click to Contact from Web Site**

**DR. JOACHIM DE POSADA —
BILINGUAL MOTIVATIONAL SPEAKER (ENGLISH/SPANISH)**
Miami, FL USA
www.jdeposada.com

Success depends on your attitude and the way you think. With over 30 years as a speaker, trainer, consultant and author, traveling to over 30 countries in the world, working with Olympic and NBA teams, and sharing the platform with celebrities from Margaret Thatcher to Dick Cheney, Dr. Posada can discuss a variety of topics such as management, change, leadership, sales, and customer service. In English or Spanish, his unique perspective on Latin America contributes to a great interview.

Dr. Joachim de Posada
*Educator*
Miami, FL
*Contact Phone:* 305-220-8398
**Click to Contact from Web Site**

## Dealing With Communications Issues?

*Discover a path to true humanity in the 21st Century from a master of communication: whether in person, in writing or on line.*

Stu Needel is the "Technology Teddy Bear" and president of Stu Needel Communications, LLC, of Baltimore, Md., whose motto is "Making The World A Small Village."

As a speaker, trainer, consultant, coach, entertainer and author, Stu Needel guides organizations to effectively communicate and pamper customers in many ways. He helps clients implement information technology and telecommunications, while always keeping people as the highest priority.

Stu Needel is also a professional drummer, percussionist and drum circle facilitator, sharing one of his greatest joys in life, rhythm and music. He conducts corporate and community events to allow groups to experience the many connections between human beings that are possible through shared rhythm and music together.

**Stuart P. "Stu" Needel**
President,
Stu Needel Communications, LLC
Baltimore, Maryland
Toll-free: 866-688-8788
Cell: 443-845-1715
www.stuartneedel.com

MEMBER NSA
NATIONAL SPEAKERS ASSOCIATION
AATH
PCFG
PERCUSSIVE ARTS SOCIETY

## ARNOLD SANOW -- THE BUSINESS SOURCE
Vienna, VA USA
www.arnoldsanow.com

Arnold Sanow, MBA, CSP (Certified Speaking Professional) is the co-author of the book, Get Along with Anyone, Anytime, Anywhere...8 keys to creating enduring connections with customers, co-workers - even kids. His keynotes and seminars focus on good interpersonal skills which are the foundation for working with customers and co-workers to create a positive, productive and profitable organization.

Arnold Sanow, MBA, CSP
*Speaker, Seminar Leader, Facilitator*
The Business Source
Vienna, VA
*Contact Phone:* 703-255-3133
*Cell:* 703-869-1881
**Click to Contact from Web Site**

## SHERI JEAVONS - POWER PRESENTATIONS, INC.
Broadview Heights, OH USA
http://www.power-presentations.com/

Sheri Jeavons, author of Tips for your Talk® and a highly regarded consultant specializing in presentation, communication skills and professional presence, has trained over 10,000 professionals from America's best known corporations. A three time recipient of the Case Western Reserve School of Management Weatherhead 100 Award, Sheri was also selected as one of the Top Ten Women Business Owners by the National Association of Women Business Owners and received the Working Woman Magazine Entrepreneurial Excellence Award.

Gayle Reese
Power Presentations, Inc.
Broadview Heights, OH USA
*Contact Phone:* 440-526-4400
**Click to Contact from Web Site**

## LAUREN THIBODEAU, PH.D. / PRINCETON CONSULTING & THERAPY, LLC
New York, NY USA
http://www.DrLauren.com

Dr. Lauren Thibodeau brings compassion, integrity, insight and the inquiring, yet skeptical mind of an academic trained in the scientific method to her work as an author, psychic medium, workshop leader, speaker, and metaphysical teacher. She holds a Ph.D. in Counseling, and masters degrees in Counseling and Business. An acclaimed practitioner, she has worked with individuals, groups and organizations for more than 15 years. Author of Natural-Born Intuition: How to Awaken & Develop Your Inner Wisdom and a member of the National Speakers Association, she speaks internationally. Regularly in the media, Dr. Lauren is a nationally certified counselor with experience in grief, bereavement and trauma and a former hospice volunteer.

Lauren Thibodeau, Ph.D., NCC, MBA
Princeton Consulting & Therapy, LLC
Princeton, NJ United State
*Contact Phone:* 609-430-9300
*Cell:* 609-430-9301
**Click to Contact from Web Site**

# *Empowering organizations to harvest market potential*

Sales and marketing are the lifeblood of any successful organization. International Business Empowerment Consultants, Inc., is a consulting organization dedicated to identifying and implementing improvement strategies for your business's customer acquisition and retention endeavors, increasing cash flow to your business both immediately and in the long term.

## IBEC, Inc., specializes in:

■ **improving** the performance of sales persons, their managers and the internal structures and systems in which they operate;

■ **fueling** individual and enterprise leadership for maximum value contribution of the organization to all of its dependents;

■ **managing** the systematic change and conflict inherent in benchmarking, continuing performance improvement and ongoing accountability

Drawing from more than 25 years of experience in sales, with an emphasis in the wireless sales and radio marketing industries, as well as having consulted with businesses of all sizes and industries, IBEC, Inc., provides your business with the foundation, resources and abilities to "reap the lion's share" in your market.

**Harmony Tenney**
**International Business Empowerment**
**Consultants, Inc.**
511 Robin Street
Staunton, Virginia 24401

Phone: (540) 255-5686
Fax:    (540) 886-2433

**Harmony**
**@BusinessEmpowerment.com**

## PATRICIA FRIPP
San Francisco, CA USA
www.fripp.com

Patricia Fripp simplifies and demystifies the process of designing a presentation for anyone who needs to speak in public. Executives, sales teams and even high-fee professionals undergo nothing less than a transformation in their presentations from both a content and delivery standpoint. Kiplinger's Personal Finance says, 'Fripp's Speaking Skills seminar is the 6th best way to invest $1,000 in you.' Meetings and Conventions magazine calls Patricia, 'One of the country's 10 most electrifying speakers.' Author of Get What You Want!, Make It, So You Don't Have to Fake It! And co-author of Speaking Secrets of the Masters and Insights into Excellence. Fripp is an award-winning speaker, executive speech coach, and sales presentation skills trainer.

Patricia Fripp, CSP, CPAE
*President*
Executive Speech Coach.com
San Francisco, CA USA
*Contact Phone:* (415)753-6556
**Click to Contact from Web Site**

## JONI WILSON, VOICE EXPERT
San Diego, CA USA
www.joniwilsonvoice.com

Joni Wilson is an internationally known voice expert, best selling author, speaker/trainer. Her books and CD's are used by business and entertainment professionals because, singing or speaking, her amazing 3-Dimensional Voice Technique brings instant results. She is a media favorite because she has the expertise of a Master Voice Trainer and the wit of a seasoned entertainer. From bedroom to boardroom, your voice alone can keep you from that special job or date. . . call Joni!

Joni Wilson
San Diego, CA USA
*Contact Phone:* 619-229-0726
**Click to Contact from Web Site**

## PATTI WOOD — COMMUNICATION DYNAMICS
Decatur, GA USA
http://www.pattiwood.net

Patti Wood, MA, CSP — the Body Language Lady — a dynamic speaker and trainer. She is an expert on Body Language, Public Speaking, Customer Service and Dealing with Difficult People, delivers keynote speeches, workshops and convention seminars, nationally recognized college teacher, books on body language, public speaking, first impressions and other topics, and private coaching.

Patti Wood
*President*
Communication Dynamics
Decatur, GA
*Contact Phone:* 404-371-8228
**Click to Contact from Web Site**

VOICE POWER
Using Your Voice to
Captivate, Persuade,
and Command Attention

## RENEE GRANT-WILLIAMS -- COMMUNICATION SKILL TRAINING EXPERT
Nashville, TN USA
http://www.morevoicepower.com

Renee Grant-Williams is a communication skill training expert, vocal coach, and author of Voice Power, (AMACOM, NY). Commentary and hot tips: Public speaking, voice mail, analysis of politicians voices, customer service and sales. Created a public speaking course for the Barnes & Noble Online University. Coached Faith Hill, Tim McGraw, Dixie Chicks, Huey Lewis, Linda Ronstadt, Quoted in Cosmopolitan, BusinessWeek, Southern Living, TV Guide, UP/AP, Chicago Tribune, Boston Globe. Appearances on ABC, CBS, NBC, FOX, PBS, BRAVO, BLOOMBERG, MTV, GAC, BBC, NPR.

Elaine Collins
*Office Manager*
ProVoice
*Contact Phone:* 615-259-4900
**Click to Contact from Web Site**

## JODI WALKER, CERTIFIED PROFESSIONAL SPEAKER

Los Angeles, CA USA
www.jodiwalker.com

Jodi was once described by an L.A. Times reporter as having seemingly endless energy. As a Certified Speaking Professional, author and trainer Jodi works with people who want to tap into their true potential and with companies who want to grow the potential of their organization by focusing on their people. Her signature programs STATUS GO and Entrepreneurial Thinking for Leaders have captured the hearts and minds of audiences all over the country.

Jodi Walker
Success Alliances
Valencia, CA USA
*Contact Phone:* 661-297-6821
**Click to Contact from Web Site**

## STREETSPEAK®, INC.

New York, NY USA
www.streetspeak.net

A former award-winning journalist, Bill Blase is street smart and market savvy. He offers more than memorable sound-bites — he can also provide insight into the strategic business importance of strong media and executive presentation skills for branding a product, positioning a corporation, or closing a deal on the 9th tee at Pinehurst. Bill can also speak to the benefits of establishing lasting relationships with print, broadcast and even Internet media.

William T. Blase
*President*
StreetSpeak®, Inc.
New York, NY
*Contact Phone:* 212-221-1079
**Click to Contact from Web Site**

## LARRY TRACY - TRACY PRESENTATION SKILLS

Alexandria, VA USA
www.Tracy-presentation.com

President Ronald Reagan described Larry Tracy as 'an extraordinarily effective speaker' due to his hundreds of successful presentations before demanding audiences. He has converted this real world experience into a highly-acclaimed communications coaching program, in either English or Spanish, providing time-pressed executives a short cut system to deliver persuasive presentations. His Web page is in the number one position on the Google, MSN and Yahoo! search engines under Presentation skills training for executives.

Larry Tracy
Tracy Presentation Skills
Alexandria, VA
*Contact Phone:* 703-360-3222
**Click to Contact from Web Site**

## JAY PLATT — INSPIRING PEOPLE TO BE UNSTOPPABLE...NO MATTER WHAT!

Jacksonville, NC USA
http://www.JayPlatt.com

He is a former U. S. Marine Corps Drill Instructor, a cancer survivor, endurance athlete, and adventurer. He knows how to succeed, despite the obstacles... No Matter What! Now, he's determined to help others do the same. Jay is the author of A Time to Walk: Life Lessons Learned on the Appalachian Trail and a co-author of Transformational Leadership and Success is a Journey. As a dynamic speaker, author, and coach, he shares his 'No Matter What' philosophy of living with Clarity, Courage and Commitment, and inspires his clients to reach for higher levels of performance and maximize their potential.

Jay Platt
Jacksonville, NC USA
*Contact Phone:* 910-346-1817
**Click to Contact from Web Site**

## MS. BERT FIFE - CONSULTANT, SPEAKER, COACH

Baton Rouge, LA USA
http://www.bertfife.com

REFINED- characterized by selective taste based upon broad knowledge, self-development, and education. Tools to make you and your company own the marketplace. Lead the Refined Life while managing the Refined Staff in the Refined Company. Selected the states Outstanding Business Owner, Bert Fife can help you be recognized for refined people, profits and productivity. Recent presentation topics; Post Katrina workplace issues, What to do if you are laid off, If you can't sell it at the top, how can you sell it in the streets? How your thoughts create your success. Moving From zero to a multimillion dollar company, start your business now. elerated Success-out of the box solutions to move you into the winner's circle. Life in the Fast Lane.

Bert Fife
The Refined Life
Baton Rouge, LA USA
*Contact Phone:* 225-281-3008
**Click to Contact from Web Site**

# FRIPP

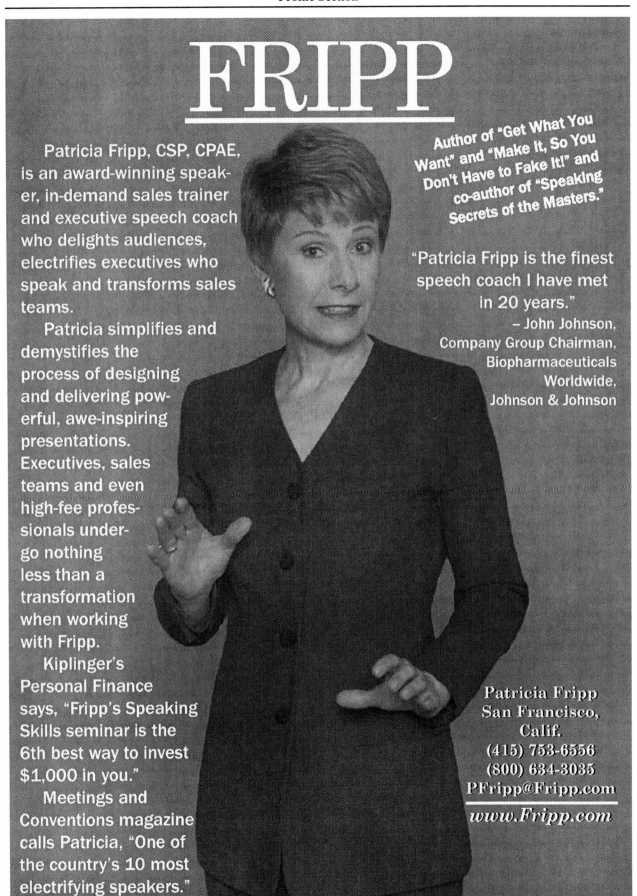

Patricia Fripp, CSP, CPAE, is an award-winning speaker, in-demand sales trainer and executive speech coach who delights audiences, electrifies executives who speak and transforms sales teams.

Patricia simplifies and demystifies the process of designing and delivering powerful, awe-inspiring presentations. Executives, sales teams and even high-fee professionals undergo nothing less than a transformation when working with Fripp.

Kiplinger's Personal Finance says, "Fripp's Speaking Skills seminar is the 6th best way to invest $1,000 in you."

Meetings and Conventions magazine calls Patricia, "One of the country's 10 most electrifying speakers."

Author of "Get What You Want" and "Make It, So You Don't Have to Fake It!" and co-author of "Speaking Secrets of the Masters."

"Patricia Fripp is the finest speech coach I have met in 20 years."
– John Johnson, Company Group Chairman, Biopharmaceuticals Worldwide, Johnson & Johnson

Patricia Fripp
San Francisco, Calif.
(415) 753-6556
(800) 634-3035
PFripp@Fripp.com

*www.Fripp.com*

## ELLEN A. KAYE AND PERFECT PRESENTATION
Scottsdale, AZ USA
http://www.ellenkaye.com

Ellen A. Kaye coaches executives in the world's most distinguished corporations in presentation and communication skills, leadership, image, and etiquette. Her clients include Boeing, Price Waterhouse, McGraw-Hill, and Bank of America. Ellen shares her knowledge on how to effectively communicate, write and deliver professional presentations, entertain for business. Ellen will bring her enthusiasm, expertise and her secrets to your readers, listeners, and viewers.

Ellen A. Kaye
Perfect Presentation
Scottsdale, AZ USA
*Contact Phone:* 480-391-9888
**Click to Contact from Web Site**

## CHERYL PERLITZ - LIFE CHANGE AND SURVIVAL EXPERT
Chicago, IL USA
http://www.soarwithme.com

Cheryl is known as the author of the popular book "Soaring through Setbacks". She is a dynamic speaker, and is a sought after talk show guest. She is a fearless mountain climber, adventurer and story teller with an insatiable spirit of adventure. Her compelling stories and 'survival tips' educate, inspire and encourage listeners and readers to push their boundaries and transform their personal and business challenges into opportunities for adventure and positive change.

Cheryl Perlitz
Soar With Me
Glenview, IL USA
*Contact Phone:* 847-609-8032
*Cell:* 847-609-8032
**Click to Contact from Web Site**

## MERYL RUNION, CSP-- COMMUNICATION, MANAGEMENT LEADERSHIP SPEAKER
Colorado Springs, CO USA
http://www.SpeakStrong.com

Meryl Runion, CSP, is the expert on Risky Conversations, Dangerous Dialogue and Courageous Confrontation. Her PowerPhrases books sold 200,000 copies worldwide. Whether you're a manager wanting to hold employees accountable, you're wondering how to tell the boss her idea is flawed, or your spouse that you want to stay home for the holidays, Runion has the words you need. Her newsletter at www.speakstrong.com offers a plethora of article ideas.

Meryl Runion, CSP
*CEO*
Speak Strong, Inc.
Cascade, CO USA
*Contact Phone:* 719-684-2633
**Click to Contact from Web Site**

## AVIVA DIAMOND — BLUE STREAK/A COMMUNICATIONS COMPANY
Los Angeles, CA USA

Aviva Diamond is President of Blue Streak/A Communications Company, a Los Angeles-based executive media and speaker training firm. She is an Emmy-winning former ABC Network correspondent with more than 20 years of experience in the media, business and academics. Clients have included top executives from: Microsoft, Symantec, Universal Studios, Expedia, Kaiser Permanente and Paramount Parks. Ms. Diamond's reports appeared on Good Morning America, World News Tonight and Nightline, and she has been quoted by the Wall St. Journal, Associated Press, Los Angeles Times, Investor's Business Daily and Business 2.0.

Aviva Diamond
Blue Streak, Inc
Los Angeles, CA USA
*Contact Phone:* 323-655-2583
**Click to Contact from Web Site**

## DIANE DIRESTA — TRAINING COACH
New York, NY USA
http://diresta.com

As a top workplace communications training coach and author of Knockout Presentations and Conversations on Success, Diane DiResta shows clients how to communicate with greater impact and project a more powerful presence. Whether coaching sports celebrities to shine in the media, developing leaders to excel at executive presentations, or helping women in Tanzania to step into their power, Diane teaches spoken word strategies to manifest results.

Diane DiResta
*President*
DiResta Communications, Inc.
New York, NY USA
*Contact Phone:* 212 481-8484
**Click to Contact from Web Site**

## THE PROCRASTINATOR'S HANDBOOK — RITA EMMETT
Des Plaines, IL USA
http://www.ritaemmett.com

In this age of self-improvement, most people know what they need to do to succeed. If they're not doing it, then they are procrastinating. Rita Emmett, media personality and author of the international bestseller, The Procrastinator's Handbook, uses humor and common sense to help people conquer procrastination and clutter. Whether an expert quote, sound bite or a popular guest, Rita's expertise appears in media throughout the world, including USA Today, Financial Times and The Today Show.

Rita Emmett
*Media personality, author, speaker*
Emmett Enterprises, Inc.
Des Plaines, IL
*Contact Phone:* 847-699-9950
**Click to Contact from Web Site**

## A PLACE FOR EVERYTHING
Maplewood, NJ USA
http://www.organizeit.com

Drowning in a blizzard of paper? File things but can't find them? No time for the things you really want in life? Want to simplify your life but don't know how? Unique, simple and practical ideas to help cope with these common problems. Member of the National Association of Professional Organizers, author and speaker on so much stuff — so little time, the rule of 80/20, time management in a nutshell and seeking serenity in today's troubled times.

Elaine Bloom
*President*
A Place For Everything
Maplewood, NJ
*Contact Phone:* 973-378-9002
**Click to Contact from Web Site**

*Organize your office, your home, your life!*

**Organizing FOR DUMMIES**

Eileen Roth with Elizabeth Miles

*A Reference for the Rest of Us!*

## EVERYTHING IN ITS PLACE ®
Scottsdale, AZ USA
http://www.everythinginitsplace.net

As author of Organizing For Dummies, Eileen Roth (Today Show, Oprah) shows people how to put everything in its P-L-A-C-E. Her simple organizing secrets are easy to remember and implement right away. Best of all, maintenance is minutes a day to stay that way! Eileen's organizing principles will reduce your stress, and save you time and money.

Eileen Roth
*Prof. Organizer/Speaker/Author*
Everything in its Place ®
Scottsdale, AZ USA
*Contact Phone:* 480-551-3445
*Contact Main Phone:* 480-551-3445
**Click to Contact from Web Site**

## DOROTHY BREININGER - CENTER FOR ORGANIZATION AND GOAL PLANNING

Los Angeles, CA USA
http://www.centerfororganization.com

ORGANIZING HEALTH, SAFETY, AND SUCCESS EXPERT — Dorothy Breininger Nationally recognized organizing expert Dorothy Breininger is a specialist on the subjects of home and office organization, clutter prevention, pack rat safety hazards, hoarding, time management, medical dangers of disorganization for seniors and more. The award winning author's latest book, The Senior Organizer: Personal, Medical, Legal, Financial Organizing for a better quality of life was released in 2006. Dorothy now appears on the Dr. Phil Show as an organizing expert and life coach. She is a professional speaker and a co-author of several books including the upcoming Chicken Soup for the Soul: Life Lessons and Organizing Tips for Busy Moms. She will tailor her high-energy and engaging presentation to fit the needs and interests of your audience -from powerful business professionals who want to succeed to ordinary people who just want their lives to be free of chaos and clutter. The current winner of the Most Innovative Organizer Award, Dorothy is a favorite on regional and national television, as well as talk radio. She was recently featured as an organizing expert on the Today Show and in Woman's Day, Forbes, Better Homes and Gardens, The Chronicle of Higher Education, Entrepreneur Magazine, and Los Angeles Times. Dorothy is a past board member for the National Association of Professional Organizers. She has nearly two decades of experience organizing homes and businesses.

Dorothy Breininger
*CEO*
Center for Organization & Goal Planning
Canoga Park, CA USA
*Contact Phone:* 818-718-0611
*Contact Main Phone:* 818-718-0611
*Cell:* 818-599-7860
**Click to Contact from Web Site**

## JAN YAGER, PH.D.

Stamford, CT USA
http://www.janyager.com

A dynamic speaker, workshop leader, consultant, and prolific author praised for her extensive original research, Dr. Yager is a member of the National Speakers Association, NAPO (National Association of Professional Organizers), ASJA (American Society of Journalists and Authors), and the American Sociological Association. She is often interviewed on national television and radio, or quoted in print, including the Associated Press, USA Today, People, The Wall Street Journal, The New Yorker, New York Times, The Oprah Winfrey Show, Good Morning, America, The Today Show, CBS This Morning, CNN, ABC Radio, National Public Radio, and CBS Radio.

Jan Yager, Ph.D.
Stamford, CT
*Contact Phone:* 203-968-8098
**Click to Contact from Web Site**

## JEFF DAVIDSON, MBA, CMA — BREATHING SPACE INSTITUTE

Chapel Hill, NC USA
http://www.BreathingSpace.com

Jeff helps organizations and individuals overcome the relentless burden of information overload. Visit www.BreathingSpace.com for more about Jeff's keynote speeches and seminars including Managing Information and Communication Overload and Prospering in a World of Rapid Change.

Jeff Davidson
*Executive Director*
Breathing Space
Chapel Hill, NC USA
*Contact Phone:* 919-932-1966
**Click to Contact from Web Site**

## C. LESLIE CHARLES, AUTHOR, SPEAKER, CONSULTANT

East Lansing, MI USA
http://www.whyiseveryonesocranky.com

Got stress? If so, you're in good company: stress is as old as humankind. We all have it (well, maybe not cats), so consider it a sign of life. After all, the only absolutely and completely stress-free zone is a cemetery — for the residents, that is! In the past, experts have advised to manage our stress, control it, release it, harness it, channel it, and transform it. But until now, no one has dared to bless it! C. Leslie Charles, who put herself on the "stress map" with the critically acclaimed "Why Is Everyone So Cranky?" has done it again. Leslie Charles and coauthor Mimi Donaldson have faced the stress bully full frontal and whittled it down to size. "Bless Your Stress" is original, imaginative, practical, profound, hilarious, and heartwarming. This fun read is guaranteed to refresh, relax, and revitalize your spirit. It's just what the doctor ordered!

C. Leslie Charles, Author, Speaker, Consultant
East Lansing, MI
*Contact Phone:* 517-675-7535
**Click to Contact from Web Site**

## F. FELICIA FERRARA, PH.D.
Tampa, FL USA
www.cecconsultants.com

Dr. Ferrara provides an informative and inspirational program to enhance interpersonal relationships and increase potential. Learn of intervention strategies that can review, modify and enhance personal life scripts. Ability to achieve or fail in personal and work settings is often a matter of self-perception, not lack of ability.

F. Felicia Ferrara, PhD.
Tampa, FL USA
*Contact Phone:* 813-259-0303
**Click to Contact from Web Site**

## NETWORKING BY IMAGES
Aldie, VA USA
www.JoeRiggio.com

Joe Riggio, Ph.D. ,USMC, Veteran, is President of Networking By Images. He is the author of The Courage to Transition (available in hard copy) and How to make a Successful Transition, (available free online as an e-book at www.JoeRiggio.com). The books include a 10-step process. Balance and alkalizing is key to your health. Networking By Images provides services and products including transition classes and seminars, executive coaching, career management, professional development, exercise equipment, etc.

Joe Riggio, Ph.D. ,USMC, Veteran
*President*
Networking By Images
Aldie, VA
*Contact Phone:* 703-327-3323
*Contact Main Phone:* 703-327-3323
**Click to Contact from Web Site**

## RON BALL — AUTHOR, SPEAKER, EFT STRESS EXPERT
Washington, DC USA
http://www.stress-sucks.com/flash-web.htm

Stress has been called a worldwide epidemic by the United Nations and the World Health Organization. It's estimated to be a $300 billion profit killer. Stress overload takes its toll in health problems, plus work and life issues. Inroads teaches people to dissolve stress and negative emotions in minutes using EFT (Emotional Freedom Techniques), a breakthrough method.

Ron Ball
*Principal*
Inroads, LLC
Fredericksburg, VA USA
*Contact Phone:* (800) 930-7434
**Click to Contact from Web Site**

## PERSONAL VIBRATIONS PUBLISHING
Austin, TX USA
www.PersonalVibrations.com

Why do some people lead a charmed life while others struggle? Do you want to change aspects of your life but cannot 'crack the code'. here is an easier way to choose and create the life you desire. Will you use it? Read Personal Vibrations: Creating Heart's Desire from Your Soul! You can shift your focus and raise your personal vibration and become a powerful magnetic attractor of the life you really want.

Cindy LaFrance
Personal Vibrations Publishing
Austin, TX USA
*Contact Phone:* 512-328-5165
**Click to Contact from Web Site**

## CONSCIOUS PURSUITS, INC.
Houston, TX USA
www.consciouspursuits.com

Conscious Pursuits, Inc. - Integrating Spirituality and Work. Cindy Graves Wigglesworth is the Founder and President of CPI. Cindy is also the co-author of Grown-Up Children Who Won't Grow Up and appeared on Oprah as an expert on helping parents deal with older children (over 18) who won't take responsibility for their lives. Cindy is an expert in integrating spirituality into the workplace via consulting, training, and use of her proprietary Spiritual Intelligence Assessment Instrument.

Cynthia Graves Wigglesworth
*President*
Conscious Pursuits, Inc.
Bellaire, TX USA
*Contact Phone:* 713-667-9824
*Cell:* 713-416-0126
**Click to Contact from Web Site**

## INTERNATIONAL PERSONAL DEVELOPMENT - IVAN BURNELL
Dover, NH USA
www.yesfactor.com

International Personal Development is an educational company, teaching, consulting and presenting seminars on business and personal relationships, parenting and marriage. We show people how to take control of their own destiny and happiness by breaking through the boundries of traditional thinking. Ivan's books and tapes are the kind you keep by your bedside for constant reaffirmation. Some have called them 'a bible to live by'.

Ivan Burnell
Center Ossipee, NH USA
*Contact Phone:* 603-539-4795
**Click to Contact from Web Site**

## DAVID M. JACOBSON, MSW
Tucson, AZ USA
http://www.humorhorizons.com

David awoke one morning to find he could not walk, but oddly enough he's been laughing ever since. Diagnosed with a severe form of arthritis at 22, he conquered the disease with humor. Internationally recognized as an authority on Humor and Health, his expertise includes the rarely discussed subjects of humor, arthritis and spirituality. His many honors include a National Hero Overcoming Arthritis Award from the Arthritis Foundation for his remarkable 50-mile unicycle ride fundraiser for the Arthritis Foundation.

David M. Jacobson, MSW
*President*
Humor Horizons
Tucson, AZ USA
*Contact Phone:* 520-370-2203
*Cell:* 520-370-2203
**Click to Contact from Web Site**

## BEVERLY SMALLWOOD, PH.D., MAGNETIC WORKPLACES
Hattiesburg, MS USA
http://www.magneticworkplaces.com

Dr. Beverly Smallwood brings over 20 years of media experience (e.g. MSNBC, CNN-fn, Fox News, Maury Povich), national and international work with organizations, and counseling with thousands of clinical clients. She can be counted on to deliver an informative, lively interview on workplace issues, trauma and stress, or family/relationship concerns. What It Really Takes to Attract and Keep the Best Employees That's Not My Job Syndrome How to Ride the Waves of Change without Losing Your Balance.

Beverly Smallwood, Ph.D.
*Psychologist*
Magnetic Workplaces
Hattiesburg, MS
*Contact Phone:* 601-264-0890
**Click to Contact from Web Site**

## WOLF RINKE ASSOCIATES
Clarksville, MD USA
http://www.wolfrinke.com

Laugh, lead, and succeed-let Wolf Rinke show you how. Just because your management practices worked yesterday, doesn't mean they work today. Break out of your old management rut and break through to greater success and productivity with the techniques found in Don't Oil the Squeaky Wheel. This humorous and instructive guide distills a lifetime of management consulting experience into 20 easy-to-digest and amusing lessons to help you become a more effective leader.

Dr. Wolf Rinke
Wolf Rinke Associates
Clarksville, MD
*Contact Phone:* 800-828-9653
**Click to Contact from Web Site**

## JAY WINNER, M.D.
Santa Barbara, CA USA
http://www.stressremedy.com

For 12 years, Jay Winner, M.D. has been teaching the stress management classes for the largest medical clinic in Santa Barbara, California. This, along with his over 13 years of experience as a family physician, has given him a deep appreciation of both the physical and psychological effects of stress. His book and CD set Stress Management Made Simple:Effective Ways to Beat Stress for Better Health, has been widely endorsed.

Jay Winner, M.D.
Santa Barbara, CA USA
*Contact Phone:* 805-563-6120
**Click to Contact from Web Site**

## CINDY KUBICA, STRESS MANAGEMENT & COMMUNICATIONS EXPERT
Nashville, TN USA
http://www.cindykubica.com

Have you ever walked into a room and forgot why you entered? Fallen asleep at your desk? Snapped at someone or just couldn't stay focused on the task at hand? If stress is sucking the life out of you, you're not alone! Billions are spent every year on stress related illnesses. Life Skills expert Cindy Kubica challenges people to redefine their normal by breaking free from limiting thoughts and unhealthy routines. Her dynamic presentations are a fusion of stress management and effective communication skills she calls The Mind*Body*Mouth Connection™.

Cindy Kubica
*President*
Studio 10 Productions, Inc.
Franklin, TN USA
*Contact Phone:* 615-771-3800
*Cell:* 615-319-0057
**Click to Contact from Web Site**

## DR. TONI LEONETTI — FOUNDER, HUMAN POTENTIAL INTERNATIONAL
Los Angeles, CA USA

Dr. Toni Leonetti, licensed psychotherapist, is dedicated to the study and communication of cutting-edge discoveries maximizing happiness and self-actualization. Wisdom acquired from years of private practice and research are shared in upcoming book Ten Traits of Happy People. Dr. Leonetti has consulted for the United States Navy, corporations, colleges. She has contributed to national newspapers, radio, and television programming, (such as Radio Free Europe, USA Today, and The Chicago Tribune) for two decades.

Dr. Toni Leonetti
*Psychotherapist, Founder*
Human Potential International
Camarillo, CA USA
*Contact Phone:* 805-484-7868, Ext.43
*Cell:* 310-951-6015
**Click to Contact from Web Site**

### DR. ELIZABETH CARLL, STRESS AND TRAUMA EXPERT
Huntington, NY USA
http://www.DrElizabethCarll.com

An internationally recognized clinical and consulting psychologist, author and speaker, Dr. Elizabeth Carll is an expert on stress and post-traumatic stress, crisis management in relationship to life events and violence, including domestic, workplace, youth and media violence. She is the author of Violence in Our Lives: Impact on Workplace, Home, and Community. She is also an authority on the mind-body connection to health/illness, body image, eating disorders, self-injury behavior, family relationships and media. Dr. Carll has responded to numerous disasters/crises, including the Persian Gulf Crisis, 1993 WTC bombing, L.I. Railroad shooting, Oklahoma City bombing, TWA 800 and the 9/11 WTC disaster. She served on the American Psychological Association's National Disaster Response Advisory Task Force for seven years and founded in 1990 the New York State Psychological Association Disaster/Crisis Response Network, the first statewide volunteer disaster response network in the nation, which she coordinated for ten years.

Elizabeth Carll, Ph.D.
PsychResources, Inc.
Huntington, Long Island, NY USA
*Contact Phone:* 917-941-5400
*Contact Main Phone:* 631-754-2424
**Click to Contact from Web Site**

### SEYMOUR SEGNIT -- CHANGE THAT'S RIGHT NOW, INC.
New York, NY USA
www.ChangeThatsRightNow.com

Seymour Segnit has never met a phobia that couldn't be overcome in less than 24 hours. From Ablutophobia (washing) to Zoophobia (animals) and hundreds like Claustrophobia, Agoraphobia, Fear of Flying and Stage Fright in between, the Oxford educated phobia expert has liberated thousands from torment. His methods work. Seymour is the author of the critically acclaimed home study CD program Vanquish Fear & Anxiety and the Founder/President of CTRN: Change That's Right Now, Inc.

Seymour Segnit
Change That's Right Now, Inc.
New York, NY USA
*Contact Phone:* 212-582-8880
**Click to Contact from Web Site**

### STEVE STENSON, M.ED., MBA — STRATEGIC CONCEPTS
Phoenix, AZ USA
www.stressman.com

Steve is a nationally recognized expert on stress management, self-care, crisis, military family readiness programs, and corporate team building. His powerful seminars have impacted hundreds of organizations throughout the United States. Steve utilizes high-energy humor combined with well-documented life empowering strategies to capture the attention of his audiences. He has developed a unique training technique that creates an environment to learn new information and have fun at the same time.

Steve Stenson, M.Ed., MBA
Strategic Concepts, Inc.
Phoenix, AZ USA
*Contact Phone:* 602-953-2555
**Click to Contact from Web Site**

### AGELESS LIFESTYLES INSTITUTE - DR. MICHAEL BRICKEY
Columbus, OH USA
http://www.DrBrickey.com

Our thinking ages us unnecessarily. Easy belief changes can give you a youthful outlook at every age. -Anti-Aging Psychologist Dr. Michael Brickey. Oprah-featured author Dr. Michael Brickey is a Board Certified Psychologist, an APA Fellow, and a dynamic speaker. His critically acclaimed book, Defy Aging, gives the research, theory, and how to for living well into your hundreds. His 2005 book, 52 baby steps to Grow Young makes it even easier—with two-page-a-week baby steps.

Michael Brickey, Ph.D.
Ageless Lifestyles Institute
Columbus, OH USA
*Contact Phone:* 614-237-4556
**Click to Contact from Web Site**

# Dr. Elizabeth Carll
## Stress and Trauma Expert

An internationally recognized clinical and consulting psychologist, author and speaker, Dr. Elizabeth Carll is an expert on stress and post-traumatic stress, crisis management in relationship to life events and violence, including domestic, workplace, youth and media violence. She is the author of "Violence in Our Lives: Impact on Workplace, Home, and Community." She is also an authority on the mind-body connection to health/illness, body image, eating disorders, self-injury behavior, family relationships and media.

Dr. Carll has responded to numerous disasters/crises, including the Persian Gulf Crisis, 1993 WTC bombing, L.I. Railroad shooting, Oklahoma City bombing, TWA 800 and the 9/11 WTC disaster. She served on the American Psychological Association's National Disaster Response Advisory Task Force for seven years and founded in 1990 the New York State Psychological Association Disaster/Crisis Response Network, the first statewide volunteer disaster response network in the nation, which she coordinated for ten years.

Frequently interviewed by national television, print and radio, Dr. Carll is a past president of the Media Psychology Division of the American Psychological Association and also chairs its News Media, Public Education, and Public Policy Committee and the Interactive Media Committee. She edited a special issue of the American Behavioral Scientist, "Psychology, News Media, and Public Policy: Promoting Social Change" and chairs the Media/ ICT Working Group for the United Nations NGO Committee on Mental Health, New York. She is also vice-president of the Communications Coordination Committee for the United Nations, one of the oldest non-governmental organizations (NGO) to work with the UN to promote civil society's role in developing solutions to global problems.

**Elizabeth Carll, Ph.D.**

PsychResources, Inc.
Huntington,
Long Island, N.Y.

Main Phone:
631-754-2424
Contact Phone:
917-941-5400

**DrCarll.com**

## MITCH ANTHONY — FUTURE OF RETIREMENT EXPERT
Rochester, MN USA
www.MitchAnthony.com

See why tens of thousands of North Americans have been inspired to discard old ideas regarding traditional retirement and to get on with their lives because of the groundbreaking work of Mitch Anthony in The New Retirementality. Because work may always be a part of your life, it's time to get engaged and start collecting a playcheck. "A life of total ease is one step from a life of disease," and "You don't have to be 62 to do what you want to do," are some of the great "retiremyths" that are liberating people from what he calls the "artificial finish line" (a social experiment that has run its course). Mitch's message is about loving your life and living your dreams. . .at any age you want. His seminal work, first published in 2001, has already had a great impact in the workplace and in financial services on how individuals prepare for this major life transition. Mitch Anthony is recognized as a leading philosopher in money/life issues and is a popular keynote speaker, author, columnist, and host of the syndicated radio feature, "The Daily Dose." Print, radio, and TV interviews welcomed.

Mitch Anthony
Rochester, MN USA
*Contact Phone:* 507-282-2723
**Click to Contact from Web Site**

## ROBERT CULLEN, RETIREMENT MANAGEMENT EXPERT
Los Angeles, CA USA
www.savingmomanddad.com

With 30 years experience as a financial journalist and financial advisor, Robert J. Cullen, CFP®, provides unique and quotable insights on financial topics of interest to consumers and professionals. Robert is a recognized authority on long-term issues as evidenced in his recently-published book, Saving Mom & Dad. . .and You. As part of his practice and detailed in his book, Robert developed innovative Put it in a Box™ models that simplify the complicated Medicaid/Medi-Cal eligibility rules.

Robert J Cullen
*Certified Financial Planner*
Upland, CA USA
*Contact Phone:* 909-920-3138
**Click to Contact from Web Site**

## BOB ADAMS -- WWW.RETIREMENTWAVE.COM
Washington, DC USA
http://www.retirementwave.com

People today are concerned that they aren't prepared for retirement. Can they afford to retire? Will they be comfortable when they do? Retirement in a low-cost nation is one increasingly popular alternative. However, there's a lot of hype about overseas retirement. Bob Adams is a global businessman who has written for journals from Barron's to the Asia Times. He believes that overseas retirement is a practical goal, one that can meet the needs of retirees far better than remaining in their expensive homelands. Bob provides a practical review of overseas retirement, focusing on Panama, at RetirementWave.com.

Robert L. Adams
*Contact Phone:* 202-361-3543
*Contact Main Phone:* 301-941-1877
*Cell:* 202-361-3543
**Click to Contact from Web Site**

## POSITIVE LIGHTS, INC. PUBLISHER ELDER CARE DIGEST
Kansas City, MO USA
http://www.positivelights.org/

Positive Lights, Inc. is a non profit organization that publishes Positive Lights Elder Care News — a free email newsletter. The publication monitors articles, news and web sites that can improve the quality of care for the residents of long term care facilities. The Editor is Vernon Jacobs. He can be reached by phone at 913-362-9667 or by email at vernjacobs@yahoo.com. Subscriptions can be made at http://groups.yahoo.com/subscribe/Positivelights/

Vernon K. Jacobs
*Editor: Elder Care Digest*
Positive Lights, Inc.
Prairie Village, KS USA
*Contact Phone:* 913-362-9667
*Cell:* 913-481-3480
**Click to Contact from Web Site**

## DUANE LEE HEPPNER — EXPERT UNIVERSAL PRESENTER
Huntington Beach, CA USA
http://thereturnofthereal.us/

Duane Lee Heppner - Author and expert universal presenter would like you to experience..... A Wonderful Journey that very few people know about Do you feel trapped on this planet like so many others, especially with what is happening with Global Warming, the 9 to 5 idea and all the turbulence that is taking place on the earth today? Do you know how many lifetimes you have been here basically doing the same routines and not knowing where you are really at and what to do about it?

Duane Lee Heppner
The Real Connection
Huntington Beach, CA USA
*Contact Phone:* 714-849-3822
**Click to Contact from Web Site**

## DR. DAVID J. DEMKO, GERONTOLOGIST AND EDITOR, AGEVENTURE NEWS
Boca Raton, FL USA
http://www.demko.com

Expert credentials and 25 years of award-winning leadership make Dr. Demko one of Aging America's most qualified gerontological news commentators. The University of Michigan doctoral graduate served two commissions of service to White House Conferences on Aging under both President Ronald Reagan and President George Bush, senior. Professor Demko's contributions to the field of aging include numerous academic and mass media publications, as well as, coining new gerontological terms.

Dr. David J. Demko, Gerontologist
*Gerontologist and Editor-in-Chief*
AgeVenture Syndicated News Service
Boca Raton, FL USA
*Contact Phone:* 561-866-8251
*Cell:* query via email 1st
**Click to Contact from Web Site**

 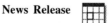

*Retirement Wave*

# Baby-boomer Retirement Planning Expert Bob Adams

People today are more concerned than ever that they are not prepared for retirement. Can they afford to retire? Will they be comfortable when they do?

Retirement in a low-cost nation of great natural beauty is one way to deal effectively with both financial concerns and the desired comfort level. Panama is one ideal example of such a nation. Although only half the size of Florida, Panama has more coastline, is less densely populated, offers a lower cost of living and welcomes retirees from every nation.

FLORIDA

PANAMA

Retirement Wave was created by Bob Adams, a businessman who has written widely for journals from Barron's to the Asia Times. He believes that overseas retirement is a practical goal and one that can meet the needs of retirees far better than remaining in their North American and European homelands. Through interviews, public speaking and his Web site, Bob Adams provides a practical, intelligent review of overseas retirement without hyperbole and exaggeration.

# www.RetirementWave.com

### Robert L. Adams
*Main Phone: 301-941-1877*
*Contact Phone: 202-361-3543*
*E-mail: RAdams@ngiweb.com*

## BARBARA MORRIS, PHARMACIST, ANTI-AGING EXPERT
Escondido, CA USA
http://www.PutOldonHold.com

Barbara Morris, R.Ph., is a 75-year-old practicing pharmacist and recognized expert on unique anti-aging strategies. Author of Put Old on Hold, her message is for Boomers who want to feel and function as a healthy 40 or 50 year old for 25 or more years. She calls it "Liberation Living" - a process she has discovered that bypasses infirmities and indignities of traditional old age.

Barbara Morris
Image F/X Publications
Escondido, CA United States
*Contact Phone:* 760-480-2710
**Click to Contact from Web Site**

## LOUIS LEVY
Bethesda, MD USA
http://www.louislevy.com

Louis Levy has been on Broadway; put on film festivals; acted in numerous feature films and plays; sung cabaret; performed voiceovers; and written reviews. He is also in the process of writing a book! He knows the secrets of how to survive the three phases of retirement: pre-retirement mental preparation, first year adjustments, and savoring life's 'second chance.' He offers passionate, sage advice spiced with humor and presented with flair. He will empower your 'Over 50' viewers, readers and listeners. A member of Toastmaster's Hall of Fame, the National Speakers Association, SAG and AFTRA.

Louis Levy
Bethesda, MD
*Contact Phone:* 301-469-8046
**Click to Contact from Web Site**

## CAROL BRADLEY BURSACK - CAREGIVING EXPERT
Fargo, ND USA
http://www.mindingourelders.com/

Columnist/author/speaker Carol Bradley Bursack, author of Minding Our Elders: Caregivers Share Their Personal Stories), is a 20 year veteran of caring for seven elderly people. She has been interviewed on countless national radio shows including Bev Smith, Radio Health Journal, The USD ElderLaw Forum, Tom Pope, Coping with Caregiving (clip on www.mindingourelders. com), Ron Thulin, Lee Michaels, Sherrie McCutcheon and Late Night with John Counsell. She is a regular guest on several national shows. Carol has also been interviewed by newspaper and magazine journalists. Carol blogs on www. healthcentral.com/alzheimers and her Web site at www.mindingourelders.com is loaded with information for caregivers and media. Carol writes a weekly elder care column. She speaks at conferences and workshops, often providing the keynote. Her book, Minding Our Elders, is used as a text to humanize the caregiving experience in college gerontology classes. Carol's mission is to carry the message that help is available to caregivers.

Carol Bradley Bursack
Minding Our Elders
Fargo, ND USA
*Contact Main Phone:* 701-241-5430
*Cell:* 701-238-0075
**Click to Contact from Web Site**

## CYNTHIA SHELBY-LANE, M.D. -- LAUGHTER IS GOOD MEDICINE
Detroit, MI USA

Laughter is Good Medicine according to Cynthia Shelby-Lane, MD, a doctor, speaker, comedienne & talk show host, who loves to laugh. Do you know a doctor, who stops to save a life, then gets up on stage to make you laugh. . .. at life. . .. at yourself . . .and at her. Well, Shelby-lane, MD is that kind of doctor. Known as the agelessdoctor, Shelby-Lane is a graduate of the University of Michigan Medical School. She trained as a surgeon at the University of Texas, in Houston and committed herself to saving lives as an emergency physician. Now, as a board certified anti-aging specialist, she keeps people young, from the inside out. Her practice, Elan Anti-Aging, incorporates alternative and complementary therapies to promote optimal health and youthful aging. She also expanded her practice to the Internet as THE Internet Doctor, answering questions for patients worldwide. Seen on national radio and television, discussing issues such as anti-aging, heart disease, weight loss, stress reduction, and cancer, Shelby-Lane speaks nationwide and is also a certified professional health coach.

Cynthia Shelby-Lane, M.D.
Second Opinion
Southfield, MI USA
*Contact Phone:* 800-584-4926
*Cell:* 248-910-8900
**Click to Contact from Web Site**

# Cynthia Shelby-Lane, M.D.
# "Laughter is Good Medicine"

"Laughter is Good Medicine," says Cynthia Shelby-Lane, M.D., a doctor, speaker, comedienne and talk show host, who loves to laugh.

Do you know a doctor, who stops to save a life, then gets up on stage to make you laugh . . . at life . . . at yourself . . . and at herself?

Well, Shelby-Lane, M.D., is that kind of doctor. Known as "the ageless doctor," Shelby-Lane is a graduate of the University of Michigan Medical School. She trained as a surgeon at the University of Texas in Houston and committed herself to saving lives as an emergency physician in Detroit. She then re-invented herself and is now a board-certified, anti-aging specialist, keeping people young and healthy from the inside out.

Her practice, Elan Anti-Aging & Longevity Center, incorporates alternative and complementary therapies to promote optimal health and youthful aging. She also expanded her practice to the Internet as "THE Internet Doctor," answering questions for patients worldwide through a detailed Internet evaluation. The doctor is also a certified, professional health coach, helping people make difficult health and life choices and create changes for optimum health and wellness.

Seen on national radio and television, discussing issues such as anti-aging, heart disease, weight loss, stress reduction and cancer, Shelby-Lane speaks nationwide and is also a certified professional health coach. She tackles tough social issues through community work and took thousands of dollars worth of drugs and medical supplies to the victims of Katrina on a solo mission in 2005.

This graduate of Second City Comedy School in Chicago and student at UCLA Motion Picture

and Television Program produces TV shows and produces a "live" comedy show called, "Laugh Attack": Stopping the #1 Killer -- Heart Disease. Appearances on the Oprah Winfrey Show and featured articles in the *New York Times*, *Ebony* and *Jet* magazines and *Women's Health Style* magazine have given her expert status as the anti-aging and comedy doc.

She can cook, too. She's no Emeril or Rachel Ray, but Dr. Shelby-Lane is now the host of her new food show, "What's Cookin', Doc?"

Trading in her stethoscope for an apron, her food show features "food remedies and foods that heal." So, if "Laughter is Good Medicine," then "great food is the cure."

---

**Cynthia Shelby-Lane, M.D.**
**Second Opinion**
**Southfield, Michigan**

**Contact Phone: 1-800-584-4926**
**Cell: 248-910-8900**
**E-mail: agelessdoctor@aol.com.**

## ROBIN THOMPSON — LEADERSHIP DEVELOPEMENT SPEAKER
Daniels, WV USA
http://www.robinthompson.com

Robin Thompson owns Thompson Training & Keynote, Inc. She works with organizations that want to keep their good people motivated and with meeting planners that want a speaker who will put fun in their next meeting or event. Robin conducts keynote speeches and workshops to increase productivity and boost morale.

Robin Thompson
Daniels, WV USA
*Contact Phone:* 304-763-3222
**Click to Contact from Web Site**

## LYNNE MARKS, IMAGE AND BRANDING
Atlanta, GA USA
http://www.LondonImageInstitute.com

Lynne is one of only six Certified Image Masters worldwide and a multi award-winning consultant on image and branding. President of London Image Institute and coach to top executives, she directed an international research study showing strong relationships between image and self-esteem. Featured in Time, Forbes, CNN, Elle, Women's day, Glamour and countless other publications and radio, she is co-author of industry best-seller, The Perfect Fit: How to Start an Image Consulting Business.

Lynne Marks
London Image Institute
Atlanta, GA USA
*Contact Phone:* 404-255-0009
**Click to Contact from Web Site**

## VINCENT MULI KITUKU, PH.D., CSP --- MOTIVATIONAL LEADERSHIP SPEAKER
Boise, ID USA
www.Kituku.com

Dr. Kituku works with organizations to increase productivity through employees and leadership development programs. A native of Kenya, Africa, he draws on his rich cultural heritage and his in-depth experience in corporate America to help others apply strategies of personal and professional success to their lives. Vincent's presentations inspire people to love what they do and understand the big picture of their contribution. He delivers authentic, informative and high-energy messages with guaranteed outcome. Audiences reach new heights of greatness.

Vincent Muli Kituku, Ph.D., CSP
Kituku & Associates
Bosie, ID USA
*Contact Phone:* 888-685-1621
**Click to Contact from Web Site**

## ASSOCIATION OF IMAGE CONSULTANTS INTERNATIONAL, AICI
Des Moines, IA USA
http://www.aici.org

The Association of Image Consultants International is a worldwide nonprofit professional association of men and women specializing in visual appearance, verbal and non-verbal communication. Our members serve individual clients in attaining authenticity, credibility and self-confidence and they serve corporate clients in attaining alignment of their employees' appearance, behavior and communication with the corporate goals.

Heather Tamminga
*Association Manager*
Association of Image Consultants International, AICI
Des Moines, IA USA
*Contact Phone:* 515-243-1558
**Click to Contact from Web Site**

## CAROLYN STRAUSS- ENTREPRENEUR/ SPEAKER
Denver, CO USA
http://www.CarolynStrauss.com

Defying society's narrow, idealized perception of beauty, Carolyn Strauss enjoyed a highly successful 20-year career as a plus size model with the Ford Modeling Agency, and she parlayed that success into The Carolyn Strauss Collection, a multimillion dollar apparel company featured on the Home Shopping Network. She has appeared on HSN many times, as well as CNN, Entertainment Tonight, Maury, and Sally Jesse Raphael. Carolyn is a powerfully compelling, effervescent, and entertaining speaker and entrepreneur.

Carolyn Strauss
Denver, CO
*Contact Phone:* 212-840-1844
**Click to Contact from Web Site**

# Lynne Marks, AICI, CIM
## *Image and Branding Expert*

Lynne Marks, President of London Image Institute, is one of only seven Certified Image Masters worldwide and a multi-award winning consultant with the Association of Image Consultants International.

Lynne has an unparalleled background in the arena of image and is among the most experienced in the world. She did pioneer postgraduate research in body language and non-verbal communication skills, when it was virtually uncharted territory. Today, her research shows a strong relationship between image consulting and increased self-esteem.

As a professor and head of one of the image and fashion departments at the London College of Fashion, she became experienced in image, color theory, design, tailoring, garment construction, fashion trends and forecasting, fashion show production, makeup and modeling. She produced and directed hundreds of fashion show and trained and consulted internationally.

As a corporate trainer and coach, Lynne provides programs in professional presence, verbal and non-verbal communication skills, business protocol and presentation skills, to companies such as American Express, The Weather Channel, Coca-Cola, AT&T and CNN Sports.

As a consultant in corporate identity design and branding she has designed and delivered courses in leadership, sales, customer service, management and executive team development, and she has consulted for companies such as United Airlines, Pacific Dunlop, Minnesota Mutual and Coca-Cola Enterprises

Her individual clients are among some of the top U.S. executives and politicians.

London Image Institute offers an international Master Training division in the U.K., U.S.A. and Asia for image entrepreneurs and corporate trainers to gain advanced skills in seminar design, business and professional development. Hundreds of consultants in more than 30 countries worldwide have graduated from the internationally acclaimed programs.

Lynne is co-author of "The Perfect Fit: How to Start an Image Consulting Business."

### *Lynne Marks: London Image Institute*

**LONDON IMAGE INSTITUTE**

4279 Roswell Road
Suite 102, PMB 318
Atlanta, Georgia 30342

404.255.0009 ■ 404.303.8818 (fax)

**info@LondonImageInstitute.com**

**www.LondonImageInstitute.com**

**NILI SACHS, PH.D.**
Minneapolis, MN USA
http://www.BoobyTrapped.com

Booby-Trapped, How to Feel Normal in a Breast-Obsessed World is Dr. Nili's recent book. Her topics on body image were featured on: The O'Reilly Factor, CNN, KABC Radio, MSN.com (personals) & Cosmopolitan. Speaker, Therapist, Author Nili Sachs, Ph.D.'s Doctorate is in clinical psychology. 28 years experience include: private practice, facilitated couples, and corporate seminars. She delivers her messages with a relevance and sense of humor. Recipient Raving Fans Award by P.A.I.R.S. International.

Nili Sachs, Ph.D.
Rockford, MN USA
*Contact Phone:* 952-471-3730
**Click to Contact from Web Site**

**DIANNE M. DANIELS, AICI**
Norwich, CT USA
http://www.imageandcolor.com

A Total Image Consultant, Dianne's advice on subjects including visual appearance, vocal presentation and verbal excellence helps clients increase their self-esteem and self-confidence, and reach new levels of success. Dianne's vibrant and charismatic personal presence is sure to interest readers and audiences of all sexes, ages and backgrounds. Call Image & Color Services at 866 618-8735 — to book this exciting and easy-to-work-with guest.

Dianne M. Daniels, AICI
*CEO*
Image & Color Services
Norwich, CT USA
*Contact Phone:* 866-618-8735
*Contact Main Phone:* 866-618-8735
**Click to Contact from Web Site**

**SANDY DUMONT -- THE IMAGE ARCHITECT**
Hampton Roads, VA USA
http://www.theimagearchitect.com

International expert in Image, Branding for People™, Crisis Management, Body Language and Impression Management. Author of Power Dressing for Men, 10-part Image System for Professional Women, and Tattletale Looks. NSA speaker and former high-fashion model, Sandy conducts Image Consultant Training Courses, and appears regularly on TV, radio and in print in the US and Europe. Recognized by her Fortune 500 clients as a pioneer in the new field of image psychology and impression strategies.

Sandy Dumont
Impression Strategies Institute
Norfolk, VA USA
*Contact Phone:* 757/627-6669
**Click to Contact from Web Site**

**MAXINE LUCILLE FIEL, B.A. -- BODY LANGUAGE EXPERT**
New York, NY USA

Expert in Body Language, Non-Verbal Behavior, and Behavioral Astrology. Photo-Analyst, Writer, Lecturer and Media Consultant. Listed in Marquis Who's Who in America/Who's Who of American Women/Who's Who in the East. Expertise: The Power of the Body in politics, terrorism, marketing and human relationships. She is a trend-spotter. She can tell you about new concepts. She's talked about The Power of Image. Dynamic First Impressions and turning off negative body signals. The East/West Culture Gap and how to bridge it in business and social situations. The Dynamics of Jury Selection and courtroom behavior.

Maxine Lucille Fiel, B.A.
New York, NY
*Contact Phone:* 718-631-3313
*Contact Main Phone:* 516-482-3700
**Click to Contact from Web Site**

**CAROLYN FINCH — BODY LANGUAGE EXPERT**
Danbury, CT USA
http://www.Electrific.com

Carolyn Finch, M.S SLP is an Author, Keynote Speaker and Expert on Body Language and the Brain -Body connection. She is a consultant to government, industry and media on BODY LANGUAGE. Carolyn energizes individuals and businesses to increase skills, change attitudes and modify behavior to improve their Health, Performance and Success. She is the author of Universal Handtalk a Survival Sign System and Reading The Body for Wellness.

Carolyn Finch
Electrific Solutions
Danbury, CT USA
*Contact Phone:* 203-775-0290
**Click to Contact from Web Site**

# MAXINE LUCILLE FIEL

## BEHAVIORAL ANALYST, BODY LANGUAGE EXPERT

"We all speak two languages . . . the language of words and the language of the body.

Yet it is too often the calculated, spoken word we believe, while the silent messages of the body scream the truth."

## *Maxine Lucille Fiel*
### *Internationally Known Pioneer*
### *of Political, Celebrity and Relationship Body Language*

Behavior and Communications Analyst, Expert in All Aspects of Body Language and Non-Verbal Behavior. Photo-Analyst, Writer, Lecturer and Media Consultant. Listed in the prestigious Marquis Who's Who in America/of American Women/in the World/in the East.

Maxine's articles and interviews appear in major magazines, newspapers, TV and other media. Her daily TV show in Japan ran for 10 years. Maxine is a consultant for political parties and sporting events as well as a trends spotter and forecaster for advertising and public relations firms.

*Maxine Lucille Fiel*
*New York,*
*New York*

*Main Phone:*
*516-482-3700*

*Contact Phone:*
*718-631-3313*

### JACK NIRENSTEIN -- RUNNING TECHNIQUE EXPERT
Myrtle Beach, SC USA
www.running-justundoit.com

ONE MAN HOLDS THE KEY TO SPEED RUNNING IS: Falling speed. Lifting speed. Twisting speed... The Nirenstein Key. You fall forward when your leg is at a backward slant (body ahead of the foot. You fall forward faster by dropping your feet farther behind the body. Gravity is the only force that pushes you forward. You lift while falling forward to keep you moving parallel to the ground. The faster you fall (run), the faster (harder) you lift. You twist the body to swing the foot to the start of the next stride. The harder you twist, the faster you are able to fall for speed. The more you do of the right thing, the faster you will run. Test the Nirenstein key against the others. Stride as long as you can and see that you can't go any faster than a slow walk. The coaches' way. Drop your feet behind your body and keep it landing there for a few steps and see that you pick up speed with a backward slanted leg. The Nirenstein way. Nirenstein's way is the new science, it can't be done at all the old way of stride length and foot speed. When your front muscles lift your back muscles can't push. Nirenstein can elaborate and answer all questions.

Jack Nirenstein
Myrtle Beach, SC USA
*Contact Phone:* 843-236-6906
**Click to Contact from Web Site**

### DR. TODD M. KAYS -- SPORTS PSYCHOLOGIST
Dublin, OH USA
www.athleticmindinstitute.com

Dr. Todd Kays, sport psychologist and founder of the Athletic Mind Institute, assists athletes and coaches in achieving their highest potential. He has consulted with Major League Soccer, PGA, LPGA, NFL, and Professional Hockey. He has co-authored two books in the area of youth and college sports, appeared with ESPN's Kirk Herbstreit in "America's Student Athlete" and trained National Champions and Olympians at The Ohio State University. He and his organization are committed to helping individuals achieve their potential both in and outside of sports. He consults regularly with athletes, coaches and parents at all levels of sport, including youth, high school, college, amateur, and professional.

Todd M. Kays, Ph.D.
*Sport and Performance Psychologist*
Athletic Mind Institute
Dublin, OH USA
*Contact Phone:* 614.874.0178
*Cell:* 614.561.4483
**Click to Contact from Web Site**

### SWIMTASTIC SWIM SCHOOL
Waukesha, WI USA
www.swimtastic.com

Sue Wainscott, founder and CEO of Waukesha, Wisconsin-based Swimtastic Swim School is recognized as a progressive leader in the learn-to-swim industry. Wainscott, a mother, former elementary school teacher and swimming instructor with more than 25 years of experience, has developed a proprietary curriculum that engages students at emotional and developmental levels to help them learn, practice and enjoy swimming. Swimtastic Corp. has two schools in Wisconsin and is now franchising its concept to share Wainscott's passion for swimming, a physical activity that can be enjoyed for a lifetime.

Susan Wainscott
*Founder and CEO*
Swimtastic Swim School
Waukesha, WI USA
*Contact Phone:* 262-549-SWIM (7946)
**Click to Contact from Web Site**

### DR. VIRGINIA BOLA
Los Angeles, CA USA
http://www.VirginiaBola.com

Dr. Bola is a licensed clinical psychologist with deep interests in employment, weight control, social psychology and politics. She has studied the effects of cultural forces, diet, and unemployment on the individual for more than 20 years. The author of two interactive workbooks: The Wolf at the Door: An Unemployment Survival Manual and Diet With An Attitude: A Weight Loss Workbook, she writes a monthly ezine on unemployment/job search and various mini-courses on weight control.

Dr. Virginia Bola
*Licensed Clinical Psychologist*
Downey, CA USA
*Contact Phone:* 562-862-9627
**Click to Contact from Web Site**

## LYNN FISCHER'S HEALTHY LIVING, INC.
Lakeland, FL USA
www.lynnfischer.com

Nutrition Expert for TV, Radio and Print - Author of seven healthy cookbooks, three best sellers, 1,000,000 books in print, Lynn Fischer has hosted and produced hundreds of her own television shows including, "The Low Cholesterol Gourmet" on The Discovery Channel, which ran for five years nationwide, Lynn Fischer's Healthy Indulgences, which ran for three on Public Broadcasting years (both in the early to late 1990's). Lynn Fischer wrote: "Low Fat Cooking for Dummies", "Quick & Healthy Cooking for Dummies", "Fabulous Fat Free cooking", and The Better Sex Diet, etc. She speaks on several nutrition subjects such as How To Have Fun With Your Hated Diet. Lynn Fischer was always anti-Atkins and pro complex carbohydrates, but she is not a vegetarian.

Lynn Fischer
Lynn Fischer's Healthy Living, Inc.
Lakeland, FL
*Contact Main Phone:* 863-644-1383
*Cell:* 863-838-5886
**Click to Contact from Web Site**

## DENISE LAMOTHE, PSY.D, H.H.D. - EMOTIONAL EATING SPECIALIST
Boston, MA USA
www.deniselamothe.com

Dr. Denise works with people who want to understand emotional eating and how to stop it. Dr. Denise Speaks from Experience! She has spent her career encouraging people to make wellness a priority in their lives. An expert in her field, she is the 'go to' person for anyone seeking to develop a healthier lifestyle and she now devotes all of her time to spreading this important message. Dr. Denise is the author of The Taming of the Chew, (Penguin 2002), which has helped thousands of people to overcome self-destructive behaviors. She is also the Emotional Eating Expert for Ann Louise Gittleman, best selling author of The Fat Flush Plan.

Denise Lamothe
Dr. Denise
Epping, NH USA
*Contact Phone:* 603-679-2432
*Cell:* 603-493-6043
**Click to Contact from Web Site**

## DR. HEATHER MACLEAN WALTERS
Long Valley, NJ USA

Dr. Walters has taught nutrition to thousands of physicians, consumers and college students, written 9 books (one bestseller), and can handle just about anything related to foods, nutrition, food safety, etc. Millions have heard her on TV or radio. She can answer accurately and with brevity. "Scientifically accurate, very helpful. . ." (about the latest book) Dr. Christiane Northrup "I knew you'd be engaging—you make your point so brilliantly in your book. . ." Dr. Jonny Bowden.

Heather Walters
Long Valley, NJ USA
*Contact Phone:* 908-876-1489
**Click to Contact from Web Site**

## BARBARA THOMPSON -- PERSONAL EMPOWERMENT EXPERT
Pittsburgh, PA USA
www.wlscenter.com

Barbara Thompson is a change agent and expert in personal empowerment. She went from a weight of 264 pounds to 139 in a year and has maintained that weight loss for 5 years. Barbara has dealt with failure, self esteem and body image - and triumphed!! She went from being an obese woman with low self esteem to becoming a healthy woman, an author and national speaker.

Barbara Thompson
WLS Center
Pittsburgh, PA USA
*Contact Phone:* 877-440-1518
**Click to Contact from Web Site**

## TIM FERRISS - FITNESS , NUTRITION & LIFESTYLE EXPERT
San Jose, CA USA
http://www.timferriss.com/

Timothy Ferriss is a guest lecturer at Princeton University and has been featured and interviewed by media worldwide, including the LA Times, Philadelphia Inquirer, MAXIM Magazine, Muscle & Fitness, and Powerlifting USA. He has designed training and nutritional programs for celebrities and over 30 professional athletes who have shattered more than 70 world records. He is a member of the American College of Sports Medicine, Institute of Food Technologists, and American Council on Exercise.

Tim Ferriss
*Director of Research and Athletic Development*
Adaptagenix Applied Biosciences
San Jose, CA USA
*Contact Phone:* 650-279-3540
**Click to Contact from Web Site**

## BYRON J. RICHARDS, CCN - LEPTIN & NUTRITION EXPERT
Minneapolis, MN USA
www.leptinexpert.com

Byron Richards, CCN, Board Certified Clinical Nutritionist is the author of Mastering Leptin. With 20 years experience, Richards leads the field of clinical nutrition and is an expert on the fat hormone leptin and its relationship to weight, disease, thyroid, metabolism, and hormone imbalance. Richards is the first to explain the relevance of leptin and its link to solving obesity. He is an acclaimed speaker who is frequently featured on television and radio programs.

Katie McClenachan
Wellness Resources
Minneapolis, MN USA
*Contact Phone:* 952-929-4575
**Click to Contact from Web Site**

## A.T. CROSS ASSOCIATES, INC.
Finesville, NJ USA

Dr. Audrey Cross delivers the real 'skinny' on difficult to decipher science. She takes the fear out of food. Dr. Audrey holds a Ph.D. in nutrition from the University of California. She is professor at Columbia University in New York and the Department of Nutrition Sciences at Rutgers University. She is the author of five books, including Nutrition for the Working Woman and The Better Body Book. Comments by and about her have appeared in such diverse publications as Time and Women's Day.

Audrey Cross, Ph.D.
A.T. Cross Associates, Inc.
Finesville, NJ
*Contact Phone:* 908-995-9073
**Click to Contact from Web Site**

## CAROLINE J. CEDERQUIST, M.D.
Naples, FL USA
http://drcederquist.com

Caroline J. Cederquist, M.D. is a wife, mother and the medical director of the Cederquist Medical Wellness Center in Naples, Florida. As one of only about 250 board certified bariatricians in the U.S. -- doctors who specialize in medical weight management -- she is on the front lines of addressing America's obesity epidemic, both at the clinical level, and thought public education efforts and participation with organizations that study and combat unhealthy weight trends and bogus diets.

Lionel Mendoza
Naples, FL USA
*Contact Phone:* 239-593-0663
**Click to Contact from Web Site**

# Lynn Fischer's Healthy Living, Inc.

## Television and Radio Nutrition Expert

Author of seven healthy cookbooks, hundreds of her own television shows, Lynn Fischer has more than 1 million books in print.

Her books include:
*Lowfat Cooking for Dummies*
*Quick & Healthy Cooking for Dummies*
*Fabulous Fat-Free Cooking*

Lynn has produced and hosted for TV, several hundred half-hour and one-hour television programs for: The Discovery Channel and Public Broadcasting, including her own series, "The Low Cholesterol Gourmet" and "Lynn Fischer's Healthy Indulgences."

Media tours include working for: Campbell's Soups; Nabisco; Shadybrook Farms; and more.

Lynn has been pictured, had recipes used or quoted in: *Forbes*; *TV Guide*; *Cooking Light*; *Reader's Digest*; *Esquire*; *Woman's World*; *Eating Well*; *Time*; *USA Today*; plus many more.

**Lynn Fischer**
*Lynn Fischer's Healthy Living, Inc.*
*Lakeland, Florida*

Main Phone: 863-644-1383
Cell: 727-422-6944

Additional Contact:
Kathy Mercier, 863-644-1383

**lynnfischer.com**

## DR. GEORGE V. DUBOUCH, PH.D. -- HEALTH & WELLNESS EXPERT
Talent, OR USA
www.glyconutrient.com

We are Dr. George & Margaret Dubouch. I am the author of the book, Science or Miracle? The Metabolic Glyconutritional Discovery...A book to educate you on health options. And co-author of The Healing Power of 8 Sugars What 20 Doctors want YOU to know about Glyconutrients. I'm happy to see you take the extra time to visit glyconutrient. com.

Dr. George V. Dubouch, Ph.D.
Inner Life Foundation
Talent, OR USA
*Contact Phone:* 541-535-9136
**Click to Contact from Web Site**

## TOPS CLUB, INC.
Milwaukee, WI USA
http://www.tops.org

TOPS (Take Off Pounds Sensibly) is an international, non-profit, non-commercial low-cost weight-loss support group, with over 240,000 members, dedicated to helping people reach and maintain their physician-prescribed weight goal. Education, fellowship and positive reinforcement available at almost 10,500 weekly meetings worldwide. Dedicated to obesity research as well as to a safe, sensible lifestyle.

Beth Maniero
*Communications Manager*
TOPS Club, Inc.
Milwaukee, WI
*Contact Phone:* 414-482-4620
**Click to Contact from Web Site**

## KAT JAMES
New York, NY USA
http://www.informedbeauty.com

Kat James, renowned holistic beauty and lifestyle expert, author, motivational speaker and public television host, has earned national acclaim for her inspiring story and her evolved approach to self-cultivation. Based on the latest research, as well as her own dramatic transformation from a "denatured," diseased, and overweight woman to the free, vital woman she has become, Kat has helped thousands of people transform their looks and lives from the inside out.

Kimberly Day
*Contact Phone:* 301-633-4010
**Click to Contact from Web Site**

**The American Society of Bariatric Physicians**
*To advance and support the physicians' role in treating overweight patients.*

## AMERICAN SOCIETY OF BARIATRIC PHYSICIANS
Denver, CO USA
http://www.asbp.org

Professional society of weight management physicians offering patients specialized programs in the medical treatment of overweight, obesity and their associated conditions. Provides reliable physician spokespersons who can knowledgeably address medical complications of overweight and obesity, plus available treatments and protocols. The first medical society to advocate for classifying obesity as a chronic disease. Responsible for the exposure of numerous weight loss scams and fraudulent products. Established and maintains bariatric practice guidelines and provides medical education.

Beth Little Shelly, CAE
*Executive Director*
American Society of Bariatric Physicians
Denver, CO USA
*Contact Phone:* 303-770-2526
*Contact Main Phone:* 303-770-2526
*Cell:* 303-995-8652
**Click to Contact from Web Site**

## AMERICAN SOCIETY FOR AESTHETIC PLASTIC SURGERY
New York, NY USA
http://www.surgery.org/

The American Society for Aesthetic Surgery is the Authoritative Source for information on cosmetic plastic surgery. Founded in 1967, ASAPS is the elite by-invitation-only organization of American Board of Plastic Surgery certified plastic surgeons that specialize in cosmetic surgery of the face and body. National network of plastic surgeon spokespersons, the most accurate statistics on cosmetic surgery, news releases, fact sheets, and position statements, B-Roll of procedures, before and after slide library and toll-free patient referrals.

Adeena Cobert
*Manager of Media Relations*
American Society for Aesthetic Plastic Surgery
New York, NY
*Contact Phone:* 212-921-0500
**Click to Contact from Web Site**

## DR. WASHINGTON BRYAN II, M. D.
Beverly Hills, CA USA
http://www.paincuremd.com

There has never been a pain relief specialist quite like Washington Bryan II, MD. That's because Dr. Bryan takes an extremely compassionate interdisciplinary approach to helping every patient fight their worst pain. Dr. Bryan is board-certified in both anesthesiology and pain management by the American Board of Anesthesiology. He has treated thousands of pain patients during over seven years in practice. And he is willing to use the full armamentarium of technology, treatments and modalities to effectively reduce or eliminate every patient's pain.

Dr. Washington Bryan II, M. D.
Dr. Washington Bryan II, M. D.
West Los Angeles, CA United States
*Contact Phone:* 310-228-3652
**Click to Contact from Web Site**

# Dr. George V. Dubouch, Ph.D.
# Health & Wellness Expert

I am Dr. George Dubouch, and I am the author of the book, "Science or Miracle? The Metabolic Glyconutritional Discovery" ... a book to educate you on health options.

And I am also a co-author of "The Healing Power of 8 Sugars: What 20 Doctors want YOU to know about Glyconutrients."

I invite you to visit www.glyconutrient.com.

If you would like to contact me, please call 1-541-535-9136, after 9am Pacific Time.

Or you can email me at: Dubouch@aol.com.

## SCIENCE or MIRACLE?
### Metabolic Glyconutritional Discovery

The "Science or Miracle" book is easy reading and has insightful information on glyconutrients and the new science called glycobiology and glycomics and how it is going to change health care as we know it. Learn what really causes chronic degenerative diseases and how to deal with them effectively without pharmaceutical drugs.

Filled with life-saving information and facts, it is written in a "science-friendly" format anyone can understand.

The book includes drawings of cellular activity, illustrating cell parts and cellular use of water and fat soluble antioxidants. Dr. Dubouch's passionate words, relating his experience and revelation will move individuals to make personal changes in improving their health -- and their lives.

George V. Dubouch, Ph.D.
Innerlife Foundation Talent, Oregon, U.S.A.

**DR. BURT ENSLEY - DERMAPLUS , INC.**
New York, NY USA
http://www.dermalastyl.com

Dr. Burt Ensley, a molecular biologist, is the creator of DermaLastyl, a high-performance tropoelastin-based skincare product line. Tropoelastin is critical to the formation of new elastin, which gives skin resilience and flexibility and is effective in delaying skin aging. DermaLastyl and Elastatropin enhance the skin's ability to repair itself, both in wound healing and tissue regeneration. For eight years, Dr. Ensley was manager of scientific affairs for Amgen, Inc. Currently, he is CEO of DermaPlus, Inc., New York.

Russ Fons
Russ Fons Public Relations
Las Vegas, NV
*Contact Phone:* 702-658-7654
**Click to Contact from Web Site**

---

**CALIFORNIA COSMETICS
CORPORATION —— BOB SIDELL**
Las Vegas, NV USA
http://www.SilkSkin.com

During 30 years as a Hollywood makeup artist, Bob Sidell became a legend for his secret formula and breakthrough work on 'The Waltons' TV series plus beauties Kathleen Turner, Joan Collins, Heather Locklear, Jaclyn Smith and Dolly Parton. He toured North America as a skin care expert for The Gillette Company and Boots Group PLC, and his patented potion led to the founding of his company, California Cosmetics Corp., with annual sales of $10 million.

Russ Fons Public Relations
Las Vegas, NV
*Contact Phone:* 702-658-7654
**Click to Contact from Web Site**

---

**WWW.YOURSPAGUIDE.COM**
Washington, DC USA
http://www.YourSpaGuide.com

Judy Colbert has been writing about spas since the 1980s. She inspects about a dozen a year and can discuss what's new, the different types of spas, various forms of massage, and trends. She is the author of 'The Spa Guide,' co-author of 'Big Bang Marketing for Spas' and a columnist for Salon City magazine and Web site. She has lectured at spa conferences and conventions.

Judy Colbert
Tuff Turtle Publishing
Crofton, MD USA
*Contact Phone:* 301-858-0196
*Cell:* 301-257-0196
**Click to Contact from Web Site**

---

**JAN MARINI -- CEO, JAN MARINI SKIN
RESEARCH, INC.**
San Jose, CA USA
http://www.JanMarini.com

Jan is the President & CEO of the skin care company, Jan Marini Skin Research Inc. She is a leading innovator and contributor to the skin care market and has worked tirelessly to develop home-based and clinical skin care management systems. Jan is a respected educator, addressing physicians about common skin disorders and non-surgical treatment alternatives and is widely regarded as an expert product and ingredient researcher, amply informed on a wide range of common skin conditions.

Claire West
*Director of Marketing*
Jan Marini Skin Reseach, Inc
San Jose, CA USA
*Contact Phone:* 800-347-2223
**Click to Contact from Web Site**

# Washington Bryan II, M.D.
## *Compassionate Medical Care*

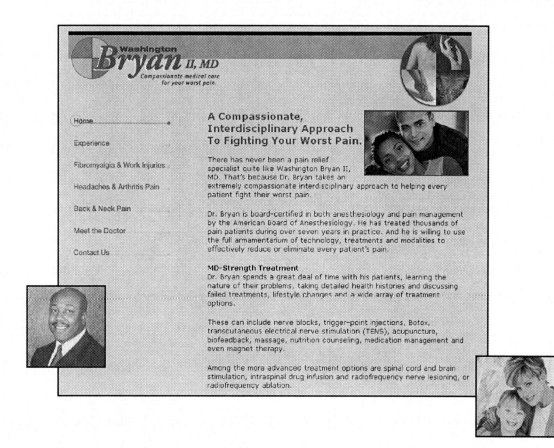

**Washington Bryan II, M.D.**
**West Los Angeles, Calif. -- U.S.A.**
**Contact Phone: 310-228-3652**

# www.paincuremd.com

### EVA SZTUPKA - SPA & SKINCARE EXPERT
Pittsburgh, PA USA
www.esspa.com

Hungarian Eva Sztupka immigrated to America in 1996 and opened ESSpa Kozmetika Skincare in 2001 (voted Best Spa in Pittsburgh - 2005). Years of training and experience in traditional European skincare methods make Eva Sztupka the leader in the creation and application of holistic, non-invasive spa treatments and organic products designed to restore, protect and maintain the skin of women, men and teenagers. Eva insists that frequent spa visits are necessary for total body health.

Eva Sztupka
*c/o: Scott Kerschbaumer, VP - Communications*
ESSpa Kozmetika Skincare, Inc.
Pittsburgh, PA USA
*Contact Phone:* 1-877-SPA-3300
*Contact Main Phone:* 412-782-3888
*Pager:* 877-713-4567
*Cell:* 412-401-4219
**Click to Contact from Web Site**

### JOSEPH PALIWODA, MBA, CAC-I — CARF ACCREDITATION EXPERT
Ann Arbor, MI USA
www.paragonconsulting.org

Mr. Joseph Paliwoda received his Masters in Business Administration from the University of Michigan with an emphasis on marketing. Mr. Paliwoda has over 16 years of experience in the behavioral health care field and currently the vice-president of a non-profit, behavioral health care corporation he co-founded in 1990. In this position, he is responsible for all marketing activities as well as the administration of the day-to-day operations. The corporation has over 27 employees, three locations and houses 52 men and women per day. In this position, Mr. Paliwoda is responsible for meeting all licensing and CARF accreditation requirements. Meeting accreditation requirements has become routine since he became a behavioral health surveyor for CARF. . .The Rehabilitation Accreditation Commission in 1995 . In this position, he provides administrative consultation with various substance abuse and mental health programs around the nation on ways of improving their services. His interest in business and improving services in behavioral health care prompted him to open his own consulting firm offering management training and consulting services through Paragon Consulting Services

Joseph Paliwoda
Paragon Consulting Services
Pinckney, MI USA
*Contact Phone:* 734-646-2502
**Click to Contact from Web Site**

### AMERICAN MASSAGE THERAPY ASSOCIATION (AMTA)
Evanston, IL USA
http://www.amtamassage.org

American Massage Therapy Association, (AMTA®), has over 55,000 member-massage therapists, with chapters in every state. Founded in 1943, AMTA promotes standards for the profession, a code of ethics and has an active Government Relations program. The best resource for information about: choosing and finding a qualified massage therapist, massage as a complement to conventional medicine, state regulation of massage therapy, research confirming benefits of massage, National Massage Therapy Awareness Week (NMTAW®) each October.

Ronald Precht
*Communications Manager*
American Massage Therapy Association (AMTA)
Evanston, IL
*Contact Phone:* 847-905-1649
*Contact Main Phone:* 847-864-0123
**Click to Contact from Web Site**

### JOAN LAFFEY - THE HEALTH CONNECTION AT CEDAR CREST COLLEGE
Allentown, PA USA
http://www.cedarcrest.edu

Joan M. Laffey is Dean of Student Affairs at Cedar Crest College and founder of the College's Health Connection—a program to improve mind, body and spirit. Laffey has appeared in national publications and on FOX News discussing The Health Connection. A respected educator and healthcare professional, Laffey is available to discuss the program's details and progress. She is a gateway to experts involved in the project in areas including Nutrition, Psychology, and Biology.

Allison Benner
Cedar Crest College Relations
Allentown, PA USA
*Contact Phone:* 610-740-3790
**Click to Contact from Web Site**

# EVA SZTUPKA:
# SPA & SKINCARE EXPERT

BORN IN BUDAPEST, ESTHETICIAN AND MODEL EVA SZTUPKA EMIGRATED FROM HUNGARY TO AMERICA IN 1996. DURING 2001, EVA FOUNDED AND OPENED ESSPA KOZMETIKA SKINCARE, VOTED "BEST SPA" IN PITTSBURGH FOR 2005.

Her years of advanced training and experience in traditional European skincare methods have made Eva Sztupka the leader in the creation and application of holistic, non-invasive spa treatments and organic products designed to restore, protect and maintain the skin of women, men and teenagers. Eva insists that frequent spa visits are necessary for total body health and is leading the beauty industry in making spa treatments accessible for younger boys and girls. It is Eva's strong belief that "Beautiful, healthy skin should never be a luxury."

**EVA SZTUPKA**

c/o: Scott Kerschbaumer,
VP, Communications
ESSpa Kozmetika Skincare, Inc.
17 Brilliant Avenue
Aspinwall, Pa. 15215

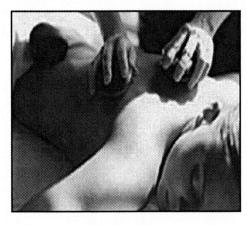

Main Phone: 412-782-3888
Contact Phone: 1-877-SPA-3300
Cell: 412-401-4219
Pager: 877-713-4567

**www.ESSpa.net**

**AGRO LABS, CHERYL RICHITT**
Dallas, TX USA
http://www.agrolabs.com

AgroLabs, Inc. manufactures and markets healthful nutritional products under the following brands: Naturally Aloe, Naturally Noni, Naturally Pomegranate, Avera Sport Nutrition and Wayless Controlled Carb Bakery and Snack Foods. These products are distributed nationwide through major mass market, grocery, drug and vitamin retailers. Marketing VP Cheryl Richitt is a leading authority on the nutraceutical industry, including the advent of noni, aloe and pomegranate juice products. AgroLabs is a subsidiary of Integrated BioPharma, Inc. (AMEX: INB).

Russ Fons
Russ Fons Pubilc Relations
Las Vegas, TX USA
*Contact Phone:* 702-658-7654
**Click to Contact from Web Site**

**TRISHA TORREY -- EVERY PATIENT'S ADVOCATE**
Syracuse, NY USA
http://www.diagKNOWsis.org

According to the US government, up to 98,000 Americans die each year from medical errors or misdiagnosis. Trisha Torrey almost became a statistic when she was diagnosed with cancer and told to begin chemo, or die within months. Instead she researched, sought second opinions, and stepped on plenty of toes, ultimately proving she had no cancer. Now she has developed tools and resources to help others be good medical consumers and decision makers.

Trisha Torrey
DiagKNOWsis :: Every Patient's Advocate
Syracuse, NY USA
*Contact Phone:* 315-446-1919
**Click to Contact from Web Site**

**LOREE TAYLOR JORDAN, C.C.H., I.D**
Campbell, CA USA
LoreeTaylorJordan.com

Loree Taylor Jordan, author of Detox for Life and Fat and Furious was personally invited by Anthony Robbins, to appear as a speaker in his Life Mastery program. As a leading health expert, Ms. Jordan has over 15 years practical and professional experience as a holistic health educator. She had hosted a two-hour radio talk show in the San Francisco Bay Area, in which her no-holds-barred message and commitment to the public's awareness made for truly outrageous radio.

Loree Taylor Jordan
Campbell, CA USA
*Contact Phone:* 408-379-9488
**Click to Contact from Web Site**

# What is the key to solving America's health crisis?

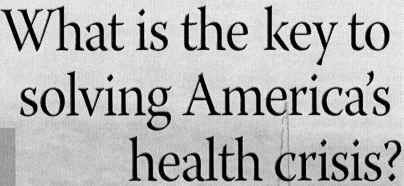

## Cedar Crest College's Health Connection and Healthy U programs are looking for answers.

Joan M. Laffey, a respected educator, administrator and healthcare professional is the Dean of Student Affairs at Cedar Crest College and the founder and co-chair of The Health Connection at Cedar Crest, a campus-wide program designed to improve mind, body

**Dean Joan Laffey is your guide.**

and spirit – and as a result, effect change at College and University campuses nationwide.

The Health Connection promotes a culture of health and wellness, emphasizing a bio-psycho-social-spiritual focus in a time when studies have suggested that many college students leave college less healthy than when they started.

The Health Connection is comprised of a number of elements including Healthy U, a 10-12 week program that encourages participants to develop healthy behaviors and meet personal health and fitness goals, ongoing research, an annual conference, and public lectures and workshops.

Joan Laffey is available to discuss the details of the progress and success of The Health Connection. She is also a gateway to the many campus experts involved in the project in specific areas such as Nutrition, Psychology, Sociology and Biology. Laffey has appeared in national and local publications and most recently on FOX News Channel discussing The Health Connection.

## BEATRICE C. ENGSTRAND, M.D., F.A.A.N.
New York, NY USA
www.doctorengstrand.com

Beatrice C. Engstrand MD is a board certified neurologist, ethicist, and geriatrician. I am a licenced physian and published author. I host my own radio show Neurology with Dr. Engstrand weekly on WOR radio.taking callers and interacting with the audience. I'm versatile with additional expertise in animal care,wildlife rehabilitation, and legal matters. Of note, I'm a single adoptive parent of 2 Russian children. I've travelled extensively throughout the world and have knowledge of several languages. I've spoken at the Diabetic association, the epilepsy foundation, NY marathon, Canyon Ranch and more. I have a well-rounded compassinate concern for the total well-being. My listeners remain faithful and trust my advice. AS a recipient of many honors Woman of Distinction, White House National Finalist,and Honary Doctorate from Lehigh University, I provide an expansive insight which adds to entertaining and expansive diaglogue.

Beatrice C. Engstrand
Huntington, NY USA
*Contact Phone:* 631-423-2100
*Cell:* 631-300-8575
**Click to Contact from Web Site**

## NATIONAL STRENGTH AND CONDITIONING ASSOCIATION
Colorado Springs, CO USA
http://www.nsca-lift.org

The National Strength and Conditioning Association is the leading authority on strength training and conditioning. For more than 26 years, the NSCA has bridged science and application to improve athletic performance and fitness by providing reliable, research-based, strength and conditioning information to its members and the general public. With nearly 30,000 members worldwide, the NSCA is the largest health and fitness association in the world.

Tom Hastings
*Director of Marketing*
National Strength and Conditioning Association
Colorado Springs, CO
*Contact Phone:* 719-632-6722
**Click to Contact from Web Site**

## NATURAL ALTERNATIVES
Oyster Bay, NY USA
www.naturalnurse.com

Ellen Kamhi, Ph.D., R.N., The Natural Nurse®, has been a leader in the wholistic health movement for over 30 years. She is on TV and radio daily, and works with medical schools as well as indigenous healers around the world. She combines integrity and clear delivery with scientific credibility. Her books include Arthritis, The Alternative Medicine Guide, The Natural Medicine Chest, Cycles of Life, Herbs for Women, and The Natural Guide to Great Sex.

Ellen Kamhi, Ph.D.,R.N.
*The Natural Nurse®*
Natural Alternatives
Oyster Bay, NY USA
*Contact Phone:* 800-829-0918
**Click to Contact from Web Site**

## DR. BILL AKPINAR, DDS, MD, PH.D. - UNIVERSITY OF NATURAL MEDICINE
New York, NY USA
http://www.universitynaturalmedicine.org/

Dr. Bill Akpinar is medical director at the Center for Healing in New York. He is a physician (M.D.), a dentist (D.D.S.), anesthesiologist and holds a doctorate in acupuncture with demonstrated excellence in auriculotherapy. Dr. Akpinar received advanced training from the personal physician to the Dalai Lama of Tibet. He is an Assistant Professor of Pain Management and Anesthesiology, and has established pain mitigation programs at numerous medical centers. He consults for many professional and college sports teams.

Dr. Bill Akpinar
Douglaston, NY USA
*Contact Phone:* 718-428-2780
**Click to Contact from Web Site**

# Health
# ┅┅ Bulletin

## WILLIAM A. KENT, THE TRUTH: DRUGS CAN KILL - FOODS CAN HEAL
New York, NY USA
www.Healthbulletin.org

For every drug there is a food, vitamin or herb that accomplishes the same positive results without the negative side effects. I can discuss the medical-scientific proof, taken strictly from medical journals. Can also discuss the Vioxx-Celebrex-Bextra fiasco, where drug companies have spun off properties of aspirin that vastly increase profits while reducing benefits. The preface of my book, What Your Doctor Doesn't Know Could Kill You, is by the Nobel Prize winner for the discovery of aspirin's action. Also, how physicians ignore solid evidence of the poor results of some surgeries and of prescription drugs--published in their own medical journals!

William A. Kent
Spuyten Duyvil, NY USA
*Contact Phone:* 718-548-5486
**Click to Contact from Web Site**

## SALLY VEILLETTE, AUTHOR AND SPEAKER

Seattle, WA USA
www.gettheglow.com

Hi, I am Sally Veillette and I want to help over-achieving women 'come to their senses', remove the 'invisible weight', and align more lightly and powerfully with their passions. I believe that the #1 problem in America is not physical, but invisible weight——the burdens that we carry on our shoulders, often the responsibilities that we assume for others. I will give you fresh choices that make life easier, more powerful, and fun.

Gloria Taylor Brown
Diva Developer
Seattle, WA USA
*Contact Phone:* 206-440-7311
**Click to Contact from Web Site**

## DAHN YOGA

Phoenix, AZ USA
http://www.dahnyoga.com

A Korean practice that dates back thousands of years is becoming a growing trend in the United States. Dahn Yoga (sometimes referred to as Dahn Hak or Dahnhak) has three components: physical exercise, accessing Ki-energy through visualization and imagery and meditation. New yoga centers are opening every month in the United States, as people strive for the total body-mind connection. Please visit www.dahnyoga.com for more information.

Martha Moyer
The Moyer Group Public Relations
Phoenix, AZ USA
*Contact Phone:* 602.861.8006
**Click to Contact from Web Site**

## COUNCIL OF COLLEGES OF ACUPUNCTURE AND ORIENTAL MEDICINE

Burtonsville, MD USA
http://www.ccaom.org

The CCAOM is an association of fifty acupuncture and Oriental medicine colleges throughout the United States that are committed to excellence in education in the field of acupuncture and Oriental medicine. Contact the CCAOM for information regarding acupuncture and Oriental medicine educational standards and opportunities.

David M. Sale, J.D., LL.M
*Executive Director*
Council of Colleges of Acupuncture and Oriental Medicine
Burtonsville, MD
*Contact Phone:* 301-476-7791
**Click to Contact from Web Site**

## JEFFREY MISHLOVE, PH.D., PARAPSYCHOLOGIST

Las Vegas, NV USA
www.intuition.org/jmbio.htm

Jeff Mishlove is the only person to have been awarded a doctoral diploma in parapsychology (the scientific study of psychic abilities and life after death) from an accredited, American university. He received his PhD from the University of California, Berkeley, in 1980. Jeff is an expert on all facets of consciousness exploration, intuition and psychic phenomena.

Jeffrey Mishlove
*President*
Intuition Network
Las Vegas, NV USA
*Contact Phone:* 702-378-0348
*Contact Main Phone:* 702-939-1800
**Click to Contact from Web Site**

## PERSONAL TRANSFORMATION PRESS
Penryn, CA USA
www.personaltransformationpress.com

Dr. Martin began his career in healing as an intern psychologist 15 years ago. In addition to conventional psychology, he studied Homeopathy, Chinese and Tibetan medicine, the Essene healings, Kahuna and many of the alternative forms of body oriented therapies. He studied with Ronald Beesley and Paul Solomon, gaining a basic understanding of the ancient laws of healing and spiritual psychology. He began developing the concepts of Neuro/Cellular therapy in 1978.

Arthur H. Martin
Personal Transformation Press
Penryn, CA USA
*Contact Phone:* 800-655-3846
**Click to Contact from Web Site**

## MCMC LLC.
Boston, MA USA
http://www.mcmcllc.com

Put Our Expertise to Work for You! MCMC is a leading source of independent health care information. Our publications include: Internet Medicine; Report of Medical Guidelines & Outcomes Research; Standards on Medical Care; and The Peer Reviewer. MCMC provides independent, objective, credible information for health care decision-making and quality improvement. MCMC is the nation's largest multi-line provider of independent, evidence-based medical reviews and related services with more than 20 years experience and more than 1000 licensed, board-certified physicians and allied health care practitioners in active practice.

Michael Lindberg
*Chief Executive Officer*
MCMC llc.
Boston, MA
*Contact Phone:* 800-227-1464
**Click to Contact from Web Site**

## NAN ANDREWS AMISH — HEALTH CARE COST EXPERT
San Francisco, CA USA
www.BigPictureHealthCare.com

Nan Andrews Amish, MBA, CLU, is a multidisciplinary, collaborative, business strategist. The Big Picture Perspective, led by Nan Andrews Amish, has three major areas of expertise: Strategic Excellence These services are designed to make sure the organization is clear about its own big picture, and that the big picture is realistic and motivating. Integrated Strategic Organizational Services The Big Picture Perspective integrates its Strategic Excellence performance systems throughout the organization. Health Care Division This division provides consulting to health care organizations who wish to address health care strategic excellence in an integrated manner. It offers all of the services available to other Big Picture Perspective clients, but with a wealth of health care expertise seldom available from other consultants.

Nan Andrews Amish
El Granada, CA USA
*Contact Phone:* 650-560-9800
**Click to Contact from Web Site**

## PATRICIA A. TRITES -- HEALTHCARE COMPLIANCE RESOURCES™
Augusta, MI USA
http://www.complianceresources.com

Patricia Trites is the Founder of Healthcare Compliance Resources, the leading healthcare compliance educational and consulting firm in the country. She presents seminars and consults nationally to physician and healthcare organizations regarding compliance issues such as, Billing and Reimbursement, HIPAA, Personnel and ERISA, OSHA, CLIA and LEP. Trites is the author of the Compliance Guide for the Medical Practice: How to Attain and Maintain a Compliant Medical Practice, recently published by the American Medical Association.

Patricia A. Trites, MPA, CPC, CHCC
*CEO*
Healthcare Compliance Resources
Augusta, MI USA
*Contact Phone:* 269-731-2561
*Cell:* 269-352-3650
**Click to Contact from Web Site**

# Get The Scoop On The
# 7 Hottest Topics In Healthcare!

**1. Who's Stealing Your Health Records?** – Healthcare Privacy/HIPAA – Hundreds of medical records are lost everyday due to neglect and theft. Are your healthcare records safe? What will happen to you if they fall into the hands of a rogue medical worker or identity thief? How can healthcare organizations and patients protect themselves?

**2. Bracing for Disaster** – The State of Emergency Care Systems in the US – How well can the current healthcare system deal with another hurricane or terrorist attack? How would the displacement of millions of Americans affect your ability to get the health services you need? How can hospitals, medical offices, and patients prevent the loss of medical records?

**3. Risky Records** – The Truth About EHRs – Following Hurricane Katrina, many healthcare providers have made the switch to Electronic Health Records. What they don't know is that many Electronic Health Record systems may be producing incomplete records that won't stand up to scrutiny in a legal or administrative proceeding. How can you tell if your records are complete and accurate? How can you fix the problem without buying a new system?

**4. Price Gouging Patients** – Healthcare Insurance – *60 Minutes* broke the story first: Uninsured patients are being charged up to 4 times that of insured patients due to a misunderstanding in the regulations. Why? And what can we do about it?

**5. Dirty Doctors** – Sexual Harassment in the Medical Environment – Hospitals and doctor's offices have some of the highest Incidents of harassment among any work environment. Why is this and what can we do as patients and workers to protect ourselves?

**6. Is Your Doctor Following the Rules?** – Healthcare Compliance – Doctors and hospitals must follow strict government regulations. Find out what they are and what to do if your healthcare provider is not following the rules.

**7. Medicare/Medicaid – What Do The Changes Mean for You?** - How do changes in Medicare/Medicaid laws affect patients and healthcare providers? Are the changes good or bad? What changes still need to be made?

**Healthcare Compliance Resources**™

## Nation's #1 healthcare compliance expert comments on breaking health news.

Patricia Trites, CHCC, CPC, CHP is one of the nation's leading experts on Medicare, Medicaid, disaster recovery, and the healthcare compliance laws protecting your health, your privacy, and your money. She is CEO of Healthcare Compliance Resources, LLC, a company that provides compliance certification, training, and resources for healthcare organizations and professionals. She sits on the editorial advisory boards of the industry's top publications, and is the author of the *Healthcare Organization and Medical Office Compliance Program Guide, Compliance Guide for the Medical Practice,* and *Due Diligence—Evaluating EHR Systems: A Hands on Manual for the Compliant EMR Before and After Purchase.*

**www.ComplianceResources.com**     **Contact:** Mike Black Media Relations • 617-230-2167 • Mike@IctusInitiative.com

## SHAPIRO HEALTHCARE MARKETING RESEARCH & MANAGEMENT CONSULTING, INC.
Maywood, NJ USA
www.jackshapiro.com

Jack M. Shapiro, President of Shapiro Healthcare Marketing Research & Management Consulting, Inc., is the well-known host of MEDI-POLITICS, the only national radio show that looks at the future of healthcare, politics, media, bioethics and the law. 31 million in audience! Based on more than 30 years in the medical field, Jack is a highly sought-after speaker on the future of American healthcare and a great resource for the media.

Jack M. Shapiro
*President*
Shapiro Healthcare Marketing Research & Management Consulting, Inc.
Maywood, NJ
*Contact Phone:* 888-331-3113
**Click to Contact from Web Site**

## AMERICAN ACADEMY OF NURSE PRACTITIONERS
Austin, TX USA
www.aanp.org

The American Academy of Nurse Practitioners (AANP) was founded in 1985 and is the oldest, largest and only full-service national professional organization for nurse practitioners of all specialties. With approximately 20,000 individual members and 110 group members, AANP represents the interests of more than 90,000 nurse practitioners around the country. AANP continually advocates for the active role of nurse practitioners as providers of high-quality, cost-effective, personalized healthcare. For more information about AANP, visit www.aanp.org

Nancy McMurrey
*Director of Communications*
American Academy of Nurse Practitioners
Austin, TX USA
*Contact Phone:* 512-442-4262
**Click to Contact from Web Site**

## M. TRAY DUNAWAY, MD, FACS, CSP, CHCO HEALTHCARE DRIVING DOCTORS CRAZY
Camden, SC USA
http://www.traydunaway.com

What physician phrustrations drive doctors crazy and are changing the fabric of American Healthcare? Dr. Dunaway practiced 16 years as an every-other-night-call surgeon until frustrations with the "business of medicine" forced him to develop a multi-million dollar business solution for physicians and hospitals. This passionate doctor's doctor gives an irreverent contrarian's insider's perspective on business issues of medicine and connects hospitals, healthcare businesses, patients, payers, and other healthcare workers to physicians in more meaningful ways.

Shawnee DeBruhl, VPoE
*VP of Everything*
Healthcare Value, Inc.
Camden, SC USA
*Contact Phone:* 803-425-8555
**Click to Contact from Web Site**

**Your Essential Connection**

## AMERICAN INDUSTRIAL HYGIENE ASSOCIATION
Fairfax, VA USA
http://www.aiha.org

Founded in 1939, AIHA represents 12,000 industrial hygiene occupational and environmental health professionals, who play an important role in worker health and safety. Members come from government, labor, industry, academia, and private business. AIHA is dedicated to improving the health and well-being of workers, the community, and the environment.

Lisa Junker
*Manager, Communications*
American Industrial Hygiene Association
Fairfax, VA
*Contact Phone:* 703-846-0734
**Click to Contact from Web Site**

## HELEN HAYES HOSPITAL
New York, NY USA
www.helenhayeshospital.org

Helen Hayes Hospital, established in 1900, is one of the nation's leading centers of excellence in physical rehabilitation medicine and research. It provides acute inpatient rehab, subacute, outpatient and transitional services to patients recovering from stroke, spinal cord and brain injury, neurological, orthopedic and cardiopulmonary diseases, helping to restore mobility and functioning. Specialties include Center for Rehabilitation Technology, Prosthetics, Orthotics, aquatic therapy and disability related research.

Mary Creagh
Helen Hayes Hospital
West Haverstraw, NY USA
*Contact Phone:* 845-786-4225
**Click to Contact from Web Site**

# THIS MAN KNOWS ABOUT THE FUTURE OF HEALTHCARE

*Jack M. Shapiro*

**TALK SHOW HOST:** Jack is the well-known host of "MEDI-POLITICS," the *only* national radio show that looks at the future of healthcare, politics, media, bioethics and the law. 31 million in audience!

**PUBLIC SPEAKER:** Based on more than 30 years in the medical field, Jack is a highly sought-after speaker on the future of American healthcare and a great resource for the media.

**AUTHOR**: Look for Jack's forthcoming book: **"A DEATH IN THE CITY: QUESTIONING THE FUTURE OF AMERICAN HEALTHCARE."**

**CONSULTANT:** Jack has assembled a team of experts to consult with healthcare organizations about their marketing and strategic planning needs.

## CONTACT: JACK M. SHAPIRO

## P.O. BOX 1025

## MAYWOOD, NEW JERSEY 07607

## 888-331-3113

## E-mail: Jack@JackShapiro.com

## Visit our Web site: www.jackshapiro.com

## DEAN KAPSALAKIS - CAKE DIET EXPERT
Roanoke, VA USA
http://www.cakediet.com/

Dean Kapsalakis, bachelor of science in Holistic Nutrition, has discovered how to create healthy snacks like cakes and cookies through a fairly simple process called extra-fortification. His new release, the Let's Eat Cake diet, a biological theory of eating, asks and answers the question, if a lion is designed to eat meat and a deer is designed to eat plants, how are humans designed? Biology ends the confusion regarding food, eliminates the guilt or denial regarding snack foods, and puts the Fun into healthy eating. Dean has done radio interviews across the country.

Dean Kapsalakis
MVPress
Catawba, VA USA
*Contact Phone:* 540-819-4666
**Click to Contact from Web Site**

## BO MARTINSEN, MD & ANNE-MARIE CHALMERS, MD — OMEGA 3 FISH OIL EXPERTS
Sarasota, FL USA
www.Omega-Cure.com

Physicians Dr. Bo Martinsen and Dr. Anne-Marie Chalmers are available to comment on the proven healing properties of Omega-3 health supplements. Omega-3 made headlines worldwide as an effective tool in the fight against heart disease, arthritis, depression, ADD/ADHD, menopausal side effects, Alzheimer's, stroke, and stress. Drs. Martinsen and Chalmer are the founders of Ambo Pharmaceutials, LLC, which markets The Omega Cure™ - the first Omega-3 fish oil sold in the U.S. that actually tastes good.

Anne-Marie Chambers, MD
Osprey, FL USA
*Contact Phone:* 941-966-7848
**Click to Contact from Web Site**

## TODAY'S CAREGIVER MAGAZINE
Hollywood, FL USA
www.caregiver.com

Caregiver Media Group is a leading provider of information, support and guidance for family and professional caregivers. Founded in 1995, we produce Today's Caregiver magazine, the first national magazine dedicated to caregivers, the Sharing Wisdom Caregivers Conferences, and our web site, caregiver.com which includes topic specific newsletters, online discussion lists, back issue articles of Today's Caregiver magazine, chat rooms and an online store. Caregiver Media Group and all of it's products are developed for caregivers, about caregivers and by caregivers.

Gary Barg
*Publisher*
Today's Caregiver Magazine
Hollywood, FL
*Contact Phone:* 954-839-0550
**Click to Contact from Web Site**

## DR GLORIA JO FLOYD
San Antonio, TX USA
http://www.DrGloriaJoFloyd.com

Nursing, Consultant, Educational and Health Services (NCEHS) was established in 1978 by Dr. Gloria Jo Floyd (Ph.D., RN). NCEHS provides nationwide the following services: Great speakers for conventins, programs and special events nationwide for Corporations Associations Women's Groups Health Care Organizations Universities, Etc. Continuing Education Courses, Live Teleseminars and Online Courses for nurses healthcare proviers, small business owenrs and related. Medical / Legal case review and analysis for plaintiffs and defendents Books, audiotapes, videotapes, manuals and guidebooks for a variety of disciplines Consultancy experts for accreditations / licensure compliance for all types of healthcare organizations Assistance with new programs or service development in nursing and healthcare organizations Three complimentary e-zine journals / magazine / newsletters The Nurses Coach™ The Peoples Coach™ The Entrepreneurs, Speaker, Consultant and Business Owners Coach™

Dr. Gloria Jo Floyd , Ph.D., R.N.
www.DrGloriaJoFloyd.com
San Antonio,, TX USA
*Contact Phone:* 210-698-8700
**Click to Contact from Web Site**

## AMERICAN ASSOCIATION OF PHARMACEUTICAL SCIENTISTS
Arlington, VA USA
http://www.aapspharmaceutica.com

The American Association of Pharmaceutical Scientists (AAPS) is a professional, scientific society of more than 13,000 individual members employed in academia, industry, government, and other research institutions worldwide. Founded in 1986, AAPS provides a dynamic international forum for the exchange of knowledge among scientists to enhance their contributions to public health. Call AAPS for expertise in the areas of drug discovery, design, development, analysis, production, quality control, clinical evaluation, and manufacturing.

Stacey May
*Director, Public Outreach*
American Association of Pharmaceutical Scientists
Arlington, VA
*Contact Phone: 703-248-4740*
*Cell: 703-864-6765*
**Click to Contact from Web Site**

## VICKI RACKNER MD FACS — DOCTOR CAREGIVER
Seattle, WA USA
http://www.MedicalBridges.com

Vicki Rackner MD is a board-certified surgeon and faculty member of the University of Washington School of Medicine who coaches patients and caregivers so they get the healthcare they want, need and deserve. Her practical tips help traverse the shortest distance between illness and health. Dr. Vicki is the author of The Personal Health Journal, The Biggest Skeleton in Your Doctor's Closet and co-author of Chicken Soup for the Soul Healthy Living Series: Heart Disease.

Vicki Rackner MD FACS
Bellevue, WA United States
*Contact Phone: 425-451-3777*
**Click to Contact from Web Site**

## UT SOUTHWESTERN MEDICAL CENTER
Dallas, TX USA
http://www.utsouthwestern.edu/home/news/index.html

The University of Texas Southwestern Medical Center at Dallas is one of the nation's leading academic medical centers, specializing in Alzheimer's and other neurological disorders; cancer; heart disease and stroke; pediatric illnesses, birth defects and inherited disorders; infectious diseases, immunology and bioterror defense; and basic genetic and molecular research, computational biology and biotechnology; as well as many other clinical and research specialties. Faculty includes four Nobel laureates, 17 members of the National Academy of Sciences.

Philip Schoch
*Assistant Vice President, News & Publications*
UT Southwestern Medical Center
Dallas, TX
*Contact Phone: 214-648-6315*
*Contact Main Phone: 214-648-3404*
**Click to Contact from Web Site**

## JAMES E. HARDY
Orlando, FL USA
http://www.mercury-free.com

James E. Hardy, D.M.D., author of the book Mercury Free has researched over 1000 scientific references including personal testimonials from people who have gone from sickness to health by becoming mercury free. He'll explain how mercury poisoning can create other disease conditions, including mood swings, short-term memory loss, headaches, kidney failure, birth defects, and other baffling symptoms.

Irene Gomulka
*Owner*
James E. Hardy
Orlando, FL
*Contact Phone: 407-898-6551*
**Click to Contact from Web Site**

## UNIVERSITY OF ILLINOIS — COLLEGE OF DENTISTRY
Chicago, IL USA
dentistry.uic.edu

The mission of the University of Illinois at Chicago College of Dentistry is to promote optimum oral and general health to the people of the State of Illinois and worldwide through excellence in education, patient care, research, and service.

Bill Bike
University of Illinois — College of Dentisty
Chicago, IL USA
*Contact Phone: 312 355-1566*
**Click to Contact from Web Site**

## AMERICAN ASSOCIATION OF ORTHODONTISTS
St. Louis, MO USA
http://www.braces.org

The American Association of Orthodontists (AAO) is a 15,000-member dental specialty organization, founded in 1900, with members in the United States, Canada and abroad. The AAO supports research and education leading to quality patient care. AAO spokespeople are uniquely qualified to discuss benefits of orthodontic treatment, trends and research.

Pam Paladin
*Communications Coordinator*
American Association of Orthodontists
St. Louis, MO
*Contact Phone: 314-993-1700*
**Click to Contact from Web Site**

## DR. JAMIE JOHNSON -- THE DENTAL DIVA
Pueblo, CO USA
http://www.Thedentaldiva.com/

Dr. Jamie Johnson has been practicing general dentistry for over 10 years. She is passionate about transforming people's fear of dentistry and created a one-of-a-kind educational DVD. Smiles for a Lifetime - how to care for your child's teeth like a mommy dentist resulted after Dr. Johnson's success in having her own son model behavior to children who were fearful of dental procedures. This DVD grows with children from birth to adolescence.

Jamie Johnson, D.D.S.
*Creator*
The Dental Diva
Pueblo, CO USA
*Contact Phone:* 888-474-6487
**Click to Contact from Web Site**

## DR. DAVID STEVENS — CHRISTIAN MEDICAL ASSOCIATION
Bristol, TN USA
www.cmdahome.org

Dr. David Stevens serves as Executive Director of the Christian Medical & Dental Associations, a movement of Christian doctors that seeks to change the heart of healthcare. From 1985 to 1991, Dr. Stevens served as executive officer of Tenwek Hospital in Bomet, Kenya. As a leading spokesman for Christian doctors in America, Dr. Stevens has conducted hundreds of television, radio and print media interviews, including NBC's Today Show, USA Today and National Public Radio. Television interviews via our satellite uplink are now available. Radio capabilites include an ISDN line.

Margie Shealy
*Director of Communications*
Christian Medical Association
Bristol, TN
*Contact Main Phone:* 423-844-1000
**Click to Contact from Web Site**

## ASSOCIATION OF AMERICAN PHYSICIANS AND SURGEONS
Washington, DC USA
http://www.aapsonline.org

Since 1943, as the voice for physicians and patients who believe in unrestricted medical freedom, the Association of American Physicians & Surgeons has spoken its mind on the tough issues. They sued the Clinton Administration to make public the secret Healthcare Task Force Records. They are against interference from the government or insurance companies. Some of the topics that concern them are Medicare Reform, Managed Care, and Patient's Rights. Nightline, Forbes and The Wall Street Journal have relied on them for stories.

Kathryn Serkes
Association of American Physicians and Surgeons
Washington, DC
*Contact Phone:* 202-333-3855
**Click to Contact from Web Site**

## MEDICAL RESEARCH ASSOCIATIES, LLC
Seattle, WA USA
www.medical-breakthroughs.com/table_of_contents.htm

The Encyclopedia of Medical Breakthroughs & Forbidden Treatments: Health Secrets & Little-Known Therapies for Specific Health Conditions from A-to-Z, puts recent breakthroughs, new treatment methods, and hard-to-find, little-known medical information, products and services directly into the hands of the reader. The Encyclopedia covers both traditional and alternative approaches, but also travels off the beaten path to uncover medical information most readers would likely never find anywhere else, even if they maintain an active interest in the fields of health and medicine. Our medical doctors are available for media interviews.

David Johnson
*Director of Media Communications*
Medical Research Associates, LLC
Seattle, WA USA
*Contact Phone:* 206-853-7799
**Click to Contact from Web Site**

## JUVENILE DIABETES FOUNDATION
New York, NY USA
JDF.org

JDRF's new billion-dollar global campaign, From Research to Reality: The Campaign to Accelerate the Cure for Diabetes, is intended to do just that: step up the transformation of research into treatments and interventions that can soon benefit people with type 1 diabetes. Focusing on JDRF's six cure therapeutic paths, this groundbreaking campaign offers you a rare chance to participate in this decisive process. Your support means helping us pay for the development of innovative therapies. It means funding the research that will culminate in a cure for diabetes. The sense of urgency is clear, yet it comes with the hope that we are nearing our goal. At JDRF dedicated to finding a cure is not just a motto—it's a call to action.

Tommi Scanlan
Juvenile Diabetes Foundation
New York, NY USA
*Contact Phone:* 212 479-7548
**Click to Contact from Web Site**

# Vicki Rackner, M.D., FACS
## *Doctor-Patient Relationship Expert*

What do you do if you just became your mother's caregiver, and you wonder if she really needs all 12 medications?

What do you say if your doctors start the exam without washing their hands, or you want an explanation of the medical condition in language you understand or you don't want to be rushed through the appointment?

What steps do you take to get a second medical opinion when the doctor says headaches are just a normal part of aging, but your intuition tells you otherwise?

Call Doctor Caregiver.

Vicki Rackner, M.D., is a board-certified surgeon and faculty member of the University of Washington School of Medicine. She left the operating room to help patients and caregivers get the health care they want, need and deserve.

Dr. Vicki believes that the most powerful medicine we have is a caring partnership between members of the health care team.  Her practical tips about what to say and what to do in challenging medical situations help patients and their caregivers traverse the shortest distance between illness and health.

Dr. Vicki is the author of "The Personal Health Journal,"  "The Biggest Skeleton in Your Doctor's Closet" and -- with Jack Canfield and Mark Victor Hansen -- "Chicken Soup for the Soul Healthy Living Series: Heart Disease."  You might see her quoted in publications that range from The Wall Street Journal to Reader's Digest to Real Simple. You might hear her on the radio, as she has been a guest on more than 100 shows.  You might consider ideas delivered in her keynote addresses.

*Test your medical advocacy savvy with a free quiz at www.DoctorCaregiver.com.*

***Ask not what your doctor can do for you; ask what you can do with your doctor.***

### *Vicki Rackner, M.D.*
*Phone: (425) 451-3777   Fax: (425) 671-0861*
*www.MedicalBridges.com   www.DrVicki.org*
*8441 SE 68th Street #298     Mercer Island, Washington 98040*

## DEBRA LACHANCE — THE HEALING PROJECT
New York, NY USA
www.thehealingproject.org

The Healing Project is a co-operative effort that reaches out to all those in need by sharing real stories about life-changing illnesses that offer strength, inspiration and hope for ourselves and others. Our objective is to develop a community whose approach to illness is GIVING in ways that can only be measured by the giver + receiver themselves. These gifts can take many forms, and we encourage you to seek within yourselves the most potent way that you can help or to click here to view our list of suggested avenues for giving.

Melissa Marr
The Healing Project
South Salem, NY USA
*Contact Phone:* 917-208-6592
**Click to Contact from Web Site**

## KERRY TUSCHHOFF, HYPNOBABIES NETWORK
Los Angeles, CA USA
www.hypnobabies.com

Kerry Tuschhoff is the foremost expert on Hypnosis for Pregnancy and Childbirth, having created the most successful hypnotic childbirth program available; Hypnobabies. She began her career in childbirth education as a Bradley natural childbirth instructor and went on to learn hypnotherapy and incorporate it into a very comprehensive natural childbirth program of her own. The results have been stunning...... and thousands of women have used Hypnobabies to give birth unmedicated and with little or no discomfort at all. The secret is Hypnobabies' hypno-anesthesia techniques which allow each Hypno-mom to move around, walk and talk and be mobile during labor, yet remain fully in hypnosis, relaxed and comfortable. She is able to take advantage of gravity and helpful relaxation positions and still maintain perfect focus, concentration and control. At Hypnobabies Kerry has developed many programs, not only for birthing mothers, but also for childbirth professionals and hypnotherapists. These include Hypnobabies childbirth classes, a self-study course, the Hypnobabies Instructor Training program, and the Hypno-Doula Program. These efforts have become immensely popular and have started a chain-reaction of interest to change the way babies get born, the way women give birth, and the way natural childbirth is perceived by the general public as well as the medical community.

Kerry Tuschhoff
Hypnobabies Network
Stanton, CA USA
*Contact Phone:* 714-898-2229
**Click to Contact from Web Site**

## ASPEN (AUTISM SPECTRUM DISORDERS)
Edison, NJ USA
AspenNJ.org

ASPEN® provides families and individuals whose lives are affected by Autism Spectrum Disorders (Asperger Syndrome, Pervasive Developmental Disorder-NOS, High Functioning Autism), and Nonverbal Learning Disabilities with: Education about the issues surrounding the disorders. Support in knowing that they are not alone, and in helping individuals with ASD's and NLD achieve their maximum potential. Advocacy in areas of appropriate educational programs, medical research funding, adult issues and increased public awareness and understanding.

Lori Shery
Aspen
Edison, NJ USA
*Contact Phone:* 732 321-0880
**Click to Contact from Web Site**

## AMERICAN KIDNEY FUND
Rockville, MD USA
www.kidneyfund.org

The American Kidney Fund (AKF) is the leading voluntary health organization serving people with, and at risk for, kidney disease. Kidney disease is among the 10 most lethal diseases in the U.S. AKF offers direct financial assistance, comprehensive education programs, clinical research fellowships, and community service programs. AKF has information about the prevention/treatment of chronic kidney disease and kidney failure, its disproportionate impact on minority communities, and organ transplantation.

Tamara Ruggiero
*Communications Director*
American Kidney Fund
Rockville, MD USA
*Contact Phone:* (301) 984-6657
*Contact Main Phone:* (301) 881-3052
**Click to Contact from Web Site**

# Kerry Tuschhoff,
## *Hypnobabies Network*

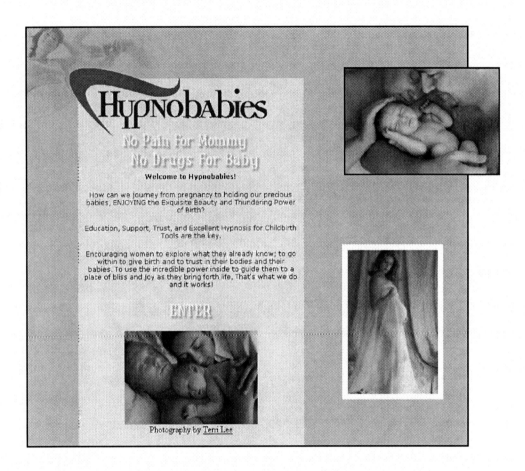

**Kerry Tuschhoff**
**Hypnobabies Network**
**Stanton, Calif. -- U.S.A.**
**Contact Phone: 714-898-BABY (2229)**

# www.hypnobabies.com

## DAVE E. DAVID, M.D.
Norfolk, MA USA
http://www.drdavedavid.com

Dave E. David is an experienced host and dynamic lecturer, whose personality and naturally-inquisitive nature make him an exciting interviewer. Dr. David, a Board Certified Obstetrician and Gynecologist as well as a weight loss specialist is a physician with over 20 years of experience. He is Harvard-trained and on the teaching faculty at Harvard University. Dr. David is available to appear on television commercials and as a spokesperson in several different venues for products he believes in.

Dave E. David, M.D.
Norfolk, MA
*Contact Phone:* 781-764-4747
*Contact Main Phone:* 800-326-4789
*Pager:* 781.764.4747
**Click to Contact from Web Site**

## NATIONAL HEADACHE FOUNDATION
Chicago, IL USA
http://www.headaches.org

NHF is the oldest and largest organization of its kind in the United States. Founded in 1970, NHF disseminates information on headache causes and treatments, funds research, sponsors public and professional education programs and has established a network of local support groups. Additionally, NHF has published Standards of Care for the Diagnosis and Treatment of Headache as well as The Therapeutic Guide for the Treatment of Headache, awards a fellowship annually, and produces NHF Head Lines, the award-winning newsletter.

Suzanne E. Simons
*Executive Director*
National Headache Foundation
Chicago, IL
*Contact Phone:* 888-643-5552
**Click to Contact from Web Site**

## MICHAEL STEFAN, M.D.
Philadelphia, PA USA
http://www.michaelstefanmd.com

Dr. Michael Stefan graduated from New York University in 1981, having double majored in both medical science and art history. Four years later, he received his doctorate from the Medical College of Pennsylvania. From there he was fellowship trained in aesthetic surgery and plastic surgery of the breast, completing his education at Georgetown University. Since then, Dr. Stefan has contributed numerous articles to medical journals. He has co-authored two book chapters on the subject of aesthetic, plastic and reconstructive breast surgery, and is regularly invited to lecture on plastic and reconstructive cancer surgery as well as cosmetic procedures. Dr. Stefan has received many awards and accolades. Most recently, he was chosen by The Consumer's Research Council of America for inclusion in their Guide to America's Top Surgeon's 2004-2005. He has been awarded Best Plastic Surgeon by the readers of Main Line Life Newspaper for the years 2001, 2002, 2003, 2004 and 2005. And he has received Top Plastic Surgeon for 2001 by Physician Poll from Main Line Today Magazine . His expertise has been cited in various newspaper articles and he has been a guest on talk shows, radio and television concerning aesthetic plastic and reconstructive surgery, as well as cancer treatment and prevention.

Michael Stefan, M.D.
Exton, PA USA
*Contact Phone:* 610-280-7900
**Click to Contact from Web Site**

## DR. EUGENE CHARLES, THE DOCTOR'S DOCTOR, HEALTH EXPERT
New York, NY USA
http://www.Charlesseminars.com

Dr. Eugene Charles DC, DIBAK, is the Doctor's Doctor. A Manhattan based author and health expert, Dr. Charles witnesses everyday the curative powers of the body and mind. He deals with the impact of living under a colored coded security alert and the deteriorating health of our society. Founder of the Charles Institute, Dr. Charles, a Diplomate in Applied Kinesiology, certifies and trains doctors of medicine and chiropractic in the diagnostic, therapeutic and inspirational tools to assist people in freeing their being from living under physical, and emotional barriers to health and happiness.

Lisa Charles
New York, NY USA
*Contact Phone:* 800-351-5450
**Click to Contact from Web Site**

## VERONA FONTE PH.D. — BIRD FLU EXPERT
Berkeley, CA USA
www.birdfluwhattodo.com

BIRD FLU WHAT TO DO: PREPARE TO SURVIVE is a concise, yet comprehensive book that outlines disaster preparation - with a particular focus on what to do if there is an influenza pandemic - for ordinary citizens. The book both consolidates resources available to the public and goes beyond what is accessible to the ordinary citizen with contributions from experts in diverse fields, and an extended appendix covering what to get, where to get it and additional information that could prove lifesaving. Rather than based on fear, Dr. Font[00e9]'s underlying premise is that disaster preparation is the most pragmatic, socially responsible thing we can do. Through relevant information and simple practical actions, individuals and neighborhoods are encouraged to empower themselves to prepare to survive in the event of any natural disaster — with added information particularly important for an avian flu pandemic.

Verona Fonte Ph.D.
*Publisher*
Iris Arts Press and Digital Media
Berkeley, CA USA
*Contact Phone:* 510 524 4150
**Click to Contact from Web Site**

 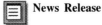

# DAVE E. DAVID, M.D.

*Do You Need a Physician As a Product Endorser, TV Spokesperson,*
*Host or Speaker?    Look no further than Dave E. David, M.D.:*
- *Obstetrician, gynecologist and weight loss/fitness specialist*
- *Can represent all types of health, fitness or medical products*

If you have a medical product, pharmaceutical product or health/fitness product that could use an endorsement by a prominent, well-known medical doctor, consider Dave E. David, M.D.

Dr. David has a warm nature and is very charismatic on camera and in person. As an experienced host and dynamic lecturer, his personality and naturally inquisitive nature make him an exciting interviewer.

Dr. David is a physician with more than 20 years of experience, treating patients and serving as assistant clinical professor at a major medical school. Harvard-trained and formerly on the teaching faculty at Harvard University, Dr. David is available to appear on television infomercials and commercials and as a spokesperson in several different venues for products he believes in.

Twenty years of media experience includes medical analyst/commentator for CNN, FOX News Channel and New England Cable News, host of his own weekly television show ("There's a Doctor in the House") and radio talk show, creator and host of "Making Womb for Baby "(full-length videotape on pregnancy and childbirth) and "Secrets to a Slimmer You" (audiotape program).

Dr. David is a SAG/AFTRA member, well-versed with teleprompter, earprompter and well-trained in commercial and dramatic acting. His appearances include infomercials with prominent celebrities and as a guest on dozens of television talk shows and extensive national exposure and recognition.

Featured on the cover of *Woman's World Magazine* and with publications in countless lay magazines and prestigious medical journals, Dr. David has treated members of the U.S. Olympic team and has acted as a medical consultant to personal fitness trainers in southern California.

As a board-certified obstetrician and gynecologist and as a weight loss specialist, Dr. David has expertise in women's health, weight loss, fitness, nutrition and herbal remedies.

DAVE E. DAVID, M.D.

NORFOLK, MASSACHUSETTS

MAIN PHONE:

800-326-4789

CONTACT PHONE:

781-764-4747

PAGER: 781-764-4747

WWW.DRDAVEDAVID.COM

## PATRICIA ANN HELLINGER, EXPERT ON IMMUNE SYSTEM DEFICIENCIES
Great Falls, MT USA
www.quasarhealing.com

Patricia Ann Hellinger, author, publisher and public speaker on Comprehensive Analysis of Natural Healing across North America. Canada and the U.K. is a strong advocate of the holistic approach to well being and brings to the public concepts, ability and methods for changing and improving ones health and the merits of the human body's immune system, which has its own perfect healing capabilities, rather than the use of harmful chemicals, prescription drugs, and medications that compromise and destroy the natural healing dynamics of the body.

Patricia Ann Hellinger
Shelby, MT USA
*Contact Phone:* 406-432-2913
**Click to Contact from Web Site**

## ZILA, INC. — ORAL CANCER DETECTION
Phoenix, AZ USA
http://www.ViziLite.com
NASDQ ZILA

The ViziLite Plus exam can help your dentist or hygienist identify abnormal tissue that might develop into oral cancer. An annual ViziLite Plus exam, in combination with a regular visual examination, provides a comprehensive oral screening procedure for patients at increased risk for oral cancer. The ViziLite Plus exam is painless and fast, and could help save your life. ViziLite Plus is performed immediately following a regular visual examination. First, you will be instructed to rinse with a cleansing solution. Next, the overhead lighting will be dimmed. Then, your dental professional will examine your mouth using ViziLite Plus, a specially designed light technology.
**Click to Contact from Web Site**

## A.P. JOHN INSTITUTE FOR CANCER RESEARCH
Jacksonville, FL USA
www.apjohncancerinstitute.org

The A.P. John Institute for Cancer Research is a non-profit organization located in Greenwich, Connecticut. Angelo P. John, Sr., a cancer scientist specializing in molecular biology has invested more than forty-five years researching cancer treatment and prevention, founded the Institute in 1978. Our cancer treatment offers healthy opportunities for cancer sufferers. The A.P. John Institute for Cancer Research functions as a conduit between you and the world of complex, confusing scientific data and studies available today. Our years of cancer research coupled with the collaboration of other researchers and our access to all of the latest scientific studies and medical information deemed necessary for understanding the whole picture in cancer prevention and treatment allow us to present this jargon in a format which is easy to comprehend and, thus, more effective in the prevention or treatment of cancer.

Angelo P. John
Jacksonville, Fl USA
*Contact Phone:* 904-260-1588
*Contact Main Phone:* 877-260-1588
**Click to Contact from Web Site**

## BREAST CARE SPECIALISTS
Roanoke, VA USA
www.breastcarespecialists.com

Dr. Alan Henry of Breast Care Specialists is a leading national expert in breast health, breast cancer, and breast cancer surgery. He is also a clinical researcher in breast cancer treatment and works with the latest technologies. He is President Emeritus of the American Society of Breast Surgeons and serves on the Society's Research and Education Committee, and is a Fellow in the American College of Surgeons and member of its Breast Advisory Panel.

Brian Gottstein
*Media Relations Manager*
Breast Care Specialists
Roanoke, VA USA
*Contact Phone:* 540-309-8255
**Click to Contact from Web Site**

## CANCER PREVENTION COALITION — SAMUEL S. EPSTEIN, M.D.
Chicago, IL USA
http://www.preventcancer.com

The Cancer Prevention Coalition (CPC) is a nationwide coalition of independent experts in cancer prevention and public health, together with citizen activists, environmental and women's health groups. CPC's goal is to reverse the escalating incidence of cancer through outreach, advocacy and public policy initiatives. CPC's Chairman, Dr. Epstein, is an internationally recognized authority on the causes and prevention of cancer. Interview topics include: modern cancer epidemic and causes; responsibility of the NCI and ACS for losing the winnable war against cancer.

Samuel S. Epstein, M.D.
*Chairman*
Cancer Prevention Coalition
Chicago, IL U.S.A.
*Contact Phone:* 312-996-2297
**Click to Contact from Web Site**

## AMERICAN SOCIETY FOR THERAPEUTIC RADIOLOGY AND ONCOLOGY
Washington, DC USA
http://www.astro.org

The American Society for Therapeutic Radiology and Oncology is the largest radiation oncology society in the world, with more than 8,500 members who specialize in treating patients with radiation therapies. As the leading organization in radiation oncology, biology and physics, ASTRO's mission is to advance the practice of radiation oncology by promoting excellence in patient care, providing opportunities for educational and professional development, promoting research and representing radiation oncology in a rapidly evolving socioeconomic healthcare environment.

Beth Bukata
*Assistant Director of Communications*
American Society for Therapeutic Radiology and Oncology
Fairfax, VA USA
*Contact Phone:* 703-839-7332
*Contact Main Phone:* 1-800-962-7876
**Click to Contact from Web Site**

# DR. MICHAEL STEFAN
### PLASTIC SURGEON

*Michael Stefan, M.D.*
*Exton, Pennsylvania*
*www.MichaelStefanMD.com*

D r. Stefan's approach to aesthetic plastic surgery is as unique as his background in both art and medicine. His training and passion for the fine arts served to hone his aesthetic sense, apparent in his work. Dr. Stefan is routinely singled out for the natural results and remarkable enhancement of his patients.

He holds board certification from both the American Board of Plastic Surgery and the American Board of Plastic and Reconstructive Surgery. He is an esteemed member of the American Society for Aesthetic Plastic Surgery, the American Society of Plastic Surgeons and the American Society of Skin Care Specialists. He is proudly affiliated with Chester County Hospital , Paoli Memorial Hospital and Bryn Mawr Hospital .

Dr. Stefan believes his medical philosophy is best summarized by Hippocrates, 400 B.C.: "Wherever the art of medicine is respected, there is also respect for humanity."

## DR MICHAEL STEFAN • AESTHETIC PLASTIC SURGEON

### 610•280•7900

### DR. PATRICK QUILLIN, CANCER & NUTRITION EXPERT
San Diego, CA USA
www.NutritionCancer.com

For 10 years, Dr. Patrick Quillin directed the nutrition program for Cancer Treatment Centers of America where he worked with thousands of cancer patients. His book, Beating Cancer with Nutrition, explains how foods and nutrition supplements can improve quality and quantity of life for medically treated cancer patients. Sugar feeds cancer and nutrients can improve the effectiveness of chemo and radiation are among the sound bites he can discuss with your viewers/listeners.

Patrick Quillin
Carlsbad, CA USA
*Contact Phone:* 760-804-5703
**Click to Contact from Web Site**

---

### DR. MICHAEL D. RABINOFF, D.O., PH.D. - UCLA / BIOGENESYS, INC.
San Jose, CA USA

Psychiatrist, author, professional speaker and media commentator. Dr. Rabinoff speaks on smoking cessation, tobacco issues, depression, anxiety disorders, weight loss and weight loss maintenance. He is board certified by the American Board of Psychiatry and Neurology. He has a faculty position at UCLA and sees patients at Kaiser Permanente. He is also CEO of Biogenesys, Inc., a biomedical research firm. He is the author of Ending The Tobacco Holocaust, to be published in November 2006.

Dr. Michael D. Rabinoff, D.O., Ph.D.
*Assistant Research Psychiatrist / C.E.O. and President*
UCLA / Biogenesys, Inc.
San Jose, CA USA
*Contact Phone:* 408-365-5525
**Click to Contact from Web Site**

---

### AMERICAN ACADEMY OF ALLERGY, ASTHMA & IMMUNOLOGY (AAAAI).
Milwaukee, WI USA
www.aaaai.org

The American Academy of Allergy, Asthma & Immunology is the largest professional medical specialty organization in the United States, representing allergists, asthma specialists, clinical immunologists, allied health professionals, and others with a special interest in the research and treatment of allergic disease. Established in 1943, the AAAAI has nearly 6,000 members in the United States, Canada and 60 other countries. The mission of the American Academy of Allergy, Asthma & Immunology is the advancement of the knowledge and practice of allergy, asthma and immunology for optimal patient care.

Michele Martinez
American Academy of Allergy, Asthma & Immunology (AAAAI).
Milwaukee, WI USA
*Contact Phone:* 414-272-6071
**Click to Contact from Web Site**

---

### DR. CHARLES BENS -- HEALTH, NUTRITION & SMOKING EXPERT
Sarasota, FL USA
http://www.thehealthysmoker.net

Dr. Bens' book The Healthy Smoker:How To Quit Smoking By Becoming Healthier First is the most controversial and most scientific book ever written on this topic. Following pioneers like Dr. Linus Pauling his books, workshops and interviews get incredible results. Best workshop ever. Better than Dr. Andrew Weil's. He stayed an hour after my show to answer the flood of calls. My patients are raving about your book. Changed my life. Never felt better.

Dr. Charles Bens
Sarasota, FL USA
*Contact Phone:* 941-377-5920
**Click to Contact from Web Site**

---

### CENTER FOR TOBACCO CESSATION
Washington, DC USA
http://www.ctcinfo.org

The Center for Tobacco Cessation (CTC) helps smokers quit by partnering with business, healthcare, and community leaders in the promotion of proven and effective tobacco cessation treatments and policies. CTC works to provide timely science-based information on treating tobacco dependence, identify emerging trends and evidence-based tobacco cessation activities, and seeks to expand access to high quality cessation services. CTC is a program supported by the American Cancer Society and The Robert Wood Johnson Foundation.

William L. Furmanski
Center for Tobacco Cessation
Washington, DC USA
*Contact Phone:* (202) 585-3200
**Click to Contact from Web Site**

## MEG JORDAN, PHD., RN
San Francisco, CA USA
megjordan.com

USA Today describes Meg Jordan, Ph.D., RN, as a 'health trendspotter'. She is a medical anthropologist, an international health journalist, radio personality, editor and founder of American Fitness Magazine, and the Global Medicine Hunter. She is the author of five books including The Fitness Instinct, (Rodale Reach 1999). Her syndicated columns, radio & television reports, and special media projects cover health, wellness, integrative medicine, indigenous healing traditions and cultural trends. She is a former health reporter for FOX, a regular media commentator for national television.

Connie St. John
St. John Group
San Francisco, CA USA
*Contact Phone:* 415-454-2243
**Click to Contact from Web Site**

## AMERICAN THORACIC SOCIETY
New York, NY USA
www.thoracic.org

The American Thoracic Society, founded in 1905, is an independently incorporated, international, educational and scientific society which focuses on respiratory and critical care medicine. Today, the Society has approximately 13,500 members, 25 percent of whom are from outside the United States. The Society's members help prevent and fight respiratory disease around the globe through research, education, patient care, and advocacy. The Society's long-range goal is to decrease morbidity and mortality from respiratory disorders and life-threatening acute illnesses.

Brian Kell
*Director of Communications and Marketing*
American Thoracic Society
New York, NY USA
*Contact Phone:* 212-315-6442
*Contact Main Phone:* 212-315-8600
**Click to Contact from Web Site**

## ADLER FOOTCARE OF GREATER NEW YORK
New York, NY USA
http://www.adlerfootcare.com

Your feet may have been hardened, even cracked, but now they can feel soft, supple, smooth, and comfortable! Renewed Podiatrist Dr. Jeff Adler has developed a remarkable two-step process to help clean, moisturize, and protect your feet. All natural and highly effective, the professional strength of Dr. Jeff Adler's footcare formulas provides you with a complete foot treatment that gives your feet real relief.

Dr. Jeffrey L. Adler
New Rochelle, NY USA
*Contact Phone:* 212-704-4310
**Click to Contact from Web Site**

## EPILEPSY FOUNDATION
Landover, MD USA
http://www.epilepsyfoundation.org

The Epilepsy Foundation is the national health agency dedicated to the welfare of nearly 3 million Americans with seizure disorders. An estimated 200,000 new cases of epilepsy occur each year. Our medical experts and spokespersons offer authoritative information on causes, symptoms, treatment, prevention, research, legal issues, social aspects, and common misconceptions concerning epilepsy.

Kimberli A. Meadows
*Director, Media Relations and Public Outreach*
Epilepsy Foundation
Landover, MD
*Contact Phone:* 301-918-3747
*Contact Main Phone:* 301-459-3700
**Click to Contact from Web Site**

AMERICAN
SPEECH-LANGUAGE-
HEARING
ASSOCIATION

## AMERICAN SPEECH-LANGUAGE-HEARING ASSOCIATION
Rockville, MD USA
http://www.asha.org

Nearly 50 million Americans have speech, language or hearing problems or disorders affecting swallowing or balance. Communication disorders can occur at any age and affect one's ability to hear, speak, understand, read or write. Contact ASHA for information about communication disorders, including hearing loss, noise, tinnitus, speech or voice problems, swallowing disorders, newborn hearing screening, language development, and accent modification. ASHA (est. 1925) is the professional, scientific, and credentialing organization for more than 123,000 audiologists, speech-language pathologists, and speech, language, and hearing scientists, the professionals who specialize in the research and treatment of communication disorders.

Mona Thomas
*Manager, Public Relations*
American Speech-Language-Hearing Association
Rockville, MD
*Contact Phone:* 301-897-0156
*Cell:* 301-592-7613
**Click to Contact from Web Site**

## MURRAY GROSSAN, MD — TOWER EAR NOSE THROAT — CEDARS SINAI
Los Angeles, CA USA
http://www.ent-consult.com

As an Otolaryngologist specializing in Scuba Diving, he innovates drug free treatments for divers and non-divers. He has published 36 peer review articles in his fields of expertise: Sinusitis, Tinnitus, Scuba Diving, Hearing Loss Prevention, and Voice. He has been interviewed for Bottom Line, Dallas News, Time, Los Angeles Times, and TV's 9, & 11. Time Magazine listed his Hydro Pulse method of sinus relief in Inventions 2000. His web site records 700,000 visitors.

Murray Grossan, MD
*Ear Nose Throat Physician*
Tower Ear Nose Throat - Cedars Sinai
Los Angeles, CA USA
*Contact Phone:* 310 659 1006
**Click to Contact from Web Site**

## THE FOUNDATION FIGHTING BLINDNESS, INC.
Owings Mills, MD USA
http://www.FightBlindness.org

The Foundation Fighting Blindness (FFB) is dedicated to finding treatments and cures for all retinal degenerative diseases. FFB is ranked as a Top-Rated charity by the American Institute of Philanthropy and is the world's leading authority on macular degeneration, retinitis pigmentosa (RP), Stargardt disease and other related diseases. Call FFB to arrange an interview with scientific experts about groundbreaking research and how it impacts millions of Americans affected by these blinding diseases.

Allie Laban-Baker
*Senior Director, Communications & Marketing*
The Foundation Fighting Blindness, Inc.
Owings Mills, MD
*Contact Phone:* 410-568-0126
**Click to Contact from Web Site**

## THE SEEING EYE
Morristown, NJ USA
http://www.seeingeye.org

The Seeing Eye is a philanthropy that helps blind people increase their independence and mobility with properly trained Seeing Eye dogs. Since 1929, it has placed more than 13,000 Seeing Eye dogs with blind people across North America. Seeing Eye is a registered trademark for dog guides of The Seeing Eye, Inc.

Teresa Davenport
*Manager of Public Relations*
The Seeing Eye
Morristown, NJ
*Contact Phone:* 973-539-4425
**Click to Contact from Web Site**

## CENTER FOR THE DEAF AND HARD OF HEARING
Milwaukee, WI USA
http://cdhh.org

CDHH, a non-profit agency, provides comprehensive services to individuals with hearing loss, from infants to the elderly. Professionals on staff have specialized training enabling them to provide practical help and support to those dealing with the challenges of hearing loss plus education on hearing loss prevention. Services include speech therapy, pre-and post-cochlear implant training, assistive listening and living device showroom and training, hearing evaluation and hearing aid fittings, communication strategies classes, sign language classes.

Kerry Malak
*Communications Director*
Center for the Deaf and Hard of Hearing
West Allis, WI USA
*Contact Phone:* 414-604-7202
*Contact Main Phone:* 414-604-2200
**Click to Contact from Web Site**

## DOGS FOR THE DEAF, INC.
Central Point, OR USA
http://www.dogsforthedeaf.org

Established in 1977, Dogs for the Deaf is a non-profit organization that rescues dogs from shelters, professionally trains them to serve as the ears of people who are deaf or hard of hearing, and places them nationwide and in Canada free of charge. The dogs are trained to alert people to environmental sounds. These dogs have been credited with saving lives, enhancing parenting skills, increasing employability, and providing the priceless gifts of freedom, independence, and love.

Robin Dickson
*President/CEO*
Dogs for the Deaf, Inc.
Central Point, OR
*Contact Phone:* 541-826-9220
**Click to Contact from Web Site**

## NATIONAL LIBRARY SERVICE FOR THE BLIND AND PHYSICALLY HANDICAPPED
Washington, DC USA
http://www.loc.gov/nls

Through a national network of cooperating libraries, NLS administers a free library program of braille and audio materials circulated to eligible borrowers in the United States by postage-free mail.

Jane Caulton
National Library Service BPH
Washington, DC USA
*Contact Phone:* 202-707-0521
**Click to Contact from Web Site**

# GLOBAL MEDICINE HUNTER™

## ...Alternative Adventures

**M**eg Jordan, Ph.D, RN, is a blend of Indiana Jones and Crocodile Hunter with an added air of mysticism unlike anyone you have interviewed.

The Global Medicine Hunter is Meg Jordan, an award-winning journalist, TV personality, author and medical anthropologist. Jordan, traverses the globe in search of ancient cures and seemingly medical magic.

Sometimes she debunks unfounded claims, but more often she reveals where modern scientists are changing their view of traditional healing remedies.

Humor pervades, despite the seriousness of the subjects. Jordan presents an interesting and insightful interview on the following topics:

- The Best Natural Pain Relievers in Existence
- The Holy Grail of Cures...A Cure For The Common Cold and Flu
- The Greatest Sleeping Remedies in the World
- The Most Powerful Aphrodisiac on Earth
- The Best Memory and Intelligence Boosters on The Planet
- The Power of Dreams and Sleep
- The Source of Fertility
- The Real Fountain of Youth
- Ways to End Teen Age Violence and Aggression
- The Magic of Music and Drumming
- The Ultimate Beauty Enhancers
- Unraveling the Mind Body Connection

Jordan will unearth the facts, expose the frauds, and dispel the myths of medicine whenever she encounters them.

Meg Jordan is...
The Global Medicine Hunter.

**Contact: The St. John Group, 415-454-2243**

## AMERICAN COUNCIL OF THE BLIND
Washington, DC USA
http://www.acb.org

ACB is a national organization of blind, visually impaired and sighted individuals working toward independence, security, equality of opportunity and improved quality of life for all blind and visually impaired people.

Sharon Lovering
*Editor*
American Council of the Blind
Washington, DC
*Contact Phone:* 202-467-5081
**Click to Contact from Web Site**

## BCCNS LIFE SUPPORT NETWORK
Cleveland, OH USA
http://www.bccns.org

BCCNS Life Support Network is a non-profit organization whose mission is to provide education and support services to children and adults manifesting inherited, metabolic or genetic disorders & diseases most commonly known as BCCNS, NBCCS, and/or Gorlin Syndrome. The Network offers essential training and educational meetings to over 400 members, their families and medical professionals. Our outreach to the special needs Gorlin Syndrome patients provides hope, self-esteem, and knowledge, together with the tools to manage their condition.

Kristi Schmitt Burr
Basal Cell Carcinoma Nevus Syndrome Life Support Network
Burton, OH USA
*Contact Phone:* 440-635-0078
**Click to Contact from Web Site**

## ENDOMETRIOSIS ASSOCIATION
Milwaukee, WI USA
http://www.endometriosisassn.org

In existence for 23 years, the Endometriosis Association is currently represented in 43 countries. It provides direct support to women and girls with endometriosis (crisis call service; chapters and support groups; educational materials) raises awareness about the disease with the medical community and the public at large; has an extensive research program, including the largest registry on endometriosis and a scientific team at Vanderbilt University School of Medicine. Links with the National Institutes of Health in research on the disease.

Mary Lou Ballweg
*President/Executive Director*
Endometriosis Association
International Headquarters
Milwaukee, WI
*Contact Phone:* 414-355-2200
*Contact Main Phone:* 414-355-2200
**Click to Contact from Web Site**

## SENSORY RESOURCES, CONFERENCES & PUBLICATIONS ON SENSORY DYSFUNCTION
Las Vegas, NV USA
www.SensoryResources.com

When a person's body misinterprets the sense of touch, movement, taste, smell, sound and/or pressure, he has "Sensory Processing Dysfunction (SPD)." One of ten children is estimated to have this condition that negatively affects learning and behavior. Sensory Resources, a totally unique U.S. company: publishes more than 25 publications on sensory integration (SI); distributes over 100 SI products; hosts over 20 workshops annually, featuring experts like Carol Stock Kranowitz.

Lyn Dunsavage
Sensory Resouces
Las Vegas, NV USA
*Contact Phone:* 888-357-5867
**Click to Contact from Web Site**

## MERCURY MASTERS — THE RUNNING TEAM FOR WOMEN 50+
New York, NY USA
http://www.mercurymasters.org/

Founded in 1995, Mercury Masters is the only team exclusively for women runners 50+ in the New York City area, established to promote a healthy lifestyle, camaraderie, and mutual support. As one of the official teams of the New York Road Runners, Mercury Masters holds first place ranking in the women's veterans division for 2002, 2003, third place for 2004, and second place in the new for 2005 established women's super veterans (age 60+) division. Members have collectively completed over 249 marathons in 23 states, 14 foreign countries on 5 continents, and raised substantial funds for charities. All levels of fitness - walkers to runners - train weekly with our coach Neil L.Cook of SLB Coaching and Training Systems. Neil was Sean P. Diddy Combs' running coach for the 2003 New York City Marathon.

Ilene Kent
Mercury Masters
New York, NY USA
**Click to Contact from Web Site**

## CURESEARCH NATIONAL CHILDHOOD CANCER FOUNDATION

Bethesda, MD USA

http://www.curesearch.org

## AMERICAN ACADEMY OF ANTI-AGING MEDICINE

Chicago, IL USA

http://www.worldhealth.net

## INTERNATIONAL ACADEMY OF ANTI-AGING MEDICINE

Los Angeles, CA USA

www.antiagingforme.com

CureSearch National Childhood Cancer Foundation proudly supports the life-saving research efforts of the world's largest and most prestigious childhood cancer research organization, the Children's Oncology Group. At more than 200 member institutions, representing every pediatric cancer program in North America, a network of over 5,000 dedicated physicians, nurses and scientists are conducting clinical trials and performing cutting-edge research to identify cancer causes and pioneer treatments and cures. Everything that we know about saving the lives of children diagnosed with cancer has come through cooperative research conducted over the past 50 years. Once considered nearly incurable; today, 78% of cancer's youngest patients overall will survive. However, in spite of this progress, childhood cancer is the #1 disease killer of children. Every school day, 46 children or two classrooms full are diagnosed with cancer, over 12,500 a year. The death of one more child to cancer is one too many. Research is the key to a cure. Our vision is to reach the day when every child with cancer is guaranteed a cure. For more information about CureSearch, please visit www.curesearch.org.

Sally Charney
*Director of Public Education*
CureSearch National Childhood Cancer Foundation
Bethesda, MD USA
*Contact Phone:* 240-235-2205
*Contact Main Phone:* 800-458-6223
**Click to Contact from Web Site**

The American Academy of Anti-Aging Medicine (A4M; www.worldhealth.net) is the world's largest professional organization dedicated to advancing research and clinical pursuits that enhance the quality, and extend the quantity, of the human lifespan. A4M is comprised of 18,500 physician, scientist, and health practitioner members from 90 nations. Since its founding in 1992, A4M's scientific educational programs have trained over 100,000 medical professionals, and the organization's education and advocacy initiatives have expanded the availability of advanced biotechnologies and leading-edge preventive healthcare throughout the world.

Catherine Cebula
*Media Spokesperson*
American Academy of Anti-Aging Medicine
Chicago, IL
*Contact Phone:* 773-528-4333
**Click to Contact from Web Site**

California 501-C non-profit educational organization; 16 board members, specialists in anti-aging, environmental and alternative medicine. Dr. Hans J. Kugler, Ph.D., President and Founder: Physiology, University of Munich Med. School under Nobel Laureate Butenandt, PhD, SUNY Stony Brook, NY; associate professor, longevity studies with cancer-prone animals, Roosevelt University, Chicago. Lecturer at medical meetings and author of seven books on aging, including Tripping the Clock, and Anti-Aging Medical Therapeutics. 500+ appearances on radio and TV.

Dr. Hans Kugler
International Academy of Anti-Aging Medicine
Redondo Beach, CA USA
*Contact Phone:* 310-540-0564
**Click to Contact from Web Site**

## KEITH NABE -- FLU EXPERT

Orlando, FL USA

www.worldhealth.net

Well, its that time of year again! Flu Season is quickly threatening our well being again, as fall is now upon us. This year, as last year, I will keep you updated on the progress of the flu, state by state by keeping in touch with the CDC (Centers for Disease Control) in Atlanta, Georgia.

Keith E. Nabe
*C.E.O & President*
Accelerated Relief
Crestview, FL USA
*Contact Phone:* 850 682 1213
*Contact Main Phone:* 850 685 3719
*Cell:* 850 685 3719
**Click to Contact from Web Site**

## MIAMI JEWISH HOME & HOSPITAL FOR THE AGED

Miami, FL USA
http://www.mjhha.org

The Southeast's most comprehensive center for geriatric care. Long/short term skilled nursing beds, assisted/independent living apartments, adult day care, Alzheimer's care, rehabilitation, chronic pain management and biofeedback, stroke prevention/education, mental health services, gerontological research, senior housing design, assistive technology and barrier-free design consultation.

Jay Sweeney
*Director, PR/Marketing*
Miami Jewish Home & Hospital for the Aged
Miami, FL
*Contact Phone:* 305-751-8626
**Click to Contact from Web Site**

## GRISWOLD SPECIAL CARE

Erdenheim, PA USA
www.griswoldspecialcare.com

GRISWOLD SPECIAL CARE is a non-medical homecare company. We refer Caregivers who provide personal care, homemaking, companionship, incidental transportation and other services to Clients wishing to remain safe and independent at home. Contact us about: Advocacy / Support / Legislation / and other issues concerning: Aging, Health care, Home care, Disability care, Family care and finances, Dementia care, Non-medical care, Criminal background checks, Home business, Eldercare, Home vs. residential care, Home care licensing, Long term care insurance.

Dot Folz
*Marketing Manager*
GRISWOLD SPECIAL CARE
Erdenheim, PA USA
*Contact Phone:* 215-402-0200
*Contact Main Phone:* 888-777-7630
**Click to Contact from Web Site**

## ALTERNATIVE LIVING FOR THE AGING

Los Angeles, CA USA
Alternative Living for the Aging (ALA) is a pioneering nonprofit organization dedicated to providing housing alternatives for older people — alternatives to living alone and to institutionalization. Janet Witkin, Founder and Executive Director of ALA, is a sought-after speaker on housing alternatives for older people — innovative housing where seniors retain their privacy and dignity, and remain active and independent. Janet started ALA in 1978, and has testified before Congressional Committees and the California and Minnesota State legislatures.

Janet Witkin
*Founder and Executive Director*
Alternative Living for the Aging
West Hollywood, CA
*Contact Phone:* 323-650-7988
**Click to Contact from Web Site**

## STONEWALL COMMUNITIES, INC. - GAY AND LESBIAN AGING ISSUES

Boston, MA USA
http://www.stonewallcommunities.com

Since 1998, Stonewall Communities' mission has been to better understand and advocate for the needs of the older members of the LBGT Community. The organization is creating more options for older people and developing residential communities that will combine quality housing with a supportive, inclusive and diverse community. Stonewall Audubon Circle in Boston, Massachusetts will be their first residence and the nation's first urban condominium community for older gay men, lesbians and their friends.

David Aronstein
Stonewall Communities, Inc.
Boston, MA USA
*Contact Phone:* 617-363-0405
**Click to Contact from Web Site**

## THE SUNBOX COMPANY

Gaithersburg, MD USA
http://www.sunbox.com

Neal Owens founded the SunBox Company in 1985 to provide information and quality phototherapy products to researchers, clinicians and the millions who struggle with seasonal difficulties sometimes referred to as SAD (Seasonal Affective Disorder). He was one of the first patients to use bright light treatment (phototherapy) for fall/winter systems of fatigue, difficulty concentrating, social withdrawal, weight gain, carbohydrate cravings and depression. He is available for interviews and lectures.

Neal Owens
*President*
The SunBox Company
Gaithersburg, MD
*Contact Phone:* 301-869-5980
**Click to Contact from Web Site**

## BIO BRITE INC.

Bethesda, MD USA
www.biobrite.com

Light affects mood, energy, sleeping and eating cycles, and other aspects of our biological clock. Scientists have shown that a lack of light can lead to health problems, including depression, weight gain, and sleeping problems. Bio-Brite's patented products, can defeat winter blues, beat jet-lag, improve sleep, and help get children up for school on time! Our experts have been featured on radio and TV and in print, including the Wall Street Journal and the Washington Post.

Mr. Kirk Renaud
*CEO*
Bio Brite Inc.
Bethesda, MD
*Contact Phone:* 301-961-5940
**Click to Contact from Web Site**

## BRAD BLANTON, PH. D., RADICAL HONESTY
Stanley, VA USA
www.radicalhonesty.com

Dr. Brad Blanton, psychotherapist, seminar facilitator, author of six books about Radical Honesty teaches that the primary cause of stress, depression and anger is living in a story and trying to maintain it by lying, and that we are all doing it to some degree all the time. Brad's media appearances include 20/20, Roseanne, Dateline-NBC, CNN, Montel Williams, Iyanla and others. articles in Cosmopolitan, Family Circle, Inner Self, Men's Health, The Chicago Herald-Tribune, The Washington Post and others. Brad Blanton is a candidate for U.S. Congress in 2006. www. blantonforcongress.com and www.radicalhonesty.com

Brad Blanton
Radical Honesty Enterprises, Inc.
Stanley, VA USA
*Contact Phone:* 540-778-2982
*Cell:* 540-421-6668
**Click to Contact from Web Site**

## AUTISM/ASPERGER'S SYNDROME
Dallas, TX USA
www.futurehorizons-autism.com

We became the leading publisher in the world in autism/Asperger's primarily because my son, Alex, was diagnosed with autism. This event led me to write a charming little book, Laughing and Loving with Autism., as I tried to show the world some of the positives and joys that a child with autism can bring. Soon other authors were bringing their books to us in numbers so large that in a short time, we stopped publishing in all other venues and focused in this field. For the first time in my life, I was blessed in that my vocation and passion were blended. Alex's perspectives constantly led me to redefine my language and outlook.

Lyn Dunsavage
Future Horizons, Inc.
Arlington, TX USA
*Contact Phone:* 800-489-0727
**Click to Contact from Web Site**

## CARON FOUNDATION
Wernersville, PA USA
http://www.caron.org

One of the nation's oldest and largest single-site addiction treatment centers specializing in treatment for adults and adolescents. Experts available on: prevention, assessment, detoxification, treatment and relapse issues; impact of addiction on families; unique issues of executives and professionals; and specialized treatment for women. Resource for addiction professionals in prevention, education and assessment in schools as well as youth tobacco cessation programs. Source of people in recovery from alcohol and all types of drugs.

Sally Orth
*Director of Communications/Public Relations*
Caron Foundation
Wernersville, PA
*Contact Phone:* 610-743-6245
*Contact Main Phone:* 800-678-2332
**Click to Contact from Web Site**

## RICK COLLINS, ESQ.
New York, NY USA
http://www.steroidlaw.com

Rick Collins, Esq., is America's foremost legal authority on anabolic steroids and other muscle-building drugs and supplements. This New York lawyer and former prosecutor is the author of the groundbreaking book, Legal Muscle, and has been interviewed on national television talk and news shows, in talk radio interviews and by countless online and print publications on the topic of athletic/cosmetic steroid use and its associated legalities and penalties.

Rick Collins, Esq.
Collins, McDonald & Gann
Carle Place, NY USA
*Contact Phone:* 516-294-0300
**Click to Contact from Web Site**

## REVEREND KAREN E. HERRICK, LCSW, CADC, PHD CANDIDATE
Red Bank, NJ USA
http://www.adult-child.com

The 9/5/2005 issue of Newsweek stated that Americans are looking for an immediate, transcendent experience of God. 30-50% of Americans have had such a spiritual experience (SE). Perhaps you have too but you don't know it? Rev. Karen Herrick names SEs, educates and helps you to add substance and meaning to your lives. Her PhD work helps other therapists understand the difference between hallucinations and spiritual experiences. She is a frequent radio guest on SEs.

Karen E. Herrick, LCSW, CADC
*Reverend*
Red Bank, NJ
*Contact Phone:* 732-530-8513
**Click to Contact from Web Site**

### JEFFREY S. WOLFSBERG & ASSOCIATES INC., ALCOHOL & OTHER DRUG PREVENTION SPECIALISTS
Boston, MA USA
www.jeffwolfsberg.com

Jeff Wolfsberg is internationally recognized as an expert in the field of the prevention of underage drinking and other drug use among adolescents. He has appeared in TIME Magazine and is a regular presenter at conferences throughout the world. His firm works with primary and secondary schools worldwide designing and implementing effective prevention programs. His firm has conducted seminars for schools and parents organizations in over eleven countries and almost every state in the United States.

Jeffrey S. Wolfsberg
*President*
Jeffrey S. Wolfsberg and Associates, Inc.
Canton, MA USA
*Contact Phone:* 781-821-6144
*Cell:* (508) 728-1706
**Click to Contact from Web Site**

### ROBERT R. BUTTERWORTH, PH.D.
Los Angeles, CA USA
http://www.drbutterworth.net

Psychologist and media commentator, Robert R. Butterworth, Ph.D., has assisted radio, TV, and print media in finding answers and providing insight to enhance understanding of psychological issues. He has conducted extensive surveys focused on youth, social, political and trauma issues. His articles have appeared in most of the major newspapers in the United States and worldwide. He is seen on NBC, CBS, ABC, FOX and CNN network news.

Robert R. Butterworth
*Director*
Robert R. Butterworth, Ph.D.
Los Angeles, CA USA
*Contact Phone:* (213) 487-7339
*Contact Main Phone:* (213) 487-7339
*Pager:* (213) 487-7339
**Click to Contact from Web Site**

### INTERNATIONAL TRANSACTIONAL ANALYSIS ASSOCIATION, INC.
Pleasanton, CA USA
http://www.itaa-net.org/contact.htm

Transactional analysis is a powerful tool to bring about human well being. In psychotherapy, transactional analysis utilizes a contract for specific changes desired by the client and involves the Adult in both the client and the clinician to sort out behaviors, emotions and thoughts that prevent the development of full human potential. Transactional analysts intervene as they work with clients in a safe, protective, mutually respectful-OK/OK— environment to eliminate dysfunctional behaviors and establish and reinforce positive relationship styles and healthy functioning. Transactional analysts are able to use the many tools of psychotherapy, ranging from psychodynamic to cognitive behavioral methods in effective and potent ways. Examples of transactional analysis psychotherapy can bee seen in our Master Therapists series, the Ellyn Bader and Peter Pearson Couples Therapy Videotapes and the Carlo Moiso-Isabelle Crespelle DVD.

Gaylon Palmer M.S.W.
*Licensed Clinical Social Worker*
International Transactional Analysis Association, Inc.
Pleasanton, CA USA
*Contact Phone:* 925-600-8110
**Click to Contact from Web Site**

### DR. JOYCE BROTHERS
New York, NY USA

Psychologist

Dr. Joyce Brothers
*Contact Phone:* 212-831-2221
**Click to Contact from Web Site**

### DR. MICHAEL NUCCITELLI, LICENSED PSYCHOLOGIST
New York, NY USA
http://www.slshealth.com

Dr. Nuccitelli is a N.Y.S. Licensed Psychologist and Executive Director of SLS Health Inc. Dr. Nuccitelli has appeared in a variety of media venues including 'O'Reilly Factor', 'CNN', 'Headline News', 'New York Times', 'Washington Post', 'Miami Herald', and 'Westwood One'. Dr. Nuccitelli is also a regularly scheduled guest on 'Court TV'. Expertise: Psychology of Terrorism, Forensic (Criminal) Psychology, Child/Adolescent, Celebrity Psychology, Women's Issues, Sexuality, Addictions, Current Events, Psychiatry, Political Analysis, Stress, and Mental Health.

Dr. Michael Nuccitelli
*Executive Director*
SLS Wellness
Brewster, NY USA
*Contact Phone:* 845-629-0205
*Contact Main Phone:* 845-279-3500
*Cell:* 845-629-0205
**Click to Contact from Web Site**

### NATIONAL ASSOCIATION OF SOCIAL WORKERS
Washington, DC USA
www.socialworkers.org

NASW is the largest organization of professional social workers in the world, with 153,000 members. Ninety percent hold master's degrees in social work. Social Workers help people in all stages of life, from children to the elderly, and in all situations from adoption to hospice care. Social Workers represent the largest number of mental health service providers in the nation. Other specialties of this "helping profession" include aging, behavioral health, health and health disparities, and children and families.

Allison Nadelhaft
*Sr. Communications Associate*
National Association of Social Workers
Washington, DC USA
*Contact Phone:* 202-336-8228
*Cell:* 410-336-0101
**Click to Contact from Web Site**

## CAROLE LIEBERMAN, M.D., MEDIA PSYCHIATRIST
Beverly Hills, CA USA
http://www.drcarole.com

The entertainment industry knows Dr. Carole Lieberman for her uncanny ability to jump in, deliver and excel in any position for which she is needed: TV/Radio Host, Commentator or Regular Guest; Author; Trial Analyst; Reality Therapist; and more! Hundreds of interviews include: Oprah, Larry King, Today, GMA, O'Reilly, ET, Court TV, Howard Stern, N.Y. Times and USA Today. Everyone puts their feet up on Dr.Carole's couch to get smart, savvy and sensitive insights on today's world!

Carole Lieberman, M.D.
Beverly Hills, CA
*Contact Phone:* 310-278-5433
**Click to Contact from Web Site**

## CAROLYN BUSHONG, LICENSED PROFESSIONAL COUNSELOR
Denver, CO USA
http://www.carolynsays.com

Carolyn Bushong, author of three relationship books, has a new book: Bring Back The Man You Fell In Love With. Bushong shows you how you can reclaim your dream man and put the magic back into your relationship. Carolyn Bushong is a practicing psychotherapist, and is an enthusiastic, knowledgeable expert who has appeared on Oprah, and other national talk shows. Carolyn Bushong has been giving relationship advice to FM morning drive-time radio listeners for years.

Carolyn Bushong, L.P.C.
Carolyn Bushong Psychotherapy Associates, Inc.
Denver, CO USA
*Contact Phone:* 303-333-1888
*Contact Main Phone:* 800-548-1888
**Click to Contact from Web Site**

## WILMA TAYLOR
Chicago, IL USA
www.WilmaTaylorMinistries.org

When Evangelist Wilma Taylor speaks, even Corporate America listens. A registered nurse, minister, motivationalist, revivalist and trainer, who has a life changing message with an unusual way of reaching people. Wilma feels listening is an art that is frequently neglected. Are we neglecting the cries of our children, our companions, our friends, the elderly and God? There are fears, delusions, depression, self destruction, substance abuse, domestic violence, illness and poverty plaguing our society.

Wilma Taylor
Wilma Taylor Ministries
Chicago, IL USA
*Contact Phone:* 773-734-4062
**Click to Contact from Web Site**

## DR. FRANK FARLEY
Philadelphia, PA USA

Internationally recognized authority in psychology and human behavior. Former president, American Psychological Association (160,000 members). Articulate and experienced in working with the media, including Time, Newsweek, U.S. News, New York Times, Wall Street Journal, USA Today, Business Week, Today Show, 20/20, Good Morning America, 48 Hours, CNN, FOX, PBS Newshour, Discovery, A & E, NPR, Leeza, and others.

Dr. Frank Farley
*The L.H. Carnell Professor*
Temple University
Philadelphia, PA
*Contact Phone:* 215-204-6024
*Cell:* 215-668-7581
**Click to Contact from Web Site**

## ASSOCIATION FOR COGNITIVE & BEHAVIORAL THERAPIES (ABCT)
New York, NY USA
http://www.aabt.org

ASSCOCIATION FOR COGNITIVE & BEHAVIORAL THERAPIES (ABCT) Formerly Know As ASSOCIATION FOR ADVANCEMENT OF BEHAVIOR THERAPY (AABT) A not-for-profit organization of 4,500+ specialists who use behavior therapy and cognitive behavior therapy, empirically-supported therapies that are usually goal-oriented, short-term, and in many instances drug free, to treat many mental health and societal problems. Assists media with experts and research. Holds a convention each November. Founded 1966.

David Teisler, CAE
*Director of Communications*
Association for Cognitive & Behavioral Therapies (ABCT)
New York, NY
*Contact Phone:* 212-647-1890
**Click to Contact from Web Site**

### NATIONAL BOARD FOR CERTIFIED COUNSELORS, INC. AND AFFILIATES
Greensboro, NC USA
http://www.nbcc.org

National Board for Certified Counselors, Inc. and Affiliates (NBCC), the largest counselor credentialing organization, certifies Master's level counselors meeting specific requirements. More than 39,000 professionals worldwide hold the National Certified Counselor (NCC) credential. NBCC's Code of Ethics governs all NCCs providing public protection. NBCC offers specialty certifications in School, Clinical Mental Health, and Addictions Counseling. The Center for Credentialing & Education, an NBCC affiliate, offers credential and board management services for counseling and other professions.

Rita Maloy, MPA
*Project Manager*
National Board for Certified Counselors, Inc.
Greensboro, NC
*Contact Phone:* 336-547-0607
**Click to Contact from Web Site**

### BARBARA BARTLEIN
Milwaukee, WI USA
http://www.barbbartlein.com

Barbara Bartlein is a relationship expert, motivational humorist and author of Why Did I Marry You Anyway? 12.5 Strategies for a Happy Marriage. She has a syndicated column, 'Success Matters,' which appears widely across the US and Canada. Barbara provides entertaining and provocative interviews and articles. She has been featured in TV/Radio and Print Media including: Fox Network, Phil Donohue Show, Chicago Tribune, Washington Post, Milwaukee Sentinel and The Business Journal.

Barbara Bartlein, RN, MSW
Great Lakes Consulting Group
Milwaukee, WI
*Contact Phone:* 888-747-9953
**Click to Contact from Web Site**

### INSTITUTE FOR CREATIVE SOLUTIONS -- RANDY ROLFE
West Chester, PA USA
http://www.instituteforcreativesolutions.com

Randy Rolfe, JD, MA, offers the newest tools for improving families, raising great kids, and bringing out the best in others. Her favorite issues include how differences attract, why spouses fight, public impact on private lives, overcoming negative influences on kids, and finding happiness. She is author of 5 titles, including The Four Temperaments; The Seven Secrets of Successful Parents, and You Can Postpone Anything But Love. A seasoned guest on Sally, Montel, Geraldo, Maury and radio.

Randy Rolfe
*President*
Institute for Creative Solutions
West Chester, PA
*Contact Phone:* 610-429-5869
**Click to Contact from Web Site**

### KERRIN CARLEEN HOPKINS - PERSONALITY PROFILE EXPERT
Skaneateles, NY USA
http://www.youresuchadave.com/

Kerrin consults all over the world on the correlation between a person's name and personality traits you can expect from a person, knowing their name. This work is studied at Universities throughout the world; Oxford, MIT, Univ of Chicago, Stanford; to name a few; it is also used at major retailers, Wal Mart, Best Buy; American Outfitters; Macy's; as they track sales and stock stores based on the names of their customers. Kerrin innately knows the strengths, weaknesses and compatibility of names. Her web site is www.youresuchadave.com

Kerrin Carleen Hopkins
One Day Corporate Workshops
Skaneateles, NY USA
*Contact Phone:* 315-263-9242
**Click to Contact from Web Site**

## HENRY JOHNSON -- MEN'S HEALTH NUTRITION & FITNESS EXPERT
Chicago, IL USA

The Men's Room -- How to grow more johnson.

Henry Johnson
Chicago, IL USA
*Contact Phone:* 312-638-0868
*Cell:* 773-456-7875
**Click to Contact from Web Site**

## MENCENTER
Washington, DC USA

Dr. Alvin Baraff knew men's thoughts, attitudes, and feelings toward current events, women, sex, family, and careers. He was an experienced psychotherapist, and an effective communicator. He gave personal and political commentary from a down-to-earth psychological angle. His well-attended seminars on domestic violence and sexual harassment offed solutions and hope. He had appeared on national and international television. Dr. Baraff had been quoted in numerous publications including USA Today and The Washington Post.

MenCenter
Washington, DC
*Contact Main Phone:* 1-866-MenCenter
**Click to Contact from Web Site**

## MARILYN REDMOND, HEALING AND SPIRITUAL GROWTH
Edgewood, WA USA
http://www.angelicasgifts.com

Professional Speaker and consultant focuses on Therapeutic Hypnotherapy/ Holistic Counseling. In Manchester's 'Who's Who' for her pioneering work in healing the causes of trauma and illness. Inspirational and knowledgeable presentations from personal understanding and study. Addresses all addictions, illness, domestic violence, rape, relationships, health, and healing. Shares over twenty years of teaching school, college, and research for solutions. Award-winning international writer, minister, and member of the National Speakers Association, American Counseling Association, and American Board of Hypnotherapy.

Marilyn Redmond
Marilyn Redmond, BA, CHT, IBRT
Edgewood, WA
*Contact Phone:* 253-845-4907
**Click to Contact from Web Site**

## GARY KARP - DISABILITY AWARENESS EXPERT
San Rafael, CA USA
http://www.lifeonwheels.org/

Gary Karp is an internationally recognized public speaker, corporate trainer, facilitator, author, and editor. He has been living — fully — with a T12 spinal cord injury since 1973 when he was injured in a fall from a tree at the age of eighteen. Since his injury, Gary has earned a graduate degree in architecture, worked for eleven years in the presentation graphics industry as a designer and production manager, then began providing ergonomics training and consultation services to companies in the San Francisco Bay Area where he lives with his wife Paula and their yellow Labrador Retriever, Nava Leah.

Gary Karp
*Author/Speaker/Trainer*
Life On Wheels
San Rafael, CA USA
*Contact Phone:* 415-491-4280
*Cell:* 415-509-6682
**Click to Contact from Web Site**

## RHONDA BORMAN, MENTAL HEALTH EXPERT
Nashville, TN USA
www.rhondaborman.com

What do I tell my children every time the terror alert is raised? Does my sales force have attention deficit disorder or are they just disorganized? My therapist makes me laugh. Which one of us is crazy? Practical mental health advice. Humorous storytelling. Short stories available from the author of Taking Mama Home and Dusty Sees The World, a book which helps children and parents talk about scary situations. Radio, magazine and TV interviews welcomed.

Rhonda Borman
*Storyteller & Licensed Clinical Social Worker*
Nashville, TN USA
*Contact Phone:* 615-327-3200
*Pager:* 615-923-4388
**Click to Contact from Web Site**

### ROSE LEE ARCHER, M.S.
Palm Beach County, FL USA
http://www.roseleearchershow.com

Elevate your career from an unknown to a distinguished expert through: How to be a Media Magnet. Discover Rose Lee's Award Winning approach to a dynamic interview. Reveal your talents and skills to light up the airwaves to create a lasting impression: Documented research reports that the delivery of a television interview impacts an audience based on 7% content, 38% voice, and 55% body language.

Rose Lee Archer
*TV Producer & Host*
Rose Lee Productions
Women Helping Women Help Themselves
Boca Raton, FL USA
*Contact Phone:* 561-241-7987
**Click to Contact from Web Site**

### DR. MICHAEL LEVITTAN, ANGER MANAGEMENT SPECIALIST
Los Angeles, CA USA
www.michaellevittan.com

Dr. Levittan is a psychotherapist, professor, expert witness, and consults for L.A. Times, Inside Edition, In-Touch Magazine, Orlando Sentinel, Golf Magazine, Riverside Press. He recently completed two Tyra Banks Shows and appeared on NBC-TV's 'Starting Over'. He is a noted Anger Management expert and has articles published on Workplace Violence. Dr. Levittan teaches seminars on Anger Management, Domestic Violence, Child Abuse, & Post-Traumatic Stress at UCLA, Loyola Marymount University, California Graduate Institute, L.A. Superior Court, U.S. Marines, Women's Shelters, Marriage & Family Therapy Associations. He is Director of the Spousal Abuse program T.E.A.M., developed a curriculum on treatment, is Editor of a California Newsletter, and presents papers on Batterer's Treatment at the International Conference on Family Violence. Dr. Levittan receives frequent requests to speak. His enthusiasm and passion make him an outstanding speaker!

Dr. Michael Levittan
*Psychotherapist/Director*
Michael Levittan, Ph.D.
Los Angeles, CA USA
*Contact Phone:* 310-556-2050
**Click to Contact from Web Site**

### PATRICK K. PORTER, PH.D. — MOTIVATIONAL KEYNOTE SPEAKER
Virginia Beach, VA USA
http://www.patrickkporter.com

Dr. Patrick Porter is an entrepreneur, award-winning author, and motivational speaker. He grew his mom & pop business to international franchise status in two short years. His electrifying keynote speeches and seminars deliver the real life, nuts 'n bolts concepts he used to take his business venture to astounding heights. He teaches entrepreneurs to think like business leaders. Corporate executives and sales professionals learn how to think like entrepreneurs.

Patrick K. Porter Ph.D.
AVA Marketing Group
Virginia Beach, VA United States
*Contact Phone:* 757-321-6213
**Click to Contact from Web Site**

### AL SIEBERT, PH.D.
Portland, OR USA
http://www.resiliencycenter.com

Dr. Al Siebert, Director of The Resiliency Center, is internationally recognized for his research into the inner nature of highly resilient survivors. He is author of The Survivor Personality and The Resiliency Advantage. Al is an ex-paratrooper with a Ph.D. in psychology. He is quoted in many publications and has been interviewed on many radio and TV programs including National Public Radio, The Discovery Channel, and OPRAH. More info at www.resiliencycenter.com.

Al Siebert, Ph.D
The Resiliency Center
Portland, OR USA
*Contact Phone:* 503-289-3295
**Click to Contact from Web Site**

# Marilyn Redmond, BA, CHT, IBRT

## International Speaker & Consultant

**Areas of Expertise Include:**

- Holistic Health and Healing
- Complimentary Medicine
- Counseling / Therapeutic Hypnosis
- Regression Therapy
- Empowerment / Self-Esteem
- Relationships
- Domestic Violence
- Addictions and the Family
- Educational Issues
- Spiritual/Metaphysical
- Inspirational

Marilyn Redmond's journey reveals the secrets to life and living, imparting reality to all areas of our lives in health, wholeness, happiness and prosperity; it is available to everyone. Experiencing addictions, mental illness, childhood and adult domestic violence are a few of the problems that became Marilyn's laboratory to understand the dynamics of life and living.

She shares this wisdom throughout her more than 20 years of speaking, writing, and counseling. In addition, her 44 years in education -- acquired through years of teaching elementary through college students -- offers solutions to educational problems.

An international lecturer, award-winning author and columnist, she appears at universities, schools, seminars, retreats and conventions. Marilyn's first book, "Roses Have Thorns," along with her videos on

Empowerment & Domestic Violence, are available. Marilyn hosted and produced her own radio show and appears on radio and television.

Marilyn Redmond is a registered counselor, holds a bachelor of arts in education and has completed three years of graduate work toward a doctor of science. An ordained minister, she recently was inducted into "Manchester's Who's Who" for pioneering work in restoring traumatic lives, healing emotional causes of illness and releasing negative energy.

Here are a few testimonials:

"She understands addictions better than most doctors," asserts psychiatrist Dr. George Zerr, M.D.

"I very much enjoyed the real life stories and examples," says Corrine Thompson, Association for Research and Enlightenment Program. "Marilyn is an excellent speaker and down-to-earth."

**AVAILABLE FOR YOUR NEXT EVENT**
Book her expertise
Transform your life

**Marilyn Redmond**
253-845-4907
marilyn@angelicasgifts.com
www.angelicasgifts.com

**MEMBER**
**NSA**
NATIONAL SPEAKERS ASSOCIATION

## MICHAEL J. MAYER -- LICENSED PSYCHOLOGIST/CONSULTANT
Columbia, MO USA
http://www.mikemayer.com

Psychologist, consultant to businesses and professionals, coach and personal guide. Offers professional perspectives to a variety of business settings that increases profit, reduces absenteeism and promotes good morale. Author of four books, the latest being, Choose a Better Road: Tips for Life's Traffic Jams. Partner in a psychological practice and consultant to many businesses. Presenter at state/national workshops on a variety of topics. Individualized training, retreats and workshops available. Presents live radio programs on the radio every two weeks and some television interviews. Focus is on helping people resolve work and home issues thus bringing positive meaning to their lives and to those they influence. Challenging informative and motivating. Likes media presentations. Answers questions relating to work and personal relationships, conflicts at home and office, employee selection, professional and executive insight into effective problem resolution and other personal and work related issues. Dr. Mayer has good and effective answers. Call him.

Michael J. Mayer
*Psychologist/Consultant*
Michael J. Mayer -- Licensed Psychologist/
Consultant
Columbia, MO
*Contact Phone:* 573-443-1177
**Click to Contact from Web Site**

## RICHARD FENTON - THE GO FOR NO GUY
Vancouver, WA USA
http://www.goforno.com/

Richard Fenton teaches others to break through self-imposed limitations and achieve their full potential by intentionally increasing their failure rate. The author of four books (including Go for No!) and over 100 published articles on sales, customer service, and management performance, Richard is a dynamic and engaging speaker who delivers keynotes and workshops across the country. He enjoys being interviewed to share what he considers to be the single greatest success strategy: failing.

Andrea Waltz
*Director of Marketing*
GoForNo.com
VANCOUVER, WA USA
*Contact Phone:* 800-290-5028
*Contact Main Phone:* 1-866-GoForNo
**Click to Contact from Web Site**

## ELAYNE SAVAGE, PH.D., THE REJECTION EXPERT
San Francisco, CA USA
http://www.queenofrejection.com

Dr. Elayne Savage is the Queen of Rejection—the ideal expert for journalists on a deadline. This media-savvy commentator provides succinct insights and realistic strategies (WebMD, BBC, The London Guardian, Sunday Observer, Maury Povich, NPR, LA Times, Chicago Tribune, Reader's Digest, Men's Health, Seventeen, Self, Cosmopolitan). International 'overcoming rejection' expert, relationship coach, and professional speaker with books published in 9 languages: DON'T TAKE IT PERSONALLY! THE ART OF DEALING WITH REJECTION and BREATHING ROOM—CREATING SPACE TO BE A COUPLE.

Dr. Elayne Savage
*The Queen of Rejection*
Relationship Coach, Professional Speaker,
Author
San Francisco Bay Area, CA USA
*Contact Phone:* 510-540-6230
**Click to Contact from Web Site**

## GINI GRAHAM SCOTT, PH.D., J.D. (EXPERT ON BUSINESS RELATIONSHIPS)
Oakland, CA USA
http://www.ginigrahamscott.com

Writer, sociologist, anthropologist, speaker, workshop/seminar leader, and consultant on work relationships, conflict resolution, creativity, popular culture, social trends, psychological profiling, privacy, and criminal justice. Author of 40+ books, including: A Survival Guide for Working with Bad Bossses, A Survival Guide for Working with Humans, A Complete Idiot's Guide to Party Plan Selling, Work With Me! Resolving Everyday Conflict in Your Organization, The Truth About Lying, and Homicide by the Rich and Famous? Featured guest on TV/radio, including Oprah, CNN, and the O'Reilly Factor.

Gini Graham Scott, Ph.D., J.D.
*Director*
Changemakers
Oakland, CA USA
*Contact Phone:* 510-339-1625
**Click to Contact from Web Site**

## COMPULSIVE GAMBLING FOUNDATION
Bradley Beach, NJ USA
www.compulsivegamblingfoundation.org

Mission Statement of the Compulsive Gambling Foundation. The mission of the Compulsive Gambling Foundation (CGF) is to provide education, awareness, prevention and assistance to those persons and family members, suffering from Compulsive Gambling. We will provide speakers, literature and outreach, as well as financial assistance to those in need of legal and treatment services in the form of scholarships. If you are interested in obtaining a speaker or literature about the legal needs and treatment of compulsive gambling, or are in need of financial assistance for the treatment of a compulsive gambling addiction, please contact us.

Sheila Wexler
Compulsive Gambling Foundation
Bradley Beach, NJ USA
*Contact Phone:* (732) 774-0019
**Click to Contact from Web Site**

## ROBERT DELETIS, ADDICTIONS EXPERT
New York, NY USA
http://www.erptherapy.com

Robert DeLetis, international and nationally certified alcohol and drug counselor (CADC). As the co-author of Kill the Craving, a book that introduces ERP to professionals and their clients, Mr. DeLetis presents a new and innovate way to deal with their addiction. He has developed presentations, seminars, as well as created a full professional ERP kits for counselors, psychologist, and doctors to learn this exciting new approach to substance abuse treatment.

Robert DeLetis
*Senior Addictions Counselor*
SLS Health
Brewster, NY USA
*Contact Phone:* 347-672-7199
*Contact Main Phone:* 845-279-5994
**Click to Contact from Web Site**

## TOM NICOLI BCH, CI - HYPNOSIS EXPERT
Woburn, MA USA
http://www.prosperusa.com

Tom Nicoli, BCH, CI, author, speaker, trainer and expert in the field of hypnotism. A Board Certified Hypnotist, Certified Instructor and 3 time award winner with the National Guild of Hypnotists. His national appearances on radio and television (Dateline NBC) support the success of his work. Harvard Medical School said, "He is an expert in his field. His presentation was thought provoking, stimulating and made a large impression. We highly recommend him for any speaking engagement."

Tom Nicoli BCH, CI
*Author, speaker & trainer*
A Better You Hypnosis, Inc.
New England Institute of Hypnosis
Woburn, MA USA
*Contact Phone:* 781-938-7779
**Click to Contact from Web Site**

## HYPNOSIS FEDERATION — SHELLEY STOCKWELL, PH.D.

Rancho Palos Verdes, CA USA
www.hypnosisfederation.com

The International Hypnosis Federation represents mind, body, and spirit practitioners, hypnotists, and motivational speakers worldwide. Spokesperson Shelley Stockwell, Ph.D, is the author of ten books including Hypnosis: How to Put a Smile on Your Face and Money in Your Pocket and Time Travel: The Do-It-Yourself Past Life Journey Handbook. Their annual conference is in California in July.

Shelley Stockwell, Ph.D.
International Hypnosis Federation
Rancho Palos Verdes, CA
*Contact Phone:* 310-377-7908
**Click to Contact from Web Site**

## SUSAN NERI-FRIEDWALD CHT. (NGH, ABH, IMDHA, IACT) BEHAVIOR MODIFICATION EXPERT

New York, NY USA
http://www.newbehaviorinstitute.net/

Author of 10 Hypnosis CDs, Behavior Modification Specialist, and a highly certified Hypnotist, Motivational Coach and Professional Speaker, Susan is Founder of The New Behavior Institute and The Language Exchange. She works with Corporations, Groups and Individuals who come from all over the world for sessions with her to make life changes. With a proven record of success and high standard of excellence, Susan helps people take back their lives and release habits that no longer serve them.

Susan Neri-Friedwald
New Behavior Institute
New York, NY USA
*Contact Phone:* 212-889-5362
**Click to Contact from Web Site**

## JEAN CIRILLO, PH.D. -- THE LOVE NANNY

Huntington, NY USA

Meet the Cool Dr. Phil -- The Love Nanny -- Appeals to younger audiences Dr. Jean Cirillo has been seen on hundreds of national talk shows as expert guest and staff psychologist. Presently consults with MTV, VHI and BET for reality shows: including Made, College Hill, Model Apartments, Kept, Flavor of Love, and the Ozzy Osbourne Ozzfest. Specialties include women's issue, teens, abuse, self-esteem and relationships.

Jean Cirillo, Ph.D.
Huntington, NY
*Contact Phone:* 516-795-0631
**Click to Contact from Web Site**

## ELAINE FANTLE SHIMBERG, HEALTHCARE, WOMEN & FAMILY ISSUES
Tampa, FL USA
www.elainesbooks.com

Elaine Fantle Shimberg, an award-winning medical writer, translates confusing medical jargon into lay language. Among her 20 books are: Coping with COPD: Chronic Obstructive Pulmonary Disease, Coping with Chronic Heartburn: What You Need to Know About Acid Reflux and GERD, Living with Tourette Syndrome Relief from IBS: Irritable Bowel Syndrome, She's also written on strokes and depression. Elaine also writes on parenting, women's and family issues and has authored several books including Another Chance for Love: Finding a Partner Later in Life, Blending Families, and Write Where You Live.

Shimberg Elaine Fantle
*Writer*
Elaine Fantle Shimberg
Tampa, FL
*Contact Phone:* 813-259-9673
**Click to Contact from Web Site**

## LENORA MADISON POE, PH.D.
Berkeley, CA USA

Addictions have rendered many parents unable to fulfill their obligations and left grandparents responsible for raising their grandchildren. Dr. Poe has done the first comprehensive study of grandparents parenting their grandchildren. She is a Licensed Marriage, Family, and Child Therapist at the West Coast Children's Center in California. She has a Ph.D. in Clinical Psychology. Dr. Poe's recent book, Black Grandparents As Parents, focuses on the enormous adjustments that grandparents must make to rescue their grandchildren from repeating the self-destructive cycle of their parents.

Lenora Madison Poe, Ph.D.
Berkeley, CA
*Contact Phone:* 510-845-7189
**Click to Contact from Web Site**

## SUSIE VANDERLIP -- TEEN & PARENTING SKILLS EXPERT
Orange, CA USA
http://www.legacyofhope.com

When people speak of SUSIE VANDERLIP, they often refer to 'The Dancer' or 'Julio, the Gangbanger!', one of her many captivating and mesmerizing characters used to illustrate some of life's most serious concerns and destructive outcomes from a life of abuse and stress. Both teens and adults remember: 'You could have heard a pin drop!' 'She really touched me...' Many adults have said: 'I wish I'd seen this when I was a teen. It would have saved me a lot of painful mistakes.' Many teens have said: 'She saved my life!'

Susie Vanderlip
Legacy of Hope
Orange, CA USA
*Contact Phone:* 714-997-2158
**Click to Contact from Web Site**

## LOVE AND LOGIC INSTITUTE
Denver, CO USA
www.loveandlogic.com

Jim Fay, Dr. Charles Fay, and all the experts at the Love and Logic Institute can provide you with important and practical insights and suggestions regarding parenting, teaching, and positive discipline techniques, such as how to: make parenting fun and rewarding; effectively use choices, consequences, and empathy; end temper tantrums and sibling rivalry; get the most out of parent/teachers relationships; and deal with specific issues facing toddlers, children, and teenagers.

Carol Thomas
Love and Logic Institute
Golden, CO
*Contact Phone:* 800-338-4065
**Click to Contact from Web Site**

## KATHY PEEL — AMERICA'S FAMILY MANAGER
Dallas, TX USA
http://www.familymanager.com

Kathy Peel is called America's Family Manager by millions of women. She's the author of 18 books and a frequent guest on television and radio programs. In her entertaining and inspiring style, she speaks from podiums across the nation giving audiences practical ideas and proven strategies for creating a smoothly running, happy home; being a great parent and raising responsible, well-rounded kids; living a balanced, personally fulfilling life, and achieving your personal dreams.

Kathy Peel America's Family Manager
*Founder and CEO*
Family Manager Network
Dallas, TX USA
*Contact Phone:* 972-818-4403
**Click to Contact from Web Site**

## ROBERT NASEEF, PH.D.
Philadelphia, PA USA
http://www.specialfamilies.com

Robert Naseef, Ph.D., is a unique psychologist, author, and father of an adult child with autism. His highly regarded book Special Children, Challenged Parents: The Struggles and Rewards of Parenting a Child with a Disability has received international recognition. He has appeared on radio and television. Dr. Naseef's specialty is working with families of children with special needs. He has a special interest and expertise in the psychology of men and fatherhood.

Robert Naseef, Ph.D.
Philadelphia, PA
*Contact Phone:* 215-592-1333
**Click to Contact from Web Site**

## DR. JOHN E. MAYER -- EXPERT ON YOUTH & PARENTING
Chicago, IL USA
www.drjohnmayer.com

The foremost national expert on teenagers often Referred to as, 'The Teen Doc' meets you needs for expert opinion/analysis from a sound bite, full interview to feature. Well known across the US, he lectures, consults and intervenes to schools, the federal government and law enforcement. He is often the expert brought into the 'Headline' cases involving youth, parenting and teenagers. He has been called to evaluate serial killers and Death Row inmates.

Dr. John E. Mayer
*Clinical Psychologist*
Chicago, IL USA
*Contact Phone:* 312-917-1240
**Click to Contact from Web Site**

## KANETA R. LOTT, DDS -- PEDIATRIC DENTIST, BANKER
Atlanta, GA USA
http://www.lottseminars.com

With the changes in parenting styles, Dr. Lott knows that it takes patience, knowledge and Lotts of Love to care for children. She also knows that in order for the dental staff to provide continuous quality services, they must feel a sense of fulfillment. Her goal is to educate, inspire and lead from her own experiences and professional knowledge. For more than 20 years, Dr. Lott has helped to shape the smiles of hundreds of children. She has taught dentists and staffs in Virginia, California, Georgia, Florida and numerous other states not to mention at Sea on a Caribbean Cruise. Dr. Lott's message is that caring for children can be profitable as well as fun. However, you must know the answers to parents' frequently asked questions. You also have to have some training in childhood behavior and at times are willing to act like a child.

Kaneta R. Lott, DDS
*President*
LottSeminars
Atlanta, GA United States
*Contact Phone:* 404-349-7777
**Click to Contact from Web Site**

## DIANNE LINDERMAN - PARENTING EXPERT & AUTHOR
Grants Pass, OR USA
http://www.thefirstmomsclub.com

David and Dianne have opened the first of the First Moms' Clubs Entrepreneurs' Market-places—a 7,000-square-foot store with more than 150 small business available for moms, dads, grandma's, granddads, and even kids to try their hands at business. This is the perfect opportunity for anyone to have a little store, starting with a 4 x 4 booth with the option to grow. Moms can come in and set up shop—and the best part is they don't have to be there! We sell everything for them! This is a great way to launch a business idea. There is also a play area in the Entrepreneurs' Marketplace to keep the kids entertained while moms stock and decorate their booths!

Dianne Linderman
*Owner*
The First Moms Club
The Moms Club Mercantile
Grants Pass, OR USA
*Contact Phone:* 541-476-5582
*Cell:* 541-761-2007
**Click to Contact from Web Site**

## INTERNATIONAL NANNY ASSOCIATION -- PAT CASCIO, PRESIDENT
Houston, TX USA
www.Nanny.org

Established in 1985, the INA is a non-profit, educational association for nannies and those who educate, place, employ, and support professional in-home child care providers. Membership is open to those who are directly involved with the in-home child care profession including nannies, nanny employers, nanny placement agency owners (and staff), nanny educators, and providers of special services related to the nanny profession.

Pat Cascio
International Nanny Association
Houston, TX USA
*Contact Phone:* 713-526-3989
**Click to Contact from Web Site**

## MARY ANN LOFRUMENTO, MD - PEDIATRICIAN AND PARENTING EXPERT
New York, NY USA
http://www.simplyparenting.com

Formerly in private practice for 18 years and a Clinical Assistant Professor of Pediatrics at Columbia University's College of Physicians and Surgeons, Dr. LoFrumento currently teaches at the Goryeb Children's Hospital in New Jersey and is the author of the Simply Parenting Childcare series of books and DVDs including: Understanding Your Newborn and Infant and Understanding Your Toddler . "Dr. Mary Ann" is dedicated to bringing childcare back to basics for parents.

Dawn Gual
Simply Parenting
New York, NY USA
*Contact Phone:* 973-701-7373
**Click to Contact from Web Site**

## MELISSA GALT, IDS, IFDA - LIFESTYLE DESIGN EXPERT
Atlanta, GA USA
http://www.melissagalt.com/

Melissa believes that your home is your external heart and that the process of defining personal style and creating your signature life follows the same path as the process of self-discovery. She is an expert guide, coach and director to those who are on this journey to create their ideal home and the life of their dreams. Her team ensures that each client receives the highest level of customization and attention to detail. Whether she is working one on one with a busy professional or a family on creating the interiors and life of their vision; or devoting her efforts to the goals of a company or association in providing its employees and members the benefit of her knowledge, programs, and motivation, Melissa and her team strive to give her clients a winning experience and lasting success.

Melissa Galt
Atlanta, GA USA
*Contact Phone:* 404-812-4613
**Click to Contact from Web Site**

## LISSA COFFEY -- LIFESTYLE DESIGNER
Los Angeles, CA USA
http://www.coffeytalk.com

Lissa Coffey is a 'Relationship Barista' who mixes up an inspiring blend of ancient wisdom and modern style! Her new book, 'What's Your Dosha, Baby? Discover the Vedic Way for Compatibility in Life and Love,' does for Ayurveda and relationships what Linda Goodman's Love Signs has done for astrology. Bright, fun, and super media-friendly, Lissa shares valuable insights to show your audiences how to enhance all aspects of their lives.

Lissa Coffey
*President*
Bright Ideas Productions
Westlake Village, CA
*Contact Phone:* 818-707-7127
*Cell:* 818-370-9025
**Click to Contact from Web Site**

## THE WOMEN'S CENTER
Vienna, VA USA
http://www.thewomenscenter.org

Providing Resources to Meet Life's Challenges -- Since 1974, The Women's Center's mission has been to improve significantly the psychological, career, financial and legal well being of women and families regardless of their ability to pay. A 501(c)(3) nonprofit organization, The Women's Center provides approximately 30,000 hours of counseling, 150 educational workshops and 15 support and therapy groups per year to clients in its Vienna, VA and downtown D.C. offices.

Nicole P. Skuba
*Marketing Manager*
The Women's Center
Vienna, VA USA
*Contact Phone:* 703-281-4928
*Contact Main Phone:* 703-281-2657
*Cell:* 703-463-4280
**Click to Contact from Web Site**

## DAVID GORDER — HIGH ENERGY WEIGHT LOSS PROGRAM
Chicago, IL USA
www.HighEnergyLifestyle.com

What Is a High Energy Lifestyle? A high energy lifestyle is when you get up each day working a job that you are passionate about along with goals and hobbies that inspire you. You have relationships with high quality people and together are creating a difference in the quality of not only your own lives but in the quality of other peoples lives. You have unlimited energy and don't suffer from the after work I am so exhausted, low energy, overweight, yawning, headache and flu, acid reflux, gas and constantly sick ailments from the follow the leader, undisciplined, short cut, mainstream, excuse-ridden human beings looking for sympathy for their self-induced conditions.

David Gorder
High Energy
Lombard, IL USA
*Contact Phone:* 630-776-2346
**Click to Contact from Web Site**

## DARY DAY
Fair Haven, NJ USA
http://www.darydayshow.com/

Dary Day is a journalist who's written for The New York Times, Harper's, New York Magazine, among other publications. She is the author of the book "Real Talk: a Savvy Guide to the Hidden Meaning Behind What People Say", hailed as "the sauciest guide to modern communication and relationships" by the New England Review of Books and as "wise and witty" by Spy Magazine. She also wrote a column on broadcasting and has given advice on relationships for Women's World for several years. Dary's been a guest and contributor on over 200 TV and radio shows. She hosts the syndicated talk show for women - The Day Show.

Ekko Productions
Fair Haven, NJ
*Contact Phone:* 732-219-0332
**Click to Contact from Web Site**

## DR. GALLATIN ON BROADWAY
New York, NY USA
alwayswin.com

Dr. Martin V. Gallatin, 'Broadway's Orator'; www.alwayswin.com; www.alwayslose.com. 'Dr. Gallatin Wipes out Rejection' in new book. Author, AlwaysWin®: Walk Away a Winner®From Any Situation or Circumstance, and Lover Shopping® for Men and Women: How to Be Married One Year From Today. Appearances on hundreds of television/radio shows, including Oprah. Featured in New York Times, Newsweek. Doctorate in sociology, New York University. Professor, Touro College, NYC; 'Instructor of the Year 2005.' Created seminar, 'Lover Shopping at Bloomingdale's'; started 'Singles Nights at The Supermarket.'

Dr. Martin V. Gallatin
*Speaker/Author/Publisher*
Dr. Gallatin on Broadway
New York, USA
*Contact Phone:* 212-989-8415
*Contact Main Phone:* 212-989-8415
**Click to Contact from Web Site**

## DR. SUSAN CAMPBELL, DATING & RELATIONSHIP COACH
San Francisco, CA USA
www.susancampbell.com

Nine-time author Susan Campbell offers audiences a blueprint for successful relationships—10 truth skills that make you a more authentic, courageous communicator. In her books, Getting Real, Truth in Dating, and Saying What's Real (2005) she offers insights from 35 years practicing psychology. A media pro, she hosted her own reality TV show for 13 weeks, and has appeared on such shows as CNN's Newsnight and Good Morning America.

Susan Campbell
Getting Real Resources
Sebastopol, CA USA
*Contact Phone:* 707-829-3646
**Click to Contact from Web Site**

## FRAN GREENE, A.C.S.W.

Commack, NY USA
http://www.frangreene.com

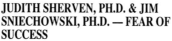

Nationally recognized, sought after expert on flirting, dating and relationships. Greene has appeared on Dateline NBC, Today Show, Bill O Reilly, The Travel Channel and Iyanla and has been featured in the New York Times, Self, Cosmopolitan and Princess Cruises. Fran Greene is a well known dating and relationship coach in private practice. Producer of Self Help Video, FlirtingWorks. An energetic, popular and inspiring speaker, her humor and charisma make her workshops a sell out. Former Director of Flirting and Dating at Match.com, the Internet's premiere matchmaking service.

Fran Greene, A.C.S.W.
Commack, NY
*Contact Phone:* 631-265-5683
*Cell:* 516-317-5818
**Click to Contact from Web Site**

## JUDITH SHERVEN, PH.D. & JIM SNIECHOWSKI, PH.D. — FEAR OF SUCCESS
Albany, NY USA
www.JudithAndJim.com

In twenty-two years of private practice as a clinical psychologist, Judith helped hundreds of women and men through dark and difficult times to create the kind of intimacy they dreamed of. As the founder of the Menswork Center in Santa Monica and is a co-founder of The Men's Health Network in Washington, D.C. Jim helped scores of men and women with issues of intimacy, especially giving and receiving love.

Judith Sherven
Windham, NY USA
*Contact Phone:* 518-734-3657
**Click to Contact from Web Site**

## DR. AVA CADELL
Los Angeles, CA USA
http://www.avacadell.com

World-renowned love and relationship expert Dr. Ava Cadell says, The meaning of life is learning how to give love and how to receive love. In the end, none of our accomplishments will mean as much as the loving memories that we have created. A media therapist and author of six books, Dr. Ava's mission is to promote the benefits of healthy love and intimacy to people around the globe. Dr. Ava has appeared on Good Morning America, Extra, Montel Williams, CNN, NBC, ABC & Fox News, various shows for MTV, VH1, Discovery, Lifetime, Learning Channel, and E! The A & E Channel recently produced and aired a personal profile featuring Dr. Ava's career. For more on Dr. Ava, visit her website at www.avacadell.com

Dr. Ava Cadell
Kudos, Inc.
Los Angeles, CA USA
*Contact Phone:* 310.276.8623
*Contact Main Phone:* 310.276.8623
**Click to Contact from Web Site**

### LEANN THIEMAN, CSP — CAREGIVER NURSE
Denver, CO USA
http://www.LeAnnThieman.com

LeAnn Thieman is an award winning speaker, author and nurse. By sharing her dramatic experiences from the Vietnam Orphan Airlift, LeAnn Thieman motivates people to balance their lives and make a difference in the world. She has been featured in Newsweek Magazine, FOX-TV, CNN, BBC, NPR and is co-author of 6 Chicken Soup for the Soul books. She is expert on the nursing shortage, caregiver stress, fathers and daughters, grandparents raising children, and parenting.

LeAnn Thieman, CSP
Denver, CO USA
*Contact Phone:* 877-THIEMAN
**Click to Contact from Web Site**

### DR. NANCY KALISH -- LOST LOVE EXPERT
Sacramento, CA USA
http://www.LostLovers.com

Psychologist Dr. Nancy Kalish is the international expert on rekindled romance. Her landmark study of 3000 couples over twelve years, and her acclaimed book, Lost & Found Lovers, has catapultedDr. Kalish into the limelight as the leading source for print & broadcast media stories on lost love, reunions, teen romance, Internet dating, marriage and affairs, and Baby Boomer relationships. Interviews welcomed.

Dr. Nancy Kalish
*Professor/ Author/ Researcher/ Consultant*
Sacramento, CA USA
*Contact Phone:* 916-278-6962
**Click to Contact from Web Site**

### BOB HECK & JIM THIELMAN -- THE THEORY OF WRONG
Richland, WA USA
http://www.wrongtreeink.com/

Womb to tomb, women get a kick out of wrong guys (sometimes a sharp kick). That won't change, because guys are wrong even before birth. Also after, says author Jim Thielman and partner Bob Heck (Theory of Wrong: Married Guys Are Wrong and That's OK.) Wrong Jim knows wrong guys—strong on stuff and systems, weak on empathy and relationships. Wrong Theory turns dense gender research into sound bites. Where's the love? Laughter over wrong guys brings couples closer together . Funny and fast paced. . .a goofy trip into the gender gap. Bookwire. See www. theoryofwrong.com.

Jim Thielman
Wrong Tree Ink, LLC
Richland, WA USA
*Contact Phone:* 509-554-2253
**Click to Contact from Web Site**

## TODAY'S RELATIONSHIPS — RUSSELL PRICE, JR.

Largo, MD USA
www.TodaysRelationships.com

Russell Price, Jr. is a speaker, author, consultant and relationship expert, specialising red flags to show women he may be stringing you along. For the past 10 years he has been providing information on male-female relationships to the community. His seminar topics are: 'You Might Not Have A Woman If' (A blue print to relationships), 'The Five Levels of Relationships', 'Are You In Relationship Jail?', 'When Your Wife Is Not Your Woman'. — His new book it titled: Is He Your Man or is Your Head In The Sand?

Russell Price, Jr.
*Relationship Expert*
Today's Relationships
Largo, MD USA
*Contact Phone:* 240-676-3959
**Click to Contact from Web Site**

## AMY SCHOEN, CPCC - DATING & RELATIONSHIP EXPERT

Washington, DC USA
www.heartmindconnection.com

Amy Schoen, CPCC, MBA is a certified professional life coach and is a dating and relationship expert who coaches singles to attract the right relationship into their lives. She speaks regularly to professional organizations and social groups in the DC and New York area and is the author of 'Motivated to Marry- A Better Method to Dating and Relationships'. In addition, Amy has been quoted in the Washington Post and the Washington Business Journal.

Amy Schoen CPCC
HeartMind Connection
Rockville, MD USA
*Contact Phone:* 240-498-7803
**Click to Contact from Web Site**

## NICOLE CASANOVA - ENTREPRENEUR & RELATIONSHIP EXPERT

Boulder, CO USA
http://www.shiftthegame.com/

Nicole Casanova is the CEO, visionary-extraordinaire, and the heart behind Shift. She started her days in a Jewish/Italian family in sunny Miami, Florida. After a stint as honor student, president of this and that, and Miami Beach party girl, Nicole went off to study Communications at Florida State University. From there the eternally driven Ms. Casanova trekked out to Boulder, Colorado to get her Masters in Integrated Marketing Communications. Because her Master's thesis (this was 1995 when her professors wondered if she'd go door to door signing people up for the World Wide Web) was on Targeted Marketing on the Web, Nicole's natural next step was to seek fortune and challenge in San Francisco's world of Internet business.

Nicole Casanova
*Founder and CEO*
Exponential Growth, LLC.
Boulder, CO USA
*Contact Phone:* 303-530-0787
**Click to Contact from Web Site**

## LAURA GILES — HEALTHY LIVING SOLUTIONS INC.

Virginia Beach, VA USA
http://healthy-living-solutions.com

Who's Your Daddy? With up to 20% of people having a parent who is not who they think it is, extramarital families is a hot topic. Could YOU be an other child? Talk to Laura Giles, author of The Other Child: Children of Affairs to find out about this previously taboo subject. Short notice radio and tv interviews welcome.

Laura Giles
Healthy Living Solutions Inc.
Virginia Beach, VA USA
*Contact Phone:* 757-313-2313
**Click to Contact from Web Site**

## RUTH HOUSTON - INFIDELITY EXPERT

New York, NY USA
www.InfidelityAdvice.com

Infidelity expert, Ruth Houston is the author of 'Is He Cheating on You? - 829 Telltale Signs.' Frequently called on by the media to comment on celebrity infidelity, high profile infidelity cases and infidelity issues in the news, Ruth has been quoted in the New York Times, Cosmopolitan, Newsday, iVillage, MSN-Lifestyle and other print and online media; and has appeared on The Today Show , Good Day New York and 200+ TV and radio talk shows worldwide.

Ruth Houston
Elmhurst, NY USA
*Contact Phone:* 718 592-6039
**Click to Contact from Web Site**

### GEORGE B. BLAKE -- SINGLE AGAIN
Sarasota, FL USA
www.geocities.com/georgeblakecolumnist/
author.html

By 2010, single U.S. adults will outnumber marrieds. Each year, 5 million become single again and face an unfamilar lifestyle. Singles newspaper columnist and author George B. Blake lends a hand by addressing the vital subjects of five best places to meet your next mate, how modern singles are different, pitfalls to avoid, overcoming loneliness and much more. Assuring a lively interview, Blake is the author of Single Again and Married Again as well as seven other books.

George B. Blake
*Author*
George B. Blake/
Bradenton, FL
*Contact Phone:* 941-755-8637
**Click to Contact from Web Site**

### DIANA KIRSCHNER, PH.D. - PSYCHOLOGIST & LOVE EXPERT
New York, NY USA
http://www.openinglovesdoor.com

Diana Kirschner, Ph.D. is a nationally-known psychologist & love expert who has appeared on OPRAH, GOOD MORNING AMERICA & NPR Radio. She is quoted in the New York Times, USA Today, Time Magazine, The New York Post, The LA Times & Cosmopolitan and numerous on- & offline publications. Her book, Opening Love's Door: The Seven Lessons has been called a 'cult classic' by Readerviews.com & her Amazon short, The Ultimate Guide to Getting the Love You Want is a #1 bestseller. Dr. Diana is the star of Love in 90 Days Boot Camp, a reality TV pilot that is an Official Selection of the New York TV Festival, webcast by MSN.

Diana Kirschner, Ph.D.
Opening Loves Door
New York, NY USA
*Contact Phone:* 212-420-8079
*Cell:* (917) 749-7791
**Click to Contact from Web Site**

### ALMA H. BOND, PH.D.
New York, NY USA
alma_bond.tripod.com

WHO SCULPTED RODIN'S SCULPTURES? Camille Claudel was institutionalized for paranoia for 30 years, insisting Rodin had stolen her work. Yet did he really? Like many sculptors of the era, Rodin used apprentices like Camille to help with his sculptures. Each of their creations was worked on by the other artist. Anyone could confuse their work. Was Camille imprisoned to enhance Rodin's career, or were her comments the content of a diseased mind? Dr. Bond's novel reveals the startling truth.

Alma H. Bond
*Dr.*
ASJA
IPTAR
New York, FL USA
*Contact Phone:* 212-786-3230
**Click to Contact from Web Site**

### DR. CAXTON OPERE
Baton Rouge, LA USA
www.DrCaxton.com

Dr. Opere is a board certified internist in Baton Rouge, Louisiana. He is a highly sought after conference speaker on high yield Divorce Prevention techniques and The Medical Complications of Divorce. He hosts a daily radio show Treasure Chest, is the author of The 36 Well Kept Secrets and offers private consultations on Mate Selection to individuals as well as corporate seminars on How Divorce Affects Productivity.

Caxton Opere, MD
Divorce Prevention
Baton Rouge, LA
*Contact Phone:* 225-923-3660
**Click to Contact from Web Site**

# Russell Price, Jr.:
## Relationship Expert,
### Specializing In Red Flags That Show Women He May Be Stringing You Along

Russell Price, Jr., is the founder and CEO of Today's Relationships, an organization for people who are married, separated, widowed, divorced or single.

Russell conducts seminars and workshops on relationships such as the five levels of relationships and how to determine if your relationship is a healthy or addictive one.

As a former police officer, Russell has had the opportunity to witness several domestic situations and many males being locked up. This inspired Russell to write his first book, "You Might Not Have A Woman If . . .," to help individuals to see the signs that would prevent domestic violence and help men and women to communicate better. For example, if you are contributing to the household financially and don't have a key, it might not be your woman.

Russell's book, "Is He Your Man Or Is Your Head In the Sand?" is the first book, written by a man, that shows women the red flags he may be stringing you along. The book is "straight-talk-no-chaser" information that is hard to swallow but good to know. Each chapter is short and straight to the point . The book is a must-read for every women and a must-give to every daughter.

Russell Price, Jr., is a speaker, author, consultant and relationship expert in the Washington, D.C., metropolitan area. For the past 10 years, he has been providing information on male-female relationships to the community. He has hosted a talk show on WOL-1450AM in Washington, D.C., and WOLB-1010 in Baltimore, Md.

## Russell's seminar topics are:

- You Might Not Have A Woman If . . . (a blueprint to relationships)

- The Five Levels of Relationships

- Are You In Relationship Jail? "When Your Wife Is Not Your Woman"

- Is He Your Man, Or Is Your Head in the Sand?

- How To Let Go (and make your life better)

## Russell Price, Jr.

**Relationship Expert**
**Today's Relationships**
**Largo, Maryland**
**240-676-3959**

**www.TodaysRelationships.com**

## JEFFERY M. LEVING — FATHERS' RIGHTS
Chicago, IL USA
www.dadsrights.com

Jeffery M. Leving is one of the country's leading family law attorneys and co-author of the Illinois Joint Custody Law. His book, "Fathers' Rights," is regarded as a definitive work on this important subject. Leving helped reunite Elian Gonzalez with his father. A fathers' rights activist, Leving is a sought after media spokesperson on legislation relating to fathers. Appointed member of the U.S. Congressional Task Force on Fathers, Families & Public Policy. President Emeritus—Fatherhood Educational Institute. Mr. Leving has been appointed Chairman of The Illinois Council on Responsible Fatherhood by Illinois Governor Rod Blagojevich.

Jeffery M. Leving
*President*
Jeffery M. Leving, Ltd.
Chicago, IL
*Contact Phone:* 312-807-3990
*Contact Main Phone:* 312-807-3990
*Cell:* (312) 296-8656
**Click to Contact from Web Site**

## NEW BEGINNINGS — SUPPORT GROUP FOR SEPARATED/DIVORCED MEN & WOMEN
Olney, MD USA
New Beginnings is a support group located near Baltimore and Washington, D.C.

Carol
New Beginnings
Olney, MD USA
*Contact Phone:* 301-924-4101
**Click to Contact from Web Site**

## NANCY R. VAN TINE
Boston, MA USA
http://www.burnslev.com/our-attorneys/
attorney-detail.asp?id=176&scrollpos=2243

Nancy Van Tine chairs the Divorce and Family Law Group, co-chairs the Private Client Group and is a member of the Probate Litigation Group. She handles diverse issues, including divorce and separation, child custody and support, as well as actions for modification and contempt. She often deals with enforcement and modification of decrees entered in other states, reciprocal child custody, and complex asset division situations. Mrs. Van Tine has been a frequent lecturer at seminars sponsored by Massachusetts Continuing Legal Education and other groups.

Nancy R. VanTine, Esq.
*Partner*
Burns & Levinson LLP
Boston, MA USA
*Contact Phone:* 617-345-3229
*Contact Main Phone:* 617-345-3000
**Click to Contact from Web Site**

## THE DIVORCE FORUM
Santa Barbara, CA USA
www.thedivorceforum.com

Susan Allan, Founder of The Divorce Forum, is America's leading Divorce Coach. Allan has created 'How to Avoid Divorce' training, 'Marital Mediation and The 7 Stages of Divorce' and is a popular media personality and lecturer. Allan writes the 'Ask The Divorce Coach' advice column and the 'Ask the Love and Relationship Coach' column in various newspapers and has created www.thedivorceforum.com and www.themarriageforum.com. Allan is a featured author of The Los Angeles Daily News' Booktalk.

Susan Allan
*Founder*
The Divorce Forum
Santa Barbara, CA USA
*Contact Phone:* 805-695-0011
*Cell:* 818-314-1200
**Click to Contact from Web Site**

## STEPFAMILY ASSOCIATION OF AMERICA
Lincoln, NE USA
http://www.SAAfamilies.org

Dr. Engel, President of the Step Familes Association is passionately committed to providing effective, creative and timely program information to avoid or minimize negative individual and family consequences from life changes. Call her if you want quotable help and resources to prepare an article or program about complicated families. Then, you will be able to say to your readers, viewers, listeners, members, employees or clients who are experiencing family changes this is what's going to happen and here are your NEW choices.

Erin Flynn
Stepfamily Association of America
Lincoln, NE
*Contact Phone:* 402 477-STEP
**Click to Contact from Web Site**

## EUTHANASIA RESEARCH & GUIDANCE ORGANIZATION (ERGO)
Junction City, OR USA
http://www.FinalExit.org

ERGO! is a non profit research group studying the subtleties and complexities of euthanasia (help with a good death) so it can be carefully carried out as and when the law permits. Derek Humphry (president), who founded the Hemlock Society, also authored the bestseller Final Exit, which sells in 12 languages. As editor of the newsletter of the World Federation of Right to Die Societies, Humphry has an international perspective on euthanasia. http://www.FinalExit.org

Derek Humphry
*President*
Euthanasia Research & Guidance Organization (ERGO)
Junction City, OR
*Contact Phone:* 541-998-3285
**Click to Contact from Web Site**

**REV. MAURICE N. HANSEN, PH.D. --
LIVING WILL EXPERT**
Los Angeles, CA USA
http://www.finaldetails.net

Dr. Maurice N. Hansen Entrepreneur, Businessman, Educator, Author. Pastor Morrie is a Marriage & Family Counselor, a Certified Anger Management Provider and Senior Pastor of SERV
Ministries whose purpose is to assist distressed
and abused women and children. He has developed courses and has taught: "Fund & Friend Raising", "Presenting Yourself in the 21st Century",
and as an Expert on Living Wills, "Final Details"
the most important list you'll ever write!

Rev. Maurice N. Hansen, Ph.D.
Hanslyn Publishing
Dana Point, CA USA
*Contact Phone:* 949-661-8020
**Click to Contact from Web Site**

**THE FUNERAL HELP PROGRAM**
Virginia Beach, VA USA
www.funeral-help.com

'The Affordable Funeral' addresses funeral arrangement from three situations: the Sudden
Death/No Notice Funeral, The Anticipated Death
Funeral, and the Pre-Planned Funeral, which includes a workbook. At each step of the process the
reader is advised what is required, what is op-
tional, and what it will cost. Appendices at the end
of the workbook offer 'tear-out-and-take-with'
checklists as well as lists of sources and resources
with their contact information.

Donald Hull
*V.P. Public Relations Director*
Funeral Help Program
Suite 102
Virginia Beach, VA United State
*Contact Phone:* 757-340-7033
**Click to Contact from Web Site**

**J. SHEP JEFFREYS, ED.D. -- GRIEF
EXPERT**
Columbia, MD USA
www.GriefCareProvider.com

With comfort, understanding and skills, you will
heal grief. His mission is "to teach the public how
normal human grief is, what to expect from grief
and skills for helping grieving people." He is the
author of Helping Grieving People -When Tears
Are Not Enough and Coping With Workplace
Grief: Dealing With Loss, Trauma and Change.
Shep uses storytelling, poems, music and his
wealth of clinical and personal life experiences in
his teaching, lecturing and consulting. Jeffreys,
licensed psychologist, is associated with Johns
Hopkins University School of Medicine, Loyola
College in Maryland and Elisabeth Kubler-Ross.

J. Shep Jeffreys, Ed.D.
Columbia, MD USA
*Contact Phone:* 410-730-3310
**Click to Contact from Web Site**

## JACQUELINE MARCELL - ELDER CARE, ALZHEIMER'S, CAREGIVING EXPERT

Irvine, CA USA
http://www.ElderRage.com

Jacqueline Marcell is a former television executive who gave up her career to care for her elderly parents, both with Alzheimer's Disease. The experience compelled her to write and self-publish her best-selling book, 'Elder Rage', a Book-of-the-Month Club selection. AARP's Bulletin featured her on their cover, CNN and TODAY interviewed her, and she was honored with 'Advocate of the Year'. She also hosts 'Coping with Caregiving', an Internet radio program heard free worldwide on wsRadio.com

Jacqueline Marcell
*Author & Publisher 'Elder Rage' and Radio Host 'Coping with Caregiving'*
Irvine, CA USA
*Contact Phone:* 949-975-1012
*Cell:* 714-878-3713
**Click to Contact from Web Site**

## NATIONAL FUNERAL DIRECTORS ASSOCIATION

Brookfield, WI USA
http://www.nfda.org

Today's public wants to be more informed about how to handle circumstances and alternatives surrounding the death of a loved one and how to plan for it. 87 percent of the 22,000 funeral homes in the United States are family-owned, community based businesses. Trends affecting the industry include greater emphasis on more personalized ceremonies, advanced planning prior to death, cremation, and greater consumer emphasis on the value of high quality, ethical service rather than merchandise.

Celine Clark
*Manager of Public Affairs & Comm.*
National Funeral Directors Association
Brookfield, WI
*Contact Phone:* 800-228-6332
**Click to Contact from Web Site**

## FRANK JAKUBOWSKY, AUTHOR

Oakland, CA USA
www.bold-books.com

Frank Jakubowsky discovered the writing pattern of authors. It is of ten parts. Each part has a particular quality, which he named: enlighten, inadequacy, expansive, fruitful, authoritative, communication, reject, sociable, spiritual, and action. The writing pattern supposes that it is a mind pattern. My Inspirational Stories is Frank Jakubowsky recent book.

Frank Jakubowsky
Oakland, CA USA
*Contact Phone:* 510-763-4324
**Click to Contact from Web Site**

## MARY ANNE AYER, SPIRITUALITY & MYSTICISM EXPLAINED

Naples, FL USA
http://www.tenthgatepublishing.com

The author spent 30 years in search of answers regarding God and soul purpose. Her search took her around the world to Temples, Ashrams, monasteries and churches, including meetings with swamis, monks, yogis, sages, Christian mystics and a living Saint. Her in-depth studies of ancient Sanskrit text and the writings of mystics around the world take all of the mystery and confusion out of the profound benefits of spiritual practices and insights. She invites you to join her as her search for answers unfolds to gain new appreciation for the role that science and the ancient systems of yoga can bring to add new purpose, meaning and happiness to life. Spiritual practices create a pathway through the brain to the soul. When one contacts soul, all of the gifts that are the birthright of humans can be appreciated. Life can be lived from a whole new level of existence of love and happiness. The kingdom is within, and can be discovered and appreciated.

Mary Anne Ayer
Tenth Gate Publishing
Naples, FL USA
*Contact Phone:* 781-820-3900
**Click to Contact from Web Site**

Rev. Maurice N. Hansen, Ph.D.
Living Will Expert

Don't Leave Your Family In the Dark

"Get your wishes written down," said Michael Schiavo on ABC's The View on March 28, 2006.

Avoiding wills and informing loved ones about post-passing desires is so popular, it's an American tradition. Perhaps if Terri Schiavo had read Dr. Maurice N. Hansen's book 20 years ago, her relatives and society would have been spared a lot of agony. The upbeat, thorough Hansen speaks from experience -- having helped families settle estates, handle funeral arrangements, and resolve angry moments during his eight years of accumulating the information for "Final Details."

In Hansen's book, "Final Details," you have a checklist to assist you in pulling together detailed information, such as personal, financial and other benefits available for your loved ones. The forms alone included in the book are worth more than $80.

With humor and dignity, Hansen talks about how you can keep the peace -- while you're resting in it! His expertise was apparent on many radios stations throughout the United States and Canada, such as the Keith Rush Show, Love & Money/XM Satellite Radio, Gary Doyle, Gomez & the Good Guys, just to name a few. Plus, he has notable reviews in *the Orange County Register*'s *Sun Post News* and *the Christian Examiner*.

Dr. Maurice N. Hansen (aka Pastor Morrie) is an entrepreneur, businessman, educator and author.

Pastor Morrie is a Marriage & Family Counselor and a Certified Anger Management Provider for the Christian Community and the California Courts System as well as Senior Pastor of SERV Ministries (a non-profit 501C3 corporation) whose purpose is to assist distressed and abused women and children. He is presently Associate Pastor with West Coast Church in Mission Viejo, California.

Give your family the greatest gift money can't buy: Comfort & Peace of Mind.

---

Order now at: www.finaldetails.net
Toll free: 866-706-5690
Email: hanslynpublish@wwdb.org

*If you're in need of an upbeat, interesting and informative expert on this subject or any of Maurice's certifications, contact him at:*
**P.O. Box 127,
Dana Point, Calif. 92629**
Email: hansenm1@sbcglobal.net

## JAMES ROBINSON — SPIRITUAL HEALER AND TEACHER

Hot Springs, AR USA
http://www.divinelightmaster.com

James is an expert on relationships, parenting, spirituality, self-improvement and especially male issues. With so many men confused about appropriate male behavior, James is a welcome guide and instructor. James has counselled individuals on numerous personal issues for decades. Being a male in today's society should be exciting, uplifting, easy and fun! James has answers for many questions men ask in today's society have about their place in the world.

James Robinson
Hot Springs, AR USA
*Contact Phone:* 501.609.0660
*Cell:* 519.596.1221
**Click to Contact from Web Site**

## SOL WEISS, AUTHOR, INVENTOR, MEDICAL DOCTOR

Los Angeles, CA USA

A hundred years after Einstein's Theory of Special Relativity in 1905, "We Are Inevitable We Are Forever" gives to the world answers to the issues of the real fate of humankind, as well as Einstein's dream of a deterministic world. Written by Dr. Sol Weiss, this thought provoking book provides scientifically based insights into important issues. . .how we came to be and where we are going. . .why life exists. . .where intuition and instinct come from. . .how prodigies happen. . . where inventions come from. . .why there is a supreme reasoning power. . .why women should control all their life decisions.

Sol Weiss, M.D.
Canoga, CA USA
*Contact Phone:* 818-346-1515
**Click to Contact from Web Site**

## FUND FOR UFO RESEARCH, INC.

Alexandria, VA USA
http://www.fufor.com

The Fund for UFO Research, a nonprofit scientific organization in Washington, D.C., is trying to find the answers to questions such as: Did the U.S. Government recover a crashed 'flying saucer' in 1947? Did President Truman appoint a high-level commission to analyze the wreckage? Have hundreds — perhaps thousands — of humans been 'abducted' by alien beings? They are interested in trying to identify unidentified aerial craft and researching questions about UFO.

Don Berliner
*Chairman*
Fund for UFO Research, Inc.
Alexandria, VA
*Contact Phone:* 703-684-6032
**Click to Contact from Web Site**

## AURELIE LAURENCE — BIO-FEEDBACK EXPERT

St. Petersburg, FL USA
www.CoachAurelie.org

Aurelie Laurence knows about bio-feedback.

Aurelie Laurence
Trinity, FL USA
*Contact Phone:* 727-232-0504
**Click to Contact from Web Site**

## PETRENE SOAMES, AUTHOR OF THE ESSENCE OF SELF-HEALING

Houston, TX USA
timeismine.com

For over twenty years Petrene has been a leading authority in Healing, Self Awarness, and Multi Dimensional Reality. Her Unique practices and insights which are drawn from every realm of human sciences studies and beyond, have helped countless numbers of people worldwide. Petrenes public radio and TV appearances have helped and inspired millions more. To date she has appeared on over thirty five TV shows, over two hundred Radio shows, has over a hundred published articles, is the author of The Essence Of self healing, How to bring health and happiness into your life and is the producer of The Positive Thought Wakeup Cards.

Janie Jones
*Media Contact*
Petrene Soames Corporation
The Woodlands, TX USA
*Contact Phone:* 281-363-9983
**Click to Contact from Web Site**

# Mary Anne Ayer:
## Spirituality & Mysticism Explained

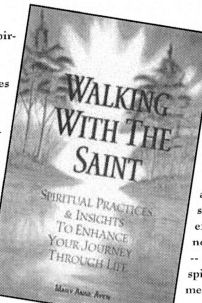

■ Gain insights into the secrets of spirituality and the journey of the soul

■ Learn to choose spiritual practices and how to perform them

■ Achieve peace, happiness and self-fulfillment

■ Have the answers to the most profound questions ever asked

In "Walking With The Saint -- Spiritual Practices and Insights to Enhance Your Journey Through Life," author Mary Anne Ayer, a spiritual practitioner and teacher, takes the reader on her journey through Christian mysticism and an exploration of Oriental religion, based upon her travels and in-depth study of ancient Sanskrit texts as well as her meetings with yogis, sages and a living saint.

Ayer provides insights and analysis of a topic rarely understood on this level. She offers explanations that readers may not get from religious institutions -- and a gateway to the benefits of spiritual practices and enlightenment.

---

*Topics which the author can discuss with you and your audience:*

■ **Author's personal journey around the world in search of God**

■ **Meetings with yogis, sages, swamis, monks and a living saint**

■ **World religions and their commonality**

■ **Spiritual practices around the world and the way to know God**

■ **A new look at Jesus as a master -- and the Christian Gnostics**

■ **Reincarnation: its proof and implications**

■ **The problem of the pursuit of happiness**

■ **A specific yoga for everyone**

■ **The science of spirituality: how science proves the world's spiritual viewpoints**

■ **Walking within the light: how spiritual practices will enhance your life**

■ **De-stress your life: how spiritual practices and insights improve your sense of well being and performance**

■ **How to gain the most out of life by spiritual practices and insights**

■ **How science proves God**

---

Mary Anne Ayer
Tenth Gate Publishing
Naples, Florida
781-820-3900
TenthGatePublishing.com

546      **Yearbook of Experts®   Vol. XXV, No. IV**
**Profile Section**
     546

**WALTER SEMKIW, MD --**
**REINCARNATION EXPERT**
San Francisco, CA USA
www.johnadams.net

Practicing physician, Walter Semkiw, MD, is arguably the pre-eminent reincarnation expert today. His remarkable book, 'Return of the Revolutionaries - the case for reincarnation and soul groups reunited,' provides scientific evidence of past lives, karma, souls. He believes the Founding Fathers/American Revolutionary leaders are back to lead us thru a spiritual revolution. He identifies past/present lives of Oprah, Halle Berry, Marilyn Monroe, Anne Frank, Ben Franklin, Bush, Clinton, Gore, JK Rowling etc. and how reincarnation explains child prodigies.

Walter Semkiw, MD
*Founder/CEO*
IISIS
San Francisco, CA USA
*Contact Phone:* 415-244-9658
**Click to Contact from Web Site**

# Petrene Soames

## World-Class Psychic, Paranormal Expert, Healer, Medium, Therapist, Author, Teacher and New Dimensional Artist

Petrene Soames, originally from England, widely traveled and based in The Woodlands Texas, has been interviewed on hundreds of radio stations, has been featured on or appeared on almost 40 TV Shows, has hundred of published articles and is the author of "The Essence of Self-Healing: How to bring health and happiness into your life." She is also the creator of the new and updated "Positive Thought Cards."

Petrene is famous for her unique insight, problem-solving abilities and being able to bring real answers and a positive spin to just about anything.

Petrene speaks about anything and everything from how to really lose weight, heal your body, despite what medicine says, time travel -- as well as the paranormal, disasters, celebrities, people alive and those who are dead and much, much more. She also offers ten-day fix-it-all retreats in The Woodlands, Texas. And following in Greece this year, she heads to Taiwan for her latest book published in Chinese.

For more information and to find out more about Petrene's one-of-a-kind therapies, including experiencing past, future and parallel time, check out her Web sites at Timeismine.com, Healyourselfnow.com and Petrenepress.com.

---

■ *Call Janie Jones or Petrene Soames directly at 281-363-9983.*

# Objective Evidence of Reincarnation
## Walter Semkiw, MD

| Anne Frank | Barbro Karlen | John B. Gordon | Fire Chief | US Diplomat | Louise | Carroll | Police Captain |
|---|---|---|---|---|---|---|---|
| Childhood Memory Case | | Civil War General | Jeff Keene | Wayne Peterson | Vanderbilt | Beckwith | Robert Snow |
| Videotape Available | | Featured on *Proof Positive* | | Former Fulbright Director | | Featured on *Proof Positive* | |

In his book, ***Return of the Revolutionaries: The Case for Reincarnation and Soul Groups Reunited***, **Walter Semkiw, MD**, has compiled compelling, **independently researched reincarnation cases (above)**, which demonstrate that facial features, personality traits and linguistic writing style stay the same across lifetimes, and that people incarnate in karmic groups. The case of Barbro Karlen, who was born into a Christian family and who has had memories since childhood of being **Anne Frank**, shows that people can change religion from lifetime to lifetime. This knowledge could have prevented the Holocaust, can help mitigate violence in the Middle East and can serve as an **"Antidote to 9/11."**

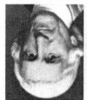      

| Charles | Ralph | James | Oprah | Kate | John | Rev. William | Neale |
|---|---|---|---|---|---|---|---|
| Thomson | Nader | Wilson | Winfrey | Fox | Edward | Walter | Donald Walsch |

Dr. Semkiw has also worked with **Kevin Ryerson**, the medium featured in Shirley MacLaine's books, who has demonstrated an ability to make accurate past life matches, as demonstrated in the cases featured above. One of the most remarkable matches involves *Conversations with God* author **Neale Donald Walsch**, who was identified as a little known 18th century minister in Boston, Rev. William Walter. Historical research revealed matching facial features and personality traits. Mr. Walsch supports this match. Celebrity cases, featured below, were also solved through Mr. Ryerson.

   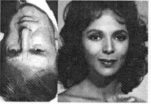   

| Angelina | Duchesse De | Comte de | Donald | Dorothy | Halle | Daniel | George W. |
|---|---|---|---|---|---|---|---|
| Jolie | Bourgogne | Ponchartrain | Trump | Dandridge | Berry | Morgan | Bush |

**World famous neurosurgeon, Norm Shealy, MD, Ph.D.**, also an independently researched reincarnation case, has stated regarding Dr Semkiw's book, **"For the survival of humanity, this is the most significant book written in 1000 years."** At a July 4, 2005 gathering hosted by Dr. Shealy, 33 people convened to support Dr. Semkiw's reincarnation research, including 6 MDs (two professors and a **Human Genome Project** scientist), 6 PhDs, 6 published authors, 2 retired US Diplomats, a JD and Navy and Army Captains, all who have past lives identified. Dr. Semkiw is also collaborating with Adrian Finkelstein, MD, whose new book presents the **reincarnation of Marilyn Monroe.**

**To Review Cases Go To:　www.johnadams.net**
**Contact Info: E Mail:　walter@johnadams.net　Phone: (415) 244-9658**

   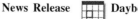

# Geographic Index

## Alabama

**Birmingham**
Civitan International, 195
Gayle Lantz - Organizational
    Development Expert, 332
**Fairhope**
Islam In Focus, 248
**Huntsville**
ADTRAN, Inc., 346
Homer Hickam, 322
**Mobile**
Foreign-Trade Zone Corporation, 205
**Montgomery**
Alabama Department of Economic and
    Community Affairs, 204

## Arizona

**Gilbert**
Stephen Fairley, M.A., RCC, --
    Today's Leadership Coaching, 449
**Lake Havasu City**
Career Coach Institute, 366
**Phoenix**
Debbie Allen — Motivational Speaker
    for Business, 438
David G. Dwinell, Master Broker, 280
Got Game Consulting, 384
Alton J. Jones -- How to Get Good
    Credit Expert, 358
Abhay Padgaonkar, 410
Dianne Post, 189
Solutions For Hiring, 377
Steve Stenson, M.Ed., MBA —
    Strategic Concepts, 476
Beth Terry - Phoenix Life Coach, 446
Tom Lee — Expert on Catholic
    Church History, 195
Dahn Yoga, 499
Zila, Inc. — Oral Cancer Detection,
    512
Joseph Zodl—World Trade, 205
**Scottsdale**
Coaching Insider, 400
Everything in its Place ®, 471
Great Potential Press, Inc., 186
Joan Johnson, B. S. - Domestic
    Violence Expert, 189
Ellen A. Kaye and Perfect
    Presentation, 470
James Spencer — Expert — Video
    Learning Library, 313
**Tempe**
Dandelion Books, LLC - Dynamic
    Literature Experts!, 307
National Speakers Association, 330
**Tucson**
David M. Jacobson, MSW, 474

## Arkansas

**Hot Springs**
James Robinson — Spiritual Healer
    and Teacher, 544

## California

**Berkeley**
Verona Fonte Ph.D. — Bird Flu
    Expert, 510
Independent Scholars of Asia, Inc., 247
Overcoming Job Burnout, 364
Lenora Madison Poe, Ph.D., 531
**Beverly Hills**
Dr. Washington Bryan II, M. D., 490
Carole Lieberman, M.D., Media
    Psychiatrist, 523
Robert Radi — Product Designer, 436
**Big Bear Lake**
Diana L. Guerrero's Ark Animals, 264
**Blue Lake**
Kevin Savetz, 348
**Campbell**
Loree Taylor Jordan, C.C.H., I.D, 496
**Campo**
National Border Patrol Council, 390
**Carlsbad**
Gemological Institute of America, 294
NAMM, The International Music
    Products Association, 298
**Citrus Heights**
Crusade Against Fire Deaths, Inc. —
    Richard M Patton, 238
**Encino**
Marta Perrone - Domestic Connections
    Publications, 252
**Escondido**
Barbara Morris, Pharmacist,
    Anti-Aging Expert, 480
**Fortuna**
C. Crane Company —- Conusmer
    Radio Experts, 344
**Gilroy**
createaway, 339
**Grand Terrace**
John Paul Mendocha - Pod Casting
    Profits, 348
**Healdsburg**
Resource Realizations, 405
**Hermosa Beach**
American Association for Career
    Education (AACE), 369
**Huntington Beach**
Duane Lee Heppner — Expert
    Universal Presenter, 478
**Irvine**
Guido Campellone — CitiPacific
    Mortgage, 278

Jacqueline Marcell - Elder Care,
    Alzheimer's, Caregiving Expert,
    542
ORYXE Energy International, 258
Angelo A Paparelli, US Immigration
    Law Specialist, 253
Son of the Soil, 279
Joseph Vranich, Author & Rail Travel
    Expert, 281
**La Quinta**
John Patrick Dolan - Negotiate like the
    Pros, 382
**Laguna Beach**
Randall Bell, Real Estate Damages,
    270
**Livermore**
Lawrence Livermore National
    Laboratory, 261
**Long Beach**
Litigation Management & Training
    Services, Inc., 234
**Los Angeles**
Accord Management Systems, 377
Alternative Living for the Aging, 520
Americans for Free Choice in
    Medicine, 364
Artists of America, 186
Gary M. Barnbaum CPA CMC, 242
Baum Hedlund, A Professional
    Corporation, 234
Jennifer Beever -- New Incite
    Marketing, 340
Hannah Bentley, Attorney at Law, 230
Esther M. Berger -- The MoneySmart
    Expert, 356
Bernstein Crisis Management, 316
Black Speakers Online, 328
Dr. Virginia Bola, 486
Rachel Bondi --
    www.EarningPower.org, 218
Dorothy Breininger - Center for
    Organization and Goal Planning,
    472
Robert R. Butterworth, Ph.D., 522
Dr. Ava Cadell, 535
The Celebrity Source, 328
The Child SHARE Program, 188
CODEPINK: Women for Peace, 250
Lissa Coffey -- Lifestyle Designer, 534
Robert Cullen, Retirement
    Management Expert, 478
Carmen Day -- Wealth4u In Spirit, 418
Patrick De Carolis, Jr. — Firm
    Specializes in Family Law, 230
Aviva Diamond — Blue Streak/A
    Communications Company, 471
Eliot Disner -- McGuireWoods LLP,
    222
Dream Merchant New Product
    Guidance, 402

Michael Dwight -- Real Estate Speaker, 276

Joel Eisenberg — How to Survive a Day Job, 380

Farmers Insurance Group, 364

Fulcrum Financial Inquiry LLP — Litigation Consulting Services, 234

Murray Grossan, MD — Tower Ear Nose Throat — Cedars Sinai, 516

Robert S. Grossman — Business Performance Expert, 388

Dr. Reese Halter — Tree Scientist, 268

Rev. Maurice N. Hansen, Ph.D. -- Living Will Expert, 541

Jeffrey Hansler, CSP, 454

The Hip Hop Educator, 184

The Institute for Effective Innovation, 416

International Academy of Anti-Aging Medicine, 519

Dave Jensen, MS - Sales & Productivity Expert, 370

John Longenecker — Author and Columnist on Personal Sovereignty., 214

Joe Kennedy — The Small Business Owners Manual, 395

Larry S. Greenfield — Mediation-Complex Business & Entertainment Law, 230

Bo Lebo -- New Life Options -- Literacy Expert, 187

Dr. Toni Leonetti — Founder, Human Potential International, 475

Levine Communications, Inc., 316

Dr. Michael Levittan, Anger Management Specialist, 526

Live the James Bond Lifestyle, 322

Magana, Cathcart & McCarthy, 234

LuAn Mitchell-Halter — Entrepreneur/Author/Motivational Speaker, 334

Nancy Gray — Gray & Associates, P.C., 232

Mr. Laurie Pane — Chasing Sunsets — Sail Around The World, 286

Geela Parish, Author, 332

Edward Poll, J.D., M.B.A.., CMC -- Law Firm Management Expert, 223

Donald Silvers, CKD--Author, Kitchen Design With Cooking in Mind,, 268

Southwestern University School of Law, 220

Kerry Tuschhoff, Hypnobabies Network, 508

Bill Thompson — TV, Inc. — Infomercial Production Company, 450

Union Rescue Mission, 195

Jodi Walker, Certified Professional Speaker, 468

Dottie Walters — Walters Speaker Services, 330

Sol Weiss, Author, Inventor, Medical Doctor, 544

World Business Exchange Network/ Global Internet Trade Course, 426

World Wide Pet Industry Association, Inc., 264

James Yang — Intellectual Property Attorney, 230

Paul Young -- Securities Arbitration Commentator, 228

Azita Zendel — Independent Hollywood Film Maker, 299

Irwin Zucker — Promotion In Motion Public Relations, 310

**Los Angelex**

Ralph Martinez — Martinez Law Group, 232

**Los Gatos**

UpLevel Strategies, 416

**Menlo Park**

SRI Consulting, 260

**Moorpark**

Rev. Roy A. Teel Jr., 196

**Newport Beach**

Dr. Marlene M. Coleman, M.D. - Harbor Pediatric Medical Group, 190

**North Hollywood**

Denise Wakeman — The Blog Squad, 339

**Oakland**

Coach and Grow R.I.C.H., 404

Dreyer's Grand Ice Cream, 268

Frank Jakubowsky, Author, 542

Jonathan Koomey, 326

Gini Graham Scott, Ph.D., J.D. (Expert on Business Relationships), 529

**Orange**

Dr. Robert Morey - Religion & Cult Expert, 198

Susie Vanderlip -- Teen & Parenting Skills Expert, 531

**Orange County**

Tom Nassif, President & CEO — Western Growers, 266

**Pacific Palisades**

Dr. Valerie Kirkgaard — Getting the Best Out of People, 392

**Palos Verdes Estates**

Angi Ma Wong, 452

**Pasadena**

June Davidson, American Seminar Leaders Association, 330

**Penryn**

Personal Transformation Press, 500

**Petaluma**

Strozzi Institute, 405

**Pleasanton**

International Transactional Analysis Association, Inc., 522

**Rancho Palos Verdes**

Hypnosis Federation — Shelley Stockwell, Ph.D., 530

**Sacramento**

Dr. Nancy Kalish -- Lost Love Expert, 536

Leonard Lewin, Furniture Consultant, 270

Lifetime Adoption Foundation — Let's Talk Adoption Radio Show, 187

**San Clemente**

Sheila Kessler, PhD-- Customer Satisfaction Expert & Executive Coach, 334

**San Diego**

BusinessOL - Search Engine Optimization Experts, 339

Institute for Business Technology --IBT-USA, 376

Greg Lawson -- Worldwide Scenic Photography, 296

R. A. Martinez, Homeowners Insurance Expert, 270

Nelson Motivation, Inc., 386

Dr. Patrick Quillin, Cancer & Nutrition Expert, 514

Threat Assessment, 239

Vistage International (formerly TEC International), 424

Gregg Ward, CMC — Workplace Diversity Expert, 398

Joni Wilson, Voice Expert, 466

**San Francisco**

Nan Andrews Amish —- Health Care Cost Expert, 500

Association of World Citizens, 250

Big Horse Incorporated, 299

Dr. Maynard Brusman - Workplace Expert, 376

Dr. Susan Campbell, Dating & Relationship Coach, 535

Michael Cannon -- Sales Consultant, 442

Ted Celentino, Business Travel Expert, 285

Chin-Ning Chu —- Asian Marketing Consultants, 428

Michael Clark -- Business and Beyond, 422

Prof. William Crossman - Futurist & Talking Computers ExpertTalking Computers Expert, 341

Expert Authors, 306

Patricia Fripp, 466

Mahash Grossman — The Authors Team, 310

Roberta Guise — Small Business Marketing Expert, 430

Institute for Childhood Resources, 292

Meg Jordan, PhD., RN, 515

Michael Levin, How to Take a Product to Market, 450

Steve Lillo, PlanetLink: Internet Solutions for Business, 348

Jill Lublin -- Networking Expert, 398

Mariposa Leadership, 405

Michael W. McLaughlin, 278

PublishersandAgents.net, 306

Elayne Savage, Ph.D., The Rejection Expert, 528

Walter Semkiw, MD -- Reincarnation Expert, 546

Ed Sherman -- Nolo Press Occidental, 232

TangibleFuture, Inc. — Richard G. Caro, 450

Jinsoo Terry: Building Self-Confidence in the Multi-Cultural Workforce, 378

Merrill Vargo, Ph.D. — Executive Director of Springboard Schools, 180

Jennifer Vessels, 432

Diana Vollmer -- Ascend Consulting Group, 440

Brian Young — Sexual Assault Prevention Instructor, 239

**San Francisco Bay Area**

Linda Popky - L2M Associates, Inc., 414

**San Francsico**

Harold Lustig — Achieve Financial Security, 350

**San Jose**

Diana Cornelius, Non-Religious Spirituality Expert, 201

Tim Ferriss - Fitness , Nutrition & Lifestyle Expert, 488

Philippa Gamse, Web Strategy Speaker, 340

Jan Marini -- CEO, Jan Marini Skin Research, Inc., 492

Dr. Michael D. Rabinoff, D.O., Ph.D. - UCLA / Biogenesys, Inc., 514

**San Rafael**

Gary Karp - Disability Awareness Expert, 525

**Santa Barbara**

The Divorce Forum, 540

Dan Poynter -- Book Publishing Industry Expert, 305

Jay Winner, M.D., 475

**Silicon Valley**

Global System Services Corporation, 428

**Sonoma**

Edward E. Morler - Management Consultant, Executive Coach, Author, 370

**South Laguna Beach**

Lola Gillebaard - Humorist & Motivational Speaker, 380

**Temecula**

Foundation for A Course in Miracles, 201

**Thousand Oaks**

Jim Lorenzen, CFP®, AIF® - The Independent Financial Group, 354

Rhonda L. Sher — Two Minute Networker, 460

**Ventura**

Mystery Shop Link, LLC, 430

**Westlake Village**

Barton Goldsmith, Ph.D., 424

# Colorado

**Boulder**

Nicole Casanova - Entrepreneur & Relationship Expert, 537

Room 214, Inc. - Social Media Experts, 436

Theresa M. Szczurek, Ph.D., Leadership Development Consultant, 449

**Colorado Springs**

National Strength and Conditioning Association, 498

Meryl Runion, CSP-- Communication, Management Leadership Speaker, 470

Small Publishers Association of North America, 306

**Denver**

American Society of Bariatric Physicians, 490

American Water Works Association, 254

Judith Lee Berg -- Human Resource Communication, 214

Carolyn Bushong, Licensed Professional Counselor, 523

Dominic A. Cingoranelli, CPA, CMC -- Specialist in Growth, Strategy and Performance Issues, 428

Creation Chamber, 341

Debra Benton -- Leadership Development Expert, 313

Love and Logic Institute, 531

NetQuote — Insurance Experts, 364

Marilyn Ross — Self-Publishing Resources, 307

Laura Stack, MBA, CSP, The Productivity PRO, 395

Carolyn Strauss- Entrepreneur/ Speaker, 482

Karen Susman — Karen Susman & Associates, 376

LeAnn Thieman, CSP — Caregiver Nurse, 536

Time Warner Telecom, Inc., 346

**LaPorte**

Doug Butler --Horseshoeing Expert, 263

**Loveland**

Terry L. Anna CDMP - Professional Business & Life Journey Coach, 448

**Pueblo**

EllynAnne Geisel -- Not So Desperate Housewife a/k/a the Apron Lady, 303

Dr. Jamie Johnson -- The Dental Diva, 506

# Connecticut

**Bridgeport**

Outsecure, Inc. Information Security Consultant, 244

**Danbury**

Carolyn Finch — Body Language Expert, 484

**Hartford**

Alderman & Alderman, 228

Cynthia Bercowetz, Identity Theft Expert, 349

Projectize Group, 428

Safe Goods Publishing, 324

**New Haven**

Association of Divorce Financial Planners, 356

**Norwalk**

Kelley Connors MPH - Women's Health & Wellness Marketing Expert, 398

**Norwich**

Dianne M. Daniels, AICI, 484

**Ridgefield**

S. G. Hart & Associates, LLC, 400

**Stamford**

JANUS Associates, Inc. -- Information Security, 244

The Volunteer Center of SW Fairfield County, 192

Jan Yager, Ph.D., 472

**Trumbull**

Susan M. Mangiero, Ph.D. AVA, CFA, FRM -- Business Consultant, 362

**Wilton**

Trade Dimensions International, Inc., 324

# Delaware

**Newark**

International Reading Association, 183

Produce Marketing Association, 266

# District of Columbia

**Washington**

Bob Adams -- www.RetirementWave.com, 478

Advocacy Associates, LLC., 216

Alliance to Save Energy, 256

American Council of Life Insurers, 362

American Council of the Blind, 518

American Foreign Service Association, 246

American Gas Association, 260

American Public Power Association, 256

American Public Transportation Association, 281

American Red Cross, 192

American Society for Therapeutic Radiology and Oncology, 512

American Society of Association Executives (ASAE), 203

Americans for Democratic Action, 208

Lois Angell, 212

Kristin J. Arnold, CMC, CPF, CSP, 396

Association of American Physicians and Surgeons, 506

Association on Third World Affairs (A.T.W.A.), 246

Ron Ball — Author, Speaker, EFT Stress Expert, 473

BellSouth Corporation, 338

Dr. Liz Berney — Training & Organizational Development, 388

Biotechnology Industry Organization, 204

BNA, Inc., 216

Travel Expert Gloria Bohan — CEO of Omega World Travel, 286

Jerry Boutcher - Residental Real Estate Investment, 274

Brady Campaign to Prevent Gun Violence, 214

Broadcast Interview Source, Inc. — Publisher of the Yearbook of Experts, 460

Renana Brooks, Ph.D, Sommet Institute for the Study of Power, 206

Brenda Campbell — Management Consulting and Information Technology, 368

TheCapitol.Net, 206

Center for Civil Society & Governance at AED, 250

Center for Tobacco Cessation, 514

Center for Women Policy Studies, 216

Judy Colbert -- Web Usability Speaker, 346

Competitive Enterprise Institute, 206

Consumer Data Industry Association, 359

Council on Hemispheric Affairs, 247

Paul Dickson — Baseball Commentator & Author, 298

Dickstein Shapiro Morin & Oshinsky, 220

Directory of Experts, 313

Dow Lohnes PLLC, 218

The Driving Company, LLC, 282

Du Plain Enterprises, Inc., 326

Edison Electric Institute, 258

Equal Justice Works (formerly NAPIL), 228

Executive Coaching & Consulting Associates, 308

Features USA — Copyright Free News, 308

Federation for American Immigration Reform (FAIR), 253

FIABCI-USA — FIABCI, the International Real Estate Federation, 272

The Financial Services Roundtable, 354

Dr. Marilyn Kern Foxworth, APR, Communications & Marketing Expert, 316

Dave Gerber — Innovative Organizational Solutions, 448

Global Academy Online, 181

Steven Roy Goodman, M.S., J.D. — College Admissions Expert, 182

Nathan Greeno, Drawing Board Consulting Group, 402

Gregg Gregory, CSP — America's Business Navigator, 384

HOMERUN SOFTWARE — 800-HOMERUN.COM, INC., 288

Honeymoon Card Corporation, 285

The Humane Society of the United States, 262

Linda Hunt — Media Critic, 301

Institute of Management Consultants USA, Inc., 411

International Society of Protocol & Etiquette Professionals, 454

Levick Strategic Communications, 318

Paul A. London, 208

Marymount University, 180

Douglas M. McCabe, Ph.D. — Employee Relations Expert, 392

MenCenter, 525

Minority Business Development Agency, 426

MinutePage.com Brand HomePage Creator, 342

Miriam's Kitchen, 195

National Association of Government Communicators, 203

National Association of Letter Carriers(AFL-CIO), 392

National Association of Social Workers, 522

National Chicken Council, 267

National Defense University Press, 247

National Education Association - NEA, 179

National Immigration Forum, 252

National Library Service for the Blind and Physically Handicapped, 516

National Multi Housing Council, 276

National Oilheat Research Alliance, 258

National Pest Management Association, 262

National Right to Life Committee, 216

National Speakers Association, Washington D.C. Area Chapter, 378

NCSJ: Advocates on Behalf of Jews in Russia, Ukraine, Baltic, etc, 196

Negative Population Growth - NPG, Inc, 253

The News Council Corporation, 300

News Release Wire, 312

The Newseum, 301

NOAA Public Affairs, 262

Nuclear Energy Institute (NEI), 258

The Ocean Conservancy, 254

Carol M. Olmstead -- Feng Shui For Real Life, 452

On This Spot Productions — Washington D.C. Historial Information, 301

Pan American Health Organization, 192

Michael J. Pangia, 234

Pet Food Institute, 264

Leon Pomeroy, Ph.D., 212

Penny Pompei — National Women's Business Center, 218

Power Media BlueBook, 312

PubCom -- Publishing Communications Group, 324

Public Relations Software, 314

Radio Free Asia, 301

Zoe Rastegar — Talk Show Host, 248

Ted Rockwell -- Engineer & Nuclear Power Experts, 258

Sailboat Incorporated, 285

Salt Institute, 267

Amy Schoen, CPCC - Dating & Relationship Expert, 537

Search Optimization News, 346

Shakespeare Oxford Society, 279

SIIA, 344

Sister To Sister - National Woman's Heart Day, 194

John M. Snyder, Gun Law Expert, 214

Speaker Bank — Your Professional Keynote Speaker Source, 326

SpeakerLeads.com, 328

Specialized Information Publishers Association, formerly NEPA, 300

St. Andrew's Foundation of Romania, 191

Sugar Association, Inc., 267

SuggestionBank.com Focus Group Services, 444

U.S. Chamber of Commerce, 205

Paul Lawrence Vann -- Motivational Speaker, Author, Trainer, 332

Vertical Search Engine, 348

Veteran's Vision, 246

Vision Strategic Marketing & Communications, 432

Washington Italia Film Festival, 298

Debbie Weil-- Corporate Blogging Expert, 349

Wharton School Club of Washington, 204

Winning Campaigns — Alan Locke, 206

Yearbook of Experts ®, 308

Yearbook Shop Web Site, 320

Young Marines, 246

www.YourSpaGuide.com, 492

Kate Zabriskie - Training Seminars, Workshops, and Keynotes, 390

# Florida

**Boca Raton**
Dr. David J. Demko, Gerontologist and Editor, AgeVenture News, 478

**Bradenton**
Humanists of Florida Association, 199
Dr. Adrian H. Krieg, CFMGE, 210

**Crestview**
Keith E. Nabe - Management Consultant/Public Speaker, 412

**Davie**
National Writers Union, 301

**Daytona Beach**
Theodore W Garrison, III - Construction Expert - Strategic Planning, 279
Dr. John M. Presley - Peace Advocate, 250

**Ft. Lauderdate**
Pete Silver — Marketing Communications Writer, 450

**Gulfport**
Centers for Excellence, 224
Stetson College of Law Centers for Excellence, 224

**Hollywood**
Debra Holtzman, J.D., M.A. — Corporate Spokesperson, 320

Debra Holtzman, J.D., M.A. -- Child Safety Expert, 191
Today's Caregiver Magazine, 504

**Jacksonville**
America's Dumbest Criminals, 226
A.P. John Institute for Cancer Research, 512
Dale Bowman — The Life and Death of Lynyrd Skynyrd bassist Leon Wilkeson, 299
Contented Cow Partners, LLC, 374
Steve Waterhouse, 460

**Jupitter**
Captain Haggerty & Babette Haggerty, 263

**Lakeland**
Lynn Fischer's Healthy Living, Inc., 487

**Miami**
Margo Berman - Creative Marketing Expert, 372
Dr. Gayle Carson, CSP, CMC -- Author of Winning Ways, 382
Cheli Cerra -- Child Success Expert, 191
Dr. Joachim de Posada — Bilingual Motivational Speaker (English/Spanish), 462
Randy Gage, 434
Connie Gordon — Gordon Global Creative Center, 298
Miami Jewish Home & Hospital for the Aged, 520
Bari Meltzer Norman, Ph.D. — College Admissions Expert, 182
PodSwap, 305
Joe Rodriguez, Global Innovation Leadership, Inc., 394
Carolyn Stein -- The Training Express, 388

**Miami Beach**
My First TradeShow, 325

**Naples**
Mary Anne Ayer, Spirituality & Mysticism Explained, 542
Connie Bransilver, Nature Photographer, Writer, Inspirational Speaker, 296
Caroline J. Cederquist, M.D., 488

**Orlando**
James E. Hardy, 505
International Association of Canine Professionals, Martin Deeley, 263
Keith Nabe -- Flu Expert, 519
National Cartoonists Society, 304

**Palm Beach**
Jay Block — Leadership Training Coach, 373

**Palm Beach County**
Rose Lee Archer, M.S., 526

**Palm Beach Gardens**
Robert Stack, CLC, APR, Fellow PRSA - The Comeback Coach, 388

**Palm Harbor**
Brad Kent -- SmartleadsUSA, LLC, 373

**Pompano Beach**
Dr. Kenneth S. Kallin PhD, 191

**Sarasota**
Dr. Charles Bens -- Health, Nutrition & Smoking Expert, 514
George B. Blake -- Single Again, 538
Bo Martinsen, MD & Anne-Marie Chalmers, MD — Omega 3 Fish Oil Experts, 504

**St. Petersburg**
David DeBatto - Former Counterintelligence Special Agent, 212
Aurelie Laurence — Bio-Feedback Expert, 544

**Sunrise**
Peter J. Fogel - Reinvention & Communications Expert, 380

**Tampa**
Bob Brown, Consulting Intelligence, LLC, 411
Hellen Davis, CLU, Master Influencer, 328
F. Felicia Ferrara, Ph.D., 473
Jim Meisenheimer — Creator of No-Brainer Selling Skills, 460
Elaine Fantle Shimberg, Healthcare, Women & Family Issues, 531
Tampa Bay Technology Forum, 342
Tim Walsh — Toy Expert, 292

**Tampa Bay**
Stetson University College of Law, 224
United Christian Services, Inc., 196

**West Palm Beach**
SIGN*A*RAMA — Start-up Your Own Business, 442

**Weston**
Gerald (Gerry) Katz, MSPA, RHU, ALHC, DABFE, 364

**Winter Haven**
Tim Kern, Economic Insight, 392

# Georgia

**Americus**
Habitat for Humanity International, 276

**Atlanta**
Around the Rings.com, 290
The Consummate Consumer, 359
Eric de Groot -- Global Problem Solver, 205
Financial Voyages, LLC., 430
Melissa Galt, IDS, IFDA - Lifestyle Design Expert, 533
Giant Leap Consulting, 448
Dr. Kathleen Hall, Stress Management and Work-Life Balance Expert, 378
William C. Head, 236
Anthony Hsieh - Loans and Personal Finance Expert, 352
LogistiCare, Non-Emergency Transportation, 281
Kaneta R. Lott, DDS -- Pediatric Dentist, Banker, 532
Lynne Marks, Image and Branding, 482
National Families in Action, 236

David Nour -- Relationship Economics Expert, 458
Roger Nunley — Customer Care Institute, 336
Readers Are Writers, Inc, 181
Greg Smith -- Chart Your Course International, 374
Mike Stewart — Internet Audio Guy, 348
Al Vivian, BASIC Diversity, Inc., 368
James A. Ziegler — Financial Prosperity Speaker, 416

**Decatur**
Patti Wood — Communication Dynamics, 466

**Kennesaw**
JoAnn Hines - The Packaging Diva, 432
Women in Packaging, Inc. — Consumer Product Packaging Expert, 432

**Norcross**
Ruth King - BusinessTVChannel.com, 422

**Ringgold**
Common Sense for Today, 201

# Idaho

**Boise**
Vincent Muli Kituku, Ph.D., CSP --- Motivational Leadership Speaker, 482

**Rathdrum**
Patrick Wood - The August Review, 210

# Illinois

**Barrington**
Michael Mercer, Ph.D., Expert on Hiring, Leadership, HR, & Management, 376

**Bartlett**
Frank C. Bucaro & Associates, Inc., 202

**Chicago**
100 Jobs For Kids & Young Adults—A Self-Empowerment Tool, 366
Abbott, Langer & Associates, Inc. — Salary and Benefits Survey Experts, 373
M. Sean Agnew Enterprises LLC, 372
Anne Aldrich — Across The Board Marketing, Inc., 318
American Academy of Anti-Aging Medicine, 519
American Academy of Matrimonial Lawyers, 232
Amnesty International, 250
Wendy Barlin CPA, 420
William S. Bike -- Political Commentator, 208
Ralph J. Bloch & Associates, Inc. -- Association Programs and Consulting, 204
Karma Brown, The Strategic Coach, 404

Cancer Prevention Coalition —
Samuel S. Epstein, M.D., 512

Challenger, Gray & Christmas, Inc.,
364

Christian-Muslim Studies Network,
199

Consumer Credit Insurance
Association, 362

Council of Residential Specialists, 274

Don Crowther -- Marketing & Internet
Marketing Expert, 436

David Gorder — High Energy Weight
Loss Program, 534

James D. Feldman, CITE, CPT, MIP,
369

Gregg Fraley, 414

Jeff Gee, Customer Service Expert,
336

Zimbabu T. Hamilton - Expert
Percussionist Jazz Radio Producer,
280

Heather Harder, Ph.D., Author,
Speaker, and Consultant, 184

Institute of Food Technologists, 267

Dale Irvin — Very Funny Speaker, 377

The John Marshall Law School, 220

Henry Johnson -- Men's Health
Nutrition & Fitness Expert, 525

Jeff Korhan -- Grow from What You
Know, 406

Al Lautenslager -- Certified Guerrilla
Marketing Coach, 372

Lawrence Hall Youth Services, 184

Jeffery M. Leving — Fathers' Rights,
540

Dr. John E. Mayer -- Expert on Youth
& Parenting, 532

Gary Moore — Direct Sales &
Marketing Expert, 254

National Headache Foundation, 510

Olson Communications, Inc., 268

Pattishall, McAuliffe, Newbury,
Hilliard & Geraldson LLP, 218

Cheryl Perlitz - Life Change and
Survival Expert, 470

Donald J. Ramsell — DUI & Drunk
Driving Defense Attorney, 236

Janet Tavakoli - President, Tavakoli
Structured Finance, Inc., 354

Wilma Taylor, 523

University of Illinois — College of
Dentistry, 505

Mikki Williams Unltd. * Vistage
International * Coaching, etc..., 330

Winston Mid East Analysis &
Commentary, 248

WomensPath—Christian Products &
Workshops for & about Women,
198

Steve Yastrow — Yastow Marketing,
434

**Des Plaines**
The Procrastinator's Handbook — Rita
Emmett, 471

**Evanston**
American Massage Therapy
Association (AMTA), 494

KHB Consulting Services, 260

**Kenilworth**
Ad College - BDNI, 436

**Lincolnshire**
Association of Legal Administrators,
224

**Schaumburg**
American Veterinary Medical
Association, 263

**Wilmette**
Joel Warady - Branding & Marketing
Expert, 368

# Indiana

**Elkhart**
Terri Kay, 307

**Fort Wayne**
Deborah C. Miller — Strategy and
Process Development Services, 420

**Indianapolis**
Jean Palmer Heck -- Executive Speech
Coach, 333

Society of Professional Journalists,
300

# Iowa

**Des Moines**
Association of Image Consultants
International, AICI, 482

**Evansdale**
XANADU Enterprises -- Get Paid to
Travel, 286

**Fairfield**
Robert Keith Wallace, Ph.D. -
Homeland Security and Conflict
Resolution Expert, 242

# Kansas

**Kansas City**
Vernon Jacobs, CPA -- President,
Offshore Press, Inc., 359

**Topeka**
Think Tank Directory, 349

# Kentucky

**Goshen**
Jonathan Cowan — Peak Achievement
Training, 426

**Lexington**
International Coach Federation, 405

Sylvia L. Lovely — Expert on Cities,
276

Stan B. Walters 'The Lie Guy', 228

**Louisville**
The Dream Factory, Inc., 188

# Louisiana

**Baton Rouge**
Ms. Bert Fife - Consultant, Speaker,
Coach, 468

Dr. Caxton Opere, 538

**New Orleans**
Rebecca O'Meara, 314

PixelPagesPlus.com (sm), 349

Liz Tahir, 420

# Maine

**Bangor**
Bernhoff A. Dahl, M.D. - Trionics
International, Inc., 395

**Portland**
Scott Simmonds — Insurance Expert,
362

# Maryland

**Annapolis**
Naval Institute, 247

Naval Institute Press -- U.S. Naval
Institute, 247

Prison Ministry Task Force, Episcopal
Diocese of Maryland, 226

Strategic Management Partners, Inc. -
Turnaround Management & Equity
Investing Experts, 410

**Baltimore**
Calvert School, 186

Stu Needel, 456

Kathryn Seifert, Ph.D., Trauma Expert,
186

Brian Taylor, Publishing Industry
Consultant & Book Marketer, 322

**Bethesda**
Robert A. Bernstein -- Families of
Value, 198

Bio Brite Inc., 520

CureSearch National Childhood
Cancer Foundation, 519

Louis Levy, 480

Bill Mead — Baseball Goes to War,
296

Jill Tanenbaum — Washington DC
Graphic Design, 340

**Burtonsville**
Council of Colleges of Acupuncture
and Oriental Medicine, 499

**Clarksville**
Wolf Rinke Associates, 475

**Columbia**
Angels Over America, 302

Fred L. Coover, Esquire, 232

J. Shep Jeffreys, Ed.D. -- Grief Expert,
541

**Frederick**
Aircraft Owners and Pilots Association
-- AOPA, 284

**Gaithersburg**
The SunBox Company, 520

**Garrett Park**
The Bonus Army — An American
Epic, 303

**Landover**
Epilepsy Foundation, 515

**Lanham**
Chika Obodozie, 272

**Largo**
Today's Relationships — Russell Price, Jr., 537

**Montgomery County**
Jamie S Lapin, CDP, CFP Risk Management Group, Inc., 278

**Olney**
New Beginnings — Support Group for Separated/Divorced Men & Women, 540

**Owings Mills**
The Foundation Fighting Blindness, Inc., 516

**Rockville**
American Kidney Fund, 508
American Speech-Language-Hearing Association, 515
Goodwill Industries International, Inc., 194
Interstate Commission on the Potomac River Basin, 254

**Silver Spring**
The Lett Group, 455
Masonic Information Center, 201
National Council for the Social Studies, 182

**Street**
SWS Security, 242

# Massachusetts

**Amherst**
UMass, Amherst, 180

**Boston**
James M. Atkinson, 242
Edward Bond, Professional Certified Construction Manager, 278
Boston Center for the Arts, 280
Dr. Pamela Brill, Peak Performance Consultant, 448
William E. Donoghue -- The Father of Safe Money Investing, 350
Germany-USA Career Center, 376
Gregory Girard -- Telecom Technology Expert, 338
Paige Stover Hague, 313
International Coalition of Art Deco Societies (ICADS), 291
Denise Lamothe, Psy.D, H.H.D. - Emotional Eating Specialist, 487
Evana Maggiore -- Fashion Feng Shui International, 452
MCMC llc., 500
Mequoda Group — Helping Publishers Harness The Internet, 342
Opera Boston, 279
Gary Patterson — Fiscal Doctor, 414
ProofreadNOW.com —- Phil Jamieson, Founder, 316
The Safety Minute Seminars, 239
David Meerman Scott -- Strategic Internet Marketing Consultant, 348
Society for Advancement of Consulting, LLC, 410
Speaking of Leadership® - Phil Holberton, CPA, CMC, 325
Stonewall Communities, Inc. - Gay and Lesbian Aging Issues, 520

Nancy R. Van Tine, 540
The Verghis Group, 334
Jeffrey S. Wolfsberg & Associates Inc., Alcohol & Other Drug Prevention Specialists, 522

**Catham**
Bob Staake, 304

**Dedham**
Milestone Consulting, 400

**Franklin**
Howard Services, Security, 244

**Hanson**
The Art and Creative Materials Institute, Inc., 291

**Norfolk**
Dave E. David, M.D., 510

**Peabody**
Possibilities at Work, 418

**Springfield**
Sports Travel and Tours, 284

**Waltham**
Massachusetts Association of Realtors, 270

**Woburn**
Tom Nicoli BCH, CI - Hypnosis Expert, 529

# Michigan

**Ann Arbor**
Carol Dunitz, Ph.D -- Effective Business Communication Expert, 333
Joseph Paliwoda, MBA, CAC-I — CARF Accreditation Expert, 494
Passporter Travel Press, 285

**Augusta**
Patricia A. Trites -- Healthcare Compliance Resources™, 500

**Detroit**
Barry Demp Coaching, LLC — Detroit Life Coach, 449
Kwasny Flooring, 271
Richard Marquis -- College Success Expert, 183
Tom Nardone — Online Privacy Expert, 340
Cynthia Shelby-Lane, M.D. -- Laughter is Good Medicine, 480

**East Lansing**
C. Leslie Charles, Author, Speaker, Consultant, 472

**Lansing**
James E. White — Honest Inventor Help, 396

**Plymouth**
Scott Lorenz, Westwind Communications, 318

# Minnesota

**Minneapolis**
Brian Carroll, CEO of InTouch, Inc., Author, Speaker, 440
International Association of Facilitators, 204

Arik Johnson — Competitive Intelligence Consultant, 244
Jill Konrath -- Selling to Big Companies, 369
Byron J. Richards, CCN - Leptin & Nutrition Expert, 488
Nili Sachs, Ph.D., 484
Amy S. Tolbert, Ph.D., CSP, Diversity Consultant, 398
Dr. Alan Zimmerman - Author, Professional Speaker, Business Consultant, 450

**Minnetonka**
Change Masters Incorporated, 396

**Rochester**
Patricia R. Adson, Ph.D., Adson Coaching and Consulting, 404
Mitch Anthony — Future of Retirement Expert, 478

# Mississippi

**Hattiesburg**
Beverly Smallwood, Ph.D., Magnetic Workplaces, 475

# Missouri

**Clayton**
SeaWorld, Busch Gardens and the Anheuser-Busch Adventure Park, 286

**Columbia**
Michael J. Mayer -- Licensed Psychologist/Consultant, 528
Don Zeman, America's Home Improvement Expert, 271

**Kansas City**
Advoates for EMS Leadership, 263
Pam Newman, 418
Positive Lights, Inc. Publisher Elder Care Digest, 478

**St. Louis**
American Association of Orthodontists, 505
Anheuser-Busch Companies, Inc., 268
Dan Coughlin, The Corporate Catalyst, 352
Nancy Friedman, Telephone Doctor, 336
Timberland Design, 270

# Montana

**Great Falls**
Patricia Ann Hellinger, Expert on Immune System Deficiencies, 512

**Missoula**
Center for Wildlife Information, 253

# Nebraska

**Lincoln**
iUniverse Inc. Book Publisher, 318
Stepfamily Association of America, 540

**Mitchell**
Mike Jay -- World's Most Innovative Coach, 406

# Nevada

**Las Vegas**
Dr Janelle Barlow says: 'Good customer service is no longer enough!', 438
California Cosmetics Corporation —— Bob Sidell, 492
CalorieLab, Inc., 266
Loren Ekroth - Conversation & Communications Expert, 460
Gail Howard -- Lottery Expert, 291
Justice On Trial, 226
Robert X. Leeds, Author/Publisher (Epic Publishing), 322
Barry Maher - Barry Maher & Associates, 453
Denise Michaels — Testosterone-Free Marketing, 368
Jeffrey Mishlove, Ph.D., Parapsychologist, 499
Sensory Resources, Conferences & Publications on Sensory Dysfunction, 518
Steve Wilson, 453

# New Hampshire

**Bedford**
PowerHouse Consulting, Inc., 336
**Dover**
International Personal Development - Ivan Burnell, 474
**Keene**
Antioch New England Graduate School, 180
**Portsmouth**
Hideaways International, Inc., 285

# New Jersey

**Bedminster**
Michael R. Martorella, Executive Coach & Advisor — MMI Communication, 408
**Berkeley Heights**
Shawn Collins — Affiliate Program Expert, 349
**Boonton**
The Insight Research Corporation, 339
**Bradley Beach**
Compulsive Gambling Foundation, 529
Arnie Wexler — Arnie & Sheila Wexler Associates, 291
**Cherry Hill**
Barbara Pachter, Communications Expert, 453
**Clifton**
Joseph F. Dunphy, M.B.A., 356
Encore Studios, 296
Alan Goldberger — Referee Law Expert, 222

**Colonia**
Tom Owen - OWL Investigations, Inc., 230
**Edison**
Aspen (Autism Spectrum Disorders), 508
**Fair Haven**
Dary Day, 534
**Finesville**
A.T. Cross Associates, Inc., 488
**Hammonton**
Aldonna R. Ambler, CMC, CSP, 462
**Hillsborough**
Global Training Systems, 428
**Little Falls**
Peter J. Killeen, 238
**Livingston**
New Jersey Pest Management Association, 262
**Long Valley**
Dr. Heather MacLean Walters, 487
**Maplewood**
A Place For Everything, 471
**Maywood**
Shapiro Healthcare Marketing Research & Management Consulting, Inc., 502
**Montclair**
Laura Berman Fortgang - The Life Blueprint Institute, 446
**Morristown**
The Seeing Eye, 516
**Mt. Freedom**
Michael G. Zey, Ph.D. -- Longevity Trends Expert., 325
**New Brunswick**
Gary Griffin - On Turnaround Management, 410
**Newark**
Cheryl L. Wild, Ph.D., Education and Certification Testing Consultant, 182
**Oakhurst**
Tom Kraeutler — Home Improvement Expert, 271
**Princeton**
Forums Institute for Public Policy, 203
Patricia D. Galloway — The Nielsen-Wurster Group, Inc., 278
Kris R. Nielsen — The Nielsen-Wurster Group, Inc., 278
**Red Bank**
Reverend Karen E. Herrick, LCSW, CADC, PhD Candidate, 521
On-Tech E-Rate Services, 181
**South Orange**
Alan Caruba — Public Relations Expert, 208
The National Anxiety Center, 254
Seton Hall University, 179
**Washington Township**
Terry Wall, Certified Management Consultant, 332

# New Mexico
**Santa Fe**
Andrew Sobel, 444

# New York
**Albany**
Bob Bloch — Facilitation Expert, 400
Judith Sherven, Ph.D. & Jim Sniechowski, Ph.D. — Fear of Success, 535
**Bronx**
Harry Husted, 306
**Brooklyn**
Howard Levy — Red Rooster Group, 316
WCFO, INC The World Canine Freestyle Organization, 264
**Buffalo**
Lauren Fix -- Automotive Expert & Consultant, 282
**Commack**
Fran Greene, A.C.S.W., 535
**East Meadow**
HomeWorkingMom.com, 373
**Head of the Harbor**
William R. O'Connell — Business Consultant, 418
**Hempstead**
Hofstra University, 180
**Huntington**
Dr. Elizabeth Carll, Stress and Trauma Expert, 476
Jean Cirillo, Ph.D. -- The Love Nanny, 530
**Lake Placid**
Susan Friedman, CSP — The Tradeshow Coach, 324
**Montauk**
Deb Capone, 190
**Naples**
Marketing Intelligence Service Ltd./ Datamonitor Naples, 453
**Nesconset**
Gestech, Inc., 455
**New Paltz**
Child Find of America, 187
**New York**
Accessory Brainstorms, 294
Adler Footcare of Greater New York, 515
Dr. Bill Akpinar, DDS, MD, Ph.D. - University of Natural Medicine, 498
Lisa Aldisert — Pharos Alliance, Inc., 395
ALMExperts, 220
American Jewish Joint Distribution Committee, Inc., 194
American Society for Aesthetic Plastic Surgery, 490
American Society of Journalists and Authors (ASJA), 300
American Thoracic Society, 515
Imran Anwar / IMRAN.TV, 248
Association for Cognitive & Behavioral Therapies (ABCT), 523

Astron Solutions - Human Resource Consulting, 386

Paul Basile — I to I LLC, 414

Alma H. Bond, Ph.D., 538

Dan Borge — Risk Consultant, 362

Amy Borkowsky, Author and Comedian, 304

Krista Bradford — Bradford Executive Research, LLC, 244

Dr. Joyce Brothers, 522

Jeff Bukantz -- US Olympic Fencing Team Captain, 290

BustedHalo.com, 196

Olivia Fox Cabane - Communications Expert & Networking Expert, 460

Dr. Alden M. Cass, President of Catalyst Strategies Group, 406

Dr. Eugene Charles, The Doctor's Doctor, Health Expert, 510

Charlotte Reed — International Pet & Media Expert, 264

CityCast Media — Podcasts, Webcasts, Blogs, & RSS Technologies, 340

Rick Collins, Esq., 521

Congress of Racial Equality — CORE, 192

Rosanne Dausilio, Ph.D.--Customer Service Expert, 338

Herbert DeGraffe, Jr., Sports & Entertainment Marketing & Advertising, 288

Robert DeLetis, Addictions Expert, 529

Diamond and Diamond LLC, Attorneys at Law, 230

Diane DiResta — Training Coach, 471

Beatrice C. Engstrand, M.D., F.A.A.N., 498

Dr. Burt Ensley - Dermaplus , Inc., 492

EPM Communications, Inc. — Entertainment Marketing Company, 322

Etiquette International, 453

Fidelifacts, 240

Maxine Lucille Fiel, B.A. -- Body Language Expert, 484

Food Allergy Initiative, 267

Eugenia Foxworth, President of The Greater New York Council of FIABCI-USA, 274

Rick Frishman -- Planned Television Arts, 314

Mary Campbell Gallagher, J.D., Ph.D. - - BarWrite Schools & BarWrite Press, 183

Dr. Gallatin on Broadway, 535

Allan Gorman — Brand Marketing Consultant, 436

Richard Gottlieb - Toy Industry Expert, 370

Christopher L. Hansen, Home-Based Business Expert, 380

Headwear Information Bureau — Bush Casey, 296

Helen Hayes Hospital, 502

Tom Hennigan — Promotions USA, LLC, 312

History Publishing Company, LLC, 303

Asuncion C. Hostin, Esq. - Evidence and Courtroom Trial Technique, 224

Ruth Houston - Infidelity Expert, 537

Human Resources Association of New York, 377

Humanity's Team, 200

Kat James, 490

Annie Jennings PR, America's Publicity Firm, 316

Juvenile Diabetes Foundation, 506

Ron Karr — Karr Associates, Inc., 446

William A. Kent, THE TRUTH: Drugs Can Kill - Foods Can Heal, 498

Kessler International, 240

Diana Kirschner, Ph.D. - Psychologist & Love Expert, 538

Debra LaChance — The Healing Project, 508

Maria Liberati, 268

Pam Little — Editor - WomensWallStreet.com, 356

Mary Ann LoFrumento, MD - Pediatrician and Parenting Expert, 533

Look Consulting International, 456

Lynda McDermott, Author, Expert on Leadership & Teams, 422

Michael Mendelsohn - Inheritance Planning of Art Assets, 358

Mercury Masters — The Running Team for Women 50+, 518

Wayne Messick, 452

National Committee on American Foreign Policy, 248

Susan Neri-Friedwald CHT. (NGH, ABH, IMDHA, IACT) Behavior Modification Expert, 530

New York State Society of CPAs, 360

Dr. Michael Nuccitelli, Licensed Psychologist, 522

Ovations International Inc. -- Matthew Cossolotto, 396

Overseas Press Club of America, 300

PartyLine, Public Relations Media Newsletter, 310

Francisco Patino — Inventor, 256

Public Patent Foundation (PUBPAT), 218

Public Relations Society of America, 320

QStat USA Inc — Dr. Philip Truscott — Statistics Expert, 302

The Research Department, 444

Peter Ressler & Monika Mitchell Ressler, 424

Frank Scoblete -- Casino Gambling Expert, 290

Seymour Segnit -- Change That's Right Now, Inc., 476

StreetSpeak®, Inc., 468

Lauren Thibodeau, Ph.D. / Princeton Consulting & Therapy, LLC, 464

Scott Travers - Rare Coin Expert, 294

The United Synagogue of Conservative Judaism, 198

Stephen Viscusi - Workplace Expert , Life Coach , Career Coach & Headhunter, 394

Volvo Group North America, 281

Walker & Co. Publishers, 320

T. J. Walker — Media Trainer/ Presentation Coach, 320

Wizard Entertainment, 292

Eric Woolf — Mailing List Expert, 440

**Oyster Bay**

Natural Alternatives, 498

**Rhinebeck**

The Newsletter on Newsletters, 320

**Riverdale**

Bash Dibra — Dog Trainer to the Stars, 264

**Rochester**

Gene C. Mage, 412

**Roslyn Heights**

Alternative Education Resource Organization, 184

**Saratoga Springs**

Barbara Garro -- Electric Envisions, Inc., 298

**Scarsdale**

Jordan E. Goodman - America's Money Answers Man, 354

**Schenectady**

RID-USA, Inc. Remove Intoxicated Drivers, 203

**Setauket**

Joseph Werner -- Creator of the term: Silent Majority, 212

**Skaneateles**

Kerrin Carleen Hopkins - Personality Profile Expert, 524

**Syracuse**

Trisha Torrey -- Every Patient's Advocate, 496

**Utica**

Utica College, 181

**Westbury**

Catholic Traditionalist Movement, Inc., 200

**Westchester**

Michael A. Covino, 276

# North Carolina

**Asheville**

R. Brent and Company Publishing, 307

Dr. John A. Henderson M.D. - God & Religion Expert, 199

**Chapel Hill**

Jeff Davidson, MBA, CMA — Breathing Space Institute, 472

**Charlotte**

Educational Adventures, 190

Scott Love — Leadership Expert, Author, Syndicated Columnist, 400

Donna Poisl, Immigrant Expert, Author, 252

Sports Media Challenge, 288

Gloria Starr, 453

Ronald George Vance — Cost Segregation Expert, 360

Michael York -- The Michael York Learning Center Inc., 408

**Franklin**

Osie Jackson & Londa Woody, Entertainment Promoter for Elvis Presley, 299

**Greensboro**
Bill Brooks -- The Brooks Group, 434
Employee Retention Survey, 390
The Herman Group -- Strategic Business Futurists, 328
National Board for Certified Counselors, Inc. and Affiliates, 524

**Jacksonville**
Jay Platt — Inspiring People To Be Unstoppable...No Matter What!, 468

**Raleigh**
Patti Fralix — Speaker, Consultant, Coach, 369

**Southport**
Stan Craig — Performance Leadership Speaker, 350

**Winston-Salem**
Elsa McKeithan — Living History Consultant, 302

# North Dakota

**Fargo**
Carol Bradley Bursack - Caregiving Expert, 480

# Ohio

**Akron**
Bill Jelen — Excel Consultant — MrExcel.com, 344
Timothy A. Dimoff — High Risk Security Expert, 238

**Broadview Heights**
Sheri Jeavons - Power Presentations, Inc., 464

**Chagrin Falls**
Michael E. Brizz, CMC, ReferralMastery.com, 394

**Cincinnati**
COLLOQUY, 434
Melvin J. Gravely, II, Ph.D. - Institute For Entrepreneurial Thinking, LTD., 422
National Coalition for the Protection of Children & Families, 189
WonderGroup Youth Marketing and Advertising, 438

**Cleveland**
BCCNS Life Support Network, 518
National School Safety and Security Services -- Ken Trump, 239

**Columbus**
Ageless Lifestyles Institute - Dr. Michael Brickey, 476
Dr. Jay Lehr — TechnoFuturist, Environmental Scientist, 326
Victoria Ring, Legal Marketing, 224

**Dublin**
Dr. Todd M. Kays -- Sports Psychologist, 486

**Hilliard**
Personal Best Consulting, LLC — Dr. Leif H. Smith, 288

**Lucasville**
Dale Powell - Christmas Storyteller, Tradition Sharer & Christmas Trivia, 302

**Pepper Pike**
Ivan Gelfand -- America's Money Man; Financial Strategist, 358

**Powell**
Jon Petz - Ohio Motivational Speaker, 462

**TIpp City**
Ben B. Graham -- Business Process Mapping Software Expert, 388

**Toledo**
Kevin Joyce, Management Consultant and Organizational Change Expert, 384
National Child Abuse Defense & Resource Center, 189

# Oklahoma

**Oklahoma City**
Express Personnel Services, 366

**Tulsa**
National Association of Legal Assistants, Inc., 223
Carl Potter, CSP, CMC, Certified Safety Professional, 192

# Oregon

**Ashland**
Dr Michael Brein... Public Transportation Tourism Expert & Travel Psychologist, 286

**Bend**
Thin Book Publishing Company, 307

**Central Oregon**
Rising Star Press, 324

**Central Point**
Dogs for the Deaf, Inc., 516

**Grants Pass**
Dianne Linderman - Parenting Expert & Author, 533

**Junction City**
Euthanasia Research & Guidance Organization (ERGO), 540

**Portland**
Senator Don Benton, Political Expert, 206
Myrna T. McCulloch, Director, The Riggs Institute, 184
Bill Shirley, Executive Leadership Coach, InSearchofEagles.com, 410
Al Siebert, Ph.D., 526
University of Portland, 180

**Talent**
Dr. George V. Dubouch, Ph.D. -- Health & Wellness Expert, 490

# Pennsylvania

**Allentown**
Joan Laffey - The Health Connection at Cedar Crest College, 494

**Blue Bell**
TASA (Technical Advisory Service for Attorneys), 220

**Carlisle**
U.S. Army War College, 247

**Erdenheim**
Griswold Special Care, 520

**Erie**
Dr. Dennis Dirkmaat — Mercyhurst College Archaeological Institute, 234
Research/Intelligence Analyst Program, 246

**Gibsonia**
Craig Conroy, Conroy Research Group, 314

**Jenkintown**
Marjorie Brody, CSP, CPAE Speaker Hall of Fame, PCC, 456

**North Wales**
Terri Levine, CEO of Comprehensive Coaching U. Inc., 408

**Philadelphia**
Amec Earth & Environmental Specialists, 261
Attention Deficit Disorder Association, 186
Dr. Frank Farley, 523
The Fellowship Press - Publishing Works by M.R. Bawa Muhaiyaddeen, 196
Friends of Libraries U.S.A., 184
Denny Hatch — Direct Mail Expert, 442
InfoCommerce Report, 349
Intelysis — Fraud Investigators, 242
Annmarie Kelly - - SkillBuilder Systems, 333
Harriet Lessy - BuzzCommunications, 318
Robert Naseef, Ph.D., 532
National Adoption Center, 188
Project Management Institute (PMI), 271
Smith Publicity, 314
Michael Stefan, M.D., 510
TeamChildren — Philadelphia Youth Charity, 190
Toll Brothers, Inc, 270

**Pittsburgh**
Steve Gilliland -- Training & Motivating Today's Professionals, 382
Dr. Audrey Guskey, 430
National Flag Foundation, 302
Eva Sztupka - Spa & Skincare Expert, 494
Technolytics -- Kevin G. Coleman, 342
Barbara Thompson -- Personal Empowerment Expert, 487

**Reading**
Marsha Egan, Success & Executive Coach, 405

**Wernersville**
Caron Foundation, 521

**West Chester**
Institute for Creative Solutions -- Randy Rolfe, 524

# Rhode Island

**Block Island**
Holland Cooke -- Podcasting Expert, 305
**East Greenwich**
Summit Consulting Group, Inc. -- Alan Weiss, Ph.D., 411
**Jamestown**
Kristin Zhivago, Revenue Coach, 446
**Newport**
Performance Research, 288
**Warwick**
Plan USA, 195

# South Carolina

**Camden**
M. Tray Dunaway, MD, FACS, CSP, CHCO Healthcare Driving Doctors Crazy, 502
**Charleston**
John Carroll, Author and Consultant, 402
**Columbia**
Jim Reed - Severe & Unusual Weather, 261
**Greenville**
Dr. Ira Williams, the Cure for Medical Malpractice, 222
**Hartsville**
Sonoco Products Company, 260
**Hilton Head Island**
Dawn Josephson -- Cameo Publications, Publishing & Editorial Services, 308
**Myrtle Beach**
Jack Nirenstein -- Running Technique Expert, 486
**North Charleston**
JK Harris & Company, 354

# Tennessee

**Bristol**
Dr. David Stevens — Christian Medical Association, 506
**Clinton**
Scot Kenkel - Sales Coaching Expert, 438
**Knoxville**
Greg Maciolek - Speaker, Author, Business Consultant, 404
Dan Stockdale — Business Relationship Expert, 402
**Memphis**
Robin L. Graham, InnerActive Consulting Group Inc., 386
Voss W. Graham — InnerActive Consulting, 368
**Nashville**
Carol Grace Anderson, M.A., 454

Christopher Bauer, Ph.D. -- Business Ethics Training, 202
Rhonda Borman, Mental Health Expert, 525
Renee Grant-Williams -- Communication Skill Training Expert, 466
Joyce Knudsen, Ph.D., AICI, CIM, Image & Assessments, 455
Cindy Kubica, Stress Management & Communications Expert, 475
Music City Community Chorus, 279
Carol M. Swain — Vanderbilt University Law School, 220
Norma Tillman -- Private Investigator, 240
Veritas Institute, Inc., 368

# Texas

**Amarillo**
Man from the Middle of Nowhere, Texas, 286
**Arlington**
Mensa, 181
**Austin**
American Academy of Nurse Practitioners, 502
Stephanie Breedlove - Household Employment Tax Expert, 360
Jeanette S. Cates, PhD - The Technology Tamer ™, 344
CommuniCard, 462
Ann Fry --- HumorU.com, 378
In the Moment Productions, Inc., 386
Cindy Lafrance - Strategy and Tactics for Revenue Growth, 414
Personal Vibrations Publishing, 473
Superb Speakers and Consultants Bureau - Joyce Scott, CEO, 395
Tim Wright - Leadership Training Expert, 449
**Corpus Christi**
Three Dimensional Development, LLC, 414
**Dallas**
AchieveMentors, Inc., Leslie Furlow, RN, Ph.D., 384
Agro Labs, Cheryl Richitt, 496
American Floral Industry Association, 266
American Lighting Association, 271
Autism/Asperger's Syndrome, 521
Customer Reference Forum, 314
Christopher Faulkner, C I Host, 342
Marc Harty -- PRTraffic.com, 342
Karyl Innis -- Career Success Expert, 374
Kathy Peel — America's Family Manager, 531
Kim Snider - Retirement Income Expert, 350
Juanell Teague, Consultant, Author, Speaker, 313
Trinity Foundation, Inc./The Wittenburg Door Magazine, 200
Roger Turner — Emergency Response Training Expert, 238
UT Southwestern Medical Center, 505

**Houston**
aha! Process, Inc. — Publishing & training on economic diversity, 187
Philip Bell, JD CPA LL.M, 223
Conscious Pursuits, Inc., 474
Dr. Bill Crawford — Performance Training Expert, 384
Donna Fisher, Author of Power Networking, 458
IAC SecureTech — Information Security Company, 239
International Nanny Association -- Pat Cascio, President, 533
Debra Kimbrough -- Child Care Safety Expert, 190
Mike Knox — Youth Violence and Gang Expert, 238
David Krueger MD, 420
Karen McCullough, CSP - Executive Presentation Coach, 382
Paul D. Slocumb, Ed.D., Educational Crisis for Boys, 186
Petrene Soames, author of The Essence of Self-Healing, 544
Cathy Stucker — The Idea Lady, 430
Linda Talley, CSP -- Texas Leadership Coach, 455
Triangle Performance, LLC, 426
WorldFest-Houston, 298
**Iredell**
Daniel New, 210
**Nacogdoches**
7FigureBusiness, 456
**San Antonio**
American Payroll Association, 378
Mark Dankof's America, 210
Dr Gloria Jo Floyd, 504
**Sugarland**
Jim Jacobus — Human Performance Improvement Expert, 424

# Utah

**Orem**
Financial Freedom International, Inc., 359
**Provo**
National Medical Foundation for Asset Protection, 223
**Salt Lake City**
Excend Hispanic Consulting, 322
Kathy Loveless — Business Productivity Expert, 400
National Association of Industrial & Office Properties — Utah Chapter, 272
Robert Paisola's Western Capital Corporate Training Services, 454
Dian Thomas — Free Publicity Expert, 325

# Vermont

**Woodstock**
Antoinette Matlins, P.G., 294

# Virginia

**Aldie**
Networking By Images, 473

**Alexandria**
APICS The Association for Operations Management, 279
Association for Supervision and Curriculum Development (ASCD), 181
Association of Fundraising Professionals, 194
ASTD, 382
Fund for UFO Research, Inc., 544
International Fresh-Cut Produce Association, 266
Jack Marshall — ProEthics, Ltd., 202
Military Officers Association of America, 244
National Association of Professional Insurance Agents, 362
National District Attorneys Association, 222
National Taxpayers Union, 205
Salvation Army National Headquarters, 195
Larry Tracy - Tracy Presentation Skills, 468
Volunteers of America, 192
Water Environment Federation, 254

**Arlington**
Aerospace Industries Association, 284
American Association of Pharmaceutical Scientists, 505
American Chemistry Council, 260
American Feed Industry Association, 266
The American Waterways Operators, 280
Animal Agriculture Alliance, 267
Association for Postal Commerce, 203
Consumer Bankers Association, 359
Consumer Electronics Association (CEA), 344
The Freedom Forum, 301
Steven Gaffney — Honesty Expert, 202
Maurer & Associates, 418
National Rural Electric Cooperative Association, 256
National Science Foundation, 261
Navy League of the United States, 246
Pantheon Software — Web Site Design Development Experts, 350

**Bristow**
PhoChron Yearbooks, 310

**Fairfax**
American Industrial Hygiene Association, 502
Ric Edelman - Radio/TV/Author/Columnist, 352
Independent Educational Consultants Association (IECA), 182
Marketing Solutions, 444

**Falls Church**
International Association of Emergency Managers (IAEM), 238

**Hampton Roads**
Sandy Dumont -- The Image Architect, 484

**Harrisonburg**
Jeffrey B. Harris, ChFC, Independent Wealth Management Consultant, 352

**Leesburg**
National Institute for Automotive Service Excellence (ASE), 281

**Machipongo**
United Poultry Concerns, Inc., 262

**McLean**
National Automobile Dealers Association, 281
National Policy Institute, 203
Jim Thomas, Negotiate to Win, 412

**Monterey**
Americans for Immigration Control, Inc., 253

**Reston**
MENC: The National Association for Music Education, 299
National Council of Teachers of Mathematics, 179
Recreation Vehicle Industry Association (RVIA), 282

**Richmond**
Council for America's First Freedom, 210
Polly Franks - Crime Victim Advocate & Child Safety Expert, 188
Bobby Lopez and the G-TEAM, 290
Julia O'Connor —- Trade Show Marketing Ideas, 325
Harmony Tenney, Sales Performance Consultant, 458

**Roanoke**
Breast Care Specialists, 512
Dean Kapsalakis - Cake Diet Expert, 504

**Round Hill**
Equissage, Inc., 263

**Stafford**
American Life League, 216

**Stanley**
Brad Blanton, Ph. D., Radical Honesty, 521

**Vienna**
Arnold Sanow -- The Business Source, 464
Dr. William S. Turner III, Project Management Consultant, 272
The Women's Center, 534

**Virginia Beach**
Tom Antion -- Internet Marketing Expert, 341
The Funeral Help Program, 541
Laura Giles — Healthy Living Solutions Inc., 537
Patrick K. Porter, Ph.D. — Motivational Keynote Speaker, 526

**Williamsburg**
Cerulean Associates LLC, 450

**Winchester**
Oakhill Press — Business and Self-Help Books, 324

# Washington

**Bellingham**
Corbin Ball, CSP, CMP, MS - Meetings & Events Technology Expert, 376

**Edgewood**
Marilyn Redmond, Healing and Spiritual Growth, 525

**Everett**
Operation Lookout ® National Center for Missing Youth, 188

**Portland**
Don Benton — Yellow Pages Expert, 448

**Richland**
Bob Heck & Jim Thielman -- The Theory of Wrong, 536

**Seattle**
Coaching Makes a Difference, 398
MAQ Software, 346
Medical Research Associates, LLC, 506
Vicki Rackner MD FACS — Doctor Caregiver, 505
Survival Center — Family Preparedness, Health, Survival Supplies, 253
Sally Veillette, Author and Speaker, 499

**Spokane**
Silver-Investor.com — Analysis for Serious Investors, 352

**Vancouver**
Richard Fenton - The Go For No Guy, 528

# West Virginia

**Daniels**
Robin Thompson — Leadership Developement Speaker, 482

**Harpers Ferry**
Appalachian Trail Conservancy (ATC), 284

**Wheeling**
Robert C. Byrd National Technology Transfer Center, 260

# Wisconsin

**Appleton**
National Association of Tax Professionals (NATP), 360

**Brookfield**
National Funeral Directors Association, 542

**Madison**
Credit Union Executives Society (CUES), 358
WTCA - Representing the Structural Building Components Industry, 271

**Milwaukee**
American Academy of Allergy, Asthma & Immunology (AAAAI)., 514
Barbara Bartlein, 524

# China

# Brazil

# Canada

# Germany

# India

# United Kingdom

# Participant Index

# K

# Know someone who should be included in the next edition of the Yearbook of Experts® and Yearbook.com?

## (It could be you.)

## Call 1-800-YEARBOOK (1-800-932-7266), or copy and fax this page to (202) 342-5411.

### Broadcast Interview Source, Inc.
2233 Wisconsin Avenue, N.W.
Washington, D.C. 20007
Tel: (202) 333-5000    Fax: (202) 342-5411

Name:_____

Title:_____

Organization:_____

Address:_____

City:_____ State:_____ Zip:_____

Phone:_____ Fax:_____

Email:_____

# What do journalists say about the Yearbook of Experts® & Yearbook.com?

"An invaluable tool."
-- *CNN*

"Dial-an-Expert."
-- *The New York Times*

"... an encyclopedia of sources."
-- *The Associated Press*

"... internet dating service of PR"
-- *PRWeek*

"The type of tool great stories are made of."
-- *Chicago Tribune*

"Something every talk show host must have."
-- *Larry King Show*

"If your clients include experts, you should make sure they are included."
-- *Public Relations Quarterly*

"... it will make your group the central point for interviews in your field."
-- *Association Trends*

"An impressive directory that produces results."
-- *Book Marketing Update*

---

**Broadcast Interview Source, Inc.**
2233 Wisconsin Ave., N.W.
Washington, D.C. 20007
(202) 333-5000
www.Yearbook.com

**Yearbook of Experts**®
Volume XXV, No. IV
ISBN: 0-934333-55-6
ISSN #1051-4058
Printed Edition: $39.95

CPSIA information can be obtained at www.ICGtesting.com
Printed in the USA
LVOW021328180911

246788LV00001B/1/A